GERRY FRANK'S

Where to
Find it,
Buy it,
Eat it
in
New York

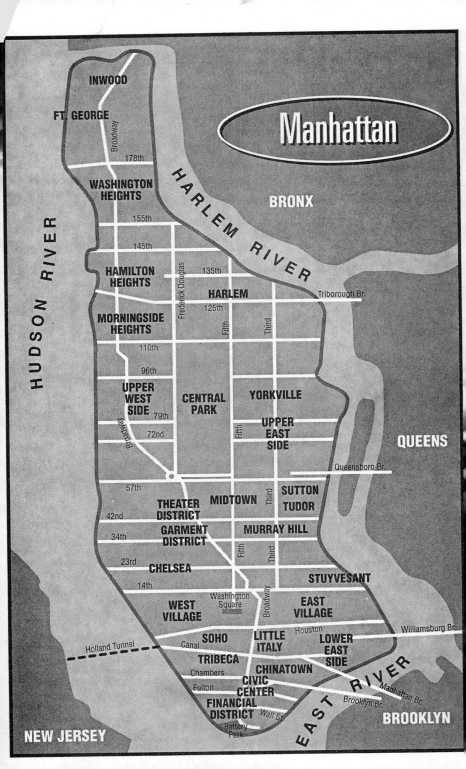

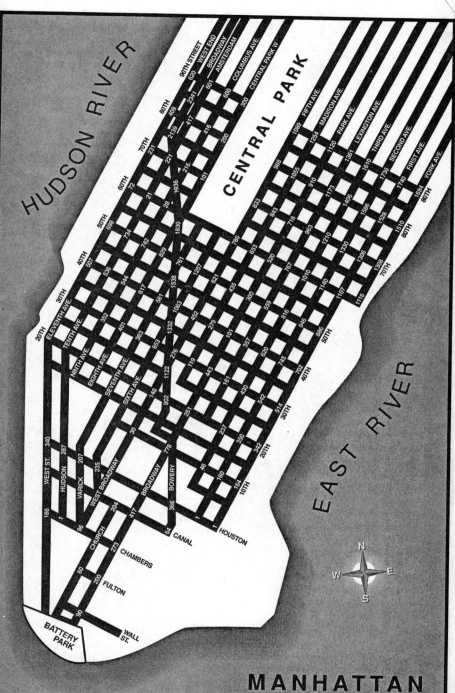

MANHATTAN
STREET ADDRESS

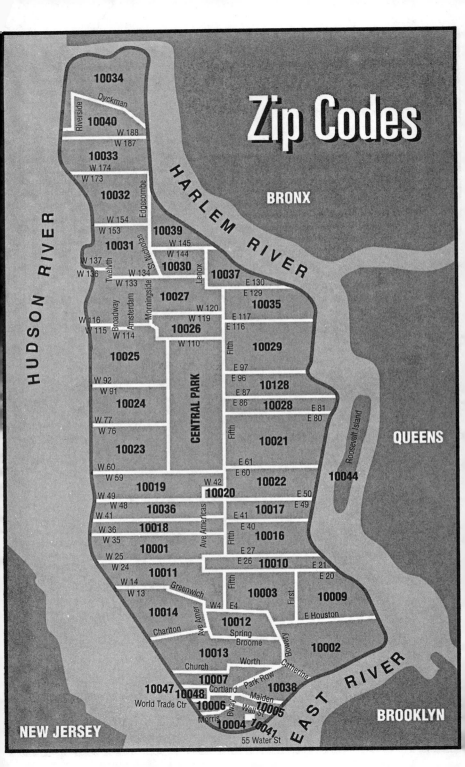

GERRY FRANK'S

Where to Find it, Buy it, Eat it in New York

For additional copies (special quantity prices available),
write or call:

Gerry's Frankly Speaking

P.O. Box 2225
Salem, Oregon 97308
503/585-8411
800/NYC-BOOK (800/692-2665)
Fax: 503/585-1076
E-Mail: gerry@teleport.com

Contents

III. WHERE TO FIND IT: MUSEUMS, TOURS, AND OTHER EXPERIENCES

IV. WHERE TO FIND IT: NEW YORK'S BEST FOOD SHOPS

V. WHERE TO FIND IT: NEW YORK'S BEST SERVICES

VI. WHERE TO BUY IT: NEW YORK'S BEST STORES

VII. WHERE TO "EXTRAS"

Preface

I love New York.

I loved it when I was a child and my family brought me here during school vacations.

I loved it when I came here as a young adult on buying trips, looking for the next big sensation for my family's department-store chain in Oregon.

I loved it when I found refuge here from Washington, D.C., on weekends, walking the streets and exploring the city during the 26 years I worked with U.S. Senator Mark Hatfield.

I loved it two decades ago when I first started publishing my personal collection of "where to" advice as a guidebook to this great city.

I loved the city's relentless energy, its mosaic of diversity, and its constant change. I loved walking up and down the streets and never knowing what I might find next. I loved all the characters who populated New York and all the stories they had to tell.

A lot has changed since I first started coming to New York. Indeed, a lot has changed since I first started publishing this guidebook. New York has become less formal, cleaner, safer, and much more welcoming to visitors. Its neighborhoods have become a bit less distinct and its divisions a bit less clearly drawn. If anything, this richly textured city of immigrants has become even more diverse.

But for all the changes, New York remains New York. And I love it now more than ever before.

The question I'm most often asked is, "How could someone from Oregon possibly know enough about New York to write a useful, best-selling guidebook?" The answer is that I've been coming here all my life. I kept a file of notes on places to eat, shop, explore, and stay in New York to share with anyone who asked. Eventually I had a lot of notes and a lot of people asking for them.

When I first proposed the idea of putting my notes together as a guidebook, all the major publishing houses laughed at the idea. So I published it myself. Despite the fact many of those same publishing houses would love to get their hands on it today, I think it's a more comprehensive and informative book because I'm my own boss. Nobody tells me what to put in it. Nobody pays to be included. And except for places I don't feel qualified to judge, like maternity stores, nobody else does the legwork for this book.

Anyone familiar with New York knows there's a lot to keep up with. The city is constantly changing. Restaurants and stores sometimes come and go quickly. But self-publishing allows me to shorten the time between finishing a new edition and its appearance on the shelves. This volume—my 11th edition in 20 years—therefore contains the most up-to-date information possible.

I'm also often asked what qualifications I have to judge the places included in this book. Part of the answer, of course, is that we're all qualified judges, since we know what we like. But I also am a former retailer with an eye for value, service, presentation, and style. As a private citizen and longtime Chief of Staff to Senator Mark O. Hatfield, I have been privileged to travel to more than 140 countries. I have a pretty good idea of what I'm experiencing and how it compares. For instance, I've dined in more than 2,200 restaurants in Manhattan alone! As the owner of a very successful restaurant and specialty-foods operation in Oregon, I've also developed a good eye for what customers are looking for in the ever-changing food world.

As I said, I do almost all of the legwork. But this book would not be possible without the help of several people. I am particularly indebted to my very talented researcher (and maternity store expert), Carrie McMillan Klein; my editor, Parke Puterbaugh; my fact checker, Cathy Shea; my extremely able book assistant, Cheryl Johnson; my incredibly organized executive assistant, Linda Wooters; and my part-time helper, Linda Chase. Tim Prock, a talented local artist, did the cover. Not to be forgotten, accolades to hard-working typesetters, Tom and Carole Stinski.

Since the first edition of this book was published two decades ago, it has been a labor of love and my attempt to share what I know and love about New York with people who live or visit here. Let me know what you think. Nothing is more valuable to me than feedback from my readers. If you have a favorite spot I haven't mentioned, let me know about it. If you went somewhere I recommended, tell me what you thought of it, pro or con.

Most of all, enjoy! I love New York. I hope you do, too!

A real New Yorker:
- never minds walking when the light is red
- just shrugs when taxis splatter dirty rain water
- always refers to his place of residence as "the city"
- grabs the early edition of the Sunday *Times* on Saturday evening
- pays absolutely no attention to horns or sirens
- is usually on the cell phone when walking down Fifth Avenue
- wouldn't be caught dead wearing a hat

I. The World's Greatest City

The millennium gives us pause to reflect on some of our great American communities. New York City is far and away the largest city in the United States. Well over 7 million people live in its five boroughs, 1.5 million of them in Manhattan. That means roughly the combined populations of Alaska, Vermont, and Wyoming live on an island 12 miles long and only 2.3 miles at its widest!

Despite tremendous improvements in recent years, its detractors continue to argue that Manhattan is the most crowded, dirty, and rude place in the world. To some extent, they're still right on all three points. It *is* crowded. More people live in a residential city block in Manhattan than in many small towns. On any given weekday, a quarter of a million people pass through the MetLife building in midtown, and enough people work in the World Trade Center to make it the fourth largest city in my home state of Oregon! Manhattan *is* dirty: New York produces 13,000 tons of garbage a day. An estimated 12,000 cigarette butts are picked up every day in and around Times Square—that's something like 4.4 million a year! And who would argue that New Yorkers aren't rude—at least some of them, some of the time? (Although what they mostly are is plainspoken and direct.) Everyone seems to be in a hurry, and chances are that anybody who smiles at you on the street isn't just being friendly.

So why visit? Because crowds, dirt, and rudeness aside, New York is the most interesting, exciting, and diverse city in the world. Although they sometimes don't act like it, most New Yorkers are proud of their city and can't imagine why anyone would want to live anywhere else. At the very least, anyone who lives in the United States or who visits this country ought to spend a week or two getting to know this incredible city. And for those who were put off by horror stories about New York in the past, it's worth repeating: New York at the dawn of the 21st century is cleaner, safer, and more welcoming than it's been in decades.

New York has something for everyone. Where else can you find a medieval garden with almost 250 different plants in it? A cafe with a kosher sushi bar? Or several nesting pairs of peregrine falcons (which makes naturalists in other parts of the country crazy)? Whether you love opera, jazz, or tribal drums; whether you're interested in history, architecture, or modern art; whether you like to shop, jog, or attend lectures; whether you live for Italian, Ethiopian, or Chinese food—whatever your interest, New York has it all. This book is all about finding *your* New York—the little slice of this magnificent pie that's just right for your tastes and appetite.

1

GETTING THERE

So you're headed for New York! Whether you're traveling 90 miles from Philadelphia or 9,000 miles from Singapore, you're in for a wonderful treat. But first you need to get here.

AIRPORTS—New York City is served by three major airports. LaGuardia is most frequently used for domestic flights, while John F. Kennedy has flights to and from just about every country on Earth. Both are in the borough of Queens. Newark Airport, across the Hudson River in New Jersey, handles an increasingly large volume of both domestic and international flights. The most common ways of traveling between Manhattan and these airports are by taxicab, shuttle bus, and private car or limousine.

Taxi lines form in front of most terminals at all three airports, and the exits to them are usually well marked. These lines are legitimate and generally move quickly. Under *no* circumstances should you go with someone either inside or outside the terminal who asks if you want a taxi. It may seem tempting if the airport is crowded, but you'll end up paying far more than you should and will have no recourse. Assuming you don't run into bad traffic, the trip between LaGuardia and midtown will take about half an hour and cost roughly $25, plus bridge toll and tip. The trip between Kennedy (also called JFK) and anywhere in Manhattan can take as long as an hour and costs a flat fee of $30, plus bridge or tunnel toll and tip (a trip *from* Manhattan *to* JFK is a metered fare of roughly $35, plus toll and tip). A trip between Newark and Manhattan also can take as long as an hour and costs roughly the same, although a $10 interstate charge is added to the fare. If you have a preference for which route to take into or out of Manhattan, tell the driver in advance. And be forewarned: although they are required by law to do so, cab drivers in Manhattan often don't like taking people to the airports because it's sometimes hard to get quick fares back. In fact, they aren't even allowed to pick up passengers at Newark.

If taxi fares seem a little steep, several companies run shuttle buses and vans between Manhattan and the airports. If you're alone and are going to a major hotel in midtown, you can really save money by taking a shuttle bus. But it may not be worth it if there are others in your party to share a cab with, if you're in a hurry, or if you're headed for a friend's apartment or an out-of-the-way hotel. Shuttle-bus tickets and schedules are available at the ground transportation desks at all three airports. Shuttle-bus options to and from LaGuardia and Kennedy airports include Carey Airport Shuttle (212/286-9766), Gray Line (212/315-3006) and New York Airport Service (718/706-9658). The shuttle bus to and from Kennedy is slightly more expensive than the one to and from LaGuardia, but both are under $20. Olympia Trails (212/964-6233) runs a shuttle bus to all the various terminals at Newark from four Manhattan locations for $10.

If you really want to save money and are in absolutely no hurry, public transportation also is an option. One and a half dollars will buy a trip on the M60 bus between the corner of Broadway and 116th Street (just outside the main gates to the Columbia University campus) and both the main terminal and the Marine Terminal at LaGuardia. The same $1.50 will get you a ride on the A train and then on a free shuttle bus from the Howard Beach subway stop through the long-term parking lots to Kennedy. (Call 800/247-7433 for specific information about departures from the Howard Beach station.)

Like everything else, these prices are subject to change, and it's worth asking about discounts for children and senior citizens. Moreover, these are by no means the only airport shuttle services. For a more complete list of options, call the Port Authority's Air-Ride recording (800/247-7433).

A third option is calling a private car or limousine service ahead of time and having a driver meet you at the gate or in the baggage claim area. The driver will hold up a sign with your last name on it—which, depending on your personality, can make you feel important, embarrassed, or a little bit of both. Be forewarned that this can get pretty pricey, particularly if the driver has to wait because your flight is delayed. (They charge for waiting time.) Costs to and from LaGuardia run anywhere from around $25 plus tip, if you just want a sedan and everything goes smoothly, to well over $100, if there are delays or you request a limousine. Prices are higher to and from Kennedy and Newark. You can go to the ground transportation desks at any of the three airports to get a sedan or limousine after you've arrived as well. (For the names and phone numbers of several large, reputable companies, see the "Transportation" section in this chapter.)

Finally, if you're coming or going from LaGuardia, you can take the Delta Water Shuttle. It ferries passengers between LaGuardia's Marine Terminal and both Pier 11 near Wall Street and several locations on the East River. You don't need to be a Delta Airlines passenger, and the shuttle often takes less time than a taxi, but it only runs hourly on weekday mornings and in the late afternoon. Tickets cost $15 one-way, $25 round-trip. Call Delta at 800/221-1212 for more information.

TRAINS—Dozens of Amtrak trains come in and out of New York City every day. The service is concentrated in the Northeast Corridor, between Washington and Boston, but you can catch a train between New York and Florida, Chicago, or even Seattle and many cities in Canada. Trains arrive and depart from Pennsylvania Station (usually called Penn Station), underneath Madison Square Garden between 31st and 33rd streets and Seventh and Eighth avenues. Penn Station is a major subway hub, but you also can find a legitimate and well-organized taxicab line immediately outside the station on Seventh Avenue. (Under *no* circumstances should you go with someone who comes up to you either inside or outside Penn Station asking if you need a taxi or help with your bags.) You can choose between the Metroliner, sleeping cars, and other kinds of service. Multi-day excursion passes are also available. Although the station is much improved and now has a separate waiting area for ticketed Amtrak passengers in the middle of the main concourse, it's still not a place you will want to spend much time. If you need to stash your luggage for a couple hours and are willing to pay $1.50 per bag, there's an efficient and safe storage area near the far left end of the Amtrak ticket windows. (Call Amtrak at 800/872-7245 for fare and schedule information.) Train service to and from Connecticut and suburban New York is run by MetroNorth through the wonderfully reborn Grand Central Station.

DRIVING—If you can avoid driving to or in New York, by all means do so. Otherwise, you will end up paying exorbitant prices for tolls and parking (and your mental health will inevitably suffer, too). The fact that most New Yorkers don't own cars ought to tell you something! Traffic in and around the metropolitan area is horrendous and drivers are very aggressive. Once you're in New York, the only time you may possibly need a car is if you want to leave for a day or two—and then you can rent one, as many New Yorkers do. The public transportation system in New York is extremely efficient and is used frequently by just about everyone.

If you still aren't convinced or have no alternative, get a map before setting out and study it carefully. The three major approaches to the city involve the New England Thruway (I-95), the New York State Thruway (I-87), and the New Jersey Turnpike (I-95). Expect long waits during rush hour at the bridges and tunnels leading in and out of Manhattan. Tune in AM radio stations 770, 880, or 1010 for area traffic reports if you're trying to decide which approach to take. Expect to pay a toll for whichever bridge or tunnel you choose, although most charge only those cars entering Manhattan.

Why is New York Called the Big Apple?

Attorney/word sleuth Barry Popick spotted two 1920s articles that clarify that John J. FitzGerald, racing editor for the *New York Morning Telegraph,* heard "the big apple" mentioned in a conversation between two African-American stable hands in New Orleans (January 1920). The term referred to the New York City racetracks as the big time in horse racing.

FitzGerald picked up the term and popularized it in his newspaper, still in reference to the NYC racetracks.

In the 1930s, black jazz musicians then applied the term to Harlem specifically, and New York City in general, as the big time in jazz.

In 1971, Charles Gillett, president of the New York Convention and Visitors Bureau, revived the term as part of a public relations campaign on behalf of New York City. He readily acknowledged deriving "the Big Apple" from the 1930s jazz scene.

The term itself goes back ultimately to the big Red Delicious apples developed in Iowa in the 1870s. And for jockeys active in the "bushes," the New York City tracks represented the big time, the big treat they looked forward to, i.e., "the Big Apple."

GETTING AROUND

In case you haven't already figured it out, this book isn't really about New York. It isn't even about New York City. It's about Manhattan. Most people (including me) use New York, New York City, "the city," and Manhattan synonymously. But New York is one of the Northeast's largest states, and New York City actually includes five separate boroughs: Manhattan, Staten Island, the Bronx, Queens, and Brooklyn. Of those five boroughs, only the Bronx is attached to the mainland. Manhattan and the other three are all islands.

A LITTLE HISTORY — Now that you know we're talking only about the island of Manhattan, a little history may help make sense of how the city is laid out. Native Americans were the first known residents of this area. Italian explorer Giovanni da Verrazano (for whom the Verrazano Narrows Bridge, between Brooklyn and Staten Island, is named) sailed into New York Harbor in 1524 and "discovered" Manhattan for his French patron, King Francis I. In 1609, a trader for the Dutch East India Company named Henry Hudson sailed into the harbor and up the river that now bears his name. The first permanent European settlement in Manhattan, a Dutch trading post called Nieuw Amsterdam, was established in 1625 at the very southern tip of the island, where Battery Park is today. The story you've probably already heard is more or less true: the island was "bought" by the Dutch West India Company a year later from local Indians with beads, cloth, and other goods worth roughly $24. It was renamed New York in 1664 after the British—in the person of Charles II's brother, the Duke of York—gained control of the still-tiny settlement.

It's hard to imagine today, but such areas as midtown and even Greenwich Village were way out in the country for another 150 years. Indeed, Wall Street is so named because a wall of logs was erected there in the middle of the 17th century to protect the farms in lower Manhattan from the wilderness beyond. New York's population—only 60,000 as late as 1800—remained concentrated on the southern tip of the island, while most of Manhattan was used for country estates and farmland or just left as forests and wilderness. When a commission headed by engineer John Randall, Jr., laid out a grid system for the largely undeveloped area from Houston Street north to 155th Street in 1807, the city's minute population laughed at the thought that it would ever be necessary.

THE RANDALL PLAN—For those of us trying to find our way around Manhattan, the so-called Randall Plan is a godsend. The streets below Houston (pronounced *House*-ton), particularly those below Canal Street, are laid out like the Dutch farm trails they once were. Even those that are relatively straight were not built for 21st-century traffic. The world-famous Wall Street, for example, is more narrow than the typical suburban driveway. Truth be told, not much about the city's layout makes sense south of 14th Street. If you're ever at the corner of West 4th Street and West 10th Street in Greenwich Village, you'll know what I mean!

Thanks to the Randall Plan, however, everything north of 14th Street is as simple as a major city can be. With the exception of Broadway—originally a well-worn footpath and now one of the country's longest streets (it extends from the southern tip of Manhattan to Albany as Route 9)—and some of the streets in northern Manhattan, the streets and avenues are laid out in a north-south, east-west grid. All of the east-west streets are numbered, as are many of the north-south avenues. In general, most avenues are one-way and are alternately northbound and southbound. Most streets are one-way as well: the even-numbered ones tend to be eastbound, and the odd-numbered ones westbound. Exceptions include such major east-west thoroughfares as Canal, Houston, 14th, 23rd, 34th, 42nd, 57th, 72nd, 79th, 86th, 96th, 110th, and 125th streets. (See the "Key to Addresses" section if you need help finding a specific address.)

EAST SIDE, WEST SIDE—Starting just north of Washington Square Park at about 8th Street in Greenwich Village, Fifth Avenue divides the city into East and West sides. Broadway acts as the east-west dividing line south of Washington Square, although it runs a little east of where Fifth Avenue would be. That east-west distinction is important, as most addresses in New York reflect it. For example, 125 East 52nd Street and 125 West 52nd Street are two distinct locations several blocks apart.

Let's start with the East Side of the city. Moving east from Fifth Avenue toward the East River, you'll cross Madison Avenue, Park Avenue (called Park Avenue South below 34th Street and Fourth Avenue below that), Lexington Avenue (called Irving Place between 14th and 20th streets), Third Avenue, Second Avenue, and First Avenue. Madison Avenue doesn't start until 23rd Street, while Lexington Avenue begins as Irving Place at 14th Street. Sutton Place starts at about 51st Street between First Avenue and the river, turns into York Avenue at 60th Street, and then stops at 92nd Street. East End Avenue runs between York Avenue and the river from 79th Street to 90th Street. All of these avenues run north-south, parallel to Fifth Avenue. FDR Drive ("The FDR" to locals) runs between the easternmost avenue and the river, along the East Side of the island.

The West Side of Manhattan is a little more confusing. Moving west from Fifth Avenue toward the Hudson River, you'll find Avenue of the Americas (or Sixth Avenue, as everyone still calls it, despite the official name change in the 1950s), Seventh Avenue, Eighth Avenue (known as Central Park West north of 59th Street), Ninth Avenue (known as Columbus Avenue north of 59th Street), Tenth Avenue (known as Amsterdam Avenue north of 59th Street), and Eleventh Avenue (known as West End Avenue north of 59th Street until it ends at 107th Street). You'll also find Broadway on the West Side above 23rd Street. Avenue of the Americas and Seventh Avenue both stop at the south end of Central Park. Riverside Drive runs between West End Avenue and the river north of 72nd Street. All of these avenues run north-south, parallel to Fifth Avenue (except Broadway, which meanders diagonally before more or less straightening out around 79th Street). The Henry Hudson Parkway (also known as the West Side Highway and sometimes called Twelfth Avenue around midtown) runs along the entire West Side of the city.

Central Park occupies land between 59th and 110th streets, further dividing Manhattan's East and West sides. Fifth Avenue runs along the East Side of the park, and everything east of it is known as the Upper East Side. Central Park West runs along the West Side of the park, and everything west of it is known as the Upper West Side. Both the Upper East Side and the Upper West Side are largely residential, although most of the north-south avenues have plenty of shops and stores.

NORTHERN MANHATTAN—The avenues on the East Side remain fairly consistent as they move north of Central Park into the area known as East (or Spanish) Harlem. Lenox Avenue (which soon becomes Malcolm X Boulevard) picks up where Avenue of the Americas left off below the park. Adam Clayton Powell, Jr. Boulevard picks up where Seventh Avenue left off. Central Park West becomes Frederick Douglass Boulevard. Amsterdam Avenue, Broadway, and Riverside Drive all extend into Northern Manhattan, while such major roads as Convent Avenue, Saint Nicholas Avenue, Edgecombe Avenue, and Fort Washington Avenue are exclusive to Harlem and the northern tip of Manhattan.

KEY TO ADDRESSES

So how do you find an address in Manhattan? I'm not sure who came up with the following system, but I do know it works and isn't as complicated as it looks.

AVENUES—If you know an address on one of the north-south avenues, you can determine the approximate cross street by canceling the last number, dividing the remainder by two, and adding or subtracting the number indicated.

Avenue A, B, C, or D	Add 3
First Avenue	Add 3
Second Avenue	Add 3
Third Avenue	Add 10
Lexington Avenue	Add 22
Fourth Avenue/Park Avenue South	Add 8
Park Avenue	Add 35
Madison Avenue	Add 26
Fifth Avenue	
Addresses up to 200	Add 13
Between 201 and 400	Add 16
Between 401 and 600	Add 18
Between 601 and 774	Add 20

Between 775 and 1286	Subtract 18
Between 1289 and 1500	Add 45
Addresses up to 2000	Add 24
Avenue of the Americas/Sixth Avenue	Subtract 12
Lenox Avenue/Malcolm X Boulevard	Add 110
Seventh Avenue	Add 12
Adam Clayton Powell, Jr. Boulevard	Add 20
Broadway	
Addresses up to 754 are below 8th Street	
Between 754 and 858	Subtract 29
Between 858 and 958	Subtract 25
Addresses above 1000	Subtract 30
Eighth Avenue	Add 10
Ninth Avenue	Add 13
Columbus Avenue	Add 60
Tenth Avenue	Add 14
Amsterdam Avenue	Add 60
Eleventh Avenue	Add 15
West End Avenue	Add 60
Convent Avenue	Add 127
St. Nicholas Avenue	Add 110
Manhattan Avenue	Add 100
Edgecombe Avenue	Add 134
Fort Washington Avenue	Add 158

Central Park West and Riverside Drive don't fit into this formula but have ones of their own. To find the cross street for a building on Central Park West, divide the address by 10 and add 60. To find the cross street for a building on Riverside Drive up to West 165th Street, divide the address by 10 and add 72.

A word of caution: because certain addresses, particularly those on Fifth, Madison, and Park avenues, are thought to be particularly prestigious, many buildings use them even if their entrances are actually on a side street. This is most common in midtown and along Fifth Avenue on the Upper East Side. If you can't find an address, look around the corner.

CROSS STREETS—Numbered cross streets run east-west. Addresses on them are easy to find. Allow for a little variation below 23rd Street (because Madison, Eleventh, and Twelfth avenues have yet to begin) and throughout the city whenever Broadway is involved.

EAST SIDE

1 to 49	Between Fifth Avenue and Madison Avenue
50 to 99	Between Madison Avenue and Park Avenue
100 to 149	Between Park Avenue and Lexington Avenue
150 to 199	Between Lexington Avenue and Third Avenue
200 to 299	Between Third Avenue and Second Avenue
300 to 399	Between Second Avenue and First Avenue
400 to 499	Between First Avenue and York Avenue

WEST SIDE BELOW 59th STREET

1 to 99	Between Fifth Avenue and Avenue of the Americas
100 to 199	Between Avenue of the Americas and Seventh Avenue
200 to 299	Between Seventh Avenue and Eighth Avenue
300 to 399	Between Eighth Avenue and Ninth Avenue

400 to 499	Between Ninth Avenue and Tenth Avenue
500 to 599	Between Tenth Avenue and Eleventh Avenue
600 and up	Between Eleventh Avenue and Twelfth Avenue

WEST SIDE ABOVE 59th STREET

1 to 99	Between Central Park West and Columbus Avenue
100 to 199	Between Columbus Avenue and Amsterdam Avenue
200 to 299	Between Amsterdam Avenue and West End Avenue
Above 300	Between West End Avenue and Riverside Drive

Odd-numbered addresses on east-west streets are on the north (uptown) side, while even-numbered ones are on the south (downtown) side.

NEIGHBORHOODS

It may be hard for visitors to think of the city this way, but New York is really a collection of small neighborhoods. Some are more famous than others, and their borders do ebb and flow over the years, but each has a history and flavor all its own. To get a full sense of this wonderful city, I encourage you to visit as many neighborhoods as possible. From north to south, they include:

INWOOD AND WASHINGTON HEIGHTS—Home to General George Washington's forces during the Revolutionary War, these neighborhoods cover all of Manhattan north of about 151st Street. Racially and ethnically mixed, they have been home to generations of immigrants and now include both middle-class and quite poor areas. Several large and remarkably unspoiled parks, Yeshiva University, the Dyckman Farmhouse, the Cloisters, Columbia Presbyterian Medical Center, and Audubon Terrace are all in this area, as is the entrance to the George Washington Bridge. As the name implies, Washington Heights contains some surprisingly steep sections.

HARLEM—There are actually two Harlems: East Harlem (also called Spanish Harlem) and Harlem proper. East Harlem begins at about 96th Street and runs on the east side of the island to its northern tip. The population of this area is almost entirely Latino, and Spanish is spoken more frequently than English here. El Museo del Barrio is on the southwestern edge of East Harlem, while La Marqueta, the oldest public market still standing in New York (and one of the best places in the city to buy fresh fruit and vegetables), is a little further north.

Harlem itself occupies a small corridor in the middle of the island at the top of Central Park (at 110th Street) and then extends north and west of the famous and always busy 125th Street. The population of Harlem is almost entirely African-American, and the historic neighborhood is known around the world as a center of African-American music, politics, and culture. As do Inwood and Washington Heights, Harlem includes both middle-class and very poor areas. You'll find the Schomburg Center for Research in Black Culture, Abyssinian Baptist Church, and the Studio Museum of Harlem here.

MORNINGSIDE HEIGHTS—This relatively small but vibrant area runs between Morningside Drive and the Hudson River from 110th Street to 124th Street. The stretch of Broadway between those streets is the neighborhood's economic heart. The area is dominated by three large and well-known institutions: Columbia University, Riverside Church, and the Cathedral Church of St. John the Divine. Grant's Tomb is also here, across the street from Riverside Church at 122nd Street in Riverside Park. The neighborhood is full of students and professors from all over the world.

UPPER WEST SIDE—A primarily residential area extending west of Central Park to the Hudson River from 59th Street all the way north to 110th Street, the Upper West Side is home to such famous apartment buildings as the Dakota and the Ansonia. The neighborhood is racially and ethnically mixed, and its residents pride themselves for being politically progressive and tending toward the bohemian (although by downtown standards, Upper West Siders are decidedly conventional). In the southern part of the neighborhood, the American Broadcasting Company's studio (where soap operas are taped) and Lincoln Center dominate the low and high ends of cultural life, respectively. The fabulous food stores Fairway and Zabar's are landmarks a bit further north. So are the American Museum of Natural History and the New York Historical Society. Barnes & Noble at Broadway and 82nd Street has become a major force in the neighborhood as well. Columbus Avenue, Amsterdam Avenue, and Broadway are lined with stores, while Central Park West, West End Avenue, and Riverside Drive are almost exclusively residential. The most elegant living areas of the Upper West Side are on Central Park West and the cross streets in the high 60s, the 70s, and the low 80s. Tourists probably won't want to wander north of 96th Street, particularly on Columbus and Amsterdam avenues.

UPPER EAST SIDE—Although it's best known for art museums, galleries, and upscale boutiques, the Upper East Side is also the city's most prestigious residential neighborhood. Most of Manhattan's elite private schools are here, too. It covers the area east of Central Park from Fifth Avenue to the East River between 59th Street and 96th Street. Fifth Avenue (also known as Museum Mile) is dominated by such famous institutions as the Metropolitan, Guggenheim, and Cooper-Hewitt museums. It is also home to a large number of expensive apartment buildings, former mansions, and foreign consulates. You'll find the Whitney Museum and lots of galleries, upscale boutiques, and the flagship stores of all sorts of chic designers on Madison Avenue. Park Avenue and most of the cross streets are home to residential buildings and such institutions as the Asia Society and the Americas Society. From Lexington Avenue east to the river above 75th Street (an area known as Yorkville), rents go down a bit. You'll find Gracie Mansion, the mayor's residence, in Carl Schurz Park, overlooking the river at about 88th Street. Bloomingdale's has long been a major retail force at the southern end of the Upper East Side.

MIDTOWN—Squarely in the middle of the island south of 59th Street, midtown Manhattan is one of the busiest places on Earth on weekdays and is almost deserted, except for tourists, on Sundays. (During Christmas season, tourists and natives alike flock to midtown.) The area extends from 42nd to 59th streets between about Third and Seventh avenues. Fifth Avenue is the heart of midtown and one of the world's most famous shopping areas. The flagship stores of Tiffany's, FAO Schwarz, Lord & Taylor, Saks Fifth Avenue, Bergdorf Goodman, and all sorts of other upscale retailers are located here, as are a number of bookstores, Niketown, the Warner Brothers Studio Store, an enormous Gap, and other new "superstores." Many stately mansions once lined this part of Fifth Avenue, but only a few remain and none still serve as residences.

St. Patrick's Cathedral and several other famous churches are also on Fifth Avenue in midtown, while St. Bartholomew's is on Park Avenue and the stately Central Synagogue is on Lexington Avenue. Landmark buildings like the Citicorp Center, Trump Tower, Rockefeller Center, and the Chrysler Building dominate the skyline here. Carnegie Hall, the Ed Sullivan Theater, and Radio City Music Hall sit on the western edge of midtown. Tony stores and galleries line both sides of 57th Street in the northern part of midtown. Many of the tourist-oriented "theme" restaurants, including Planet Hollywood, the Hard Rock Cafe, and the Motown Cafe, occupy the west side of 57th Street. Grand Central Station, the New York Public Library, and Bryant Park mark midtown's southern edge.

CLINTON—Home to the Hell's Kitchen Gang in the late 19th and early 20th centuries, this neighborhood was once among the most violent and dangerous in the nation. It stretches south from 59th Street to about 34th Street between Eighth Avenue and the Hudson River. Although the hype surrounding the ongoing rejuvenation of 42nd Street and the X-rated area around the Port Authority Bus Terminal sometimes outstrips the reality, the area is significantly cleaner and more family-friendly than it was even a year or two ago. In and around Times Square itself, a giant Disney store, a Warner Brothers Studio store, the Virgin Records superstore, and several newly renovated theaters will soon be joined by a fancy new hotel, a multiplex, and all sorts of splashy tourist draws. Ninth Avenue, particularly in the high 30s and low 40s, is home to a lot of ethnic grocers, bakers, and butchers, and the west end of 42nd Street boasts some very good off-Broadway theaters. The Jacob K. Javits Convention Center and most of the city's passenger ship terminals are located here along the Hudson River.

MURRAY HILL—Covering the east side from 42nd Street to 34th Street, Murray Hill begins at Park Avenue and runs to the East River. This area is almost entirely residential, with the nicest part around Park Avenue in the upper 30s. The only real visitor attractions are the Morgan Library and the incredible Science, Industry, and Business Library in the old B. Altman building at Madison and 34th Street.

CHELSEA—As it has been for the past several years, this area remains one of Manhattan's hottest. Another largely residential neighborhood, it extends from 34th Street to 14th Street between Avenue of the Americas and the Hudson River. Madison Square Garden, Penn Station, and the city's main post office are all in the northeast corner of Chelsea, but it's the southern part of the neighborhood that has really taken off. Surprisingly quiet and relatively clean, the southwestern part of Chelsea has lots of turn-of-the-century townhouses and small apartment buildings. It's also home to the lovely grounds of the General Theological Seminary and the Chelsea Piers development, as well as a good many galleries (on and around the far west end of 22nd Street) and the Dia Center for the Arts. The southeastern edge of Chelsea, particularly where Chelsea and the Flatiron District overlap along Avenue of the Americas in the high teens and low 20s, has become what it was a century ago: a retailing hub. Such superstores as Bed Bath & Beyond, Barnes & Noble, and Burlington Coat Factory occupy buildings that once housed famous department stores.

FLATIRON DISTRICT—Named for the historic Flatiron Building, an architectural curiosity at the intersection of Broadway and Fifth Avenue at 23rd Street, this area was known in the late 19th century as Ladies' Mile for its elegant department stores. (A famous jingle at the time went "From 8th Street down, the men are earning it/From 8th Street up, the women are spending it.") Those department stores went out of business at the beginning of this century, but the buildings and the neighborhood are again alive and well, thanks in large part to an influx of "superstores." The Flatiron District runs between Park Avenue South and Avenue of the Americas, from 23rd Street to 14th Street.

Avenue of the Americas is really thriving now, and parts of Fifth Avenue in this area also have undergone a resurgence in the past decade. The Church of the Transfiguration (affectionately known as "the Little Church Around the Corner"), the Marble Collegiate Church, and the Empire State Building are all just north of here.

GRAMERCY PARK — This aging but still pleasant neighborhood was once the city's most elegant residential area. It covers the area from Park Avenue South to Second Avenue between 34th Street and 14th Street. The nicest part is around Gramercy Park itself. The city's only remaining private park, it is bounded by Park Avenue South and Third Avenue and by 20th and 21st streets. A stroll down Irving Place, which runs from the park south to 14th Street, can be very pleasant indeed. The Flatiron District and the Gramercy Park area meet at Union Square, a lively area that serves to divide them from Greenwich Village and is home to the city's largest and most popular Greenmarket. The New York Police Academy and Theodore Roosevelt's birthplace are on the western edge of Gramercy Park, and Stuyvesant Park occupies both sides of Second Avenue between 15th and 17th streets. Two sizeable residential areas, Stuyvesant Town and Peter Cooper Village, abut the East River, as does Bellevue Hospital.

MEATPACKING DISTRICT — This is one of the city's most bizarre and fascinating neighborhoods. Don't get me wrong: I'm not suggesting you wander around here. But the neighborhood west of Ninth Avenue from 15th Street south to Gansevoort Street between Chelsea and the West Village is being shaped by a collision of interesting forces. Traditionally this dirty, architecturally uninteresting area has been the home of New York's meatpacking industry, as well as a great deal of prostitution. But the number of meat businesses has been cut in half in recent years and community action has forced at least some of the prostitution to move elsewhere. Meanwhile, artists, bar owners, and even young families are attracted by the neighborhood's cheap rents. Unfortunately, the sort of X-rated places that used to populate Times Square are also attracted by those rents and the neighborhood's unrestrictive zoning regulations. The result is a weird mix of trendy bars, wholesale meatpacking plants, studios, transvestites, and families with small children. Only in New York!

EAST VILLAGE — About 150 years ago the Astors, the Vanderbilts, and much of the rest of the city's elite lived here, but today the East Village is among the city's funkiest neighborhoods. It sits between Avenue B and Broadway from 14th Street down to Houston Street. Alphabet City (the avenues that in the eastern part of the East Village that have letters for names) and Tompkins Square are much tamer than they were a decade ago, and some parts have become downright family friendly, but they're still home to a great many offbeat and colorful nightclubs, shops, and people. The area around 6th Street between First and Second avenues is a thriving ethnic enclave known as Little India, while the area around 7th Street and Third Avenue is home to a great many Ukrainian immigrants. The Ukrainian Museum, St. Mark's in the Bowery, and Grace Church are all in the northern part of the East Village. Old Merchant's House, the last remnant of the East Village of yesteryear, is on the neighborhood's western edge.

GREENWICH VILLAGE — Although Greenwich Village is best known today for the beatniks and jazz clubs of the 1950s, it's also true that Edgar Allan Poe, Walt Whitman, Edna St. Vincent Millay, Frederic Church, and Edward Hopper all lived here at one time or another. In fact, this area has been among the city's most vibrant centers of culture since relatively affluent New Yorkers began moving here in the early part of the 19th century to avoid the epidemics of the increasingly crowded city to the south. Greenwich Village covers most of the area from Broadway west to the Hudson River between 14th Street and Houston Street. The section from Seventh Avenue to the river is known to locals as the West Village, and the part above Ninth Avenue is the Meatpacking District (see above). The beautiful Jefferson Market Library, the Forbes Magazine Galleries, New York University, and lots of interesting shops and nightclubs are located here, as is the always lively Washington Square Park and its famed arch.

SOHO – Short for *So*uth of *Ho*uston, Soho went from being the center of New York in the middle of the 19th century to an almost entirely abandoned wasteland in the middle of this century. Discovered by artists looking for inexpensive space in the 1960s and by upscale boutiques and retailers like Banana Republic in the 1990s, it's now so trendy – that is to say, crowded and overrun with designer boutiques and tourists – that many galleries have moved to 57th Street in midtown and to the gallery area at the western edge of Chelsea. That said, it's still an energetic and dynamic neighborhood. Soho begins several blocks south of Washington Square Park on Houston Street and runs south to Canal Street between Broadway and Avenue of the Americas. The neighborhood is most alive on weekends and in the evening. Almost everything down here stays open later than similar establishments in the rest of the city. You'll find the Alternative Museum, the Museum for African Art, the New Museum of Contemporary Art, and the Guggenheim Soho on the same block of Broadway between Houston and Prince streets. Many of the neighborhood's commercial galleries are concentrated on and around West Broadway (a separate street four blocks east of Broadway) between Houston and Broome streets.

TRIBECA – Shorthand for *Tri*angle *Be*low *Ca*nal, Tribeca used to be a rather dull and dirty commercial district but is becoming both residential and every bit as chic as Soho. It covers the area from Canal Street south to Chambers Street between Broadway and the Hudson River. Although it doesn't look as upscale as you might expect, Tribeca is home to emerging and established artists, commercial galleries, converted loft apartments, movie stars (Robert DeNiro's Tribeca Film Center has been a boon), some good restaurants, and a growing number of boutiques.

CHINATOWN – This neighborhood's 150,000 residents in roughly 40 square blocks make up the largest concentration of Chinese outside of Asia. Because it is always growing and increasingly overlaps such neighborhoods as Little Italy and the Lower East Side, Chinatown has boundaries nobody can quite agree how to define. I'll use the Chinatown Tourism Council's definition: from Grand Street south to Worth Street, between Broadway and Allen Street. Its busiest streets are Canal, Mott, and Pell. If you've ever been to Hong Kong or southern China, you'll be overwhelmed by the similarities between those places and this neighborhood. Look for all sorts of wonderful food stores down here, as well as the Museum of Chinese in the Americas and the marvelous Chinese New Year parade and celebration.

LITTLE ITALY – No longer home to many Italian immigrants and seemingly shrinking every year as Chinatown expands, this area nonetheless remains the emotional heart of the entire region's Italian-American population, many of whom return for weddings, funerals, holidays, and other special occasions. Mulberry Street (better known as Via San Gennaro) between Canal and Prince streets is the heart of Little Italy and is known for its restaurants and festivals.

LOWER EAST SIDE—Many people use the Lower East Side as a geographic umbrella for Chinatown, Little Italy, and the Bowery, but I know it as a distinct neighborhood where generations of Eastern European and other immigrants first settled in overcrowded tenements and worked in sweatshops so their children could have better lives. (Many newer immigrants still live and work here in conditions that are not as much improved as you might think.) I also know it as the best place in Manhattan to shop for high-quality clothing, household goods, and accessories at a discount. Because some of the area's businesses still are run by observant Jews, they are closed on Friday afternoon and Saturday. Sunday is *the* shopping day here. Canal and Orchard streets are the area's heart, but it extends broadly from Houston to Canal streets and from the Sara D. Roosevelt Parkway east to Ludlow Street. The area still looks pretty run-down and some of the old stores are really struggling these days, but it is being reborn thanks to some very hip clubs, chic boutiques, and other stores that have been attracted by lower rents. Make sure to stop by the Lower East Side Tenement Museum and the Eldridge Street Synagogue to get a sense of the area's rich history. The perenially rundown area known as the Bowery is just west of the Lower East Side.

DOWNTOWN—This area is a little hard to define except to say that it's centered around City Hall. Very roughly speaking, it runs from Chambers Street south to Fulton Street and from West Broadway east to Pearl Street. Lots of mom and pop stores as well as major chains are sited here, and its streets are always busy. However, the beautiful St. Paul's Chapel, the Woolworth Building, and the entrance to the Brooklyn Bridge pedestrian walkway are virtually the only reasons for a tourist to come down here. It's not a dangerous area, but it always seems dirtier than the rest of the city. The South Street Seaport is located just east of here.

LOWER MANHATTAN—Extending from Wall Street and other parts of the Financial District south to Battery Park, this is the oldest part of New York City. Things are very compact and vertical down here: the streets are as narrow as the buildings are tall. The boat to the Statue of Liberty and Ellis Island leaves from near Castle Clinton National Monument in Battery Park, and the Staten Island Ferry's terminal is just east of the park. Look for the exceptional Museum of the American Indian, Trinity Church, the Federal Hall National Memorial, Fraunces Tavern Museum, and the New York Stock Exchange in Lower Manhattan.

BATTERY PARK CITY—A relatively new residential area built entirely on landfill, this collection of high-rise apartment buildings sits on the western side of Manhattan's southern tip, starting a bit north of Battery Park itself. The World Financial Center, where a lot of its residents work, is planted squarely in the middle of this neighborhood, and the Museum of Jewish Heritage is at its southern tip.

SHOPPING DISTRICTS

If you were going to open a specialty store, would you choose a location right between two existing stores that specialize in exactly the same thing? No? Then you're not a real New Yorker. Unlike other cities where the whole idea is to move into a neighborhood that doesn't have whatever you're selling, New York is full of areas like the four-block stretch of Canal Street in Chinatown that's lined with virtually nothing but stores selling cheap gold jewelry. The city also has wonderful shopping districts for everything from diamonds to flowers, beads, and trimming. The merchants seem to thrive on the competition.

Two basic rules govern shopping in New York: you should never pay retail, and the best deals are often in "the districts." While there are not as many cohesive districts in New York as there once were, the ones that remain are well worth a visit.

Let's begin with an insider's guide to a baker's dozen of hot bargains:

Athletic facility: **Asser Levy Gym** (FDR Dr at 23rd St)
Books: **Strand Book Store** (828 Broadway)
Burger: **Big Nick's** (2175 Broadway)
Caviar: **Rush 'n Express** (111 E 23rd St)
Designer labels: **Century 21** (22 Cortlandt St)
Doughnuts: **Rebecca's Bakery** (Ave C at 8th St)
Home, gift items: **Mikasa Home Store Clearance Center** (30 W 23rd St)
Kitchenware: **Broadway Panhandler** (477 Broome St)
Lingerie: **A.W. Kaufman** (73 Orchard St)
Liquor: **Warehouse Wine and Spirits** (735 Broadway)
New York tour: **Howard Goldberg's Adventure on a Shoestring** (212/265-2663)
Watches: **Chelsea Watch Outlet** (62 W 22nd St)
Wine: **Best Cellars** (1291 Lexington Ave)

ANTIQUES—Because rents are so expensive and the antiques market is pretty soft, many dealers have either moved in together or moved out to the Bronx. If you're looking for really elegant pieces and money is not a concern, try some of the galleries in the somewhat fading two-story underground Place des Antiquaires (135 57th Street) and in the tri-level Manhattan Art & Antiques Center (Second Avenue at 50th Street). You'll also find lots of individual stores of varying quality along Broadway just south of Union Square, in Soho, and sprinkled on and around 60th Street and Madison Avenue on the Upper East Side. More adventurous shoppers ought to try Bruckner Boulevard in the Mott Haven section of the South Bronx.

DIAMONDS—This is the epitome of a New York shopping district and one of those places you have to see to believe. Concentrated on 47th Street between Fifth Avenue and Avenue of the Americas, the Diamond District glitters with great deals on diamonds and other jewelry. Be careful, however. I've recommended a couple of places in the "Jewelry" section of Chapter VI, and I urge you to stick with them. Insist on seeing the Gemological Institute of America's report on any stone you're thinking about buying. All diamonds have one. Many of the businesses in the Diamond District are run by observant Jews, which means they're closed on Friday afternoons and Saturdays.

FABRIC, BEADS, AND TRIMMING—Part of the spillover from the garment district, this area is in the upper 30s and lower 40s, between Avenue of the Americas and Seventh Avenue. A lot of stores are up a flight or two of stairs, where rents are cheaper. In addition to every imaginable kind of fabric, bead, and trimming, you'll find hats, feathers, buckles, and bangles here. A couple of good fabric stores can also be found in the Lower East Side and on Broadway between Leonard and Broome streets. Look in the "Fabrics, Trimming" section of Chapter VI for particularly good ones.

FISH—Despite a major fire in 1995 and talk of a possible move, the Fulton Fish Market continues to thrive as the city's source of fresh fish and seafood. They say 125 million pounds of seafood are sold here annually. The market operates between midnight and 8 a.m. in the South Street Seaport at the eastern end of Fulton Street, just above the Financial District. They will sell to individuals and prices are great, but 6 a.m. is considered late for a shopping expedition. If you want fresh fish but can't face those hours, look on Grand and Canal streets in Chinatown for significantly better prices than you'll find anywhere else in Manhattan.

FLOWERS—Roses are sold at deep discounts in specialty stores all over the city. Some of the biggest flower wholesalers have moved out to the South Bronx because of escalating rents in Manhattan. Still, the area from 26th to 30th streets between Avenue of the Americas and Seventh Avenue remains *the* place to get the best prices on flowers and plants. Business is done here very early, but wholesalers usually will sell to individuals who show up by 7 a.m. Planters, soil, and other supplies also are sold in this area.

FUR—Go to the wholesale fur district between 27th and 30th streets on and around Seventh Avenue if you want some great buys. As with diamonds, be careful. (I've listed some particularly good stores under "Furs" in the "Clothing and Accessories" section in Chapter VI.) While animal-rights advocates have made significant inroads into this market in recent years, many men and women still wear furs in New York in the winter. If you have questions, call the American Fur Council at 212/564-5133.

FURNITURE—The wholesale furniture warehouses and showrooms are located on Lexington Avenue between 29th and 33rd streets, but the public is not welcome at most of them. However, some showrooms have special sales when they change their displays, and a few will let you in. Another good bet is the North Carolina Furniture Showroom (Fifth Avenue at 21st Street), where the public is welcome. More specialized furniture stores have begun creating their own district in the area around Varick and Spring streets in Tribeca.

GALLERIES—Three areas in Manhattan are home to the vast majority of art galleries: 57th Street in midtown, West Broadway and surrounding streets in Soho, and the area between 20th and 26th streets west of Ninth Avenue in Chelsea. The 57th Street galleries tend to sell works by more established and conventional artists, while more innovative work is shown in the Chelsea galleries. "Gallery hopping" is a favorite New York pastime. (See the "Galleries" section of Chapter III for information about specific galleries.)

HANDBAGS—The area in the high 20s and 30s off Fifth Avenue has all sorts of good handbag stores. Look up, as most of them are on upper floors. A few stores on the Lower East Side also offer good discounts on fine leather and other handbags. (I've listed some of the stores in both areas under "Women's Accessories" in the "Clothing and Accessories" section of Chapter VI.)

INTERNATIONAL FOOD—A lot of people write off Ninth Avenue in the high 30s and low 40s as nothing more than the dull, dirty back door to Port Authority Bus Terminal. A closer look, however, reveals a startling concentration of ethnic grocery stores, butcher shops, restaurants, and bakeries. Whether you're looking for fresh Italian bread, West African casabas, or West Indian spices, this is a great place. The Ninth Avenue International Food Festival is held here on the third weekend in May.

MEN'S DISCOUNT CLOTHING – Look in the Flatiron District on and around Fifth Avenue between 18th and 21st streets for some really good deals on men's clothing. This is another neighborhood where you need to look up to find most stores, although the people handing out flyers for them will happily give you directions. (I've listed some of the best stores in this area under "Men's, General" in the "Clothing and Accessories" section of Chapter VI.)

SUPERSTORES – Whether you love them or hate them, the invasion of the so-called superstores is now a part of Manhattan's history. Several national chains and corporations, including Nike, Coca-Cola, Warner Brothers, the Gap, and even the National Basketball Association have superstores along Fifth Avenue in the 50s. A great many high-end designers, including Armani, Prada, Valentino, and Vuitton, have superstores on 57th Street near Madison Avenue. Some of the more suburban chains, including Burlington Coat Factory, Old Navy, Bed Bath & Beyond, now dominate Avenue of the Americas and Seventh Avenue in Chelsea. And Virgin Records, Disney, and Warner Brothers are just some of the high-profile superstores in and around Times Square.

THRIFT SHOPS – You can find some offbeat thrift shops in the East Village, while the more upscale ones are in Gramercy Park, on Madison Avenue in the 80s, and in the Yorkville section of the Upper East Side (First, Second, Third, and Lexington avenues in the upper 70s, 80s, and lower 90s). We aren't talking Salvation Army here, but as a general rule the quality goes down the further north and east you go. (I've included some good ones under "Thrift Shops" in the "Clothing and Accessories" section of Chapter VI.)

USED BOOKS – The area on and around 18th and 19th streets between Fifth Avenue and Avenue of the Americas has become a mecca for folks hunting for used and out-of-print books. While the Strand Book Store, which lies a little further south, remains the grandfather of all used bookstores, this neighborhood now boasts scores of small and not-so-small shops and stores where you can find just about any book imaginable. Academy Book Store, Skyline Books, and the frequent book fairs at the Arts and Antiques Pavilion are just a few places to look.

WOMEN'S DISCOUNT CLOTHING – Probably the greatest concentration of decent discount women's clothing stores (and shoe stores) is on Orchard Street in the Lower East Side, from Houston Street south to Grand Street. (Look under "Women's General" and "Shoes" in the "Clothing and Accessories" section of Chapter VI for some of my favorites.) Because many of these stores are run by observant Jews, they are closed on Friday afternoons and Saturdays. Sunday is definitely *the* shopping day in this area. Along 8th Street between Fifth Avenue and Avenue of the Americas is also a good place to look for women's shoes.

OTHER DISTRICTS

FINANCIAL DISTRICT – Better known as Wall Street, the Financial District covers many other streets, too. The older part of the district sits between Broadway and Water Street from Maiden Lane south to Exchange Place. (To get an idea of what I mean when I say "older," consider that Maiden Lane was named for the women who once gathered there to wash clothes!) The New York Stock Exchange, the Federal Reserve Bank of New York, the Fraunces Tavern Museum, Trinity Church, Federal Hall National Memorial, and all sorts of financial institutions are located here. So, too, at least for now, is the Skyscraper Museum. The newer part of the Financial District extends from Church Street east to the Hudson River, between Vesey and Albany streets. Adjacent to the northwest corner of the original district, it includes both the World Trade Center and the World Financial Center.

GARMENT DISTRICT—This district, also referred to simply as Seventh Avenue or Fashion Avenue, is dedicated to one thing: the wholesale dressing of American women. It runs between Broadway and Seventh Avenue from 42nd Street to 34th Street. Fashion models, clothing racks, and trucks filled with fabric jam the streets, especially in summer. Make sure to look (usually up, where rents are a bit lower) for stores selling such Garment District overflow as fabrics, beads, and trimmings throughout this area.

MUSEUM MILE—Beginning at 70th Street and running north for almost 40 blocks along Fifth Avenue, Museum Mile is actually closer to two miles. Regardless, it is the most stunning concentration of museums anywhere in the world. The highlights, from south to north, are the Frick, the Metropolitan, the Guggenheim, the National Academy of Design, the Cooper-Hewitt, the Jewish Museum, the International Center for Photography, the Museum of the City of New York, and El Museo del Barrio.

THEATER DISTRICT—Broadway is on Broadway. Right? Wrong, at least for the most part. And it's not on 42nd Street either, although some excellent off-Broadway theaters are clustered on 42nd Street between Ninth and Tenth avenues. The heart of the Theater District is between Broadway and Eighth Avenue from 44th Street to 48th Street. While it has become much more of a daytime destination than it was even a year or two ago, the Theater District really comes alive at night with theatergoers, restaurant patrons, marvelous street performers, and lots of lights.

I didn't include a couple of districts because they are not so easily defined and because I've covered them extensively elsewhere in the book. If you're interested in art, look in the "Auctions" and "Galleries" sections of Chapter III. General-interest bookstores also are listed in Chapter VI under "Books." If you want a personal touch and good discounts on audio and video equipment, try **Kaufman's Electronics** on the Lower East Side. Finally, whatever it is you're looking for, make sure to check the exclusive shopping list at the beginning of Chapter VI.

TRANSPORTATION

Because it is an island and cannot sprawl outward, New York is very compact and easier to navigate than most of the world's other large cities. You have a range of choices for how to get around, listed here in order of my own preferences.

WALKING—Without question, this is my favorite way to get around New York. It may seem a little overwhelming at first (particularly in midtown at rush hour), and you'll stick out like a sore thumb if you wait on the curb for the "walk" signs, but walking is definitely the best way to see the city and get a sense of its neighborhoods. If you're walking north-south (uptown or downtown), 20 blocks are equivalent to one mile. Most east-west (crosstown) blocks, particularly those between Fifth and Seventh avenues, are much longer. Unless you have small children or are trying to get from Columbia University (at 116th Street) to New York University (at 4th Street), walking is the least expensive and most interesting way to travel. Just be very cautious about the traffic and make sure to bring along comfortable walking shoes!

SUBWAY — Some visitors and New Yorkers alike love to ride the subway, while others will do anything to avoid it. The over one billion rides taken each year prove that it's simply the fastest and most efficient way to travel. As those numbers suggest, the subway can get very crowded. If you get claustrophobic, stay away from the subway around rush hour. And whatever time you travel, hold on tightly to the hands of any children who are with you. Thanks to an ongoing anti-grafitti campaign, a beefed-up police presence, an increasingly well-enforced ban on panhandling, and lots of renovations in recent years, it also has become significantly more pleasant.

The subway system is the result of a merger of private lines like the BMT and the IRT that sprang up at the turn of the century. Most of the stations and some of the cars are quite old, so don't expect the relative luxury of BART in San Francisco or the Metro in Washington, D.C. Its 714 miles of track and 468 stations connect every borough except Staten Island. In Manhattan, the system is concentrated south of 110th Street (particularly below 59th Street). Maps of the system are available at token booths inside the stations and are posted in most subway cars and stations. If you need to study a map, I suggest doing so in your hotel room or some other private place so as not to advertise that you don't know where you're going. You'll also find a detailed map of the subway system in the front section of the Manhattan Yellow Pages.

The stairs leading down to most subway stations are marked by signs with a big M. Unlike some of the other boroughs, Manhattan's subway stations are underground. You'll find the token booths at the bottom of the stairs. Inside the station, signs point to the appropriate platform for the uptown (sometimes "Bronx-bound") or downtown (sometimes "Brooklyn-bound") train you want. Keep an eye out for "express" trains—they're great time-savers if you want to go where they're going, but they make a limited number of stops. The line number or letter, "local" or "express," and the name of the last stop are written on the side of each subway car.

If you pay per ride, the subway costs $1.50 (75 cents for senior citizens). Thanks to the new MetroCard system, you can buy an unlimited seven-day pass for $17—or a 30-day one for $63. You can also buy a one-day Fun Pass for $4. Finally, you can buy pre-paid, per-ride cards for between $3 and $80. For every $15 you buy on such cards, 10% is automatically added (which essentially means you get 11 rides for the price of 10). Of course, you also can still buy a token, although it will not get you the free bus transfer automatically available to people using a MetroCard. Both MetroCards and tokens can be purchased at token booths (for cash only). MetroCards are also available at Rite Aid stores, Sloan's and Gristede's supermarkets, Hudson News branches, and other locations.

For all its great features, the MetroCard has two not-so-great ones that are worth mentioning. The first is that you cannot use the unlimited use Fun Pass or any multiday pass again within 18 minutes of leaving a subway station. That can be frustrating if you get off at the wrong stop or are just running a quick errand. The second irritating feature of MetroCard is that, at least for now, you can only "read" information about how many rides are left on it or its expiration date on bus fare boxes and special MetroCard readers at certain subway stations. Subway turnstiles do not give you such information but *will* refuse your card if it is no longer valid.

Some general subway rules: As many as three children under 44 inches tall can ride free if they're accompanied by an adult. Once you've passed through the turnstiles and are inside the station, you can transfer between lines or ride for as long as you like. And if you're using a MetroCard, you can even transfer for free onto a bus within two hours! Stops usually are announced inside the cars over a public address system; a planned upgrade with fiber-optic technology hopefully will mean that those announcements are no longer garbled and hopelessly confusing. Look for signs posted in the station as you pull in if you need to know where you are. Some lines stop running for a couple hours in the early morning, and many have less frequent or different service at night and on weekends, but the system itself runs 24 hours a day, seven days a week. If you have questions or a problem, call the Metropolitan Transit Authority any day between 6 a.m. and 9 p.m. at 718/330-1234. (Non-English speakers can call 718/330-4847 between 7 a.m. and 7 p.m.)

Two tricks that frequent subway riders use also are worth mentioning. One is taking an express to the stop closest to your destination and then waiting for a local to take you the rest of the way. You can always get on one line at the stop that's most convenient for you and then switch trains at a stop served by another that will take you to your destination. This works particularly well on the 4, 5, and 6 lines on the East Side, for example, as only the 6 makes local stops in midtown but the 4 and 5 go down to Bowling Green. The obvious thing to do, then, is get on the 6 in midtown and switch to a 4 or 5 at 42nd Street, 34th Street or wherever else the lines meet. A second trick is simply waiting for the next train if the one that arrives is packed full. If you've been waiting for awhile, chances are there's a less crowded train right behind the first one. Your ride could be significantly more pleasant if you just wait a minute or two. (This is also true for buses.)

Finally, a word about safety. Despite real improvements in recent years, an emphasis by the Metropolitan Transit Authority on cleaning up stations and the *art* in them, and significantly fewer breakdowns than a decade ago, stations and the cars themselves are sometimes dirty and all sorts of strange people wander through them. Statistically, however, the system is no more dangerous than any other mode of transportation. Indeed, like crime in New York generally, crime in the subway has been cut drastically in recent years. But do use common sense. *Don't* ride late at night or very early in the morning, particularly if you're alone. *Don't* enter deserted stations. *Don't* ride in an otherwise empty car. *Don't* wear flashy jewelry. *Don't* wander around aimlessly. *Don't* stand too close to the tracks. *Don't* use the bathroom inside any station. *Do* stick close to the designated off-hours waiting area if you're riding at an off-peak hour so that the attendant can keep an eye on you. And *do* watch your wallet or purse, particularly when riding in crowded cars.

TAXIS—All of the officially licensed medallion taxicabs in New York are yellow, have the words "NYC Taxi" and fare information written on their side doors, and post their medallion number in a box on the roof. Inside you'll see a meter and the driver's license (with his or her picture) and medallion number displayed on the dashboard, usually on the passenger's side. The city, particularly outside midtown, is full of unregulated "cars for hire" (a.k.a. "gypsy cabs") that are not legally allowed to pick up people south of 96th Street. Still, they sometimes try to do that. I strongly encourage you to stick with the medallion cabs. The cost of a ride in a medallion cab is calculated per trip rather than per person, which means that a short trip for four adults in a cab can actually be cheaper than a bus or subway ride. That said, however, fares can add up quickly, particularly if you're stuck in heavy traffic. The charge begins at $2 the moment you get in and costs 30 cents for every one-fifth of a mile or 90 seconds stopped or slowed in traffic. In general, the meter should "click" every four blocks when you're going north-south and every block when you're going east-west. You pay for any tolls, and there's a 50 cent surcharge for rides made between 8 p.m. and 6 a.m. The meter in the front keeps a running total of the fare, and the driver is required to give you a receipt if you request one. A tip of between 15% and 20% of your fare is expected, and you probably will need to pay in cash. Drivers often cannot make change for bills larger than $20 (and are not required to).

Drivers *are* required to take you anywhere within the five boroughs of New York City, to Westchester and Nassau counties, and to Newark Airport. That's the law, but the reality is that many cab drivers will make a fuss if you want to go to one of the airports, out to one of those suburban counties, or even to lower-income neighborhoods in Manhattan. If you have such a problem, jot down the driver's name and medallion number and write or call the New York City Taxi and Limousine Commission (221 West 41st Street, New York, NY 10036; 212/221-8294) to complain. These folks take their oversight responsibilities seriously.

So how do you go about hailing a cab? Stand on or just off a curb and stick your arm up and out. If the number (but not the "off-duty" sign) is lit in the rectangular box on a cab's roof, it's empty and looking for business. Finding a cab in a snowstorm or in midtown on a rainy Friday afternoon is difficult, but you usually won't have trouble finding one in most parts of the city at most times of day. If you do have trouble, go to a major hotel or join the cab line at Penn Station, Grand Central Station, or Port Authority Bus Terminal. If you want the driver to take a particular route (it's a good idea to know exactly where you're going), say so when you get in. Assuming it isn't raining, I also suggest giving the driver the closest intersection rather than a street address as your destination. This will save you both time and money. Passengers ride in the back seat, although the driver will usually let one person ride up front if there are four in your party.

BUSES—In the first several editions of this book, I wrote that the only reason to take a city bus is if you have a lot of time and are afraid of the alternatives. A friend who rode the bus every day objected strongly. First of all, she pointed out, most buses are wheelchair-accessible (which the subway decidedly is not) and "elderly friendly" in that the driver can lower the stairs at the entrance (called "kneeling") for anyone who has trouble climbing high steps. Buses are also "stroller friendly" insofar as the doors don't close automatically and there are only a few steps to climb and descend. Precisely because the people who take the bus aren't in a hurry, they tend to be friendlier than subway riders and often will give an older person or a harried parent their seat. The buses are very safe and usually don't attract the strange people who still sometimes habituate subway cars and stations. Because there is a driver, you can ask questions or get directions. And because the bus stops frequently and you can always see where you're going, it's a good and relatively cheap way to get a flavor of the city. Finally, there's a new bonus: unlike subway turnstiles, bus fareboxes tell when a MetroCard will expire and how many rides are left on it. I still find the system frustratingly slow, but buses do have some redeeming features, and their popularity in recent years has increased dramatically.

Buses run up and down most avenues and on most major cross streets. Uptown buses stop every two or three blocks, and crosstown buses stop on every block — assuming someone is waiting at a bus stop or a bus rider has pushed the tape to alert the driver that a stop is requested. Many bus lines have a limited "express" version that stops only every ten blocks or so; an orange "limited" sign is clearly visible in their front windshields. At a minimum, you can spot a bus stop by its blue sign and route numbers. But the city recently renovated some "Guide-a-Ride" signs and route maps, and added many more, making the entire system much more user-friendly. Many stops are used by more than one route, so check the screen on the front or side of each bus for its route number or simply ask the driver. Your fare entitles you to one transfer, and you should request the transfer ticket from the driver when you board. The transfer is good only for a continuous trip, but you actually have at least an hour to make a connection. You cannot, however, get off and then reboard another bus on the same route. If you're using a MetroCard, you can even transfer onto a subway within two hours.

A ride on the bus costs $1.50 (75 cents for senior citizens and free for small children when accompanied by a fare-paying adult). As with the subway, however, you can buy an unlimited seven-day pass for $17 or a 30-day one for $63. You can also buy a one-day Fun Pass for $4. Finally, you can buy pre-paid, pay-per-ride cards for between $3 and $80. For every $15 you buy on such cards, 10% is automatically added (which essentially means you get 11 rides for the price of 10). You also can still pay your fare with a token, although it will not get you the free subway transfer automatically available to MetroCard users. You also can pay with exact change (bills and pennies are not accepted). Both MetroCards and tokens can be purchased at subway station token booths (for cash only). MetroCards are also available at Rite Aid stores, Sloan's, and Gristede's supermarkets, Hudson News branches, and other locations. Many buses run all night, although service is less frequent on weekends, late at night, and early in the morning.

You can get a map of Manhattan bus routes on most buses (ask the driver or look for boxes by the front and back doors) and at most subway token booths. You will also find a detailed map of the bus system in the Manhattan Yellow Pages. The map details where buses run, frequency of service, and which bus to take to major museums and other attractions. If you have questions about how to get from one place to another on the bus, call the Metropolitan Transit Authority between 6 a.m. and 9 p.m. at 718/330-1234. (Non-English speakers can call 718/330-4847 between 7 a.m. and 7 p.m.)

CAR SERVICES — If you notice a large number of Lincoln Town Cars and other black sedans in midtown and the Financial District, they are car services. Unlike taxicabs, which cruise the streets looking for business, car services are available only by reservation and often exclusively for corporate clients. If you're in New York on business, your company may arrange to have you picked up from the airport and shuttled around town by one of these services. Chances are you will be given an account number and pay with a voucher provided either by your company or the driver. A client's name and car number will typically be posted in the window of the car, and you'll be told in advance what to look for.

Some car services (limousine companies, too) take reservations from individuals. Carey Limousine (212/599-1122 or 800/336-4646) and Sabra (212/777-7171) are among the larger and more reputable companies. You can have a car meet you at the airport, be shuttled around town for a day, or simply arrive and depart from the opera in style. The cost is calculated by the hour or the trip rather than by mileage, so make sure you agree on a price before making a commitment. Reservations are required. Make them at least a day in advance and call to confirm several hours before you expect to leave. If you want a specific kind of car or limousine, say so when you're making reservations. These car services are on the high end of the business. You'll find lots of gypsy cabs and low-end car services in the outer boroughs and outside midtown, but I suggest avoiding them. Just so you know, licensed limousines are required to have a diamond-shaped decal on the right side of their windshield. On it will be an eight-digit number starting with T and ending with C.

DRIVING—If you read my comments earlier in this chapter, you already know that I strongly recommend against driving in New York. Leave the hassles and headaches to cab and bus drivers. The parking regulations alone ought to discourage you. There are alternate-side rules, special rules for several dozen official holidays, and weekend rules. And that's if you can find a space. Illegal parking can cost you upwards of $200 after you've paid for the towing and impoundment of your vehicle. If you can't find a space on the street or want the security of a garage, you're going to pay big bucks. I once was charged $18 per half hour at a garage in midtown. On top of that, they cheated on the clock!

If all that's not bad enough, consider this: 750,000 cars come into Manhattan every day and 80,000 more than that congest midtown during the Christmas season! It's little wonder that the average speed of traffic going uptown or downtown is 8.2 miles an hour . . . and the average crosstown speed is 5.2 miles per hour! Moreover, it's illegal for anyone under 18 to drive in New York City. If you must drive, I *highly* recommend becoming a member of AAA or some other major automobile club and getting all the information they have about traffic laws and driving in the city. Whatever else you do, make sure you know where you're going and be prepared for a lot of honking. Drivers in New York are not very patient people.

SAFETY

It makes sense that there are more crimes committed in New York than any other city, because more people live here than any other city. But New York is not nearly as dangerous as people think. In fact, fewer crimes are committed per capita in New York than in more than 20 other U.S. cities, and the violent crime rate has plummeted in the last several years and continues to fall.

The percentages definitely are with you, especially if you observe a few common-sense "don'ts":
- Don't display big wads of money or flashy watches and jewelry. In fact, don't even carry them with you. Leave most of your cash and all of your valuables at home or in the hotel safe.
- Don't open your wallet in public.
- Don't use automated teller machines (ATMs) when no one else is around.

- Don't leave those machines until you've put your money in a wallet and then put the wallet in your pocket or purse.
- Don't keep your wallet in your back pocket unless it's buttoned. Better yet, carry your wallet in a front pocket, along with keys and other important items.
- Don't wear your purse slung over one shoulder. Instead, put the strap over your head and keep your purse in front of you or to the side.
- Don't doze off on the subway or bus.
- Don't take the subway late at night or very early in the morning.
- Don't walk down empty streets or enter empty subway stations.
- Don't jog in Central Park or anywhere else after dark.
- Don't let yourself believe that staying in "good" neighborhoods protects you from crime. The only time I was ever mugged was on Park Avenue at 62nd Street, and you can't find a better neighborhood than that!
- Don't let anybody in your hotel room, even if they claim to work for the hotel, unless you've specifically asked them to come or have checked with the front desk.
- Don't talk to strangers who try to strike up a conversation unless you're very sure of their motivations.
- Don't leave bags unattended. If you're going to put a bag or backpack on the floor at a restaurant or even in a bathroom stall, put your foot through the strap.
- Don't hang your purse or anything else on the back of the door in a public bathroom stall.
- Don't walk around with your mouth open, your camera slung over your shoulder, and your map out while saying things like "Gee, honey, they sure don't have buildings this big back home!"
- Don't be afraid to cross the street if a situation doesn't feel right or to shout for help if somebody is bothering you.

A final word of warning that has nothing to do with crime per se: watch where you walk. Manhattan has an incredible amount of traffic, and the struggle among cars, taxis, trucks, buses, and pedestrians is constant. The city has tried with limited success to erect pedestrian barriers at some of the most dangerously crowded intersections, like the one on Fifth Avenue between Rockefeller Plaza and Saks Fifth Avenue. Other particularly dangerous spots include Park Avenue at 33rd Street, Avenue of the Americas and Broadway as they intersect 33rd and 34th streets at Herald Square, and 42nd Street and Eighth Avenue around Port Authority Bus Terminal. It sounds silly to repeat a warning from childhood, but look both ways before stepping into the street, wherever you are.

If there's an emergency, don't hesitate to call 911. If you need more general assistance, try the Travelers' Aid Society at Broadway and 42nd Street in Times Square, or give them a call at 212/944-0013. These kind folks will help with medical referrals, emergency flight changes, and anything else you might need in a pinch.

SMOKING

Like many cities and states, New York has become increasingly hostile to smokers in recent years. Indeed, there has been a massive change in society's attitude toward smoking in the two decades since I started writing this book. Thanks to the city's 1995 Smoke-Free Air Act, New Yorkers and visitors alike now will find the number of places where they can smoke severely limited.

Even before the new city law was enacted, New York state banned smoking in airports, train stations, bus stops, and similar public areas. Now that ban extends to restaurants that seat more than 35 people, many bars where food is served, the seating areas of both indoor and outdoor sports arenas, and the public spaces of all buildings. Most hotels maintain rooms (and sometimes entire floors) for smokers and nonsmokers.

STROLLERS AND WHEELCHAIRS

New York is a walker's city. Walking in New York is not only the best way to see the city but also often the fastest way to get around. However, as anybody who has tried traversing the city with a baby stroller or in a wheelchair will tell you, New York is not a paradise for anybody who has trouble climbing steps or curbs and navigating through stopped or slowed traffic.

If you're coming to New York with a stroller in tow, make sure it's a durable one and be prepared for obstacles. Because space is at a premium in New York, the aisles of grocery stores, boutiques, and even restaurants are often much narrower than they are in the suburbs. Despite the requirements of a variety of laws and significant improvements in recent years, many of New York's older buildings are not equipped with ramps or easily accessible elevators. While people use strollers on the subway system all the time, carting them up and down stairs can be a pain, and wheeling children on them between platforms and subway cars is downright dangerous. Be forewarned that some places, including the United Nations and the Metropolitan Museum of Art (on Sundays), ban strollers altogether.

Obstacles for wheelchairs are even greater. Although most of the city's buses are equipped with special lifts and spaces for wheelchairs, much of the subway system is completely inaccessible. (Exceptions include some major stops, like Grand Central Station and the World Trade Center, where elevators are safe and functioning.) If you're coming to New York in a wheelchair, you ought to know about a couple of resources. First, make sure to get a copy of "Access for All," an exceptional guide to the city's cultural institutions that describes in detail what sorts of facilities those institutions have for people in wheelchairs (as well as the blind and deaf). This invaluable guide is available from Hospital Audiences, Inc. (220 West 42nd Street, New York, NY, 10036) for $5 a copy. This organization also runs a hotline (888/424-4685) on weekdays. Second, the Metropolitan Transit Authority has a special phone number (718/596-8585) for information about routes accessible to people in wheelchairs, and offers postage-paid fare envelopes to disabled riders. Finally, the City of New York's Office for People with Disabilities publishes an access guide. Call 212/788-2830 to request that publication or for general information. One piece of good news: many Broadway theaters offer deeply discounted tickets for folks in wheelchairs and their companions. Call the individual theaters for more information.

TIPPING AND OTHER EXPENSES

Be forewarned: New York is expensive. *Really* expensive. Most nice hotel rooms in midtown run upwards of $250 a night. The average meal at a decent restaurant can easily run upwards of $50 per person, and most theater and opera tickets are just plain outrageous. Everybody expects a tip. It's up to you, of course, but $1 per bag to the bellman, between 15% and 20% of your fare to the cab driver, and between 15% and 20% of your pre-tax restaurant bill (just double the tax—it's 8.25% on just about everything) to your waiter is expected. Most people also tip wine stewards (10% of the wine bill), parking valets ($2), private tour guides (at least $5 a day), and doormen who hail cabs ($1), among others.

The good news is that prices have not risen much is recent years. The average cost of a meal, while still the highest in the nation, actually has gone down a bit. With a little effort, you *can* find cheaper hotels, less expensive restaurants, and even some free events and activities. (Make sure to check the "Manhattan for Free" section in Chapter VII, and look in the "Tickets" section of Chapter III for information about how to get bargains on theater tickets.) You don't always have to spend a lot to get what you want. After adding tax, an automatic gratuity, and a hotel surcharge to the cost of the item itself, a friend calculated the difference between buying a single bagel through room service in one midtown hotel and buying it in a deli a block away at more than $10! But in general my advice is be prepared to spend money—and lots of it—if you're here for a special visit. Don't nickel-and-dime yourself out of enjoying what could be a once-in-a-lifetime experience!

CHECKLISTS

If you're planning a trip to New York a couple months in advance, I suggest thinking ahead about what you want to do and reading the relevant sections of this book carefully. Pay special attention to the "Tours" and "Tickets" sections of Chapter III and the "Annual Events" and "Resources" sections of Chapter VII. Some things—tickets to certain events, Broadway shows, television show tapings, and tours, for example—require advance planning. Other things—special sales or events, for example—require that you visit at certain times of year. Weather is always a consideration. Average temperatures range from highs in the 30s and 40s in December, January, and February to highs in the 80s and 90s in June, July, and August. Whenever you come and whatever you plan to do, however, I recommend packing these key items:

- Comfortable walking shoes
- An umbrella and raincoat
- A jacket and tie or nice dress
- Opera glasses
- An address book and postcard stamps
- Prescriptions and an extra pair of glasses
- Traveler's checks
- A fanny pack or money belt
- Tickets (airplane and otherwise)
- An AARP and/or Medicare card
- Student identification card

All the little items that you may want in your hotel room or when you're out and about cost a lot less at home than they do in New York. Most hotels will supply small sewing kits, and some will let you borrow an umbrella or hair dryer for free. But consider packing things like film, aspirin, instant coffee, snacks, and gum. Plan what you're going to need for the day before leaving the hotel room. Put a couple of credit cards, driver's license, and some money in a secure pocket, fanny pack, or money belt and then stash everything else in a shoulder bag so there's no worrying about a stolen purse or wallet. I suggest leaving your room key at the front desk for the same reason. Depending on the time of year, here's a list of things I might take with me for a day of exploring:

- Addresses and phone numbers of places you plan to visit and details about how to get there
- Address and phone number of your hotel
- Bus and subway maps
- Tissues
- A list of public bathrooms in the areas you'll be going (see Chapter VII)
- An umbrella
- A coat or sweater
- An unlimited-use MetroCard (for subways and buses)
- Some loose change and small bills
- Finally, don't forget this book!

Do you want to be *in* at your favorite restaurant? You know, impressing your guests by being called by name, being seated at the best table, getting extra-attentive service! Here's how: go often to that restaurant; call a day in advance and speak to the owner or maitre d'; write a confirming note for your reservations; dress appropriately; arrive on time; if you don't like where you are seated, say so; thank the manager if the meal was good; and don't forget that big tips are remembered!

II. Where to Eat It: Manhattan a la Carte

No section of this book is more popular than "Where to Eat It." I get literally hundreds of comments, suggestions, and ideas from readers, restaurant operators, and the wide world of "foodies." My job is to put all the material in a form that is useful, accurate, and timely; I hope I have succeeded.

What you will read in this section is the result of years of work, if you call trying out over 2,200 eating establishments work! When you combine the meals with visits (and sampling) at hundreds of food shops, from street vendors to the elegant halls of the finest gourmet shops, you are able to get a feel of what the food scene in Manhattan is all about. I pass along my comments—and they are mine alone—to help you find your way in this bewildering scene.

Let me set the guidelines. I make no pretense of being a professional food critic. However, I am presenting information from my own informed perspective: that of someone who has spent over a quarter of a century in the food-service field, who owns and operates his own restaurant and gourmet cake shop in Oregon, and who has had the opportunity to make judgments based on dining experiences in over 140 nations.

The New York restaurant scene is in constant change. *Prix-fixe* meals have become very popular, and even the fanciest places have taken a second look at their out-of-sight tabs. A sizable number of newer restaurants are priced in the lower and moderate ranges. This is because fewer New Yorkers and visitors are eating at home. Lack of time plus the trouble and expense of food preparation in one's own kitchen have contributed to this noticeable trend. Since people dine out so much, they want to do so affordably.

Expense accounts are being carefully monitored. Food has become simpler and healthier. Casual attire is now taken for granted; it is the rare establishment that sticks to a serious dress code. Trendiness rules, as the mob hops from one new hot spot to another. In the restaurant biz, it is truly survival of the fittest.

Many restaurant guides give stars or ratings, but I have chosen not to do so. Only those establishments that I feel are especially commendable (for food, ambience, service, and price) are included herein. The also-rans are not included, except in the "Don't Bother" section, where I think you should know my feelings about some of the better-known places.

There is a diner's code of conduct, just as there are rules and regulations for restaurant personnel. A few suggestions, if you want the best service:

- Become a regular patron.
- Tell the maitre d' if it is a special occasion.
- Write a confirming note if your reservation is several weeks in advance.
- Dress appropriately.
- Arrive on time.
- If you don't like something (location of table, service, food item), tell the person in charge in a friendly manner.
- Be smart by making reservations well in advance of holidays.

We all have our beefs about food service. I have a number of them. I don't like dirty menus or ones with prices crossed out. I don't like to have to ask repeatedly for the check. I don't like waiters who are syrupy friendly and proceed to tell you all of *their* favorites. I object to restaurant personnel who scrape remains off a dish in front of diners. I don't like to be interrupted over and over during a meal with the query "Is everything all right?" I don't like "background" music played so loudly that you can't hear conversation across the table. I don't like to be seated next to the kitchen or rest room. Paper tablecloths turn me off. I have a real problem with too much food on a plate; it is unappetizing to see a huge mound of meat and veggies heaped together. Beware of dishes that combine several ethnic flavors—like a French, Japanese and Brazilian mixture—because you won't really get a true taste of anything. Cleanliness, above all, is a must.

The first part of this chapter lists the outstanding places I have found. Each listing, organized by districts, includes the address, type of cuisine, and whether or not the establishment is open on Sunday. The next section features listings for different kinds of meals and occasions, such as breakfast, brunch, late evening, outdoor cafes, bistros, coffeehouses, personal favorites, burgers, seafood, ethnic specialties, and more. In the following section, I have compiled a listing of major food items and dishes, indicating where the best can be found. Rest assured this is the cream of the crop, and the prices are right! Finally, I list and describe in detail more than 260 restaurants that deserve special attention. These reviews include important information (location, phone number, pricing, meals served) and a general feel for ambience. In most cases I have purposely not been too specific on menu items, as they tend to change almost overnight. I have eliminated trendy establishments that I suspect will not survive in this fast-changing environment.

The Smoke Free Air Act went into effect in New York City in 1995, and it has created much confusion for both operators and customers of local restaurants. The bottom line is that a number of restaurants have become creative in their rules and regulations, allowing those who want to light up to do so in designated areas. Arrangements change, so a smoker's best strategy is to pick out a restaurant and then call ahead to find out their rules. In most cases, you will be accommodated, although you might have to sit at the bar or in a lounge, private dining room, or outdoor setting.

A few housekeeping details: "Inexpensive" means under $15 per person for a meal without drinks. "Moderate" is roughly $16–$34. "Moderately expensive," $35–$45. "Expensive," $46 and up. Most establishments take all major credit cards, although a few accept American Express only. Sometimes cash only is taken. Some establishments will take a check, if proper identification is presented.

I am not a wine expert, therefore commentary on wine lists is not included. If you have a question about dress codes, call the establishment. If a gentleman forgets his jacket and the dress code requires one, most places will provide a loaner.

In many cases, reservations are essential. An increasingly annoying habit is for the establishment to ask for a telephone contact or reconfirmation. I strongly object to the latter.

A few words about service. How does the restaurant handle phone reservations? Are you put on hold indefinitely? Are you greeted promptly and properly when you enter an establishment? Are food items and drinks served on a timely basis? Can your server describe dishes in an adequate and informed way? When constructive comments are made, do restaurant personnel receive them graciously or respond defensively?

A very unattractive practice has developed at some of the more trendy places. Reservation agents will tell you nothing is available until three weeks from next Tuesday or until after 10 p.m. That is baloney, in all likelihood. If you are persistent or show up at the door, you will stand a good chance of being seated at a more convenient time. If you feel you are not being treated fairly on the phone, ask to speak to the maitre d' or manager.

About tipping:

- If the service was appalling and the manager unresponsive, leave nothing.
- If service was poor to fair, tip 10% to 14%.
- If service was good, meaning prompt and accurate, tip 15%.
- If service was very good, meaning an attentive server with good knowledge of the menu, leave up to 18%.
- If service was excellent, above and beyond the expected, tip up to 20%.
- If service was extraordinary, meaning unforgettable, tip 21% to 25%.

Restaurants are increasingly offering off-menu daily specials. Be careful, because the prices for these are usually considerably higher than printed menu items. Don't be afraid to ask your server for prices.

Again I must mention how volatile the dining scene is in Manhattan. Chefs and owners come and go. Restaurants change formats overnight. What is great one day can be not-so-great the next day. Because I self-publish, my information is more current than guidebooks provided by large publishers, but listings can become out-of-date before the next volume. If this happens, please accept my apologies. If you disagree with an evaluation, bear in mind that this is an informed but personal opinion. I would like to hear from you about a particularly good or bad dining experience.

Quick Reference Guide

CENTRAL PARK AREA

CHELSEA

MIDTOWN WEST

SOHO/LITTLE ITALY

THEATER DISTRICT/TIMES SQUARE

TRIBECA/DOWNTOWN/FINANCIAL DISTRICT

WEST SIDE/UPPER WEST SIDE

An Exclusive List: Hundreds of the Best Taste Treats In New York City (Eat In and Takeout)

Almond cream: Aquavit (13 W 54th St)

Antipasti, hot: Pasta Amore Trattoria (315 W 57th St)

Antipasto bar: Trattoria dell'Arte (900 Seventh Ave) and Da Umberto (107 W 17th St)

Appetizers, gourmet: Russ & Daughters (179 E Houston St)

Apple ring: Lafayette (26 Greenwich Ave)

Artichoke: La Lunchonette (130 Tenth Ave)

Babka: Gertel's (53 Hester St)

Bacon: The Kitchenette (80 West Broadway)

Baguettes: Amy's Bread (75 Ninth Ave and 672 Ninth Ave), Tribakery (186 Franklin St), and Flatiron Diner & Baking Co. (18 W 18th St)

Baked Alaska: Union Square Cafe (21 E 16th St)

Baskets, gift and corporate: Basketfull (1123 Broadway, Suite 718), Manhattan Fruitier (105 E 29th St), and Petrossian (182 W 58th St)

Beef, fillet of: King's Carriage House (251 E 82nd St)

Beef, Kobe: Two Two Two (222 79th St)

Beef (when price matters): Florence Meat Market (5 Jones St)

Beef and veal (when price is no object): M. Lobel & Sons (1096 Madison Ave)

Beef rolls, Saigon: La Soirée d'Asie (156 E 64th St)

Beef Wellington: One If By Land, Two If By Sea (17 Barrow St)

Belgian nut squares: Duane Park Patisserie (179 Duane St)

Bialys: Kossar's Bialystoker Kuchen Bakery (367 Grand St)

Bigoli (Venetian pasta): Remi (145 W 53rd St)

Biscotti (savory): Vesuvio Bakery (160 Prince St)

Biscotti (sweet): Ecce Panis (1120 Third Ave, 1260 Madison Ave, and 282 Columbus Ave)

Biscuits, blueberry-peach: Taylor's Prepared Foods (523 Hudson St, 228 W 18th St, and 175 Second Ave)

Biscuits, pepper: Vesuvio Bakery (160 Prince St)

Blintzes: Cafe Edison (228 W 47th St), Ratner's (138 Delancey St), and Kiev (117 Second Ave)

Boeuf Bourguignon (menu special): Country Cafe (69 Thompson St)

Bomboloncini (fried doughnuts with fillings): Osteria del Circo (120 W 55th St)

Borscht: Andrusha (1370 Lexington Ave)

Bouillabaisse (winter only): Gotham Bar & Grill (12 E 12th St)

Bratwurst: Schaller & Weber (1654 Second Ave)

Bread, chocolate: Amy's Bread (75 Ninth Ave and 672 Ninth Ave) and Ecce Panis (1126 Third Ave and 1260 Madison Ave)

Bread, fruit: Anglers & Writers (420 Hudson St)

Bread, general: Hot & Crusty (various locations, including Third Ave at 17th St, Second Ave at 44th St, Second Ave at 63rd St, and Broadway at 87th St)

Bread, Indian: Akbar (475 Park Ave) and Dawat (210 E 58th St)

Bread, Irish soda: Zabar's (2245 Broadway)

Bread (just baked): Pasha (70 W 71st St)

Bread, raisin nut: E.A.T. (1064 Madison Ave)

Bread pudding: Le Cirque 2000 (455 Madison Ave)

Bread, Semolina raisin fennel: Amy's Bread (672 Ninth Ave and 75 Ninth Ave)

Bread, whole wheat: Bread Shop Cafe (3139 Broadway) and Dean & Deluca (560 Broadway)

Brioche: Bonte Patisserie (1316 Third Ave), Chez Laurence Patisserie (245 Madison Ave), and Lipstick Cafe (885 Third Ave)

Brownies (best): Charles and Laurel Desserts (537 Greenwich St), Fat Witch Bakery (75 Ninth Ave), and Sarabeth's Kitchen (several locations)

Brownies, zebra: Hudson Caterers Cafe (145 Hudson St)

B'stilla: Lotfi's Moroccan Restaurant (358 W 46th St)

Buns, sticky: William Greenberg Jr. Desserts (1100 Madison Ave) and Sarabeth's Kitchen (423 Amsterdam Ave)

Burritos: Burritoville (1606 Third Ave and other locations), California Burrito Company (295 Park Ave and other locations), Harry's Burrito Junction (241 Columbus Ave and other locations), Nacho Mama's Burritos (2893 Broadway), Samalita's Tortilla Factory (1429 Third Ave), and Taqueria de Mexico (93 Greenwich Ave)

Burritos (to go): Benny's Burritos (113 Greenwich Ave and 93 Ave A)

Butcher: Balducci's (424 Ave of the Americas)

Butcher, Eastern European: Kurowycky Meat (124 First Ave)

Butcher, French: Les Halles (411 Park Ave S)

Cabbage, pickled with pork and noodles: Ollie's Noodle Shop and Grill (200 W 44th St)

Cacik: Turkish Kitchen (386 Third Ave)

Cake: Edgar's Cafe (255 W 84th St) and Ferrara (195 Grand St)

Cake, Belgian chocolate: King's Carriage House (251 E 82nd St)

Cake, blackout: Gertel's (53 Hester St) and Serendipity 3 (225 E 60th St)

Cake, Bohemian: Cupcake Cafe (522 Ninth Ave)

Cake, butter cream and chocolate: Moishe's Bakery (181 E Houston St and 115 Second Ave)

Cake, carrot: Carrot Top Pastries (3931 Broadway and 5025 Broadway)

Cake, chocolate: Second Avenue Kosher Delicatessen and Restaurant (156 Second Ave), Hard Rock Cafe (221 W 57th St), Soutine Bakery (104 W 70th St), and Jo Jo (160 E 64th St)

Cake, chocolate devil's food: An American Place (2 Park Ave)

Cake, chocolate ganache: Gramercy Tavern (42 E 20th St)

Cake, chocolate meringue with chocolate mousse: Soutine Bakery (104 W 70th St)

Cake, chocolate mousse (individual): City Bakery (22 E 17th St)

Cake, chocolate mud: Umanoff & Parsons (467 Greenwich St)

Cake, chocolate raspberry: Caffe Roma (385 Broome St)

Cake, chocolate soufflé: Taylor's Prepared Foods (523 Hudson St, 228 W 18th St, 175 Second Ave, and 156 Chambers St)

Cake, chocolate-peanut graham: Mesa Grill (102 Fifth Ave)

Cake, fruit, Milanese Italian: Bleecker Street Pastry (245 Bleecker St)

Cake, fudge layer: Caffe Bianco (1486 Second Ave)

Cake, gourmet: Salon de Thé (712 Fifth Ave, at Henri Bendel)

Cake, handmade and all natural: Umanoff & Parsons (467 Greenwich St)

Cake, Venetian wine: Canard & Co (1292 Madison Ave)

Cake, white coconut and marshmallow meringue: Magnolia Bakery (401 Bleecker St)

Calzone: Little Italy Gourmet Pizza (65 Vanderbilt Ave) and Piatti Pronti (1221 Ave of the Americas and other locations)

Candy, bonbons: Teuscher Chocolates (620 Fifth Ave and 25 E 61st St)

Candy, butter crunch: Mondel Chocolates (2913 Broadway)

Candy, caramels: Fifth Avenue Chocolatiere (510 Madison Ave)

Candy, caramel apples (by order): Philips Candy Shop (1237 Surs St, Brooklyn)

Candy, fruit jellies: La Maison du Chocolat (1018 Madison Ave)

Candy, jelly beans: Myzel Chocolates (140 W 55th St)

Cannelloni: Piemonte Homemade Ravioli Company (190 Grand St) and Giambelli (46 E 50th St)

Cannoli: Caffe Vivaldi (32 Jones St) and De Robertis Pastry Shop and Caffe (176 First Ave)

Cappuccino: Sant Ambroeus (1000 Madison Ave)

Carpaccio: Downtown (376 West Broadway)

Cassoulet: Cafe Crocodile (354 E 74th St), L'Absinthe (227 E 67th St), and Trois Jean (154 E 79th St)

Caviar: Caviar Russe (538 Madison Ave), Caviarteria (Delmonico Hotel, 502 Park Ave), Firebird (365 W 46th St), Lenox Room (1278 Third Ave), Match Uptown (33 E 60th St), and Petrossian (182 W 58th St)

Caviar (best prices): Russ & Daughters (179 E Houston St)

Ceviche (marinated seafood): Patria (250 Park Ave S) and Rosa Mexicano (1063 First Ave)

Champagne: Garnet Wines & Liquor (929 Lexington Ave) and Gotham Liquors (2519 Broadway)

Cheese, mozzarella: DiPalo Dairy (206 Grand St)

Cheese, ricotta: Alleva Dairy (188 Grand St)

Cheese cart: Parioli Romanissimo (24 E 81st St)

Cheese selection: Grace's Marketplace (1237 Third Ave), Zabar's (2245 Broadway), and Murray's Cheese Shop (257 Bleecker St)

Cheesecake, apple-mascarpone: Remi to Go (145 W 53rd St)

Cheesecake: Mitchel London Foods (22-A E 65th St)

Cheesecake, combination fruit: Eileen's Special Cheese Cake (17 Cleveland Pl)

Cheesecake, ricotta: Primavera (1578 First Ave)

Cheesecake, vanilla: Miss Grimble (909 E 135th St)

Chicken, beggar's: Shun Lee Palace (155 E 55th St) and Shun Lee West (43 W 65th St)

Chicken, dijon: Zabar's (2245 Broadway)

Chicken dishes: International Poultry (1133 Madison Ave and 983 First Ave)

Chicken, fried: All-State Cafe (250 W 72nd St), Lola (30 W 22nd St), M&G Diner (383 W 125th St), and Jezebel (630 Ninth Ave)

Chicken, grilled: Da Nico (164 Mulberry St), El Pollo (1746 First Ave), and Rainbow Chicken (2801 Broadway)

Chicken hash: 21 Club (21 W 52nd St)

Chicken-in-the-pot: Fine & Schapiro (138 W 72nd St)

Chicken, Murray's free-roaming: sold in top-quality meat markets all over the city

Chicken, parmesan: Il Mulino (86 W 3rd St)

Chicken, Peruvian style: El Pollo (1746 First Ave)

Chicken pot pie: Between the Bread (141 E 56th St and 145 W 55th St)

Chicken, roasted: Mitchel London Foods (22-A E 65th St) and Montrachet (239 West Broadway)

Chicken salad: China Grill (60 W 53rd St) and Michael's (24 W 55th St)

Chicken salad, coriander: Petak's (1246 Madison Ave)

Chicken salad, sesame: Indiana (80 Second Ave)

Chicken, Southern: Charles' Southern Style Kitchen (2839 Frederick Douglass Blvd) and Lola (30 W 22nd St)

Chicken, tandoori: Curry in a Hurry (119 Lexington Ave)

Chicken wings: Shun Lee Palace (155 E 55th St)

Chili: Manhattan Chili Company (1500 Broadway)

Chinese vegetables: Kam Man (200 Canal St)

Chocolate Bruno: Blue Ribbon Brasserie (97 Sullivan St)

Chocolate desserts: Four Seasons Hotel (57 E 57th St)

Chocolate, gratin of (seasonal): Daniel (60 E 65th St)

Chocolate indulgence: Josephina (1900 Broadway)

Chocolate tasting: Payard Patisserie (1032 Lexington Ave)

Chocolate tasting plate: Gramercy Tavern (42 E 20th St)

Chocolate truffles: La Maison du Chocolat (1018 Madison Ave)

Cholent: Second Avenue Kosher Delicatessen and Restaurant (156 Second Ave)

Chops, mutton: Keens Steakhouse (72 W 36th St)

Choucroute garni: Maureen's Passion (1200 Lexington Ave)

Clams, baked: Frank's Trattoria (371 First Ave)

Cobbler, apple: Yura (1645 Third Ave and 1292 Madison Ave)

Cobbler, strawberry rhubarb: Gramercy Tavern (42 E 20th St)

Cod, roast: Gramercy Tavern (42 E 20th St)

Coffee beans: Porto Rico Importing Company (201 Bleecker St, 107 Thompson St, 50 Grove St, and 40½ St. Marks Pl) and Zabar's (2245 Broadway)

Coffee, iced: Oren's Daily Roast (Third Ave at 30th St, 1144 Lexington Ave, 31 Waverly Pl, and 1574 First Ave)

Coffeecake: Sticky Fingers (121 First Ave)

Congee (occasionally): Lobster Club (24 E 80th St)

Cookies, butter: CBK of New York (226 E 83rd St)

Cookies, chocolate chip: Taylor's Prepared Foods (523 Hudson St, 228 W 18th St, 175 Second Ave, and 156 Chambers St) and Cookie Jar at Moomba (133 Seventh Ave S)

Cookies, chocolate chubbie: Sarabeth's Kitchen (423 Amsterdam Ave, 1295 Madison Ave, and 945 Madison Ave, at Whitney Museum) and Sarabeth's Bakery (75 Ninth Ave)

Cookies, chocolate hazelnut meringue: De Robertis (176 1st St)

Cookies, chocolate turtles: Yura (1645 Third Ave and 1292 Madison Ave)

Cookies, Mexican wedding: Word of Mouth (1012 Lexington Ave)

Corn: Popcorn Store (1275 Lexington Ave)

Cornbread: Moishe's Bakery (181 E Houston St and 115 Second Ave) and 107 West (2787 Broadway)

Corn on the cob, cheese-smeared: Cafe Habana (17 Prince St)

Corned beef: Katz's Delicatessen (205 E Houston St)
Corned beef hash: Broadway Diner (1726 Broadway and 590 Lexington Ave) and Carnegie Delicatessen and Restaurant (854 Seventh Ave)
Couscous: Provence (38 MacDougal St, Sunday only), Cafe Crocodile (354 E 74th St), and Scarabee (230 E 51st St)
Crab: Pisacane Midtown (940 First Ave)
Crab, soft shell: New York Noodle Town (28 Bowery)
Crab cakes: Tropica (200 Park Ave) and Acme Bar & Grill (9 Great Jones St)
Crème brûlèe: Le Cirque 2000 (455 Madison Ave), Tribeca Grill (375 Greenwich St), La Métairie (189 W 10th St), and Barbetta (321 W 46th St)
Crème brûlèe, coffee: Lumi (963 Lexington Ave)
Crème caramel, mocha: Etats-Unis (242 E 81st St)
Crepes: Palacinka (28 Grand St)
Croissants: City Bakery (22 E 17th St) and Paris Croissant (1776 Broadway and other locations)
Croissants, almond: Marquet Patisserie (15 E 12th St)
Cupcakes: Cupcake Cafe (522 Ninth Ave) and Magnolia Bakery (Bleecker St at 11th St)
Curry: Baluchis (193 Spring St) and Tabla (11 Madison Ave)
Custard, frozen: Custard Beach (World Financial Center, 225 Liberty St, and Grand Central Terminal, lower food court)
Danishes: Chez Le Chef (127 Lexington Ave)
Delicatessen assortment: Dean & Deluca (560 Broadway)
Dessert, all natural frozen: PAX Gourmet Deli (109 E 59th St)
Dessert, frozen, low-calorie: Tasti D-Lite (Lexington Ave at 86th St and other locations)
Doughnuts: Fisher & Levy (875 Third Ave) and Krispy Kreme (265 W 23rd St)
Doughnuts (doughnut plant): Dean & Deluca (560 Broadway) and Balducci's (424 Ave of the Americas)
Doughnuts, filled brioche: Circo Take Out (120 W 55th St)
Doughnuts, Sally Darr's: Mitchel London Foods (542 Ninth Ave)
Doughnuts, whole wheat: Cupcake Cafe (522 Ninth Ave)
Duck: Apple Restaurant (17 Waverly Pl)
Duck, Beijing: Shun Lee Palace (155 E 55th St)
Duck, braised: Quatorze Bis (323 E 79th St) and Tang Pavilion (65 W 55th St)
Duck, Peking: Home's Kitchen (22 E 21st St), Peking Duck House Restaurant (22 Mott St), Shun Lee Palace (155 E 55th St), and Shun Lee West (43 W 65th St)
Duck, roasted: La Bohême (24 Minetta Lane) and Four Seasons (99 E 52nd St)
Dumplings: Joe's Shanghai (9 Pell St), Chef Ho Dumpling House (148 W 49th St), Chin Chin (216 E 49th St), Excellent Dumpling House (111 Lafayette St), and Great Shanghai (27 Division St)
Egg cream: Gem Spa (131 Second Ave), Carnegie Delicatessen and Restaurant (854 Seventh Ave), EJ's Luncheonette (447 Amsterdam Ave and 1271 Third Ave), Mill Luncheonette (2895 Broadway), and Tom's Restaurant (782 Washington Ave, Brooklyn)
Eggs, fresh Jersey: (72 E 7th St, Thurs only: 7 a.m. to 5:30 p.m.)
Eggs, Jersey (extra large): 1750 Second Ave
Eggs, Scotch: Myers of Keswick (634 Hudson St)
Empanadas: Ruben's (64 Fulton St, 15 Bridge St, and 505 Broome St) and Empanada Oven (826 Seventh Ave)

Espresso: Chez Laurence Patisserie (245 Madison Ave) and Caffe Dante (79-81 MacDougal St)

Fada's capretto: San Domenico (240 Central Park S)

Fajitas: Zarela (953 Second Ave)

Falafel: Moshe's Falafel (442 W 45th St), Sahara East (184 First Ave), and Pita Cuisine of Soho (65 Spring St)

Fish, fresh: Citarella (2135 Broadway) and Central Fish Company (527 Ninth Ave)

Fish, gefilte: Citarella (1313 Third Ave and 2135 Broadway)

Fish (pickled herring): Sable's Smoked Fish (1489 Second Ave)

Fish, smoked: Russ & Daughters (179 E Houston St) and Barney Greengrass (541 Amsterdam Ave)

Fish steaks: Foley's Fish House (714 Seventh Ave)

Fish (sturgeon): Barney Greengrass (541 Amsterdam Ave)

Flatbreads: Kalustyan's (123 Lexington Ave)

Foie gras: Gascogne (158 8th St), Gramercy Tavern (42 E 20th St), La Caravelle (Shoreham Hotel, 33 W 55th St), Le Périgord (405 E 52nd St), and Veritas (43 E 20th St)

Fondue: Swiss Inn (311 W 48th St)

Food and kitchen equipment (best all-around in the world): Zabar's (2245 Broadway)

"Forbidden Broadway" (monstrously awesome sundae!): Serendipity 3 (225 E 60th St)

Frico (savory filled pancake-like envelope): Frico Bar (402 W 43rd St)

Fries, Tuscan: Coco Pazzo (Paramount Hotel, 23 E 74th St)

Frites (French fries with mayonnaise): Le Frite Kot (148 W 4th St) and Pommes Frites (724 Seventh Ave)

Fruits and vegetables, fresh: Fairway (2127 Broadway) and Balducci's (424 Ave of the Americas)

Fruit dessert plate: Primavera (1578 First Ave)

Game: Ottomanelli's Meat Market (285 Bleecker St) and Da Umberto (107 W 17th St)

Gateau Charlene Blanche: Patisserie J. Lanciani (414 W 14th St)

Gelati: Caffe Dante (81 MacDougal St)

Gift basket: Petrossian (182 W 58th St)

Gingerbread house: Chez Le Chef (127 Lexington Ave)

Goat, roast baby: Primavera (1578 First Ave)

Groceries, discount: Gourmet Garage (453 Broome St, 301 E 64th St, 2567 Broadway, and 117 Seventh Ave S)

Guacamole: Manhattan Chili Company (1500 Broadway) and Rosa Mexicano (1063 First Ave)

Haggis: St. Andrews (120 W 44th St)

Halibut, poached: Le Bernardin (155 W 51st St)

Ham, baked: Little Jezebel Plantation (529 Columbus Ave)

Ham, peach-glazed: Word of Mouth (1012 Lexington Ave)

Hamburgers: Jackson Hole Burgers (232 E 64th St and other locations), Corner Bistro (331 W 4th St), and Hamburger Harry's (145 W 45th St)

Hamburgers, roquefort: Burger Heaven (9 E 53rd St)

Hen, Cornish: Lorenzo and Maria's Kitchen (1418 Third Ave)

Hen, grilled Guinea: Babbo (110 Waverly Pl)

Heros: Italian Food Center (186 Grand St) and Hero Boy (492 Ninth Ave)

Heros, sausage: Manganaro Grosseria Italiana (488 Ninth Ave)

Hors d'oeuvres, hot: Dufour Pastry Kitchen (25 Ninth Ave)
Hot chocolate: City Bakery (22 E 17th St)
Hot dogs: Brooklyn Diner USA (212 W 57th St), Old Town Bar (45 E 18th St), Gray's Papaya (8th St at Ave of the Americas, 2090 Broadway), and Papaya King (86th St at Third Ave)
Huitlacoche (Mexican specialty): Rosa Mexicano (1063 First Ave)
Ice cream: Serendipity 3 (225 E 60th St)
Ice cream, caramel: Gramercy Tavern (42 E 20th St)
Ice cream, coffee: Starbucks (many locations)
Ice cream, white pepper: Vong (200 E 54th St)
Ice cream soda: Judson Grill (152 W 52nd St)
Ice cream sundae: Brooklyn Diner USA (212 W 57th St)
Jambalaya: 107 West (2787 Broadway)
Kebabs: Turkish Cuisine (631 Ninth Ave) and Turkish Kitchen (386 Third Ave)
Kielbasa: First Avenue Meat Products (140 First Ave)
Kielbasa spring roll: Pat Pong (93 E 7th St)
Knishes: Murray's Sturgeon Shop (2429 Broadway)
Lamb, rack of: Cafe des Artistes (1 W 67th St) and Gotham Bar & Grill (12 E 12th St)
Lamb shank: Bolo (23 E 22nd St) and Molyvos (871 Seventh Ave)
Lamb stew: Bouterin (420 E 59th St) and Pamir (1437 Second Ave)
Lasagna: Barocco (301 Church St)
Latkes: Just Like Mother's (110-60 Queens Blvd, Forest Hills, Queens)
Lemonade: Lexington Candy Shop (1226 Lexington Ave)
Liver, chopped: Fischer Brothers (230 W 72nd St) and Second Avenue Kosher Delicatessen and Restaurant (156 Second Ave)
Lobster: Docks Oyster Bar and Seafood Grill (2427 Broadway and 633 Third Ave) and Wilkinson's Seafood (1573 York Ave)
Lobster bisque (catering): Neuman & Bogdonoff (173 Christie St)
Lobster, live: Blue Ribbon Sushi (119 Sullivan St)
Lobster risotto: Le Cirque 2000 (455 Madison Ave)
Lobster Roll: Pearl Oyster Bar (18 Cornelia St)
Macaroni and cheese: E.A.T. (1064 Madison Ave)
Mahi-mahi (grilled): American Park (Battery Park at State St)
Marinara sauce: Patsy's (236 W 56th St)
Marzipan: Elk Candy (1628 Second Ave) and La Maison du Chocolat (1018 Madison Ave)
Matzoh Brei: Lobster Club (24 E 80th St)
Meat (best prices): Empire Purveyors (901 First Ave)
Meat (best service): H. Oppenheimer Meats (2606 Broadway) and Jefferson Market (450 Ave of the Americas)
Meat (cold-cut selection): Schaller & Weber (1654 Second Ave)
Meat (designer sausage): Salumeria Biellese (376-378 Eighth Ave)
Meat (German deli): Schaller & Weber (1654 Second Ave)
Meat (grill-ready): Les Halles (411 Park Ave S)
Meat, kosher (grilled): Cafe Masada (1239 First Ave)
Meatloaf: Lobster Club (24 E 80th St), Mortimer's Restaurant (1057 Lexington Ave), and Word of Mouth (1012 Lexington Ave)
Meat (pork): H. Oppenheimer Meats (2606 Broadway)
Meat (prime): Jefferson Market (450 Ave of the Americas)
Meat (steak, price no object): Old Homestead (56 Ninth Ave)
Meat (tandoori): Curry in a Hurry (119 Lexington Ave)

Meat (wholesale): Old Bohemian Meat (452 W 13th St)
Meats and poultry (reasonably priced): Empire Purveyors (901 First Ave)
Mediterranean foodstuffs: Mezze (10 E 44th St)
Mexican foodstuffs: Kitchen Market (218 Eighth Ave)
Middle Eastern foodstuffs: Soho Provisions (518 Broadway) and Turkish Grill (193 Bleecker St)
Milkshake: Comfort Diner (214 E 45th St)
Moussaka: Periyali (35 W 20th St)
Mousse, chocolate (the best!): Bistro Margot (26 Prince St)
Mousse, white chocolate, in a bittersweet chocolate basket: Manhattan Ocean Club (57 W 58th St)
Mozzarella: Distasi (484 Ninth Ave) and Melampo Imported Foods (105 Sullivan St)
Mozzarella and ricotta (homemade): Russo and Son (344 E 11th St)
Muffins: Between the Bread (145 W 55th St and 141 E 56th St), My Favorite Muffins (11 John St), Lee & Elle (336 Madison Ave), and Connecticut Muffin (206 Elizabeth St)
Muffins, corn: 107 West (2787 Broadway)
Muffins, nonfat: Brooklyn Diner USA (212 W 57th St)
Muffins, pear-walnut: Soutine Bakery (104 W 70th St)
Mushrooms, grilled portobello: Giovanni 25 (25 E 83rd St)
Mushrooms, wild: Grace's Marketplace (1237 Third Ave)
Mussels: Jubilee (347 E 54th St)
Nachos: Benny's Burritos (93 Ave A and 113 Greenwich Ave)
Napoleon: Montrachet (239 West Broadway) and Ecco (124 Chambers St)
Natural foods: Whole Foods Markets (117 Prince St and 2421 Broadway)
Noodles: Honmura An (170 Mercer St) and Sammy's Noodle Shop & Grill (453 Ave of the Americas)
Noodles, Asian: Republic (37 Union Sq W)
Noodles, buckwheat: Honmura An (170 Mercer St)
Noodles, cold, with hot sesame sauce: Sung Chu Mei (615 Hudson St)
Noodles, Shanghai-style: Shun Lee Palace (155 E 55th St)
Noodles soba: Honmura An (170 Mercer St)
Nuts: A.L. Bazzini Co. (339 Greenwich St)
Nuts and packaged dried fruits (great prices): J. Wolsk and Company (81 Ludlow St)
Oatmeal: Sarabeth's Kitchen (1295 Madison Ave, 423 Amsterdam Ave, and 945 Madison Ave, at Whitney Museum)
Olives: International Grocery (529 Ninth Ave)
Omelets: Romaine de Lyon (132 E 61st St)
Onion rings: Home Restaurant (20 Cornelia St), Palm (837 Second Ave), and Lola (30 W 22nd St)
Orange juice, fresh-squeezed: hole-in-the-wall stand at 1428 Ave of the Americas
Organic foods: Angelica's (147 First Ave) and Urban Organics (718/499-4321, home delivery)
Oyster stew: Grand Central Oyster Bar Restaurant (Grand Central Station)
Oysters, Louisiana: Cafe des Artistes (1 W 67th St)
Oysters Rockefeller: City Hall (131 Duane St)
Paella: Bolo (23 E 22nd St) and Sevilla (62 Charles St)
Panna cotta (dessert): Gramercy Tavern (42 E 20th St)
Pancakes: Friend of a Farmer (77 Irving Pl) and Vinegar Factory (431 E 91st St)

Pancakes, blue corn (weekends): Mesa Grill (102 Fifth Ave)
Pancakes, kimchi: Dok Suni's (119 First Ave)
Pancakes, potato: Rolf's (281 Third Ave)
Pasta: Arqua (281 Church St), Artusi (36 W 52nd St), Bottino (246 Tenth Ave), Cafe Pertutti (2888 Broadway), Caffe Buon Gusto (236 E 77th St), Cinque Terre (22 E 38th St), Col Legno (231 E 9th St), Follonico (6 W 24th St), Fresco by Scotto (34 E 52nd St), Gabriel's (11 W 60th St), Il Valentino (330 E 56th St), Paola's (343 E 85th St), and Todaro Bros. (555 Second Ave)
Pasta, angel hair: Piemonte Homemade Ravioli Company (190 Grand St) and Nanni's (146 E 46th St)
Pasta, handmade egg: Balducci's (424 Ave of the Americas)
Pasta (inexpensive): La Marca (161 E 22nd St)
Pasta, Venetian: Remi (145 W 53rd St)
Pastrami: Carnegie Delicatessen and Restaurant (854 Seventh Ave)
Pastrami, salmon: Park Avenue Cafe (100 E 63rd St)
Pastries: Bleecker Street Pastry (245 Bleecker St)
Pastries, charlotte russe: Jon Vie Pastries (492 Ave of the Americas)
Pastries, French: La Bergamote (169 Ninth Ave)
Pastries, Hungarian: Hungarian Pastry Shop (1030 Amsterdam Ave)
Pastries, Italian: LaBella Ferrara Pastry & Caffe (108-110 Mulberry St) and Rocco Pastry Shop (243 Bleecker St)
Paté: Les Trois Petite Cochons (453 Greenwich St)
Peanuts, candied: A.L. Bazzini Co. (339 Greenwich St)
Penne with prosciutto: Petak's (1246 Madison Ave)
Pickles: Pickle-Licious (580 Amsterdam Ave)
Pickles, sour or half-sour: Russ & Daughters (179 E Houston St)
Pie, apple: William Greenberg Jr. Desserts (1100 Madison Ave) and Yura (1645 Third Ave and 1292 Madison Ave)
Pie, apple crumb: Cupcake Cafe (522 Ninth Ave)
Pie, banana cream: Sarabeth's Kitchen (several locations)
Pie, caramel-nut crunch: Houlihan's (729 Seventh Ave and other locations)
Pie, cheddar-crust apple (fall only): Little Pie Company (424 W 43rd St)
Pie, cherry crumb (summer only): Magnolia Bakery (401 Bleecker St)
Pie, duck shepherd's: Balthazar (80 Spring St)
Pie, key lime: Little Pie Company (424 W 43rd St) and Union Square Cafe (21 E 16th St)
Pie, pecan: Magnolia Bakery (401 Bleecker St)
Pie, shepherd's: Landmark Tavern (626 Eleventh Ave)
Pie, walnut sour-cream apple: Little Pie Company (424 W 43rd St)
Pies: Bespeckled Trout (422 Hudson St)
Pig sandwich (pulled pork): Hard Rock Cafe (221 W 57th St)
Pig's feet: Cafe Boulud (20 E 76th St) and Daniel (60 E 65th St)
Pizza and calzone: House of Pizza and Calzone (132 Union St, Brooklyn)
Pizza, designer: Paper Moon Milano (39 E 58th St)
Pizza, Neopolitan slice: Sal's & Carmine Pizza (2671 Broadway) and Stromboli Pizzeria (112 University Pl)
Pizza, Sicilian: Sal's and Carmine Pizza (2671 Broadway)
Pommes frites (French fries): Cafe de Bruxelles (118 Greenwich Ave)
Popcorn: Popcorn Store (1275 Lexington Ave)
Popovers: Popover Cafe (551 Amsterdam Ave)
Pork: 69 Mott Street (69 Mott St)
Pork, braised breast: Daniel (60 E 65th St)

Pork, European-style cured: Salumeria Biellese (376 Eighth Ave)
Pork chops, smoked: Yorkville Packing House (1560 Second Ave)
Pork shank: Maloney & Porcelli's (37 E 50th St)
Pot de crème: Verbena (54 Irving Pl)
Potato chips: Vinegar Factory (431 E 91st St)
Potatoes (Belgian-style fries): Le Frite Kot (148 W 4th St)
Potatoes (French fries): Cafe de Bruxelles (118 Greenwich Ave), Cafe de Paris (924 Second Ave), Grand Salon (158 E 23rd St), Michael's (24 W 55th St), Petite Abeille (466 Hudson St), Steak Frites (9 E 16th St), and Tout Va Bien (311 W 51st St)
Potatoes, huge stuffed baked: Citarella (2135 Broadway)
Potatoes, mashed: Lenox Room (1278 Third Ave) and Union Square Cafe (21 E 16th St)
Pot-au-feu: Bouterin (420 E 59th St; seasonal), Cafe des Artistes (1 W 67th St), and Le Bernardin (155 W 51st St)
Pretzels: Pennsylvania Pretzel Company (295 Greenwich St)
Pretzels and cookies, hand-dipped chocolate: Evelyn's Chocolates (4 John St)
Prime rib: Fresco by Scotto (34 E 52nd St), Two Two Two (222 W 79th St), and Smith & Wollensky (201 E 49th St)
Produce, fresh: Fairway Market (2127 Broadway)
Profiteroles: Chez Ma Tante (189 W 10th St)
Pudding, rice: Marti Kebab (238 E 24th St), Marti's Turkish Restaurant (1269 First Ave), and Word of Mouth (1012 Lexington Ave)
Quiche: Chez Laurence Patisserie (245 Madison Ave)
Raspberry Charlotte: Dolci on Park (12 Park Ave)
Ravioli: Russo's (344 E 11th St), Osteria del Circo (120 W 55th St), Ravioli Store (75 Sullivan St), Piemonte Homemade Ravioli Company (190 Grand St), and Di Palo Fine Food (206 Grand St)
Ravioli, steamed Vietnamese: Indochine (430 Lafayette St)
Red snapper, roasted (seasonal): Daniel (60 E 65th St)
Ribollita (hearty Tuscan bean soup): Trattoria Dopo Teatro (125 W 44th St)
Ribs: Hog Pit (22 Ninth Ave), Tennessee Mountain (121 W 45th St), Sylvia's Restaurant (328 Lenox Ave), Wylie's Ribs and Company (891 First Ave), and Brother Jimmy's Bar-B-Q (1461 First Ave)
Ribs, baby back: Baby Buddha (753 Washington St), Emily's (1325 Fifth Ave), Mesa Grill (102 Fifth Ave), and Ruby Foo's Dim Sum & Sushi Palace (2182 Broadway)
Ribs, beer-braised: Verbena (54 Irving Pl)
Ribs, braised, short beef: Daniel (60 E 65th St; seasonal) and Spartina (355 Greenwich St)
Rice: Rice (227 Mott St)
Rice, sticky, with mango: Vong (200 E 54th St)
Risotto: Four Seasons (99 E 52nd St)
Rogoleh: Royale Pastry Shop (237 W 72nd St)
Rugalach: Ruth's Cheesecake and Rugalach Bakery (75 Ninth Ave)
Salad bar: Azure (830 Third Ave), Mezze (10 E 44th St)
Salad bar (Greenmarket-driven): City Bakery (22 E 17th St)
Salad, Caesar: Post House (28 E 63rd St)
Salad, egg: Murray's Sturgeon Shop (2429 Broadway)
Salad, lobster: Sable's Smoked Fish (1489 Second Ave) and Hurricane Island (1303 Third Ave)
Salad, potato, Nicoise: Manny Wolf's (145 E 49th St)

Salad, seafood: Gotham Bar & Grill (12 E 12th St)
Salad, tuna: Murray's Sturgeon Shop (2429 Broadway), Cosi Sandwich Bar (numerous locations), and Todaro Bros. (555 Second Ave)
Salad, veal Oscar: Oscar's at the Waldorf-Astoria (301 Park Ave)
Salad, warm white bean: Caffe Grazie (26 E 84th St)
Salad, whitefish: Barney Greengrass (541 Amsterdam Ave)
Salmon: Jo Jo (160 E 64th St)
Salmon cakes: All-State Cafe (250 W 72nd St)
Salmon filets, Norwegian: Sea Breeze (541 Ninth Ave)
Salmon, marinated: La Réserve (4 W 49th St)
Salmon, smoked: Aquavit (13 W 54th St) and Murray's Sturgeon Shop (2429 Broadway)
Salmon, truffle-crusted: Montrachet (239 West Broadway)
Sandwich, bacon, lettuce & tomato: Bread & Butter (229 Elizabeth St)
Sandwich, beef brisket: Smith's Bar & Restaurant (701 Eighth Ave) and Second Avenue Kosher Delicatessen and Restaurant (156 Second Ave)
Sandwich, chicken: Ranch 1 (62 Pearl St and other locations)
Sandwich, Thai chicken: Cosi Sandwich Bar (numerous locations)
Sandwich, grilled portobello: Zoë (90 Prince St)
Sandwich, grilled chicken breast: Island Burgers & Shakes (766 Ninth Ave) and Ranch 1 (684 Third Ave and other locations)
Sandwich, loin of pork: Bottino (246 Tenth Ave)
Sandwich, croque monsieur: Payard Patisserie (1032 Lexington Ave)
Sandwich, po' boy: Two Boots (37 Ave A)
Sandwich, poulet roti: Chez Brigitte (77 Greenwich Ave)
Sandwich, puff-pastry: Dufour Pastry Kitchen (25 Ninth Ave)
Sandwich, tuna: Melampo Imported Foods (105 Sullivan St)
Sandwich, turkey: Viand Coffee Shop (1011 Madison Ave)
Sandwich wraps: Emerald Planet (2 Great Jones St)
Sardines, marinated: Oceana (55 E 54th St)
Satays: Typhoon Brewery (22 E 54th St)
Sauerkraut: Katz's Delicatessen (205 E Houston St)
Sausage, East European: Kurowycky Meat Products (124 First Ave)
Sausage, Italian: Corona Heights Pork Store (107-04 Corona Ave, Queens)
Sausage, Tuscan: Toscana (843 Lexington Ave)
Scallops: Bouley (165 Duane St) and Le Bernardin (155 W 51st St)
Schnecken: William Greenberg Jr. Desserts (1100 Madison Ave)
Scones: Tea & Sympathy (108-110 Greenwich Ave), Muffin Shop (Columbus Ave at 70th St), and Mangia (50 W 57th St and 16 E 48th St)
Seafood dinners: Pisces (95 Ave A), Wilkinson's Seafood (1573 York Ave), Le Bernardin (155 W 51st St), and Le Pescadou (18 King St)
Seafood platter: Mezzogiorno (195 Spring St)
Shabu-Shabu: Seryna (11 E 53rd St)
Shrimp Creole: Jezebel (630 Ninth Ave)
Shrimp, roasted: Periyali (35 W 20th St)
Singing waiters: Asti (13 E 12th St)
Skate: Butterfield 81 (170 E 81st St)
Sliders (mini burgers): Sassy's Sliders (163 First Ave)
Smorgasbord starter: Christer's (145 W 55th St)
Snacks, soups and sandwiches: Serendipity 3 (225 E 60th St)
Snails (menu special): Lutèce (249 E 50th St)
Sole, Dover: Parioli Romanissimo (24 E 81st St)
Sorbet: La Boite en Bois (75 W 68th St)

Soufflé: Capsouto Frères (451 Washington St), La Caravelle (33 W 55th St), and La Côte Basque (60 W 55th St)

Soufflé, chocolate: Jean Georges (1 Central Park W) and La Réserve (4 W 49th St)

Soufflé, chocolate mint: La Caravelle (Shoreham Hotel, 33 W 55th St)

Soufflé, glace pistache (seasonal): Daniel (60 E 65th St)

Soufflé, Grand Marnier: La Grenouille (3 E 52nd St)

Soufflé, lemon: Gramercy Tavern (42 E 20th St)

Soup, black bean: Union Square Cafe (21 E 16th St) and International Poultry (1133 Madison Ave and 983 First Ave)

Soup, chestnut & fennel (seasonal): Picholine (35 W 64th St)

Soup, chestnut with mushroom ravioli: Jean Georges (1 Central Park W)

Soup, chicken: Brooklyn Diner USA (212 W 57th St) and Second Avenue Kosher Delicatessen and Restaurant (156 Second Ave)

Soup, Chinese: Chao Chow (111 Mott St)

Soup (clam chowder): Aquagrill (210 Spring St)

Soup (clam chowder, Manhattan): Rosedale Fish and Oyster Market (1129 Lexington Ave)

Soup, duck: Kelley & Ping (127 Greene St)

Soup, French onion: La Bonne Soupe (48 W 55th St)

Soup, homemade: Kiev (Second Ave at 7th St)

Soup, hot and sour: Shun Lee Cafe (43 W 65th St)

Soup, lobster (seasonal): Peacock Alley (Waldorf-Astoria Hotel, 301 Park Ave)

Soup, Mandalay fish: Road to Mandalay (380 Broome St)

Soup, minestrone: Il Vagabondo (351 E 62nd St) and Trattoria Spaghetto (232 Bleecker St)

Soup, mushroom: Flavors (8 W 18th St)

Soup, noodle: New Chao Chow (111 Mott St)

Soup, parmentier (seasonal): Peacock Alley (Waldorf-Astoria Hotel, 301 Park Ave)

Soup, pumpkin (seasonal): Mesa Grill (102 Fifth Ave)

Soup, raison d'être: Shopsin's General Store (63 Bedford St)

Soup, tomato: Sarabeth's Kitchen (423 Amsterdam Ave, 1295 Madison Ave, and 945 Madison Ave at Whitney Museum)

Soup, yellow squash and rosemary: Yura (1645 Third Ave and 1292 Madison Ave)

Spaghetti: Paolucci (149 Mulberry St)

Spareribs, Chinese: Fu's (972 Second Ave)

Spices: Aphrodisia (264 Bleecker St), International Grocery (529 Ninth Ave), and Kalustyan's (123 Lexington Ave)

Spicy food: Hot Stuff (227 Sullivan St)

Spinach pies, Greek: Poseidon Greek Bakery (629 Ninth Ave)

Spring rolls, crab: Vong (200 E 54th St)

Squid, grilled stuffed: I Trulli (122 E 27th St)

Steak, Black Angus, and French fries: Steak Frites (9 E 16th St)

Steak, Cajun rib: Morton's of Chicago (551 Fifth Ave and 90 West St) and Post House (28 E 63rd St)

Steak, pepper: Chez Josephine (414 W 42nd St)

Steak, Porterhouse: Manhattan Cafe (1161 First Ave) and Morton's of Chicago (551 Fifth Ave and 90 West St)

Steak, strip: Restaurant Charlotte (145 W 44th St)

Steak fries: Balthazar (80 Spring St)

Steak tartare: 21 Club (21 W 52nd St)

Strawberry shortcake: An American Place (2 Park Ave)

String beans, Chinese-style: Tang Tang (1328 Third Ave)

Striped bass (menu special): Cellini (65 E 54th St)

Strudel: Big Apple Strudel (1652 Second Ave) and Mocca Hungarian (1588 Second Ave)

Sushi: Takahachi (85 Ave A), Kuruma Zushi (7 E 47th St, 2nd floor), Sushihatsu (1143 First Ave), Avenue A Sushi (103 Ave A), Iso (175 Second Ave), Ten Kai (20 W 56th St), Hatsuhana (17 E 48th St), and Nippon (155 E 52nd St)

Swordfish, grilled (menu special): Chez Ma Tante (189 W 10th St)

Tabbouleh: Benny's (321½ Amsterdam Ave)

Tacos: Fresco Tortilla Grill (36 Lexington Ave, 253 Eighth Ave, 769 Ave of the Americas, and 125 W 42nd St)

Tamales: Rosa Mexicano (1063 First Ave, seasonal) and Zarela (953 Second Ave)

Tapas, Spanish: Domingo (209 E 49th St), El Cid (322 W 15th St), ñ (33 Crosby St), Solera (216 E 53rd St), and Tapestry (575 Hudson St)

Tart, a la banane (seasonal): Daniel (60 E 65th St)

Tart, apple: Gotham Bar & Grill (12 E 12th St), Marquet Patisserie (15 E 12th St), and Quatorze Bis (323 E 79th St)

Tart, chocolate: Le Bernardin (155 W 51st St)

Tart, fruit: Ceci-Cela (55 Spring St) and Payard Patisserie (1032 Lexington Ave)

Tart, fruit and vegetable: Once Upon a Tart (135 Sullivan St)

Tart, lemon: Margot Patisserie (2109 Broadway)

Tarts and logs, stuffed puff pastry: Dufour Pastry Kitchen (25 Ninth Ave)

Tartufo: Erminia (250 E 83rd St) and Il Corallo (172-176 Prince St)

Tempura: Inagiku (Waldorf-Astoria, 111 E 49th St)

Tiramisu: Torre di Pisa (19 W 44th St), Mezzogiorno (195 Spring St), Caffe Dante (79 MacDougal St), and Biricchino (260 W 29th St)

Tong shui (Chinese soup): Sweet-n-Tart Cafe (76 Mott St)

Tonkatsu: Katsu-Hama (11 E 47th St)

Torta Milanesa: Mexico Lindo (459 Second Ave)

Torte, chocolate raspberry: Ecce Panis (1126 Third Ave)

Torte, sacher: Duane Park Patisserie (179 Duane St)

Torte, toffee: Circa (103 Second Ave)

Torte, Viennese chocolate: Peacock Caffe (24 Greenwich Ave)

Tripe (menu special): Les Halles (411 Park Ave S)

Truffles: Black Hound (170 Second Ave) and La Maison du Chocolat (25 E 73rd St)

Truffles, champagne: Teuscher Chocolates (25 E 61st St and 620 Fifth Ave)

Tuna, seared: Two Two Two (222 W 79th St)

Tuna steak: Union Square Cafe (21 E 16th St)

Tuna tartare: Tropica (MetLife Building, 200 Park Ave) and Le Cirque 2000 (455 Madison Ave)

Turbot: Jean Georges (1 Central Park W) and Montrachet (239 West Broadway)

Turnover, apple: La Boulangere (49 E 21st St)

Veal: Pierre au Tunnel (250 W 47th St)

Veal chops: Aperitivo (29 W 56th St), Daniel (60 E 65th St), and La Réserve (4 W 49th St)

Veal cutlet: Trastevere (309 E 83rd St)

Veal scaloppini (special): Zinno's (126 W 13th St)

Veal stew (menu special): Pierre au Tunnel (250 W 47th St)

Vegan baking: Whole Earth Bakery & Kitchen (130 St. Marks Pl)

Vegetable terrine: Montrachet (239 West Broadway)
Vegetarian combo: Hudson Falafel (516 Hudson St)
Vegetarian items: Vegetarian's Paradise (144 W 4th St)
Vegetarian meals: Natural Gourmet Cookery School (48 W 21st St)
Veggies, raw: Estiatorio Milos (125 W 55th St)
Venison (seasonal): Chanterelle (2 Harrison St)
Waffles, Belgian: Le Pain Quotidien (1131 Madison Ave), Petite Abeille (107 W 18th St), and Cafe de Bruxelles (118 Greenwich Ave)
Waffles, pumpkin: Sarabeth's Kitchen (1295 Madison Ave, 423 Amsterdam Ave, and 945 Madison Ave, at Whitney Museum)
Wagashi (Japanese sweets): Minamoto Kitchoan (49th St at Fifth Ave)
Whiskeys, malt: Soho Wines & Spirits (461 West Broadway)
Wine, European: Quality House (2 Park Ave)
Wine, French: Park Avenue Liquors (292 Madison Ave) and Quality House (2 Park Ave)
Wine, German: First Avenue Wines & Spirits (383 First Ave)
Yogurt, "Only 8" frozen: Peppermint Park Cafe (1225 First Ave)
Zabaglione: Il Monello (1460 Second Ave)

Appetizers

Barney Greengrass (541 Amsterdam Ave): sturgeon king
Caviarteria (502 Park Ave): a small caviar heaven
Murray's Sturgeon Shop (2429 Broadway): old-time reliability
Russ & Daughters (179 E Houston St): the very best, with a personal touch
Zabar's (2245 Broadway): There's no place in the world like it!

Bagels

Absolute Bagels (2788 Broadway)
Bagel City (720 W 181st St)
Bagel Works (1229 First Ave)
Bagelry (1324 Lexington Ave, 1380 Madison Ave, and 1228 Lexington Ave)
Columbia Hot Bagels (2836 Broadway)
Daniel's Bagel Corp. (569 Third Ave)
Ess-a-Bagel (359 First Ave and 831 Third Ave)
H&H Bagels (2239 Broadway and 639 W 46th St)
H&H Bagels East (1551 Second Ave)
Hot Bagels (168 Madison Ave)
Lenny's (2601 Broadway)
Mom's Catering (15 W 45th St)
Murray's Bagels (500 Ave of the Americas)
Pick-a-Bagel (1083 Lexington Ave)

Barbecues

Big Wong (67 Mott St): Chinese style
Brother's Bar-B-Q (228 W Houston St): smoked ribs
Churrascaria Plataforma (Belvedere Hotel, 316 W 49th St)
Copeland's (547 W 145th St): Harlem setting
Dallas BBQ (1265 Third Ave, 27 W 72nd St, 21 University Place, and 132 Second Ave): big and busy, but only fair in quality
Shun Lee Cafe (43 W 65th St): classy Chinese
Sylvia's Restaurant (328 Lenox Ave): reputation is better than the food
Virgil's Real Barbecue (152 W 44th St): big, brassy, mass-production

Bistros

Alison on Dominick Street (38 Dominick St)
Balthazar (80 Spring St)
Cafe Boulud (20 E 76th St)
Chelsea Bistro & Bar (358 W 23rd St)
Jean Claude (137 Sullivan St)
Jo Jo (160 E 64th St)
Le Gigot (18 Cornelia St)
Le Jardin Bistro (25 Cleveland Pl)
Montrachet (239 West Broadway)
Payard Patisserie and Bistro (1032 Lexington Ave)
Raoul's (180 Prince St)
Rive Gauche (560 Third Ave)
Trois Jean (154 E 79th St)

Breakfast

Breakfast is a big deal in New York. Some folks use it for a business setting, others for a social get-together. More and more people look at their first meal of the day as something healthy before or after a morning workout. Still others want something tasty and quick at a good price.

For the real *power* scenes, hotels are the preferred locations. The biggest names are the **Regency** (540 Park Ave), the **Peninsula New York** (700 Fifth Ave), **Fifty-seven Fifty-seven,** at the **Four Seasons** (57 E 57th St), the **Paramount** (235 W 46th St), and the **Royalton** (44 W 44th St).

Other recommended places with excellent day-starters include **Aggie's** (146 Houston St), **Balthazar** (80 Spring St), **Bubby's** (120 Hudson St), **Cafe Botanica** (Essex House, 160 Central Park S), **Cafe Word of Mouth** (1012 Lexington Ave), **Comfort Diner** (214 E 45th St), **EJ's Luncheonette** (447 Amsterdam Ave), **Ellen's Stardust Diner** (1377 Ave of the Americas), **Jerry's** (101 Prince St), **Le Gamin** (50 MacDougal St), **Noho Star** (330 Lafayette St), **Payard Patisserie** (1032 Lexington Ave), **Popover Cafe** (551 Amsterdam Ave), **Sarabeth's Kitchen** (423 Amsterdam Ave, 1295 Madison Ave, and 945 Madison Ave, at Whitney Museum), **Tivoli** (515 Third Ave), and **Tramway Coffee Shop** (1143 Second Ave).

The breads are great (and expensive) at Eli Zabar's **E.A.T.** (1064 Madison Ave), and the pancakes at **Fifty-seven Fifty-seven** (57 E 57th St) are excellent. **Aggie's** (146 W Houston St) has home fries that are hard to beat (so are her bacon and omelets), **Friend of a Farmer** (77 Irving Pl) has a late pancake feast, and the **Columbus Bakery** (474 Columbus Ave) offers sinful cheese danishes and yummy croissants. **Carnegie Delicatessen and Restaurant's** (854 Seventh Ave) trio of cheese blintzes only have half-a-million calories, while **Serafina on the Run** (38 E 58th St) has great egg dishes. Of note is the exuberant all-day breakfast at **Norma's** (118 W 57th St), in the Parker Meridien Hotel. One of the more popular places for breakfast is **Cafe Europa** (1177 Ave of the Americas).

Insider Breakfast Tip!

Look like you belong there as you stroll into the **Pfizer** (yes, the Viagra maker) cafeteria (235 E 42nd St, bet Second and Third Ave, 2nd floor; 7:30 a.m. to 10 a.m.). The food is good and healthy, and the price is right. Just don't tell 'em I sent you!

Brunch

Aquagrill (210 Spring St)
Amici Miei (472 West Broadway): outdoor garden in summer
Cafe Botanica (Essex House Westin, 160 Central Park S)
Cafe des Artistes (1 W 67th St): Both ambience and food are classy.
Canal House (310 West Broadway, parlor floor)
Capsouto Frères (451 Washington St)
Cendrillon (45 Mercer St): Filipino flavors
Chelsea Bistro & Bar (358 W 23rd St)
Crystal Fountain (Grand Hyatt Hotel, Park Ave at Grand Central Station)
Cub Room (131 Sullivan St)
Cupping Room Cafe (359 West Broadway)
Danal (90 E 10th St): luscious French toast
Emily's (1325 Fifth Ave): soul food
Friend of a Farmer (77 Irving Pl)
Iridium (44 W 63rd St): live gospel music
Julian's (802 Ninth Ave)
Lobster Club (24 E 80th St)
Lola (30 W 22nd St)
Mark's Restaurant (25 E 77th St): classy
Match Uptown (33 E 66th St and 160 Mercer St)
Mesa Grill (102 Fifth Ave)
Miracle Grill (112 First Ave)
Odeon (145 West Broadway)
Paris Commune (411 Bleecker St): Bohemian West Village bistro
Park Avenue Cafe (100 E 63rd St): American dim sum, Saturday only
Peacock Alley (Waldorf-Astoria Hotel, 301 Park Ave)
Provence (38 MacDougal St)
River Cafe (1 Water St, Brooklyn)
Sarabeth's Kitchen (423 Amsterdam Ave, 1295 Madison Ave, and 945 Madison Ave, at Whitney Museum): dependably good food in a relaxed environment
Soho Steak (90 Thompson St): high-protein bistro fare
Tapika (950 Eighth Ave): Southwestern
Tartine (253 W 11th St)
Tavern on the Green (Central Park at 67th St): for entertaining out-of-town guests
Vinegar Factory (431 E 91st St)
Voulez-Vous (1462 First Ave): marvelous steak tartare
Water Club (500 E 30th St)

Some brunch bargains:

Arlo's (1394 York Ave)
EJ's Luncheonette (433 Amsterdam Ave)
Landmark Tavern (626 Eleventh Ave)
Popover Cafe (551 Amsterdam Ave)

Burgers

Aggie's (146 W Houston)
All-State Cafe (250 W 72nd St)
Alva (36 E 22nd St)

Baby Jake's (14 First Ave)
Bar 89 (89 Mercer St)
Big Nick's (2175 Broadway): You'll love it!
Billy's (948 First Ave)
Blue Ribbon Bakery (33 Downing St)
Bolivar (206 E 60th St)
Brew's (156 E 34th St)
Burger Heaven (20 E 49th St)
Cafe de Bruxelles (118 Greenwich Ave)
Cal's (55 W 21st St): excellent
Chelsea Grill (135 Eighth Ave)
Chumley's (86 Bedford St)
Corner Bistro (331 W 4th St)
Diane's Downtown (249 Columbus Ave)
Fanelli (94 Prince St)
44 (Royalton Hotel, 44 W 44th St)
Hamburger Harry's (145 W 45th St)
Hard Rock Cafe (221 W 57th St): The action is as tasty as the burgers!
Home Restaurant (20 Cornelia St)
Jackson Hole Burgers (232 E 64th St, Third Ave at 35th St, and Second Ave
     at 84th St)
Keens Steakhouse (72 W 36th St)
Knickerbocker Bar and Grill (33 University Pl)
Madison Pub (980 Madison Ave)
McDonald's (160 Broadway): This one has class.
Michael Jordan's, the Steak House (Grand Central Terminal)
P.J. Clarke's (915 Third Ave)
Patroon (160 E 46th St)
Planet Hollywood (150 W 57th St)
Popover Cafe (551 Amsterdam Ave)
Prime Burger (5 E 51st St)
Quilty's (177 Prince St)
Sassy's Sliders (163 First Ave): small, tasty burgers
Silverspurs (771 Broadway)
Smith & Wollensky (797 Third Ave)
21 (21 W 52nd St)
Union Square Cafe (21 E 16th St)
Wollensky's Grill (201 E 49th St)
World Cafe (201 Columbus Ave)
Zoë (90 Prince St)

Cheap Eats

Some of the better deals in town:

Aggie's (146 W Houston St)
Alley's End (311 W 17th St)
Alouette (2588 Broadway)
Avenue (520 Columbus Ave)
B&H Dairy (127 Second Ave)
Bar Six (502 Ave of the Americas)
Barking Dog Luncheonette (1678 Third Ave)
Bendix Diner (219 Eighth Ave)
Bereket (187 E Houston St)

Big Nick's (2175 Broadway)
Bistro Margot (26 Prince St)
Boca Chica (13 First Ave)
Bona Fides (60 Second Ave)
Bus Stop Cafe (597 Hudson St)
Cabana Carioca (123 W 45th St)
Cafe Lalo (201 W 83rd St)
Cafe Pertutti (2888 Broadway)
Cafe Riazor (245 W 16th St)
Caffe Buon Gusto (236 E 77th St)
Caffe Lure (169 Sullivan St)
Caffe Vivaldi (32 Jones St)
Carmine's (2450 Broadway)
Casa Adela (66 Ave C)
Chantale's Cajun Kitchen (510 Ninth Ave)
Chelsea Grill (135 Eighth Ave)
Chez Brigitte (77 Greenwich Ave)
Christine's (208 First Ave)
City Bakery (22 E 17th St)
Coffee Mug (233 Broadway)
Coffee Shop (29 Union Sq W)
Col Legno (231 E 9th St)
Comfort Diner (214 E 45th St)
Confetti (5 E 38th St)
Corner Bistro (331 W 4th St)
Cucina (256 Fifth Ave)
Cucina di Pesce (87 E 4th St)
Cucina Della Fontana (368 Bleecker St)
Cucina Stagionale (275 Bleecker St)
Cupcake Cafe (522 Ninth Ave)
Dallas BBQ (1265 Third Ave, 27 W 72nd St, 21 University Pl, and 132 Second Ave)
Danal (90 E 10th St)
Da Nico (164 Mulberry St)
Diane's Downtown (249 Columbus Ave)
Dining Commons (City University of New York Graduate Center, 365 Fifth Ave, 8th floor)
Edgar's Cafe (255 W 84th St)
Eighteenth & Eighth (159 Eighth Ave)
El Cid (322 W 15th Ave)
El Pollo (1746 First Ave)
Elvie's Turo-Turo (214 First Ave)
Emerald Planet (2 Great Jones St)
Festival Mexico (120 Rivington St)
Film Center Cafe (635 Ninth Ave)
First (87 First Ave)
Flor de Mayo (2651 Broadway)
Frank (88 Second Ave)
Frank's (85 Tenth Ave)
Fresco Tortilla Grill (36 Lexington Ave)
Gabriela's (685 Amsterdam Ave)
Golden Unicorn (18 East Broadway)

Gray's Papaya (2090 Broadway)
Hallo Berlin (402 W 51st St)
Home (20 Cornelia St)
Hurley's (1240 Ave of the Americas)
Hurricane Island (1303 Third Ave)
Il Bagatto (192-E Second Ave)
Island Burgers & Shakes (766 Ninth Ave)
Isola (485 Columbus Ave)
Jean Claude (137 Sullivan St)
Jo-An Japanese (2707 Broadway)
Joe, Jr's (482 Ave of the Americas)
Joe's Shanghai (9 Pell St)
John's Pizzeria (several locations)
Katz's Delicatessen (205 E Houston St)
Key West Diner & Cafe (2532 Broadway)
Kiev (117 Second Ave)
Kitchen Club (30 Prince St)
Kitchenette (80 West Broadway)
L'Ardoise (1207 First Ave)
La Bonne Soupe (48 W 55th St)
La Cocina (217 W 85th St)
La Conquista (236 Lafayette St)
La Foccaceria (128 First Ave)
La Taza de Oro (96 Eighth Ave)
Le Gamin (183 Ninth Ave)
Le Tableau (511 E 5th St)
Lemon Tree Cafe (769 Ninth Ave)
Little Havana (30 Cornelia St)
Mama's Food Shop (200 E 3rd St)
Margon (136 W 46th St)
Marnie's Noodle Shop (466 Hudson St)
Mavalli Palace (46 E 29th St)
McDonald's (160 Broadway)
Mee Noodle Soup (795 Ninth Ave)
Mill, The (2895 Broadway)
Mingala West (325 Amsterdam Ave)
Miss Elle's Homesick Bar and Grill (226 W 79th St)
Moondance Diner (80 Ave of the Americas)
New York Noodle Town (28½ Bowery St)
Nha Trang (87 Baxter St)
Ollie's Noodle Shop and Grill (190 W 44th St)
107 West Restaurant (2787 Broadway)
Pad Thai (114 Eighth Ave)
Panna II (93 First Ave)
Papaya King (179 E 86th St)
Patsy's Pizza (2287 First Ave and 509 Third Ave)
Pepe Rosso to Go (110 St. Mark's Pl)
Persepolis (1423 Second Ave)
Pintaile's Pizza (26 E 91st St)
Pisces (95 Ave A)
Pitchoune (226 Third Ave)
Pò (31 Cornelia St)

Pommes Frites (123 Second Ave)
Popover Cafe (551 Amsterdam Ave)
Prime Burger (685 Amsterdam Ave)
Rainbow Chicken (2801 Broadway)
Rao's (455 E 114th St)
Rose of Bombay (326 E 6th St)
Royal Siam Thai (240 Eighth Ave)
Sapporo (152 W 49th St)
Second Avenue Kosher Delicatessen and Restaurant (156 Second Ave)
Seventh Regiment Armory Mess Hall (643 Park Ave)
Sevilla (62 Charles St)
Shopsin's General Store (63 Bedford St): an original!
Soho Kitchen & Bar (103 Greene St)
Spring Street Natural Restaurant (62 Spring St)
Sweet-n-Tart Cafe (76 Mott St)
Sylvia's Restaurant (328 Lenox Ave)
Symposium Greek Restaurant (544 W 113th St)
Tanti Baci Cafe (163 W 10th St)
Taqueria de Mexico (93 Greenwich Ave)
Tartine (253 W 11th St)
Tea & Sympathy (108-110 Greenwich Ave)
Teresa's (103 Firs Ave)
Tibetan Kitchen (444 Third Ave)
Topaz Thai (127 W 56th St)
Tossed (295 Park Ave S)
Tres Aztecas (66 Rivington St)
Turkish Cuisine (631 Ninth Ave)
Uncle Nick's (747 Ninth Ave)
Urban Roots (51 Ave A)
Veronica (240 W 38th St)
Veselka Coffee Shop (144 Second Ave)
Viand Coffee Shop (1011 Madison Ave, 673 Madison Ave, and 300 E 86th St)
Vietnam Restaurant (11 Doyers St)
Wong Kee (113 Mott St)
Zula Restaurant (1260 Amsterdam Ave)

— Millennium Note —
The city's first printer, William Bradford, who set up shop at 81 Pearl Street in 1693, established New York's first newspaper, the *New York Gazette,* and started Manhattan's great book-publishing industry.

Cheese

Babbo (110 Waverly Pl)
Chanterelle (2 Harrison St)
Georgia's (597 Metropolitan Ave): fresh mozzarella made daily
Gramercy Tavern (42 E 20th St)
Jean Georges (1 Central Park W)
La Caravelle (33 W 55th St)

La Grenouille (3 E 52nd St)
Monzu (142 Mercer St): make a meal of cheese
Osteria del Circo (120 W 55th St): vertical tasting of the classic Italian pecorino
    (sheep's milk) cheeses
Parioli Romanissimo (24 E 81st St)
Solera (216 E 53rd St)

Cigar Friendly

Alva (36 E 22nd St)
American Park at the Battery (Battery Park)
Angelo and Maxie's (233 Park Ave S)
Asia De Cuba (Morgan's Hotel, 237 Madison Ave)
Cigar Room at Trumpets (Grand Hyatt Hotel, Park Ave at Grand Central
    Station)
City Wine & Cigar Company (62 Laight St)
Club Macanudo (26 E 63rd St)
Cub Room (131 Sullivan St)
Delmonico's (56 Beaver St)
Hudson Bar and Books (636 Hudson St)
King Cole Bar at St. Regis Hotel (2 E 55th St)
Lattanzi (361 W 46th St)
Monkey Bar (60 E 54th St)
Oak Room at Plaza Hotel (768 Fifth Ave)
Onieal's (174 Grand St)
Parlour, the, at Cafe des Artistes (1 W 67th St)
Patroon (160 E 46th St)
Pravda (281 Lafayette St)
Remi (145 W 53rd St)
Skybox at Windows on the World (1 World Trade Center)
Tatou Le Cigar (151 E 50th St)

Coffeehouses

You can relax, enjoy good company, and drink various coffee beverages at the
following:

Basset Coffee & Tea Company (123 West Broadway)
Big Cup (228 Eighth Ave)
Bleecker Street Pastry (245 Bleecker St)
Bodum (673 Madison Ave)
Broadway Bagels Deli (2658 Broadway)
Cafe La Fortuna (69 W 71st St)
Cafe Lalo (201 W 83rd St)
Cafe Orlin (41 St. Mark's Pl)
Caffe Biondo (141 Mulberry St)
Caffe Dante (79 MacDougal St)
Caffe del Corso (19 W 55th St)
Caffe Novocento (33 West Broadway)
Caffe Reggio (119 MacDougal St)
Caffe Roma (385 Broome St)
Caffe Vivaldi (32 Jones St)
Chez Laurence Patisserie (245 Madison Ave)
City Bakery (22 E 17th St)

Coffee Arts (5 World Trade Center)
Coffee Bar (2151 Broadway)
Cupcake Cafe (522 Ninth Ave)
Cupping Room Cafe (359 West Broadway)
Daily Caffe (Rockefeller Center)
Dean & Deluca (560 Broadway)
Dolci on Park (12 Park Ave)
DT.UT (1626 Second Ave)
Espresso Madison (33 E 68th St)
Eureka Joe (168 Fifth Ave)
Ferrara (195 Grand St)
French Roast (458 Ave of the Americas)
Golden Frog Coffee Company (564 Third Ave)
Hungarian Pastry Shop (1030 Amsterdam Ave)
Jonathan Morr Espresso Bar (133 Greene St)
Le Gamin (50 MacDougal St)
Lipstick Cafe (885 Third Ave)
New World Coffee (449 Ave of the Americas)
Newsbar (366 West Broadway)
Once Upon a Tart (135 Sullivan St)
Oren's Daily Roast (many locations)
Pane & Cioccolato (10 Waverly Pl)
Philip's Coffee (155 W 56th St)
Sant Ambroeus (1000 Madison Ave)
Sarabeth's Kitchen (1295 Madison Ave, 423 Amsterdam Ave, and 945 Madison
   Ave, at Whitney Museum)
Scharmann's (386 West Broadway)
Sensuous Bean (66 W 70th St)
Starbucks (many locations)
Timothy's Coffees of the World (100 Park Ave): reading material, too!
Uncommon Grounds (533 Third Ave)
Veniero Pasticceria (342 E 11th St)
Veselka Coffee Shop (144 Second Ave)
Xando Coffee and Bar (2160 Broadway)

Crepes

Jean Georges (1 Central Park W)
Le Gamin (183 Ninth Ave)
Le Gamin Buvette (410 West Broadway)
Lespinasse (St Regis Hotel, 2 E 55th St)
Serendipity 3 (225 E 60th St)
Vong (200 E 54th St)

Delis

Barney Greengrass (541 Amsterdam Ave)
Carnegie Delicatessen and Restaurant (854 Seventh Ave)
E.A.T. (1064 Madison Ave)
Fine & Schapiro (138 W 72nd St)
Katz's Delicatessen (205 E Houston St)
Second Avenue Kosher Delicatessen and Restaurant (156 Second Ave)
Third Avenue Delicatessen (276 Third Ave)

Desserts

Cafe Lalo (201 W 83rd St): the best European-style cafe!
Caffe Biondo (141 Mulberry St): Little Italy's star
Caffe Bondi (7 W 20th St): Italian tortes
Caffe Pertutti (2862 Broadway): a waist-expanding experience
Carnegie Delicatessen and Restaurant (854 Seventh Ave): Everything here is big.
Delices de France (289 Madison Ave): The name says it all.
Dolci on Park Caffe (12 Park Ave): undiscovered gem
Eclair Pastry Shops (Grand Central Terminal, Herald Square, 54th St at First Ave, and 141 W 72nd St): good selection
Ferrara (195 Mulberry St): Italian gelati
Gindi (935 Broadway): great pastries
Halcyon (151 W 54th St): spectacular!
Hard Rock Cafe (221 W 57th St): all-American treats
Le Cirque 2000 (New York Palace Hotel, 455 Madison Ave): world famous!
Les Delices West (370 Columbus Ave): fine French pastries
Les Friandises (972 Lexington Ave): fabulous chocolate mousse cake
Lo Spuntino (117 Mulberry St): ice cream specialties
Madeline's (117 Prince St): end of a great meal
Palm Court (Plaza Hotel, 768 Fifth Ave): vintage New York
Sant Ambroeus (1000 Madison Ave): rich and classy
Serendipity 3 (225 E 60th St): an institution for the young-at-heart
Tavern on the Green (Central Park W and 67th St): There's nothing like it back home!
Zabar's Cafe (2245 Broadway): big treats, low prices

Dim Sum

The serving of small tea pastries called dim sum originated in Hong Kong and has become a delicious Chinatown institution. Although dim sum is usually eaten for brunch, some restaurants also serve it as an appetizer before dinner. The food is rolled over to your table on carts, and you simply point at whatever looks good. This eliminates the language barrier and encourages experimentation. When you're finished, the small plates you've accumulated are counted, and the bill is drawn up. Some of the most popular dim sum dishes:

Cha Siu Bow (steamed barbecued pork buns)
Cha Siu So (flaky buns)
Chun Guen (spring rolls)
Dai Tze Gau (steamed scallop and shrimp dumplings)
Don Ta (baked custard tart)
Dow Sah Bow (sweet bean paste-filled buns)
Fancy Fans (meat-filled wonton skins)
Floweret Siu Mai (meat-filled dumplings)
Four-Color Siu Mai (meat- and vegetable-filled dumplings)
Gau Choi Gau (pan-browned chive and shrimp dumplings)
Gee Cheung Fun (steamed rice-noodle rolls)
Gee Yoke Go (savory pork triangles)
Ha Gau (shrimp dumplings)
Jow Ha Gok (shrimp turnovers)
Pot Sticker Kou The (meat-filled dumplings)
Pot Sticker Triangles (meat-filled wonton skins)

Satay Gai Tran (chicken satay)
Siu Mai (steamed pork dumplings)
Tzay Ha (fried shrimp ball on sugarcane)

For the most authentic and delicious dim sum in New York, I recommend:

Golden Unicorn (18 East Broadway): serves an especially fine selection
H.S.F. (46 Bowery and 578 Second Ave)
Jing Fong (20 Elizabeth St)
Mandarin Court (61 Mott St)
Nice Restaurant (35 East Broadway)
Oriental Pearl (103 Mott St)
Shun Lee Cafe (43 W 65th St)
Silver Palace (50 Bowery)
Sun Hop Shing Tea House (21 Mott St)
Tai-Hong-Lau (70 Mott St)
Triple 8 Palace (59 Division St)

Diners

There are not many classic diners left in Manhattan. The best of the survivors:

Aggie's (146 W Houston St)
Broadway Diner (590 Lexington Ave)
Brooklyn Diner USA (212 W 57th St): outstanding
Ellen's Stardust (1650 Broadway)
Empire Diner (210 Tenth Ave)
Market Diner (Eleventh Ave at 43rd St)
Moondance Diner (80 Ave of the Americas)

Dining and Dancing

Cafe Pierre (Pierre Hotel, 2 E 61st St): refined
Decade (1117 First Ave): modern food, 1960s and 1970s music
Delia's (197 E 3rd St): alphabet-land French-Caribbean dancing
Supper Club (240 W 47th St): vintage 1940s with big bands
Tavern on the Green (Central Park W at 67th St): great setting
Well's (2247-49 Seventh Ave): Harlem soul food and jazz
World Yacht Cruises (Pier 81, 41st St at Hudson River): nonstop party

Dining Solo

Some of these restaurants have dining counters, while others are tranquil and suitable for single diners.

Babbo (110 Waverly Pl)
Broadway Diner (590 Lexington Ave and 1726 Broadway)
Cafe de Bruxelles (118 Greenwich Ave)
Cafe SFA (Saks Fifth Ave, 611 Fifth Ave)
Carnegie Delicatessen and Restaurant (854 Seventh Ave)
Caviar Russe (538 Madison Ave)
Chez Napoleon (365 W 50th St)
Coffee Shop (29 Union Sq W)
Elephant & Castle (68 Greenwich St and Seventh Ave at 11th St)
Grand Central Oyster Bar Restaurant (Grand Central Station, lower level)
Hosteria Fiorella (1081 Third Ave)
J.G. Melon (1291 Third Ave)

Jackson Hole Burgers (232 E 64th St, Third Ave at 35th St, and Second Ave at 84th St)
La Bonne Soupe (48 W 55th St)
Lexington Avenue Grill (Loews Summit Hotel, 569 Lexington Ave)
Lipstick Cafe (885 Third Ave)
Mme. Romaine de Lyon (132 E 61st St)
Raoul's (180 Prince St)
Republic (37 Union Square W)
Sarabeth's Kitchen (1295 Madison Ave, 423 Amsterdam Ave, and 945 Madison Ave, at Whitney Museum)
Second Avenue Kosher Delicatessen and Restaurant (156 Second Ave)
Trattoria dell'Arte (900 Seventh Ave)
Tropica (MetLife Bldg, 200 Park Ave)
Union Square Cafe (21 E 16th St)
Verbena (54 Irving Pl)
Viand Coffee Shop (300 E 86th St, 1011 Madison Ave, and 637 Madison Ave)
Zoë (90 Prince St)

Dog Friendly

Brew Bar (327 W 11th St)
Cafe Pick Me Up (145 Ave A)
Chelsea Lobster Company (156 Seventh Ave)
Christina's (606 Second Ave)
Girasole (151 E 82nd St)
Indian Delhi (392 Columbus Ave)
Time Cafe (87 Seventh Ave)
Verbena (54 Irving Pl)

Don't Bother

Too many restaurants spoil the real reason for dining out: to get a good meal in a comfortable setting at a fair price. With so many great restaurant choices in Manhattan, why waste time and money on poor or mediocre ones? Many on the following list are well known and popular, but I feel you can get better value elsewhere.

Angelo of Mulberry Street: The portrait of President Reagan is their only claim to fame.
Bice: very "in," very noisy, very unimpressive
Bowery Bar: The servers are as disinterested as you will be in the food.
Cafe Lure: The smell is enough to take away your appetite.
Charley O's: the Benetton of the food scene
Chiam: charming in every way except the most important—the food
City Crab: The amateurish service and mediocre food is enough to make anybody crabby.
City Hall: Like so many buildings with this name, the place looks good at first glance, but the rest of the experience is a real letdown.
Demarchelier: very ordinary
Destinee: pretentious
El Teddy's: Only the desserts are worth the effort.
EQ: overpriced
Ernie's: The pickup scene must be awfully good.
Flowers: This place has not yet bloomed.

Gage & Tollner: great ambience and reputation, but really not worth the trip to Brooklyn
Giovanni Venti Cinque: haughty treatment and high prices
Great American Health Bar: Ugh!
Grill Room: consumer unfriendly
Harley Davidson Cafe: Let's stick to the cycles.
Houlihan's: places of the past
Island: There are better ones in the Caribbean.
Jekyll & Hyde: for ghoulish appetites
Le Bar Bat: even the name turns me off
Le Veau d'Or: Heaven help the stranger trying to get a table.
Lexington Avenue Grill: poor service
Mickey Mantle's: a strikeout
Official All-Star Cafe: Joe Montana 10, Diners 1
Old Homestead: "Old" is the best description.
Park View Restaurant: The setting is special, but the food isn't.
Ratner's: Why pay to get insulted?
Sardi's: once great; twice bad; thrice, coming back slowly
Savoy: uncomfortably "cute," unappealing plates
Union Pacific: The culinary ride isn't always smooth.
Wylie's Ribs: Pass the Pepto-Bismol.

Eating at the Bar

Beekman, The (15 Beekman St)
China Grill (52 W 53rd St)
Christer's (145 W 55th St)
Delmonico's (56 Beaver St)
Fanelli (94 Prince St)
Gotham Bar & Grill (12 E 12th St)
Gramercy Tavern (42 E 20th St)
Lobster Club (24 E 80th St)
Mesa Grill (102 Fifth Ave)
Monkey Bar (60 E 54th St)
Old Town Bar & Restaurant (45 E 18th St)
Palio (151 W 51st St)
Patroon (160 E 46th St)
Penang (109 Spring St)
Petrossian (182 W 58th St)
Pravda (281 Lafayette St)
Rain (100 W 82nd St)
Redeye Grill (890 Seventh Ave)
Tapika (238 W 56th St)
Union Square Cafe (21 E 16th St)
Zoë (90 Prince St)

Family-Style Dining

Carmine's (2450 Broadway)
Coco Pazzo (23 E 74th St; Fri, Sat, and Sun)
Drovers Tap Room (9 Jones St)
Marchi's (251 E 31st St)
Sambuca (20 W 72nd St)
Szechuan Hunan (1588 York Ave)

Fireplaces

American Park at the Battery (Battery Park)
Barbetta (321 W 46th St)
Christer's (145 W 55th St)
Gramercy Tavern (42 E 20th St)
Hunter's (1397 Third Ave)
I Trulli (122 E 27th St)
Keens Steakhouse (72 W 36th St)
La Bohême (24 Minetta Lane)
March (405 E 58th St)
Marchi's (251 E 31st St)
Marylou's (21 W 9th St)
One If By Land, Two If By Sea (17 Barrow St)
René Pujol (321 W 55th St)
Savoy (70 Prince St)
Water Club (500 E 30th St)
Ye Waverly Inn (16 Bank St)

Foreign Flavors

Afghan: Afghanistan Kebab House (764 Ninth Ave) and Pamir (1437 Second Ave)
African: La Baraka (153 Broadway), Metisse (239 W 105th St), and Sugar Bar (354 W 72nd St)
Arabian: Layla (211 West Broadway)
Argentine: Chimichurri Grill (606 Ninth Ave)
Asian: Pacific East (318 W 23rd St) and Rain (100 W 82nd St)
Belgian: Cafe de Bruxelles (118 Greenwich Ave), Markt (401 W 14th St), Petite Abeille (400 W 14th St), and Waterloo Brasserie (145 Charles St)
Burmese: Mingala West (325 Amsterdam Ave)
Caribbean: Bambou (243 E 14th St), Cabana (1022 Third Ave), Caribe (117 Perry St), Caridad (4311 Broadway), and Tropica (200 Park Ave)
Chilean: Pomaire (371 W 46th St)
Chinese: Au Mandarin (250 Vesey St), Baby Buddha (753 Washington Ave), Big Wong (67 Mott St), Broadway Cottage (2690 Broadway), Chin Chin (216 E 49th St), China Fun West (246 Columbus Ave), First Taste (53 Bayard St), Fu's (1395 Second Ave), Golden Unicorn (18 East Broadway), H.S.F. (46 Bowery), Joe's Shanghai (9 Pell St), Kam Chueh (40 Bowery), Mr. K's (570 Lexington Ave), Natural Restaurant (88 Allen St), New Hong Kong City (11 Division St), New York Noodle Town (28½ Bowery), Oriental Garden (14 Elizabeth St), Oriental Pearl (103 Mott St), Shanghai Cuisine (89-91 Bayard St), Shun Lee Palace (155 E 55th St), Shun Lee West (43 W 65th St), Sunny East (21 W 39th St), Tang Pavilion (65 W 55th St), 10 Pell St (10 Pell St), 20 Mott Street (20 Mott St), Wu Liang Ye (36 W 48th St), and Zen Palate (34 Union Sq E, 663 Ninth Ave, and 2170 Broadway)
Cuban: La Caridad (2199 Broadway), Little Havana (30 Cornelia St), and Victor's Cafe (240 Columbus Ave)
East European: Firebird (365 W 46th St)
Ethiopian: Ghenet (248 Mulberry St) and Zula (1260 Amsterdam Ave)
Filipino: Elvie's Turo-Turo (214 First Ave)
French: (see restaurant listings)
French-Moroccan: Chez Es Saada (42 E 1st St)

German: Hallo Berlin (402 W 51st St), Heidelberg Restaurant (1648 Second Ave), Roetelle A.G. (126 E 7th St), and Rolf's (281 Third Ave)

Greek: Artos (307 E 53rd St), Estiatorio Milos (125 W 55th St), Gus' Place (149 Waverly Pl), Ithaka (48 Bararow St), Likitsakos Market (1174 Lexington Ave), Meltemi (905 First Ave), Molyvos (871 Seventh Ave), Periyali (35 W 20th St), Uncle Nick's (747 Ninth Ave), and Viand Coffee Shop (1011 Madison Ave, 673 Madison Ave, and 300 E 86th St)

Hungarian: Mocca Hungarian Restaurant (1588 Second Ave)

Indian: Akbar (475 Park Ave), Bay Leaf (49 W 56th St), Bengal Express (789 Ninth Ave), Bombay Dining (320 E 6th St), Chola (232 E 58th St), Dawat (210 E 58th St), Haveli (100 Second Ave), Jewel of India (15 W 44th St), Marichu (342 E 46th St), Mavalli Palace (46 E 29th St), Pondicherry (8 W 58th St), Pongal (110 Lexington Ave), Rose of India (308 E 6th St), Salaam Bombay (317 Greenwich St), Shaan (57 W 48th St), Surya (302 Bleecker St), Tabla (11 Madison Ave), and Taj Mahal (328 E 6th St)

Indonesian: Bali Nusa Indah (651 Ninth Ave)

Irish: Landmark Tavern (626 Eleventh Ave), Neary's (358 E 57th St), and Thady Con's (915 Second Ave)

Italian: (see restaurant listings)

Jamaican: Jamaican Hot Pot (2260 Adam Clayton Powell, Jr. Blvd)

Japanese: Benihana (120 E 56th St), Bond Street (6 Bond St), Chikubu (12 E 44th St), Hatsuhana (17 E 48th St), Honmura An (170 Mercer St), Iso (175 Second Ave), Jo-An Japanese (2707 Broadway), Japonica (100 University Pl), Kiiroi Hana (23 W 56th St), Kuruma Zushi (7 E 47th St), Menchanko-Tei (39 W 55th St), Nadaman Hakubai (Kitano Hotel, 66 Park Ave), Nobu (105 Hudson St), Next Door Nobu (105 Hudson St), Omen (113 Thompson St), Sakagura (211 E 43rd St), Seryna (11 E 53rd St), Sugiyama (251 W 55th St), Sushihatsu (1143 First Ave), Sushisay (38 E 51st St), and Toraya (17 E 71st St)

Korean: Bop (325 Bowery), Cho Dang Gol (55 W 53rd St), Clay (202 Mott St), Dae Dong Restaurant (17 W 32nd St), Dok Suni's (119 First Ave), Han Bat (53 W 35th St), Hangawi (12 E 32nd St), Kang Suh (1250 Broadway), Korea Palace (127 E 54th St), Won Jo (23 W 32nd St), and Woo Chon (8-10 W 36th St)

Latin: Calle Ocho (446 Columbus Ave)

Lebanese: Al Bustan (827 Third Ave)

Malaysian: Malaysia and Indonesia (18 Doyers St), Malaysia Restaurant (48 Bowery), Penang (109 Spring St)

Mediterranean: Agora (1586 First Ave), Gus' Place (149 Waverly Pl), Mezze (10 W 44th St), Provence (38 MacDougal St), Savoy (70 Prince St), and Spartina (355 Greenwich St)

Mexican: El Parador Cafe (325 E 34th St), El Rey del Sol (232 W 14th St), El Teddy's (219 West Broadway), Ernesto Restaurant (2277 First Ave), Fresco Tortillas (766 Ninth Ave), Gabriela's (685 Amsterdam Ave), La Hacienda (219 E 116th St), L-Ray (64 W 10th St), Maya (1191 First Ave), Mi Cocina (57 Jane St), Rinconcito Mexicano (307 W 39th St); Rosa Mexicano (1063 First Ave), Taqueria de Mexico (93 Greenwich Ave), Tortilla Flats (767 Washington St), and Zarela (953 Second Ave)

Middle Eastern: Al Bustan (827 Third Ave), Cleopatra's Needle (2485 Broadway), Habib's Place (438 E 9th St), Layla (211 West Broadway), Lemon Tree Cafe (769 Ninth Ave), and Scarabee (230 E 51st St)

Moroccan: Acquario (5 Bleecker St), Anda-Lousia (28 Cornelia St), Cafe Fes (246 W 4th St), Chez Es Saada (42 E First St), Lofti's (358 W 46th St), and L'Orange Bleue (430 Broome St)

Nordic: Christer's (145 W 55th St)

Nuevo Latino: Bolivar (206 E 60th St), Cafe Habana (17 Prince St), Calle Ocho (446 Columbus Ave), Ideya (349 West Broadway), and L-Ray (64 W 10th St)

Persian: Persepolis (1423 Second Ave)

Peruvian: Felipe's Peruvian Restaurant (688 Tenth Ave)

Polish: Christine's (438 Second Ave and 208 First Ave), Teresa's (103 First Ave), and Veselka Coffee Shop (144 Second Ave)

Portuguese: O Padeiror (641 Ave of the Americas), O Lavrador (138-40 101st Ave), and Pão (322 Spring St)

Puerto Rican: La Taza de Oro (96 Eighth Ave)

Russian: Firebird (363 W 46th St), Moscow (137 E 55th St), Pravda (281 Lafayette St), Russian Samovar (256 W 52nd St), and Uncle Vanya (315 W 54th St)

Scandinavian: Christer's (145 W 55th St)

Senegalese: Africa (247 W 116th St) and Keur-Famba (126 W 116th St)

South American: Bolivar (206 E 60th St), Cabana Carioca (123 W 45th St), Calle Ocho (446 Columbus Ave), Campo (89 Greenwich Ave), Churrascaria Plataforma (316 W 49th St), Circus (808 Lexington Ave), El Pollo (1746 First Ave), Emporium Brazil (15 W 46th St), Ipanema (13 W 46th St), L-Ray (64 W 10th St), Patria (250 Park Ave S), Rice and Beans (744 Ninth Ave), and Riodizio (417 Lafayette St)

Spanish: Bolo (23 E 22nd St), Cafe Riazor (245 W 16th St), El Cid (322 W 15th St), El Faro (823 Greenwich St), Solera (216 E 53rd St), and Toledo (6 E 36th St)

Sri Lanka: Lakruwana (358 W 44th St)

Swedish: Aquavit (13 W 54th St) and Christer's (145 W 55th St)

Swiss: Roettele A.G. (126 E 7th St)

Thai: Kin Khao (171 Spring St), Pongsri Thai (244 W 48th St), Rain (100 W 82nd St), Regional Thai Sa-Woy (1479 First Ave), Royal Siam Thai (240 Eighth Ave), Siam Cuisine (1411 Second Ave), Siam Grill (586 Ninth Ave), Thailand Restaurant (106 Bayard St), Topaz Thai (127 W 56th St), Thai House Cafe (151 Hudson St), and Vong (200 E 54th St)

Tibetan: Lhasa (96 Second Ave), Tibetan Kitchen (444 Third Ave), Tibetan on Houston (136 West Houston St), Tibetan Shambala (488 Amsterdam Ave), and Tsampa (212 E 9th St)

Turkish: Deniz (400 E 57th St), Layla (211 West Broadway), Uskudar (1405 Second Ave), Turkish Cuisine (631 Ninth Ave), and Turkish Kitchen (386 Third Ave)

Ukrainian: Ukrainian East Village (1240 Second Ave)

Vietnamese: Cyclo (203 First Ave), La Soirée d'Asie (156 E 64th St), Le Colonial (149 E 57th St), Me Kong (44 Prince St), Miss Saigon (1425 Third Ave), Monsoon (435 Amsterdam Ave), Nam Phuong (19 Ave of the Americas), New Viet Huong (77 Mulberry St), Nha Trang (87 Baxter St), Orienta (205 E 75th St), River (345 Amsterdam Ave), and Vietnam (11 Doyers St).

Want to eat and have access to the Internet? Visit the **Internet Cafe** at 82 East 3rd Street.

Ordering a Chinese Meal

Get together a large party in order to sample a wide variety of dishes. While everyone's taste should be taken into account, it is advisable to let one person organize the order. A well-balanced meal comprises the five basic tastes of Chinese cuisine: acid, hot, bitter, sweet, and salty. Texture should vary between dry and sauced, crisp and tender. A good rule of thumb is to order one dish per diner, plus one soup. Your utensils will be chopsticks, which are ideal for the small pieces of food commonly found in Chinese cooking. Most restaurants will, however, gladly supply chopstick novices with knives, forks, and spoons.

A Chinese meal usually starts with a cold meat dish and is then followed by fish or seafood, red or white meat, vegetables, and soup. Steamed white rice is the typical accompaniment, but you can also order a fried noodle or rice dish to be served at the end of the meal. In Northern Chinese-style restaurants, bread or noodles often replaces rice.

Asian food tips

- **Chinese:** The most popular Chinese cuisines are: Cantonese (heavy on fish, dim sum a specialty); Chiu Chow (thick shark's fin soup, sliced goose, the "Sicilians" of China); Hakka (salted, use of innards); Hunan (very spicy, try fried chicken with chili); Peking (Peking duck and beggar's chicken are best-known); Shanghai (freshwater hairy crab is very popular); and Szechuan (spiciest of all, simmering and smoking are common cooking methods).

- **Indian:** Not necessarily hot. Northern Indian food features wheat bread and curries. Fish or chicken is cooked in tandoor clay oven.

- **Indonesian:** Satay (skewered chicken or beef, barbecued and served with peanut sauce) is the main dish.

- **Japanese:** Most popular is sashimi (slices of fresh, raw fish), sushi (raw fish served atop vinegary rice or in rolls), tempura (deep-fried vegetables and fish), and teppanyaki (beef, seafood, garlic, and veggies cooked at a central griddle). And, of course, sake (rice wine).

- **Korean:** Table-top griddles are used for barbecuing beef slices for a dish called *bulgogi.*

- **Malaysian:** Best-known specialty is *laska,* a creamy, coconut-based soup with noodles, shrimp and chicken.

- **Singaporean:** A combination of cultures: fried *mee* (thick yellow noodles) and satay (skewered and barbecued meat). Coconut is featured in sweet rice cakes and *laska* noodle soup.

- **Taiwanese:** Full-flavored, heavy on fish and other seafoods cooked in hot pots and enhanced by chili and sesame-flavored oil condiments.

- **Thai:** Spicy! National dish is *tom yum gung,* a soup made with chili, lemon grass and coriander and topped with shrimp, chicken or squid.

- **Vietnamese:** French-inspired dishes like fried frog legs, sausage, and salami cold cuts platter. Spring rolls wrapped in lettuce leaves are traditional.

Game

Aquavit (13 W 54th St)
Aureole (34 E 61st St)
Barbetta (321 W 46th St)

Bouterin (420 E 59th St)
Cafe Boulud (Surrey Hotel, 20 E 76th St)
Cafe des Artistes (1 W 67th St)
Chanterelle (2 Harrison St)
Hudson River Club (4 World Financial Ctr)
Il Cantinori (32 E 10th St)
Il Mulino (86 W Third St)
Jo Jo (160 E 64th St)
La Caravelle (Shoreham Hotel, 33 W 55th St)
La Réserve (4 W 44th St)
Le Cirque 2000 (New York Palace Hotel, 455 Madison Ave)
Le Périgord (405 E 52nd St)
Les Halles (411 Park Ave S)
Mesa Grill (102 Fifth Ave)
Monkey Bar (Hotel Elysee, 60 E 54th St)
Montrachet (239 West Broadway)
Park Bistro (414 Park Ave)
Primavera (1578 First Ave)
Terrace, The (400 W 119th St)
Union Square Cafe (21 E 16th St)

Healthy Fare

You can find healthy fare at the following restaurants, some of which have special menus:

Akbar (475 Park Ave): Indian
American Cafe and Health Bar (160 Broadway)
Angelica Kitchen (300 E 12th St)
Blanche's Organic Cafe (22 E 44th St and 972 Lexington Ave)
Dine by Design (252 Elizabeth St)
Four Seasons (99 E 49th St): expensive
Fraunces Tavern Restaurant (54 Pearl St): historic
Heartbeat (149 E 49th St)
Herban Kitchen (290 Hudson St)
Honmura An (170 Mercer St)
Josie's Restaurant and Juice Bar (300 Amsterdam Ave)
Marylou's (21 W 9th St)
Nosmo King (54 Varick St)
Popover Cafe (551 Amsterdam Ave)
Quantum Leap Natural Food (88 W 3rd St)
Republic (37 Union Sq W)
Spring Street Natural Restaurant (62 Spring St): your best bet
Time Cafe (380 Lafayette St)
Zen Palate (663 Ninth Ave and others)

Hi-Tech Eateries

How about cyber-cafes? Not surprising in the Internet world. Computer terminals make food seem secondary at these:

Alt.coffee (137 Ave A)
Cyber Cafe (273-A Lafayette St)
Internet Cafe (82 E 3rd St)

Hotel Dining

One of the biggest changes on the restaurant circuit in Manhattan is the resurgence of hotel dining. No longer are on-premises eateries just for the convenience of guests. Now they are bonafide destinations for anyone who desires a bit more atmosphere and a less trendy scene. Following are some of the best:

Algonquin (59 W 44th St): Round Table Room and Oak Room (evening cabaret)

Carlyle (35 E 76th St): Cafe Carlyle (features Bobby Short, very expensive)

Elysee (60 E 54th St): Monkey Bar (great history, great American cuisine)

Essex House Westin (160 Central Park S): Cafe Botanica (casual) and Les Célébrités (very expensive)

Four Seasons (57 E 57th St): Fifty-seven Fifty-seven (superb dining)

Grand Hyatt (Grand Central Station at Park Ave): Crystal Fountain and Sun Garden (nice setting)

Hilton New York (1335 Ave of the Americas): Etrusca (Tuscan) and New York Marketplace (all day dining)

Inn at Irving Place (54 Irving Pl): Verbena (charming)

Intercontinental (112 Central Park S): Fantino

Kitano (66 Park Ave): Nadaman Hakubai (Japanese) and Garden Cafe

Lowell (28 E 63rd St): Pembroke and Post House (very good meat and potatoes, next door)

Mark, The (25 E 77th St): Mark's Restaurant (one of the very best, French cuisine)

Marriott Marquis (1535 Broadway): The View (top floor, revolving), Encore (casual), and J.W. Steakhouse

Millenium Hilton (55 Church St): Taliesin (classy)

New York Palace (455 Madison Ave): Le Cirque 2000 (a New York one-and-only by Sirio Maccioni) and Istana (lobby)

Omni Berkshire (21 E 52nd St): Kokachin (good seafood)

Pierre (2 E 61st St): Cafe Pierre (stately and beautiful)

Plaza (768 Fifth Ave): Palm Court (vintage New York), Oak Room (serious), and Oyster Bar (seafood)

Plaza Athenee (37 E 64th St): Le Régence

Regency (540 Park Ave): 540 Park Avenue Restaurant (power scene) and the Library (informal)

RIHGA Royal (151 W 54th St): Halcyon (beautiful appointments and fine food)

Royalton (44 W 44th St): 44 (chic, favorite of publishing moguls)

St. Regis (2 E 55th St): Lespinasse (you can't do better)

Sheraton Manhattan (790 Seventh Ave): Russo's Steak & Pasta

Sheraton New York (811 Seventh Ave): Streeter's (café) and Hudson's Sports Bar & Grill

Sheraton Russell (45 Park Ave): Club Lounge

Shoreham (33 W 55th St): La Caravelle (elegant French)

Stanhope (995 Fifth Ave): Cafe M (French Mediterranean, casual)

Surrey Hotel (20 E 76th St): Cafe Boulud (French/American)

Trump International (1 Central Park W): Jean Georges (The Donald's personal gem)

Waldorf-Astoria (301 Park Ave): Bull & Bear (British atmosphere), Inagiku (Japanese), Peacock Alley (it has come back to life), and Oscar's (cafeteria)

Wales (1295 Madison Ave): Sarabeth's Kitchen (delightful) and Busby's (upscale diner, next door)

Warwick (63 W 54th St): Ciao Europa

Japanese Bars

Angel's Share (8 Stuyvesant St, 2nd floor)
Decibel (240 E 9th St)
J&A Pub (214 E 49th St)
New Tokyo 18 (113 E 18th St)
Riki (248 E 52nd St)
Sai Kai (141 E 45th St)
Tomi Jaz (216 E 10th St)

Kosher

There is a tremendous variety of kosher restaurants in the city. In fact, kosher dining choices mirror the fare in other restaurants. They include Indian, vegetarian, Italian, and steakhouses. The caveat that restaurants are the most mercurial of businesses in the city is especially true of kosher eateries. The list below represents the best and the longest-lived of Manhattan's kosher restaurants.

Abigail's (9 E 37th St and 1407 Broadway): two of the finest, classiest, and best restaurants in town
All-American Cafe (24 E 42nd St): a dairy cafe
Cafe 1-2-3 (2 Park Ave): great fish grill, salads and focaccia pizza
China Shalom II (686 Columbus Ave): kosher Chinese with a sidewalk cafe
Colbeh (43 W 39th St): glatt kosher authentic Persian cuisine
Deli Kasbah (251 W 85th St): one of the best grills in the area
Diamond Dairy (4 W 47th St, mezzanine overlooking Diamond Exchange): traditional Jewish dairy
Domani Ristorante (1590 First Ave): Italian meat menu
Dougie's Bar-B-Que & Grill (222 W 72nd St): kosher ribs, buffalo wings, and steak
Estihana (221 W 79th St): Oriental restaurant and sushi bar
Galil Restaurant (1252 Lexington Ave): continental, Israeli/Moroccan grill
Gan-Asia (691 Amsterdam Ave): authentic kosher Thai
Glatt Dynasty (1049 Second Ave): kosher Chinese, with a sushi bar
Gotham Kosher Grill (127 W 72nd St): kosher fast food
Haikara Grill (1016 Second Ave): upscale Japanese sushi/steakhouse
Infini (193 Second Ave): French continental
Jasmine (11 E 30th St): Persian glatt kosher
Kosher Delight (1359 Broadway and 1156 Ave of the Americas): glatt kosher fast food
Le Marais (150 W 46th St): good kosher French steakhouse
Levana Restaurant (141 W 69th St): one of the best buys in town; elegant
Mendy's Steak House, Delicatessen & Bar (61 E 34th St): kosher sports bar
Mendy's West (208 W 70th St): kosher sports bar
My Most Favorite Dessert Company, Restaurant & Cafe (120 W 45th St): The desserts are the stars here.
Polanco (502 Amsterdam Ave): authentic Mexican cuisine
Ratner's (138 Delancey St): historic
Tevere 84 (155 E 84th St): glatt kosher Roman-accented meat dinners
Va Bene (1589 Second Ave): Pasta is the star attraction.
Wolf & Lamb Steakhouse (10 E 48th St): steakhouse

Late Hours (See also "Manhattan at Night")

The city that never sleeps . . .

24 hours:
Big Nick's (2175 Broadway)
Cafeteria (119 Seventh Ave)
Coffee Shop (29 Union Square W)
Empire Diner (210 Tenth Ave)
Gray's Papaya (2090 Broadway)
Greenwich Cafe (75 Greenwich Ave)
Kum Gang San (49 W 32nd St)
Odessa (119 Ave A)
Sarge's Deli (548 Third Ave)
Veselka Coffee Shop (144 Second Ave)
Viand Coffee Shop (1011 Madison Ave, 673 Madison Ave, and 300 E 86th St)
Woo Chon (8-10 W 36th St)

Open until about four a.m.:
Blue Ribbon (97 Sullivan St)
Brooklyn Mod (271 Adelphi St, Brooklyn)
Cafe Noir (32 Grand St)
Corner Bistro (331 W 4th St)
Florent (69 Gansevoort St)
Joe's Pizza (7 Carmine St)
Kam Chueh (40 Bowery St)
Medusa (239 Park Ave S)
P.J. Clarke's (915 Third Ave)

Open until about three a.m.:
Casa la Femme (150 Wooster St)
Clementine (1 Fifth Ave)
Gold Rush Bar & Grill (449 Tenth Ave)
Katch (339 E 75th St)
Lucky Strike (59 Grand St)
Moomba (133 Seventh Ave S)
Pravda (281 Lafayette St)
Tapas Lounge (1078 First Ave)
Waterloo Brasserie (145 Charles St)

Open until about two a.m.:
Balthazar (80 Spring St)
Big Cup (228 Eighth Ave)
Broome Street Bar (363 West Broadway)
Cafe Lalo (201 W 83rd St)
Elaine's (1703 Second Ave)
First (87 First Ave)
Garage Cafe (99 Seventh Ave S)
Match (160 Mercer St)
Merchants, N.Y. (1125 First Ave)
Odeon (145 West Broadway)
Opaline (85 Ave A)
Papaya King (179 E 86th St)
Spy (101 Greene)

Tio Pepe (168 W 4th St)
White Horse Tavern (567 Hudson St)
Wollensky's Grill (205 E 49th St)

Open until about one a.m.:
America (9 E 18th St)
Brooklyn Diner USA (212 W 57th St)
Caffe Vivaldi (32 Jones St)
Chumley's (86 Bedford St)
I Tre Merli (463 West Broadway)
Il Cortile (125 Mulberry St)
Jackson Hole Burgers (232 E 64th St, Third Ave at 35th St, and Second Ave at 84th St)
Jekyll & Hyde (91 Seventh Ave S)
Metro Diner (2641 Broadway)
Mezzaluna (1295 Third Ave)
Motown Cafe (104 W 57th St)
Nirvana (30 Central Park S)
Planet Hollywood (140 W 57th St)
Tatou Le Cigar (151 E 50th St)
Windows on the World (1 World Trade Ctr, 107th floor)

Munching at the Museums

Some of the more appealing possibilities while you digest a bit of art and culture:

American Museum of Natural History (Central Park W at 79th St): Garden Cafe and the Whale's Lair (weekends only)
Guggenheim Museum (1071 Fifth Ave): Museum Cafe
Jewish Museum (1109 Fifth Ave): Cafe Weissman
Metropolitan Museum (Fifth Ave at 82nd St): Museum Restaurant, Great Hall Balcony Bar, Museum Bar and Cafe, and Roof Garden Espresso and Wine Bar (warm weather only)
Morgan Library (29 E 36th St): Morgan Court Cafe
Museum of Modern Art (11 W 53rd St): Garden Cafe and Sette MoMA
Sotheby's (1334 York Ave): The Cafe
Whitney Museum (945 Madison Ave): Sarabeth's Kitchen

Offbeat

Looking for someplace a bit different? Here are some ideas:

Acme Bar & Grill (9 Great Jones St): swinging
Afghan Kebab House (764 Ninth Ave and 1345 Second Ave): kebab
Barney Greengrass (541 Amsterdam Ave): You're in the 1940s.
Becco (355 W 46th St): family dining
Brother Jimmy's Bar-B-Q (1461 First Ave): great ribs
Coco Pazzo (23 E 74th St): crazy chef!
Frank's (85 Tenth Ave): meat and potatoes
Great Jones Cafe (54 Great Jones St): eclectic
Khyber Pass (34 St Mark's Pl): Afghan
Landmark Tavern (626 Eleventh Ave): historic
Next Door Nobu (105 Hudson St)
Nobu (105 Hudson St): Oriental delight
Noho Star (330 Lafayette St): diner
Nosmo King (54 Varick St): organic

Rao's (455 E 114th St): way uptown
Ruby's River Road Cafe (1754 Second Ave): Cajun
Sammy's Roumanian (157 Chrystie St): Lower East Side
Seventh Regiment Armory Mess Hall (643 Park Ave): unusual setting
Sylvia's (328 Lenox Ave): soul food
Veselka Coffee Shop (144 Second Ave): Polish-Ukrainian

Some of the younger generation like noisy hangouts! For them I recommend **Motown Cafe** (104 W 57th St), **Carmine's** (2450 Broadway), **Coffee Shop** (29 Union Square W), **Blue Ribbon** (97 Sullivan St), **Balthazar** (80 Spring St), and **Park Avalon** (225 Park Ave S).

For those who have more sensitive ears and like to be able to carry on a reasonable conversation, here are a few suggestions: **Union Square Cafe** (21 E 16th St), **Cafe des Artistes** (1 W 67th St), **La Côte Basque** (60 W 55th St), **Four Seasons** (99 E 52nd St), **Gramercy Tavern** (42 E 20th St), **La Réserve** (4 W 49th St), **Nobu** (105 Hudson St), and **Primavera** (1578 First Ave).

Old-timers

How far back do you want to go?

1763: Fraunces Tavern Restaurant (54 Pearl St)
1854: McSorley's Old Ale House (15 E 7th St)
1864: Pete's Tavern (129 E 18th St)
1865: Landmark Tavern (626 Eleventh Ave)
1868: Old Homestead (56 Ninth Ave)
1870: Billy's (948 First Ave): oldest family-run restaurant in Manhattan
1879: Gage & Tollner (372 Fulton St, Brooklyn)
1885: Keens Steakhouse (72 W 36th St)
1887: Peter Luger (178 Broadway, Brooklyn)
1888: Katz's Delicatessen (205 E Houston St)
1890: P.J. Clarke's (915 Third Ave)
1905: Ratner's (138 Delancey St)
1906: Barbetta (321 W 46th St)
1907: Plaza Hotel restaurants (768 Fifth Ave)
1912: Frank's (85 Tenth Ave)
1913: Grand Central Oyster Bar Restaurant (Grand Central Station, lower level)
1914: Cafe des Artistes (1 W 67th St)
1920: Ye Waverly Inn (16 Bank St)
1926: Palm (837 Second Ave)
1927: Minetta Tavern (113 MacDougal St)

Outdoor Dining

A taste of the outdoors in a garden, patio, or on the sidewalk:

Aquagrill (210 Spring St)
Aureole (34 E 61st St)
Barbetta (321 W 46th St)
Barolo (398 West Broadway)
Blue Water Grill (31 Union Sq W)

Bottino (246 Tenth Ave)
Bouterin (420 E 59th St)
Bryant Park Grill (25 W 40th St)
Cafe la Fortuna (69 W 71st St)
Caffe Bondi (7 W 20th St)
Caffe Bianco (1486 Second Ave)
Caffe Dante (79 MacDougal St)
Chelsea Commons (242 Tenth Ave)
Cheyenne Diner (411 Ninth Ave)
Chez Ma Tante (189 W 10th St)
Cloister Cafe (238 E 9th St)
Da Silvano (260 Ave of the Americas)
Demi (1316 Madison Ave)
Dia Center for the Arts (548 W 22nd St)
Druids (736 Tenth Ave)
Empire Diner (210 Tenth Ave)
Fletcher Morgan Provisions (864 Lexington Ave)
Gascogne (158 Eighth Ave)
Grove (314 Bleecker St)
Hatsuhana (17 E 48th St)
Home (20 Cornelia St)
I Coppi (432 E 9th St)
I Trulli (122 E 27th St)
Il Monello (1460 Second Ave)
Jackson Hole Burgers (232 E 64th St)
Jean Georges (1 Central Park W)
La Bohême (24 Minetta Lane)
La Cigale (231 Mott St)
Le Jardin Bistro (25 Cleveland Pl)
Le Madri (168 W 18th St)
Lombardi's (32 Spring St)
Luna Park (1 Union Sqare E)
March (405 E 58th St)
Mezzogiorno (195 Spring St)
Miracle Grill (112 First Ave)
Moustache (405 Atlantic Ave)
Museum of Modern Art (11 W 53rd St)
One If By Land, Two If By Sea (17 Barrow St)
Orson's (175 Second Ave)
Park View at the Boathouse (Central Park Lake)
Patroon (160 E 46th St, 3rd floor)
Pete's Tavern (129 E 18th St)
Provence (38 MacDougal St)
Restaurant Raphael (33 W 54th St)
Rialto (265 Elizabeth St)
River Cafe (1 Water St, Brooklyn)
Saloon, The (1920 Broadway)
San Pietro (18 E 54th St)
Spring Street Natural Restaurant (62 Spring St)
Tavern on the Green (Central Park W at 67th St)
Time Cafe (380 Lafayette St)
Trattoria dell'Arte (900 Seventh Ave)

Verbena (54 Irving Pl)
Vince & Eddie's (70 W 68th St)
Vinegar Factory (431 E 91st St)
Water Club (East River at 30th St)
White Horse Tavern (567 Hudson St)
Yaffa (97 St Mark's Pl)

Oyster Bars

Blue Ribbon (97 Sullivan St)
Docks Oyster Bar and Seafood Grill (2427 Broadway and 633 Third Ave)
Grand Central Oyster Bar Restaurant (Grand Central Station, lower level)
Plaza Oyster Bar (768 Fifth Ave)

A Guide to Oysters

Blue Point (Connecticut side of Long Island Sound): juicy, briny, firm and plump, clean finish
Caraquet (Nova Scotia): small, sweet, thin meat with a clean, mild finish
Dabob Bay (Washington): slightly sweet, small, firm, briny, fruity finish
Elkhorn (Washington): deep cup, salty, medium texture, mild aftertaste
Fanny Bay (British Columbia): sweet, very briny, plump, firm with a clean finish
Hood Canal (Puget Sound, Washington): mildly briny, delicate texture, sweet
Glidden Point (Maine): sweet, slightly briny, plump, full of flavor, mild finish
Malpeque (Prince Edward Island): small, thin firm meat, clean and juicy texture
Nantucket (Cape Cod, Massachusetts): small to medium, briny finish
Narragansett (Rhode Island): briny, plump, juicy with a clean finish
Oysterville Select (Washington): briny, delicate texture, fruity finish
Pearl Point (Netarts Bay, Oregon): sweet, plump, mildly briny with a clean finish
Point Reyes (California): deep cup, mildly salty, meaty with a sweet finish
Saltaire (Nova Scotia): medium size, juicy, plump with a clean, briny taste
Skookum (Puget Sound, Washington): deep cup, exceptionally sweet, briny, firm texture
Spinney Creek (Maine): plump, full meat, sweet with a salty finish
Wellfleet (Cape Cod, Massachusetts): juicy, slightly briny, plump with a salty finish

---

People Watching

Aureole (34 E 61st St)
Babbo (110 Waverly Pl)
Bice (7 E 54th St)
Bryant Park Grill (25 W 40th St)
Cafe Centro (MetLife Bldg, 200 Park Ave)

Chanterelle (2 Harrison St)
Coco Pazzo (23 E 74th St)
Daniel (20 E 76th St)
Ecco (124 Chambers St)
44 (44 W 44th St)
Four Seasons (99 E 52nd St)
Gotham Bar & Grill (12 E 12th St)
Gramercy Tavern (42 E 20th St)
Harry Cipriani (Fifth Ave at 59th St)
Il Mulino (86 W 3rd St)
Jo Jo (160 E 64th St)
La Côte Basque (5 E 55th St)
La Grenouille (3 E 52nd St)
La Réserve (4 W 49th St)
Le Cirque 2000 (New York Palace Hotel, 455 Madison Ave)
Le Madri (168 W 18th St)
Le Périgord (405 E 52nd St)
Le Rivage (340 W 46th St)
Mercer Kitchen (Mercer Hotel, 99 Prince St)
Mezze (10 E 44th St)
Mickey Mantle's (42 Central Park S)
Osteria del Circo (120 W 55th St)
P.J. Clarke's (915 Third Ave)
Palio (151 W 51st St)
Palm (837 Second Ave)
Palm Court (Plaza Hotel, Fifth Ave at Central Park S)
Paper Moon Milano (39 E 58th St)
Park Avalon (225 Park Ave S)
Planet Hollywood (140 W 57th St)
Provence (38 MacDougal St)
Remi (145 W 53rd St)
San Domenico (240 Central Park S)
Sette Mezzo (969 Lexington Ave, on Sunday nights)
Tavern on the Green (Central Park W at 67th St)
Trattoria dell'Arte (900 Seventh Ave)
Tribeca Grill (375 Greenwich St)
21 (21 W 52nd St)
Union Square Cafe (21 E 16th St)
Vong (200 E 54th St)
Windows on the World (2 World Trade Center)
Zoë (90 Prince St)

Personal Favorites

Everybody has a list of favorite places, and I am happy to share mine:

Adrienne (Peninsula New York Hotel, 700 Fifth Ave): elegance
Alison on Dominick Street (38 Dominick St): a hand-holding charmer
Blue Ribbon (97 Sullivan St): value for your buck
Cafe des Artistes (1 W 67th St): restful
Cafe des Sports (329 W 51st St): homey French
Cent Anni (50 Carmine St): consistent
Etats-Unis (242 E 81st St): homey
Gabriel's Bar & Restaurant (11 W 60th St): sophisticated

Gotham Bar & Grill (12 E 12th St): Everything is good.
Gramercy Tavern (42 E 20th St): the "in" place
Il Mulino (86 W 3rd St): Italian heaven!
Jackson Hole Burgers (various locations): best burgers
La Bohême (24 Minetta Ln): unpretentious
La Caravelle (33 W 55th St): Everything and everyone seems important.
La Grenouille (3 E 52nd St): beautiful
La Métairie (189 W 10th St): cozy
La Réserve (4 W 49th St): perfection!
Le Périgord (405 E 52nd St): impeccable
Lespinasse (St Regis Hotel, 2 E 55th St): grand
March (405 E 58th St): imaginative
Mark's (Mark Hotel, 25 E 77th St): hotel dining as it should be
Montrachet (239 West Broadway): very professional
One If By Land, Two If By Sea (17 Barrow St): romantic
Park Side (107-01 Corona Ave, Queens): Come here to eat!
Piccolo Angolo (621 Hudson St): like family friends
Primavera (1578 First Ave): superb service
River Cafe (1 Water St, East River, Brooklyn): Oh, that view!
Rosemarie's (145 Duane St): intimate
Sonia Rose (150 E 34th St): The place to propose!
Terrace, The (Columbia University, 400 W 119th St): great outlook
Toscana (843 Lexington Ave): quality folks
Union Square Cafe (21 E 16th St): justly famous
Wong Kee (113 Mott St): basic Chinatown

A bet, a bite, a beer

You'll be able to place orders for all three at the **Winners Circle** (515 Seventh Ave, 212/730-4900). Off-Track Betting (OTB) activity can be conducted here while you enjoy a steak.

Pizza

You can't go wrong with any of these:

Allegria (66 W 55th St)
Angelo's (117 W 57th St)
Antonio Restaurant (140 W 13th St)
Arturo's Pizzeria (106 Houston St)
Barocco (297 Church St)
Broadway Grill (Holiday Inn Crowne Plaza, 1605 Broadway)
California Pizza Kitchen (201 E 60th St)
Candido (1606 First Ave)
Coffee Shop (29 Union W Sq)
Da Ciro (229 Lexington Ave)
Da Nico (164 Mulberry St)
Don Giovanni's (210 Tenth Ave)
Figaro Pizza (1469 Second Ave)
Fisher & Levy (875 Third Ave)
Fred's at Barney's (10 E 61 St)
Galleria (600 Metropolitan Ave)
Grimaldi's (19 Fulton St)

Hosteria Fiorella Seafood Grill (1081 Third Ave)
Il Corallo (176 Prince St)
Isola (485 Columbus Ave)
John's Pizzeria (278 Bleecker St, 48-50 W 65th St, 260 W 44th St, and 408 E 64th St)
Koronet Pizzeria (Broadway at 111th St)
La Bohême (24 Minetta Lane)
La Traviota (461 W 23rd St)
Le Madri (168 W 8th St)
Lemon Tree Cafe (769 Ninth Ave)
Lento's (7003 Third Ave)
Lombardi's (32 Spring St)
Lula Lounge (220 Ave B)
Martini's (810 Seventh Ave)
Mezzogiorno (195 Spring St)
Mona Lisa (190 Bleecker St)
Nick & Toni's Cafe (100 W 67th St)
Nick's Pizza (108-26 Ascan Ave, Forest Hills, Queens)
Orso (322 W 46th St)
Osteria al Doge (142 W 44th St)
Osteria del Mezzaluna (75 Fifth Ave)
Patsy's Pizza (2287 First Ave)
Pintaile's Pizza (26 E 91st St)
Pizza Joint Too (70 W 71st St)
Pizzeria Uno (432 Columbus Ave)
Polistina's (2275 Broadway)
Pronto Pizza (6 E 42nd St)
Sal's & Carmine Pizza (2533 Broadway)
Stromboli Pizzeria (112 University Pl)
Totonno's Pizzeria Napolitano (1544 Second Ave)
Trattoria dell'Arte (900 Seventh Ave)
Two Boots (36 Ave A, 514 2nd St, and 75 Bleecker St)
Vinnie's Pizza (285 Amsterdam Ave)
Zito's East (211-13 First Ave)

Power Meals

Cafe des Artistes (1 W 67th St)
Cafe Pierre (Pierre Hotel, Fifth Ave and 61st St)
Campagna (24 E 21st St)
Carlyle Hotel (35 E 76th St)
Four Seasons (99 E 52nd St)
Gabriel's Bar & Restaurant (11 W 60th St)
Il Mulino (86 W 3rd St)
Jean Georges (1 Central Park W)
La Grenouille (3 E 52nd St)
La Réserve (4 W 49th St)
Le Bernardin (155 W 51st St)
Le Cirque 2000 (New York Palace Hotel, 455 Madison Ave)
Lespinasse (St Regis Hotel, 2 E 55th St)
Maloney & Porcelli (37 E 50th St)
Michael's (24 W 55th St)
Monkey Bar (60 E 54th St)

Morton's of Chicago (551 Fifth Ave)
Next Door Nobu (105 Hudson St)
Nobu (105 Hudson St)
Palm (837 Second Ave)
Paramount Hotel (235 W 46th St)
Park Avenue Cafe (100 E 63rd St)
Peninsula New York Hotel (700 Fifth Ave)
Primavera (1578 First Ave)
Regency Hotel (540 Park Ave)
Sette Mezzo (969 Lexington Ave)
Smith & Wollensky (797 Third Ave)
21 (21 W 52nd St)

Pre-Theater

It is best to let your waiter know when you sit down that you are planning to go to the theater so that service can be properly adjusted. Also, if it is raining, be sure to allow extra time for getting a taxi. Some restaurants have specially priced pre-theater dinners.

Aquavit (13 W 54th St)
Arqua (281 Church St)
Barbetta (321 W 46th St)
Cafe Botanica (Essex House Westin, 160 Central Park S)
Cafe des Artistes (1 W 67th St)
Cafe Un Deux Trois (123 W 44th St)
Carmine's (2450 Broadway and 200 W 44th St)
Chez Josephine (414 W 42nd St)
Dawat (210 E 58th St)
Fifty-seven Fifty-seven (57 E 57th St)
44 (Royalton Hotel, 44 W 44th St)
Four Seasons (99 E 52nd St)
Garrick, The (242 W 49th St)
Gino (780 Lexington Ave)
Indochine (430 Lafayette St)
La Boite en Bois (75 W 68th St)
La Caravelle (33 W 55th St)
La Réserve (4 W 49th St)
Marchi's (251 E 31st St)
Ollie's Noodle Shop and Grill (200B W 44th St, 2315 Broadway, and 1991 Broadway)
Orso (322 W 46th St)
Picholine (35 W 64th St)
Tavern on the Green (Central Park W at 67th St)
Tropica (MetLife building, 200 Park Ave)

Prix-Fixe Lunches

Gotham Bar & Grill (12 E 12th St)
La Caravelle (Shoreham Hotel, 33 W 55th St)
Le Cirque 2000 (New York Palace Hotel, 455 Madison Ave)
Nobu (105 Hudson St)
21 (21 W 52nd St)
Vong (200 E 54th St)

Pubs and Good Bars

To feel the real flavor of New York, visit a pub on St. Patrick's Day. However, these spots feature good brew, good times, and good company every day:

Billy's (948 First Ave)
Blarney Rock Pub (137 W 33rd St)
Blind Tiger Ale (518 Hudson St): olde flavor, every beer described
Brewsky's (43 E 7th St): top-quality beer
Burp Castle (41 E 7th St): Don't you love the name?
Chelsea Brewing Company (Pier 59, West St at 18th St): big place, big steaks
Chumley's (86 Bedford St)
Commonwealth Brewing Company (35 W 48th St): German lagers
Coup (509 E 6th St)
d.b.a. Forty One First Ave (41 First Ave): relaxed, good drinking, best beer list
Ear Inn (326 Spring St)
East Side Ale House (961 Second Ave): upstairs
Eleven Madison Park (11 Madison Ave)
Elsie's Oke Doke (304 E 84th St): memorabilia collection
Frank's (85 Tenth Ave)
Full Moon Saloon (735 Eighth Ave): rough-hewn honky-tonk
Ginger Man (11 E 36th St): huge beer selection
Great Jones Cafe (54 Great Jones St)
Greenwich Pizza & Brewing Co (418 Ave of the Americas)
Heartland Brewery (35 Union Square W): try the charcoal (stout)
Jack Dempsey (61 Second Ave): books plus fireplace
Jeremy's Ale House (254 Front St)
Jimmy Armstrong's (875 Tenth Ave)
Jimmy Day's (186 W 4th St)
Joe's Pub (425 Lafayette St)
Keens Steakhouse (72 W 36th St)
KGB (85 E 4th St): once a speakeasy
Landmark Tavern (626 Eleventh Ave): good afternoon bar
McQuaid's Public House (589 Eleventh Ave)
McSorley's Old Ale House (15 E 7th St)
Monkey Bar (60 E 54th St)
Morgan's Bar (235 Madison Ave): great ambience
Neptune Brewery (448 W 16th St): first microbrewery in Manhattan
No Idea (30 W 20th St)
North Star Pub (93 South St): authentic English style
Old Town Bar (45 E 18th St)
Peculiar Pub (145 Bleecker St): imagine . . . 500 beers!
Peter McManus Cafe (152 Seventh Ave)
Pete's Tavern (66 Irving Pl): New York's oldest continuously operating pub
PG Kings (18 W 33rd St): a beautiful bar
P.J. Clarke's (915 Third Ave)
Pugsley's Pub (Albany and Washington St)
Rao's (455 E 114th St)
Rudy's Bar & Grill (627 Ninth Ave)
Smith's (701 Eighth Ave): drink standing up
Soho Kitchen & Bar (103 Greene St)
Subway Inn (143 E 60th St): cheap
Swift Hibernian Lounge (34 E 4th St): 26 choices on tap

Tabla (11 Madison Ave)
Tavern at the Tonic (108 W 18th St)
Telephone Bar & Grill (149 Second Ave)
Temple Bar (332 Lafayette St)
Times Square Brewery (160 W 42nd St): in the middle of it all
Wall Street Kitchen & Bar (70 Broad St): 128 beers on tap
Waterfront Ale House (540 Second Ave): great Belgian beer, good food
Westside Brewing Company (340 Amsterdam Ave)
White Horse Tavern (567 Hudson St)
Wollensky's Grill (205 E 49th St)

New York's best bartenders:

Dale DeGroff at Blackbird (60 E 49th St)
Wolfgang Hauck at King Cole Bar and Lounge (St. Regis Hotel, 2 E 55th St)

Romantic

Some great places for hand-holding romance:

Alison on Dominick Street (38 Dominick St)
Aureole (34 E 61st St)
Barbetta (321 W 46th St)
Bouterin (420 E 59th St)
Bridge Cafe (279 Water St)
Cafe des Artistes (1 W 67th St)
Cafe Pierre (Pierre Hotel, 61st St at Fifth Ave)
Cafe Trévi (1570 First Ave)
Caffe Vivaldi (32 Jones St)
Capsouto Frères (451 Washington St)
Casa la Femme (150 Wooster St)
Chanterelle (2 Harrison St)
Enoteca at I Trulli (122 E 27th St)
Four Seasons (99 E 52nd St)
Hudson River Club (4 World Financial Center)
Il Cortile (125 Mulberry St)
La Bohême (24 Minetta Ln)
La Caravelle (33 W 55th St)
La Côte Basque (5 E 55th St)
La Grenouille (3 E 52nd St)
La Métairie (189 W 10th St)
La Réserve (4 W 49th St)
Le Cirque 2000 (New York Palace Hotel, 455 Madison Ave)
Le Périgord (405 E 62nd St)
Les Célébrités (160 Central Park S)
March (405 E 58th St)
Mark's (Mark Hotel, 25 E 77th St)
One If By Land, Two If By Sea (17 Barrow St)
Palm Court (Plaza Hotel, Fifth Ave and Central Park S)
Paola's (347 E 85th St)
Provence (38 MacDougal St)
River Cafe (1 Water St, Brooklyn)

Rosemarie's (145 Duane St)
Savoy (70 Prince St)
Sonia Rose (150 E 34th St)
Tavern on the Green, Crystal Room (Central Park W at 67th St)
Terrace, The (Columbia University, 400 W 119th St)
Windows on the World (1 World Trade Ctr)
Zoë (90 Prince St)

Rotisseries

Cafe Centro (MetLife Bldg, 200 Park Ave)
Daniel (60 E 65th St)
Mercer Kitchen (Mercer Hotel, 99 Prince St)
Patroon (160 E 46th St)
Zoë (90 Prince St)

Sandwiches

There are thousands (yes, thousands) of places that serve sandwiches in Manhattan, and most of them are pretty ordinary. But the following turn out exceptionally good combinations for eating in or taking out:

America (9-13 E 18th St)
Amy's Bread (672 Ninth Ave)
Azuri Cafe (465 W 21st St)
Barocco (301 Church St)
Bread & Butter (220 Elizabeth St)
Bread Market & Cafe (485 Fifth Ave)
Cafe Gitane (242 Mott St)
Cafe Journal (47 E 29th St)
Carnegie Delicatessen and Restaurant (854 Seventh Ave)
Casanas & Sons (461 Columbus Ave)
Chez Bernard (323 West Broadway)
City Bakery (22 E 17th St)
Cleaver Company (229 West Broadway)
Cosi Sandwich Bar (many locations)
Cucina & Company (200 Park Ave)
Deb's (200 Varick St)
Delices de France (289 Madison Ave)
Devon & Blakely (461 Fifth Ave)
E.A.T. (1064 Madison Ave)
Ecce Panis (1120 Third Ave and 1260 Madison Ave)
Eisenberg's Sandwich Shop (174 Fifth Ave)
Hudson Caterers Cafe (145 Hudson St)
Kathy's Kitchen (645 Hudson St)
La Boulangère (49 E 21st St)
La Fromagerie (1374 Madison Ave)
Lyn's Cafe (12 W 55th St)
Mama Joy's (2893 Broadway)
Manganaro's Hero Boy (492 Ninth Ave)
Mangia (50 W 57th St)
Market (230 Mott St)
Melampo Imported Foods (105 Sullivan St)
Old Navy Coffee Shop (610 Ave of the Americas): in the store
Olive's (120 Prince St)

Once Upon a Tart (135 Sullivan St)
Pepe Rosso to Go (149 Sullivan St)
Picnic (52 Irving Pl)
Popover Cafe (551 Amsterdam Ave)
Sandbox (289 Madison Ave)
Sosa Borella (460 Greenwich St)
Souperman (77 Pearl St and 55 Liberty St)
Sullivan Street Bakery (73 Sullivan St)
Telephone Bar & Grill (149 Second Ave)
Terramare (22 E 65th St)
Union Square Cafe (21 E 16th St)

Seafood
Aquagrill (210 Spring St)
Aquavit (13 W 54th St)
Bridge Cafe (279 Water St)
Blue Ribbon (97 Sullivan St)
Blue Ribbon Sushi (119 Sullivan St)
Blue Water Grill (31 Union Square W)
Captain's Table (860 Second Ave)
Christer's (145 W 55th St)
Docks Oyster Bar and Seafood Grill (2427 Broadway)
Estiatorio Milos (125 W 55th St)
Grand Central Oyster Bar Restaurant (Grand Central Station)
King Crab (871 Eighth Ave)
Kokachin (21 E 52nd St)
Le Bernardin (155 W 51st St)
Manhattan Ocean Club (57 W 58th St)
Marylou's (21 W 9th St)
Ocean Grill (348 Columbus Ave)
Oceana (55 E 54th St)
Oriental Town Seafood (14 Elizabeth St)
Pearl (18 Cornelia St)
Primola (1226 Second Ave)
Remi (145 W 53rd St)
Tropica (MetLife Building, 200 Park Ave)
Wilkinson's (1573 York Ave)

Shopping Breaks
To replenish your energy, here are some good places to eat in the major Manhattan stores:

ABC Carpet & Home (881 and 888 Broadway): Parlour Cafe (contemporary American) and Colina (upscale)
Barney's Uptown (660 Madison Ave): Fred's (upscale)
Bergdorf Goodman (men's store, 745 Fifth Ave): Cafe 745
Bergdorf Goodman (women's store, 754 Fifth Ave): Cafe on 5 (5th floor)
Bloomingdale's (1000 Third Ave): 59 & Lex (mid-level), Le Train Bleu (6th floor), and Showtime Cafe (7th floor)
Felissimo (10 W 56th St): Tea Room (4th floor)
Henri Bendel (712 Fifth Ave): Salon de Thé (tearoom; the Lalique windows are magnificent!)

Lord & Taylor (424 Fifth Ave): Cafe 424 (1st floor; coffee and pastries), Restaurant Cafe (American style), and Soup Bar
Macy's (151 W 34th St): Eatzi (cellar level), Emack and Bolio (4th floor), and 34th Street Diner (8th floor)
Old Navy (610 Ave of the Americas): Old Navy Coffee Shop
Saks (611 Fifth Ave): Cafe SFA (tasty and classy; 8th floor) and Espresso Bar (3rd floor)
Takashimaya (693 Fifth Ave): Tea Box Cafe (Oriental flavor)

By law, smoking is permitted at the bar of a restaurant if the dining tables are at least six feet away, or if the bar area is separated from the dining area by a solid floor-to-ceiling partition. Some restaurants are able to accommodate a small number of smokers because smoking is permitted in 15% of seating as long as that seating is in the same area as the bar. But if the bar is in the same area where patrons wait for their tables, then smoking is prohibited at the bar. Stand-alone bars are also exempt from the measure.

The following restaurants allow cigar smoking in their bar areas: **Campagna, Gallagher's, Keens Steakhouse, La Caravelle, Mark's, Morton's of Chicago, Post House,** and the **21 Club.** The following also have areas where you can enjoy a puff: **Cafe Tabac** (232 E 9th St), **Lucky Strike** (59 Grand St), **Match** (160 Mercer St), and **Viceroy** (160 Eighth Ave). They are all aptly named, eh?

Smoker-friendly

Angelo and Maxie's (233 Park Ave)
Avenue A Sushi (103 Ave A)
Blue Water Grill (31 Union Square W)
Bowlmor Lanes (110 University Pl)
City Wine & Cigar Co. (62 Laight St): cigar club
Clementine (1 Fifth Ave)
Corner Bistro (331 W 4th St)
Downtown (376 West Broadway)
Grand Bar (Soho Grand Hotel, 310 West Broadway)
Kelley & Ping (127 Greene St)
Les Deux Gamins (59 Grand St)
Lucky Strike (59 Grand St)
Panna (330 E 6th St)
Patroon (158 E 46th St)
Rain (100 W 82nd St)
Republic (37 Union Square W)
Rio Mar (1 Ninth Ave)
Screening Room (54 Varick St)
Smalls (183 W 10th St)
Sparks Steakhouse (210 E 46th St)
Tapas Lounge (1078 First Ave)
Vong (200 E 54th St)
Zarela (953 Second Ave)

Soups

Al Yeganeh (259-A W 55th St)
Chez Laurence Patisserie (245 Madison Ave)
Daily Soup (many locations)
Hale and Hearty Soups (849 Lexington Ave)
Mr. Soup (120 W 44th St and 108 E 23rd St)
Seaport Soup Company (76 Fulton St)
Second Avenue Kosher Delicatessen and Restaurant (156 Second Ave)
Soup Kitchen International (259-A W 55th St)
Soup Nutsy (148 E 46th St)
Soupcon (226 E 53rd St)
Souperman (55 Liberty St)
Sweet-n-Tart Cafe (76 Mott St)
Tea Den (940 Eighth Ave)
Veselka Coffee Shop (144 Second Ave)

Southern Flavors and Soul Food

Acme Bar & Grill (9 Great Jones St)
Cafe Con Leche (424 Amsterdam Ave)
Cajun (129 Eighth Ave)
Chantale's Cajun Kitchen (510 Ninth Ave)
Copeland's (547 W 145th St)
Emily's (1325 Fifth Ave)
Great Jones Cafe (54 Great Jones St)
Jezebel (630 Ninth Ave)
Londel's (2620 Frederick Douglass Blvd)
Louisiana Community Bar & Grill (622 Broadway)
Manna's (2331 Frederick Douglass Blvd)
Mekka (14 Ave A)
107 West (2787 Broadway)
Pink Tea Cup (42 Grove St)
Savannah Club (2420 Broadway)
Shark Bar (307 Amsterdam Ave)
Sister's Cuisine (1931 Madison Ave)
Sylvia's (328 Lenox Ave)
T.J.'s Southern Gourmet (92 Chambers St)
Well's (2247 Adam Clayton Powell, Jr. Blvd)

Southwestern

These places are a good distance from the Wild West, but they deliver a taste of cattle country!

Canyon Road (1470 First Ave)
El Rio Grande (160 E 38th St)
Mesa Grill (102 Fifth Ave)

Sports Bars

Boomer's Sports Club (349 Amsterdam Ave): football
Jimmy's Bait Shack (1644 Third Ave): football
Mccormack's (365 Third Ave): soccer
Mustang Sally's (324 Seventh Ave): basketball

Park Avenue Country Club (381 Park Ave S)
Play-by-Play (4 Penn Plaza)
Runyon's (932 Second Ave)
Sporting Club (99 Hudson St): basketball
Vazac's Horseshoe Bar (108 Ave B): hockey

Steaks

For meat-and-potato lovers, here are the best steaks in town:

Angelo and Maxie's (233 Park Ave S): reasonable prices
Ben Benson's (123 W 52nd St)
Bistro le Steak (1309 Third Ave): inexpensive and good
Bull & Bear (Waldorf-Astoria, 301 Park Ave)
Churrascaria Plataforma (Belvedere Hotel, 316 W 49th St)
Cité (120 W 51st St)
Dan Maxwell's Steakhouse (1708 Second Ave): good value, good eating
Frank's (85 Tenth Ave)
Frankie and Johnnie's (269 W 45th St)
Gage & Tollner (372 Fulton St, Brooklyn)
Gallagher's (228 W 52nd St)
Keens Steakhouse (72 W 36th St)
Le Marais (150 W 46th St): kosher
Les Halles (411 Park Ave S)
Maloney & Porcelli (37 E 50th St)
Manhattan Cafe (1161 First Ave)
Michael Jordan's, the Steak House (Grand Central Terminal)
Morton's of Chicago (551 Fifth Ave and 90 West St)
Old Homestead (56 Ninth Ave)
Palm and Palm Too (837 Second Ave and 840 Second Ave)
Patroon (160 E 46th St): outrageously expensive
Peter Luger (178 Broadway, Brooklyn): a tradition since 1887
Pietro's (232 E 43rd St)
Post House (28 E 63rd St)
Ruth's Chris Steak House (148 W 51st St)
Seryna (11 E 53rd St)
Smith & Wollensky (797 Third Ave)
Sparks Steakhouse (210 E 46th St)
Steak Frites (9 E 16th St)

Sushi

During the 1980s boomtime, sushi bars were the fast-food joints of the fashionable set. To this day, New Yorkers love to wrap their chopsticks around succulent bits of raw fish on rice. Although many are content to order the assortment plates concocted by the chef, true aficionados prefer to select by the piece. To tailor your next sushi meal to your specific tastes, here's what you need to know:

Amaebi (sweet shrimp)
Anago (sea eel)
California roll (avocado and crab)
Hamachi (yellowtail)
Hirami (halibut)

Ika (squid)
Ikura (salmon roe)
Kappa maki (cucumber roll)
Maguro (tuna)
Nizasakana (cooked fish)
Saba (mackerel)
Sake (salmon)
Tekka maki (tuna roll)
Toro (fatty tuna)
Umeshiso maki (plum roll)
Unagi (freshwater eel)
Uni (sea urchin)

Give any of these a try for sushi:

Avenue A Sushi (103 Ave A)
Blue Ribbon Sushi (119 Sullivan St)
Bond Street (6 Bond St)
Catch 21 (31 E 21st St)
Genki Sushi New York (565 Fifth Ave)
Hatsuhana (17 E 48th St and 237 Park Ave)
Iso (175 Second Ave)
Japonica (100 University Pl)
Kuruma Zushi (7 E 47th St)
March (405 E 58th St)
Match (160 Mercer St)
Nippon (155 E 52nd St)
Nobu and Next Door Nobu (105 Hudson St)
Otabe (68 E 56th St)
Ruby Foo's Dim Sum & Sushi Palace (2128 Broadway)
Sapporo East (245 E 10th St)
Sushi Bar (256 E 49th St)
Sushi Hana (1501 Second Ave)
Sushihatsu (1143 First Ave)
Sushi Rose (248 E 52nd St)
Sushi Zen (57 W 46th St)
Takahachi (85 Ave A)
Takino Japanese (1026 Second Ave)
Ten Kai (920 W 56th St)
Tomoe Sushi (172 Thompson St)
Yama (122 E 17th St)

In the best sushi bars . . .
- The tuna looks fresh.
- The ginger is ivory.
- The seaweed wrap is crisp.
- The menu has many different items.
- The rice is not cold.
- The restaurant uses Dungeness or snow crab.
- The sashimi comes with fresh-grated wasabi.

Teatime

Afternoon tea is usually served between 3 and 6 p.m. The common story is that the Duchess of Bedford started the practice in the 18th century because it helped fortify her ladysmith between lunch and dinner. It is common practice to serve tea sandwiches, scones, and a sweet.

Some tips:
- Tea bags are definitely *out*.
- Weak tea is diluted with hot water from a separate pot.
- Sugar (never more than two cubes) and milk (not cream) can be added.
- Paper-thin tea sandwiches (two only) should be put on your tea plate, not on the saucer.
- Never butter an entire scone at once.

Now you're ready for an invitation to take tea with the Queen!

ABC Carpet & Home's Parlour Cafe (38 E 19th St)
Adrienne at the Peninsula New York Hotel (700 Fifth Ave)
Algonquin Hotel (59 W 44th St)
Anglers & Writers (420 Hudson St)
Barclay Restaurant at the Intercontinental Hotel (111 E 48th St)
Cafe SFA at Saks Fifth Avenue (611 Fifth Ave)
Carlyle Hotel Gallery (35 E 76th St)
Ceci-Cela (55 Spring St)
Cocktail Terrace at the Waldorf-Astoria (301 Park Ave)
Danal (90 E 10th St)
Felissimo Tea Room (10 W 56th St)
Fifty-seven Fifty-seven (Four Seasons Hotel, 57 E 57th St)
Firebird (365 W 46th St)
Four Seasons Hotel (57 E 57th St)
Gold Room at the New York Palace (455 Madison Ave)
Gotham Lounge at the Peninsula New York Hotel (700 Fifth Ave)
King's Carriage House (251 E 82nd St)
Kitano Hotel (66 Park Ave)
Lady Mendl's (56 Irving Pl)
Le Salon at the Stanhope (995 Fifth Ave)
Le Salon de Thé at Henri Bendel (712 Fifth Ave)
Le Train Bleu at Bloomingdale's (1000 Third Ave)
Lowell Hotel (28 E 63rd St)
Mark (25 E 77th St)
Mayfair Regent Hotel (610 Park Ave)
Oak Room at the Algonquin Hotel (59 W 44th St)
Palm Court at the Plaza Hotel (768 Fifth Ave)
Payard Patisserie (1032 Lexington Ave)
Pembroke Room at the Lowell Hotel (28 E 63rd St)
Plaza Athenee (37 E 64th St)
Regency Hotel (540 Park Ave)
Rotunda at the Hotel Pierre (2 E 61st St)
Sant Ambroeus (1000 Madison Ave)
Serendipity 3 (225 E 60th St)
Stanhope Hotel (995 Fifth Ave)
Sweet Melissa (276 Court St)
Sweet Tea Room at Mackenzie-Childs (824 Madison Ave)

T Salon & Emporium (11 E 20th St)
Tea & Symphathy (108 Greenwich Ave)
Tea Box Cafe (Takashimaya, 693 Fifth Ave)
Toraya (17 E 71st St)
21 (21 W 52nd St)
Waldorf-Astoria Hotel (301 Park Ave)
Wild Lily Tea Room (511 W 22nd St)

Top-Rated Restaurants

The following appear in most listings as the best of the best.
Aureole (34 E 61st St)
Bouley Bakery (120 West Broadway)
Cafe des Artistes (1 W 67th St)
Chanterelle (2 Harrison St)
Daniel (20 E 76th St)
Four Seasons (99 E 52nd St)
Gotham Bar & Grill (12 E 12th St)
Gramercy Tavern (42 E 20th St)
Il Mulino (86 W 3rd St)
Jean Georges (1 Central Park W)
La Caravelle (33 W 55th St)
La Côte Basque (60 W 55th St)
La Grenouille (3 E 52nd St)
La Réserve (4 W 49th St)
Le Bernardin (155 W 51st St)
Le Cirque 2000 (New York Palace Hotel, 455 Madison Ave)
Lespinasse (St. Regis Hotel, 2 E 55th St)
Lutèce (249 E 50th St)
March (405 E 58th St)
Montrachet (239 West Broadway)
Morton's of Chicago (551 Fifth Ave and 90 West St)
Next Door Nobu (105 Hudson St)
Nobu (105 Hudson St)
Oceana (55 E 54th St)
Peter Luger (178 Broadway, Brooklyn)
Primavera (1578 First Ave)
River Cafe (1 Water St, Brooklyn)
Sushisay (38 E 51st St)
Union Square Cafe (21 E 16th St)

Vegetarian

Angelica Kitchen (300 E 12th St)
Bachué (36 W 21st St)
Benny's Burritos (113 Greenwich Ave and 93 Ave A)
Candle Cafe (1307 Third Ave)
City Bakery (22 E 17th St and 550 Madison Ave)
Good Earth (167 Amsterdam Ave)
Good Health Cafe (324 E 86th St)
Hangawi (12 E 32nd St)
Indian Delhi (392 Columbus Ave)
Integral Yoga (229 W 13th St)
Le Potager at Cafe Boulud (20 E 76th St)

Lespinasse (St. Regis Hotel, 2 E 55th St)
Nature Works (200-A W 44th St)
Planet One (76 E 7th St)
Quantum Leap (88 W 3rd St)
Ratner's Dairy Restaurant (138 Delancey St)
Souen (28 E 13th St and 210 Ave of the Americas)
Spring Street Natural Restaurant (62 Spring St)
Two Boots (37 Ave A)
Union Square Cafe (21 E 16th St)
Vegetable Garden (15 E 40th St and 233 Bleecker St)
Vege Vege II (544 Third Ave)
Village Natural (46 Greenwich Ave)
VP 2 (144 W 4th St)
Whole Earth Bakery and Kitchen (130 St. Marks Pl)
Zen Palate (663 Ninth Ave and 2170 Broadway)

Cheese boards are *in!* No one does them better than the **Gramercy Tavern** (42 E 29th St). Here's a sampling of their offerings, from which you can choose three, five, or seven cheeses of your liking:
Artavaggio (tangy cow's milk cheese from Italy)
Boer Piet (sharp, nutty, raw cow's milk cheese from Holland)
Camembert (soft-ripened cow's milk cheese from France)
Chimay (cow's milk cheese washed in beer from Belgium)
Explorateur (triple-cream cow's milk cheese from France)
Garroxta (aged goat's milk cheese from Spain)
Gorgonzola (tangy cow's milk blue cheese from Italy)
Manouri (buttery, tart, young sheep's milk cheese from Vermont)
Pavé Sauvage (young goat's milk cheese with herbs from France)
Round Caraway (aged goat's milk cheese from New York)
Selles-Sur-Cher (aged goat's milk cheese from France)
Shropshire Blue (earthy cow's milk blue cheese from England)
Valdeon (piquant cow's milk blue cheese from Spain)
Vermont Shepherd (sharp, raw sheep's milk cheese from Vermont)

View

Contrary to the axiom that good food does not come with a good view, the food at all of these "rooms with a view" is terrific.

American Park (inside Battery Park, off State St)
Delegates Dining Room (United Nations, First Ave at 42nd St, visitor's entrance)
Hudson River Club (4 World Financial Center, 250 Vesey St)
Peninsula New York Hotel Bar (700 Fifth Ave, 23rd floor)
River Cafe (1 Water St, Brooklyn): A window seat affords that famous view of the downtown skyline you've seen on postcards and in movies.
Tavern on the Green (Central Park W at 67th St): Magical!
Terrace, The (400 W 119th St): The windows here show what the city looks like from uptown.
Top of the Tower (3 Mitchell Pl): An art deco penthouse delight
View, The (Marriott Marquis Hotel, 1535 Broadway): You're high above Times Square and revolving.

Water Club (East River at 30th St): Try the view with Sunday brunch.
World Yacht Cruises (Pier 81, 41st St at Hudson River): Manhattan from the water

Wine Bars

Harry's at Hanover Square (1 Hanover Sq)
I Tre Merli (463 West Broadway)
Soho Kitchen & Bar (103 Greene St)

New York Restaurants: The Best of the Lot

ACAPPELLA
1 Hudson St   212/240-0163
Lunch: Mon-Fri; Dinner: Mon-Sat
Moderately expensive

Acappella is a very classy, upscale (in atmosphere, food, and pricing) Tribeca Northern Italian dining room that provides the kind of background and highly professional staff for a very special dining experience. It's a good place for a romantic interlude, an important business lunch, or to experiment with some unique Italian dishes. You'll find pastas, risotto, calamari, veal scaloppine, veal chops, breaded breast of chicken and prime steak on the menu. Forget the ordinary desserts (tiramisu or crème brûlée) and splurge on the homemade Italian cheesecake or chocolate truffle torte.

ACROSS THE STREET
444 E 91st St (at York Ave)   212/722-4000
Dinner: Mon-Sat
Moderately expensive

There are three things you can say about Eli Zabar (the proprietor of Across the Street): (1) He makes some of the best bread in town (and does it right across the street from this restaurant). (2) The quality of his food is very good. (3) He knows how to charge for his goodies. Across the Street, in appearance very much like an upscale coffee shop, fits the bill in all three catgeories. Every night the inventive chef offers six rather unique appetizers, six delicious entrees, a cheese selection, and four desserts. Of course, there is Eli's crusty bread on the table to start. The menu changes seasonally, but there are some new items daily. The name of this novel eatery comes from the fact that the Vinegar Factory, another of Eli's enterprises (which features more reasonably priced gourmet items) is just a hop, skip, and jump away.

ADRIENNE
The Peninsula New York
700 Fifth Ave (at 55th St)   212/903-3918
Breakfast: Daily; Lunch: Mon-Fri; Dinner: Tues-Sat;
Brunch: Sun
Moderately expensive

The Peninsula New York has had a very successful face lift, and Adrienne has a contemporary new look also. It is a charming room, in keeping with a classy hotel, where you will feel much more comfortable dressed up than in jeans. The menu is in keeping with the atmosphere: wonderful lobster bisque, crayfish and Yukon Gold potato tart, and a napoleon of roasted veggies for the health addict—all great appetizers. Upscale entrees include crispy ahi tuna in rice paper and seared squab. Of course, there are also popular dishes like rack of lamb and tenderloin of beef. For those who are hungry for sandwiches, try the hotel's Bistro. Afternoon tea, a Peninsula tradition, is available in the Gotham lounge. No matter where you go in this extremely well-run hotel, you will be delighted with the personal attention.

AKBAR
475 Park Ave (bet 57th and 58th St)   212/838-1717
Lunch: Mon-Fri; Dinner: Daily
Moderate

If you are interested in northern Indian cuisine, you can't do better than Akbar. You'll get a real taste of the region in a distinguished atmosphere, where *muglai* cooking at its very best is featured. The nice part is that the food is not too hot or oily. Wonderful tandoori breads, baked in a traditional clay oven, are real treats. There are other tandoori specials: several chicken dishes (chicken fritters are excellent), minced lamb, cubes of fish, and large prawns. You can taste them all in a mixed-grill plate. At noontime there are set menus. In the evening, you can choose from delicious vegetarian dishes (very reasonably priced), traditional lamb entrees, and mildly spiced seafood specialties. Try a lassi with your meal; it is a yogurt drink that comes salted or sweet. The Chai Salon features exotic teas. Although most folks don't come to an Indian restaurant for desserts, the cottage cheese and milk flavored with rose water is surely different!

ALISON ON DOMINICK STREET
38 Dominick St   212/727-1188
Dinner: Daily
Expensive

Genteel is the appropriate word here. Nothing trendy. No hip waiters. No complicated multi-ethnic dishes. It is right for a special evening out, when you want to bring a bit of class back into your life. There have been constant rumors that Alison intends to move this tiny and romantic French bistro. This West Soho address is hard to find; most taxi drivers have never heard of the street. But insist! The menu changes often; you will probably find special delights like smoked salmon, roast chicken, or roast cod. Servers (and all personnel) are especially friendly and efficient. Pricey desserts are worth every buck. The rich bittersweet chocolate gratin is superb.

ALLEY'S END
311 W 17th St (bet Eighth and Ninth Ave)   212/627-8899
Dinner: Daily
Moderate

If you blink, you'll miss this place! A set-back door does indeed take you back through an alleyway into a cozy room with a distinctly friendly and upbeat atmosphere. The glassed-in patio area gives this popular neighborhood restaurant a homey feel. The only down side is the feeling that if an emergency occurred, the two exits might become a problem! But let's concentrate instead on the really good food and really good prices. Wonderful homemade soups are a great start. On to curried portabello mushrooms, pan-roasted black sea bass with pecans, or a pan-roasted prime ribeye steak with marinated beefsteak tomatoes! The menu changes with the season. If strawberries are in season, don't miss the classic strawberry shortcake.

ALVA
36 E 22nd St   212/228-4399
Lunch: Mon-Fri; Dinner: Mon-Sat
Moderate

I'd go back here anytime for one reason: Alva's personnel are extremely friendly without being overbearing. Owner Charles Palmer sets the upbeat mood. The room is small, manageable, and attractively done, but the emphasis is in the quality of the American bistro-type food and the reasonable pricing. You'll find a continental menu complete with delicious burgers, salads, and fish dishes at noon. In the evening there's chicken, steak, and everything else the American palate desires. Desserts? Try the banana ice cream sandwich or homemade chocolate pudding.

AMERICA
9-13 E 18th St   212/505-2110
Lunch, Dinner: Daily; Brunch: Sat, Sun
Inexpensive to moderate

There is just one word to describe this place: *big!* The room is big, the menu is big, the portions are big, the noise level is big. The good news is that the tab is relatively small. Kids will love it: burgers, chili, pasta, pizza, great sandwiches. Mom and Dad have their items, too: omelets, Boston brown bread, Cincinnatis (shoestring french fries drenched in gravy), deep-fried crawfish tails, Buffalo chicken wings, New Mexican black-bean cakes, roast turkey, shrimp jambalaya, and South Carolina crab cakes. Super desserts include Toll House cookies, Death by Chocolate, key lime pie, ice cream, and more. This is not gourmet dining, but it's vintage America-at-the-dinner-table—a really big dinner table.

AMERICAN PARK
Battery Park (off State St)   212/809-5508
Lunch: Mon-Fri; Dinner: Mon-Sat;
Outside grill open daily in summer
Moderate

This is one of those good news/bad news operations. First the good news: the setting is spectacular, overlooking the harbor and the Statue of Liberty in the distance. The menu, with its emphasis on American and seafood items, offers some excellent choices, and the raw bar is appealing. Braised short ribs are excellent. The wood-burning oven does bass, lobster, and squab to perfection. Now the bad news! The place is difficult to find; the best point of reference is the vehicle entrance to the Staten Island Ferry. But the major drawback is unprofessional service. The poorly trained personnel will surely improve as the operation matures. I'd recommend American Park on a nice day, when the outdoor patio grill is particularly appealing. And try the La Liberté dessert, a takeoff on the statue based in a delicious mocha torte.

AN AMERICAN PLACE
565 Lexington Ave (bet 50th and 51st St)   212/888-5650
Lunch, Dinner: Daily
Moderately expensive to expensive

From sparkling new quarters in the Benjamin Hotel, respected chef Larry Forgione continues his patriotic Yankee love affair with classic regional American cuisine. Wonderful dishes include warm potato crisp Napoleon with

Hudson Valley foie gras; a terrine of three smoked fish with caviars and champagne dressing; and cedar-planked Atlantic salmon with toasted corn sauce. The strawberry shortcake, banana Betty, and double chocolate pudding desserts would surely have pleased George Washington himself.

ANGELS
1135 First Ave (bet 62nd and 63rd St)   212/980-3131
Daily: 11:30-11:30
Inexpensive

Wouldn't you expect two people named Angela and Angelo to open a place called Angels? Well they did, and it has heavenly food at heavenly prices. Angels is a non-fancy pastaria, with angels all over the place—on the plain tables and on the plain walls. The food is contemporary Italian, with a heavy emphasis on delicious pastas, salads, and chicken. You are treated here as a member of the family with informal service and loving care. It is no wonder that the place is busy all day and evening. Desserts include gelati, Oreo cheesecake, and a wonderfully rich Mississippi (in an Italian restaurant?) mud cake. The goodies don't stop here. Make sure you go around the corner to their takeout at 365 E 62nd St (212/371-8484), where you will find an absolutely fantastic assortment of bakery and prepared foods, pastas, sandwiches, and salads. The prices are extremely reasonable, the quality exceptional. Catering services are available, and so is delivery.

ANNIE'S
1381 Third Ave (bet 78th and 79th St)   212/327-4853
Breakfast: Mon-Fri; Lunch, Dinner: Daily; Brunch: Sat, Sun
Inexpensive to moderate

Doesn't anyone go out for breakfast or lunch on Saturdays? It would seem that way in Manhattan, with most restaurants pulling the shades until dinnertime. Not at Annie's. The Saturday brunch finds this place hopping with neighborhood regulars who know they can get a good meal at a sensible price. On the brunch menu are tasty eggs, omelets, frittatas, cereals, and homemade baked items. The regular lunch and dinner menus feature tasty soups and salads, sandwiches, pastas, steaks, chicken, burgers, seafood, and delicious short ribs of beef. If you can imagine desserts under $6 at today's inflated New York prices, look at what Annie offers: homemade apple pie, tarts, old-fashioned strawberry shortcake, gelati, and sorbets. No wonder this is such a popular place. Even standing in line is a pleasure when you get value like this! Free delivery is available from 65th to 96th Streets, between East End and Fifth avenues.

ANTON'S
259 W 4th St (at Perry St)   212/675-5059
Dinner: Wed-Mon
Moderate

On a quiet corner in the West Village, Anton's provides a welcome change from the noise and frantic atmosphere of so many Manhattan restaurants. Outside, a white picket fence surrounds several spaces that appeal during nice weather (although the view is not the greatest). Inside, a dozen tables covered with paper cloths are the setting for casual dining at its home-style best. You'll find a nice selection of salads, different daily pastas, and several fresh fish dishes, all done with chef-owner Anton Linder's personal touch. There are several other choices: chicken breast, Viennese schnitzel, rack of lamb, and New York shell steak. Homemade tarts and filling Viennese apple strudel will complete a pleasant and affordable meal.

AQUAVIT
13 W 54th St   212/307-7311
Lunch: Mon-Sat; Dinner: Daily; Smorgasbord: Sun (12-3)
Expensive

Aquavit presents an attractive, wholesome background for some very tasty (and expensive) Scandinavian dishes. The setting is a feast for the eyes, while the platters are a feast for the tummy. One has a choice of eating upstairs in the slightly less expensive cafe or in the several areas downstairs, including a covered patio with a waterfall. From here, the diner looks eight stories skyward in a dramatic atrium (the former John D. Rockefeller townhouse). Major alterations have been made to the menu, which is now prepared by chef Marcus Samuelsen. Cafe specialties include herring, gravlax, and delicious salmon (poached or pan-fried). Danish open-faced sandwiches are also available. Outstanding dishes in the dining room include pan-roasted loin of beef, loin of Arctic venison, Arctic char (like salmon trout), and rack of lamb. For dessert, how about a warm chocolate ganache?

ARQUA
281 Church St   212/334-1888
Lunch: Mon-Sat; Dinner: Mon-Sun
Moderate

To be outstanding in New York, an Italian restaurant must have something special going for it. Arqua is special because the staff does things so plainly, simply, and well. This is not a fancy, pricy restaurant of the moment. Arqua (named for a small city near Venice) is situated in an old warehouse with high ceilings, which adds to the noisy atmosphere. The folks who run this place are not fancy, either. It shows in the TLC they give all their patrons, and the food is exceptional. Choose from homemade pastas, Venetian dishes, marinated salmon, and ravioli with butternut squash. Squab and duck are specialties. There are also excellent veal dishes. The flourless espresso chocolate cake is wonderful.

A TAVOLA
1095 Lexington Ave (at 77th St)   212/744-1233
Breakfast, lunch, dinner: daily
Inexpensive to moderate

An inexpensive Italian diner in the midst of the high-rent Upper East Side? Yes sir, and they serve excellent food. An unbelievably small kitchen turns out dozens of hot and cold appetizers, soups, stews, seafood, sandwiches, poultry, steaks and chops, pastas, and much more. They serve complete Italian meals with very tasty Italian breads and just about anything else your heart desires. There's nothing fancy in the decor, the service is homey and informal, and the owners seem sincerely happy to welcome you. The breakfast menu offers the whole gamut: juices, fresh fruit, omelets, lox and bagels, cereals, and griddle items. Don't ask me how they manage to do it all so well, but this is a real find . . . and the price is right. Their tartufo is as good as any I have tasted in Italy.

AUREOLE
34 E 61st St (bet Madison and Park Ave)   212/319-1660
Lunch: Mon-Fri; Dinner: Mon-Sat
Expensive

I am not a big fan of Aureole. Not that it isn't a fine restaurant; at the prices they charge, it should be. Owner-chef Charlie Palmer usually does a fine job with the preparation of his dishes. They are beautifully served by personnel who are more than a little bit impressed that they work for this establishment. If you manage to get seated (without questionable waits at the bar) and are lucky enough to sit on the first floor, with its seasonal garden views, you are fortunate. Best bets are the game dishes, signature plates like smoked salmon with cucumber salad and sea scallop sandwiches in crisp potato crusts, and roast pheasant. Desserts look better than they taste. Personally, I can think of other places to spend your hard-earned bucks where the staff will appreciate your business, although the four-course *prix fixe* luncheon is a good value.

AU TROQUET
328 W 12th St   212/924-3413
Dinner: Daily
Moderate

Allow extra time if you're arriving here by taxi since most drivers will have trouble delivering you to the front door. And be sure to call for reservations. The place is small and very popular with neighbors as well as knowledgeable diners who have previously enjoyed Au Troquet's delights. This is a no-nonsense French country restaurant where food is prepared professionally. Your plate is flamboyant in presentation and exceptional in taste. Au Troquet deserves special mention for its seasonings; they know how it's done. The soups are all delicious, as is the *pate de foie de canard.* You can go on to fillet of sole, grilled salmon, lobster, or a fabulous rabbit dish. There is almost always a fine selection of lamb dishes available. Homemade desserts include a great mousse and sorbets. This is the kind of place to go to when you feel like having a relaxed, cozy dinner for two.

✗ BABBO
110 Waverly Pl (nr Washington Square)   212/777-0303
Dinner: Daily
Moderate to moderately expensive

In past days one of my very favorite dining spots was the Coach House, in Greenwich Village. Alas, due to the demise of its owner, the place closed and legions of New Yorkers, along with me, lost one of the city' s best. But not to worry! Now with the new owners and a completely new look, 110 Waverly Place has been reborn as Babbo (which means "daddy" in Italian). Babbo is one of the most delicious establishments in the city. It's difficult to say what is best in the ever-changing menu: perhaps the marinated anchovies in vinaigrette, the spaghettini with spicy artichokes, or the fabulous grilled guinea hen. Then again, Copper River salmon (if available) is sensational. The desserts get my five-star rating! Delicious chocolate hazelnut cake, pistachio and chocolate *simifreddo,* and the cheese plate are all outstanding. But best of all is the assortment of homemade gelati and *sorbetti,* served in six small cups that delight the eye as well as the taste. Babbo is a winner!

BALTHAZAR
80 Spring St (at Crosby St)   212/965-1414
Breakfast, Lunch, Dinner: Daily; Brunch: Sat, Sun; afterhours menu
after midnight
Moderate

A certain chemistry hurtles some restaurants into the big time very early in their existence. This happened in spades at Balthazar. Despite the overtaxing of every aspect of their operation, they stuck to a basic necessity: the food must be good, even very good, if popularity was to last. In a comfortable setting with tile floors, old mirrors, ceiling fans, and an unattractive yellow tin roof, the harried help scoot around trying to please diners, who should wear earplugs in order to concentrate on tasty dishes. Seafood—steamed halibut, grilled brook trout, seared salmon, and the like—is especially good. An attractive baked goods section is right at the front door, and a seafood bar serves oysters, clams, and lobster until the wee hours. A nice selection of cheeses is available, along with tasty desserts like apple and caramelized banana ricotta tarts. I went for the bittersweet chocolate torte with chocolate malted ice cream. If you want to see or be seen, this is a hot spot. The takeout menu includes soups, salads, and sandwiches on delectable breads.

BARBETTA
321 W 46th St (bet Eighth and Ninth Ave)   212/246-9171
Lunch, Dinner, Supper: Tues-Sun
Moderate to expensive

Barbetta is one of those special places you can only find in New York. It is an elegant restaurant serving Piemontese cuisine. Piemonte is located in the northern part of Italy, and the cuisine reflects that charming part of the country. You can dine here in European elegance. One of New York's oldest restaurants, celebrating its 100th anniversary in 2006, Barbetta is still owned by the family who founded it. One of the special attractions is dining alfresco in the garden during the summer. The main dining room and private party rooms are magnificent! There is an a la carte luncheon menu, as well as a six-course before-theater dinner menu, which offers fish specialties, *scottiglia,* and a number of other selections served expeditiously so that you can make opening curtain. If you have more time and can enjoy a leisurely dinner, think about the minestrone (which is almost a meal in itself), handmade ravioli, or the fabulous *finocchio e parmigiano* salad. Barbetta specializes in fish and game dishes that vary daily. Try the squab prepared with glazed chestnuts and leeks. Other selections include rabbit, beef braised in red wine with polenta, and a delicious rack of venison. Desserts include several chocolate offerings and an assortment of cooked fruits, as well as *panna cotta*—one of the best in the city. Added attractions: a pianist during pre-theater dinner every night and lunchtime fashion shows on Wednesday. (P.S. Ask for Jay Frank for your waiter.)

BAROCCO
301 Church St   212/431-1445
Lunch: Mon-Fri; Dinner: Daily
Moderate

If you are looking for simple and well-prepared food in the Tribeca area, this *trattoria* with a Tuscan flavor is your best bet. Barocco has a special way with seasonings that make their dishes light and easy to digest. This style of dining attracts many celebrities, who are so mindful of their figures! Specialties include wonderful homemade grilled bread with garlic and olive oil (*fettunta*), lasagna, spinach ravioli, grilled Norwegian salmon, grilled lamb chops, roast chicken, and prime New York strip steak. Top it all off with Tuscan almond cookies. Many items served in the restaurant are available for takeout next door.

BELLINI
208 E 52nd St   212/308-0830
Lunch: Mon-Fri: Dinner: Mon-Sat
Moderately expensive

You might call the cuisine in this new classic Italian beauty "all in the family." The head lady at Bellini is Donatella Arpaia; her father, the well-known chef Lello Arpaia, and her brother Dino are also in the restaurant business. But Donatella has stepped out on her own to create an instant success. Her menus take into account the current interest in healthy platters. Specialties of the house include thinly sliced raw tuna with dill, grilled sirloin steak, a number of specialty pastas, and a great Dover sole. Even the appetizers, like grilled portabello mushrooms, and the fresh salads are a treat. For traditionalists, the Bellini gnocchi, served with a Bolognese sauce, is sure to please. For dessert, how about warm chocolate hazelnut cake? Besides the glamorous owner, other attractions include businesslike waiters, tables far enough apart to enable patrons to carry on a conversation, and an acoustically advantageous ceiling, missing in so many of today's better restaurants. Cigar lovers will feel right at home at the Bellini bar; Donatella handpicked the offerings herself!

BEN BENSON'S
123 W 52nd St   212/581-8888
Lunch: Mon-Fri; Dinner: Daily
Moderately expensive

With all the excitement of a number of new steakhouses in Manhattan, it is easy to overlook the old reliables. For years, Ben Benson's has been a favorite of the meat-and-potatoes set, and with justification. The atmosphere is very macho-clubby, the air is nicely tinged with cigar smoke from boys having an evening out on the town, and the food is uniformly good. Unlike some other steakhouses, service here is courteous and efficient. The menu is what you would expect: sirloin steak, filet mignon, T-bone, prime rib, chops, and the like. But there is much more. Ben Benson's also offers seafood, chicken, calves liver, and chopped steak. Wonderful potatoes, onion rings, or healthy spinach complete the stomach-filling experience. Lunchtime specials include lobster cakes, grilled chicken breast, roast beef hash, and chicken pot pie. Don't come here looking for bargains. Ben treats you well, and you pay well for what you get!

BERGER'S DELICATESSEN AND RESTAURANT
44 W 47th St (bet Fifth Ave and Ave of the Americas)   212/719-4173
Mon-Fri: 6 a.m.-7:30 p.m.; Sat: 7-5

Berger's has been serving delicious deli items since 1952. It is easy to understand why this unfancy place is so popular with folks in the jewelry district. You'll find great omelets and pancakes for breakfast, fantastic sandwich combinations for lunch, and a full dinner menu as well. There are daily specials, deli platters to go, wonderful salads, and a full range of afternoon snacks. All items are prepared in their own kitchen.

BIENVENUE
21 E 36th St   212/684-0215
Lunch: Mon-Fri; Dinner: Mon-Sat
Moderate

The neighborhood knows and loves this reliable, smallish French bistro that serves exceptionally good food in large portions at very moderate prices. There is absolutely no service "attitude" here, just informed and gracious folks taking care of the busy tables. Snails, large and fresh salads, delicious onion soup, and specialty patés all make good starters (be sure to bring a healthy appetite). On to chicken in red wine sauce, striped bass, crab cakes, beef bourguignon, roast loin of pork, or other daily specials. When I saw profiteroles on the menu, I made that my dessert choice. This comfortable, professional operation has been doing things right since 1971, and that is quite an accomplishment!

Be forewarned: Monday is not a good day to order seafood at New York restaurants; it may not be fresh.

BIG NICK'S
2175 Broadway (at 77th St)   212/362-9238
24 hours
Inexpensive

For those readers who feel this volume deals only in pricy places, that is simply not true! Take Big Nick's, for example. This place is unfancy, unexpensive, untrendy, and practically unknown . . . except for those who want really good food at really low prices and don't care about atmosphere! The burgers are sensational. There is a special selection for diet-watchers. Meat pies, cheese pies, spinach pies, and filo pastries are all specialties. There are lots of pizzas, baked potatoes served any way you want, delicious cakes and pies, homemade baklava, and yogurt. The service is super-friendly, and they offer free delivery. Oh yes, breakfasts are super, too, and they serve lots of salads and sandwiches for lunch. They've been at it since 1962 with no publicity. Now the secret is out!

BILLY'S
948 First Ave   212/753-1870, 212/355-8920
Lunch, Dinner: Daily; Brunch: Sat, Sun
Moderate

This is New York's oldest family-owned restaurant! For those who like old-fashioned setups, complete with white-tiled floors, checkered tablecloths, and a busy bar right in the center of the dining area, Billy's is your kind of place. Established in 1870, this bustling pub/restaurant has been in the same family since opening day. It is a First Avenue institution where the food is as inviting as the atmosphere. Their weekend brunch is a must. No menus, just a blackboard listing steaks, scallops, chops, hamburgers, and the like. All are well prepared, with large portions accompanied by French fries, homemade mashed potatoes, or baked potatoes. Cole slaw is served when you are seated. The waiters are vintage New York. The ethnic mix of the Big Apple makes for exceptional talent in baking, and that is evident in the fine breads served at restaurants like Billy's. Desserts include delicious ice cream, cheesecake, pies, and homemade rice pudding. Top it all off with Irish coffee. There is a *prix fixe* menu for early evening, and a late-evening menu is available as well.

BISTRO MARGOT
26 Prince St   212/274-1027
Dinner: Daily; Brunch: Sat, Sun
Moderate
Cash or checks only

You have heard of a sliver of a place . . . well, Bistro Margot fits the description very well! An open kitchen in the middle with a garden in the back and some cozy tables make up the entire establishment. Small though it is, Bistro Margot turns out excellent French bistro plates: fresh salads, homemade soups, patés, charcuterie, smoked salmon, and a nice assortment of cheeses. A number of sandwiches and entrees are featured, with beef stew in red wine the big winner. What a dish for a chilly evening! Dress down, bring cash only (along with your appetite), and you'll have a superior meal. The chocolate mousse and crème brûlée are as good as I've ever tasted at any of Manhattan's pricier rooms.

BLUE RIBBON
97 Sullivan St (bet Spring and Prince St)   212/274-0404
Tues-Sun: 4 p.m.-4 a.m.
Moderate

Put a star by this one! This place is aptly named. It deserves a blue ribbon in just about every respect . . . except for quiet, leisurely dining. Blue Ribbon is one of the most popular spots in Soho, with a bustling bar scene and a line waiting for its limited number of tables. The regulars know of the exceptional food served in this unpretentious restaurant. There is a raw bar to attract seafood lovers, along with clams, lobster, crab, boiled crawfish, and the house special, the "Blue Ribbon Royale." One can choose from two dozen appetizers, including barbequed ribs, smoked trout, caviar, and chicken wings. Entrees are just as wide-ranging: sweetbreads, sesame-glazed catfish, tofu ravioli, fried chicken and mashed potatoes, burgers, and much more. How the smallish kitchen can turn out so many different kinds of dishes is amazing, but they certainly do it well. Don't come here for a relaxed evening; this is strictly an all-American culinary experience. Note the hours for those who experience hunger pangs after midnight.

BLUE RIBBON BAKERY
33 Downing St (at Bedford St)   212/337-0404
Tues-Sun: 12 noon-2 a.m.
Moderate

I am impressed with both the Blue Ribbon restaurant and sushi bar. They know what they are doing, and the quality is high. Now, a new operation for them: a cafe and bakery, The rustic breads are excellent, as you would expect, but there is much more. Downstairs, a brick oven was unearthed; customers may dine in this fantastic space, complete with two small dining rooms, a wine cellar, and wonderful fresh-bread aroma. All of this in a grotto-like atmosphere. The menu upstairs and downstairs features sandwiches, grill items, veggies and yummy desserts, including profiteroles. The wonderful veal stew is a must! There is a good selection of soups, salads, and cheeses at the deli counter. Ask for the belly-buster sandwich . . . it has everything, and I mean that literally!

BLUE WATER GRILL
31 Union Square W 212/675-9500
Lunch, Dinner: Daily
Moderate

Here is a seafood restaurant that really knows the ocean and all the creatures that inhabit it! The Blue Water Grill is a highly professional operation, with superbly trained personnel operating in a building that once served as a bustling bank and is now a *very* bustling restaurant. Wonderful appetizers include lobster bisque, Cape Cod steamers, and real Maryland crab cakes. Tuna, salmon, swordfish, and mahi-mahi are prepared several different ways. Lobsters and oysters (several dozen varieties) are fresh and tasty. For those who want to stick to shore foods, there are pastas, chicken dishes, and a grilled filet mignon. A half dozen sensibly priced desserts include frozen espresso toffee mousse on a hazelnut crust, and lemon, lime, and orange filling on a lemon spongecake with raspberry sorbet (only 2 grams of fat per serving). A jazz room downstairs is available for listening, dining, and cigar smoking six nights a week.

BOLO
23 E 22nd St 212/228-2200
Lunch: Mon-Fri; Dinner: Daily
Moderate to moderately expensive

The menu here is not a copy of the namesake restaurant at the Ritz Hotel in Madrid, but it does encompass contemporary Spanish flavors in an attractive and comfortable setting. The atmosphere and personnel are upbeat, and the folks want your meal to be both fun and tasty. The logistics are a miracle, with a tiny kitchen that is able to turn out a bevy of wonderful dishes. The menu changes seasonally.

BONDI
7 W 20th St (nr Fifth Ave) 212/691-8136
Lunch, Dinner: Mon-Sat; Brunch: Sat, Sun
Moderate

In the mood for Sicilian cuisine? Well, this is the place. Lunches and dinners are excellent, and desserts are superb. You can sit indoors or on the outside patio and savor every one of those delicious calories in the shape of marvelous tortes and cakes. It's a convenient place for meeting friends if you are working near Broadway or Fifth Avenue in the 20s. The baked goods are special. *Prix fixe* lunches and dinners are available, and historical menus are a unique treat.

BOULEY BAKERY
120 West Broadway (at Duane St) 212/964-2525
Lunch, Dinner: Daily
Moderately expensive

When David Bouley does something, he does it right and people respond. This has certainly been the case with Bouley Bakery, an adventure that has been so successful that seating has been doubled. Breads are one of the attractions here; to say that they are special is an understatement. But nearly everything here is special: wonderful chicken dishes, rack of lamb, breast of duckling.

In the seafood category, David's touch is magic: lobster, oysters, clams, codfish, and sea bass are all done to perfection with the sauces and accompaniments of a master. At lunch, the sandwiches are unusual and satisfying. I loved the organic chicken with avocado and tomato on mountain bread. The menu here changes from time to time; I'd suggest that you come prepared to try whatever the master has in mind. And by all means, don't leave without trying the chocolate brioche pudding. There is no pretension here; there need not be, because the food speaks for itself.

BOULEY

No name excites more interest in the food world than David Bouley. Not only is he a master chef and perfectionist, but he has an uncanny ability to spot (and create) new trends.

Bouley Bakery (120 West Broadway, 212/964-2525) has been a big hit from the start, so much so that it has doubled in size. The interesting menu, plus a wonderful selection of baked items, has made this place a must-visit (if you can get in).

Next on the schedule is the long anticipated opening of **Danube,** an Austrian restaurant at 30 Hudson St. It has been years since Manhattan had a fine home for truly great Austrian food, and now, with the help of master designer Jacques Garcia, David Bouley will initiate what he feels will become a major new culinary trend. In addition to the main room, there will be seating for 65 at the bar, where food will also be available. The wine cellar will provide a unique space for private parties.

Finally, the opening of David's signature restaurant, **Bouley** (163 Hudson St), is scheduled for late 2000. Patrons can expect the ultimate in cuisine and service at the establishment.

BOUTERIN
420 E 59th St (near First Ave)   212/758-0323
Dinner: Daily
Moderately expensive

In one of the most pleasant dining settings in Manhattan, Antoine Bouterin has put his culinary skills to work in creating a French country restaurant with style and class. The flowers and accessories in the room add to the enjoyment of the *provençal* theme. And what goodies he produces: crab cakes with red pepper sauce; hearty lamb stew; red snapper with shallot crust; and bouillabaisse Marseille-style are just a few of the treats. By all means save a corner for the signature dessert: Grandmother's Floating Island with fresh berries. For those who are health conscious, vegetarian dishes are available. Smoking is permissible in the intimate bar area.

BRAVO GIANNI
230 E 63rd St   212/752-7272
Lunch: Mon-Fri; Dinner: Mon-Sun
Moderately expensive

Fans of Bravo Gianni—and there are many—may be upset that I'm mentioning it in this book. They want to keep it a secret. It's so comfortable and the food is so good that they don't want it to become overcrowded and spoiled.

But it doesn't look like there's any real danger of that happening as long as Gianni himself is on the job. The not-too-large room is pleasantly appointed, with beautiful plants on every table. The intimate atmosphere makes it seem as though you're in your own private dining room. And what tastes await you! You can't go wrong with any of the antipasto selections or soups. But do save room for the *tortellini alla panna* or the *fettuccine con ricotta*; no one does them better. I can recommend every dish on the menu, with top billing going to the fish dishes and rack of lamb. Marvelous desserts, many of them made in-house, will surely tempt you. Legions of loyal customers come back again and again; it's easy to see why. But please, keep all this to yourself!

BRIDGE CAFE
279 Water St (north of South Street Seaport, under Brooklyn Bridge)
212/227-3344
Lunch: Mon-Fri: Dinner: Daily; Brunch: Sun
Moderate

Who knows? You might see former mayor Ed Koch in here; like so many other true New Yorkers, he knows that this place is one of Manhattan's treasures. As a matter of fact, the Bridge Cafe has been in operation (under a number of different owners) since 1826, making it the oldest business establishment in the city. Over the decades it has housed its share of brothels and saloons. The mahogany bar stocks 40 single-malt Scotches! Great dishes here include grilled shrimp salad, pumpkin ravioli, and braised brisket of beef, along with numerous other specialties. There is nothing fancy about this place, just good food with especially pleasant personnel. Don't leave without trying the key lime pie. On Sundays, the buttermilk pancakes will get you off to a great start!

BROOKLYN DINER USA
212 W 57th St   212/977-1957
Breakfast, Lunch, Dinner, Late Supper: Daily
Moderate

The Brooklyn Diner USA (which is located in Manhattan) is worth a visit. With an excellent location, all-day dining, expansive menu, pleasant personnel, better-than-average diner food, and reasonable prices, the place is a winner. You can find just about anything your heart desires: typical breakfast fare, sandwiches (the Reuben is a must), salads, hearty lunch and dinner plates, homemade desserts, and good drinks. Their muffins are moist, flavorful, and outrageously good. A tile floor, comfortable booths, and old-time movies add to the ambience.

BRYANT PARK GRILL
25 W 40th St   212/840-6500
Lunch, Dinner: Daily; Brunch: Sat, Sun
Moderate

A handy location in midtown, a refreshing view of Bryant Park, and a sensible menu with prices that are comfortable for families make this grill a popular destination. Although the menu changes every season, one can count on a good selection of soups, salads, seafood items, and steak at lunch and dinner. Twice-baked potatoes, not found in too many restaurants these days, make a nice accompaniment. A *prix fixe* pre-theater menu is available daily from 5-7 with three courses—handy for those going to shows nearby. The *prix fixe* $15 weekend brunch is very popular, too. Besides the usual items, special treats include banana pancakes, a roasted chicken wrap, and fresh asparagus frittata with roasted Yukon Gold potatoes. Personnel here are unusually friendly and are especially child-oriented.

CAFE BOTANICA
Essex House Westin
160 Central Park S   212/247-0300, 212/484-5120 (direct)
Breakfast, Lunch, Dinner: Daily (Brunch on Sunday)
Moderate

Chalk up another winner for the increasing number of good dining spots in Manhattan hotels. The Essex House features two excellent top-quality restaurants. Cafe Botanica overlooks Central Park, with the added pleasure of magnificent table settings to go along with the tasty fare. Villeroy and Boch's "Botanica" pattern is the theme for the serving pieces. Along with the colorfully backed chairs and the light and airy feel of the room, the china makes the terrace area of the restaurant one of Manhattan's most attractive dining rooms. Spicy crab cakes or a selection of cold appetizers will get you started well. There are great pizzas and pastas, and excellent grilled tuna and swordfish steaks. It's a wonderful spot for a very special lunch—the closest thing to a private dining room in Central Park!

CAFE BOULUD
Surrey Hotel
20 E 76th St   212/772-2600
Lunch: Tues-Sat; Dinner: Daily
Moderately expensive

If you are one of the "ladies who do lunch" or like to look at those who do, then this is the place for you. It's not that the food isn't quite good (it is); it is the attitude that I find unappealing. Once seated, however, the menu is innovative: there are vegetarian selections (like veggie couscous), world cuisines (every month a different area), traditional French classics and country cooking, and what Daniel calls the "rhythm of the seasons" (crab salad with avocado and fennel is an example). A two- or three-course *prix fixe* menu is available at lunch. Dinner prices are a bit higher, but remember this place belongs to *the* Daniel Boulud. The room is rather drab, but then again you are in the home of one of the nation's best chefs. Too bad he isn't in the kitchen, but he is doing great things at Daniel instead.

CAFE CENTRO
MetLife Building
200 Park Ave (45th St at Vanderbilt Ave)   212/818-1222
Lunch: Mon-Fri; Dinner: Mon-Sat
Moderate

In a rather large room that's very attractively appointed and broken up into appealing spaces, Restaurant Associates (a major player in the city) has created a purely American restaurant. One is greeted by a gas-fired working rotisserie and a beautiful open kitchen that's spotlessly clean and very efficient. There are *prix fixe* dinners, if you so desire. The chicken pie *bisteeya* (with almonds, raisins, and orange-flower essence) is worth a trip to Cafe Centro in itself; it is not a normal chicken pot pie, but a very tasty and light dish. There is a raw bar, a hefty seafood platter, excellent steaks and French fries, and daily roasts.

Crusty French bread is laid out right in front of you. Other specialties include sea bass, penne pasta, and a moist and flavorful half roasted chicken. The pastry chef obviously has a chocolate bias (good for him): *la marquise au chocolat,* bittersweet chocolate mousse, *souffle chaud au chocolat,* valrhona bittersweet chocolate ice cream, and crème brûlée with caramel sauce are just a sampling. Adjoining the dining room is a very busy beer bar that serves light sandwiches and appetizers.

You might get a kick out of the comments by some restaurant operators about us, their customers. These were printed in *Town and Country* magazine. Their main beefs: intoxicated customers; diners who race through meals (I accept this criticism personally); those who demand menu substitutions; diners with unruly children; and customers who table-hop, use cellular phones, and don't follow smoking policies. However, the real problems are very costly no-shows; those among us who haggle about tables (the food really tastes the same no matter where you sit); the discourtesy shown by those who appear in inappropriate dress; staff abuse; complaints made to friends and not to management; and finally, the press (like me) who think they know it all. I assure you we don't, and I agree it can be unfair at times. Sorry about that.

CAFE DES ARTISTES
1 W 67th St   212/877-3500
Lunch: Mon-Fri; Dinner: Daily; Brunch: Sat, Sun
Moderate

George Lang has created an absolute masterpiece on the West Side, just off Central Park. It's truly a landmark. There are several dining levels and some hidden tables, giving each diner the impression of being in a small, cozy establishment. Beautiful murals by Christy complement the charming decor. The personnel are wonderfully accommodating, and the food is absolutely delicious. Try the unusual Sunday brunch. Some of the mouth-watering selections include smoked salmon Benedict, asparagus omelet, crisp salmon-scallop cakes, and delicious stuffed French toast. Dinner appetizers include salmon four ways: smoked, poached, dill-marinated, and tartare; assorted planked *cochonnailles;* foie gras de Canard; and an array of delightful salads. For the main course, there is swordfish, rack of lamb with basil crust, duck confit, a variety of pasta dishes, and much more. By all means don't overlook desserts. The selection changes but includes mouth-watering choices from cheesecake sorbet to Ilona torte. A great dessert plate features samples several different treats. Three-course, *prix-fixe* lunches and dinners are offered, and the menu selection changes often. This is a lovely, romantic place at any time, but I especially recommend it for an after-theater supper. A new addition is the Parlor, an extension of Cafe des Artistes. It is most attractive, with a turn-of-the-century zinc bar brought over from Paris, plus several inlaid chessboard tables on which you may play. The room offers coffee and sweets all day, plus snacks and full bar service from noon until midnight. Smokers note: cigars and cigarettes are permitted here.

CAFE FIORELLO
1900 Broadway (at 63rd St)   212/595-5330
Lunch, Dinner: Daily; Brunch: Sat, Sun
Moderate

The big attraction here is the antipasto bar; it is attractive, varied, and reasonably priced. You can choose from vegetable, mixed, or seafood selections. The nice part is that you may pick out your own platter as you peruse the goodies or have your waiter do it for you. A number of fresh pastas are made on the premises, like cannelloni, tortelloni, *gnocchi alla bolognese,* and polenta. Their clay pot-roasted baby chicken, with roasted veggies and potatoes, is delicious. A half dozen Etruscan pizzas are available. A side dish of fried artichokes can set off the meal. Desserts are much what you would expect at an Italian restaurant.

CAFE MARGAUX
175 Ave B (at 11th St)   212/260-7960
Dinner: Daily
Moderate

I knew I'd like this place when the waiter brought iced tea served the right way: a glass of ice, and a pot of delicious hot tea! You don't find that very often, even in the classiest Manhattan eateries. You'd hardly describe Cafe Margaux as classy, either in location or physical appearance. The two dining areas are rustic and comfortable enough. The garden patio is the more appealing for warm-weather dining. The varied menu is uniformly delicious, whether it is pasta, seafood, crepes filled with vegetables ratatouille, oven-roasted chicken, or bouillabaisse. I like the steak au poivre with hand-cut French fries. The menu accent is definitely French. The triple-chocolate mousse cake with strawberry sauce is definitely a triple-bypass dessert, but we only live once!

CAFE UN DEUX TROIS
123 W 44th St   212/354-4148
Lunch, Dinner: Daily; Brunch: Sat, Sun
Moderate

Want to see one of your favorite actors? This cafe could be his or her hangout! Paper tablecloths seem like a stingy way to dress a restaurant table, but at this bustling cafe, there's a reason. Two reasons, in fact. One is that it helps keep the tab down. The other is to provide drawing paper; crayons are furnished on every table. Doodling helps pass the time, and isn't it something you've always wanted to do since childhood? The surroundings (an old hotel lobby) are plain, but the location is handy if you're going to the theater. Service is prompt and cordial, and prices are moderate. Though the menu is limited, each item is handled with obvious attention to quality and taste. Begin with a hearty onion soup, salade nicoise, or *paté de canard.* Seafood *en papillote* is an excellent selection. The steak tartare is the best in the city. This spot is also popular with the recording industry and young people. Desserts are all made on premises and are excellent.

CAFFE GRAZIE
26 E 84th St   212/717-4407
Lunch, Dinner: Daily; Brunch: Sun
Moderate

Caffe Grazie is another of those smallish, inviting neighborhood Italian cafes that serves very good food and is known mainly to those who live nearby. All the Italian staples are available, including minestrone (hearty vegetable soup), portabello mushroom or warm goat cheese salad, and carpaccio served over arugula with capers and shaved parmesan cheese. Their linguine is as good as it comes. The unusual grilled chicken lasagna (layered pasta with ricotta cheese, pesto, and tomato sauce) is popular. My favorite dish is shrimp *alla limone:* jumbo shrimp served with lemon caper sauce and mashed potatoes. Don't pass up the homemade garlic bread. Bread puddings are very "in," and Grazie's homemade variety is delicious. Otherwise, opt for the rich blackout cake. This is a perfect spot for a casual Sunday evening meal with the family.

CAMPAGNA
24 E 21st St   212/460-0900
Lunch: Mon-Fri; Dinner: Daily
Moderate

The Flatiron District is the home of this trendy Northern Italian restaurant, where food is primary and atmosphere is secondary. The surroundings are rather nondescript, but that certainly is not the case with the food. Assorted antipasti from the market table is the way to start. Their fresh pastas are terrific: ravioli, great lasagna (like Grandma used to make), spaghetti, rigatoni, and much more. Fresh fish and the mixed grill are popular entrees. You'll find a good selection of desserts: bittersweet chocolate mascarpone cake with chocolate espresso sauce, plus gelati and tarts.

CANAL HOUSE
Soho Grand Hotel
310 West Broadway   212/965-3588
Breakfast, Lunch, Dinner: Daily; Brunch: Sat, Sun
Moderate to moderately expensive

In a somewhat gloomy high-ceilinged room in the high-tech Soho Grand Hotel, waiters with equally gloomy and unattractive black outfits serve food that does much to brighten the atmosphere. Canal House's American comfort food literally melts in your mouth. The popular weekend brunch features all the usual entrees, along with burgers, seafood chowder, and pastas that will make you wish Sunday came around more often. The Hartz Mountain folks have even installed a doggie fountain out front so you can bring along the family pet! Don't leave without a slice of the warm chocolate cake and chocolate sorbet. While you are here, check out the rooms in this popular addition to Soho. The bar scene is booming!

CANDELA
116 E 16th St   212/254-1600
Dinner: Mon-Sun; Brunch: Sun
Moderate

All that is missing here is King Arthur arriving on horseback with his Knights of the Round Table! As you might guess from the name of this unique establishment in the Union Square area, the place is awash with candles . . . everywhere. The effect is quite dramatic, with a high ceiling and brick walls, and with waiters dressed in fitting (and ugly) black outfits. But the American menu is special, the service is prompt and efficient, and the dishes are fairly priced. I would rate this establishment a must-visit for those who want to prove that Manhattan has just about everything when it comes to eating establishments. The winners here: excellent salads, a superb seafood platter (three tiers for two or more hungry patrons), pesto couscous cake and especially tasty homemade pasta dishes. The warm valrhona chocolate cake, with malted milk ball ice cream and dark chocolate and milk chocolate malt sauces speaks for itself! Despite the high energy and noise levels, you'll not regret your visit. Private parties may be held here during the day.

CANTON
45 Division St   212/226-4441, 212/966-7492
Lunch, Dinner: Wed-Sun (closed five weeks during summer)
No credit cards
Moderate

For those in the know, Canton has been a favorite spot for over 40 years. Why? The place is clean, and the personnel are friendly and polite. But most of all, unlike so many Chinese restaurants, the cooking is done on an individual basis. It's almost like stepping into the kitchen of a Chinese family. Tell your waiter the kind of Cantonese delicacies you wish to have. You will be delighted with the results! I would suggest butterfly shrimp, diced chicken with vegetables and mushrooms, or fried young squab. All the seafood is fresh and tasty. So gather up a group of friends for a special Chinese treat. You'll be pleased with the quality of the food *and* the moderate bill.

CAPSOUTO FRÈRES
451 Washington St (one block south of Canal St)   212/966-4900
Lunch: Tues-Fri; Dinner: Daily; Brunch: Sat, Sun
Moderate

Capsouto Frères gets better and better. In 1891, when the building in which it is located was constructed, this might have been an "in" area. But, alas, times (and neighborhoods) have changed. The Landmark Building is still a beauty; however, the surroundings aren't the greatest. Inside, it's another story. Serving contemporary French cuisine, three brothers and their mother team up to operate a classic establishment, opened in 1980, complete with ceiling fans, wooden tables, good cheer, and tasty plates. At noon a special *prix fixe* lunch is offered, or you can order from an a la carte menu laden with salads, fish, meat, and pasta dishes. In the evening, they offer more of the same, along with quail, duckling, and first-rate sirloin steak. They are known for their dessert soufflés, a signature of the restaurant. This bistro is a great setting for a casual, let-your-hair-down evening with good friends who like to live it up!

CARMINE'S
2450 Broadway (bet 90th and 91st St)   212/362-2200
Lunch, Dinner: Daily

200 W 44th St (bet Seventh and Eighth Ave)   212/221-3800
Lunch, Dinner: Daily

American Express
Moderate

Time to treat the whole gang? Or the whole family? The first thing you want to do is round up at least six of your heavy-eating friends, call Carmine's for reservations, and show up famished wearing loose clothing. You won't be disappointed! Carmine's presents Southern Italian family dining fare with *huge* portions and zesty seasonings that come with the territory. Not only are the platters full, they are delicious. If you go with fewer than a half-dozen friends, my advice is to go early. The wait can be as long as an hour, as they will not reserve tables for smaller parties. The menu choices run the gamut of pizzas, pastas, chicken, veal, seafood, and tasty Italian appetizers such as calamari. Oh, yes, there is no printed menu. Wall signs explain the offerings.

CARNEGIE DELICATESSEN AND RESTAURANT
854 Seventh Ave (at 55th St)   212/757-2245, 800/334-5606
Breakfast, Lunch, Dinner: Daily (6:40 a.m.-4 a.m.)
No credit cards
Moderate

There's no city on earth with delis like New York's, and the Carnegie is one of the best. Its location in the middle of the hotel district makes it perfect for midnight snacks. Everything is made on the premises, and Carnegie offers free delivery between 7 a.m. and 3 a.m. within a five-block radius. Where to start? Your favorite Jewish mother didn't make chicken soup better than the Carnegie's homemade variety. It's practically worth getting sick for! It comes with matzo balls, garden noodles, rice, homemade kreplach, or real homemade kasha. There's more: Great blintzes. Open sandwiches, hot and delicious. Ten different deli and egg sandwiches. A very juicy burger with all the trimmings. Lots of fish dishes. Corned beef, pastrami, and rare roast beef. A choice of egg dishes unequaled in New York. Salads. Side orders of everything from hot baked potatoes to potato pancakes. Outrageous cheesecake topped with strawberries, blueberries, pineapple, or cherries (or just served plain). Desserts from A to Z—even Jell-O.

CHANTERELLE
2 Harrison St (at Hudson St)   212/966-6960
Lunch: Tues-Sat; Dinner: Mon-Sat
Expensive

For over twenty years I have been a customer and great admirer of Chanterelle. In my mind, Karen and David Waltuck have created something unique and special for Manhattan diners. All the ingredients are here: magnificent decor, extremely professional service, wonderful food, and owners who look after every detail. Of course, nothing this good comes cheaply, and Chanterelle dinners can be tough on the pocketbook. However, the *prix fixe* lunch is a real treat. As the menu changes often, there are many specials; I'd ask Karen (who is out front) or David (who is in the kitchen) to suggest your menu. The seafood dishes are extra special. Their grilled seafood sausage is rightfully famous. If you have room for dessert, the cheese selection is superb, as is the cheesecake. As if all of this were not enough, the petit fours (served with coffee) make all others seem very mundane.

CHELSEA BISTRO & BAR
358 W 23rd St   212/727-2026
Dinner: Daily
Moderate

Cozy up to a working brick fireplace! Chelsea now offers a number of trendy eating establishments; this is one of the best. It used to be a cave, but now it is a bustling bistro. In a comfortable space that includes a front room as well as an attractive glass-enclosed French garden room, this well-run house has a menu that will please both adventurous and conservative diners. For appetizers, there is a cassoulet of snails, sea scallops, or a tart of goat cheese and onions. Seafood entrees include crispy roasted cod or Chilean sea bass. The nicoise salad is hard to beat; other specialties include hanger steak in red wine sauce, dry-aged ribeye steak for two, roasted duck, and marinated chicken. It is in the tart department that this place really shines. Ask about daily specials.

CHEZ JACQUELINE
72 MacDougal St   212/505-0727
Lunch: Mon-Fri; Dinner: Daily
Moderate

Chez Jacqueline is a very popular neighborhood French bistro, and no wonder. The atmosphere and service are appealingly relaxed. All ages seem to be happy here: young lovers hold hands, and seniors have just as good a time on a special evening out. Popular appetizers are fish soup, snails, and goat cheese salad. As you might expect from a French house, the rack of lamb and veal dishes are excellent. My favorite is the hearty beef stew in a red wine, tomato and carrot sauce. For dessert? Caramelized apple tart, of course!

CHEZ LE CHEF
127 Lexington Ave (bet 28th and 29th St)   212/685-1888
Breakfast, Lunch, Dinner: Daily
Moderate

Chef Frederic has put together big things in this French-German bistro located in a very small space. Here you will find top-of-the-line homemade custom cakes (like black forest, soufflé cakes, cheesecakes, charlottes, and mousse cakes), delicious fresh fruit tarts, petit fours, napoleons, gingerbread houses, wedding cakes . . . and that isn't all. There is a complete health food line: veggie soups, health breads, sugar-free croissants, dietetic muffins, and tarts and cookies for diabetics. International dishes are also featured. Catering is provided (you can even order a delivered breakfast in bed), and the hungry shopper or worker on the go can buy breads, great sandwiches, and a nice selection of quiches.

CHEZ LOUIS
74 W 50th St (at Rockefeller Center)   212/333-3388
Lunch, Dinner: Daily
Moderate

Long before there were chocolate chip cookies on nearly every food counter, the big name in Manhattan was David's Cookies. And who is David? Why, David Liederman, of course. No one in the city knows the food business better than this hard-charging gentleman, and now he is at it again with the reincarnation of Chez Louis, for years one of the city's most popular dining spots. Closed since 1991, the new home brings back fond memories of some of the house's best: great burgers, all sorts of items done on a wood-fired grill, roast chicken, escargos, superb goose and duck, foie gras, hanger steak, and of course, David's Cookies. But the real treat is David's unique garlic potato pie. The ambience is pleasant, the location right in the heart of it all, and the upstairs private party room (with a great view) is outstanding for private affairs. By all means, meet Susan and David Liederman; they are one of New York's unique couples.

CHEZ MA TANTE
189 W 10th St (bet 4th and Bleecker St)   212/620-0223
Dinner: Daily; Brunch: Sun
Moderate

You don't have to be big and expensive to be good. Chez Ma Tante proves that. Friendly and cozy in the winter, the place is just as charming in the summer as the bistro opens onto the sidewalk. Manager Joseph Sutton and chef Denis Whittun handle the duties up front and in the kitchen; hordes of regular customers will attest to their capabilities. Main dishes include the "favorite French dish" (steak, French fries, and green salad), and grilled snapper and tuna are specialties of the house. Dessert? Profiteroles topped with white and dark chocolate sauce (and served warm) are a delicious variation on this popular French dish.

CHEZ MICHALLET
90 Bedford St (at Grove St)   212/242-8309
Dinner: Daily; Brunch: Sun
Moderate

Imagine you are sitting at the window of a quaint little restaurant in a picturesque village in the French countryside. The place has 17 tables, the decor is eclectic, the kitchen tiny . . . but the food and service are wonderful. All this is true, except you are looking out on the corner of Bedford and Grove streets in Greenwich Village! What a charming place this is. The friendly waiters couldn't be more helpful in explaining the varied menu: steak, salmon, duck, lamb, veal, chicken, fish . . . anything your heart desires. The desserts are good as well. Choose from tarts, a great chocolate truffle cake, crème brûlée, profiteroles, or fresh berries. For a perfectly satisfying and relaxing evening, this spot is hard to beat. There is also a special pre-theater menu.

CHEZ NAPOLEON
365 W 50th St   212/265-6980
Lunch: Mon-Fri; Dinner: Mon-Sat
Inexpensive to moderate

Happy 40th birthday, Chez Napoleon! With all the problems of daily life, it's fun to go to a place where the atmosphere is cheerful. Chez Napoleon is just the spot. The owner greets you like a long-lost friend and seats you in a small, clean dining area. It's an old house—warm, cozy, and a neighborhood favorite for many years. The cooking is dependable and hearty. The chef is 78-year-old Grandma Marguerite! My top recommendations from the large menu are coquille St. Jacques, bouillabaisse (served only on weekends), rabbit with mustard sauce, and sweetbreads. Many of the desserts are homemade. But the big plus is the freshness of the dishes and the gracious hospitality. A *prix fixe* menu is available.

CHIANTI
1043 Second Ave (at 55th St)   212/980-8686
Lunch: Sun-Fri; Brunch: Sun; Dinner: Daily
Moderate

Chianti bills itself as a new-age Italian restaurant featuring flavors of the Tuscany region. It succeeds in a charming manner. One can always tell a restaurant that serves a consistently good menu reflecting seasonal changes, as the neighborhood steadily patronizes such an establishment. The inventive chef here offers small and large salads, sandwiches, pastas, and a variety of fish dishes. The braised boneless short ribs of beef over *farro* and vegetable risotto is one of the best appetizers I have ever tasted. In the evening, there are a number of stuffed pasta dishes, double-thick rack veal chops, and from the wood-burning charcoal grill, black Angus skirt steak and wood-grilled Atlantic salmon. Try a side of Yukon Gold potato puree or spiced Tuscan fries. The dessert gelato selection brought back visions of Rome. A *prix fixe* espresso lunch is a regular feature, with a number of choices including a tasting plate of Chianti's market antipasto and several salads or sandwiches.

CHIN CHIN
216 E 49th St (bet Second and Third Ave)   212/888-4555
Lunch: Mon-Fri; Dinner: Daily
Moderate to moderately expensive

Chin Chin is a very classy Chinese restaurant whose ambience and price reflect a superior cooking style. There are two rooms and a garden in back. The soups and barbecued spareribs are wonderful for starters. The Szechuan jumbo prawns are sensational. As a matter of fact, I'd concentrate on the seafood dishes. But you might also try the wonderful Peking duck dinner, with choice of soup, crispy duck skin with pancakes, fried rice, poached spinach, and homemade sorbet and ice cream. The menu is much the same for lunch or dinner. A reasonable *prix fixe* lunch is available.

COACH HOUSE
16 E 32nd St   212/696-1800
Lunch: Mon-Fri; Dinner: Daily
Moderately expensive (lunch) to expensive (dinner)

For years one of my very favorite dining rooms in Manhattan was the Coach House. Former proprietor Leon Lianides was a jewel in the culinary world, highly respected by everyone in the industry. Now Larry Forgione, who was a close friend of both Lianides and the legendary James Beard, has re-created a room dedicated to some of the great dishes of the Coach House (as well as many of his own delights). You will find the classic bean soup, pot pie, wonderful roast rack of Shenandoah Valley lamb, pecan pie, mocha *dacquoise,* and a chocolate cake the likes of which you only dream about. There is even Dungeness crab (from my part of the world) done in a salad, spring roll, or tamale toasts. Both the lunch and dinner menus are *prix fixe* ($29 for two courses at noon, $59 for three courses at dinner). A bar menu is available all day.

COCO PAZZO
Paramount Hotel
235 W 46th St   212/827-4222
Lunch: Mon-Sat; Dinner: Mon-Sun
Moderate to moderately expensive

It is nice to know that there is a spot right in the center of the Theater District where you can get a really good meal in a pleasant atmosphere with beautiful dinnerware and quick service, if you desire. Coco Pazzo meets all of these requirements—as well it should with highly experienced owner Pino Luongo behind the scenes. Lunch is mainly pastas, pizzas, salads, and light fish. The dinner menu is essentially Italian, with a good selection of salads, seafoods, and pastas. Signature dishes include a lobster presentation in two acts . . . delicious! To insure that you stay awake for the entire performance, you may want to skip the delicious desserts . . . but you'd be making a real mistake by passing up the baked Alaska or chocolate-covered ginger tartufo. Just tell your server you have a curtain deadline, and you will be treated to very special service. A smoking section is available.

COUNTRY CAFE
69 Thompson St (bet Spring and Broome St)   212/966-5417
Lunch, Dinner: Daily; Brunch: Sat, Sun
Moderate
Cash only - they took my MC on 2/4/02 ~ Emily Rosen

You have to know about this tiny Soho establishment to find it! But once inside, you'll appreciate the no-nonsense approach to real French country dining. The service and atmosphere could easily be transplanted to any small village in France. The menu would fit right in as well, with items like homemade country paté with onion and fruit chutney; a fabulous country salad with croutons, lardons, blue cheese, and walnuts; vegetable couscous; snails in garlic butter; and steak au poivre with homemade French fries. The latter are the real thing, believe me! I love the informality of the place, the sizable portions, and the obvious delight the young staff has in showing guests what it is like to be treated by some real homebodies. Bon appetit!

CUCINA & CO.
MetLife Building Lobby
200 Park Ave   212/682-2700
Breakfast, Lunch, Dinner: Mon-Fri
(takeout open 7 a.m.-9 p.m.; Sat: 8-4)
Moderate

Hidden between two hyped restaurants (Tropica and Cafe Centro) in the bowels of the huge MetLife Building, Cucina & Co. is an undiscovered treasure. The takeout is one of the best in mid-Manhattan: all sorts of prepared foods, sandwiches, salads, great cookies and cakes, breads, and whatever else you might want to take home or to the office. Adjoining is a bustling, crowded, noisy cafe that serves first-class food at very reasonable prices for such a prime location. Daily specials feature many items available for carryout. You will also find delicious burgers (served on sesame brioche rolls), baked pastas, quiches, seafood, health dishes, and a good selection of dessert items. The service is extremely fast, the quality of the food top-notch, and the personnel highly professional. They have to be in order to serve so many people in the rush hours. I'd heartily recommend this place, especially for lunch.

CUCINA STAGIONALE
275 Bleecker St   212/924-2707
Lunch, Dinner: Daily
No credit cards
Inexpensive

When you serve good food at a low price, word gets around. So it's no wonder there's a line in front of this small Village cafe almost any time of day. Its name translates as "seasonal kitchen," and the seasonal specialties are real values. It's a bare-bones setup, with seating for only several dozen hungry folks. Service is impersonal and nonprofessional, but who cares at these prices? Innovative Italian cuisine is served here—tasty, attractive, and filling—and you can do very well on a slim budget. Recommended appetizers include smoked salmon with endive and radiccio, and sauteed wild mushrooms. For a few pennies more, you can get a large dish of vegetarian lasagna, linguini, or ravioli. I'm constantly asked about inexpensive places that serve quality food, and I have no hesitation recommending this spot. One word of warning: don't go if it's raining, because you'll probably have to wait outside to get seated.

DANAL
90 E 10th St   212/982-6930
Lunch: Mon-Fri; Dinner: Daily; Brunch: Sat, Sun;
Tea: Fri-Sat (by reservation)
Moderate

Here are Gerry Frank's guidelines to a good eating spot: The bread is fresh, crisp, and warm. Vegetables are not overcooked. Salads are cool, and the house salad is not just a bunch of lettuce. If homemade ice cream is served, it is rich and creamy and has no ice particles in it. Finally, the owner is on the job. Danal passes all of the above with flying colors. The location is the East Village, on a quiet and safe street. The atmosphere is what the owner calls "country French." I would call it homey mix-and-match. The service is understated and friendly, with no pretense. The dishes are uniformly delicious, served in right-sized portions. The menu varies every day but features something tasty for any appetite. An upstairs lounge offers a full bar and light menu. A special find!

DANIEL
60 E 65th St   212/288-0033
Lunch, Dinner: Mon-Sat
Expensive

Daniel Boulud should be immensely proud of his new $10 million French country restaurant. Despite all the hype and intense introspection of every aspect of his dream, this most accomplished chef has achieved perfection. If you are ready to have an absolutely superb dining experience and bucks don't matter, then join the often long waiting list for a table in the space of the former Mayfair Hotel lobby and Le Cirque restaurant. The setting is a reminder of the original 1920s look, with neoclassical details. The result is an unusually pleasant feeling, with the light and the hum of the room adding to the joy of each delicious platter. As befits such a room, the wait staff is highly professional and knowledgable. Signature dishes change by the season. It might be a duo of roasted beef tenderloin and braised short ribs (the best I have ever tasted), morels filled with braised duck and lamb's quarter greens, roasted quail, or roasted fillet of venison. Desserts are a work of art. Every time I visit this restaurant I don't want the meal to end. I can't think of a higher compliment.

DA UMBERTO
107 W 17th St (at Ave of the Americas)   212/989-0303
Lunch: Mon-Fri; Dinner: Mon-Sat
Moderate to moderately expensive

Da Umberto is for serious Italian diners! This Florentine bistro is a feast for the eyes as well as the palate. A groaning table of inviting antipasto dishes greets guests; one could easily make an entire meal just from this selection. All of the platters look so fresh and healthy! Umberto Assante himself is around much of the time, insuring that the service is as good as the food. One can look into the glass-framed kitchen at the rear to see how real professionals work. What to have? The three-color salad is a house specialty. On to well-prepared pastas, fish, veal, or chicken. Your waiter will have many specials to detail. If you have room, the chocolate truffle cake and tiramisu are the best of the dessert selections.

DAWAT
210 E 58th St   212/355-7555
Lunch: Mon-Sat; Dinner: Daily
Moderate

Dawat is a quality operation with a top chef. It serves tasty, reasonably priced Indian food in a refined atmosphere with superior service. There are a number of wonderful seafood choices, including a sensational shrimp entree cooked with herbs and spices. You'll also find chicken dishes, goat and lamb offerings, and such vegetarian selections as homemade cheese cubes with delicious vegetables, eggplant with sweet-and-sour tamarind sauce, and stir-fried cauliflower with ginger and cumin seeds. One of the trademarks of an Indian restaurant is its bread, and at Dawat they do it to perfection. Different varieties are offered, and no meal is complete without trying a couple. The desserts here have vastly improved.

— Millennium Note —

The first City Hall in Manhattan began its career as the town's first hotel and tavern. Governor Willem Kieft had it built at 71 Pearl Street in 1642, when he tired of entertaining visitors and traveling traders at his home.

DEGREZIA
231 E 50th St   212/750-5353
Lunch: Mon-Fri; Dinner: Mon-Sat
Moderate to moderately expensive

For sure this hidden treasure has only been discovered by the natives. Look around the two packed dining areas; there is not a touristy type in sight. Maybe mention herewith will change all that, for everything about DeGrezia is absolutely first-class. From the moment you are cordially greeted, the service and plates are without peer. The professional waiters want you to have a good time, and that is exactly what will happen. Lots of pastas are offered, but the real treats are the Northern Italian specialties, like whole chicken breast topped with eggplant prosciutto or double-cut veal chops sauteed with fresh sage and white wine. For lunch or dinner, this charmer rates high with your author. Private party rooms are available.

DELMONICO'S
56 Beaver St   212/509-1144
Lunch, Dinner: Mon-Fri
Moderately expensive

Delmonico's has been a New York tradition for decades, and it has had its ups and downs. Now, with new personnel and energy, it is again worth a visit for great pastas, grilled meats, and fresh fish. Potato lovers will go for the excellent mashed, hash brown, or baked. The specialty "tribute" dishes include lobster Newburg, grilled steak, duck, chicken cordon bleu, scallops, and one of my favorite desserts, chocolate-pistachio blackout. Daily specials are offered. I'd suggest lamb shanks on Wednesday or French-style bouillabaisse on Friday. Portions are king-sized! If you're in the Financial District and want a restaurant with a real Manhattan feel, this is the place.

DINING COMMONS
City University of New York Graduate Center
365 Fifth Ave (at 34th St), 8th floor   212/817-7000
Mon-Fri: 9-3
Inexpensive

The Dining Commons offers excellent food in comfortable surroundings and at a comfortable price. Continental breakfasts, featuring muffins, danishes, croissants, bagels, and more, are available. Lunches feature deli sandwiches, salads, and some hot entrees. It is possible to eat heartily for under $10, and both eat-in and takeout are available. The facility is open to faculty, students, and the general public, with students getting a discount with CUNY identification cards. This is not your run-of-the-mill fast-food operation. Restaurant Associates does a particularly good job of offering tasty, adequate portions without fancy touches.

DOCKS OYSTER BAR AND SEAFOOD GRILL
2427 Broadway (bet 89th and 90th St)   212/724-5588
Lunch: Mon-Sat; Dinner: Daily; Brunch: Sat, Sun

633 Third Ave (at 40th St)   212/986-8080
Lunch: Mon-Fri; Dinner: Daily; Brunch: Sun

Moderate

For those who appreciate a great raw bar, Docks is the place to anchor! Sail right up Broadway or to Docks' larger location on Third Avenue. At both lunch and dinner, you'll find fresh swordfish, lobster, tuna, Norwegian salmon, red snapper, and other seafood specials of the day. The crab cakes are outstanding. In the evening, you can enjoy a raw bar with four oyster varieties and two selections of clams. All this comes with Docks' cole slaw and choice of potatoes. Vegetables are a la carte. For a lighter meal, try steamers in beer broth or mussels in tomato and garlic. Delicious smoked sturgeon and whitefish are available. Docks has a special New England clambake on Sunday and Monday nights. For dessert, the chocolate mud fudge is a fitting way to finish your culinary cruise. The atmosphere is congenial, and so are the professional waiters.

DUANE PARK CAFE
157 Duane St (bet West Broadway and Hudson St)   212/732-5555
Lunch: Mon-Fri; Dinner: Mon-Sat
Moderate

If you find yourself in Tribeca, take advantage of some of the interesting places to eat in the area. Many are located on or near Duane Street. Duane Park Cafe is one of them. The menu is eclectic, as you might expect from chef-owner Seiji Maeda. There is a touch of Italian, a heavy emphasis on seafood, and a nod to Cajun and Japanese influences. The dishes sparkle, especially because of the tasty manner in which herbs are used. Even some of the delicious homemade breads have herbal flavors. A selection of pasta is offered at all times. The desserts are done on the premises, showing off the vivid imagination of pastry chef John Dudek. Seasonal wine-tasting dinners are featured.

EDGAR'S CAFE
255 W 84th St (bet Broadway and West End Ave)   212/496-6126
Lunch, Dinner: Daily (open late)
No credit cards
Moderate

Folks on the Upper West Side claim this place as their secret. One can understand why. Edgar's place isn't very big, but the selection, value, and quality certainly are. They offer great coffees and hot drinks, an unusually large selection of iced drinks, and a fine assortment of salads and sandwiches. Cakes and pies are sinfully rich and wonderful. All are available for takeout (or eat-in). Gelati and sorbetti fans will also be in seventh heaven.

EL PARADOR
325 E 34th St (nr First Ave)   212/679-6812
Lunch, Dinner: Daily
Moderate

When you have been in the restaurant business for four decades in New York, you are obviously doing something customers like. El Parador is doing just that: serving delicious Mexican food in a fun atmosphere at down-to-earth prices. Besides all that, they are some of the nicest folks in the city. Warm nachos are put on the table the minute you arrive; from there, you have a choice of specialties. There are quesadillas, Spanish sausages, and black-bean soup to start. Delicious shrimp and chicken dishes follow. Create your own tacos and tostaditas if you like. How about stuffed jalapenos? You'll probably want some tequila to make the evening complete. El Parador has over 30 brands of premium tequilas and what many consider the best margaritas in New York. It is really the granddaddy of New York Mexican restaurants.

ELEVEN MADISON PARK
11 Madison Ave (at 24th St)   212/889-0905
Lunch: Mon-Fri: Dinner: Mon-Sat
Expensive

When Danny Meyer opens a restaurant, you know it will have class. Eleven Madison Park is no exception. In a soaring space previously used for business meetings, an attractive dining facility has been created with an intimate bar and several superb meeting rooms. The cuisine is described as "New York with a French accent." Premium wines and a world-class selection of Calvados are available. Appetizers are heavy on the seafood side: a seasonal shellfish assortment, roasted sea scallops, tuna "cru," and a salad of Maine lobster. Foie gras is a specialty. Braised shoulder of pork, choucroute of salmon and trout, and prime aged rib of beef are excellent main-course choices. Save room for the dark chocolate terrine or the bittersweet chocolate pistachio cake! A meal here would not be complete without a journey into the past glory of this building and area by studying the pictures featured throughout.

ERMINIA
250 E 83rd St (bet Second and Third Ave)   212/879-4284
Dinner: Mon-Sat
American Express
Moderate

The Lattanzi family now has five branches, and Erminia, the smallest, is the jewel in the crown. It has about a dozen tables in a pleasant and rustic atmosphere that's just right for a leisurely, intimate dinner. I've found it an absolutely charming spot with helpful personnel and outstanding food. To start, try the artichokes cooked in olive oil. In the pasta category, you can't go wrong ordering tender dumplings with potatoes and tomatoes or large noodles with ricotta cheese. Some of the best selections are grilled and served with delicious vegetables. There is grilled chicken, seafood items on skewers (great shrimp), a special fish dish, and lamb or veal chops. Dessert selections vary daily. Note: jackets are required!

ETATS-UNIS
242 E 81st St (bet Second and Third Ave)   212/517-8826
Dinner: Daily
Moderate to moderately expensive

Etats-Unis is more like a large family dining room, with just a dozen tables and a busy kitchen where the Rapp family produces some of the best food this side of your grandmother's! The family is represented by father and son in the kitchen and an attractive daughter out front (what a charmer she is). There is no point in talking about individual items on the menu, as the appetizers, entrees, and desserts (usually about five of each) change every evening. They are uniformly delicious. It's very wholesome food, not cute or fancy but served in a professional manner and in portions that are substantial but not overwhelming. Fresh homemade bread is an additional attraction. Try the date pudding or chocolate soufflé for dessert. The tab is not cheap, but in order to support this type of operation—with limited hours and few tables—the Rapps have to make every meal count. The entire room is available for private parties.

FIFTY-SEVEN FIFTY-SEVEN
Four Seasons Hotel
57 E 57th St (bet Fifth and Madison Ave), lobby level   212/758-5757
Breakfast, Lunch, Dinner: Daily; Brunch; Sat, Sun
Moderate to moderately expensive

When the name Four Seasons is on the door, you can be assured that the service on the inside is going to be something special. And so it is at Fifty-Seven Fifty-Seven, one of Manhattan's stars in the continuing trend toward excellence in hotel dining rooms. The room is highlighted by handsome cherry floors with mahogany inlays, ceilings of Danish beechwood paneling, and bronze chandeliers. The table tops match the floor in both material and design. In an informal yet elegant atmosphere, the food presentation has the authority of classic American cooking. The menu changes by season, featuring big-time flavors, such as some exceptionally well-thought-out pasta entrees. Cured swordfish is a winner! This is a room where taste and personal attention, not the ego of a famous chef, are the names of the game. A thoughtful touch is the offer of rapid service for breakfast guests.

FOUR SEASONS
99 E 52nd St (bet Park and Lexington Ave)   212/754-9494
Lunch: Mon-Fri; Dinner: Mon-Sat
Expensive

I am always entranced by this place. If you were entertaining someone who had just arrived from overseas, a person of style and substance who had never before tasted an American meal, the magnificent Four Seasons restaurant would be the obvious choice. The place is very big, cool, and comfortable—elegant and awe-inspiring in its simplicity and charm. There are two separate dining areas—the Grill Room and the Pool Room—and they are different in both menu and appeal. You will find the dark suits (translation: the business and media heavy hitters) at noon in the Grill Room, where the waiters know each of them and what they like (baked potatoes, great salads, steak tartare, burgers). The Pool Room, set beside an actual marble pool, is romantic and more feminine. Here the ladies who "do" lunch and the couple who wants to dine with the stars are right at home with superb service, wonderful duck, and a dessert menu that can only be described as obscene, with individual soufflés in coffee cups a splendid treat.

FRANK'S
85 Tenth Ave (at 15th St)   212/243-1349
Lunch: Mon-Fri; Dinner: Daily
Moderate

The Molinari family—the third generation in a business that started in 1912—has kept up the quality and appeal of this popular spot. Customers are usually large folks with large appetites! Reservations are suggested, as the place is very popular. There are great pastas, huge steaks, superb prime rib, fresh fish, veal, lamb, and really good French fries. New York cheesecake is the best dessert.

FRANK'S TRATTORIA
379 First Ave (at 22nd St)   212/677-2991
Lunch, Dinner: Daily
Inexpensive

It's true in New York, just as it is anywhere in the country: no one knows the great, cheap places to eat better than the boys in blue. Manhattan's finest are some of the best customers of this modest *trattoria,* and it is easy to see why. The menu runs the gamut of Florentine dishes, each one prepared to order and served piping hot. And so is the bread, which is always a good sign. There is a large seafood selection, plus steaks, chops, and chicken. You can choose from over 20 pizzas, served whole or in individual pieces. Everyone here is very informal and friendly, and Frank, the boss, is delighted that the good word about his place has spread beyond the neighborhood regulars.

FRAUNCES TAVERN RESTAURANT
54 Pearl St   212/269-0144
Breakfast, Lunch, Dinner: Mon-Fri
Moderate

General George Washington is supposed to have said goodbye to his officers at a reception at Fraunces Tavern in 1783. George obviously had good taste if the tavern was as top-notch then as it is now. It's an inviting, historic spot serving authentic American fare in a charming part of lower Manhattan. It has been in the same family since 1937. The dining areas are spacious and comfortable, the service is professional, prices are reasonable, and the menu (with daily specials) is sizable. A specialty of the house is baked chicken a la Washington (cubes of tender chicken and mushrooms baked *en casserole* au gratin). Absolutely delicious! I'd suggest making a beeline here on Wednesdays for the Yankee pot roast with red cabbage and potato pancakes. On Tuesdays you can sample ales from around the world. And don't overlook dessert! The cheesecake, Georgia pecan pie, and chocolate mousse are well worth investigating. After your meal, go upstairs and visit the Fraunces Tavern Museum. It is one of the oldest museums in the city and a historic landmark. There you'll find exhibits focusing on 18th- and 19th-century life in America. By the way, the breakfast menu offers a fine selection of omelets, eggs, fruit, and muffins. It's one of the best buys in New York.

FRESCO BY SCOTTO
34 E 52nd St   212/935-3434
Lunch: Mon-Fri; Dinner: Mon-Sat
Moderate to moderately expensive

Things are hopping at Fresco, especially during the noon hour. Even with the pressure of folks in a hurry, the staff here is courteous and efficient. They take rightful pride in serving the outstanding dishes prepared by executive chef Stefano Battistini. His background shows with the kinds of plates offered: delicious homemade original pastas, a number of grilled dishes (including great grilled veal chops), and braised short ribs that will melt in your mouth. Wonderful potato side dishes include garlic mashed, basil whipped, smashed Yukon Gold, and mashed sweet potatoes. For dessert, try the novel apple plate: apple fritters, brandied apple custard, and apple cinnamon cake. After a meal here, you will understand why modern Tuscan cuisine is so "in"! Fresco-to-Go is right next door.

GABRIEL'S BAR & RESTAURANT
11 W 60th St (bet Broadway and Ninth Ave)   212/956-4600
Lunch: Mon-Fri; Dinner: Mon-Sat
Moderate

There is something special when you walk into a restaurant, are greeted by an extremely friendly host (who happens to be Gabriel, a co-owner with chef Ralph Perroti), along with background music that in this case is "Gabriel . . . Gabriel"! But there is much more. Wonderful homemade pepper biscuits and delicious bread. Fresh melon and blood orange juice. A bowl of fresh fruit on the bar. A fine assortment of Italian appetizers. Then on to really first-class pastas (like *tagliatelle* with pesto), chicken, steaks, and grilled seafood dishes. The in-house gelati creations are among New York's best, as is the chocolate espresso torte. To cap it all off, Gabriel's offers a selection of nine unusual teas (like peach melba, raspberry, and French vanilla). Gabriel doesn't have to blow his own horn; his satisfied customers do it for him!

GASCOGNE
158 Eighth Ave (at 18th St)   212/675-6564
Lunch: Mon-Fri; Dinner: Daily; Brunch: Sun
Moderate

Hearty appetites and southern French cooking spell happiness with a capital

H at this intimate Chelsea bistro. No fuss or fancy affectations by the capable and friendly waiters, all of whom are only too happy to explain the fine points of the rather limited menu. Salads are popular: roquefort with warm duck tenderloins, warm goat cheese and puree of shallots, warm scallops and garlic confit. *Foie gras* lovers will be in heaven. The main-course menu features duck, cassoulet, quail, and roasted rabbit. Seafood dishes are especially tasty. All desserts are made in-house, and they show imagination. There are sorbets, fruit tarts, soufflés, and some unusual ice cream flavors (prune, Armagnac, and chocolate mint). A small dining area is available downstairs, but it is rather claustrophobic. The garden is charming. If you are really longing for an extensive French dining experience, take a look at the *prix fixe* menu. By the way, Gascony is the only region in the world where Armagnac is produced.

GENNARO
665 Amsterdam Ave (bet 92nd and 93rd St)   212/665-5348
Dinner: Daily
Cash only
Moderate

When patrons line up and wait outside in the freezing rain or blistering heat, you know that what's inside has to be particularly good. And it is at Gennaro, a 12-table sliver of a place on the Upper West Side. Besides delicious food, known mainly to those who inhabit the neighborhood, this find offers superbly friendly service and very moderate prices. There is a $20 minimum per person, and no credit cards are accepted. You'll want to listen to the evening specials before ordering, as there are always some attractive possibilities. The menu is mainly Italian-Mediterranean, with specialties like Tuscan cannelloni bean soup, potato gnocchi, grilled Italian sausage, and grilled salmon with honey mustard sauce. Even if you hated spinach as a kid, Gennaro's is delicious, and the mashed potatoes melt in your mouth. For old timers who remember the flourless chocolate cake at the Coach House, the Gennaro taste-alike is equally superb.

GINO
780 Lexington Ave (at 61st St)   212/758-4466
Lunch, Dinner: Daily
Cash only (checks accepted if known on premises)
Moderate

As you look around the crowded dining room of this famous New York institution, you can tell immediately that the food is great. Why? Because this Italian restaurant is filled with native New Yorkers. You'll see no tourist buses stopping out front. The menu has been the same for years: a large selection of popular dishes (over 30 entrees) from antipasto to soup, pasta to fish. There are daily specials, of course, but you only have to taste such regulars as chicken a la Capri, Italian sausages with peppers, or scampi a la Gino, and you are hooked. Gino's staff has been here forever, taking care of patrons in an informed, fatherly manner. The best part comes when the tab is presented. East Side rents, as you know, are always climbing, but Gino has resisted the price bulges by taking cash only and serving delicious food that keeps the tables full. No reservations, so come early.

GOLDEN UNICORN
18 East Broadway (at Catherine St)   212/941-0911
Lunch, Dinner, Dim Sum: Daily
Inexpensive

Golden Unicorn serves the best dim sum outside of Peking! This bustling, two-floor Hong Kong-style Chinese restaurant serves delicious dim sum every day of the week. Besides the delicacies from the rolling carts, diners may choose from a wide variety of Cantonese dishes off the regular menu. Pan-fried noodle dishes, rice noodles, and noodles in soup are house specialties. Despite the size of the establishment (they can take care of over 400 diners at one time), you will be amazed at the fast service, the cleanliness, and (most of all) the price. This has to be one of the best values in Chinatown.

GOOD ENOUGH TO EAT
483 Amsterdam Ave (at 83rd St)   212/496-0163
Breakfast, Lunch: Mon-Fri; Dinner: Daily, Brunch: Sat, Sun
Inexpensive

New York is a weekend breakfast and brunch town, and I suggest you cannot do better than Good Enough to Eat in both categories. Savor the morning opportunities: apple pancakes, four-grain pancakes with walnuts and fresh bananas, and chocolate chip and coconut pancakes. There is more: French toast, waffles, six different omelets, four scrambled egg dishes, corned beef hash, homemade Irish oatmeal, fresh squeezed orange juice, and homemade sausage. The lunches in this homey and noisy room (with tile floor and wooden tables and bar) feature inexpensive and delicious salads, burgers (juicy and delicious), pizzas, and sandwiches. More of the same for dinner, plus meatloaf, turkey, pork chops, fish, and roast chicken plates. This is comfort food at its best, along with wonderful homemade pies, cakes, and ice creams for dessert.

GOTHAM BAR & GRILL
12 E 12th St   212/620-4020
Lunch: Mon-Fri; Dinner: Daily
Moderately expensive

There are some restaurants worth getting excited about revisiting. The Gotham is one of them. It has not always been this way. This place has painstakingly worked itself up into the ranks of New York's best. It is not inexpensive, but every meal I have had here has been worth the tab. However, there is a really good *prix fixe* lunch deal. The talented chef, Alfred Portale, is one of the best in the city. The modern, spacious, high-ceilinged space is broken by direct spot lighting on the tables. Fresh plants lend a bit of color. There are great salads (try the seafood), excellent free-range chicken, and superior grilled salmon and roast cod. Each entree is well seasoned, attractively presented, and delicious. The rack of lamb is one of the tastiest served in the area. Desserts are all made in-house; try the vanilla crème brûlée or the Gotham chocolate cake. Dining here can be summed up in one word: exciting!

GRAMERCY TAVERN
42 E 20th St (bet Park Ave S and Broadway)   212/477-0777
Lunch: Mon-Fri; Dinner: Daily (Tavern until midnight)
Moderately expensive

It is no mystery why the Gramercy Tavern is one of New York's most popular restaurants. It deserves to be. When you combine an outstanding and innovative operator like Danny Meyer, a highly trained staff, an unusually attractive space and reasonable prices with excellent food, the public will respond. Every detail is in superb taste. The ceiling is a work of art, the private party room is magnificent, and there isn't a bad seat in the house. Singles are in heaven here; the light menu (including a fabulous cheese selection) adds strength to possible conquests. As the menu changes often, it is difficult to suggest any favorites, but you can't go wrong with the large selection of seafood appetizers and entrees. If the roasted loin and braised shank of lamb is on your menu, grab it! How does a chocolate caramel tart with caramel ice cream sound for dessert? If you are entertaining out-of-town guests, I'd highly recommend this place for your "showcase" dinner. The Tavern menu also has some delicious suggestions, like a wood-grilled veggie Dagwood or a grilled pork tenderloin sandwich.

GRAND CENTRAL OYSTER BAR RESTAURANT
Grand Central Station (lower level)   212/490-6650
Mon-Sat: 11:30-9:30
Moderate

Native New Yorkers know about the 85-year-old institution that is the Oyster Bar at Grand Central. A midtown destination once popular with commuters and residents, it has been restored and is doing quite nicely again, thank you. (They serve over 2,000 folks a day!) The young help are most accommodating, and the drain on the pocketbook is minimal. The menu boasts more than 80 seafood items (with fresh new entrees daily), 20-30 varieties of oysters, a super oyster stew, clam chowder (Manhattan and New England), oyster pan roast, bouillabaisse, coquille St. Jacques, Maryland crab cakes, Maine lobsters, 75 wines by the glass, and marvelous homemade desserts.

GRANGE HALL
50 Commerce St (at Barrow St)   212/924-5246
Lunch: Mon-Fri; Dinner: Daily; Brunch: Sat, Sun
Moderate

Hidden away on a picturesque corner in the West Village is this charmer, an ex-speakeasy! Inside you will find peace and relaxation in addition to excellent "comfort" food! The menu changes by season, but you can count on homemade soups, a large selection of small dishes (as appetizers or in addition to your main dish), fresh salads, and ample, delicious entrees. The latter can be ordered simple (entree and accompaniment as listed on the menu) or complete (with soup or salad). Things start off right with a loaf of warm homemade bread, and all other items are served either piping hot (all entrees cooked to order) or chilly cold, as they should be. I was particularly taken with the appetizer selection: unusual items like spicy string beans, hand-cut yam fried potatoes, freshly made sausage, wild rice and wheat berry medley, and baked eggplant steaks. Your choices may not be the same, but will no doubt be equally inventive! Desserts are also made in-house, and the accommodating help makes the experience almost like eating at home. You'll love the ambience.

GUIDO'S (SUPREME MACARONI CO.)
511 Ninth Ave (at 39th St)   212/502-4842
Lunch: Mon-Fri; Dinner: Mon-Sat
No credit cards
Inexpensive

You might ask yourself what a nice person would be doing in the middle of Ninth Avenue, having lunch in the back room of a macaroni factory? Well, this is no usual back room and no ordinary macaroni factory! Up front, as you walk in, you'll see a display of 23 brands of macaroni. That was the original business (they have been open over a half century), but now it's just a sideline. The real draw is the smallish restaurant in the back, which is as busy as Times Square. Tom Scarola is the third-generation family member who runs this unusual operation. Whether you're coming for lunch or dinner, make sure you have a reservation. You might rub shoulders with some celebrities. Even if they're not here in person, their pictures (along with the blue-checkered tablecloths and wine bottles on the ceiling) help create a special atmosphere at Guido's. You don't want to miss the lobster, rigatoni with vodka sauce, shrimp *francese,* veal sorrentino, or the house specialty, chicken *alla* Guido. The pasta is freshly made, authentic, inexpensive, and delicious. Finish with an assortment of mixed pastries and fresh cakes, along with a special espresso, and you will have had a marvelous meal. Lunch specials include four different chicken, veal, and shrimp entrees, as well as linguini or spaghetti with all the trimmings.

HALCYON
RIHGA Royal Hotel
151 W 54th St   212/468-8888
Breakfast, Lunch, Dinner: Daily
Moderately expensive

This is an oasis of civility for dining. The restaurant has a dual life: a free-standing room of its own that also serves as the dining area for the adjoining hotel. The room is spacious and elegant, quiet and calming. Table settings are enhanced by beautiful Villeroy and Boch French Garden plates, and fresh flowers adorn each table. The menu is contemporary American: salads, soups, pastas, seafoods, and grilled items. There is a pre-theater dinner, a popular late light supper (10:30 p.m.– 1 a.m.), and a Sunday brunch served in the 53rd floor Gershwin Penthouse, with its fabulous view of Manhattan. The kitchen will accommodate deviations from the set menu—a nice touch in these days of restricted ordering. It is in the dessert area, however, that the operation really shines. Each plate is an absolute work of art, with the signature name drizzled on the presentation dish. Ask to see the daily selection, as well as the set dessert menu, which changes by season. Nightly entertainment is an additional feature (except on Sunday).

HARRY'S
Woolworth Building
233 Broadway   212/513-0455
Lunch, Dinner: Mon-Fri
Moderate

Never mind that you're not a member of the Harvard or Yale Club or that you don't have a gold pass to the private dining room of Citicorp or Chase Manhattan. Just head for the lower level of the Woolworth Building, and you'll find a remarkable eating spot called Harry's. You would probably never know about it unless you worked in a nearby office—or read this book! What with all the wood and leather (a very masculine atmosphere), good food, and reasonable prices, it's a real find. Although dinner is served until 10:30 p.m., this is basically a luncheon spot. Ladies are certainly welcome, but the clientele is predominantly males of the important-looking, three-piece-suit variety. While big deals are being made at the surrounding tables, you can feast on clams, smoked trout, marinated herring, and smoked sturgeon. Omelets and homemade pastas are available, as well as selections from the cold buffet, including chicken salad, sliced turkey, and tuna salad platters. There are also grilled items, cold sandwiches, seafood, and several specials each day. If you drop by on Tuesday, try the braised sauerbrauten, and if you visit on Friday, the corned beef and cabbage is outstanding. This is an ideal place to take business associates; they will, no doubt, be pleasantly surprised to learn about it. Harry's is open on weekends for private events only.

HATSUHANA
17 E 48th St   212/355-3345
237 Park Ave   212/661-3400
Lunch: Mon-Fri; Dinner: Mon-Sat
Moderate

Hatsuhana has deservedly become known as the best sushi house in Manhattan. One can sit at a table or at the bar and get equal attention from the informed help. There are several dozen appetizers, including broiled eel in cucumber wrap; steamed egg custard with shrimp, fish, and vegetables; squid mixed with Japanese apricots; and chopped fatty tuna with aged soybeans. Next, try the salmon teriyaki (fresh salmon grilled with teriyaki sauce) or any number of tuna or sushi dishes best described by the personnel. Forget about the desserts and concentrate on the exotic appetizer and main-dish offerings.

HEARTBEAT
W Hotel
149 E 49th St   212/407-2900
Breakfast, Lunch, Dinner: Daily
Moderate to moderately expensive

What a winning combination: a menu overflowing with dishes that are good for you, and an overseer like Drew Nieporent, one of America's culinary greats. Here in the newly opened W Hotel, Heartbeat looks as good as it tastes! The place is cozy and comfortable, an extension of the lounge area just outside. I have to admit that this is not my kind of food, but for you who pose in front of the mirror every morning, this is the place to visit. There are chilled oysters, sliced raw tuna, and wild mushroom ravioli for lunch. For dinner you will find some meat dishes like beef tenderloin and mustard-roasted pork tenderloin. Berries and yogurt for dessert? Hmm. I'm off to the closest burger and ice cream palace. But for those of you who have exercise machines in your bedroom, come to Heartbeat; the cuisine is healthy, pure, and full-flavored.

HEARTLAND BREWERY
35 Union Square W   212/645-3400
1285 Ave of the Americas (at 51st St)   212/582-8244
Lunch, Dinner: Daily
Moderate

There is much more to these hot spots than brews. Yes, there are plenty of those, but you'll also enjoy darn good food (and eight different home brews) at attractive prices in a fun and relaxed atmosphere. The menu can best be described as "classic American": Buffalo chicken wings, Cajun popcorn, buttermilk smashed potatoes, salads, burgers, sandwiches, and filling main courses. Chef Andy's crab cakes are a winner, as is Farmer Jon's Ma's meatloaf, served with wild mushroom ale sauce. Dessert has to be Aunt Bee's chocolate mud cake! The personable wait staff seems to have as much fun as their guests. Stay-at-homes can take advantage of a full delivery-service menu (including beer). By the way, this Farmer Jon must be quite a fellow. His oatmeal stout has hints of java with a rich dark chocolate sweetness, and it won the bronze medal at the Great American Beer Festival!

HUDSON RIVER CLUB
4 World Financial Center, lobby level (250 Vesey St)   212/786-1500
Lunch: Mon-Fri; Dinner: Mon-Sat; Brunch: Sun
Moderate to moderately expensive

Here you can have dinner with the Statue of Liberty almost at your table! The setting for the Hudson River Club is magnificent: spacious, high ceilings, great views of the river and harbor. This is not really a "club"; it is open to the public, although residents of Battery Park City are the most frequent customers. The menu is strictly American, with an emphasis on food from the fertile Hudson valley. A seven-course tasting menu will give you a feel for the marvelous foodstuffs that come from this area. For less hungry diners, I'd suggest the wonderful foie gras club sandwich or the braised short ribs that have been marinated in wine for five days for starters. What next? How about roast chicken with garlic mashed potatoes? Warm chocolate flourless cake will make your visit complete!

HUDSON'S SPORTS BAR & GRILL
Sheraton New York Hotel & Towers
811 Seventh Ave (at 53rd St)   212/581-1000
Lunch: Sat, Sun; Dinner: Daily
Moderate

The quintessential sports bar and grill, Hudson's offers continuous entertainment for the sporting enthusiast. There's satellite coverage of local, national, and worldwide sporting events on 30 monitors (including two wide screens), autographed memorabilia, and interactive programming. Complementing bar-food favorites like Buffalo wings, nachos, burgers, and steaks, Hudson's serves over 25 varieties of beer from around the world, as well as a full bar.

IL BAGATTO
192 E 2nd St (bet Ave A and B)   212/228-0977
Dinner: Tues-Sun (closed Aug)
Inexpensive
Cash only

One of Manhattan's best bargains, Il Bagatto is the place to come if you're feeling adventurous. Housed in tiny digs in an area you would hardly call compelling, the doors open on this extremely popular Italian *trattoria*. The owners have discovered the rule of success: being on the job, insuring that every dish tastes just like it came out of mama's kitchen. About a dozen tables upstairs (and one downstairs) are always filled, so it's best to call ahead for reservations. There's delicious spaghetti, homemade gnocchi with spinach, tortellini with meat sauce made from their own secret recipe, and wonderful *tagliolini* with seafood in a light tomato sauce. And there's more: chicken, thin slices of beef, salads, and always a few specials.

IL CORTILE
125 Mulberry St (bet Canal St and Hester St)   212/226-6060
Lunch, Dinner: Daily
Moderate

Little Italy is more for tourists than serious diners, but still there are some exceptions. Il Cortile is an oasis of tasty Italian fare in an attractive and romantic setting. A bright and airy garden area in the rear is the most pleasant part of the restaurant. The menu is typical Italian, with just about anything you could possibley want. Entree listings are heavy on the chicken and veal dishes, plus excellent spaghetti, fettuccine, and ravioli. Sauteed vegetables, like bitter broccoli, hot peppers, mushrooms, spinach, and green beans, are specialties of the house. One thing is for certain here: the waiters act like they are on roller skates. No wasted time; service is excellent. If you can fight your way through the gawking visitors, you will find Il Cortile to be worth the effort!

IL GIGLIO
81 Warren St (bet West Broadway and Greenwich St)   212/571-5555
Lunch, Dinner: Mon-Fri
Moderate

Il Mulino's "little brother" is doing well. So well, in fact, he might be even more handsome than his father! If you can find the place (the neighborhood is drab and dull, to say the least), you will be delighted to discover a bright, clean, classy operation that serves absolutely great Northern Italian food. Smallness is a virtue here, as the two dozen tables are looked after by a crew of highly trained, tuxedo-clad waiters, most of whom have been on the premises since its opening. The specials are almost as numerous as the menu items (be sure to ask for prices), and by all means look over the display of fresh fruits, desserts, and other goodies by the entrance. The scampi and veal dishes are superb, and few places in Tribeca (or elsewhere in Manhattan) do pasta any better. Moreover, all desserts are made in-house.

IL MULINO
86 W 3rd St (bet Sullivan and Thompson St)   212/673-3783
Lunch: Mon-Fri; Dinner: Mon-Sat
Moderately expensive

Don't try to get them on the phone—it's impossible! Those who live to eat will want to pay attention to this entry. Never mind that reservations usually must be made a week or so in advance. Never mind that it's always crowded, the noise level is intolerable, and the waiters nearly knock you down as you wait to be seated. It's all part of the ambience at Il Mulino, one of New York's best Italian restaurants. Your greeting is usually "Hi, boss," which gives you the distinct impression that the staff are accustomed to catering to members of the, uh, "family." When your waiter finally comes around, he reels off a lengthy list of evening specials with glazed-over eyes. On the other hand, a beautiful, mouth-watering display of daily specials is arrayed on a huge table at the entrance. Once you're seated, the waiter delivers one antipasto after another while he talks you into ordering one of the fabulous veal dishes with portions bountiful enough to feed King Kong. Osso buco is a favorite dish. By the time you finish one of the luscious desserts, you'll know why every seat in the small, simple dining room is kept warm all evening.

IL VAGABONDO
351 E 62nd St   212/832-9221
Lunch: Mon-Fri; Dinner: Daily
Inexpensive

Il Vagabondo is a good spot to recommend to your visiting friends. This bustling restaurant has been a favorite with knowledgeable New Yorkers for more than 30 years. The atmosphere is strictly old-time, complete with checkered tablecloths, four busy rooms, and an even busier bar. No menus are offered; the pleasant but harried waiters reel off the regular items and daily specials. You may have spaghetti or ravioli, an absolutely marvelous mine-strone, chicken parmesan, or sliced beef. I can also heartily recommend the Friday scampi or pasta *pescatore*. There is no pretense in this place. It is a great spot for office parties and folks with slim pocketbooks. You will see happy faces, compliments of a delicious meal and the extremely reasonable bill. Save room for the great "bocce-ball dessert" (*tartufo*). Il Vagabondo, you see, is the only restaurant in New York with an indoor bocce court!

INDIGO
142 W 10th St   212/691-7757
Dinner: Daily
American Express
Moderate

The clientele and menu go together at this eclectic West Village hideaway. You will see three-piece suits and fashionable ladies, and at the next table will be tank tops, green hair, and earrings. Everyone seems to feel comfortable, and that is one of the charms of the place. The menu, which changes seasonally, is also a mixed bag, with an international flavor leaning heavily toward healthy dishes. Owner Scott Bryan features braised pork, roast leg of lamb, and several seafood dishes (like monkfish and grilled salmon) for main courses. Healthy-minded diners will want to try the apple crisp. As for me, I opted for the deca-dent chocolate torte with mocha sauce and coffee ice cream. For those who want to dawdle over their meals, a huge selection of after-dinner drinks is available. Smokers may puff away in the front bar area.

Egg Cream

A New York invention, the egg cream is generally credited to Louis Auster, a Jewish immigrant who owned a candy store at Stanton and Cannon streets during the early part of the century. Mostly to amuse himself, he started mixing carbonated water, sugar, and cocoa together until he got a drink he liked. It was such a hit that Schrafft's reportedly offered him $20,000 for the recipe. Auster wouldn't sell and secretly continued making his own syrup in the back room of his store. When he died, his recipe went with him. Some years later, Herman Fox created another chocolate syrup, which he called Fox's U-Bet. Fox's brand is regarded as the definitive egg cream syrup to this day.

JACKSON HOLE BURGERS
232 E 64th St   Third Ave at 35th St   Second Ave at 84th St
212/371-7187   212/679-3264   212/737-8788

1270 Madison Ave (at 91st St)
212/427-2820

517 Columbus Ave (at 85th St)
212/362-5177

35-01 Bell Blvd, Bayside
718/281-0330
Inexpensive

69-35 Astoria Blvd, Flushing
718/204-7070

You might think that a burger is a burger is a burger. But having done hamburger taste tests all over the city, I've chosen Jackson's as one of the best. Each one weighs in at seven juicy, delicious ounces. You can get all types of hamburgers, along with great coffee and French fries. You can have a pizza burger, an Swiss burger, an English burger, or a Baldouney burger (mushrooms, fried onions, and American cheese). Or try an omelet, if you prefer. A Mexican menu has been added, as well as salads and grilled chicken breast. The atmosphere isn't fancy, but once you sink your teeth into a Jackson Hole burger, accompanied by great onion rings and a homemade dessert, you'll see why I'm so enthusiastic. Free delivery and catering are available.

JACQUES' BISTRO
204 E 85th St (bet Second and Third Ave)   212/327-2272
Dinner: Daily; Brunch: Sat, Sun
Moderate

It is easy to understand why this bistro is so popular with folks in the neighborhood. It is cozy, friendly, moderately priced, and serves great food. In addition, Jacques himself is one of the friendliest proprietors in town. All of the classic French dishes are available: onion soup, calves liver, steak au poivre, great fries, crème brûlée, cheeses, and a wonderful chocolate soufflé with Tahitian vanilla ice cream. Of course, there are also several outstanding seafood dishes and a whole lot more. An added treat: this bistro is small and intimate, and it makes a great place for private parties.

JEAN GEORGES
Trump International Hotel
1 Central Park W (bet 60th and 61st St)   212/299-3900
Lunch: Mon-Fri; Dinner: Mon-Sat (cafe open daily for breakfast)
Very expensive

Jean-Georges Vongerichten has created a new French dining experience in a setting that can only be described as cool, calm, and calculating. I mean *calculating* in the sense that one is put into a frame of mind to sample *haute cuisine* at its best in a very formal dining room that's awash with personnel who seem to be looking for something to do. In keeping with any operation bearing the Trump name, the hype at Jean Georges has been momentous. But to be honest, if price is unimportant, you just can't do better. The cafe and outdoor terrace are a bit less intimidating. The menu changes regularly. Come ready to be educated!

JIMMY SUNG'S
219 E 44th St (bet Second and Third Ave)   212/682-5678
Lunch, Dinner: Daily
Moderate

For over two decades Jimmy Sung has been a talented player in the highly competitive world of Chinese restaurants in Manhattan. Recently redecorated, Jimmy Sung's house can seat over 250 customers in the main area and in seven exceptionally attractive private dining rooms that can accommodate groups of all sizes. The cuisine includes Hunan, Canton, Shanghai, and Manchurian dishes that range from mild to very spicy. Some of Jimmy's favorites: vegetarian pie with house pancake, spicy golden chrysanthemum chicken, sauteed frog legs with garlic sauce, and seafood combination in a bird's nest. An experienced staff of chefs and waiters provides a personal touch to this busy spot. The next time the office gang plans a get-together, put Jimmy Sung's at the top of the list. On top of everything, prices are very affordable.

JOHN'S PIZZERIA
278 Bleecker St   212/243-1680
408 E 64th St (bet First and York Ave)   212/935-2895
48-50 W 65th St (bet Broadway and Central Park)   212/721-7001
260 W 44th St (bet 8th St and Broadway)   212/391-7560
Daily: Noon-11:30 p.m. (Fri, Sat until 12:30 a.m.)
Moderate

Pete Castelotti (there is no John) is known as the "Baron of Bleecker Street." However, he has expanded to the Upper West Side and the Upper East Side so that more New Yorkers can taste some of the best brick-oven pizza in the city. Pete offers 55 (count 'em) varieties, from cheese and tomatoes to a gourmet extravaganza of cheese, tomatoes, anchovies, sausage, peppers, meatballs, onions, and mushrooms. If homemade spaghetti, cheese ravioli, or manicotti is your preference, John's is also the place for you. The surroundings on Bleecker Street are a bit shabby; things are higher-class uptown. The 44th Street location is in a former church. The renovation is spectacular and the space huge. Imagine tackling a giant pizza *bianca* on the floor of a former altar!

JO JO
160 E 64th St (bet Lexington and Third Ave)   212/223-5656
Lunch: Mon-Fri: Dinner: Mon-Sat
Moderate to moderately expensive

Jean-Georges Vongerichten has become a real entrepreneur in the Manhattan restaurant world. He deserves the acclaim he is receiving from all sides. However, I like to compliment him on Jo Jo, one of his earlier successes, where he has shown he can do good things even at reasonable prices. This townhouse is a bustling place. It is a happy establishment where the extra touches that make you want to come back are so apparent. The bread is warm and wonderful. Personnel are well trained. Diners may choose from a menu of about half a dozen appetizers, entrees, and desserts. Recommended appetizers include tuna spring roll, and the goat cheese and potato tureen roast chicken is a popular entree. They are all worth a try. By all means save room for the superb warm chocolate cake.

JUBILEE
347 E 54th St (bet First and Second Ave)   212/888-3569
Lunch: Mon-Fri; Dinner: Daily; Brunch: Sun
Moderate

Jubilee is a pleasant, satisfying, and unique French bistro, serving well-prepared food in a refined atmosphere. On Thursday evenings a jazz trio adds to the fun. Authentic French plates include lamb shanks, grilled steak with marvelous French fries, and duck cassoulet. Mussels are a specialty of the house, served several ways: curried, with chicken-mushroom sauce, *mariniare*, vinaigrette, or *farcies a la Provencale*. Try the cozy and romantic table in the rear for tasty desserts like a lemon tart or a Cointreau crème brûlée.

JUDSON GRILL
152 W 52nd St   212/582-5252
Lunch: Mon-Fri; Dinner: Mon-Sat
Moderate (bar); moderately expensive (main room)

What a difference a new chef makes! My early reviews of Judson Grill were not all that positive. However, with chef Bill Telepan in the kitchen, this huge operation has taken on a decidedly upbeat feel. The place is now constantly packed. If a lighter meal is what you want (handy for pre-theater), try eating in the bar area. You'll find sirloin burgers, barbequed spare ribs (seasonal), tuna tartare, and ravioli, plus other special treats like great onion rings and a hearty cheese selection. For heavier lunches or dinners, a most interesting selection of appetizers is offered: grilled garlic-duck sausage, egg fettucine with asparagus, terrine of New York State foie gras, and a nice selection of salads. For entrees, there is a wide choice of seafood, roasted veal loin chops, duck breast, and some healthy veggie dishes. Don't pass up the Judson French fries! My dessert favorite: warm bittersweet chocolate cake with praline ice cream. Keep up the good work!

KATZ'S DELICATESSEN
205 E Houston St (at Ludlow St)   212/254-2246
Sun-Wed: 8 a.m.-10 p.m.; Thurs: 8 a.m.-11 p.m.;
Fri, Sat: 8 a.m.-12 p.m.
No credit cards
Inexpensive

Lower East Side hunger pangs? Try Katz's Delicatessen. It is a super place with some of the biggest and best sandwiches in town, hand-carved and overstuffed. The atmosphere goes along with the great food, and the prices are reasonable. Go right up to the counter and order—it is fun watching the no-nonsense operators slicing and fixing—or sit at a table where a seasoned waiter will take care of you. Try dill pickles and sauerkraut with your sandwich. Incidentally, Katz's is a perfect way to sample the unique "charm" of the Lower East Side. While you wait for a table or discover that the salt and pepper containers are empty and the ketchup is missing, you'll know what I mean. Catering (at attractive rates) and private party facilities are available.

KEENS STEAKHOUSE
72 W 36th St   212/947-3636
Lunch: Mon-Fri; Dinner: Mon-Sat
Moderate

Some of the best old restaurants in New York tend to get lost in the shuffle. With glamorous new places opening every week and people always wanting to know which places are "in," we sometimes forget about dependable restaurants that consistently do a good job. One of them is Keens Steakhouse, a unique New York institution. I can remember going there decades ago when those in the garment trade made Keens their lunch headquarters. This has not changed. Keens still has the same attractions: the bar reeks of atmosphere, and there are great party facilities and fine food to match. Keens opened in 1885, and it has been a fixture in the Herald Square area ever since. For some time it was a "gentlemen only" place, and although it still has a masculine atmosphere, ladies now feel comfortable and welcome. The famous mutton chop with mint is the house specialty, but other delicious dishes include veal, steaks, lamb, and fish. For the light eater, especially at lunch, there are some great salads. Lobster has been added to the menu. They do monthly single single Scotch tastings from fall to spring and possess one of the largest single Scotch collections in New York. If you have a meat-and-potatoes lover in your party, this is the place. Make sure you save a little room for the deep-dish apple pie.

KIN KHAO
171 Spring St (nr Thompson St)   212/966-3939
Dinner: Daily
Moderate

There are a lot of hole-in-the-wall Thai restaurants all over Manhattan. They are increasingly popular because the food is light and the price is right. Kin Khao, in Soho, is one of the best. It is clean, attractive, and professional. Best of all, the regional Thai and Bangkok dishes are authentic and uniformly delicious. The spring rolls are a special treat, healthy and tasty. You may choose from a number of meat, seafood, and chicken dishes, some rather hot and others sweet and mild. Their sticky rice is a special feature of the restaurant. You'd have to travel several thousand miles to find any better!

KING'S CARRIAGE HOUSE
251 E 82nd St   212/734-5490
Lunch: Mon-Sat; Dinner: Daily
Moderately expensive

You've made a discovery! Even folks in the immediate neighborhood don't know about this sleeper. It is indeed an old carriage house, remade into a charming two-story dining salon that your mother-in-law will love. The mood is Irish, with the menu changing every evening. In this quaint setting, with real wooden floors, one dines by candlelight in a very civilized atmosphere. The luncheon menu stays the same: salads, sandwiches, and lighter fare. Afternoon tea is a treat. The continental menu in the evening may feature grilled items (like loin of lamb or red snapper); on Sundays, it is a roast dinner (leg of lamb, loin of pork, chicken, or tenderloin of beef). The menu is *prix fixe,* and it is really a good value. Personally, I found the Stilton cheese with a nightcap of ruby port absolutely perfect for dessert, but you may prefer chocolate truffle cake or rhubarb tart. For a fleeting dinner hour, you can be taken back a century or so, with nary a thought of computers, answering machines, or the dismaying nightly news.

KIOSK
1007 Lexington Ave (bet 72nd and 73rd St)   212/535-6000
Lunch, Dinner: Daily; Brunch: Sat and Sun
Moderate

Kiosk is well-named! The place is not much bigger than a couple of telephone booths, but don't let that deter you from a very pleasurable meal. In a skinny room with a two-stool bar in the center, diners sit at copper-topped tables. They are served by some of the more pleasant personalities on the Manhattan food scene and have the added advantage of a fascinating people-watching experience. Lunchtime offerings include burgers, great French fries, grilled chicken and organic salad, several seafood dishes, a quiche and a pasta item, and a special soup everyday. Grilled chicken, steak, and varying specials are added for the evening diner. Mashed potatoes are very "in" these days, and those at the Kiosk are excellent. Rich desserts (like double chocolate gelato) are available in the afternoon, as well as at mealtime.

LA BOHÊME
24 Minetta Lane (Ave of the Americas bet 3rd and Bleecker St)
212/473-6447
Dinner: Tues-Sun; Brunch (and full menu): Sat, Sun
Moderate

Pari Dulac likes people and food, and it shows. The part-Iranian, part-French hostess is right on the job in her cozy, informal Bohemian bistro, dispensing delicious edibles at moderate prices. The setting is a quiet, charming street in the Village. When the front doors are open in warmer weather, you get the impression of being in a quaint European town. Inside, soothing music puts you in the mood to enjoy some of the best pizza you have ever tasted. In the back, an open kitchen puts out pasta, salads, and French dishes done to perfection. On Sundays, you can't beat the Country French brunch or the unique omelet selection. Dessert specialties include tarts made in-house, as well as first-class chocolate mousse cake and lemon soufflé with raspberry sauce. Pari has been wise to use only the best ingredients in her dishes, and she has resisted the temptation to raise prices to a point where value is questionable.

LA BOITE EN BOIS
75 W 68th St   212/874-2705
Dinner: Daily
No credit cards
Moderate

You don't have to be able to pronounce the name of this restaurant properly to have a good time! It packs them in every evening for obvious reasons. Owner Alain Brossard, an ex-chef, has hit upon that winning combination: delicious food, personal service, and moderate prices. The salads are unusual; the country paté is a great beginner. For an entree, I recommend fillet of snapper, roast chicken with herbs, or *pot-au-feu,* La Boite en Bois style. The atmosphere is intimate, and all the niceties of service are operative from start to finish. Desserts are made in-house; I suggest one of their sorbets. Call for reservations, since La Boite en Bois is very small and popular.

LA CARAVELLE
Shoreham Hotel
33 W 55th St (bet Fifth Ave and Ave of the Americas)
212/586-4252
Lunch: Mon-Fri; Dinner: Mon-Sat
Expensive

With the incessant hype of new places and new dishes, it is comforting to know that there are still some places where things haven't changed. And why should they, when it has always been so good? Such is La Caravelle, where chef Cyril Renaud still offers many of the same dishes that have made this deluxe French palace famous: quinelles in a rich lobster sauce, roasted crispy duck, fillet of Dover sole, mouth-watering roast chicken, and a very popular crab salad. Of course, there are newer dishes, but every time I go here I opt for something tried and true. If you happen by on Friday, don't pass up the bouillabaisse Marseillaise! This goes for the service, too; it is, as you would expect, extremely gracious, fitting in with the warm and luxurious interior of the room. It would be hard to leave without trying one of the rich soufflés or the *bavaroise* of yogurt and rhubarb. If you want to leave it up to the chef, he'll take good care of you with his fabulous *menus d'inspiration!* Congratulations to Rita and Andre Jammet for keeping a great tradition going.

LA CÔTE BASQUE
60 W 55th St   212/688-6525
Lunch: Mon-Sat; Dinner: Mon-Sun
Expensive

Yes, it's expensive. Quite expensive *(prix fixe).* But dining at La Côte Basque is an experience worth every dollar. I doubt whether there is any room, anywhere in the world, more attractive and comfortable than this one. With gorgeous murals, superb lighting, and a magnificent open setting (no high banquettes), La Côte Basque is a feast for the eyes as well as the stomach! The service is ultra-professional, as one would expect. Of course there are marvelous appetizers like Petrossian caviar, sauteed wild mushrooms, seared duck liver, and oak-smoked salmon. For entrees, on to a magnificent black bass fillet, roasted duckling with honey, or a special cassoulet by chef-owner Jean-Jacques Rachou. The desserts belong in a museum of beauty and good taste. Lemon-grass ice cream with lemon sorbet is mighty refreshing, but the chocolate cube with espresso sherbet is out-of-this-world. As if this weren't enough, a box of dessert goodies is placed temptingly in front of you. What an evening!

LA FOURCHETTE
1608 First Ave (bet 83rd and 84th St)   212/249-5924
Dinner: Daily; Brunch: Sat, Sun
Expensive

The place is charming. The personnel are charming. The food is charming. But the prices . . . that's another subject. Whether or not this relatively new French beauty on the Upper East Side can continue to survive with their check shock remains to be seen. One of the most attractive parts of this restaurant is that the portions are not unappetizingly large; they are very ample and most attractively presented. The menu is in constant flux, but a few items are usually available: for an appetizer, terrine of carrots with goat-cheese mousse; for the main course, fillet of beef with braised short ribs; for dessert, banana tart or a napoleon of exotic fruits. An extravagant tasting menu, complete with a wonderful cheese selection, goes for $75 ($115 if wine is included). The place is described as "an upscale French restaurant housed in a super-luxury skyscraper." I'd add, "Lean wallets need not apply!"

If a day of Madison Avenue window and wallet shopping has worn you out, I'd suggest a respite at **La Goulue** (746 Madison Ave, 212/988-8169). The people-watching is superb, espeially in nice weather when tables are on the sidewalk. By the way, the food is really quite good!

LA GRENOUILLE
3 E 52nd St (at Fifth Ave)   212/752-1495
Lunch, Dinner: Tues-Sat
Expensive

After charming Manhattan for nearly four decades, La Grenouille remains a special place that one really has to see to believe. It's impossible to describe. The beautiful fresh flowers are but a clue to a unique, not-to-be-forgotten dining experience. The food is as great as the atmosphere, and although prices are high, it's worth every penny. Celebrity-watching adds to the fun. You'll see most of the famous faces in the front of the room; also-rans are delegated to rear tables. The French menu is complete, the staff professional. Be sure to try their cold hors d'oeuvres; they're a specialty of the house, as are the lobster dishes, sea bass, and poached chicken. Nowhere in New York are sauces any better. Don't miss the superb dessert soufflés. The tables are very close together, but what difference does it make when the people at your elbows are so interesting?

LA LUNCHONETTE
130 Tenth Ave (at 18th St)   212/675-0342
Lunch: Mon-Fri; Dinner: Daily: Brunch: Sat, Sun
Inexpensive to moderate

This is hardly a place to please the eyes, but it does please the stomach and pocketbook. In a small and very modestly equipped kitchen, the personnel turn out really delicious food that can be as sophisticated as that of much fancier places uptown. At lunch there are salads and omelets, even *escargot au cognac* and sweetbreads. The dinner menu, which changes frequently, usually offers free-range chicken, steak, sea scallops, and pan-seared trout.

LA MÉTAIRIE
189 W 10th St (bet 4th and Bleecker St)   212/989-0343
Lunch: Sat-Sun; Dinner: Daily
Moderate

Once just a tiny hole in the wall, La Métairie ("a small communal farm") has expanded into a delightful place to dine in the Village. The atmosphere is still cozy, the food exceptional, the service prompt and accommodating— and the price is right! The kitchen offers a wide choice of French dishes. Specialties of the house include couscous, wild boar stew with fresh noodles, bouillabaisse, and rack of lamb.

LANDMARK TAVERN
626 Eleventh Ave (at 46th St)   212/757-8595
Daily: Noon-midnight; Brunch: Sun
Inexpensive

How about a cozy meal by a fireplace or potbellied stove? Landmark Tavern is open friendly hours for sandwich platters, a variety of salads, fresh seafood, steaks, and roast prime rib of beef. The real treat here is Sunday brunch. A tradition in the city since 1868, the Landmark is not content to copy everyone else's fare. Indeed, normal brunch items are available, but so is shepherd's pie (ground lamb sauteed with herbs), delicious lamb steaks, and English-style fish and chips. There is the added pleasure of sampling their famous soda bread, made fresh every hour and served with imported jams and marmalade. Corned beef hash is a favorite. And those great homemade desserts like Irish soda bread pudding and Jack Daniel's cake will make you want to come back every Sunday. The bar is friendly, the help is harried, and the atmosphere reeks of nostalgia. More important, the food is delicious, and prices are a bargain.

LA RÉSERVE
4 W 49th St   212/247-2993
Lunch: Mon-Fri; Dinner: Mon-Sat
Expensive

I have sent hundreds of diners here, and they all report on the experience in glowing terms. There are all sorts of reasons for this top billing: the food, the ambience, the consistency. But the main plus is the host and owner, Jean-Louis Missud, one of the most charming and talented hosts in the business. New York has no shortage of fine rooms, but this one shines with appealing lighting, gracious and informed service, and the feeling that you are an honored guest. What to eat? Whatever your heart desires! I would suggest letting Jean-Louis or one of his talented captains order for you. Then sit back and enjoy your journey to culinary heaven. If romance is the name of the game, you can't do better than this French charmer. A pre-theater dinner is available. Private party facilities are yours for the asking, including taking over the whole restaurant on Sundays.

Those Darned Cell Phones!

Sure they are handy, and they keep you in touch with your kids and broker and mother-in-law. But there is a time and place for everything, and their use in a restaurant is not only in bad taste but is extremely distracting to restaurant personnel and guests. Leave it in the car or at home!

LA RIPAILLE
605 Hudson St (at 12th St)   212/255-4406
Dinner: Daily
Moderate

This small, bright, romantic Parisian-style bistro makes a cozy spot for an informal dinner. The tables are rickety, but the chef puts his heart into every dish. Entrees are done to perfection; the seafood is always fresh (I recommend bass in champagne and fine herbs), and they do an excellent job with rack of lamb and duck *magret*. White chocolate is a house favorite; at least half of the dessert offerings use it as an ingredient. Proudly displayed at the front of the room are rave notices from a number of New York gourmets. They can add my enthusiastic endorsement, too!

LAYLA
211 West Broadway (at Franklin St)   212/431-0700
Lunch: Mon-Fri; Dinner: Daily
Moderate to moderately expensive

Leave it to Drew Nieporent to do something different. His exotic Layla´s just that: good food with a Turkish flair. Don't be put off by the unusual menu, as the very patient personnel will work with you to make sure you have an exotic meal. There is falafel, tabbouleh, hummus, and all the other dishes from this part of the world you may have heard about. You'll also find grilled baby chicken and grilled salmon, wonderful yogurt-glazed lamb chops, and even a grand dish of couscous royale. Dessert? Baklava, of course! A family-style Layla feast is available, as well as a belly dancing show. You may feel out-of-shape after seeing the performers!

LE BERNARDIN
155 W 51st St   212/489-1515
Lunch: Mon-Fri; Dinner: Mon-Sat
Expensive

There has to be one place that is at the top of every list, and when it comes to seafood palaces, Le Bernardin holds that spot. Owner Maguy LeCoze and chef Eric Ripert have combined talents to make this house extremely attractive to the eye and very satisfying to the stomach. Wonderfully fresh oysters and clams are a great way to start. Whatever your heart desires from the ocean is represented on the entree menu. What differentiates Le Bernardin is the way the dish is presented. Signature dishes (a different one each night) include yellowfish tuna (appetizer), pizza Bernardin with broiled shrimp (also an appetizer), roasted monkfish, poached halibut, poached skate, and spicy red snapper. Prix fixe lunch is $42; dinner is $70. Desserts change regularly but usually include an assortment of cheeses and superb chocolate dishes like layers of milk chocolate, whipped cream, and ganache on chocolate sable with honey-orange sauce and blood orange sorbet.

LE BIARRITZ
325 W 57th St (bet Eighth and Ninth Ave)   212/245-9467
Lunch: Mon-Fri; Dinner: Mon-Sat
Moderate

Nothing changes here . . . happily. New York is full of neighborhood restaurants, and Le Biarritz is one of the best. It seems like home every evening as regulars claim most of the seats in this warm, smallish eatery. The place has been at the same location and in the same hands for over three decades. Gleaming copper makes any eating establishment look inviting, and here you can see a first-rate collection of beautiful French copper cooking and serving pieces. If you're in the mood for *escargots* to start, the chef knows how to prepare them well. You might also try French onion soup or crepes a la Biarritz (stuffed with crab meat). You can't go wrong with either. Entrees include frog legs *provençale,* duck in cherry sauce with wild rice, and roast goose with chestnuts. The menu includes all kinds of chicken, lamb, beef, veal, and fish dishes, each served with fresh vegetables. Although there are no unusual desserts, all are homemade and very good. The reasonably priced dinners include soup, salad, and choice of dessert. I recommend Le Biarritz if you are going to a Broadway show or an event at Lincoln Center.

LE CIRQUE 2000
New York Palace Hotel
455 Madison Ave (bet 50th and 51st St)   212/303-7788
Lunch: Mon-Sat; Dinner: Daily
Expensive

There are restaurants that are legends, and Le Cirque is one of them. There are also restaurateurs who are legends, and Le Cirque owner Sirio Maccioni is one of those. His personality, combined with a reputation for outstanding food and beautiful people as guests, has made this establishment a must-do. This man is pure genius: showman, culinary master, superb host. The theme is circus: colorful blue and red decor, magnificent china, fun touches in the two dining rooms, outdoor cafe, bar, and banquet facilities (for 250). Chef Sottha Khunn presides over a superb kitchen staff of 55 (including 9 pastry chefs), $250,000 stoves, and a private area for special guests to eat in the midst of it all. The Sultan of Brunei (you know, the wealthiest guy in the world) footed most of the bill for the $3 million kitchen and furnishings. The food can only be discribed in one word: superb. Even the soufflés, which usually take extra time to prepare, appear at a moment's notice. Don't miss a chance to have a memorable meal at this legendary palace!

L'ÉCOLE
French Culinary Institute
462 Broadway (at Grand St)   212/219-3300
Lunch: Mon-Fri; Dinner: Mon-Sat
Moderate

Class is in session at the kitchen of L'École, the dining room of the French Culinary Institute. The students, eager and excited, are preparing daily meals under the watchful eyes of the dean of culinary studies, their head chef, and his team. They are learning their lessons well. Out front, the neighborhood is hardly inviting, and the maitre d' adds little to the effort inside. The room itself is attractive enough, if you can keep your eyes at table height and forget about the tall, unbecoming ceiling. But meals here are a real bargain! Dinner consists of a *prix fixe* four- or five-course gourmet presentation. It is obvious that the instructors are watching very carefully, for each dish is delicious and beautifully presented. Because there is a limited menu, the would-be chefs are able to concentrate on a few dishes. There is also a three-course *prix fixe* and an a la carte menu at noon.

LE GIGOT
18 Cornelia St (bet Bleecker and 4th St)   212/627-3737
Lunch, Dinner: Tues-Sun
Moderate

I can't imagine a more pleasant dinner on a chilly New York evening than one prepared at this tiny, 30-seat bistro in the bowels of the Village. Most taxi drivers have never heard of Cornelia Street, so if you plan to come here by cab, be sure to allow extra time. Once here, the cozy atmosphere and almost unbelievably warm hospitality of the ladies who greet and serve, combine with hearty dishes that will please even the most discerning diner. My suggestion for a memorable meal: *le boeuf Bourguignon* (beef stew in red wine with shallots, bacon, carrots, mushrooms, and potatoes). All of this for a truly modest price. There's much more, like roasted leg of lamb and roasted loin of pork. Snails or patés make delicious starters. Equally tasty desserts like upside-down apple tarts or flambéed bananas with cognac are offered. Le Gigot is a lot less expensive than its counterpart in Paris and just as appealing in every way.

LE GRENADIN
13 E 37th St   212/725-0560
Lunch: Mon-Fri; Dinner: Mon-Sat
Moderate

When I ordered an artichoke (my favorite food), and it arrived with the heart already fixed in the center, with each leaf spread out in a circle around the edge of the plate, I knew I had arrived in gastronomic heaven! The location of Le Grenadin in a clutter of awnings and tawdry storefronts doesn't accurately foretell what one finds inside this extremely gracious and professional restaurant. Claudine and Christian Piques have decorated their establishment in sexy pale tones, with fresh flowers on each table. For lunch there are oysters, patés, snails in garlic butter, pastas, and seafoods. In the evening try the seafood casserole with champagne sauce. On to wonderful rack of lamb or veal sweetbread with wild mushrooms. Be sure to order one of the fabulous soufflés at the start: you have a choice of Grand Marnier, chocolate, *framboises*, or *citron*. A superb cheese plate is also offered. I can't remember an evening I have enjoyed as much as the last one in this charming...and tasty...dining room.

Feel in the mood for some real Southern fried chicken or Carolina shrimp creole, or baked beef short ribs? A good bet is **Little Jezebel Plantation** (529 Columbus Ave, 212/579-4952). The place is immaculate, the service friendly, and takeout, delivery, and catering are available. Just thinking about their honey chicken, seared in a sweet and pungent sauce with yams, sends my taste buds into high gear!

LENOX ROOM
1278 Third Ave (at 73rd St)   212/772-0404
Lunch: Mon-Fri; Brunch: Sun; Dinner: Daily
Moderate to moderately expensive

Many diners feel this is the place to see and be seen. Lenox Room is an attractive and cozy retreat with Tony Fortuna making sure that everyone is properly taken care of. Oysters, clams, jumbo shrimp, lobsters, and osetra caviar are offered at the raw bar. Best appetizers include foie gras and chicken liver parfait (don't get on the scales tomorrow) and a great crabmeat timbale with grapefruit sauce. If you are a seafood lover, you'll be in heaven with the main dishes: roasted skate, crisped salmon, seared tuna steak, and blackened mahimahi are among the selections. A different risotti is offered daily. Save room for one of their lemon custard or chocolate tarts for dessert.

LE PÉRIGORD
405 E 52nd St (bet First Ave and East River)   212/755-6244
Lunch: Mon-Fri; Dinner: Daily
Expensive

Some things just get better with age (especially after 35), and Le Périgord is one of them. In spruced-up surroundings, but with the same style and class that only Georges Briguet can provide, Le Périgord offers a French dining experience of perfection. This is a dress-up place, and my advice is to come prepared to enjoy one of the rare joys in civilized dining. The waiters are so helpful you really should leave the ordering in their hands. They will probably suggest such goodies as duck foie gras, Dover sole meuniere, veal kidneys, potato-crusted salmon, or any of the beef dishes. By all means, don't leave without experiencing the Grand Marnier mousse or a soufflé! I am a sentimental fellow; every time I talk to Georges, I think how great it would be if everyone were like him! In fact, if my memory is correct, they used to be. The *prix fixe* dinner is $52.

What is the theme?

For awhile theme restaurants were very hot in Manhattan. Kids especially loved them. Their parents were less excited about the various presentations, especially when it came to eating what could best be described as very ordinary food at inflated prices. Well, things have changed a bit. Some of the shakier places have closed, and others are having trouble filling their colorful seats. Still the best of the lot is the **Hard Rock Cafe** (221 W 57th St), where the proprietors wisely have concentrated on food as well as atmosphere. Less successful are the **Harley Davidson Cafe** (1370 Ave of the Americas), where the cycles are more interesting than the food; **Jekyll & Hyde Club** (1409 Ave of the Americas), hardly an appetizing atmosphere; **Motown Cafe** (104 W 57th St), where the music is better than the eats; and **Planet Hollywood** (Times Square in early 2000), the big-name hangout with small-time platters. All of them seem more interested in selling their merchandise than training their kitchen crews. Take the kids to the **Brooklyn Diner USA** (212 W 57th St) or **Serendipity 3** (225 E 60th St), where the food is just as good as the atmosphere.

LE REFUGE
166 E 82nd St (bet Third and Lexington Ave)   212/861-4505
Lunch, Dinner: Daily; Brunch: Sat, Sun
Moderate

In any city other than New York this would be one of the hottest restaurants in town. But aside from folks in the neighborhood, few seem to have heard of Le Refuge, a charming, three-room French country restaurant that offers excellent food, professional service, and delightful surroundings. The front room is cozy and comfortable, and the rear two sections provide nice views and pleasant accommodations. A back garden is open in the summer. This is another house where the owner is the chef, and as usual, it shows in the professionalism of the presentations. Specialties of the house: duck with fresh fruit, bouillabaisse *de crustaces,* and couscous Mediterranean with shrimp. Finish off the meal with the flourless *gateau soufflé au chocolate.* A delightful *prix fixe* brunch is served on weekends.

LES CÉLÉBRITÉS
Essex House Westin
155 W 58th St (bet Ave of the Americas and Seventh Ave)
212/484-5113
Dinner: Tues-Sat
Expensive

You, too, can be a celebrity! That is, a food celebrity. Close your eyes for a moment and forget you are in a hotel dining room on Central Park in the midst of teeming Manhattan. Imagine yourself in the grand dining room of a luxurious estate in the early part of the century. This is as fine and magnificent a room as there is in New York. Decorated in superb taste, it is small enough to be intimate and large enough to convey the feeling that dining here is a grand occasion. The name comes from the artwork that adorns the walls. All are paintings created by American celebrities, including Phyllis Diller, Van Johnson, Peggy Lee, and Elke Sommer. The works are for sale; proceeds go to local charities. The menu matches the decor in splendor. New chef Luc Dimnet presents dishes that justify the high prices. A six-course menu degustation is available, as well as seasonal specialty *prix fixe* dinners. The a la carte menu changes but usually offers the kind of dishes you wouldn't prepare at home: sauteed foie gras with apricots or seafood-steamed turbot with lemon risotto and a late harvest wine sauce. What else but chocolate soufflé with praline ice cream for dessert? You won't want to wake up after this sumptuous culinary dream.

LES HALLES
411 Park Ave S (bet 28th and 29th St)   212/679-4111
Daily: noon to midnight
Moderate

Les Halles has struck a responsive note on the New York restaurant stage. Perhaps it is because France remains the most romantic scene to many gourmets or that bistros have become the "in" thing in Manhattan. But probably it is because this establishment provides the necessary ingredients in today's restaurant sweepstakes: tasty food in an appealing atmosphere at reasonable prices. Specialties like blood sausage with apples, lamb stew, or fillet of beef are served in hefty portions with a fresh salad and delicious French fries on the side. Harried waiters try their best to be polite and helpful, but they are not always successful, as tables turn over more rapidly than at most fast-food outlets. If a week in Paris is more of a dream than a reality, you might settle for snails, onion soup, and classic cassoulet at this busy establishment. Unless you love tarts, the dessert selection is a disappointment. (Note: An attractive butcher shop right by the front door is open Monday through Saturday.)

LESPINASSE
St. Regis Hotel
2 E 55th St (at Fifth Ave)   212/339-6719
Breakfast, Lunch, Dinner: Tues-Sat
Expensive

If dining in grand style is what you want, look no further. Lespinasse is not just a meal but an experience. The magnificent room, with its high ceilings and beautiful floral arrangements, is serviced by a spectacular kitchen (ask to see it). When top-rated chef Gray Kunz left, some felt that Lespinasse would never be the same. Wrong. Master chef Christian Delouvrier has been trained in some of Europe's best kitchens and spent time at some great Manhattan restaurants, including Les Célébrités. He is known for his expertise with sauces, a fine complement for almost any dish. Service here is what you would expect: highly professional, with personnel disappearing into the background when necessary. Special *prix fixe* menus are available, along with a la carte suggestions. Vegetarians will find special items listed. The chef's seven-course menu degustation is memorable. From caviar to ragout of miniature vegetables to truffles to foie gras to suckling pig to chocolate soufflé, it is perfection. Just don't have your cholesterol checked the next day!

Now You'll Know

Chinese

Dim sum: a whole meal of succulent nibblers, such as steamed dumplings, shrimp balls, and savory pastries

Egg foo yong: thick, savory pancakes made with eggs, vegetables, and meat. Often slathered with a rich, broth-based sauce

General Tso's chicken: breaded and deep-fried chicken chunks sauteed with vegetables and tossed in a spicy-sweet sauce

Moo shu: stir-fried shredded pork, vegetables, and seasonings, scrambled with eggs and rolled (usually by the diner) inside thin pancakes

Peking duck: After the chef pumps air between the duck's skin and flesh, the bird is coated with honey and hung up until the skin dries and hardens. The duck is then roasted, cut into pieces, and served with scallions and pancakes or steamed buns.

French

Bouillabaise: French seafood stew

Confit: goose, duck, or pork that has been salted, cooked, and preserved in its own cooking fat

Coulis: a thick, smooth sauce, usually made from vegetables but sometimes from fruit

En croute: anything baked in a buttery pastry crust or hollowed-out slice of toast

Foie gras: goose liver, usually made into a paté

Tartare: finely chopped and seasoned raw beef, often served as an appetizer with raw egg yolk

Italian

Bruschetta: slices of crispy garlic bread, usually topped with tomatoes and basil.

Carpaccio: thin shavings of raw beef topped with olive oil and lemon juice or mayonnaise

Risotto: creamy rice-like pasta, often mixed with chicken, shellfish, and/or vegetables

Saltimbocca: Thinly sliced veal is topped with prosciutto (Italian ham) and sage, then sauteed in butter and slow-simmered in white wine. The name means "jumps in your mouth."

Zabaglione: a dessert sauce or custard made with egg yolks, wine, and sugar; also known as *sabayon* in France

Japanese

Sashimi: sliced raw fish served with *daikon* (Japanese radish), wasabi (Japanese horseradish), fresh ginger, and soy sauce

Sukiyaki: stir-fried pieces of meat (and sometimes vegetables, noodles, or tofu) flavored with soy sauce, *dashi* (Japanese fish stock), and *mirin* (sweet rice wine)

Sushi: pieces of raw fish or vegetables placed atop vinegared rice or served inside rolls wrapped in *nori* (sheets of dried seaweed)

Tempura: fried battered seafood and vegetables

Teriyaki: beef or chicken marinated in a sauce of rice wine, soy sauce, sugar, and seasonings, then grilled or stir-fried

Mexican

Fajitas: marinated beef, shrimp, chicken, and/or vegetables served in warm tortillas (often wrapped by the diner)

Ceviche: citrus-marinated raw fish

Chilis rellenos: mild to spicy chili peppers stuffed with cheese and fried in egg batter

Chorizo: spicy pork sausage

Empanadas: Mexican meat-filled pastries, usually made with vegetables and surrounded by a fat-laden crust

Enchiladas: soft corn tortillas filled with meat, vegetables, or cheese, and topped with salsa and cheese

Paella: an elaborate Spanish or Mexican saffron-flavored rice dish that includes a variety of seafood and meats

Tamale: chopped meat and vegetables encased in cornmeal dough

LES ROUTIERS
568 Amsterdam Ave (bet 87th and 88th St)   212/874-2742
Dinner: Mon-Sun
Moderate

This charming small French bistro set amid scruffy-looking storefronts is a happy find on the Upper West Side. This is no carbon-copy French establishment; it is the real thing, with a French menu and genuine ambience. There are snails and mussels with wine, skewered sea scallops, patés, duck, breast of chicken, veal stewed in white wine sauce—all those things you might find in the heartland of France. Wonderful salads are almost a meal in themselves. An enticing selection of sweet things is available; take a look at the dessert table as you come in.

LIBRARY
Regency Hotel
540 Park Ave (at 61st St)   212/759-4100
Breakfast, Lunch, Tea, Dinner, Dessert: Daily
Moderate

The Regency Hotel exudes class, and the Library restaurant provides more of that special ingredient without inflated prices. The setting is cordial, comfortable, and clubby, with magazines and papers to keep you informed while you wait or as you dine. The service is professional and friendly, in keeping with the tradition of hotel manager Chris Knable. Luncheons offer soups, salads, seafood, burgers, and great club sandwiches. The dinner menu expands to American favorites, including steaks, additional seafood dishes, and pasta. Save room for the Jack Daniels pecan tart or the double-chocolate pudding for dessert.

LOBSTER CLUB
24 E 80th St   212/249-6500
Lunch: Mon-Sat, Dinner: Daily
Moderately expensive

Talented chef Anne Rosenzweig has created her own club for the Upper East Side! But non-East Siders are certainly welcome in this warm and inviting charmer, complete with a nautical flair and magnificent marble bar. Diners are served on two levels, as well as in the bar. Lots of seafood appetizers are offered on the changing menu. There are soups, salads (like smoked trout with endive), pastas, and mashed potatoes with wild mushroom gravy and truffled bourbon. Of course, there's no shortage of lobster dishes. One of the best is the entree-sized lobster club. I was particularly intrigued with the grilled short ribs and the different daily meatloaf entrees—delicious! Anne has outdone herself with unusual desserts, like warm chocolate bread pudding, pecan caramel tart, and cool apple soup with carmelized apple (seasonal). The downstairs room is the most inviting. Visit with the gregarious bartender, who sets the tone for this delightful operation.

LUTÈCE
249 E 50th St (bet Second and Third Ave)   212/752-2225
Lunch: Tues-Fri; Dinner: Mon-Sat
Expensive

The image of Lutèce was embodied in the person of Andre Soltner. He created not just a restaurant but an institution. How does anyone follow a legend? Well, Eberhard Müller is doing it very well. Housed in an old brownstone, this place reeks of class, composure, and comfort. The garden room is not super-attractive; the upstairs dining rooms have more appeal. The classics are still there: rack of lamb, duck, roasted lobster. The menu changes seasonally, as Eberhard is keen on fresh products (especially in the seafood category, from his background at Le Bernardin). One of their signature soufflés will top off a grand meal.

MALONEY & PORCELLI
37 E 50th St (bet Park and Madison Ave)   212/750-2233
Lunch, Dinner: Daily
Expensive

The lawyers whose names appear on the masthead should first insist that these folks get reasonable with their prices. No argument that the food is very good, but the tab is simply outrageous. Maybe that is because their bread basket is so exceptional. Pizzas and crabcakes with ratatouille or pastrami salmon are delicious appetizers. I have seldom tasted a better sirloin steak. (It *should* be, at that price!) Lobster, equally tasty, is even more expensive. Don't pass up the "angry lobster"! If this is a business meal, go for it. And include some cowboy onion rings or a portabello potato pie. Don't leave without trying the chocolate brownout cake. The supervisory staff here could lower their noses a notch or two, but the floor staff is pleasant and try to be accommodating (though they're not very well trained). I hope these talented foodies don't go the way of one of their former tenants (Gloucester House), who found out that pockets do indeed have a bottom!

MANGIA È BEVI
800 Ninth Ave (at 53rd St)   212/956-3976
Lunch, Dinner: Daily
Inexpensive to moderate

This is definitely not the spot for a relaxing, intimate, refined meal. But it is definitely a top choice for delicious food at unbelievably low Manhattan prices. The noise level is almost unbearable, the tables allow you to instantly become friendly with some new folks, and the waiters are all very casual and surprisingly helpful. The abundant antipasto platter, overflowing with nearly a dozen choices, is a house specialty. This rustic trattoria also features a large selection of pastas, fish, many meat dishes, salads and a bevy of in-season veggies.

Brick-oven pizza lovers will be in seventh heaven with pleasing combinations and equally pleasing prices. There's nothing special about desserts, except that the overexposed tiramisu served here is homemade. It is easy to see why colorful Mangia è Bevi is one of the most popular destinations along Ninth Avenue.

MANHATTAN GRILLE
1161 First Ave (at 64th St)   212/888-6556
Lunch: Mon-Fri; Dinner: Daily; Brunch: Sun
Moderate to expensive

Steakhouses are "in" — and the classy, continental Manhattan Grille has been in for quite some time. It is indeed an attractive, pleasant place to dine. But it is more than that! The steaks are large and delicious, as are the lamb chops and prime rib. Even the seafood, especially the filet of sole, is worth trying. A number of veal dishes are available, with veal piccata being particularly good. Accompany your choice with excellent cottage-fried potatoes. For dessert, the *tartufo* equals any I've tasted in Italy (except Tre Scalini's in Rome), and the cheesecake melts in your mouth. A pre-theater menu is available daily before 6:15 p.m. Manhattan Grille is a cigar-friendly restaurant with a separate smoking and cigar room featuring a built-in humidor.

MARCH
405 E 58th St (bet First Ave and Sutton Pl)   212/754-6272
Dinner: Mon-Sun
Expensive

If you want to be spoiled, start here. In this attractive and romantic townhouse with high ceilings and teak floors, you will dine in one of three rooms in absolutely regal style. Executive chef Wayne Nish and partner Joseph Scalice (who oversees the front house) have raised the art of dining to perfection. Wayne has abandoned the common practice of serving appetizers and entrees in large portions in favor of presenting smaller portions of all his dishes. Create your own four-course *prix fixe* meal from over 30 choices or a seven-course menu available after 8 p.m. It is well worth the tab, for the sky is the limit when it comes to service and quality. The fact that it is so busy is a tribute to the format. An attractive, glass-enclosed back porch overlooks a small garden in this Sutton Place neighborhood.

MARCHI'S
251 E 31st St   212/679-2494
Dinner: Mon-Sat (special hours for private parties)
Moderate

This must be one of the best-kept secrets in New York. Though there's no sign out front, Marchi's has been a New York fixture since 1930, when it was established by the Marchi family in an attractive brownstone townhouse. The Marchis, joined by their three sons, are still on hand, giving a homey flavor to the restaurant's three dining rooms and garden patio (a great spot for a private dinner). It's almost like going to dinner at your favorite Italian family's house, especially since there are no menus. Be sure to bring a hearty appetite so you can take full advantage of a superb feast. The first course is a platter of antipasto, including radishes, *finocchio,* and Genoa salami, plus a salad of tuna, olives, and red cabbage. The second is an absolutely delicious homemade lasagna. The third is a crispy deep-fried fish. The side orders of cold beets and string beans are light and tempting. The entree is delicious roast chicken and veal served with fresh mushrooms and a tossed salad. For dessert, there is a healthy bowl of fresh fruit, cheese, lemon fritter, and sensational *crostoli* (crisp fried twists sprinkled with powdered sugar). The price tag is reasonable. Come to Marchi's for a unique, leisurely meal and an evening you will long remember.

MARK'S RESTAURANT
Mark Hotel
25 E 77th St   212/879-1864
Breakfast, Lunch, Dinner: Daily; Brunch, Sun
Moderately expensive

One of the best! You can enjoy a fine meal here in a sedate atmosphere reminiscent of an English club. Adding to the pleasure of delicious food are the refined, professional service, solid wood tables, beautiful flowers, gorgeous china, and a feeling of being particularly welcome. For appetizers: warm Maine lobster and Japanese mushroom salad or Hudson Valley foie gras. For entrees: whole roasted black sea bass wrapped in sage and pancetta or grilled fillet of beef with oxtail rillettes, baby carrots, and turnips. For dessert: warm chocolate gourmandise or Grand Marnier soufflé with *crème anglaise*. Many Upper East Siders who are not guests of the hotel make this dining room a frequent stop. It is not difficult to understand why.

MAZZEI
1564 Second Ave (at 81st St)   212/628-3131
Dinner: Daily
Moderate

This small Upper East Side hideaway (it has had several previous lives under different names) now takes its cue from Philip Mazzei, an Italian-American diplomat of the 18th century who was active in furthering relations between this country and Italy. Restaurant Mazzei certainly keeps on that track, cementing the love affair between New Yorkers and good, hearty Italian fare. The brisk, professional service, the energy created by full tables of neighborhood diners (out-of-towners would have a hard time finding this jewel), and the vast assortment of daily specials make a visit here memorable. There are different appetizers from the wood-burning oven each evening. Recommended dishes include an excellent veal chop, baked prawns, and boneless breast of chicken. Be sure to ask for some of the small specialty potatoes, which are as tender and tasty as you'll ever encounter.

MERCER KITCHEN
Mercer Hotel
99 Prince St (at Mercer St)   212/966-5454
Breakfast, Lunch, Dinner: Daily
Moderate to moderately expensive

After much hype, Jean-Georges Vongerichten has opened another see-and-be-seen establishment, this one located in Soho at a newish hotel that has set the style for that area. One literally sits in an area that was under sidewalk grates where legions of New Yorkers went about their daily tasks. Now they can take comfort in an unusual downstairs space that features a raw bar, a salad bar, a pizza oven, a rotisserie, and all the other features that made up turn-of-the-century dining a la Jean-Georges. As you sit at attractive heavy wooden tables, you are offered some of Barry Wine's pizzas (like raw tuna and wasabi), baked squab, or green risotto with shrimp. All are delicious, despite being served by personnel in hideous black outfits. (Why can't someone design classy uniforms to go with classy food?) With your outstanding dessert of chocolate cake with caramel ice cream (not all of them are that great), take advantage of the large assortment of black teas.

METISSE
239 W 105th St (bet Amsterdam Ave and Broadway)   212/666-8825
Dinner: Mon-Sun
Moderate

In the neighborhood surrounding Columbia University, good dining is not easy to find. So it is with pleasure that I can heartily recommend Metisse, a small French bistro. Metisse will be a comfortable destination for both palate and pocketbook. The place is quiet and restful, the waiters unobtrusive, and the cuisine light and satisfying. A number of salads are available as appetizers, but I'd suggest the corn-breaded shrimp with spicy dipping sauce. Delicious! Entrees are slanted on the seafood side (grilled tuna, sauteed cod, black bass, red snapper), along with steak and chops. And the French fries are first rate! Their warm chocolate cake with vanilla ice cream is the most popular dessert, although less filling fruit specialties are available. It's a delightful spot for a casual meal if business or pleasure brings you to the Upper West Side.

MEZZOGIORNO
195 Spring St   212/334-2112
Lunch, Dinner: Daily
Moderate

One of the most charming cities in the world is Florence, Italy, not only for its abundance of great art but also for the wonderful small restaurants on every street corner. At Mezzogiorno, a Florence-style *trattoria* in New York, the food is just as good (though some of the art is questionable). The place is busy and noisy, and tables are so close together that conversation is impossible. The decor is best described as "modern Florence"; check out the unusual writing on the ceiling done by master fresco artist Pontormo. Better yet, keep your eyes on the food. The salad selection is outstanding, as are all the meat carpaccios. If you like lasagna, theirs is one of the best. Mezzogiorno is also famous for the pizzas it serves. You'll find all the ingredients for a wonderful make-believe evening in Florence.

MICHAEL JORDAN'S, THE STEAK HOUSE
Grand Central Terminal
23 Vanderbilt Ave   212/655-2300
Lunch, Dinner: Daily
Moderately expensive

Grand Central Station has come back to life, and Michael Jordan's new establishment gives one more reason to visit this historic building even if you are not catching a train. Michael and his partners have provided another good New York steakhouse (they are very "in" at the moment), along with an opportunity to gaze upon the sea of humanity that flows through this building. The menu? Very much what you would expect: steaks, chops, delicious braised prime short ribs, chicken, lobster, and salmon. You'll fill up with the sizable portions, but if you feel especially hungry, try the sliced tomatoes and sweet onion appetizer. Forget the calories and try the huge special French fries as a side dish. For a change, desserts are reasonably priced. They include chocolate mud cake, an ice cream sundae the kids will love, and pastries from the esteemed Payard Patisserie.

MINETTA TAVERN
113 MacDougal St   212/475-3850
Lunch, Dinner: Daily
Moderate

Do you want to take your guests to a Northern Italian restaurant in the Village where the coat-and-tie, meat-and-potatoes set feels comfortable? Well, Minetta Tavern—established in 1937 and serving excellent food for generations—is the place to go. Located on the spot where Minetta Brook wandered through Manhattan in the early days, this tavern was made famous by Eddie "Minetta" Sieveri, a friend of many sports and stage stars of yesteryear. Dozens of old pictures adorn the walls of this intimate, scrupulously clean tavern, where professional personnel serve no-nonsense Italian food at attractive prices. Grilled mushrooms, steamed clams, or *pasta e fagioli* are good ways to get the juices flowing. If you'd like something a bit heftier, veal is available. Chocolate mousse cake, profiteroles, and other pastries make a wonderful cap to a satisfying meal. By the way, if you have to wait, the bar stools are among the most comfortable in New York.

MME. ROMAINE DE LYON
132 E 61st St   212/758-2422
Lunch: Daily; Dinner: Mon-Sat
Moderate

The best omelets in New York are served at Mme. Romaine's. If you can't find what you want from their 545 varieties, it probably doesn't exist. How about a lobster, spinach, or chicken omelet? They will make any combination you want. When you're in the mood for a light lunch or dinner, this is the place to go. If omelets are not your preference, try the chef's salad or smoked salmon. At dinnertime, a full menu of continental cuisine is available, plus piano music each evening.

MONKEY BAR
Hotel Elysee
60 E 54th St   212/838-2600
Lunch: Mon-Fri; Dinner: Daily
Moderately expensive

It would be difficult to imagine that New Yorkers ate as well in the early decades of this century as they do presently at the art deco Monkey Bar, in the Hotel Elysee. Yet, reminders of those days abound in this comfortable and memory-filled room. Of course, that is only part of the pleasure. The rest is in the superb cooking of chef Kurt Gutenbrunner, who has had excellent training at the arm of legendary David Bouley. A three-course market lunch offers a choice of five items for each course at a reasonable $28. What wonders come out of that kitchen: hot smoked Atlantic salmon, crab meat and shrimp with cucumbers and asparagus, lobster salad, venison ragout, and much more. For dinner, try the oysters, the tuna tartare, any of the lobster dishes, or the Hudson Valley foie gras. A *prix fixe* pre-theater menu is available. Dessert? The Austrian chef would certainly suggest the linzer torte or the apple strudel.

MONTRACHET
239 West Broadway (bet White and Walker St)   212/219-2777
Lunch: Fri; Dinner: Mon-Sat
Moderately expensive

Thriving and exciting places like Montrachet draw discerning diners to Tribeca. Once you're inside Montrachet, the neighborhood's drabness dissipates. You can concentrate without distraction on fine modern French dishes such as seafood, game, and meat prepared to perfection by the restaurant's super-chef, Remi Lauvand. The menu changes regularly; exciting things are done with fresh produce. If you are lucky enough to find bouillabaisse on the menu, go for it. Foie gras, warm oysters, and roast chicken are outstanding choices. Salmon and tuna dishes are done to perfection. The three simply decorated rooms do not detract from the main reason you are here: good eating. Having tasted many napoleons, I can say with authority that Montrachet's is top-notch.

MORTON'S OF CHICAGO
551 Fifth Ave (at 45th St)   212/972-3315
90 West St   212/732-5665
Lunch: Mon-Fri; Dinner: Mon-Sun
Moderately expensive to expensive

Now this is a real steakhouse. Forget about the "of Chicago"—this is New York at its best! These folks are experts, as well they should be: they have units all over the country. Every member of the highly efficient staff has been trained in the Morton's manner. At the start you are shown a cart with samples of entree items, fresh vegetables, lobster, and whatever else they happen to be featuring. Every dish is fully explained by your waiter. Appetizers are heavy in the seafood department: shrimp, oysters, smoked salmon, sea scallops. Attractive and appetizing salads include one with sliced beefsteak tomatoes and purple onions. The steaks and chops are so tender you can cut them with a fork. Best of all, they arrive promptly, unlike so many steakhouses. Potatoes come in several styles, including wonderful hash browns. Sauteed spinach and mushrooms or steamed broccoli and asparagus are fresh and tasty. Top it all off with a delicious soufflé—chocolate, Grand Marnier, lemon, or raspberry—that is big enough for two hefty diners.

MR. K'S
570 Lexington Ave (at 51st St)   212/583-1668
Lunch, Dinner: Daily
Moderately expensive to expensive

During the many years I lived in Washington, D.C., Mr. K's was my favorite Chinese restaurant in that city. Now the operation has expanded to Manhattan with a dining palace that's not quite up to the standards of the original. However, it's still very good. The gourmet dishes are from every region of China, served in a classy style with imperial flatware. There are dumplings, tasty soups, vegetarian meals, popular lemon chicken, broiled rack of lamb, scallops, sesame prawns, herbal duck, and on and on. Of course, Peking duck is offered, served with crepes, scallions, and hoisin sauce. Stir-fried soft noodles and stir-fried fluffy rice are specialties of the house. Service can be a bit haughty; some of the captains act as if guests have never dined in such "regal" surroundings before. If this happens, call on manager John Fong, and you'll have a great meal!

NICOLA'S
146 E 84th St (bet Lexington and Third Ave)   212/249-9850
Dinner: Daily
Moderately expensive

Upper-crust New Yorkers who like a clubby atmosphere and good food (which are not often found together) love this place! In a setting of rich wood and familiar faces on the walls, and a noise level that sometimes reaches that of a Broadway opening, no-nonsense waiters serve delicious platters of pasta, veal, chicken, fish, and steak. There are daily specials in every category, and each is inviting. It is difficult to come up with really good home fries in a busy restaurant, but Nicola's has the secret . . . theirs are sensational! Concentrate on the early part of your meal, as the desserts show little imagination.

At a smallish Village place called **EQ** (the initials of the owner), at 267 West 4th Street, to say the menu is overpriced is being kind; one smallish bowl of lukewarm corn chowder had a price tag of $10.

NOBU
105 Hudson St (near Franklin St)   212/219-0500
Lunch: Mon-Fri; Dinner: Daily

NEXT DOOR NOBU
105 Hudson St (near Franklin St)   212/334-4445
Dinner: Mon-Sat

Moderately expensive

Now there are two! When you combine the culinary talents of chef Nobu Matsuhisa, the restaurant management expertise of Drew Nieporent, and a sensational setting done by the David Rockwell Group, you have a winning combination. So it is at these Japanese beauties in Tribeca. A loud Oriental shout greets diners as they enter Nobu, a comfortable and appealing sushi bar awaits those so inclined, and airy seating completes the scene. A full menu will please the traditional Japanese food lover while offering those with less adventurous tastes items they can enjoy. Besides the sushi and sashimi, there is tempura, kushiyaki (beef, chicken, veggies, and seafood on skewers), and a large selection of daily specialties that run heavily on the seafood side. Service has been refined to perfection. The ambience is unique—surely not that of a typical Tokyo establishment. And the pastry chef has created some trans-Pacific specialties: orange tart with bitter chocolate sorbet, yellow plum and sake sorbet, green tea crème caramel, and cherry walnut and red bean spring roll. Nobu is not a bargain, but the experience of dining in a truly professional ethnic restaurant is worth the extra bucks. Taking advantage of the popularity of Nobu, a more casual stepbrother, Next Door Nobu, provides a similar menu with a no-reservations policy. There is also a raw bar and a great selection of noodle dishes.

OCEAN GRILL
384 Columbus Ave (bet 78th and 79th Ave)   212/579-2300
Lunch, Dinner: Daily; Brunch: Sat, Sun
Moderate

Busy, busy, busy best describes this popular seafood house on the Upper West Side. The usual packed house is more an indication of the lack of good seafood restaurants in the area than in the excellence of Ocean Grill. However, one can have a very good meal if dishes are carefully selected. Tasty crab cakes and sesame crusted lobster rolls are good starters. Lobsters are a specialty that are offered steamed, broiled, or grilled. My chicken Cobb salad was delicious; a lobster Cobb is also offered. Entrees from the wood-burning grill are uniformly well-prepared and include salmon, tuna, swordfish, halibut, mahi-mahi, shrimp and scallops. Oyster lovers will be in heaven at the Ocean Grill. On the downside, desserts can only be described as poor.

OCEANA
55 E 54th St (bet Park and Madison Ave)   212/759-5941
Lunch, Dinner: Mon-Sat
Expensive

The only time you might get seasick here is when you receive the check! Otherwise, the setting, service, and food are all in the superior category. On several floors of a midtown townhouse that once was Le Cygne, talented chef Rick Moonen (formerly at the Water Club), prepares seafood dishes that rival those served aboard the *Queen Elizabeth*. The three-course price-fixed menu has a $65 tab; if you really splurge on a six-course feast, the tab is $90. The appetizer selection is staggering: grilled baby octopus, jumbo lump crab cakes, and lobster ravioli are among the selections. Entree favorites include a wonderful bouillabaisse, pan-seared striped bass, and a grilled salmon filet. All entrees are garnished with special vegetables and potatoes, the likes of which you may have never seen before! I could make a meal out of the dessert selection. Pastry chef David Carmichael offers such treats as sticky toffee pudding, pineapple upside-down cake with pineapple sorbet, and several heavenly pastry chef's samplers.

ONE IF BY LAND, TWO IF BY SEA
17 Barrow St (bet Seventh Ave and 4th St)   212/228-0822
Dinner: Daily
Expensive

If romance is the key word for the evening, then I heartily recommend this restaurant. The candlelight, fireplace, flowers, and background piano music all add to the enjoyment. One If By Land is housed in an 18th-century carriage house that reportedly was once owned by Aaron Burr. It is a very good idea to allow yourself some extra time to find this place, as Barrow Street (one of the West Village's most charming) is generally not known to taxi drivers. Besides, there is no sign out front! The tables at the front of the balcony are particularly appealing. Although some folks take exception to the food (Ruth Reichl is one), I have always found it very satisfactory. You can't go wrong with their rack of lamb or breast of duck. Beef Wellington is usually excellent. A six-course tasting menu is available, if you're extra hungry. Crème brûleé is a favorite dessert.

ONIEAL'S
174 Grand St (bet Centre and Mulberry St)   212/941-9119
Dinner: Daily
Moderate

Now here is a charmer, and talk about atmosphere! From magnificent wood ceilings with carved devil's heads to the storybook tunnel that connects the building to an old police station (the tunnel is now used to store wine), this small establishment is just the spot for a special New York evening. There are only 35 seats in the dining room, and cigar and cigarette smoking is allowed, so be prepared if smoke bothers you. An attractive bar area is full of smokers, too! But on to the food: caviar, oysters, or smoked salmon to start. Barbecued venison pot pie or roasted quail as appetizers. Lamb shanks, grilled vegetable roulade or striped sea bass for entrees. If pot roast is on the menu, go for it! The soufflé chocolate cake with fresh berries and ice cream is a dessert winner, as is the espresso float, a sinful ice cream dish with chocolate, caramel, and citrus dust. The folks here are as friendly as the ambience is inviting. Forget about the grungy buildings nearby and steep yourself in an establishment whose home has been a New York institution for over 125 years.

OPALINE
85 Avenue A (bet 5th and 6th St)   212/475-5050
Dinner: Daily
Moderate

Opaline is an only-in-New-York experience from start to finish. The location is in what is known as alphabet land, which was for years a haven for druggies and undesirable elements. Fortunately, the region has been cleaned up, but there remains an air of mystery and intrigue. Opaline is reached down a flight of stairs; you almost feel like someone behind the doors is checking you out for a visit to a speakeasy. But you enter a restaurant that is unique: a lounge that looks like it belongs in a bawdy house, a large dining room with ceiling fans, and a raised area for entertainment. You came for good food, too, and you won't be disappointed. There are mussels steamed in tomato garlic broth and braised lamb shanks with roasted garlic whipped potatoes and chocolate soufflé cake with *crème fraiche* ice cream. Prices are so low they will astound you. The image of the old Absinthe House (from which Opaline gets its name) is that of an intimate and slightly sinister meeting place where elegant people gathered. Tonight it is your dining room. The scene has been transferred to the bowels of this great city, and you will have an evening you'll never forget.

ORSO
322 W 46th St (bet Eighth and Ninth Ave)   212/489-7212
Mon, Tues, Thurs, Fri, Sun: noon–11:45;
Wed, Sat: 11:30 a.m.–11:45 p.m.
Moderate

This restaurant features the same menu all day, which is great for those with unusual dining hours and handy for those going to the theater. Orso is one of the most popular places on midtown's "restaurant row," so if you're thinking about a six o'clock dinner, be sure to make reservations. The smallish room is cozy and comfortable. It's watched over by a portrait of Orso, a Venetian dog who is the mascot for this Italian bistro. The kitchen is open in the back and visible to diners. You can see for yourself just how experienced the staff is. The changing menu includes many good appetizers, like cold roast veal and fried artichokes. A variety of pizzas and some excellent pasta dishes are also offered. For an entree, you can't go wrong with the very popular calves liver. The chocolate devil's cake, one of many homemade desserts, will finish off a great meal.

OSTERIA DEL CIRCO
120 W 55th St   212/265-3636
Lunch: Mon-Sat, Dinner: Mon-Sun
Moderately expensive

Were it not for the fact that the owners here are the sons of leqendary Sirio Maccioni (of Le Cirque) fame, this establishment might just be written off as another Italian restaurant. But here we have three brothers: Mario, Marco, and Mauro (and mother Egidiana) operating a classy establishment with a very friendly ambience, and, incidentally, not the usual Italian menu. There is a circus theme to the decor that it is well done but could be far more dramatic. Hopefully, time will cure this. The tastiest items include great pizzas, satisfying soups, unusual pastas (the ravioli is superb), and a wonderful flash-seared beef carpaccio. A unique dessert is an Italian favorite called *bomboloncini:* very small vanilla, chocolate and raspberry filled doughnuts.

Eating in **Nolita** . . . Do you know where that is? The neighborhood north of Little Italy!

Bread & Butter (220 Elizabeth St): sandwiches and lunches
Chibe's (30 Spring St): sake, caviar, and oysters
Ghenet (284 Mulberry St): Ethiopian

PALM
837 Second Ave (at 44th St)
212/687-2953

PALM TOO
840 Second Ave (at 44th St)
212/697-5198

Lunch: Mon-Fri; Dinner: Mon-Sat; Sun: 2-10 (Palm Too)
Expensive

Even with all the excellent new Manhattan steakhouses, steak and lobster lovers in Manhattan still have a special place in their hearts for the Palm and Palm Too. The Palm started as a speakeasy in 1926. These restaurants are located across the street from each other, and both have much the same atmosphere. They're noted for huge, delicious steaks, chops, and lobsters, but don't miss the terrific Palm fries—homemade potato chips—or try a combination order of fries and onion rings. It's an earthy spot, so don't get too dressed up. Indolent waiters are part of the scene.

PAMIR
1437 Second Ave (bet 74th and 75th St)   212/734-3791
1065 First Ave (at 58th St)   212/644-9258
Dinner: Tues-Sun
Moderate

The two Pamirs are among Manhattan's best ethnic restaurants! Turnovers are an Afghan specialty, and Pamir offers several. If you like extra-spicy food (like that served in the native country), they will gladly oblige. Great Afghan bread comes with each entree. Lamb is the order of the day: seasoned lamb with rice, almonds, and pistachios; chunks of lamb in an onion-and-garlic-flavored spinach sauce; lamb and eggplant cooked with tomatoes, onions, and spices; lamb on a skewer, marinated in spices; lamb chops broiled on a skewer. All are worth a try. Several vegetarian dishes are also available. Eat heartily from the start, because desserts are zilch. Folks here are unpretentious, the desire to please is sincere, and the prices are modest.

PAOLA'S
245 E 84th St   212/794-1890
Dinner: Daily
Moderate

Though it's relocated to new quarters, Paola is still a prime spot for a romantic evening. The Italian home cooking is first-class, with Paola in the kitchen taking care of the food. Great homemade filled pastas, superb veal dishes, and tasty, hot vegetables (like baby artichoke hearts) are house specialties. Take along a breath mint if romance is in the air, because they don't spare on the garlic. Mirrors reflect the warmth and flicker of candles, and the lady of the house will charm any guest. To top off the reasonably priced dinner, try a dish of rich chocolate mousse.

PAPER MOON MILANO
39 E 58th St   212/758-8600
Lunch, Dinner: Mon-Sat
Moderate

This offshoot of the well-known Milan House bills itself as a "restaurant-pizzeria." It does a good job in both departments. In a high-rent area, the atmosphere is friendly and casual; patrons in jeans and sportswear will feel perfectly comfortable. Decor is simple and appealing. The harried help tries its best to be accommodating. A fine selection of salads and pastas is offered, each presented with finesse that comes from years of experience in Italy. The full menu includes fish, meat, and poultry dishes, as well as several carpaccio dishes (thin slices of raw beef with various toppings). But you will be missing something special if you don't try the pizzas. A talented young Italian pizza chef turns out some of the lightest, tastiest combinations you will ever savor. Each is a meal in itself. A refreshing dish of gelati will top off a wonderful lunch or dinner.

Another "only in New York"!

Take note, all you peanut butter fans. Now you have your own place! **Peanut Butter & Co.**, located in the heart of Greenwich Village at 240 Sullivan Street, offers gourmet peanut butter sandwiches and snacks, as well as selling its signature line of gourmet peanut butters. They grind their own peanut butter fresh every day and are open from 11 a.m. to 11 p.m. Some items you won't want to pass up: the Fluffernutter (peanut butter on one side, marshmallow fluff on the other), and the Elvis (grilled peanut butter sandwich drizzled with honey and stuffed with sliced bananas), plus spicy, cinnamon-raisin, white chocolate, or chocolate-chip peanut butter sandwiches. You can have your choice of smooth or crunchy peanut butter!

PARIS COMMUNE
411 Bleecker St   212/929-0509
Dinner: Daily; Brunch: Sat, Sun
Moderate

The Paris Commune is a popular Village gathering spot with a Mediterranean-American menu (pastas, salads, steaks, seafood) where regulars outnumber visitors every night. There are only 17 tables, and the staff is prompt and efficient. Dining by candlelight with an adjoining fireplace is the attraction! The weekend brunch features spectacular French toast, along with the usual fare. Delicious omelets include cheddar cheese and bacon, apples and Jarlsberg cheese, and marinated artichoke hearts with mozzarella. Their homemade cheesecakes are good and rich.

PARK AVENUE CAFE
100 E 63rd St (at Park Ave)   212/644-1900
Lunch: Mon-Fri; Dinner: Daily; Brunch: Sat (Sept-May), Sun
Moderately expensive

A beautiful room that once housed Le Périgord Park and later Hubert's is now a showpiece for Alan Stillman (who has his tasty fingers in the Post House, Cité, Manhattan Ocean Club, and Smith & Wollensky). He obviously is a man of eclectic interests. Here, chef David Burke does unusual things that please most diners while puzzling some with less sophisticated tastes. The basically American menu is served by very professional waiters who appear to have been influenced sartorially by Larry King. The signature dish is a swordfish chop served with a tart lemon sauce. The people watching is great, and the conversation at the next table can be fascinating. (It's not eavesdropping when you can't help it.) Desserts are sensational!

PARK BISTRO
414 Park Ave S (bet 28th and 29th St)   212/689-1360
Lunch: Mon-Fri; Dinner: Mon-Sun
Moderate

These days it is special fun to go to a place with smiling faces, and the Park Bistro is that! This small, homey dining room specializes in cuisine from the Provence region of France. It's a jewel. From the start, when warm and tasty bread is placed before you, to the finishing touch of rich and luscious homemade desserts (like crème brûlée, tortes, and a sinful chocolate gateau), you are surrounded by attentive service and magnificent food. Don't miss the hanger steak or braised lamb shank. A professional team runs this place, and it shows.

PARK SIDE
107-01 Corona Ave (51st Ave at 108th St, Corona, Queens)
718/271-9274
Lunch, Dinner: Daily
Moderate

Do you want to show the person who claims to know everything about New York something he or she doesn't know? Do you want to eat on your way to or from La Guardia or Kennedy airport? Do you want a special meal in an unusual setting? Well, all of the above are excellent reasons to visit Park Side, in Queens. I make an exception in including a restaurant not in Manhattan because it *is* exceptional. Joseph Oliva runs a first-class, spotlessly clean restaurant that serves wonderful Italian food at prices that make most New York restaurateurs look like highway robbers. Start with garlic bread and then choose from two dozen kinds of pasta and an opulent array of fish, steak, veal, and poultry dishes. The meat is all prime cut and fresh—nothing frozen here. You'll also find polite, knowledgeable waiters in an informal atmosphere. Get a table in the garden room or the Marilyn Monroe room upstairs. Eat until your heart's content, and then be amazed at the tab.

Go to Hell! Hell's Kitchen, that is! Some interesting eateries:

Cafe Brasil (Brazilian), 746 Ninth Ave
Chantale's Cajun Kitchen (Cajun), 510 Ninth Ave
Chez Gnagna Koty's African Restaurant (African), 530 Ninth Ave
Kashmir (Pakistani), 478 Ninth Ave
Los Dos Rancheros Mexicanos (Mexican), 507 Ninth Ave
Mitchel London Foods (European), 542 Ninth Ave
Thai Jasmine (Thai), 860 Ninth Ave

PATROON
160 E 46th St   212/883-7373
Lunch: Mon-Fri, Dinner; Mon-Sat
Expensive

At Patroon, you might imagine you were in the original 21, where the food was first-class, the diners first-class plus, and the conversations world-class. So it is at Patroon today and sadly not at 21 anymore. Chef Geoffrey Zakarian rescued this spot from rather inauspicious beginnings; now it is a power scene worthy of capable restaurateur Ken Aretsky. Patroon's offerings include foie gras, lobster bisque, clams and oysters, risottos, stuffed ravioli, and skate. The side dishes (especially onion rings and creamed spinach) are excellent. Caramelized banana tart is the winner for dessert. This place is big time: big plates, big deals, big prices!

PATSY'S
236 W 56th St (bet Broadway and Eighth Ave)   212/247-3491
Lunch, Dinner: Daily
Moderate

For over half a century, the Scognamillo family has operated this popular eatery, specializing in Neapolitan cuisine. At the moment the son and a grandson are taking care of the front of the house, while another grandson is following the family tradition in the kitchen. "Patsy" was an immigrant gentleman chef whose nickname was soon attached to a New York tradition that has now grown into a two-level restaurant. Each floor has its own cozy atmosphere and convenient kitchen. The family makes sure that every guest is treated as if they are in a private home; courtesy and concern are the name of the game. A full Italian menu is available, with numerous specials that include a different soup and seafood entree each day. If you can't find what you like among the two dozen pasta choices, you are in deep trouble!

PAYARD PATISSERIE
1032 Lexington Ave (bet 73rd and 74th St)   212/717-5252
Lunch, Tea, Dinner: Mon-Sat (bakery opens at 7 a.m.)
Moderate

Francois Payard has created a winner! Everything about this place is appetizing: the look of the bakery cases as you enter, the attractively presented appetizers and entrees, the appealing and informed service by the well-trained staff. Payard is a combination French bistro and pastry shop, and it works to perfection. When you put an expert pastry chef like Francois together with executive chef Philippe Bertineau, you know you're going to find the very best. If you just want to take some goodies home, you can choose from croissants, muffins, tea cakes, seasonal tarts, individual pastries, *gateaux,* petit fours, biscuits, handmade candies, and superb chocolates. Classic and seasonal ice creams and sherbets are offered. Prepared soups, salads, sandwiches, and other goodies are also available for takeout. But don't miss the opportunity to dine here, as Payard offers terrific appetizers, superb salads, homemade foie gras, seafood dishes, traditional bouillabaisse, caramelized sweetbreads, steaks, and more.

PEACOCK ALLEY
Waldorf-Astoria Hotel
301 Park Ave (at 50th St)   212/872-4895
Breakfast: Mon-Fri; Dinner: Tues-Sat;
Brunch: Sun
Expensive

In keeping with the trend of superior dining at hotels, the Waldorf has spruced up this very attractive room just off the lobby. Best of all, you have breathing room around your table. A sparkling new menu has added a rich dimension to this room, named after the space between the former Waldorf and Astoria hotels, where Manhattan society paraded in all their finery. Although the presentations are certainly of the first order, the place has a precocious air about it, both in the service and in the food. It does not in any way compare with the superlative Les Célébrités at the Essex House or Lespinasse at the St. Regis Hotel. Their desserts are sensational, however! The real treat is on Sunday, where a spectacular buffet brunch is a sight to behold and to taste. It is centered around the famous clock in the middle of the magnificent lobby.

It's back again! The **Russian Tea Room** (150 W 57th St, 212/974-2111) offers four floors, including the original cafe and a grand ballroom. The modern Russian menu is varied, with an international influence. Don't miss the dancing bears!

PETER LUGER STEAK HOUSE
178 Broadway (at Driggs Ave), Brooklyn   718/387-7400
Lunch, Dinner: Daily
Expensive

Despite all the new steakhouses that have opened in Manhattan in recent years, readers of the popular Zagat's guide to New York restaurants have rated this Brooklyn institution tops in the city for ten years running. The place is a bit of a dump and nobody goes here for the ambience or the service. But if it's steak you want, you simply can't do better. And the menu makes it simple: your choices are steak for one, steak for two, steak for three, and steak for four. The creamed spinach and steak sauce are out of this world, although the French fries are uninspired and the wine selection is slim. Tell your waiter to go easy on the whipped cream if you order dessert. For those of you who find the thought of leaving Manhattan a bit intimidating, it's really only a stone's throw away from this borough (take the very first right off the Williamsburg Bridge), and the staff is quite accustomed to ordering cabs. Reservations are suggested before making the trip!

PICHOLINE
35 W 64th St   212/724-8585
Lunch: Tues-Sat; Dinner: Daily
Moderate

Make note: lunch is a good deal here. Terrance Brennan is a workhorse, and it shows in his attractive restaurant. The rustic atmosphere is a perfect backdrop for the Mediterranean-inspired plates. The many pluses here besides outstanding service include delicious homemade breads, perfectly done fish dishes, superbly prepared game, and one of the best cassoulets in the city. If you're having a party at Lincoln Center, the small private party room is a fabulous setting for a memorable evening. There are daily classic cuisine specials, like *civet* of duck. I always look forward to the magnificent cheeses for dessert.

PIETRO'S
232 E 43rd St (bet Second and Third Ave)   212/682-9760
Lunch: Mon-Fri; Dinner: Mon-Sat
Expensive

Pietro's is a steakhouse with Northern Italian cuisine; everything is cooked to order. The menu features great salads (they claim to make New York's best Caesar salad), steaks, chops, seafood, chicken, and an enormous selection of veal. Tell your companion not to bother getting dressed up. Bring an appetite, however, because portions are huge. Although steaks are the best known of Pietro's dishes, you will also find ten chicken dishes and ten veal selections (marsala, cacciatore, scaloppine, piccata, *francaise,* etc.). For meat-and-potatoes lovers, there are nine different potato dishes. Prices border on expensive and the service is boisterous, but you'll certainly get your money's worth. By the way, Pietro's is very child-friendly.

PLAZA HOTEL PALM COURT
Plaza Hotel
768 Fifth Ave (at 59th St)   212/759-3000
Breakfast, Lunch: Mon-Sat; Tea, Supper: Daily; Brunch: Sun
Moderate

Feeling nostalgic? Some rooms, like some people, just get better with age, and happily this is one of them. If just one place in the city could be singled out as the embodiment of all that folks dream of as the New York of yesteryear—romantic and carefree, delicious and proper—it would have to be the Palm Court at the Plaza Hotel. The great and near-great have laughed and loved here with the likes of Eloise and Auntie and Uncle, creating thousands of memories of special times. You can enjoy breakfast, luncheon salads, wonderful teas with tea sandwiches, and caloric goodies, all to the accompaniment of classic piano and violin music. There are also super snacks, seafood salads, assorted smoked fish, and some unusual sandwiches and pastries. The fabulous Sunday buffet—the largest and most glamorous in the city—is a popular New York tradition. Many three-generation families show the young ones where they used to go in the "good old days." A real treat, day or night, and a must for visitors.

PÒ
31 Cornelia St (bet Bleecker and 4th St)   212/645-2189
Lunch: Wed-Sun; Dinner: Tues-Sun
Moderate

Mario Batali and Steve Crane have found the formula for a successful eating establishment. The space is crowded, but tables are not on top of each other. The service is family-friendly, informed, and quick. The food is hearty, imaginative and unusually tasty. The portions are king-size. The prices are right. No wonder the place is always busy. As I have noted before, if the bread is good, chances are what follows will be also. Pò has hearty, crunchy, fresh Italian bread. The pastas are huge: tagliatelle, tortellini, linguine, and always a special or two. Great values on tasting menus: five-course pastas for $25 and a six-course meal for $35. Pastas and some heavier entrees (like grilled salmon) are available for lunch, along with inventive sandwiches like marinated portabello with roasted peppers. An unusual and satisfying dessert called *affogato* consists of coffee gelato in chilled cappuccino with chocolate sauce.

POST HOUSE
28 E 63rd St   212/935-2888
Lunch: Mon-Fri; Dinner: Daily
Moderately expensive

This great restaurant, not on the list for calorie counters, is an "in" social and political hangout on East 63rd Street that serves excellent food in comfortable surroundings. The guest list usually includes many well-known names and easily recognizable faces. They are attracted, of course, by the good food and warm ambience. Hors d'oeuvres like crabmeat cocktail, lobster cocktail, and stone crabs are available in season, but the major draws are steak and lobster. Prices for the latter two entrees are definitely not in the moderate category; ditto for lamb chops. However, the quality is excellent, and the cottage fries, fried zucchini, hash browns, and onion rings are superb. Save room for the chocolate box (white and dark chocolate mousse with raspberry sauce). If you can walk out under your own steam after all this, you're doing well!

PRIMAVERA
1578 First Ave (at 82nd St)   212/861-8608
Lunch: Mon-Fri; Dinner: Daily
Expensive

This is one of my very favorite places! So many times an establishment reflects a proprietor's personality and talent; nowhere is this more apparent than at Primavera. Nicola Civetta, the owner, is the epitome of class. He knows how to make you feel at home and how to present a superb Italian meal. Don't go if you're in a hurry, though. This place is for relaxed dining. I could wax eloquently with descriptions of the dishes, but you can't go wrong no matter what you order. Let Nicola choose for you, as there are specials every day. To top it all off, they have one of the most beautiful desserts anywhere: a gorgeous platter of seasonal fruit that looks too good to eat. Primavera is always busy, so reservations are a must. Pre-theater and after-theater dinners are offered.

PROVENCE
38 MacDougal St (at Prince and Houston St)   212/475-7500
Lunch, Dinner: Daily
Moderate

A bit of France in Manhattan! You won't quickly forget a visit to Provence, a bustling region of France that has been transported in a charming manner to Greenwich Village. Tasty and wholesome food is professionally served at sensible prices. Garlic is another reason you won't forget this bistro. If you like its taste, you'll love Provence! The French country menu is served in several spaces: one noisy room by the bar overlooking the Village streets; another more romantic area in the back; and a comfortable outside patio. You'll find dishes typical of the region (fish and steamed vegetables) on the menu. If you like some of the signature dishes (*pot-au-feu*, cassoulet, bouillabaisse, couscous), I'd suggest calling to find out what item is being featured that evening. Wonderful French fries come with some dishes. Top it all off with a Provence tart.

QUILTY'S
177 Prince St (bet Sullivan and Thompson St)   212/254-1260
Lunch: Tues-Sat; Brunch: Sat, Sun; Dinner: Daily
Moderate

Quilty's just gets better and better. And the service here can't be beat. In stark white surroundings and a relatively tiny space, all attention is on what is called new contemporary American cooking, with menu changes every season. This means appetizers like gulf shrimp steamed in parchment and country salad with fennel and blood oranges. My favorite is char-grilled baby artichokes on a skewer. Even spinach, one of my least favorite dishes, is done so well that I would have to call it a winner! The presentation of the main courses—grilled pork tenderloin, braised rabbit, rack of Colorado lamb—is first-rate. Chef Katy Sparks has a taste for superb sauces, and it shows. From the warm bread basket to the tasty apple tart (for two) or the chocolate banana empanada with a caramel-rum sauce, you won't be disappointed. Crowds make reservations a must.

RAFAELLA
381 Bleecker St   212/229-9885
Dinner: Daily
Moderate

One gets a bit nervous looking at a huge menu in a small establishment. How can they do well by all of those dishes? Well, have no worry here, though the menu is indeed all-encompassing. There are a dozen appetizers, from baked oysters to stuffed mushrooms, four different soups, and over two dozen pasta dishes. Their risotto is especially delicious. There are also a dozen entrees, many from the grill. Choosing from a half-dozen tasty dessert dishes will complete your opportunity for a great meal at a reasonable price. This Village find is very popular with locals, so reservations are highly recommended. The youngish staff seem pleased to be of service and are particularly helpful in guiding you through the maze of goodies. Takeout is available.

RAIN
100 W 82nd St (at Columbus Ave)   212/501-0776
1059 Third Ave (bet 62nd and 63rd St)   212/223-3669
Lunch, Dinner: Daily
Moderate

There's no need to cross the Pacific Ocean; a culinary visit to Rain will do the trick—if it is only food you are concerned with, that is! You will be treated to Vietnamese, Malaysian and Thai fare . . . some of it, naturally, quite spicy. Spring (and summer) rolls are a personal favorite, and the ones here are superb. Of course, there is more to start with: soups, broths, noodles, and Thai crab cakes. Lots of seafood on the entree menu: popular crispy snapper, stir-fried spicy jumbo shrimp, stir-fried prawns, cracked lobster, shrimp, and green curry chicken. Forget about desserts, however—they just don't cut it with most American palates.

RAO'S
455 E 114th St   212/722-6709
Dinner: Mon-Fri
No credit cards
Inexpensive

Your taste buds are stimulated as you walk in; there is no kitchen door here! After a devastating fire, all ten tables at Rao's are back in business. Don't be put off by rumors, such as two-month waits for reservations. If you want to go to Rao's—an intimate old-time (1896) Italian restaurant—you should plan a bit in advance, however. The place is crowded all the time for two good reasons: the food is great, and prices are ridiculously low. Don't walk or take a car; hail a taxi and get out in front of the restaurant, which is in Spanish Harlem. When you're ready to leave, have Frankie call a local taxi service to pick you up. Frankie is a gregarious and charming host who makes you feel right at home; he'll even sit at your table while you order. Be prepared for leisurely dining. While you're waiting, enjoy the excellent bread and warm atmosphere. I've enjoyed such especially tasty offerings as the pasta and *piselli*. Veal marsala and piccata are excellent choices, as are any number of shrimp dishes. Believe it or not, the Southern fried chicken (Rao's style) is absolutely superb; it would be my number-one choice. (Hint: Try appearing unannounced at the door or call the same day, as tables are often available on the spur of the moment.)

RAOUL'S
180 Prince St (bet Sullivan and Thompson St)   212/966-3518
Dinner: Daily
Moderate

There are dozens of good places to eat in Soho, and Raoul's is one of the best. The long, narrow restaurant used to be an old saloon. There are paper tablecloths and funky walls covered with a mishmash of posters, pictures, and calendars of every description. The bistro atmosphere is neighborly, friendly, and intimate, the prices moderate, and the service attentive. The trendy clientele runs the gamut from jeans to mink. The house specialties are steak au poivre and paté *maison*. Raoul's is a natural for those whose days begin when the rest of us are ready to hit the sack.

RAYMOND'S CAFE
88 Seventh Ave (bet 15th and 16th St)   212/929-1778
Lunch, Dinner: Daily; Brunch: Sat, Sun
Moderate

If some of the old haunts in the Chelsea area have lost their appeal, Raymond's still has a lot going for it. Chef Raymond is obviously a perfectionist.

The place is spotlessly clean with an up-to-date look, and the food is well presented and very tasty. Choices run the gamut from pastas and sandwiches at noon to delicious hot and cold appetizers and fresh seafood items at dinner. The weekend brunch features omelets, various linguini dishes, and warm chicken salad. A renovated private dining room is available, and there is free delivery within eight blocks. The early-bird dinner is a three-course bargain!

(THE FAMOUS) RAY'S PIZZA OF GREENWICH VILLAGE
465 Ave of the Americas (at 11th St)   212/243-2253
Sun-Thurs: 11 a.m.-2 a.m.; Fri, Sat: 11 a.m.-3 a.m.
No credit cards
Inexpensive

You must be named "Ray" to be in the pizza biz in Manhattan—or so it seems. None of the pizzerias in the Big Apple are any better than this one, supposedly featuring the *real* Ray. The pizza is gourmet at its best, and you can create your own from the many toppings offered. You can have a slice, a whole pizza, or a Sicilian square, all fresh. Kids love the baby pizzas. You won't leave hungry, as pizzas are a generous 18 inches. Take-and-bake personal pizzas—ten-inch pies that are all natural and handmade, with 100% real cheese—bake in your oven in 12 minutes and are sold only at this location! Free delivery is available.

REDEYE GRILL
890 Seventh Ave (at 56th St)   212/541-9000
Lunch: Mon-Fri; Dinner: Daily; Brunch: Sat, Sun
Moderately expensive

From the day it opened, this "home of the dancing shrimp bar" has been a busy place! The name attracted my attention, because I am a frequent coast-to-coast redeye flyer. When I first entered the place, I could see I had a lot of company. The room is huge, with an attractive shrimp and seafood bar (where you can eat if you desire) near the entrance. Owner Sheldon Fireman knows how to appeal to the eye, taking a cue from his very successful nearby Trattoria dell'Arte antipasto bar. Specialties include shrimp done in all shapes and sizes, smoked salmon, a huge seafood appetizer platter (at a huge price), a smoked maki and sashimi bar, grilled fish and pastas. You can even find weiner schnitzel, burgers, smoked fish, and egg dishes. The personnel are hip and helpful, but the scene is the major attraction here.

REMI
145 W 53rd St (bet Ave of Americas and Seventh Ave)   212/581-4242
Lunch: Mon-Fri; Dinner: Daily
Moderate

Remi operates in a spectacular space in midtown, handy to hotels and theaters. In an unsually long room dominated by a dramatic 120-foot Venetian wall painting by Paulin Paris, the food soars as high as the setting. In warm weather, the doors open up and diners can enjoy sitting at tables in the adjoining atrium. Waiters, chairs, and wall fabrics all match in attractive stripes. Antipasto, like shrimp and crab cakes or roasted quail wrapped in bacon, will get you off to a delicious start. Main dishes are not of the usual variety; the spaghetti, linguine, and ravioli (stuffed with ginger and tuna) can match any house in Venice. Of course, there are fish and meat dishes for more mainstream appetites. The caramelized banana tart, served with toasted almond ice cream and caramel sauce, is enough to make anyone feel guilty. Being a gelati lover myself, I found the homemade cappuccino flavor sensational. Paddle on down (Remi means "oar") for a first-class experience!

RENÉ PUJOL
321 W 51st St   212/246-3023
Lunch, Dinner: Mon-Sat
Moderate

First things first: order a chocolate soufflé right away for dessert! René Pujol is a very attractive French restaurant that makes an ideal spot for a pre-theater dinner. It's always busy, and it's obvious that a large number of customers are regular patrons, which always speaks well of a restaurant. One reason for René Pujol's success is that it's a family enterprise. The owners (daughter and son-in-law of the retired René Pujol) are on the job, and the waiters are superb. Housed in an old brownstone, the restaurant has two warmly decorated, cozy, and comfortable dining rooms, complete with a working fireplace in winter. There are attractive private party rooms upstairs, too. The menu is vintage French, with filet mignon, grilled Atlantic salmon, couscous, and tasty tarts being the specialties of the house. They boast an award-winning wine list, too!

RESTAURANT RAPHAEL
33 W 54th St   212/582-8993
Lunch: Mon-Fri; Dinner: Mon-Sat
Expensive

You don't have to worry about quality when you take guests here. Restaurant Raphael is expensive but worth it! This elegant, intimate French restaurant, which does a few things very well, is for the serious diner. Tasty smoked salmon, gnocchi, or onion tart get you off to a great start. Main courses of lamb, veal, duck, and house-smoked red snapper are served imaginatively, with superb seasonings and sauces. There is no on-the-job training for the servers; they all know what is expected in a first-class operation. Take your time, savor the contemporary French cooking, and finish with a warm, crusty chocolate cake that is as rich and delicious as any you have tasted.

RISTORANTE GRIFONE
244 E 46th St (bet Second and Third Ave)   212/490-7275
Lunch: Mon-Fri; Dinner: Mon-Sat
Moderate to moderately expensive

It's sad but true: New Yorkers get so hyped up about trendy new places that they tend to forget about some of the old-timers that have quietly been around for awhile. Grifone is one of those. If you are looking for an attractive, comfortable, and cozy place to dine—one with impeccable service and great food—then try Grifone. Seemingly only neighborhood regulars have heard of it. The menu is Northern Italian; there are so many daily specials that you probably won't even look at the printed sheet. Quality never goes out of style.

RIVER CAFE
1 Water St (Brooklyn Bridge), Brooklyn   718/522-5200
Lunch, Dinner: Daily
Moderately expensive

I look forward to every visit here. The River Cafe isn't in Manhattan, but it *overlooks* Manhattan. And that's the main reason to come here. The view from the window tables is fantastic, awesome, romantic—you name it. There's no other skyline like it in the world. And so, just across the East River in the shadow of the Brooklyn Bridge, the River Cafe remains an extremely popular place. Call at least a week in advance to make reservations, and be sure to ask for a window table. This is a true Yankee, flag-waving restaurant, proud of its American cuisine. There's no point in describing the dishes in detail, since you'll be looking out the window more than down at your plate. However, the seafood, lamb, and game entrees are particularly good, and desserts are rich and fresh. The Brooklyn Bridge, done in dark chocolate, is a dessert you will never forget . . . take along your camera.

ROLF'S
281 Third Ave (at 22nd St)   212/477-4750
Lunch, Dinner: Daily
Moderate

In a city without really good German restaurants, Rolf's is a German restaurant worth remembering. A colorful spot, its several dozen tables and wooden benches fit in perfectly with the eclectic decor. Faux Tiffany lampshades, old pictures, tiny lights, strings of beads, and what-have-you add up to a charming and cozy spot for tasty German dishes. The schnitzels, goulash, sauerbraten, boiled beef, veal shanks, and bratwurst are served in ample portions with delicious potato pancakes and sauerkraut. For pancake lovers there are German, apple, and potato varieties, with applesauce on the side. For dessert, save room for the homemade apple strudel or the Black Forest cake.

ROSA MEXICANO
1063 First Ave (at 58th St)   212/753-7407
Dinner: Daily (open late)
Moderate to moderately expensive

No touristy Mexican dive, this is the real thing. If you are lusting for classic Mexican cuisine, an evening here will be something special. Start with the guacamole *en molcajete;* prepared fresh at the table, it is the best around. There are also great appetizers, like small tortillas filled with sauteed shredded pork, small shrimp marinated in a mustard and chili vinaigrette, and raviolis filled with sauteed chicken and served with tomato and onion. Main-course entrees include tasty (and huge) crepes filled with shrimp and a multi-layered tortilla pie with all manner of goodies. Grilled specialties like beef short ribs and skewered marinated shrimp are tempting possibilities. Even the desserts are first-class. Choose from a traditional flan, cornmeal custard smothered with chocolate sauce, or layered chocolate mousse cake with a hint of chile. The atmosphere is friendly, the energy level high, and the dining top-drawer.

ROSEMARIE'S
145 Duane St (bet West Broadway and Church St)
212/285-2610
Lunch: Mon-Fri; Dinner: Mon-Sat
Moderate

This is one of those hidden treasures that regulars don't talk about. Rosemarie's is indeed hidden in the junky atmosphere of a Tribeca street. Leaving the real world behind, you enter a smallish establishment that seems more like a private dining room than a restaurant. Both the lunch and dinner menus, which change seasonally, provide an excellent choice of Italian dishes, all done with the tender care of a loving kitchen. The risotto with wild mushrooms is first-class; so are the seared salmon and grilled red snapper. A *prix fixe* menu is offered at noon. Indulge yourself with homemade gelati for dessert.

ROY'S NEW YORK
Marriott Financial Center Hotel
130 Washington St   212/266-6262
Breakfast, Lunch, Dinner: Daily
Moderate to moderately expensive

Whenever I am in Hawaii, I try to dine at one of Roy Yamaguchi's restaurants, not just because the food is uniformly appealing, but also because of the trained staff. I have never seen operations run as efficiently as Roy's, and this large one in Manhattan's Financial District makes 14 that he oversees, spread all over the globe. The menu can best be described as blending European ideas (where Roy was trained) with popular ingredients from Asia and the Pacific. There's wonderful coconut shrimp on a stick with pineapple chile sauce. Grilled Szechuan baby back pork ribs. Chinese-style barbecued chicken pizza. Hong Kong steamed fish with wok veggies. Hawaiian seared mahi-mahi. Mongolian rack of lamb. You get the idea! Top it all off with a hot chocolate soufflé or a sorbet sampler. Seats at the counter overlooking the kitchen provide an extra dimension to the meal.

RUSSO'S STEAK & PASTA
Sheraton Manhattan Hotel
790 Seventh Ave at 51st St   212/621-8537
Lunch: Mon-Fri; Dinner: Daily
Moderate

Conveniently located and attractively priced, this signature restaurant of the Sheraton Manhattan serves delicious steaks and pastas in an unusually friendly atmosphere. The American-Italian menu features antipasto plates, Italian specialties, a wonderful sandwich board (try the meatball parmigiana hero), seafood and chops, and roasted veggies.

SARABETH'S KITCHEN
423 Amsterdam Ave (at 80th St)   212/496-6280
Breakfast, Lunch, Dinner: Daily

1295 Madison Ave (at 92nd St)   212/410-7335
Breakfast, Lunch, Dinner: Daily
Moderate

SARABETH'S AT THE WHITNEY
Whitney Museum of American Art
945 Madison Ave (bet 74th and 75th St)   212/570-3670
Lunch: Tues-Fri; Brunch: Sat, Sun
Moderate

One is reminded of the better English tearooms when visiting one of Sarabeth's locations. Swinging, it is not. Reliable, it is. The big draw is the homemade quality of all the dishes, including the baked items and excellent desserts. They also make gourmet preserves and sell them nationally. Menu choices include excellent omelets for breakfast, a fine assortment of light items for lunch, and fish, game, or meat dishes for dinner. The chocolate truffle cake, chocolate soufflé, and homemade sorbets and ice cream are splendid desserts. Service is rapid and courteous. This would be an ideal place to take your mother-in-law.

SAVORE
200 Spring St   212/431-1212
Lunch, Dinner: Daily; Brunch: Sat, Sun
Moderate

Soho has no shortage of restaurants, many of them with an attitude that goes along with the area. Savore has none of this. You come here for good food served in a casual and friendly atmosphere. It is a particularly attractive destination in nice weather, when tables are placed outside for people-watching along with dining. The menu offers a large selection of pastas, from buckwheat tagliatelle with pheasant ragout to hand-cut spaghetti with basil and roasted tomato. On to fresh fish, filet mignon, or even wild boar! In true European fashion, they offer salads after the main course. I am partial to their crème brûlée, which features a wonderful coffee flavor.

SCREENING ROOM
54 Varick St (below Canal St)   212/334-2100
Lunch: Tues-Fri; Dinner: Daily; Brunch: Sun
Moderate

Movie lovers and gourmets can satisfy both of their passions at this innovative Tribeca watering hole that serves both great food and entertainment. The atmosphere is informal and congenial, with an emphasis on traditional American dishes that look and taste terrific. As a starter, I loved the pan-fried artichokes. But there's also smoked trout, pan-roasted quail, a number of healthy salads, and very popular macaroni done with spinach, leeks, tomatoes, and Parmesan. On to salmon, grilled duck, or venison (get some crushed baked potatoes, too). The lounge menu includes many of the above dishes, plus burgers, and the dessert selections are topped by a great lemon-caramel ice box cake and a scrumptious "fallen chocolate cake" with white chocolate sauce and milk chocolate sherbet. (You might go to sleep in the flicks.) A late-night menu is available.

SECOND AVENUE KOSHER DELICATESSEN AND RESTAURANT
156 Second Ave (at 10th St)   212/677-0606
Sun-Thurs 7 a.m.-midnight (Fri, Sat till 3 a.m.)
Inexpensive

You've heard all about the great New York delicatessens; now try one of the really authentic ones, located in the historic East Village. From the traditional k's—knishes, kasha varnishkes (buckwheat groats with pasta), and kugel— to boiled beef or chicken in the pot (with noodles, carrots, and matzo balls), no one does it quite like the Lebewohl family. Portions are enormous. Homemade soups, three-decker sandwiches (tongue and hot corned beef are sensational), deli platters, complete dinners—you name it, they've got it. The smell is overwhelmingly appetizing, the atmosphere is "caring Jewish mother," and they don't mind if you take out your meal instead of dining in the colorful back room. Don't leave without trying the chopped liver or warm apple strudel.

SERENDIPITY 3
225 E 60th St   212/838-3531
Sun-Thurs: 11:30 a.m.-12:30 a.m.;
Fri: 11:30 a.m.-1 a.m.; Sat: 11:30 a.m.-2 a.m.
Moderate

The young and young-at-heart rate Serenpidity 3 *numero uno* on their list of "in" places, as it has been for over 45 years. In an atmosphere of nostalgia set in a quaint, two-floor brownstone, this full-service restaurant offers a complete selection of delicious entrees, sandwiches, salads, and pastas. The real treats are the fabulous desserts, including favorites like hot fudge sundaes and frozen hot chocolate. Now frozen hot chocolate mix is available to take home! An added pleasure is the opportunity to browse a shop loaded with trendy gifts, books, clothing, and accessories. If you are planning a special gathering for the teen members of your clan, make this the destination!

SETTE MEZZO
969 Lexington Ave (at 70th St)   212/472-0400
Lunch, Dinner: Daily
Cash only
Moderate

It's small, professional, very busy, and a great spot for people-watching on Sunday evenings! There are no affectations at Sette Mezzo in decor, service, or food preparation. This is strictly a business operation, with the emphasis where it should be: on serving good food at reasonable prices. Don't worry about wearing your best gown or a suit and tie; many diners are informally dressed, enjoying a variety of Italian dishes done to perfection. At noon the menu is tilted toward lighter pastas and salads. In the evening, all of the grilled items are excellent. Fresh seafood is a specialty. Ask about the special pasta dishes; some of the combinations are marvelous. For more traditional Italian plates, try the breaded rack of veal, stuffed baked chicken, grilled boneless quail, or fried calamari and shrimp. All desserts are made in-house. They include several caloric cakes, tasty lemon tarts, sherbet and ice cream, and (take it from an expert) one of the best *tartufos* you've ever sinned over.

Of course, the first place to look for suggestions about where to eat is in the volume you now have in your hands. The **Zagat Survey** is another source; the reviews contained in that volume are pithy comments from hundreds of diners. Another source is **Foodphone** (212/777-FOOD). You will be able to hear information about hundreds of Manhattan restaurants by type of cuisine, location, and price range.

SHUN LEE CAFE/SHUN LEE WEST
43 W 65th St   212/769-3888
Lunch: Sat, Sun; Dinner: Daily
Moderate

Dim sum and street-food combinations are served in an informal setting adjoining Shun Lee West, an excellent old West Side Chinese restaurant. A large selection of special items is offered by a waiter who comes to your table with a rolling cart and describes the various goodies. The offerings vary from time to time, but don't miss the stuffed crab claws, if they are available. Go on to the street-food items: delicious roast pork, barbecued spare ribs, a large selection of soups and noodle and rice dishes, and a menu full of both mild and spicy entrees. Sauteed prawns with ginger and boneless duckling with walnut sauce are great choices. A vegetarian dish of shredded Chinese vegetables is cooked with rice noodles and served with a pancake (like moo shu pork, but without the meat). It's a fun place where you can try some unusual and delicious Chinese dishes. For heartier appetites, the adjoining Shun Lee West restaurant is equally good. Some of the best Chinese food in Manhattan is served here. If you come with a crowd, family-style dining is available. Prices are a bit higher in the restaurant than in the cafe.

SHUN LEE PALACE
155 E 55th St (bet Lexington and Third Ave)   212/371-8844
Lunch, Dinner: Daily
Moderate to moderately expensive

There are all manner of Chinese restaurants in Manhattan: The colorful Chinatown variety. The mom-and-pop corner operations. The over-Americanized establishments. The grand Chinese dining rooms. Shun Lee Palace belongs in the latter category, possessing a very classy and refined look. Here you are offered a delicious journey into the best of this historic cuisine. You can dine rather reasonably at lunch; a four-course *prix fixe* experience is available. Ordering from the menu (or from your captain) can be a bit pricier, but the platters are worth it. Specialties include beggar's chicken (24 hours advance notice required), South Sea turtle in rock candy (48 hours required), crispy prawns with passion fruit, and Kung Po frog legs with hot pepper (24 hours required). There's much more, including casserole specials and spa cuisine. Yes, this is just about the nearest thing Manhattan has to a real Chinese palace.

SISTINA
1555 Second Ave (at 80th St)   212/861-7660
Lunch, Dinner: Daily
Moderate

Because the atmosphere is pretty plain Jane, one comes to Sistina for the food, and it can't be beat. Four brothers run this outstanding Italian restaurant; one is in the kitchen, the others are out front. The specialty of the house is seafood; the Mediterranean red snapper and salmon are excellent dishes. There are also the usual choices of pasta, veal, and chicken, as well as daily specials. The philosophy of this family operation is that the joy is in the eating, not the surroundings, and for that they get top marks.

SOHO KITCHEN & BAR
103 Greene St   212/925-1866
Lunch, Dinner: Daily
Inexpensive to moderate

With over 100 wines by the glass and 21 cold draft beers, this is one of the busiest bar and restaurant scenes in the lower canyons of Manhattan. They offer wine "flights," which are servings of from four to eight glasses of wine from a particular group (French, Spanish, chardonnays, and the like). Beer tastings are also offered. The Soho Kitchen shines in food, too. Besides soups, salads, and pastas, there are great hamburgers, steaks, and omelets. A delicious fruit and cheese plate is a welcome change from heavy eating. The real treat here is the pizza, made with homemade dough. You can choose from wild mushroom, pesto, vegetarian, or a fantastic Italian combination of sausage, roasted peppers, grilled eggplant, mozzarella, and provolone. Prices are very reasonable, making Soho Kitchen a good place for a casual encounter.

SONIA ROSE RESTAURANT
150 E 34th St (bet Lexington and Third Ave)   212/545-1777
Lunch, Dinner: Daily
Moderate

Even though these folks have moved, this is still one of my favorite places. Named after a coral peach rose, Sonia Rose has only about a dozen tables, each with a single rose and a flickering candle. The menu is *prix fixe* for both lunch and dinner, with supplemental charges for several special items. Diane is in the front, always charming and helpful; Gary Thompson is in the kitchen, dishing up some of the most attractive and delectable continental-style dishes you could imagine. The charm is in the exceptional attention to detail in both service and food. There is plenty of well-trained help. And the food plates are a sight for the eyes, as if an artist had arranged each bite. From the time you start with a refreshing hot towel to the ending selection of a half-dozen dessert samples, this is perfection. An outdoor garden is available during nice weather.

SPARKS STEAKHOUSE
210 E 46th St   212/687-4855
Lunch: Mon-Fri; Dinner: Mon-Sat
Moderately expensive

You come here to eat, period. This is a well-seasoned and popular beef restaurant with little ambience. For years, businessmen have made an evening at Sparks a must, and the house has not let time erode its reputation. In the meat category, you can choose from veal and lamb chops, beef scaloppine, and medallions of beef, as well as a half-dozen steak items, like steak *fromage* (with Roquefort cheese), prime sirloin, sliced steak with sauteed onions and peppers, and top-of-the-line filet mignon. Seafood dishes are another specialty; the rainbow trout, filet of tuna, and halibut steak are as good as you'll find in most seafood houses. The lobsters are enormous, delicious, and expensive. Skip the appetizers and dessert, and concentrate on the main dish.

SPRING STREET NATURAL RESTAURANT
62 Spring St (corner Lafayette St)   212/966-0290
Daily; 11:30 a.m.-midnight; Fri-Sat until 1 a.m.
Inexpensive

Even before eating "naturally" was a big thing, the Spring Street Natural Restaurant was a leader in the field. That tradition continues today after 25 years of experience. In attractive surroundings, their kitchen provides meals prepared with fresh, unprocessed foods, and most everything is cooked to order. Neighborhood residents are regular customers here, so you know the food is top-quality. Specials are offered every day, with a wide variety of organically grown salads, pastas, vegetarian meals, free-range poultry, and a large selection of fresh farm-fed and line-caught fish and seafood. Try wonderful roasted salmon with creamy risotto and baby asparagus stalks. The best is saved for last: Spring Street believes in great desserts, like chocolate walnut pie, honey raspberry blueberry pie, and honey pear pie. The latter two are made without sugar and dairy products.

T SALON & EMPORIUM
11 E 20th St   212/358-0506
Daily: 10:30-8
Moderate

With renewed interest in tea, the unusual and enchanting T Salon will captivate those who are tea addicts, or who just want to experiment on an occasional basis. Here you will find green teas (light-colored Oriental tea with a delicate taste), oolong teas (distinctively peachy flavor), and black teas (heavy, deep flavor and rich amber color). A specialty here is blending teas. Proper afternoon tea, with scones, sandwiches, and pastries, is served daily. One can choose from 499 different teas. Upstairs is one of Manhattan's largest tea selections, and all kinds of tea accessories, attractively displayed and reasonably priced. This is one of the more unusual operations in Manhattan, again proving that no other city in the world offers specialties like the Big Apple!

TABLA
11 Madison Ave (at 25th St)   212/889-0667
Lunch: Mon-Fri: Dinner: Mon-Sun
Expensive

Danny Meyer, Tabla's proprietor, is a fine person and a superb restaurateur. I want to make it clear that I think Tabla is one of the most sensuous and attractive dining establishments I have ever visited. Even the rest rooms have been done with admirable taste. I know I am going against the conventional wisdom, as a reservation at Tabla is one of the toughest tickets in the city, but in my opinion, most of the dishes don't work, are too high-priced, and just don't satisfy the average palate. True lovers of Indian food, especially Indian breads, will be disappointed with the flacid output of the three Tandoori ovens at the bread bar, the more casual and less expensive room on the first floor. I am a great fan of crab cakes but the ones here described as "goan-spiced Maine crab cakes" are so overpowered with cumin (as are several other entrees) that the crab is almost indistinguishable. (And where, by the way, is the accompanying avocado salad?) Strangely enough, the desserts are the best part of the meal, especially the warm chocolate date cake. Maybe you will be turned on by "rawa-crusted shrimp" and "Maine sweet shrimp with curry leaf braised cabbage." Sorry, but I was not.

TAPIKA
950 Eighth Ave (at 56th St)   212/397-3737
Lunch: Mon-Fri; Dinner: Daily
Moderate

The Marlboro man would feel right at home here. In a steakhouse atmosphere, with a distinct Southwestern twist to the menu, Tapika is doing things right for those who love New Mexico and Arizona cuisine. Executive Chef David Walzog wants you to table-share appetizers. Buttermilk biscuits and pan gravy, spicy black bean puree, and lemon-marinated shrimp are excellent suggestions. Tapika classics are novel and uniformly delicious; I like the bacon-wrapped organic turkey and seared rare tuna. Cowboy-size steaks run the gamut from New York strip to sirloin to porterhouse, all at reasonable prices. The fried onions are great. For dessert, the sweet potato and toasted pecan cheesecake is the winner!

TARTINE
253 W 11th St (at 4th St)   212/229-2611
Lunch: Tues-Fri; Dinner: Tues-Sun; Brunch: Sat, Sun
Cash only
Moderate

Tartine is your type of place if you don't mind: (1) waiting outside in the rain, cold, or heat; (2) bringing your own drinks; (3) paying cash; and (4) having your fork laid back down in front of you for the next course. All of this, of course, is secondary to the fact that this tiny spot (about 30 chairs) serves some of the tastiest dishes in the Village. There are soups, salads, quiches, and omelets plus chicken, meat, and fish entrees at pleasing prices. The French fries are a treat. Desserts, danish, and all pastries are baked on the premises. For about half the price of what you would pay uptown, you can finish your meal with splendid custard-filled tarts, a fabulous hazelnut-covered chocolate ganache, strawberry shortcake, or thinly sliced warm apples with cinnamon on puff pastry with ice cream. There is always a wait at dinner. That is a good sign, as neighbors know what is best!

TAVERN ON THE GREEN
Central Park W (at 67th St)   212/873-3200
Lunch, Dinner: Daily
Moderate to moderately expensive

Tavern on the Green is not just another place to eat; proprietor Warner LeRoy has created a destination attraction. The setting in Central Park, with twinkling lights on nearby trees and the glamour of the inside fixtures, makes for an occasion residents and visitors alike will never forget. Even though the place is big and busy, the food and the service are usually first-rate. Chef Sam Hazen has a big job to keep this place hopping. If you are planning an evening that has to be extra special, make reservations in the Crystal Room. Your relatives will love it!

We all know the history of conglomerates. Most of them have not been very successful. Now we are seeing more of the restaurant-cum-retail store, with neither operation being very special. **Tuscan Square** (16 W 51st St, 212/977-7777) is an ambitious operation undertaken by culinary showman Pino Luongo. The setting is vast and dramatic, on several levels, with handy access from Rockefeller Center for quick takeouts. The merchandise is well-chosen and attractive, if rather spendy. But you really come here to be fed, and on that count Tuscan Square is a major disappointment. The food service and many of the dishes are just plain amateurish. Come take a look around—it *is* a feast for the eyes—but let your stomach feast better elsewhere.

THE TERRACE
400 W 119th St   212/666-9490
Lunch: Tues-Fri; Dinner: Tues-Sat
Moderate to moderately expensive

Don't be put off by the address! The Terrace is located on the roof of a Columbia University building, providing a superb view of Manhattan. A table by the window is absolutely enchanting. An outdoor roof garden is a special feature! You'll be impressed by the classy atmosphere, beautiful table settings (attractive china, candlelight, and a single red rose), and soft dinner music. The tables are spaced nicely apart, giving one a chance to talk confidentially. Indeed, if there's one word that describes this operation, it's *style*. The food is as good as the atmosphere. The menu is classical French with some Mediterranean touches. Special services include free valet parking and a glass-enclosed greenhouse for private parties.

THE TONIC
108 W 18th St (bet Ave of the Americas and Seventh Ave)
212/929-9755
Lunch, Dinner: Mon-Sat
Moderate (tavern) to expensive (dining room)

In a large space that for years was the home of Harvey's Chelsea, a new winner has emerged with the unusual name of The Tonic. With a new American cuisine and a choice of venues (tavern, restaurant, party space), diners are offered excellent food with big portions at reasonable prices. The original back bar has been left in place; it is magnificent and worth a look. The tavern floor is old-time tile, and the service goes along with the friendly old-time attitude. Executive chef Chris Gesualdi offers appetizers like truffle, sweetbread, and salsify ravioli and Maryland crabmeat salad. Entrees include delicious seafood dishes: truffle-crusted salmon, foie gras-stuffed guinea hen, and a saddle of venison. Apple crumb pie and chocolate mousse cake make excellent dessert choices. The expansive dining room, with huge floral pieces, makes The Tonic a special place for either a casual or formal meal.

TOSCANA
843 Lexington Ave (bet 64th and 65th St)   212/517-2288
Lunch, Dinner: Mon-Sat
Moderate

Cozy and comfortable, Toscana has been serving delicious Tuscan food for over two decades. Great dishes like *pappardelle* with duck—a signature Tuscan pasta dish made fresh daily at Toscana—brings loyal customers back no matter what the restaurant location may be. What really impresses me about this house is the friendly family feeling exhibited by all the personnel. It comes right from the top! Assisting Sergio Bitici in providing that TLC are two of his daughters. Besides providing care to diners, Bitici and his staff present some pasta dishes you won't find on most Italian restaurant menus. What else to order? Calamari in ink sauce, sweetbreads with capers, Tuscan sausage. Dessert is also a special happening, with ricotta cheesecake or *zabaglione* being my choices. Takeout, delivery, and catering are available.

TRATTORIA DELL'ARTE
900 Seventh Ave (at 57th St)   212/245-9800
Lunch: Mon-Fri; Dinner: Daily; Brunch: Sat, Sun
Moderate

Just because you don't hear a lot about a restaurant doesn't mean that it isn't of star quality. This is the case with Trattoria dell'Arte, a bustling spot across the street from Carnegie Hall. The natives surely know about it, as the place is bursting at the seams every evening. A casual cafe is at the front, seats are available at the antipasto bar in the center, and the dining room is in the rear. One would be hard-pressed to name a place at any price with tastier Italian food than is served here. The antipasto selection is large, fresh, and inviting; you can choose a platter with various accompaniments. There are daily specials, superb pasta dishes, grilled fish and meats, *focaccia* sandwiches, and salads. Wonderful pizzas are available every day. Special spa cuisine from Italy is a feature. The atmosphere and personnel are warm and pleasant. I recommend this place without reservation—although you'd better have one if you want to sit in the dining room.

TREEHOUSE
436 Hudson St   212/989-1471
Lunch: Mon-Fri; Dinner: Daily; Brunch: Sat, Sun
Moderate

Here's a great place to take the family! With a treehouse in the window and mix-and-match chairs and tables for only several dozen guests, Treehouse has all the ingredients to make everyone feel right at home. The food goes right along with the pleasant surroundings. There are crab cakes, French onion soup, fried calamari, and escargot to start. The specialty salad of the house is roast portabello mushrooms over spinach. It's warm and delicious. Entrees include a real old-fashioned turkey dinner with all the trimmings, oven-roasted loin of pork with prunes and raisins, country-style stew, a selection of risottos and pastas, and various fish and chicken dishes. Kids will love their delicious Treehouse burgers. There's nothing special about the desserts (except the sorbets), but by then you'll feel plenty full. The service is a bit disorganized, but then I guess treehouses are supposes to be like that!

TRIBECA GRILL
375 Greenwich St (at Franklin St)   212/941-3900
Lunch: Mon-Fri; Dinner: Daily; Brunch: Sun
Moderate

It hardly seems possible this place is a decade old! Please note the address is Greenwich *Street,* not Avenue. The setting is a Tribeca warehouse. The inspiration is Robert De Niro. The bar comes from the old Maxwell's Plum restaurant. The kitchen is first-class. The genius is savvy Drew Nieporent. Put it all together, and you have a winner. A huge old coffee-roasting house in a refurbished neighborhood plays host to a very glamorous clientele. They enjoy a spacious bar and dining area, fabulous private movie-screening room upstairs, a collection of paintings by Robert De Niro, Sr., and banquet facilities for private parties. The food is stylish and wholesome. Excellent salads, seafood, veal, steak, and first-rate pastas are house favorites. So are the potato pancakes! The tarts, tortes, and mousses rate with the best.

TROPICA
200 Park Ave (MetLife Building)   212/867-6767
Lunch, Dinner: Mon-Fri
Moderate

In a hurry? Realizing that most New Yorkers have limited time to spend over lunch, Tropica provides speedy and efficient service in addition to very tasty food. Dinner hours are a bit more relaxed in this bright, charming, tropical seafood house, which is hidden away on the concourse of the MetLife building in midtown. Featured entrees include excellent tuna (in the sushi and sashimi assortment), citrus honey shrimp, and seafood salads. The bittersweet chocolate soufflé cake easily wins best-dessert honors. Stick to the fish and shellfish, and you'll be more than satisfied here.

TURKISH KITCHEN
386 Third Ave (bet 27th and 28th St)   212/679-1810
Lunch: Mon-Fri; Dinner: Daily
Moderate

This Turkish delight has great ethnic food and is absolutely spotless.
Moreover, the staff literally exudes TLC! There are all kinds of Turkish
specialties, like zucchini pancakes, *istim kebab* (baked lamb shanks wrapped
with eggplant slices), hummus, and a number of tasty baked and grilled fish
dishes. You can wash it all down with sour cherry juice from Turkey or *cacik,*
a homemade yogurt. (Turkish music is the Tuesday entertainment feature.) This
family-run Gramercy-area operation is one of the best.

TWO TWO TWO
222 W 79th St (bet Broadway and Amsterdam Ave)   212/799-0400
Lunch: Tues-Fri; Dinner: Daily
Moderate

This one is a surprise for several reasons. First, the location, which is hardly
the center of great Manhattan dining. Second, the size: a smallish townhouse,
with one crowded and very noisy room and several dozen tables. Oh yes, there
is also a miniature cubicle (if you really want togetherness) that takes care of
four persons . . . just barely. But put all that aside. Dinners are great, and
service is of the same caliber. Grilled dishes are featured: tuna steak, sirloin
steak, breast of chicken. Rack of lamb is one of my favorite dishes, and they
do it very well at Two Two Two. The crème brûlée is superb. An early-bird
prix fixe dinner is a good value. All in all, this is a good choice if you want
to rub shoulders with Manhattan's "dining out" crowd and leave the tourists
behind.

Quick lunch? Quick order for the office? At **Tossed** (295 Park Ave
S, 212/674-6700, fax 212/674-4950), you can create your own salad
from eight different kinds of lettuce, 15 different dressings, and 50 or
so toss-ins (avocado, coconut, pine nuts, lobster) at a very reasonable
price. There are also ready-mades and tossed sandwiches, too. The
quality is amazingly good. **Tossed** also offers home and office delivery.

TYPHOON BREWERY
22 E 54th St   212/754-9006
Lunch, Dinner: Mon-Sat
Moderate

A bit of Bangkok has been brought to Manhattan with a booming Thai eatery
and brewery in midtown. The ground floor houses a huge bar with a vast selection of handcrafted American beers on draught and others (domestic and
imported) in bottles. There must be several dozen of them, and they even serve
a "flight" of three. Chef James Chew provides quite a culinary selection upstairs,
with tasty satays like beef with penang curry glaze and wonderful shrimp with
spicy tamarind glaze. A raw bar offers oysters from both coasts, as well as
Littleneck clams. All five Thai flavors—salty, sweet, sour, bitter and spicy—
are featured on the menu. Take your choice of five selections in each category.
Family-style platters add to the fun: great squid with garlic, delicious lemon-

grass chicken, superb seared monkfish in sour tamarind broth, tasty soft-shell crab. Desserts? Not bad, for a Thai house. "Banana nana na" (warm boxes of surprises, with banana ice cream) and typhoon brûlées (Thai coffee crème, coconut jelly, apple tofu) head the list. It's crowded and fun but no place for those wearing hearing aids.

UNION SQUARE CAFE
21 E 16th St   212/243-4020
Lunch: Mon-Sat; Dinner: Mon-Sun
Moderate

This is one of New York's most popular restaurants—and with good reason. The Stars and Stripes fly high here, as Union Square Cafe is very much an American restaurant. The clientele is as varied as the food, with conversations often oriented toward the publishing world, as well-known authors and editors are sometimes in attendance at lunch. The menu is creative, the staff unusually down-to-earth, and the prices very much within reason. Owner Danny Meyer offers such specialties as oysters Union Square, hot garlic potato chips, and wonderful black bean soup. For lunch, try the tuna club or hamburger served on a homemade poppyseed roll. Dinner entrees from the grill are always delicious (tuna, shell steak, or veal). I go here just for the homemade caramel and mocha ice cream *tartufo* or warm banana tart with honey-vanilla ice cream and macadamia nut brittle. A Yankee winner!

UNITED NATIONS DELEGATES DINING ROOM
United Nations Headquarters
First Ave at 46th St   212/963-7626, 212/963-7099 (banquets)
Lunch: Mon-Fri (open nights and weekends for special functions)
Moderate

Don't let the name put you off! The public can eat here and enjoy the special international food and atmosphere. Conversations at adjoining tables are conducted in almost every language. The setting is charming, overlooking a patio and the river. The room is large and airy, the service polite and informed. Although there is a large selection of appetizers, soups, salads, entrees, and desserts on the regular menu, the best deal is the Delegates Buffet. A huge table of salads, baked specialties, seafoods, roasts, vegetables, cheeses, desserts, and fruits await the hungry noontime diner. Some rules do apply: jackets required, no jeans permitted, and a photo ID is needed. (The room is used for private gatherings in the evening.) There isn't a more appetizing complete daily buffet available in New York than this one. All of the dishes are attractively presented and very tasty. After a tour of the United Nations building, this is a great place to relax, dine, and discuss world affairs!

VERITAS
43 E 20th St (near Park Ave S)   212/353-3700
Lunch: Mon-Fri; Dinner: Mon-Sat
Moderately expensive

In the case of this restaurant, good things come in small packages! With only 65 seats (every one of them kept warm for every meal), getting a chance to enjoy Scott Bryan's refreshingly simple dishes is worth the wait. The world-class wine cellar is reputed to have 1,300 bottles, ranging in price from $18 to $25,000. (Maybe the latter awaits a visit from the Sultan of Brunei.) Like the food, the room is done in superb taste; every color and surface spells quality, including the restrooms. Top dishes include seared foie gras, sauteed sweetbreads, warm oysters, and tender chicken that will melt in your mouth. Warm chocolate cake is a must for dessert. The praline parfait and cheese selection are also top-notch. Veritas proves that someone is finally getting the word that complex food combinations, in most cases, just don't work. Simple is best!

VERONICA RISTORANTE
240 W 38th St   212/764-4770
Breakfast, Lunch: Mon-Fri
Inexpensive to moderate

Some time ago a friend who works in the Garment District told me about a fantastic Italian restaurant in the area but wouldn't give me the name or location because he was afraid I'd put it in my book. This piqued my interest, so I did some investigating. The restaurant turned out to be Veronica, a tiny place in the heart of the Garment District that's open only for breakfast and lunch. Run by Andrew Frisari and his wife, Ceil Hermes, this marvelous cafeteria-style restaurant serves sensational home-cooked food. What wonders they serve up! There is veal piccata, mouth-watering homemade lasagna, delicious tortellini, and chicken salad. Other favorites are pasta primavera and chicken *florentina* (breast of chicken with creamed spinach, prosciutto, mozzarella, and mushrooms in cream sauce). Low-fat and cholesterol-free items are featured. The clientele is sophisticated, the atmosphere informal and homey. Try the cheesecakes or other great homemade desserts. Most items are available for takeout, individual orders, parties, and special occasions.

VINCE & EDDIE'S
70 W 68th St   212/721-0068
Lunch: Mon-Sat; Dinner: Daily; Brunch: Sun
Moderate

Eddie and Vince have taken rooms that housed several now-defunct operations and created a homey, well-priced bistro that is at once charming and professional. The long, narrow quarters mean you must pass by the rest rooms and kitchen to reach the rear dining room and garden. But never mind. The cozy fireplace near the entrance will make you feel wanted, even if the help seem a little overpowered by their attentive customers. The menu selections will please most any taste; it's nothing fancy, just good home cooking.

VIVOLO
140 E 74th St   212/737-3533
Lunch: Mon-Fri; Dinner: Mon-Sat
Moderate

Angelo Vivolo has created a neighborhood classic in an old townhouse that has been converted into a charming two-story restaurant with cozy fireplaces and professional service. Now he has expanded his empire to include a specialty food shop (Cucina Vivolo) next door at 138 East 74th Street. There are great things to eat in both places. You can sit down and be pampered, have goodies ready for takeout, or place an order for delivery to your front door free of charge (from 66th to 80th streets between York and Fifth avenues). The Cucina menu offers wonderful Italian specialty sandwiches, made with all kinds of breads, as well as soups, cheeses, sweets, espresso, and cappuccino. In the restaurant proper there are daily specials, pastas, stuffed veal chops, and much more. The capellini primavera pasta is the house favorite. At Vivolo, there are over 60 scaloppine preparations. Their secret is simple: they use vegetable oil when sauteing the scaloppine and add butter later when finishing the sauce. (Butter alone burns at the high temperatures required.) To romance your taste buds, this is a great choice. Save room for the *cannoli alla Vivolo,* a pastry filled with ricotta cream. A special *prix fixe* menu is available after 9 p.m.

VONG
200 E 54th St (bet Second and Third Ave)   212/486-9592
Lunch: Mon-Fri; Dinner: Daily
Moderate to moderately expensive

The atmosphere here is Thai-inspired, with romantic and appetizing overtones. The ladies will love the colors and sexy lighting, and the gentlemen will remember the great things Vong does with peanut and coconut sauces. I could make a meal on just the appetizers, like chicken and coconut milk soup, prawn satay with oyster sauce, and raw tuna wrapped in rice paper. If crispy squab or venison medallions are available, stop right there! Of course, there is rice for dessert: sticky rice with mango and coconut milk or crispy rice crepes with raspberries and coconut cream. Dining here is a lot cheaper than a week at Bangkok's Oriental Hotel and is honestly just as delicious!

WALKER'S
16 N Moore St (at Varick St)   212/941-0142
Lunch, Dinner: Daily
Inexpensive

If you are looking for atmosphere and a glimpse of what old Manhattan was like, you'll love Walker's. In three crowded rooms, at tables covered with plain white paper so that diners can doodle with crayons, you will be served hearty food at agreeable prices. The regular menu includes homemade soups, salads, omelets (create your own), sandwiches, and quiches. Their burgers are big and satisfying. A dozen or so daily specials include fish and pasta dishes, as well as full entree meals. Homemade desserts (ask what's been freshly made) are unusually tasty and easy on the palate and the pocketbook. For those coming from uptown, it is a bit of a project to get here. For those in the neighborhood, it is easy to see why Walker's is a community favorite, especially on Sunday jazz nights.

WATER CLUB
500 E 30th St (at East River)   212/683-3333
Lunch: Mon-Sat; Dinner: Daily; Buffet Brunch: Sun
Moderately expensive

Warning! Do not fill yourselves with the marvelous small scones that are made fresh in the Water Club's kitchen and served warm. They are absolutely the best things you have ever tasted, but they can be devastating to your appetite for what will be an excellent meal to follow. The Water Club presents a magnificent setting right on the river. The place is large and noisy but has a fun atmosphere that is ideal for special occasions. (They also have excellent private party facilities.) There is nightly entertainment, as well as accommodations for a drink or meal on the roof, if weather permits. A large selection of seafood appetizers is available, including a great seafood gumbo served in a cast-iron crock. Entrees include numerous fish dishes, but you can also find meat and poultry items, as well as a special pasta dish. Homemade ice cream and sorbet, along with dessert soufflés and a fresh-baked apple tart, will round off a special meal. The Water Club's flourless chocolate cake, served with devil's-food ice cream and mango sauce, competes favorably with the famous one originally served at the Coach House. Be advised that getting here from the north can be confusing. (Exit FDR Drive at 23rd Street and make two left turns.)

WILKINSON'S SEAFOOD RESTAURANT
1573 York Ave (bet 83rd and 84th St)   212/535-5454
Dinner: Daily
Moderately expensive

If you are looking for a top-grade seafood house and can't quite bear the prices of Le Bernardin, then venture to Yorkville for an evening at this intimate restaurant. The designers have done everything with lighting to make guests and meals look especially good. Chef Thomas Duncan does wonders with really fresh seafood: oysters, grilled shrimp, or tuna tartare to start. Entrees run the gamut from scallops to snapper to sauteed skate to sole almondine. If someone in your party is averse to seafood, delicious filet mignon and roast chicken are available. Wilkinson's has over a half-dozen refreshing salads. I like the poached pear and Stilton cheese. For dessert, besides a nice selection of fresh fruit and cheeses, the warm bananas Foster filling in phyllo cup with vanilla ice cream is awesome.

WINDOWS ON THE WORLD
One World Trade Center (107th Floor)
212/524-7000 or 212/524-7011 (reservations)
Dinner: Daily; Brunch: Sun
Note: The Windows on the World bar (bar menu and sushi), Sky Box, and Wild Blue (an American chophouse) have different hours; call for updated information.
Expensive

The view is the thing here. Although the food and service can be quite good, most diners are so enthralled with the scene that the plates take second place. The sophisticated menu offers a diverse opportunity: lobster cocktail, oak-smoked salmon, braised short ribs, or caviar (watch the price) to start. On to a delicious lobster pot pie, an unusual potato lasagne of mushrooms and veggies, or a hearty double-cut venison chop. As is fitting for a destination room, desserts amply fill the bill: pear strudel, baby banana split, rice pudding, and homemade ice creams and sorbets. A $35 three-course sunset menu is offered. There is a great wine list; you might need a stiff drink after the elevator ride. Please make note that jackets are required for gentlemen.

Wild Blue (1 World Trade Center, 107th floor, 212/524-7107) boasts a magnificent view, attractive surroundings, and an exceptional wine list. The food, however, is sadly mediocre.

WOO CHON

8 W 36th St (off Fifth Ave)   212/695-0676
Daily: 24 hours
Moderate

Sparkling clean, friendly, and inviting describe this Korean restaurant, which never closes. For a group dinner, order a variety of beef, pork, or shrimp dishes and have fun broiling them right at your table. The sizzling seafood pancake is a winner! All of the accompanying dishes add a special touch to your meal. Besides the marinated barbecue items, there are such tasty delights as Oriental noodles and veggies, traditional Korean herbs and rice served in beef broth, a variety of noodle dishes, and dozens of other Far East treats. If you are unfamiliar with Korean food, the helpful personnel will explain what you are eating and how to eat it. Woo Chon is a different style of dining that is fun to experience.

YE WAVERLY INN

16 Bank St   212/929-4377
Lunch: Mon-Fri; Dinner: Daily; Brunch: Sat, Sun
Moderate

Looking for a great garden setting? Ye Waverly Inn, a picturesque Village restaurant in confined quarters, dates from the early part of the century. There are four rooms with three working fireplaces. An outside eating area has adequate though uncomfortable furnishings, but the atmosphere is truly delightful. It's a given that the food is good, because the place is always crowded and a number of famous folks often dine here. If all this is not reason enough to come to Ye Waverly, their chicken pot pie is one of the best I have ever tasted. Other possibilities include sauteed calves liver, crispy fried chicken, barbecued rack of ribs, boiled beef and horseradish sauce, and boneless chicken breast. Try the fresh fruit and cheese, corn pudding, or baked brie with sour cherry preserves. The dessert selection is excellent, especially the tasty pecan pie. I can see why legions of Village regulars flock here, and you should join the crowd.

ZARELA

953 Second Ave (bet 50th and 51st St)   212/644-6740
Lunch: Mon-Fri; Dinner: Daily
Moderate

If you want the very best Mexican meal in New York, get yourself invited to the home of Zarela Martinez. Failing that, head for her charming and busy restaurant, a two-story building on Second Avenue. Don't let them seat you downstairs, because the second-floor dining room, complete with fireplace, is much more quaint and colorful. You'll understand how Zarela has earned her reputation for some of the best south-of-the-border cuisine when you taste her *antojitos*, which include wonderful daily chile rellenos. And there is much more: seafood dishes, such as shrimp sauteed in a spicy jalapeno sauce; grill-smoked salmon; delicious seared tuna with a sesame seed sauce; roasted half duck with a sauce of red chiles and dried fruit; chicken dishes; and delicious meat entrees, like stewed pork in a chipotle sauce. There's also a great selection of Mexican side dishes like refried black beans, golden-fried cauliflower, and fried plantain slices with mole sauce. Even the desserts are special. The chocolate crepes are heaven-sent. But if you're going Mexican all the way, try the Mexican fruit bread pudding with applejack brandy butter sauce.

ZOË
90 Prince St   212/966-6722
Lunch: Tues-Fri; Dinner: Daily; Brunch: Sat, Sun
Moderate

Soho has come alive; it is a thriving area with many new galleries, stores, and restaurants. Zoë fits right into the picture in its old building with original tiles and columns still visible. Adding to the visual enjoyment are a wood-burning grill, wood-fueled pizza oven, and rotisserie. The menu is contemporary American, with seasonal changes. If the grilled loin of Pennsylvania lamb with wonderful iron-skillet potatoes and truffled mushrooms is on the menu, order it! Pizzas, pastas, and sandwiches are offered at noon, and Zoë has an outstanding wine selection. My favorite dessert: warm chocolate bread pudding with brandy-toffee ice cream.

JAMES BEARD HOUSE
167 W 12th St   212/675-4984

This is a real chef's place! The legendary James Beard had his roots in Oregon, so anything to do with his life is of special interest to this author. He was a familiar personality on the Oregon coast, where he delighted in serving the superb seafood for which the region is famous. When Beard died in 1985, his Greenwich Village brownstone was put on the market and purchased by a group headed by Julia Child. Now the home is run by the nonprofit James Beard Foundation as a food and wine archive, research facility, and gathering place. It is the nation's only such culinary center. There are already nightly dinners anyone can attend where some of our country's best regional chefs show off their talents. For foodies, this is a great opportunity to have a one-on-one with some really interesting folks. Call for scheduled dinners.

You have a special occasion off premises, and you'd like some special take-out food? Try these:

Aquagrill (210 Spring St): seafood
Astra (979 Third Ave): soups, salads, steaks
Bouley Bakery (120 West Broadway): breads, salads, tarts
Coco Pazzo (23 E 74th St): veal chops, ravioli, grilled veggies
Patria (250 Park Ave): clams, beef tenderloin, vanilla flan
Shun Lee Palace (155 E 55th St): exotic Chinese dishes

III. Where to Find It: Museums, Tours, and Other Experiences

You could live in New York your entire life and still never see and do everything this great city has to offer. If you're interested in American social history and the urban immigrant experience, spend the morning on Ellis Island and the afternoon at the Lower East Side Tenement Museum. If you're interested in the history of Broadway, stand where the Ziegfeld girls once stood on a tour of the renovated New Amsterdam Theater. And if it's a night at the opera that really rings your bell, there's no place in the world like the Metropolitan Opera House at Lincoln Center.

The pages of this chapter are bursting with possibilities. Whoever you are and whatever you like, I defy you to sit back and turn on the television instead of getting out and enjoying the wonderful diversity of this magnificent city.

Auction Houses

Whether you're in the market for rare antiques or just looking for a fun experience, New York's auction houses can be a real treat. Look in the Weekend section of the Friday *New York Times* or the Arts and Leisure section of the Sunday *Times* for advertisements about auctions and previews at the auction houses listed below and others. The classified section of the *New York Times* also has an auction section, and all of Manhattan's auction houses are listed in the Manhattan Yellow Pages under "Auctioneers."

Before you go, think carefully about what it is that you're doing. If you just want to learn a little about the art world, simply show up, hang back, and take it all in. If you're even remotely serious about making a purchase, however, make sure you know the rules of the game. I strongly encourage you to get your hands on the auction's illustrated catalog and to take full advantage of auction previews. Attend some of the lectures and courses offered at the auction houses listed below to learn about a particular period or medium.

Finally, a word of warning: the people you will find at most auctions in New York are professionals. They know what they are looking for, they know what they want to pay, and sometimes they know each other. Auctions in New York are a one-of-a-kind experience and can be lots of fun. Just don't go expecting to beat the professionals.

The fine art and antiques market in New York (and indeed throughout the world) is dominated by two houses: Christie's and Sotheby's. I've added William Doyle Galleries, a third quite reputable one, to that list.

Christie's—Located at 502 Park Avenue, this British auction house specializes in fine arts and antiques. For information about upcoming auctions, previews, and viewings, look for the Christie's advertisement in the *New York Times*, call its 24-hour recording at 212/371-5438, or talk to a representative at 212/546-1000 during business hours. For information about lectures and courses, call 212/546-1092.

Christie's East—Located at 219 East 67th Street, this is the junior version of Christie's. It sells what a lady at the reception desk once described to me as anything of value that "would not pass the clientele at the big Christie's." Christie's East also advertises its upcoming previews and auctions in the *New York Times*. Call 212/606-0400 during business hours for more information.

Sotheby Parke Bernet—Located at 1334 York Avenue, Sotheby's is arguably the most elite auction house in the world. Like Christie's, it's British and specializes in fine arts and antiques. Sotheby's also has a junior version, Sotheby's Arcade, where more affordable pieces are sold. For information about upcoming previews, auctions, and exhibitions at both places, look for Sotheby's advertisement in the *New York Times*. For information about Sotheby's, call its 24-hour recording at 212/606-7245 or talk to a representative at 212/606-7000 during business hours. Out-of-towners can call 800/444-3709 to order catalogs or register for special courses and events. For information about Sotheby's Arcade, call 212/606-7409.

William Doyle Galleries—Located at 175 East 87th Street, this American-owned auction house specializes in American and British estates. For information about upcoming previews and auctions at a variety of price levels, look for its advertisement in the *New York Times* or call 212/427-2730.

Films

Like any city, New York has lots of theaters for first-run movies. Indeed, many movies open in New York and Los Angeles before they open anywhere else (and, depending on the size of the crowds they draw, some never do open anywhere else). The *New Yorker, Time Out New York, New York Magazine,* and the *New York Times'* Friday Weekend section and its Sunday Arts and Leisure section are all good places to look for what is playing and where at any given time. You can also call 212/777-FILM (3456) for information about what movies are showing at virtually every theater in Manhattan and, if you have a credit card, to purchase tickets in advance at many of those theaters. (If you're on-line, try www.moviephone.com.)

If you want to combine an excellent dinner with a first-run movie for a surprisingly reasonable price, head for the **Screening Room,** at 54 Varick Street in Tribeca (212/334-2100). Two other places where you can combine a meal and a movie are **City Wine & Cigar Company,** at 62 Laight Street (call 212/334-2274 for details on their every-other-Monday-night Armchair Film Festival), and in the basement of **Two Boots Pizzeria and Video,** at 44 Avenue A on weekends (call 212/254-1441 for details). If you're looking for an old movie, a foreign film, an unusual documentary, a 3-D movie (in the Sony IMAX Theater), or something out of the ordinary, try calling one of the following theaters. Most of the phone numbers connect you with a recording that tells what is playing, how much tickets cost, and how to get there.

American Museum of Natural History's IMAX Theater: Central Park West bet 77th and 81st St (212/769-5034)

Angelika Film Center: 18 W Houston St (212/995-2000)
Anthology Film Archives: Second Ave at 2nd St (212/505-5110)
Cinema Village: 12th St bet University Pl and Fifth Ave (212/924-3363)
Film Forum, Film Forum 2, and **Film Forum 3:** 209 W Houston St (212/727-8110)
Florence Gould Hall at the French Institute: 55 E 59th St (212/355-6160)
Lincoln Center Plaza Cinemas: Broadway bet 62nd and 63rd St (212/757-2280)
Millennium Film Workshop: 66 E 4th St (212/673-0090)
Museum of Modern Art: 11 W 53rd St (212/708-9480)
Museum of Television and Radio: 25 W 52nd St (212/621-6800)
Quad Cinema: 13th St bet Fifth Ave and Ave of the Americas (212/255-8800)
Sony IMAX Theater: Broadway at 68th St (212/336-5000)
Symphony Space: 2537 Broadway (212/864-5400)
Village East Cinemas: 189 Second Ave (212/529-6799)
Walter Reade Theater at Lincoln Center: 165 W 66th St (212/875-5600)
Whitney Museum of American Art: 945 Madison Ave (212/570-3676)

Like everything else, the price of movie tickets in New York tends to be higher than anywhere else in the country. (If, like tens of thousands of other people in New York every week, you purchase tickets over the phone and thus incur a $1.25 per ticket surcharge, you'll spend more than $20 for two adults!) The second-run theaters, film societies, and museums usually charge a little less than the first-run theaters, however. It's also worth finding out what's playing in the seven theaters at **Cineplex Odeon's Worldwide** (50th Street bet Eighth and Ninth Ave). Every seat in the house is $3 and the movies, while not brand new, are surprisingly recent releases. Call 212/777-3456 (ext. 610) for more information and showtimes.

Finally, New York is home to several popular film festivals. The best known is the Film Society of Lincoln Center's **New York Film Festival,** held in late September and early October. This annual event showcases 20 films and gets more popular every year. Call 212/875-5600 for more information. The Society also cosponsors a **New Directors/New Films** series (212/708-9400) with the Museum of Modern Art in late March. The American Museum of Natural History showcases documentaries at the **Margaret Meade Film Festival** (212/769-5650) in early November. The **New York Underground Festival** at Anthology Film Archives (212/505-5181) in March features an oddball assortment of films you probably won't see elsewhere. Those who want to see the work of famous-directors-in-the-making should check out the work of New York University's film school students at their **First-Run Film Festival** (212/924-3363) in early April. Both the **Lesbian and Gay Film Festival** at the Public Theater (212/598-7171) and the **Human Rights Watch Film Festival** at the Walter Reade Theater in Lincoln Center (212/875-5620) are held in June.

Flea Markets

Craft and street fairs pop up all over New York on weekends in spring, summer, and fall. If you hear about or just stumble onto one, by all means do some browsing. Real New Yorkers go to these, so you'll get a very different sense of the city and the people who live here than you would walking around midtown on a weekday. You'll also find everything from woven baskets made by somebody's relatives in Nigeria to socks and underwear sold at steep discounts. You'll also find some great food. That said, however, many street fairs have begun to look alike in recent years, and some neighborhoods have grown weary of them. Moreover, I suggest watching your pockets in a crowd. If you're online, try accessing the city's website at www.ci.nyc.ny.us for a complete listng of upcoming street fairs.

In addition to these craft and street fairs, New York also has several regularly scheduled **flea markets,** as well as **Greenmarkets.** (See the "Fruits, Vegetables" section of Chapter IV for more information on these wonderful markets.) Take cash, don't be embarrassed to haggle a bit, and look around before buying anything — sometimes you'll see the same item at more than one place. Collectors and treasure hunters often go at the beginning of the day, when selections are best, while bargain hunters usually wait until the end of the day, when dealers may lower prices. Remember there are no guarantees and no refunds.

The flea markets in the following list all are relatively well-established. Be forewarned that virtually all of them shrink a bit in the colder months and some may disappear without notice. You might look under "Flea Markets" in the special "Antiques" classified listing in the Friday *New York Times'* Weekend section before setting out.

Annex Antiques Fair and Flea Market — Assuming developers haven't bought out all the real estate, you'll find this sprawling market in parking lots on both sides of Avenue of the Americas from 24th to 27th streets. The antiques section is closer to 27th Street and is open from 9 a.m. to 5 p.m. on Saturdays and Sundays, while the flea market is closer to 24th Street and is open from 9 a.m. to 5 p.m. on Sunday only. Admission to the antiques section is $1, but the flea market is free.

Intermediate School 44 Flea Market — Inside and outside Public School 44 on Columbus Avenue between 76th and 77th streets, this very popular market is held on Sundays from 10 a.m. to 5:30 p.m. Look for one of the city's Greenmarkets here, too.

Public School 183 Flea Market — Open Saturdays from 9 a.m. to 5:30 p.m., this decidedly upscale flea market is known for antiques. It's held at Public School 183, on 67th Street between First and York avenues.

Soho Antique Fair and Collectibles Market — Held at the intersection of Broadway and Grand Street, this market is open Saturdays and Sundays from 9 a.m. to 5 p.m.

Union Square Farmers Market — This is the grandfather of all Greenmarkets. Held all year on Wednesdays, Fridays, and Saturdays at the north end of Union Square (between Broadway and Park Ave S on 17th St), this popular market offers all sorts of fresh goodies: seasonal produce, baked goods, jams, jellies, and flowers.

Galleries

When people think of art, they sometimes think only of museums. While the art museums in New York are exceptional, anybody interested in art ought to think about visiting commercial galleries, too. Galleries are places where potential buyers and admirers alike can look at the work of what are usually contemporary and other 20th-century artists (a few galleries specialize in older work) at their own pace and without charge. Let me stress "admirers alike." A lot of people are afraid to go into galleries because they think they'll be expected to buy something or be treated poorly if they don't know everything there is to know about art. That just isn't true, and an afternoon of "gallery hopping" can be lots of fun.

First decide what kind of art you want to see. New York has long been considered the center of the contemporary art world, and it follows that the city is home to literally hundreds of galleries of all sizes and styles. In general, the more formal and conventional galleries are on or close to Madison Avenue on the Upper East Side and along 57th Street. (You need to look up to find a lot of them, particularly on 57th Street.) Some of the less formal, avant-garde galleries tend to be in Soho on West Broadway between Broome and Houston streets, on Greene Street between Prince and Houston streets, and on Prince Street between Greene Street and West Broadway. Some of the latter are also in Tribeca. In recent years, the west end of Chelsea, around the Dia Center for the Arts at 22nd Street and Tenth Avenue, as well as the northwest corner of the West Village (also known as the Meatpacking District) on 14th Street have become the city's latest hot gallery spots.

If you want to get a sense of the diversity of the New York gallery scene, sample a couple galleries in each neighborhood. In Soho, you can try **Artists Space** (38 Greene St), **Pace Wildenstein** (142 Greene St), **Tony Shafrazi Gallery** (119 Wooster St), the **Thread Waxing Space** (476 Broadway), and the **Jack Tilton Gallery** (49 Greene St). In midtown, try **Mary Boone** (745 Fifth Ave), **Marlborough** (40 W 57th St), **Galerie St. Etienne** (24 W 57th St), and **Andre Emmerich** (41 E 57th St). In Chelsea, check out **Matthew Marks** (522 W 22nd St), **Barbara Gladstone** (513-523 W 24th St), and **Greene/Naftali** (526 W 26th St). Of course, you can just wander the neighborhoods and enter whatever galleries appeal to you!

For a free directory of galleries that belong to the Art Dealers Association of America (not all of them do) and their specialties, write the association at 575 Madison Avenue, New York, NY, 10022 or call 212/940-8590. You can also ask at any gallery for a free copy of the *Art Now Gallery Guide,* a monthly listing of exhibits at several hundred Manhattan galleries.

Galleries are typically known for the artists they showcase. If you are interested in the work of just one artist, both the *New Yorker* and *New York Magazine* contain listings of gallery shows by artists' names. Be sure to look at the dates, as shows sometimes change quickly. *Time Out New York* has a geographical list of galleries in its "Arts" section, complete with descriptions of current shows. The Sunday *New York Times'* Arts and Leisure section devotes several pages of advertisements from various galleries and reviews of new shows. The *Times'* Friday Weekend section also contains reviews, as do *Art in America* and *Arts* magazines.

Most galleries are open Tuesday through Saturday from 10 or 11 a.m. to 5 or 6 p.m. Some close for a couple of weeks during the summer.

Western art collectors should not miss visiting the **J. N. Bartfield Galleries** at 30 West 57th Street, 3rd floor, 212/245-8890. Hours: Monday through Friday from 10 to 5, Saturday from 10 to 3 (summer hours by appointment).

Museums

New York is home to some of the most famous, most interesting, and most unusual museums in the world. With one exception, I've limited the following list to museums in Manhattan, but that does not mean that museums in the other boroughs aren't worth exploring. The **Brooklyn Museum** (718/638-5000), for example, is among the oldest and largest art museums in the country and has one of the best Egyptian collections in the world. The **New York Hall of Science** in Queens (718/699-0005), the **Museum of the Moving Image** in Queens (718/784-0077), the **Staten Island Children's Museum** (718/273-2060), the **Bronx Zoo** (212/369-1010), and the **New York Botanical Garden** (718/817-8700) also have lots of fans. I've also not included some of the smaller museum gallery spaces in Manhattan, such as the **American Indian Community House Gallery** (212/360-8111), the **French Institute-Alliance Francaise** (212/355-6100), and **Tibet House** (212/807-0563). They, too, are worth visiting, and you'll find a listing of their current exhibitions in the "Museums" section of *Time Out New York.*

Even if you aren't a museum person, take a look through the following museum outlines. I can't imagine that you won't find at least one place that strikes a chord. Most of them have gift shops, the larger and more interesting of which I've described in the "Museum and Library Shops" section in Chapter VI. For a list of the best museums for children, see the "Manhattan for Children" section in Chapter VII. And for a complete list of museums offering free admission or special free hours, see the "Manhattan for Free" section in Chapter VII. For museums off the beaten tourist path, I've provided suggestions about how to get there.

As a general rule, I suggest calling ahead. Some of the smaller museums and galleries close for a couple days or even a couple weeks when exhibits are being changed, and all sometimes change their hours. If you want to find out about current exhibits, look in the front of the *New Yorker,* the back of *New York Magazine,* the "Museums" section of *Time Out New York, Museums New York,* or *Where New York* magazine, distributed free in most Manhattan hotel rooms.

ABIGAIL ADAMS SMITH MUSEUM AND GARDENS
421 E 61st St (bet First and York Ave)   212/838-6878

This little (and little-known) gem will transport you back to the days when midtown Manhattan was a country escape for New Yorkers living at the southern end of the island. Constructed in 1799 as a carriage house for a 23-acre estate and converted into the Mount Vernon Hotel in 1826, this stone building sits on land originally owned by Colonel William Smith and his wife, Abigail Adams Smith, daughter of President John Adams. The house is run by the Colonial Dames of America, the oldest women's genealogical society in the United States, and preserved in its hotel incarnation. Because both staff and volunteers are as enthusiastic as they are knowledgeable, part of the pleasure of a visit is that someone walks around the house with guests to answer any questions about the hotel or the period. You'll also find changing exhibits and educational programs for adults, children, and families throughout the year. Anyone interested in social history or antiques ought to put this well-run and interesting museum at the top of the itinerary. The tour lasts about half an hour. **Hours:** Tuesday through Sunday from 11 to 4 (Tuesday evenings in June and July until 9). The museum is closed in August. **Admission:** $3 for adults, $2 for senior citizens and students, free for children under 12.

ALTERNATIVE MUSEUM
594 Broadway (bet Houston and Prince St)   212/966-4444

Located in Suite 402 of a building largely occupied by commercial galleries, this small, artist-run museum definitely merits a visit if you're spending time in Soho and are interested in contemporary art. (Also check out the New Museum of Contemporary Art across the street.) The Alternative Museum was founded in 1975 and is dedicated to exhibiting "the work of emerging and mid-career artists who have been under-recognized or disenfranchised because of ideology, race, gender, or economic inequality." In addition to its changing exhibits, the museum sponsors a variety of lectures, concerts, and other events. **Hours:** Tuesday through Saturday from 11 to 6. **Admission:** free (although a contribution to this nonprofit museum is encouraged).

AMERICAN BIBLE SOCIETY
1865 Broadway (at 61st St)   212/408-1200

The American Bible Society is an organization dedicated to making the Christian Bible readily available to people in this country and around the world. Founded in 1816, ABS has distributed more than 6.9 billion Bibles and other portions of Scripture. If you're interested in religious history, the small gallery on the second floor of its recently remodeled headquarters is well worth the trip. Changing exhibits offer insight into various biblical subjects as well as such related topics as the art and purposes of stained glass. In the adjacent research library, you'll find a portion of a Torah scroll that was found after the flooding of Kai Feng Fu in China in 1643. A wide assortment of Bibles— everything from annotated study Bibles to richly illustrated ones for children—is available in the first-floor gift shop. **Hours:** Monday through Wednesday from 10 to 6, Thursday from 10 to 7, and Saturday from 10 to 5. **Admission:** free.

AMERICAN CRAFT MUSEUM
40 W 53rd St (bet Fifth Ave and Ave of the Americas)   212/956-3535

This is one of those museums that you'll either love or wonder why you came. Its modern galleries are wide open and well lit, and the atmosphere is decidedly unhurried. Both its changing displays and permanent collection are dedicated to crafts of the 20th century—quilts, baskets, pottery, clay sculpture, and other media that fit under that umbrella. If your definition of art is limited to the great masters, stick to Museum Mile along Fifth Avenue or go out on a limb at the Museum of Modern Art across the street. But if art also means innovative crafts or you just want to expand your horizons, by all means make time for a visit here. Call before coming and ask for the Information Department if you're interested in taking a tour. The helpful folks there or at the front desk can also give you information about upcoming lectures, films, and family workshops. **Hours:** Tuesday through Sunday from 10 to 6 (Thursday until 8). **Admission:** $5 for adults, $2.50 for senior citizens and students with ID cards, free for children under 12.

AMERICAN MUSEUM OF NATURAL HISTORY
Central Park West bet 77th and 81st St   212/769-5100

If ever there was a perfect answer for what to do with children on a rainy day, this sprawling collection of 30 million (yes, *million*!) artifacts and specimens is it. You could spend an entire day on any one of the museum's four floors. (The main entrance puts you on the second floor.) I suggest getting a floor plan at the information desk and planning what you want to see, if time is limited. I also suggest going during the week to avoid what are often overwhelming weekend crowds. Exhibits include dinosaur and fossil halls; a hall of ocean life, complete with a whale suspended from the ceiling; one devoted to African mammals, complete with elephants; gems and minerals (keep an eye out for the Star of India sapphire); the new Hall of Biodiversity; and fascinating displays about different cultures and people from all over the globe. On top of all that, a new planetarium and the Center for the Earth and Space are scheduled to open soon after this book goes to press. Guided tours of the museum's highlights are scheduled frequently throughout the day. You'll find a decidedly downscale cafeteria and the more pleasant Garden Cafe on the lower level, and the Whale's Lair for drinks and snacks under the whale (where else?) on weekends and holidays. Request information about the IMAX Theater (212/769-5034) at the information desk. It costs extra, but whatever is showing is bound to be excellent. **Hours:** Sunday through Thursday from 10 to 5:45, Friday and Saturday from 10 to 8:45. **Admission:** $8 for adults, $6 for students and senior citizens, and $4 for children between 2 and 12 is "suggested" (indeed presented as if required, but pay whatever you feel is appropriate).

AMERICAN NUMISMATIC SOCIETY
Audubon Terrace (Broadway bet 155th and 156th St)   212/234-3130

Audubon Terrace in Washington Heights isn't exactly on most New York tourist maps, particularly since the National Museum of the American Indian moved into its new location at the other end of Manhattan. Besides, a place with a name like the American Numismatic Society certainly isn't going to attract great crowds. But if you're interested in the history of money or just like unusual museums, put this fascinating place on your list of places to visit. Founded in 1858, the Society is dedicated to the study of money and maintains an unusually large and diverse collection of more than half a million coins and medallions. Call ahead to express an interest in a particular period or region, and one of the museum's curators will personally arrange to show you certain pieces. You can take either the M4 bus up Madison Avenue or the M5 bus up Avenue of the Americas to get to the museum and then take either back down to Fifth Avenue in midtown. You can also take the 1 subway line from the West Side to 157th Street. **Hours:** Tuesday through Saturday from 9 to 4:30, Sunday from 1 to 4. **Admission:** free.

AMERICAS SOCIETY ART GALLERY
680 Park Ave (at 68th St)   212/249-8950

This classy operation is housed in a beautiful neoclassical townhouse that once served as home to the Soviet Union's delegation to the United Nations. Its relatively small gallery showcases a variety of changing exhibits of art from Latin America, the Caribbean, and Canada. The Americas Society has no permanent collection of its own, so the work in the exhibitions is all on loan from museums and other collections. Call for information on its various public programs. **Hours:** Tuesday through Sunday from 11 to 6. **Admission:** free.

ASIA SOCIETY GALLERY
725 Park Ave (bet 70th and 71st St)   212/288-6400

The Asia Society is a nonprofit organization founded in 1956 to foster mutual understanding between Asian nations and the United States. One of the many ways it reaches out to the public is through changing art exhibitions in its marvelous gallery. Gallery talks are held Tuesday through Saturday at 12:30, Thursdays at 6:30, and Sunday at 2:30. Call ahead to make sure an exhibition is showing when you plan to visit. For information about concerts, lectures, and other special programs, drop by the information desk in the lobby or call the event line at 212/517-ASIA. The Asia Society also runs a shuttle service on Saturday to and from the impressive Isamu Noguchi Garden Museum in Long Island City. (Call that museum from the beginning of April through the end of October at 718/721-1932 for details.) **Hours:** Tuesday through Saturday from 11 to 6 (Thursday until 8), and Sunday from noon to 5. **Admission:** $4 for adults, $2 for students and senior citizens, and free for members and children under 12 accompanied by a parent or guardian.

BARD GRADUATE CENTER FOR STUDIES IN THE DECORATIVE ARTS
18 W 86th St (bet Central Park W and Columbus Ave)
212/501-3023

A welcome newcomer to the New York art world, the Bard Graduate Center devotes the first two floors of its elegant *beaux-arts* townhouse to changing exhibitions of home furnishings and other decorative arts. As is the case in many smaller museums and galleries in New York, half the pleasure of a visit here is simply being inside the building itself. Call ahead to learn about tours and public lectures. **Hours:** Tuesday through Sunday from 11 to 5 (Thursday until 8). **Admission:** $2 for adults, $1 for students and senior citizens, free for children under 12 accompanied by an adult.

CHILDREN'S MUSEUM OF MANHATTAN
212 W 83rd St (bet Broadway and Amsterdam Ave)   212/721-1234

"C-Mom," as the locals call it, has experienced a real growth spurt since I complained about its cramped spaces and confusing layout in my last edition. Despite a few associated growing pains, the results are terrific, as the museum has doubled in size! There are still lots of buttons to push; ladders to climb; all sorts of things to sort, touch, and examine; an early childhood center and play space; and even an imaginative exhibit and exploration space for babies and toddlers devoted to language and its development. Older preschoolers and kids in early elementary school will appreciate the new Body Odyssey exhibit as well as the interactive media center. Strollers must be checked at the entrance and food is not allowed in the museum. **Hours:** Wednesday through Sunday from 10 to 5. **Admission:** $5 for adults and children, $2.50 for senior citizens, free for children under one. Many workshops and performances cost an additional dollar or two.

CHINA INSTITUTE GALLERY
125 E 65th St (bet Lexington and Park Ave)   212/744-8181

This extremely small but interesting gallery is run by the non-partisan China Institute in America and is housed on the first floor of the institute's lovely brownstone. In addition to the changing exhibits of Chinese art and artifacts, the gallery has a tiny gift shop specializing in books about China and Chinese art. The China Institute itself offers a wide array of educational programs, lectures, tours, performances, and language courses. **Hours:** Monday through Satuday from 10 to 6 (Tuesday and Thursday until 8), and Sunday from 1 to 5. **Admission:** $3 for adults, $2 for students and seniors.

THE CLOISTERS
Fort Tryon Park   212/923-3700

Perhaps the finest medieval art museum in the world, the Cloisters is also one of the quietest and most beautiful places in all of Manhattan. Built on land donated by John D. Rockefeller, Jr., in the late 1930s, the museum incorporates large sections of cloisters and other pieces of buildings brought to the United States from southern France by sculptor George Grey Barnard. His collection was purchased by the Metropolitan Museum of Art with money donated for that purpose by Rockefeller in 1925, making the Cloisters a branch of the Metropolitan. The truly spectacular collection also includes carved wood and ivory, tapestries, and sculptures. The museum is quiet, peaceful, and rarely crowded, and its outdoor terrace and medieval gardens offer a great view of the Hudson River and the Palisades. Though it takes about an hour each way, the M4 bus brings you right to the front entrance from Madison Avenue in midtown and back again via Fifth Avenue (the A subway line to 190th Street takes half the time). **Hours:** Tuesday through Sunday from 9:30 to 5:15 (4:45 from November through February). **Admission:** $10 for adults, $5 for students and senior citizens, free for children under 12 when accompanied by an adult. The fee entitles you to same-day admission to the Metropolitan Museum of Art.

COOPER-HEWITT NATIONAL MUSEUM OF DESIGN
2 E 91st St (bet Fifth and Madison Ave)   212/849-8400

Founded by three granddaughters of Peter Cooper (their last name was Hewitt) as the Cooper Union Museum for the Arts of Decoration just before the turn of the century, this exceptional museum became part of the Smithsonian Institution in 1967 and moved into Andrew Carnegie's Fifth Avenue mansion in 1976. Drawing from a permanent collection of almost a quarter million pieces involving every imaginable aspect of design, the museum's exhibitions change frequently. Outstanding lectures, workshops, tours, and special gallery talks are developed around the exhibitions. They often are free but usually require advance reservations (call 212/849-8389 for more information). Of course, part of the pleasure of a visit to the recently renovated Cooper-Hewitt is seeing the Carnegie Mansion itself, including the spectacularly beautiful Great Hall (where an organ was once played at 8 a.m. every morning to wake up the household!). **Hours:** Tuesday from 10 to 9, Wednesday through Saturday from 10 to 5, and Sunday from noon to 5. **Admission:** $5 for adults, $3 for senior citizens and students over 12, free for children under 12 accompanied by an adult and for Smithsonian Associates. It's also free to everybody on Tuesday evening from 5 to 9.

DAHESH MUSEUM
601 Fifth Ave (bet 48th and 49th St), 2nd floor   212/759-0606

A new museum in New York? On Fifth Avenue in midtown? Thanks to the late Lebanese writer and philosopher after whom the museum is named, this tiny space is a showcase for popular French and other European artists of the 19th and early 20th centuries. Dr. Dahesh, who died in 1984, was an art collector extraordinaire who dreamed of opening a public museum for European art in Beirut. Sadly, that never came to pass, but his wondrous collection found its way to New York, and the result is this museum. The changing exhibits, most of them drawn from the Dahesh collection, are consistently interesting, and the gallery space itself offers a quiet respite from the hustle of midtown. If you're interested in gallery talks, lectures on related subjects, or the museum's programs for families, be sure to ask for a copy of the latest *Dahesh Muse*. **Hours:** Tuesday through Saturday from 11 to 6. **Admission:** free.

DIA CENTER FOR THE ARTS
548 W 22nd St   212/989-5566

This renovated warehouse is the anchor for the growing art scene in Chelsea and an exhibition space for large-scale projects designed specifically for it. Those interested in Minimalism, Conceptualism, and Earth Art know that the Dia Center—and the Dia Art Foundation before it—has been a major force in supporting the careers of many of the world's most innovative contemporary artists. If those schools are your thing, the four floors of this museum and its rooftop will be a real treat. The Dia Center also sponsors lectures, poetry readings, and conferences, as well as several long-term installations. These include the Dan Flavin Art Institute in Bridgehampton, the Cy Twombly Gallery in Houston, and the Andy Warhol Museum in Pittsburgh. A new 160,000-square-foot facility in an old factory up the Hudson River in Beacon, New York, is scheduled to open in 2001. **Hours:** Wednesday through Sunday from noon to 6. **Admission:** $6 for adults, $4 for students and senior citizens.

DYCKMAN FARMHOUSE
4881 Broadway (at 204th St)   212/304-9422

This is the last surviving example of the sort of farmhouse built all over New York well into the 19th century. It is a real treat for anybody interested in the city's history or the Revolutionary War period. The Dyckman family emigrated to what were then the American colonies from the Netherlands in the 17th century and had a thriving orchard in this area before the Revolutionary War. They were forced to flee during the war, however, and both their home and orchard were occupied and ultimately destroyed by British troops. When they returned to the area in 1784, the Dyckmans built this home and later used the surrounding area for grazing cattle on their way to market downtown. The adjoining buildings housing the slave quarters and outdoor kitchen no longer exist, but the house itself has been preserved much as it was then. You'll find several rooms with period furniture (some of which actually belonged to the Dyckmans) on the first and second floors and a kitchen in the basement. Probably the most interesting room in the house is the Relic Room, which houses a display of such Revolutionary War artifacts as a general's uniform, a tattered American flag with 13 stars, cannonballs, and bayonets. All of the items on display in this room were excavated from around the house at the beginning of this century. The cherry tree and flowers on the lovely grounds surrounding the house come alive during the spring and early summer. You can get to Dyckman House from midtown by taking the M1 bus up Madison Avenue to 125th Street and transfering to the M100 bus, which will drop you off in front of Dyckman House and pick you up again on the corner of 204th Street and Broadway for a return trip down Fifth Avenue). You can also get there by taking the A subway line to 207th Street and walking south to 204th Street on Broadway. It's actually only a block, as there are no 205th and 206th Streets. **Hours:** Tuesday through Sunday from 11 to 4. **Admission:** free.

EL MUSEO DEL BARRIO
1230 Fifth Ave (near 105th St)   212/831-7272

El Museo del Barrio—Spanish for "Museum of the Neighborhood"—is the only museum in New York and one of only several in the United States devoted to the art and culture of Puerto Rico and all of Latin America. Located at the southern end of Spanish Harlem and the northern tip of Museum Mile, El Museo is in the northern part of the old Heckscher Building, which runs the length of the block between 104th and 105th streets. El Museo, a special place clearly devoted to the people and cultures of the surrounding community, is currently in the process of expanding and renovating its children's theater. It features both permanent and changing exhibitions of contemporary and traditional art, and sponsors all sorts of festivals, lectures, workshops, and other outreach programs. **Hours:** Wednesday through Sunday from 11 to 5. Call for extended summer hours May through September. **Admission:** free, but a "suggested contribution" of $4 for adults, $2 for students with ID and senior citizens, $1 for children under 12.

ELLIS ISLAND MUSEUM OF AMERICAN IMMIGRATION
Ellis Island   212/363-3200

Think of immigration to the United States, and Ellis Island instantly comes to mind. At least one in every four Americans today can trace one or more relatives who came through the immigration processing center on the island between 1892 and 1954. Whether or not you're one of them, this is one of New York's "must see" museums. Located in the shadow of the Statue of Liberty in New York Harbor, Ellis Island was all but abandoned until it was restored and opened to the public in 1990. Walk through the moving display of photographs and artifacts brought to this country by immigrants, and you'll inevitably come across someone telling his children or grandchildren about what his family brought when they came to this country. Other displays include one that retraces the steps the immigrants took once they arrived on the island and another discussing immigration in the U.S. through the present. An Academy Award-winning film by Charles Guggenheim—*Island of Hope, Island of Tears*—is shown frequently and is well worth watching. To get to Ellis Island, take the Circle Line ferry from Battery Park. The ticket booth is in Castle Clinton, and the ferry makes stops at both Ellis Island and the Statue of Liberty. The best time to go is early in the morning on a weekday, as lines can get pretty long in the afternoon and on Saturday and Sunday. The least expensive and most efficient way to get to Battery Park is by taking the 1 or 9 subway line to the South Ferry stop (be sure to get in one of the front cars, as only a few doors open at this stop) or the 4 or the 5 to the Bowling Green stop. **Hours:** 9:30 to 5 in winter and 9:30 to 5:30 in summer, although the last ferry leaves at about 3 or 3:30. **Admission:** $7 for adults, $6 for senior citizens, and $3 for children between 3 and 17. Admission to both Ellis Island and the Statue of Liberty is included in the price of a ferry ticket.

EQUITABLE GALLERY
787 Seventh Ave (bet 51st and 52nd St)   212/554-4818

Perhaps the nicest of several gallery spaces in the lobbies of midtown office buildings, this one is located in the righthand corner of the Equitable Center's soaring atrium. It consists of four interconnected rooms that play host to a variety of consistently well-conceived exhibitions. While you're here, make sure to rest your feet in the unusually pleasant and peaceful sitting area in the building's atrium while looking at Roy Lichtenstein's five-story *Mural with Blue Brushstroke*. The Brooklyn Museum runs a small shop to the right of the gallery entrance. **Hours:** Monday through Friday from 11 to 6, Saturday from noon to 5. **Admission:** free.

FORBES MAGAZINE GALLERIES
62 Fifth Ave (bet 12th and 13th St)   212/206-5548

What do 10,000 toy soldiers, 12 Faberge eggs, documents written by Abraham Lincoln and other American presidents, and an Imperial Russian diadem have in common? They're in the Forbes Magazine Galleries (on the first floor of the *Forbes* magazine building). Assuming you're among the 900 people allowed in on a first-come, first-served basis every day, you can view them for free. These small galleries can get a little cramped on Saturdays, but the collections assembled over the years by the late Malcolm Forbes and his sons definitely have something for everyone. Strollers are prohibited, children under 16 are not allowed in without an adult, and no more than four children can accompany one adult. **Hours:** Tuesday, Wednesday, Friday, and Saturday from 10 to 4. Call ahead to make a reservation if you want to take one of the guided tours offered on Thursdays. **Admission:** free.

FRAUNCES TAVERN MUSEUM
54 Pearl St (at Broad St)   212/425-1778

If you're interested in Colonial and early U.S. history and culture, you'll really enjoy this often overlooked museum. The site of General George Washington's farewell address to his officers in 1783 and an anti-British meeting place before and during the Revolutionary War, this tavern has seen many generations and a lot of history come and go through its doors. If you open the front door of the Fraunces Tavern only to find yourself in a restaurant, don't think you've gone to the wrong place! The first floor of the building is home to one of Wall Street's more pleasant places to eat. Just proceed straight ahead and up the stairs. On the second and third floors, you'll find period rooms (including the room in which General Washington gave his address) with changing exhibitions on all sorts of different topics in early American history and culture. Make sure to ask about movies, special events, and walking tours. **Hours:** Monday through Friday from 10 to 4:45, Saturday and Sunday from noon to 4. **Admission:** $2.50 for adults, $1 for students, senior citizens, and children under 6.

FRICK COLLECTION
1 E 70th St (bet Fifth and Madison Ave)   212/288-0700

The home of the late Henry Clay Frick, this exceptionally elegant and peaceful mansion displays Frick's collection of paintings, sculpture, rugs, furniture, porcelain, and other artwork. Take time to wander around and look at the mansion itself—the moldings, the floors, the ceilings, the light fixtures, and the stairs—as well as the art. Built in 1914, this is one of the last great mansions on Fifth Avenue. Unlike the guards at a lot of other museums, the sentinels here are very knowledgeable and obviously proud of the building and the collection. If you ask, they'll even tell you about the giant heat lamps that are brought out every night for the plants and flowers in the inner garden! Because the museum's temperature is kept at a constant 70 degrees, you'll be glad they require you to check your coat (at no charge). A special exhibition is often held downstairs, so be sure to ask about it. Although not a place to take children (those under ten are not allowed), this exceptionally beautiful and uncrowded museum is a real treat for art buffs and oglers alike. A free Artphone audiotour of the permanent collection is available in several languages, and a 22-minute slide presentation about the collection runs throughout the day. **Hours:** Tuesday through Saturday from 10 to 6, Sunday from 1 to 6. **Admission:** $7 for adults, $5 for students with ID and senior citizens.

GROLIER CLUB
47 E 60th St (bet Madison and Park Ave)   212/838-6690

You won't find any bells or whistles here, and it's definitely not for the kids. Dedicated to the study and preservation of books, the Grolier Club is an old, reserved, and elegant institution. It mounts a variety of exhibits on such esoteric topics as the history of Greek translation in a small gallery on the first floor of its townhouse for its members and anybody else who happens to be interested. Check in with the receptionist immediately inside the front hall before heading back to the gallery. **Hours:** Monday through Saturday from 10 to 5. **Admission:** free.

— Millennium Note —

The first Jewish holiday services conducted anywhere in what became the United States were held in New York in observance of Rosh Hoshanah on September 12-13, 1654, a week after the arrival of 23 Jews from Brazil.

GUGGENHEIM MUSEUMS
1071 Fifth Ave (bet 88th and 89th St)   212/423-3500
575 Broadway (at Prince St)

Housed in an enormous white spiral designed by Frank Lloyd Wright, the Solomon R. Guggenheim Museum is as famous for its building as for its collection. That is saying a lot, given a collection of 20th-century art that is arguably the best in the world. A second Guggenheim location in Soho opened in 1992 to showcase parts of the museum's permanent collection, as well as special exhibitions designed to complement those at the Fifth Avenue location. A third Guggenheim museum, the Peggy Guggenheim Collection, is located in Venice —but that's another trip! The works displayed at these museums offer a who's who of 20th-century art: Chagall, Miro, Calder, Kandinsky, Picasso, and Gauguin are just a few of the artists whose work you'll come across. Both museums mount special exhibits featuring world-renowned collections and artists, as well as gallery talks and other special events. As this book was going to press, the Soho branch was closed for renovations. **Hours:** The Fifth Avenue location is open Sunday through Wednesday from 10 to 6, Friday and Saturday from 10 to 8. The Soho location is open Sunday, Wednesday, Thursday, and Friday from 11 to 6, Saturday 11 to 8. **Admission:** $12 for adults, $7 for senior citizens over 65 and students with ID at the Fifth Avenue location; $7 for adults, $5 for senior citizens over 65 and students with ID at the Soho location. Children under 12 are admitted free at both places. If the Soho branch has reopened and you're interested in visiting both museums, check to see if discount admission to both is offered. Admission on Friday between 6 and 8 is "pay-what-you-wish" at the Fifth Avenue location.

HISPANIC SOCIETY OF AMERICA
Audubon Terrace (Broadway bet 155th and 156th St)   212/926-2234

Founded as a public museum and research library in 1904, this little-known place is home to a diverse and impressive collection of art and artifacts from the Iberian Peninsula (Spain and Portugal). The building itself, located directly across from the dramatic El Cid statue in the middle of Audubon Terrace, is beautiful, but the lighting in the galleries is awful and descriptions of most things are less than complete. That said, however, the Hispanic Society is well worth a visit. You'll find seals from the Roman Empire, a 15th-century silver processional cross from Barcelona, and paintings by such masters as Goya, Valazquez, and El Greco. Make sure to look at the beautiful tiles and mosaics in the walls on your way up the stairs between floors. You can take either the M4 bus up Madison Avenue or the M5 bus up Avenue of the Americas to get to the museum and then take either back to Fifth Avenue in midtown. You can also take the 1 subway line from the West Side to 157th Street. **Hours:** The museum and library are open Tuesday through Saturday from 9 to 4:30; the museum only is open on Sunday from 1 to 4. The library is closed in August. **Admission:** free.

INTERNATIONAL CENTER OF PHOTOGRAPHY
1130 Fifth Ave (at 94th St)   212/860-1777
1133 Ave of the Americas (at 43rd St)   212/768-4680

If you're interested in photography, put the International Center of Photography (ICP) galleries at the top of your list of places to visit. Devoted to displaying photography as both art and historical record, these galleries have changing exhibits of work by photographers from all over the world, as well as ones drawn from the center's permanent collection. The main ICP gallery on Fifth Avenue is in a relatively small townhouse, but its unhurried, quiet atmosphere allows you to take in exhibits at your own pace. The newer gallery in midtown is almost twice the size, but the atmosphere is every bit as pleasant. **Hours:** Tuesday through Thursday from 10 to 5, Friday from 10 to 8, and Saturday and Sunday from 10 to 6. **Admission:** $6 for adults, $4 for senior citizens and students, $1 for children under 12, and "pay-what-you-wish" for everyone from 5 to 8 on Friday.

INTREPID SEA-AIR-SPACE MUSEUM
Pier 86 (46th St at Hudson River)   212/245-0072

The water in the Hudson River is not particularly inviting, and you'll find few pedestrians in this area, but a trip down here can be lots of fun if you're interested in aircraft carriers, submarines, space exploration, and the like. The centerpiece is the giant *U.S.S. Intrepid,* an aircraft carrier that served in both World War II and the Vietnam War. The *U.S.S. Edison* (a destroyer used in Vietnam), the Coast Guard cutter *Tamoroa,* and the *U.S.S. Growler* (a guided-missile submarine) are also here. You must take a guided tour of the *Growler,* but for everything else you can choose between a tour or wandering around by yourself. Galleries, display halls, and theaters are scattered throughout the complex. You won't have much trouble finding the museum, as the *Intrepid* dominates along this part of the river. The ticket booth and gift store are right inside the main entrance, past the tanks. The best ways to get to the museum from midtown are by taxi or M42 bus (make sure it says "Piers" on the front) all the way to the west end of 42nd Street. **Hours:** Monday through Saturday from 10 to 5 and Sunday from 10 to 6 between April 1 and September 30; Wednesday through Sunday from 10 to 5 the rest of the year. The ticket booth closes at 4 (5 on Sunday in summer), and the last tours finish at 6. **Admission:** $10 for adults; $7.50 for veterans, reservists, students between 12 and 17 with ID cards, and senior citizens; $5 for children between 6 and 11; $1 for children under 6.

JEWISH MUSEUM
1109 Fifth Ave (at 92nd St)   212/423-3200

Operated by the Jewish Theological Seminary of America and housed in yet another elegant Fifth Avenue mansion, the Jewish Museum displays the largest collection of Jewish art and Judaica in the United States. Much of the museum's collection was rescued from European synagogues before World War II, and all of it is extremely well displayed. Renovated in the early 1990s, the museum has a large permanent exhibit tracing the Jewish experience that's entitled "Culture and Continuity: the Jewish Journey," as well as a variety of changing exhibits. Families will also want to visit the children's gallery and ask about special family programs and workshops. Cafe Weissman in the museum's basement is a pleasant place for a light lunch or snack. **Hours:** Sunday through Thursday from 11 to 5:45 (Tuesday until 8). The museum is closed on most Jewish holidays. **Admission:** $8 for adults, $5.50 for students and senior citizens, free for children under 12 (and for everyone between 5 and 8 on Tuesday).

LOWER EAST SIDE TENEMENT MUSEUM
90 Orchard St (at Broome St)   212/431-0233

Founded in 1988, this unique museum is making an enormous contribution to the preservation of American social history and the urban immigrant experience. In the visitor's center itself are permanent and changing exhibits, an oral-history video, and a slide show tracing the history of the tenement building across the street at 97 Orchard Street. The really exciting part of this museum, however, is the tenement building itself. Home to as many as 7,000 people from more than 20 nations between 1863 and 1935, the tenement has had four of its apartments restored to different periods in their history. Together, they offer a glimpse of what life in one of these incredibly crowded places must have been like (or what it is like for hundreds of thousands who still live this way). The museum's docents—who lead tours of the tenement Tuesday through Friday at 1, 2, 3, and 4 and on Sundays every 30 minutes between 11 a.m. and 4:15 p.m.—are enormously interesting, well-informed, and dedicated. The Confino Program, a living-history tour, is also offered on Saturdays and Sundays at noon, 1, 2, and 3. Reservations are stongly encouraged (and required well in advance for groups of more than ten). **Hours:** Tuesday through Friday from noon to 5, Saturday and Sunday from 11 to 6. **Admission:** $8 for adults, $6 for senior citizens and students, free for children under five. That fee includes admission to an audiovisual history of the site as well as a tour of the tenement building. Exceptionally well-conceived and educational walking tours are offered on weekends for an additional charge.

MERCHANT'S HOUSE MUSEUM
20 E 4th St (bet Broadway and Lafayette St)   212/777-1089

Once home to a hardware merchant and his family, this 1832 rowhouse now offers its visitors a glimpse of life in an age when Greenwich Village was considered the suburbs. The house is filled with all the latest "modern" equipment of the period, including pipes for gas lighting. A self-guided tour is available inside the front door, and you can wander around at your own pace. A docent-guided tour is available Sunday afternoons. **Hours:** Sunday through Thursday from 1 to 4. **Admission:** $5 for adults, $3 for students and senior citizens, free for children under 12.

METROPOLITAN MUSEUM OF ART
Fifth Ave bet 80th and 84th St   212/535-7710

The Met, as it is known to New Yorkers (not to be confused with the Metropolitan Opera), is one of those places you can visit a hundred times and never see the same thing twice. Whether you're interested in Egyptian tombs, Greek and Roman sculpture, paintings by the great Renaissance masters, African masks, Chinese and Asian art, Tiffany windows, or arms and armor from the Crusades, the Met has a lot you'll want to see. Start by picking up a floor plan at one of the information desks in the main hall and mapping out your visit. Make sure to ask for a "Dining Guide" of the museum's five restaurants, bars, and cafes. Although the Met often has extremely popular special exhibits, I sometimes head for places with fewer people so I can wander and gaze at my own pace. If you want to avoid the crowds (almost 5 million people come through the Met every year), the best time to visit is on a weekday morning. Self-guided audio tours in English and other languages are available at an extra charge. The Met also sponsors an incredible number of films, lectures, gallery talks, concerts, and other special programs. Call 212/879-5500 for information on gallery and museum tours, as well as upcoming schedules and programs, or pick up a seasonal program at one of the information desks. If you come to New York frequently and like to visit the Met and its gift shops, consider becoming a National Associate. For a small annual fee, people who live outside a 200-mile radius of New York City can get free admission to both the Met and the Cloisters, a 10% discount at the Met's many gift shops, seasonal schedules, and a subscription to the museum's magazine. **Hours:** Sunday, Tuesday, Wednesday, and Thursday from 9:30 to 5:15; Friday and Saturday from 9:30 to 8:45. **Admission:** $10 for adults, $5 for senior citizens and students, free for children under 12. The fee entitles you to same-day admission to the Cloisters.

MORGAN LIBRARY
29 E 36th St (at Madison Ave)   212/685-0610   7/02 superb

Have you ever wondered where to find a copy of the Gutenberg Bible? Wonder no more. You'll find one of the few original Gutenberg Bibles, as well as a remarkable collection of medieval and Renaissance manuscripts, books, drawings, and art here in the Morgan Library. Built at the turn of the century by financier J. Pierpont Morgan to house his personal collection, the library was opened to the public by his son in 1924. It's now a scholarly research center and museum with changing and permanent exhibitions. By far the most exciting thing here is "Mr. Morgan's Library," a study and private three-story library connected by a rotunda. Free tours are offered of these rooms, which contain an unbelievable collection of mostly Italian Renaissance carvings, furniture, paintings, tapestries, mosaics, and other marvels. Call 212/685-0610 for recorded information about guided tours, current exhibitions, and special events. The Morgan Court Cafe and the museum's gift shop are both well worth a visit. **Hours:** Tuesday through Thursday from 10:30 to 5, Friday from 10:30 to 8:30, Saturday from 10:30 to 6, Sunday from noon to 6. **Admission:** $7 for adults, $5 for students and senior citizens.

MORRIS-JUMEL MANSION
160th St (bet Edgecombe and Amsterdam Ave)   212/923-8008

Built in 1765 as a summer house for Colonel Roger Morris and his wife, this graceful Georgian country house sits atop a hill overlooking the East River. It briefly served as General George Washington's headquarters in 1776 and later was home to Madame Eliza Jumel and her second husband, Aaron Burr. (Rumor has it that Madame Jumel's ghost has been spotted yelling at neighborhood children to be quiet from the second floor balcony!) Throughout the house you'll find exceptional period furniture, including a 19th-century French mahogany *directoire* sleigh bed said to have belonged to Napoleon Bonaparte when he was First Consul of France. The surrounding neighborhood has definitely seen better days, but the mansion itself has recently been renovated. The grounds are particularly pretty in the spring and early summer. Take the M2 bus up Madison Avenue to the front of the mansion on Edgecombe Avenue. Getting back to midtown is a little more complicated. I recommend taking a taxi or coming here on a tour (look under Harlem in the "Tours" section of this chapter). **Hours:** Wednesday through Sunday from 10 to 4. **Admission:** $3 for adults, $2 for senior citizens over 60 and students with ID, free for children under 10.

MUSEUM FOR AFRICAN ART
593 Broadway (bet Houston and Prince St)   212/966-1313

Although both the Metropolitan Museum of Art and the American Museum of Natural History have African collections, this is the only museum in New York and one of only a few in North America devoted exclusively to African art. In a space designed by Vietnam War Memorial architect Maya Lin, the museum's two floors house changing exhibits from all over the continent. It is entered through part of the eclectic gift shop and bookstore. (Check out the magnificent coffee-table books and the children's books to the right of the reception desk.) The museum sponsors gallery talks, special events, and trips to Africa and other places abroad. **Hours:** Tuesday through Friday from 10:30 to 5:30, Saturday and Sunday from noon to 6. **Admission:** $5 for adults, $2.50 for children, senior citizens, and students.

MUSEUM OF AMERICAN FOLK ART
2 Lincoln Sq (Columbus Ave bet 65th and 66th St)   212/595-9533

You'll find a lot of what I call Americana here: weather vanes, quilts, whirligigs, wooden carrousel horses, and some marvelous paintings. The gallery is quite small but has lots of benches and can be a very pleasant place just to sit and think. Best of all, it's free. The museum, which eventually will move to a new home in midtown, next to the Museum of Modern Art, also sponsors lectures, educational programs, and demonstrations. The gift shop next door is well worth a visit. **Hours:** Tuesday through Sunday from 11:30 to 7:30 **Admission:** free.

MUSEUM OF AMERICAN ILLUSTRATION
128 E 63rd St (bet Park and Lexington Ave)   212/838-2560

On the first floor of the Society of Illustrators' townhouse offices, this gallery houses changing exhibits of advertising, artistic, and other works by professional illustrators. Most of the exhibits center around the Society's annual juried competitions for illustrators in a variety of categories. A small museum shop offers books by and for illustrators, exhibition catalogs, and other items. **Hours:** Tuesday 10 to 8, Wednesday through Friday from 10 to 5, Saturday noon to 4. **Admission:** free.

MUSEUM OF CHINESE IN THE AMERICAS
70 Mulberry St (at Bayard St), 2nd floor   212/619-4785

Designed in the shape of a 15-sided traditional Chinese lantern, this recently opened successor to the Chinatown History Museum is a small but wonderfully interesting place in the heart of Chinatown. Its stated mission is to reclaim, preserve, and broaden the understanding of the incredibly diverse story of Chinese people in the Americas. The museum's fascinating permanent exhibit—

"Where Is Home? Chinese in the Americas"—combines the extraordinary with the ordinary to give visitors a glimpse into that story. If you're visiting Chinatown, this museum offers some perspective on the world bustling around you on the streets below. **Hours:** Tuesday through Saturday from 10:30 to 5. **Admission:** $3 for adults, $1 for senior citizens and students, free for children under 12.

MUSEUM OF THE CITY OF NEW YORK
1220 Fifth Ave (bet 103rd and 104th St)   212/534-1672

This treasure is often overlooked by tourists and New Yorkers alike because of its location at the far north end of Fifth Avenue's Museum Mile. It's dedicated to the history of the city from the earliest European settlement through the present, and it offers something for just about everyone. Permanent exhibits include period rooms, an exquisite silver collection, toys and dollhouses, a fire-fighting gallery, and an enormous number of model ships. Thanks to popular demand, what was a temporary exhibit on Broadway now seems to have become a permanent one. The actual bedroom and dressing room from the home of John D. Rockefeller, Sr., on the museum's fifth floor are a truly breathtaking pleasure for anyone who likes antiques. Changing exhibits cover everything from the history of theater in New York to the city's different ethnic groups. The museum also offers an exceptionally diverse array of walking tours, children's programs, lectures, classes, and other events. Call the Education Department (ext. 206) for more information, or pick up a seasonal schedule at the information desk right inside the entrance. **Hours:** Wednesday through Saturday from 10 to 5, Sunday from noon to 5. Call before going, as the museum plans to upgrade and expand in the near future and may temporarily move out of its current home altogether. **Admission:** free, but contributions of $5 for adults; $4 for senior citizens, students, and children; and $10 for families are strongly encouraged.

MUSEUM OF JEWISH HERITAGE: A LIVING MEMORIAL TO THE HOLOCAUST
18 First Pl (adjacent to Battery Park)   212/968-1800

A newcomer to the New York museum scene, this exceptional place fills a real void in the city. In addition to being a museum, it is also a memorial to Holocaust victims and survivors. New York is, after all, the heart of Jewish history and culture in the United States, and it is fitting that such a thoughtfully conceived and carefully constructed museum has its home here. The museum is composed of three parts, one on each floor. The first floor is dedicated to Jewish life a century ago, the second to the persecution of Jews and the Holocaust, and the third to modern Jewish life and renewal. An eight-minute video is remarkably well done and sets the tone for your visit. This may not be a place for young children, and visitors should be prepared to take their time. Two additional notes: the view of New York Harbor, Ellis Island, and the Statue of Liberty from the museum's third floor is extraordinary, and a visit to the gift shop is worthwhile. Security here is very tight, and the rule against food in the galleries is strictly enforced. The museum itself looks a bit like a layered cupcake and is surrounded by a black gate adjacent to Battery Park at the southern end of Battery Park City. **Hours:** Sunday through Friday from 9 to 5 (Thursday until 8). The museum closes early on Friday during winter and is closed on all Jewish holidays. **Admission:** $7 for adults, $5 for students and senior citizens.

MUSEUM OF MODERN ART

11 W 53rd St (bet Fifth Ave and Ave of the Americas)   212/708-9480

Affectionately known as "MoMA" to New Yorkers, the Museum of Modern Art is among the most important museums in the world devoted to modern art. If a major contemporary work is not at one of the two Guggenheims, chances are it's at MoMA. This is a big museum, and wandering through its many galleries takes time. MoMA does host some traveling exhibits, but its permanent collection is as enormous as it is impressive. If you need to rest, spend some time in the sculpture garden behind the front entrance on the ground floor or head for the very pleasant and not terribly expensive (although sometimes quite crowded) Garden Cafe at the far northeastern corner of the ground floor. Sette MoMA, an Italian restaurant overlooking the sculpture garden, is a popular place for lunch and dinner. (Call 212/708-9710 for reservations.) MoMA also offers lectures, workshops, films, and a weekly "Conversations with Contemporary Artists" series on Friday evenings, as well as jazz in the Garden Cafe. Information and schedules are available at the information desk in the main lobby. **Hours:** Daily except Wednesday from 10:30 to 6 (Friday until 8:30). **Admission:** $9.50 for adults, $6.50 for students with ID and senior citizens, free for children under 16 accompanied by an adult, and "pay-what-you-wish" for everybody on Friday evenings between 4:30 and 8:30.

MUSEUM OF TELEVISION AND RADIO

25 W 52nd St (bet Fifth Ave and Ave of the Americas)   212/621-6800

Television fans of all ages will definitely not want to miss this terrific place (or its West Coast branch, opened in 1996 in Beverly Hills!). Its extensive collection includes thousands of radio and television programs and commercials, many of which are periodically shown to the public and all of which are available for individual viewing. Indeed, the museum's computerized catalog makes six decades worth of television immediately accessible. Several galleries display changing exhibits on every imaginable aspect of television and radio, but most people come to watch their favorite shows. Check the schedule in the lobby or give the museum a call to find out what is going on at any given time. The International Children's Television Festival, held every spring, is particularly fun. I suggest going on a weekday, as the museum gets crowded on weekends. **Hours:** Tuesday through Sunday from noon to 6 (Thursday until 8). The theater stays open on Friday until 9. **Admission:** $6 for adults, $4 for students with ID and senior citizens, $3 for children under 14.

NATIONAL ACADEMY OF DESIGN

1083 Fifth Ave (bet 89th and 90th St)   212/369-4880

Founded in 1825, this museum, fine-arts school, and artists association was modeled after the Royal Academy in London. In addition to workshops and classes for artists, the Academy has changing exhibits of American and European paintings and other art. During the Academy's "Annual Exhibition," some of the work is actually for sale. The museum is in a surprisingly large townhouse, and wandering through its three floors of galleries is a real pleasure. Winslow Homer, Thomas Eakins, and John Singer Sargent are just a few of the artists who have been members of the academy and whose work is part of its permanent collection. A small museum shop featuring work by artist members sits inside the museum's lobby. For information on lectures and other programs, call 212/369-4880 or pick up a seasonal schedule at the museum's information desk in the lobby. For information about the school itself, call 212/996-1908.

Hours: Wednesday, Thursday, Saturday, and Sunday from noon to 5, Friday from 10 to 6. **Admission:** $8 for adults, $4.50 for students, children under 16 and senior citizens.

NATIONAL MUSEUM OF THE AMERICAN INDIAN
1 Bowling Green (at the foot of Broadway)   212/668-6624

Opened in late 1994, this replaces the old Museum of the American Indian on Audubon Terrace and is the first of three planned museums showcasing the Smithsonian's enormous collection of North, Central, and South American Indian art and artifacts. (Assuming budget cuts don't scuttle the plan, the other two will be in Washington, D.C.) The museum's permanent exhibit—"Creation's Journey: Masterwork of Native American Identity and Belief"—offers insight into the histories and cultures of the incredibly diverse Native American community. A second exhibit—"All Roads Are Good: Native Voices on Life and Culture"—is the result of 23 Native American artists, scholars, elders, story-tellers, and others from throughout the Western Hemisphere who got together to choose artifacts for display and discuss what those artifacts mean to them. As if the exhibits weren't special enough, the spectacular building—the former U.S. Customs House—is worth visiting in and of itself. Take time to look up at the intricate detail in the ceilings, and make sure to go down the exquisite staircase to one of the museum's two gift shops. **Hours:** daily (except Christmas) from 10 to 5 (Thursday until 8). **Admission:** free.

— Millennium Note —

What may be the smallest chunk of real estate in Manhattan is a triangle in the sidewalk on Seventh Avenue South between Waverly Place and Perry Street. Designated Block 12, Lot 46, it measures one foot three inches, two feet one and a half inches, and one foot nine and an eighth inches on its three sides.

NEW MUSEUM OF CONTEMPORARY ART
583 Broadway (bet Houston and Prince St)   212/219-1222

This showcase for contemporary artists is definitely worth a visit if you're in Soho. Its changing exhibits feature individual artists and thematic collections, which tend to be unusually well displayed and conceived. The museum is known for its multidisciplinary approach to art, focusing on group and solo shows accompanied by educational public programs. The museum, which recently doubled its size, offers gallery talks and group tours tailored to the age and interest of the participants. **Hours:** Wednesday and Sunday from noon to 6, Thursday through Saturday from noon to 8. **Admission:** $5 for adults; $3 for artists, students, and senior citizens; free for those under 18 and for everyone from 6 p.m. to 8 p.m. on Thursday.

NEW YORK CITY FIRE MUSEUM
278 Spring St (between Hudson and Varick St)   212/691-1303

This museum, located in a turn-of-the-century firehouse, is dedicated to the history of fire-fighting and fire prevention. In addition to a relatively modern fire engine, a quite old ladder truck, a hand-pulled hand pump from 1820, and many other fire apparatuses, the museum displays pictures from fire stations all over New York, a collection of 19th-century leather fire buckets, and an assortment of badges. You'll also find collections of presentation shields, trumpets, and Currier and Ives prints. Older kids will love looking at the equipment, and most things are quite well displayed. But be forewarned: although the museum hopes to create a climbing and "hands-on" exploring space for younger children in the future, "hands-off" is the rule now. The museum is a bit out of the way, although less so since Soho has become a major tourist destination. Call ahead to make sure your visit isn't going to coincide with that of a large school group. **Hours:** Tuesday through Sunday from 10 to 4. **Admission:** a "suggested contribution" of $4 for adults, $2 for students and senior citizens, and $1 for children under 12.

NEW YORK HISTORICAL SOCIETY
Central Park West bet 76th and 77th St   212/873-3400

For two centuries, the New York Historical Society has been what the *New York Times* once described as "New York City's archive and attic." The grand old institution is a real treasure trove, with more than half a million books; 2 million maps, manuscripts, and other documents; thousands of pieces of art; and even John James Audubon's watercolor "Birds of America" series. Unfortunately, however, the Historical Society fell on hard times and was forced to close its doors in 1993. Thanks to an innovative director and some rather unorthodox fundraising, those doors and the galleries inside were reopened several years ago. While I'm a big fan of the Museum of the City of New York and encourage anyone interested in New York's history to spend time there, the Historical Society also has tremendously deep archives and mounts a wide array of interesting exhibits. The Luman Reed Gallery (complete with Thomas Cole's *The Course of the Empire* and many of Audubon's works) and the library (open only to those 18 and older) are great treats. Children, particularly those who live in New York, will be interested in Kid City, a new hands-on exhibit designed to compare life on the Upper West Side in 1901 to life there today. **Hours:** Tuesday through Sunday from 11 to 5 (library closed on Sunday). **Admission:** a "suggested donation" of $5 for adults and $3 for senior citizens and children.

NEW YORK TRANSIT MUSEUM
Boerum Pl at Schermerhorn St, Brooklyn   718/243-8601

Anybody interested in New York's amazing subway system will understand why I've made an exception to my "only in Manhattan" rule to include this wonderful museum. It is run by the Metropolitan Transit Authority and is technically devoted to both buses and subways. Old subway cars and exhibits detailing the system's history are the real draws here. Kids will love getting on and off the cars, while history buffs will get a kick out of the old signs and ads like those publicizing the Miss Subways competition. At least for now, the entire museum is housed in an abandoned station a couple of blocks from Brooklyn's Borough Hall. (It may move to another abandoned station in Manhattan in the future.) Take the 2, 3, 4, or 5 subway line to the Borough Hall Station, and then look at the neighborhood map by the token booth to get your bearings. On weekends and in summer, the museum offers a wide range of popular workshops and other programs for adults, children, and families. If you're going on a weekday during the school year, call ahead to make sure your visit doesn't coincide with that of a large school group. A small Transit Museum gallery recently opened in Grand Central Station as well. (Monday through Friday from 8 to 8, 10 to 4 on Saturday). **Hours:** Tuesday through Friday from 10 to 4 (Wednesday till 6), and Saturday and Sunday from noon to 5. **Admission:** $3 for adults, $1.50 for children under 17 and senior citizens.

NEWSEUM/NY
580 Madison Ave (bet 56th and 57th St)   212/317-7596

A branch of the Newseum in Arlington, Virginia, Newseum/NY is a bit of an oasis in the hustle and bustle of midtown. Its programs—everything from photography exhibits to lectures, films, and panel discussions—are all designed to enhance the general public's understanding of journalism and the First Amendment. Its gallery space is small but exhibits are consistently provocative and well conceived. Tours are offered at 2:30 on weekday afternoons and by appointment. **Hours:** Monday through Saturday from 10 to 5:30. **Admission:** free.

NICHOLAS ROERICH MUSEUM
319 W 107th St (just off Riverside Dr)   212/864-7752

Located in an aged but still elegant townhouse on an unusually pleasant block between Riverside Drive and Broadway, this museum is dedicated to the life and work of Russian-born artist-philosopher-author-educator Nicholas Roerich. History buffs may remember him as author of the Roerich Pact, a 1935 agreement signed by President Franklin Roosevelt and the leaders of 20 Latin American countries stipulating that a banner be flown over museums, monuments, and other cultural institutions in times of war and peace alike. You'll find a number of books written by and about Roerich in several languages, but the real reason to come to this museum is the large collection of unusual paintings of the Himalayas, various religious scenes, and other subjects by Roerich. Very little is labeled and the displays are quite informal, but it's a pleasant place off the beaten track. Seasonal schedules of poetry readings, concerts, and other events are available in the front hall, as are postcards with reproductions of some of Roerich's paintings. **Hours:** Tuesday through Sunday from 2 to 5. **Admission:** free.

PAINEWEBBER GALLERY
1285 Ave of the Americas (bet 51st and 52nd St)   212/713-2885

The folks at PaineWebber have set aside the east end of their wood-paneled lobby for a variety of changing exhibits. Much like those at the gallery in the Equitable Center's lobby, the exhibits here are often high quality. Look for printed exhibit information on either side of the lobby immediately inside the entrance. **Hours:** Monday through Friday from 8 to 6. **Admission:** free.

ROSE MUSEUM
Carnegie Hall (Seventh Ave at 57th St)   212/903-9629

Actually just a handsome, wood-paneled room with well-lit display cases, this small museum is home to a permanent exhibit on the history of Carnegie Hall and the people who have made their careers here as well as an annual temporary exhibit coinciding with a special event or anniversary. The museum, on the second floor of Carnegie Hall, is open during intermissions of performances, but it's also accessible to the general public during the day. The entrance is at 154 West 57th Street (take the elevator in the Weill Recital Hall lobby to the second floor). **Hours:** daily except Wednesday from 11 to 4:30. **Admission:** free.

THE SKYSCRAPER MUSEUM
16 Wall St   212/968-1961

Think of New York, and one of the first images that comes to mind is the skyline, with its many skyscrapers. New York doesn't have the tallest building anymore. It may not even have the most tall buildings of any city. But this is where skyscrapers were born, and it's only fitting that the city is home to a museum dedicated to the subject. The Skyscraper Museum has moved around a bit and eventually may find a home in a new hotel in Battery Park City. Wherever it lands, however, the museum is an interesting place to poke around. **Hours:** Tuesday through Saturday from noon to 6. **Admission:** free (a small donation is suggested).

SOUTH STREET SEAPORT MUSEUM
east end of Fulton St   212/748-8600

This is not a museum in the traditional sense but rather a collection of exhibits, ships, stores, and restaurants spread throughout 11 square blocks of what was once the city's bustling port and economic center. You can walk around the South Street Seaport complex and look at everything from a distance without paying a dime, a fact that has spelled financial trouble for the museum in recent years. That museum includes the four-masted *Peking,* a light ship called the *Ambrose,* a tall ship called the *Wavertree* (which is now being restored), several galleries with changing exhibitions, a printer's shop, and a children's center with all sorts of hands-on workshops and displays. Paying admission to visit these places is worth it, particularly since your money goes to support educational outreach, historical research and preservation, and urban archaeological programs. Stop by the visitors center a block and a half down Fulton Street from the main entrance on your right or the ticket booth on Pier 16 to get a map and more information. On any given day (particularly in the warmer months), you'll find all sorts of special tours and activities throughout this fascinating complex. **Hours:** daily from 10 to 6 (Thursday until 8) between April 1 and September 30; daily except Tuesday from 10 to 5 from October 1 to March 31. Restaurants and some stores stay open longer in summer. **Admission:** $6 for adults, $5 for senior citizens over 65, $4 for students with ID, $3 for children under 12.

STUDIO MUSEUM IN HARLEM
144 W 125th St (bet Malcolm X and Adam Clayton Powell, Jr. Blvd)
212/864-4500

This light and modern space is a real jewel. The name reflects its original mission to be a studio for working artists. Since its inception more than three decades ago, it has evolved into a premier museum of contemporary and traditional African, Caribbean, and African-American art. The museum mounts exhibits from its permanent collection and plays host to traveling ones. It also offers lectures, gallery talks, performances, and other programs throughout the year. (To get to the museum from midtown, take the M101 bus up Third Avenue to the corner of 125th Street and Malcolm X Boulevard. To return, board the M101 bus downtown from the opposite corner of what becomes Lexington Avenue.) **Hours:** Wednesday, Thursday, and Friday from 10 to 5, Saturday and Sunday from 1 to 6. **Admission:** $5 for adults, $3 for students and senior citizens, $1 for children under 12.

THEODORE ROOSEVELT BIRTHPLACE
28 E 20th St (bet Broadway and Park Ave)   212/260-1616

Tucked on a side street in a neighborhood often overlooked by New Yorkers and visitors alike (although the street was once among the city's most elegant), this wonderful brownstone is a reconstruction of Theodore Roosevelt's childhood home. The original building was torn down in 1916 but rebuilt by the president's sisters and wife using original blueprints and the house next door as a model. The rooms were then furnished and decorated largely as they had been in Teddy's childhood. You come in at what was once the servants' entrance on the ground floor and browse through a collection of pictures, clothing, and other items that belonged to the Roosevelt family in a wonderful wood-paneled room. Then you are taken through the living quarters on the second and third floors by a National Park Service guide. (This is a National Historic Site run by the U.S. Park Service.) If you're interested in presidential history and the late 19th and early 20th centuries, or if you just want to see how the wealthy lived in the 1850s and 1860s, put this museum on your itinerary. Tours are given on the hour. **Hours:** Wednesday through Sunday from 9 to 5 (final tour begins at 4). **Admission:** tours cost $2 for adults, free for senior citizens and children under 17.

UKRAINIAN MUSEUM
203 Second Ave (bet 12th and 13th St)   212/228-0110

Founded by the Ukrainian National Women's League of America in 1976 and housed in the top two floors of a townhouse on the northern edge of the East Village, this out-of-the-way place is a real find for anybody interested in the Ukraine and the heritage of its people. The best time to visit is the roughly two-month period around Easter, when the museum displays its extraordinary collection of *pysanky,* the elaborately decorated Ukrainian Easter eggs that were once used as talismans to ward off evil spirits. The museum also sponsors demonstrations and classes during this period and around Christmas. You'll find Ukrainian costumes and crafts on display all year round and a small gift shop on the fifth floor. The museum is very much a part of New York's Ukrainian immigrant community. **Hours:** Wednesday through Sunday from 1 to 5. **Admission:** $1 for adults, 50 cents for senior citizens and students, free for children under 12.

WHITNEY MUSEUM OF AMERICAN ART
945 Madison Ave (at 75th St)   212/570-3676

This museum has a decidedly modern focus, although the Whitney's collection includes works by American artists from throughout this country's history. Several exhibits run concurrently, some focusing on a single artist and others built around a theme. If you're interested in gallery talks, special events, or what's on display at any given time, pick up a "This Week at the Whitney" schedule outside the museum's main entrance or drop by the information desk just inside the front door. Also look here for some innovative family programs. A branch of Sarabeth's Kitchen, long a popular East Side restaurant, is located on the museum's lower level. **Hours:** Wednesday, Friday, Saturday, and Sunday from 11 to 6, Thursday from 1 to 8. **Admission:** $9 for adults, $7 for students with ID and senior citizens over 62, free for children under 12 and for everybody on Thursday evening from 6 to 8.

The small **Whitney Gallery and Sculpture Court** is located in the lobby of the Philip Morris Building (120 Park Avenue). The gallery is open weekdays from 11 to 6 (until 7:30 on Thursday evening), and admission is free. The sculpture court, which doubles as a pleasant sitting area, is open Monday through Saturday from 7:30 a.m. until 9:30 p.m., Sunday from 11 to 7. Call 917/663-2453 for more information.

YESHIVA UNIVERSITY MUSEUM
2520 Amsterdam Ave (at 185th St)   212/960-5390

Located on the main campus of Yeshiva University, this often overlooked museum houses an exceptional collection of paintings, books, religious artifacts, and other things related to Jewish life and culture. It mounts one major exhibit each year, in addition to smaller exhibits that change throughout the year. Ask about special holiday events and workshops for adults and children. Before heading up here, you ought to know that the university campus is safe but the surrounding neighborhood can get rough after dark. It's also full of steep hills, in case you're thinking about walking around. The M101 bus will take you up Third Avenue to the museum and back down again via Lexington Avenue. **Hours:** Tuesday, Wednesday, and Thursday from 10:30 to 5, Sunday from noon to 6. The museum is closed on Jewish holidays. **Admission:** $3 for adults, $2 for senior citizens and children, free for children under 4.

Parks

As hard as it may be to believe when you're standing amidst the skyscrapers of midtown, Manhattan has almost 2,600 acres of parkland. That means 17% of the city is grass, rocks, lakes, playgrounds, and walking trails. Spanning 843 acres in the middle of the island, Central Park is the biggest and certainly the most famous. Smaller ones like Carl Schurz Park and Lighthouse Park on Roosevelt Island can sometimes be more peaceful, however, because fewer people know about them. Inwood Hill Park and Fort Tryon Park on Manhattan's northern tip are so wooded and hilly that you won't believe you're in New York.

Unless you are going to a scheduled event such as a play or concert, you probably don't want to walk around in any park at night. (It is worth noting, however, that the Central Park police precinct is the safest in all of Manhattan.) If you are by yourself, stay away from isolated areas and dense shrubs even during the day. Unfortunately, funds for park upkeep have been cut and some areas of the larger parks are looking a bit shabby these days. All that said, however, the parks are real treasures to explore and enjoy—and they offer a wonderful respite from the concrete and chaos.

The following is an annotated listing of some of the city's biggest parks, as well as some personal favorites among the lesser known:

Battery Park—Named for the gun battery built along its old shoreline during the War of 1812, this 23-acre park sits at the very southern tip of Manhattan, below State Street and Battery Place. Castle Clinton, a National Monument originally built as a fort during the War of 1812, is located here. This is the place to buy tickets for trips to the Statue of Liberty and Ellis Island. One of the last remaining kiosks for the original subway system is in Battery Park, too. The Staten Island Ferry Terminal is adjacent to the park's eastern edge. The marvelous new National Museum of the American Indian is directly north of the park, and the Museum of Jewish Heritage is on the park's northwest edge. You'll find lots of benches and pathways here, as well as an excellent view of New York Harbor. A major renovation of the park recently got underway and may culminate with a rebuilding of the Castle Clinton fort itself.

Bryant Park—Behind the New York Public Library (from 40th to 42nd streets between Fifth Avenue and Avenue of the Americas), this was the site of the 1853 World's Fair, where Isaac Singer unveiled his sewing machine and Elisha Otis introduced his elevator. After years of neglect, the park underwent a multimillion-dollar renovation in the early 1990s and is now a real gem. The benches are great resting spots, and you'll find lots of vendors and a fine garden in the spring and summer. You'll also find games like checkers and Scrabble for rent, toy boats to rent and sail in the fountain, and free movies on Monday nights in summer. Bryant Park even has clean and safe public bathrooms (just off 42nd Street, behind the library), complete with security guards, attendants, and fresh flowers in the ladies' room. There is also a good restaurant, the Bryant Park Grill.

Carl Schurz Park—Between East End Avenue and the East River from 84th to 90th streets, this is probably the safest public park in the city. Named for a German immigrant-turned-U.S. Senator and Secretary of the Interior, the park includes Gracie Mansion, the official residence of New York's mayor. In addition to a great view of barge traffic along the East River, the park offers plenty of benches and playgrounds.

Central Park—Designed in 1858 by Frederick Law Olmsted, the same landscape architect who designed the U.S. Capitol Grounds in Washington, D.C., this is the ultimate urban park. Its 843 acres are bounded on the south and north by 59th and 110th streets, and on the east and west by Fifth Avenue and Central Park West. The park has two ice-skating rinks (in winter), lakes, ponds, a marvelous wildlife conservation center, theaters, jogging tracks, a reservoir, baseball diamonds and other playing fields, playgrounds, tennis courts, a miniature golf course (in summer), and a castle. You can even find a wonderful restaurant (Park View at the Boathouse, near 72nd Street on the east side), a more downscale cafe (near 65th Street on the west side), and two warm-weather sidewalk Italian cafes (inside the Columbus Circle entrance). There's lots of open space and 58 miles of paths. For maps and a current schedule of events, stop by the Visitor Information Center at the Dairy, just behind Wollman Rink at about what would be 65th Street and Avenue of the Americas (if those roads went into the park); the Henry Luce Nature Observatory, in Belvedere Castle at mid-park near 79th Street; or at the Charles A. Dana Discovery Center, in the park's northeast corner, near 110th Street and Fifth Avenue. You can also call 212/794-6564 between 10 and 4 from Tuesday to Sunday for current information. If you ever get lost in the park, it might help to know that the first digits of the number plate on the lampposts correspond to the nearest cross street. Particularly in warmer months and on weekends, the park is a paradise for walkers, joggers, bike riders, and rollerbladers. In summer, Central Park is home to a wide variety of cultural events, including Shakespeare in the Park, various concerts on the "Summer Stage," and free concerts by the New York Philharmonic and the Metropolitan Opera.

Fishers Park—One of what are commonly called "vest-pocket parks," because of their small size, this pleasant surprise is tucked between Avenue of the Americas and Seventh Avenue off 54th and 55th streets. It has a fountain, trees, greenery, tables, seats, and working pay phones.

Fort Tryon Park—This 66-acre gift from John D. Rockefeller, Jr., extends from Riverside Drive to Broadway and from 192nd Street to Dyckman Street. Home to the Cloisters, this hilly and wooded park offers magnificent views of the Hudson River and the Palisades. Make sure to visit the beautiful but little known Heather Garden, the largest public garden in Manhattan. Take a friend along, however, if you plan on exploring off the beaten path here.

Greenacre Park — Another vest-pocket park, this was a gift from the daughter of John D. Rockefeller, Jr. It's located on 51st Street between Second and Third avenues. On a nice day during the work week, follow the lunchtime crowds.

Hudson River Park — In Battery Park City, stretching from the World Financial Center down to the Museum of Jewish Heritage, this delightful riverside park opened in 1992. You'll find great playgrounds, walkways, and wide open spaces. Particularly in warmer months, the park's spectacular views of the Hudson River, New York Harbor, and the Statue of Liberty make a trip here well worth the effort.

Inwood Hill Park — The second largest park in Manhattan, Inwood Hill Park is at the northwest tip of Manhattan. Bordered by the Harlem River to the north and the Hudson River on the west, this rugged park of nearly 200 acres is home to a marsh, caves once used by Algonquin Indians, and the island's last remaining stands of virgin timber (most of the original forests were cut down by British troops during the Revolutionary War). Hiking and climbing enthusiasts will love its relatively unspoiled wilderness, but I suggest going in groups for safety sake. Drop by the Urban Ecology Center (inside the park at 218th St) for information on nature walks and other scheduled events.

Lighthouse Park on Roosevelt Island — If you really want to get away but only have a little time, go to Lighthouse Park. Located on the northern tip of Roosevelt Island in the middle of the East River, this park has picnic facilities and clean, open space, as well as the lighthouse for which it is named. The view of the Manhattan skyline from the west side of the park is among the best in the city. A tram to Roosevelt Island leaves frequently from its own station on Second Avenue between 59th and 60th streets. It costs $1.50 each way, and the bus that takes you from the tram station to the northern end of the island costs another dime.

Riverside Park — Running between Riverside Drive and the Hudson River from 72nd to 159th streets, this is another one of Frederick Law Olmsted's creations. In addition to playgrounds, great paths for walking, jogging, and bicycling, popular clay tennis courts at 92nd Street, and a terrific view of the Hudson River, the park is home to the new Eleanor Roosevelt statue (at 72nd Street), the 79th Street Boat Basin, the Soldiers and Sailors Monument (at 89th Street), and Grant's Tomb (at 122nd Street). People used to complain about erosion and vandalism in the park, but those who live around it now take adoptive responsibility for its upkeep (including Bette Midler, who has hired people to make sure its more remote reaches are kept clean!).

Stuyvesant Square Park — This park was given to the city by Peter Stuyvesant, the last Dutch governor of "Nieuw Amsterdam" in the mid-17th century. Once among the most elegant places in the city, it still has a little charm and a lot of benches. You'll find it on both sides of Second Avenue at the southern end of the Gramercy Park neighborhood, between 15th and 17th streets.

Union Square Park — Once known for its drug scene, this old park has really come back to life. It stretches from 14th to 17th streets between Broadway (called Union Square West through here) and Park Avenue South (Union Square East). It is home to the city's most popular Greenmarket, and you'll also find playgrounds, picnic benches, and, in warmer months, an outdoor bar and cafe near the Abraham Lincoln statue at the park's north end. The George Washington statue at the south end was erected in 1856 to commemorate the 80th anniversary of the signing of the Declaration of Independence.

Washington Square Park—Long considered the emotional if not geographic center of Greenwich Village, this park sits at the foot of Fifth Avenue and is best known for the Washington Memorial Arch. The park was constructed in 1827, but the marble arch was not dedicated until 1895. (It replaced a wooden one.) The park is near New York University, and its chess tables, playgrounds, and other features are much used by students and other neighborhood residents.

For recorded information on what's happening on any given day in the parks around Manhattan and the other boroughs, call 212/360-3456.

Places of Worship

Manhattan is home to some of the oldest, largest, and most famous churches and synagogues in the United States. These places, many of which are Episcopal churches—a relic of the city's life under British colonial rule—are integral to the social and architectural history of the city. Many of them allow people to come in and look around. You should always behave respectfully and remember that you are in a place of worship. Here are some of my favorites.

Abyssinian Baptist Church—Located at 132 West 138th Street (between Frederick Douglass and Adam Clayton Powell, Jr. boulevards), this church is one of the oldest in Harlem, and it boasts one of the city's largest congregations. Made famous by the late U.S. congressman, the Rev. Adam Clayton Powell, Jr., the church has a display of pictures of Powell and memorabilia from his career. Call 212/862-7474 for information about services and programs.

Cathedral Church of St. John the Divine—Facing Amsterdam Avenue at 112th Street near Columbia University, this magnificent Episcopal cathedral has been under construction for more than a century and will be among the largest Christian houses of worship in the world when (and if) it is completed sometime in this new century. The stonework, art, and stained glass are exceptional, as is the combination of Gothic, Romanesque, and Byzantine architectural styles. Even if you are not particularly interested in cathedrals, architecture, or religion, this somewhat out-of-the-way marvel is a must-see. To give you some sense of its scale, the Statue of Liberty could fit comfortably inside the main sanctuary. The rose window over the entrance is 40 feet in diameter! The Cathedral Shop, in what will one day be the cathedral's north transcept, has an eclectic assortment of books and gifts (see the "Museum and Library Shops" section in Chapter VI for more information). Call 212/316-7540 for information about services and other programs, including the annual blessing of the animals. If you visit in spring or summer, be sure to explore the fountains, peacocks, and rose garden tucked in the grounds immediately south of the cathedral. (For information about tours, see the "Tours" section later in this chapter, or call 212/932-7314.)

Central Synagogue—On the southwest corner of Lexington Avenue and 55th Street, this reform synagogue is the oldest continuously used synagogue in the city. Completed in 1872, it was designed by Henry Fernbach and is a rare example of early Victorian religious architecture. The beautiful Moorish Revival exterior, complete with magnificent carved wooden doors, is well worth a look. A fire several years ago did extensive damage, but the congregation wasted no time rebuilding this gem. Call 212/838-5122 for information about services and programs.

Church of the Holy Trinity — Near Gracie Mansion at 316 East 88th Street (between First and Second avenues), this Episcopal church is a French Gothic marvel that dates back a hundred years. It's a favorite of classical music lovers because of its frequent winter concerts. Call 212/289-4100 for information about services, concerts, and programs.

Church of the Transfiguration — On the north side of 29th Street between Fifth and Madison avenues, this Episcopal church is known to older generations as "the little church around the corner." It's known to younger generations for its marvelous programs of the music of Vivaldi and other composers throughout the year. You'll find a lovely garden in front of this low-lying brick church and beautiful stained-glass windows inside. Call 212/684-6770 for information about services, concerts, and programs.

First Presbyterian Church — On the west side of Fifth Avenue between 11th and 12th streets, this church is the direct decendant of the first Presbyterian congregation in the United States. The building itself was built in 1846 (the original church was on Wall Street). The sanctuary has wooden pews with doors, a beautifully carved wooden pulpit that towers over the congregation, and a glorious blue rose window. Call 212/675-6150 for more information about services and programs.

Grace Church — On Broadway between 10th and 11th streets, this exquisite Episcopal church was built in 1846 and is one of several in New York designed by James Renwick, Jr. It is an elegant Gothic presence in the neighborhood and one of the most important examples of early Gothic Revival architecture in the country. The church is best known for its daily prayer services, carved pulpit, and outstanding music. Call 212/254-2000 for information about services and programs.

Holy Trinity Greek Orthodox Cathedral — Located on the north side of 74th Street between First and Second avenues, this magnificent brick cathedral may not look like much from the outside. Once inside the lovely wooden doors, however, you'll think you're in ancient Greece. Call 212/288-3215 for information about services and programs.

Islamic Center of New York — Opened in 1991, this sleek mosque and its grounds are hard to miss, as they dominate Third Avenue between 96th and 97th streets. The mosque, a gift to New York's Muslim community from several Islamic countries, was built at an angle so that it faces Mecca. Call 212/722-5234 for information about services and programs or to arrange a visit.

Marble Collegiate Church — At the northwest corner of Fifth Avenue and 29th Street, this stately church was designed by Samuel Warner in 1854 and made famous by Dr. Norman Vincent Peale. It is an example of Early Romanesque Revival, and it draws its name from the Tuckahoe marble used in its construction. Its congregation is quite large and socially active. Call 212/686-2770 for information about services and programs.

Riverside Church — A gift of John D. Rockefeller, Jr., this interdenominational church was inspired by the famous Chartres cathedral in France and can seat up to 2,500 people. Its 22-story bell tower dominates the northern end of Morningside Heights, and the 74-bell carillon can be heard throughout the area. (For $2 and a lot of energy, you can climb to the top!) Known for its beauty as well as the congregation's social activism, the church is located at 490 Riverside Drive, between 120th and 122nd streets. Call 212/870-6700 for information about services and programs.

St. Bartholemew's Church—Complete with a carved triple-arched portico (designed by architect Sanford White) and a mosaic dome, this brick and stone Episcopal church sits between 50th and 51st streets on Park Avenue. It has fallen on hard financial times in recent years but remains one of the most dramatic and beautiful sights in midtown. Call 212/751-1616 for information about services and programs.

St. Mark's in the Bowery—Constructed on the site of Peter Stuyvesant's personal chapel in 1799, this understated but elegant Episcopal church has lovely yards on either side. It is located on the northwest corner of 10th Street and Second Avenue in what is now the East Village but what was once Stuyvesant's farm. ("Bouwerie" is *farm* in Dutch.) Call 212/674-6377 for information about services.

St. Patrick's Cathedral—Designed by James Renwick, Jr., more than a century ago, this astonishing building is the largest Roman Catholic church in the United States and the seat of the archdiocese of New York. It takes up the entire block from 50th to 51st streets between Fifth and Madison avenues. The main organ alone has 9,000 pipes! Its steps along Fifth Avenue are a great place to rest your feet and watch the world go by. Call 212/753-2261 for information about services.

St. Paul's Chapel—On Broadway between Fulton and Vesey streets, this Episcopal parish is housed in the oldest church building in the city. Its construction began in 1764 when New York was New Amsterdam and America was a British colony, as the dates on the gravestones in the surrounding cemetery suggest. The interior may initially strike visitors as surprisingly plain but is, in fact, exceptionally elegant, understated, and lit by Waterford crystal chandeliers. (Look for George Washington's pew in the north aisle.) This is yet another church known for its music programs, often held on weekdays at lunchtime. Call 212/602-0874 for information about services, concerts, and programs.

St. Peter's Lutheran Church—The only really modern church on this list, St. Peter's is nestled under the towering Citicorp Center at the southeast corner of 54th Street and Lexington Avenue. The church has an extensive program of jazz, opera, and other music on Sunday and during the week. Look for a posted schedule outside the main entrance or call 212/935-2200 for information about services, concerts, and programs.

St. Thomas Episcopal Church—On the northwest corner of Fifth Avenue and 53rd Street, this beautiful church is best known for its magnificent music programs. The incredibly ornate stone carvings on the church's exterior, its lovely doors, and its stately bell tower make it a real presence on Fifth Avenue. Call 212/757-7013 for information about services, concerts, and programs.

Spanish and Portuguese Synagogue—Home of the orthodox Congregation Shearith Israel, founded in 1654 by descendents of Jews who fled the Spanish Inquisition, this synagogue was built in 1897 but contains remnants from its congregation's original synagogue, built on the Lower East Side in 1730. The Tiffany stained-glass windows are particularly impressive. The synagogue is located at 8 West 70th Street, near Central Park West. Call 212/873-0300 for information about services and programs.

Temple Emanu-El—Built in 1929 and capable of seating 2,500 people, this is the largest Reform synagogue in the world. Stained-glass windows and mosaics grace the interior, and the limestone facade is a beautifully carved combination of Eastern and Western architectural styles. While the entrance is at 1 East 65th Street, be sure to look at the doors on Fifth Avenue. Call 212/744-1400 for information about services and programs.

Trinity Church—At the intersection of Broadway and Wall streets in the heart of the Financial District, this is the third building of an Episcopal church founded in 1698 on land donated by King William III of England. This building was completed in 1846, although the oldest headstones in its 2.5-acre graveyard date back to 1681. Alexander Hamilton is among the many historic figures buried here. Believe it or not, Trinity Church was the tallest building in Manhattan for much of the 19th century. The church offers a small museum, guided tours (see "Tours" later in this chapter), and concerts, in addition to daily services. Call 212/602-0800 for information.

If you want to find out when services are held at churches, synagogues, and other places of worship, the first section of the Saturday *New York Times* includes advertisements for Catholic, Protestant, Ethical Culture, Hindu, and Jewish services under the heading "Religious Services." The Manhattan Yellow Pages' extensive listings can be found under the headings "Churches," "Synagogues," and "Religious Organizations."

Recreation

Visitors sometimes see Manhattan as nothing but concrete and can't imagine what those who live here do for exercise other than walking. The people who live here, however, know that you can do just about anything in New York that can be done anywhere else—and then some! Whether it's miniature golf, horseback riding, or scuba diving, chances are that New York has got it if you just know where to look. Unless otherwise noted, call the Manhattan Department of Parks and Recreation (212/360-8133) for information.

Baseball—There are seven public baseball diamonds in Central Park and at least a dozen more in other parts of Manhattan.

Basketball—Between schoolyards and city parks, you'll find more than a thousand public basketball courts in Manhattan. You can also try Basketball City, down by the Chelsea Piers Complex at Pier 63 (212/924-4040).

Bicycling—You can ride bikes on the 6.2-mile loop in Central Park, in Riverside Park, or on the 5.5-mile route that runs along the Hudson River down to Battery Park. You can even pedal the city's streets, if you have the nerve! One caveat: off-road mountain biking in New York is illegal and punishable with a $50 fine. Bicycles are available for rent during warmer months at Loeb Boathouse (212/517-2233) in Central Park for $10 an hour and at most bicycle shops in the city.

Billiards—Manhattan has several dozen pool and billiards halls. Chelsea Billiards (212/989-0096), at 54 West 21st Street, is the largest. You can also try the Billiard Club (212/206-7665), at 220 West 19th Street, or the Amsterdam Billiard Club (212/496-8180), at 344 Amsterdam Avenue.

Birdwatching—Believe it or not, Central Park is a tremendous spot for birdwatching. Of the roughly 800 species of birds in North America, nearly 300 have been spotted here. There's even a hotline reporting rare and interesting sightings (212/979-3070). Call the New York Audubon Society (212/691-7483) for information about outings, or check in at the Charles A. Dana Discovery Center (212/860-1370) or the Henry Luce Nature Observatory in Belvedere Castle (212/772-0210) in Central Park.

Boating and Sailing—Rowboats are rented at the Boathouse (212/517-2233) in Central Park between May and early October. Believe it or not, you can also rent a Venetian gondola, complete with gondolier, here on summer evenings. Other on-the-water alternatives include kayaking in New York Harbor with Atlantic Kayak Tours (914/246-2187) or through the Downtown Boathouse (212/966-1852); taking sailing lessons at North Cove Sailing School in Battery Park City (800/532-5552), Great Hudson Sailing Center at Chelsea Piers (212/741-7245), or Chelsea Sailing School (212/627-7245). For $2, boaters can take to the water from the Parks and Recreation Department's three launch sites in Manhattan (212/360-8131). (For information about bigger boats, see the "Manhattan on the Water" section of Chapter VII.)

Bowling—Try Bowlmor Lanes (212/255-8188) at 110 University Place (between 12th and 13th streets) or Leisure Time Bowling (212/268-6909), on the second floor of Port Authority Bus Terminal. There's also a new state-of-the-art facility in the Chelsea Piers Complex (212/835-2695).

Boxing—The city is full of boxing gyms, but boxers and fans alike seem to favor Church Street Boxing Gym (212/571-1333), at 25 Park Place.

Chess, Checkers, and Backgammon—For $4 an hour, you can play to your heart's content at the Backgammon Chess Club (212/787-4629), at 212 West 72nd Street. You can often find a game of chess in the afternoon and evening (it's open until midnight) at the Chess Shop (212/475-9580), at 230 Thompson Street. In warm weather, games of checkers are usually going at Washington Square Park, at the Chess and Checkers House in Central Park, or at Bryant Park.

Climbing—The city maintains an indoor climbing wall at the West 59th Street Recreation Center (212/397-3166), at 533 West 59th Street. Sports Center at the Chelsea Piers has a 10,000-square-foot rock-climbing wall (212/336-6000).

Fencing—If you're looking for a partner, try the New York Fencers Club (212/874-9800), at 154 West 71st Street, after 5 p.m. If you're looking for lessons, give the folks at Metropolis Fencing a call (212/463-8044). They can be found on the second floor at 45 West 21st Street.

Fishing—If you want to borrow poles and fish with the kids in the well-stocked Harlem Meer in Central Park in spring, summer, and fall, bring your picture ID to the Charles A. Dana Discovery Center (212/860-1370), near Fifth Avenue at 110th Street.

Golf—Unsurprisingly, Manhattan has not a single golf course. However, duffers can play at some of the nation's great courses, thanks to video technology, or go down to Chelsea Piers and hit a bucket of balls at the four-tiered driving range on Pier 59. If you have your heart set on a real golf course, call the Metropolitan Golfer's Club (800/463-8465). They have access to more than 20 public and semi-private courses throughout the area and will arrange for you to play and even rent clubs. The best public course in the outer boroughs is Split Rock, in the Bronx (718/885-1258). Legendary pro Jack Nicklaus is currently designing another course in the Bronx, as well!

Handball—Try the outdoor courts in Central Park near 97th Street and Transverse Road or in St. Vartan's Park at Second Avenue and 35th Street.

Horseback Riding—If you know how to ride, you can rent a horse at Claremont Riding Academy (175 West 89th Street, 212/724-5101) for $35 an hour and ride in either Central Park or the academy's ring. The academy offers lessons, too. You can also check out the Chelsea Equestrian Center on Pier 63, next to the Chelsea Piers complex at the west end of 23rd Street (212/367-9090).

Ice Skating—The most famous rink in New York and probably the world is the one in front of Rockefeller Plaza (212/332-7654), just off Fifth Avenue between 49th and 50th streets. Central Park also has rinks at its south and north ends: Lasker Rink (212/534-7639), near 110th Street and Lenox Avenue, and Wollman Rink (212/396-1010), near what would be 62nd Street and Avenue of the Americas. For a small, uncrowded rink, try Rivergate Rink (212/689-0035), at 401 East 34th Street. You can also try the clean, spacious rink in Riverbank State Park (212/694-3642), at 145th Street and Riverside Drive. Sky Rink (212/336-6100) used to be on the 16th floor of a building (hence, the name) but has moved to Chelsea Piers. Sky Rink is open all year, but the others have limited seasons, so call ahead to make sure they're open. All of them rent skates.

Model Boats—Model boats can be sailed on the Conservatory Water in Central Park, near Fifth Avenue at 74th Street. Regattas are held on Saturday in summer, and remote-controlled boats can be rented for $10 an hour. Model boats can also be found at the fountain at Bryant Park.

Ping Pong—Real players head to Fat Cat Billiards (212/675-6056), at 75 Christopher Street.

Racquetball—Try the Manhattan Plaza Racquet Club (212/594-0554), at 450 West 43rd Street, or Club La Raquette (212/245-1144), in the Parker Meridean Hotel at 119 West 56th Street.

Rollerblading—The proper name for this sport is "in-line skating," as Rollerblade is actually a brand name. Whatever you call it, it's still all the rage in Manhattan. You can rent skates by the hour or day from Blades Board & Skate West (212/787-3911), at 105 West 72nd Street; Blades Board & Skate East (212/996-1644), at 160 East 86th Street; Manhattan Sports (212/580-4753), at 2188 Broadway; and at a variety of other skating stores.

Roller Skating—Try the Lezly Dance and Skate School (212/777-3232), at 622 Broadway, or the Chelsea Piers Roller Rinks (212/336-6100).

Running—Two of Manhattan's most popular places to run are Riverside Park and the 1.5-mile trail around the reservoir in Central Park. If you want some other jogging routes or company (the latter is always a good idea), call the

New York Road Runners Club (212/860-4455). The Road Runners can also tell you about upcoming races.

Scuba Diving—PanAqua Diving (212/496-2267), at 166 West 75th Street, runs certification courses at various sites throughout the city. Also try Sea Horse Divers (212/517-2055), at 1416 Second Avenue.

Soccer—Central Park has four public soccer fields. One is on the Great Lawn, behind the Metropolitan Museum of Art, and three are in the North Meadow, near the park's north end.

Squash—Try the Park Avenue Athletic Complex (212/686-1085), at 3 Park Avenue; City Hall Squash Club (212/964-2677), at 25 Park Place; or Club La Raquette (212/245-1144), in the Parker Meridien Hotel at 119 West 56th Street.

Swimming—You can find public beaches in the other boroughs and out on Long Island, but swimming in Manhattan is almost entirely limited to pools. Believe it or not, endurance swimmers circumnavigate the island for the annual Manhattan Island, Marathon and plans are in the works to open a 400-yard strip of imported sand off the Gansevoort Pier on the Hudson River in 2003. Until then, however, inexpensive indoor options include the Asser Levy Pool (212/447-2020), at 23rd Street and Avenue A; the pool at the 59th Street Recreation Center (212/397-3166), at 533 West 59th Street; the pool at the John Jay College of Criminal Justice; and the pool in Riverbank State Park (212/694-3665), on Riverside Drive at 145th Street.

You can find a little bit of just about everything at the Ys in Manhattan. They include the **92nd Street YMHA** (212/427-6000), at 1395 Lexington Avenue; the **West Side YMCA** (212/875-4100), at 5 West 63rd Street; the **YWCA** (212/735-9753), at 610 Lexington Avenue; and the **McBurney YMCA** (212/741-9210), at 215 West 23rd Street.

For $25 a year ($10 for senior citizens over 55 and children 12 to 17), you can find all sorts of facilities and classes at the 13 recreation centers in Manhattan run by the Department of Parks and Recreation. Among the better ones are the **Asser Levy Recreation Center** (212/447-2020), at Avenue A and 23rd Street; the **59th Street Recreation Center** (212/397-3166), at 533 West 59th Street; and the **Carmine Recreation Center** (212/242-5228), at 1 Clarkson Street. Seasonal passes to **Riverbank State Park,** on Riverside Drive at 145th Street (212/694-3600), are inexpensive, and the facilities are excellent.

For information about gyms and fitness centers, see the "Health and Fitness" section of Chapter IV.

Tennis—Manhattan has more than a hundred public tennis courts. Permits cost $50 and can be purchased at the Arsenal (Fifth Avenue at 64th Street). For more information, call 212/360-8133. To find out about lessons at the Central Park Tennis Center, call 212/280-0201. A few of the many private facilities include Manhattan Plaza Racquet Club (212/594-0554), Sutton East Tennis (212/751-3452), and Columbus Tennis Club (212/662-8367). Believe it or not, you can even play tennis on one of two indoor courts tucked into the third floor of Grand Central Station. Call the Tennis Club at Grand Central (212/687-3841) for details.

Yoga—Try the Integral Yoga Institute in Greenwich Village (212/929-0586), at 227 West 13th Street, or on the Upper West Side (212/721-4000), at 200 West 72nd Street.

Sights and Other Pleasant Places

Some of the places that make New York unique don't fit neatly into "Museums," "Places of Worship," or any of the other categories included in this book. Many can be visited without a guide or a formal agenda—indeed, simply walking around and gazing is pleasurable. A diverse lot, the following list includes some of the most famous, interesting, and unusual sights and places in Manhattan. Unless otherwise noted, admission is free.

Alwyn Court Apartments—Of all the magnificent apartment buildings in New York, this is my favorite to look at from outside. Built between 1907 and 1909, it's a block from Carnegie Hall on the corner of 58th Street and Seventh Avenue. You could spend hours studying the elaborate carved terra-cotta exterior. Its features include a crowned salamander, the symbol of Renaissance art patron Frances I, in whose style the building was built. For the best view, cross the street.

Brooklyn Bridge—Spanning the East River between Manhattan and Brooklyn, this was the world's longest suspension bridge when built, and it remains one of the most spectacular. The 5,989-foot bridge took 15 years (1868-1883) and two generations of Roeblings to construct. After John Roebling, the engineer who designed the bridge, died from injuries sustained in an accident, his son Washington and wife Emily finished the project. An incredible view of New York Harbor and the city's skyline can be had by taking a stroll on the bridge's historic promenade. To reach it, go through the Municipal Building, just off Park Row on the southeast side of City Hall, and follow signs in the subway tunnel. Better yet, ask one of the police officers patroling the area for directions.

Carnegie Hall—On the corner of Seventh Avenue and 57th Street, this magnificent concert hall opened in 1891 with the American conducting debut of Peter Ilyich Tchaikovsky. Named for steel magnate Andrew Carnegie, it underwent a $60 million renovation several years ago that has improved its acoustics dramatically. Actually, it *restored* the acoustics of old by taking out a piece of concrete that was added during an earlier renovation! In addition, the seating capacity has been expanded to accommodate more than 2,800. The latest renovation will create an 800-seat performance space underground! If you want to visit during the day, take a tour or stop by the new Rose Museum at Carnegie Hall. (See the "Tours" and "Museums" sections of this chapter for more information.) For box-office information, call 212/247-7800 or drop by the lobby after 11 a.m. **Hours:** weekdays and Saturdays between 11 and 6, Sunday between noon and 6.

Castle Clinton National Monument—Probably the best known of Manhattan's seven National Parks—it's the gateway to two others and headquarters for them all—Castle Clinton is a red circular building in Battery Park, at the southern tip of Manhattan. Built on what was once an island as part of a series of forts designed to defend New York Harbor at the beginning of the 19th century, Castle Clinton has been different things through the years: an entertainment center, an immigrant receiving station (8 million came through between 1855 and 1890), and home to the New York Aquarium. Castle Clinton is best known as the place to buy tickets for the short boat rides to Ellis Island and the Statue of Liberty, but take a few minutes to visit the small museum detailing the site's history inside the door to your right. If all goes according to plan, a recently initiated renovation of Battery Park will culminate in the rebuilding of the fort built on this site during the War of 1812. **Hours:** daily from 9 to 5.

Central Park Wildlife Conservation Center — When people in New York hear the word *zoo*, they tend to think of the big one in the Bronx. But the Central Park Wildlife Conservation Center — the animal-friendly replacement for the dilapidated and depressing Central Park Zoo — is well worth a visit for kids and grownups alike. Divided into three sections by climate, the center includes an indoor rain forest, an outdoor temperate zone, and an indoor "Edge of the Icepack" exhibit. You'll find everything from a bat cave and a colony of leaf-cutter ants to Japanese snow monkeys and chinstrap penguins in this well-designed and manageably sized place. There are even a couple of polar bears! The new Tisch Children's Zoo will be a big hit with preschoolers. The center is located in Central Park at Fifth Avenue and 64th Street, behind the Arsenal. It sponsors classes, workshops, and other events for children and families on weekends and in warmer months. A visit on a winter weekday can be enjoyable, too. Call 212/861-6030 for general information or 212/439-6538 for information on classes and workshops. The gift shop is nothing special, but the hot-dog-and-French-fries crowd will love the small cafe. **Hours:** daily from 10 to 5:30 (4:30 from November through March). The last tickets are sold half an hour before closing. **Admission:** $3.50 for adults, $1.25 for senior citizens, 50¢ for children between 3 and 12, free for children under 3.

Chelsea Piers — When built at the beginning of the 20th century, Piers 59, 60, 61, and 62 on the Hudson River in Chelsea quickly became the destination for such elegant passenger ships as the *Lusitania* and the *Ile de France*. Indeed, the *Titanic* was headed for the Chelsea Piers when she sank in 1912. But when the length of ships increased in the 1930s and 1940s, new piers were built near 44th Street and the ones in Chelsea were largely abandoned. Thanks to a visionary developer, the Chelsea Piers have sprung back to life. Running between 17th and 23rd streets on the Hudson River, the Chelsea Piers Sports & Entertainment Complex encompasses 1.7 million square feet of golf (yes, there's a year-round, outdoor driving range in Manhattan!), ice skating, roller-blading/skating rink, rock climbing, gymnastics, and other activities in the gym and sports center. There's more: two restaurants, a 1.2-mile esplanade, a maritime center, and Silver Screen Studios (home to NBC's *Law and Order*). It's really an amazing place. Whether you're interested in classes for all ages and skill levels in just about every sport, membership at the sports center, or a one-time visit, call 212/336-6000. For more information about specific facilities at the Chelsea Piers, look in the "Recreation" section of this chapter.

Chrysler Building — One of New York's most recognizable sights, this art deco building on Lexington Avenue between 42nd and 43rd streets was built as the home of the Chrysler Corporation between 1928 and 1930 at the dawn of the automobile age. Its stainless-steel spire is easy to spot, but take a closer look at the radiator-cap gargoyles, based on the 1929 Chrysler, and the racing cars built into the relief. The Chrysler Corporation no longer maintains offices here and the interior isn't particularly interesting, but the lobby is open to the public.

Citicorp Center — A relative newcomer to the New York skyline, this 59-story building from 53rd to 54th streets between Lexington and Third avenues opened in 1977. Its slanted roof and modern design allow the Citicorp building to stand out among its more traditional neighbors, and its diverse shops, restaurants, and food court have made it a favorite with the midtown lunch crowd. Its large and pleasant atrium is often used for concerts, workshops, and other events on weeknights and weekends.

Conservatory Garden – In warmer months, this elegant and peaceful spot is alive with color – and, as a popular site for wedding pictures, with wedding parties as well. There are fountains, benches, and entrance gates that once were part of Cornelius Vanderbilt's Fifth Avenue mansion. The park, just off Fifth Avenue at 105th Street, is open from 8 in the morning to dusk.

Eldridge Street Synagogue – New York is full of time capsules, but this one must be seen to be believed. It is located at 12 Eldridge Street in what was the largely Jewish Lower East Side but is now the edge of Chinatown. This magnificently elaborate synagogue was home to more than a thousand worshipers at the turn of the century. Although the orthodox Congregation K'hal Adath Jeshurun hasn't missed a Sabbath since the synagogue opened in 1887, its numbers steadily shrank in the middle of this century, and the building fell into such disrepair that pigeons were living in the sanctuary. Thanks to a few visionary and committed people, the sanctuary has been saved, and an $8.5 million capital campaign is now underway. Call 212/219-0888 for more information or to schedule a tour of this special place. **Hours:** Drop-in tours are given Sunday at 11, noon, 1, 2, and 3, plus Tuesday and Thursday at 11:30 and 2:30. **Admission:** $4 for adults, $2.50 for students, senior citizens, and children. All money goes to the synagogue's restoration.

Empire State Building – When people think of New York, this 102-story building is often the first image that comes to mind. Conceived as a great office building but almost bankrupted when it opened in 1931 because of the Great Depression, the Empire State Building soars above its neighbors on Fifth Avenue between 33rd and 34th streets. The neighborhood and the building itself are a bit grimy these days, most of the staff is alternately bored and rude, and the deadly gunfire that erupted here in early 1997 still weighs heavily on everyone's mind. All that said, however, this New York landmark still draws almost 3 million visitors a year, and the views from the top live up to every expectation (assuming it's a relatively clear day or night). For more information about the outdoor terrace on the 86th floor and the indoor observation deck on the 102nd floor, call 212/736-3100, ext. 347. Although many people beg off, I urge you to make the trip to the 102nd floor – the views are spectacular. **Hours:** daily from 9:30 to midnight (the last tickets are sold at 11:25 p.m.). **Admission:** Tickets to the terrace and observation deck cost $6 for adults, $3 for children under 12, military personnel, and senior citizens over 62.

Federal Hall National Memorial (Here's a history test: where was the nation's first capital? Not Washington, D.C., or even Philadelphia. It was New York City. And the building that housed it (yes, one building housed the entire federal government!) occupied this site. George Washington took his first oath of office and Congress debated the Bill of Rights here. Earlier, this site was home to New York's first city hall (dating back to 1703). Federal Hall – a grand structure at the corner of Wall and Nassau streets that was built in 1842 as the U.S. Customs House – is now a National Monument run by the National Park Service with exhibits on the site's incredible history. It's also the starting point for wonderful walking tours of the area run by Heritage Trails New York. (See the "Tours" section of this chapter for more information.) Call 212/825-6888 for more information. **Hours:** weekdays from 9 to 5.

Flatiron Building—This 22-story architectural oddity was built at the intersection of Fifth Avenue and Broadway (at 23rd Street) in the early years of this century. The prow of the building is said to sit on the windiest street corner in Manhattan. Its triangular shape and terra cotta exterior have made it a familiar landmark, and the thriving neighborhood around it—the Flatiron District—carries its name.

Ford Foundation Gardens—The warm, multilevel garden in the Ford Foundation's glorious atrium is one of New York's great escapes, especially in the winter. The plants are watered with rain and steam condensation gathered in a cistern on the building's roof, and any coins thrown into the little pool are donated to UNICEF. The building is at 320 East 43rd Street (between First and Second avenues). You also can enter the atrium from 42nd Street. **Hours:** weekdays from 9 to 5.

Grand Central Terminal—This stunningly beautiful *beaux-arts* station was built at the turn of the century during the great age of railroads. It replaced a station built on the spot by Cornelius Vanderbilt after steam engines were banned south of 42nd Street in 1854. Scores of commuter trains to Westchester County and Connecticut arrive and depart here. But the real reason for visitors to come here is the incredible cleaning and renovation it recently underwent. To say that the project was long overdue is an understatement—the ceiling hadn't been cleaned since 1944! And the results are amazing! Retail space has doubled. Newcomers like Michael Jordan's the Steak House (yes, *that* Michael Jordan), have joined famous eateries like the Grand Central Oyster Bar Restaurant, and all sorts of great shops line the Lexington Avenue passageway and other spots throughout this grand place. Moreover, purists need not fear: Grand Central does not feel like a giant shopping mall. With its breathtaking ceiling, chandeliers, and carved marble details, this is first and foremost an elegant peephole into New York's past, present, and future. The Municipal Art Society offers a fascinating free tour of the station at 12:30 on Wednesdays. (See the "Tours" section of this chapter for more information.) The most dramatic entrance to Grand Central Station is through the driveway off Vanderbilt Avenue (a small street just east of Madison Avenue) at 43rd Street. Incidentally, the original waiting room off Park Avenue was cleaned and renovated, too, and is well worth a visit. While you're at it, spend a couple minutes at the Whisper Gallery outside the Oyster Bar. Stand in opposite corners facing the wall, and try to hear each other whisper! **Hours:** daily, from 5:30 a.m. to 1:30 a.m.

Grant's Tomb—If you're an American history buff, you'll want to venture to the far reaches of the Upper West Side to visit this not-so-subtle final resting place of President (and General) Ulysses S. Grant and his wife, Julia. When you're up at this lonely place in Riverside Park at 122nd Street, inspired by Napoleon's tomb in Paris and run today by the National Park Service, it's hard to imagine that a quarter million people filed through City Hall during the 48 hours Grant lay in state there and that a million more lined Broadway to watch his coffin being taken here. For anyone who remembers Grant's Tomb as being a bit seedy, the interior and exterior were cleaned and restored in 1997 as part of the centennial marking the dedication of this monument. Call 212/666-1640 for more information. **Hours:** daily from 9 to 5.

Haughwout Building—Considered by many architectural historians to be the finest example of cast-iron construction in the country, this building at the corner of Broadway and Broome Street was built in 1857 and contained one of

Elisha Otis' first elevators. Originally home to E. V. Haughwout (how-it) & Company—a silver, china, and porcelain manufacturer and retailer—the building fell on hard times around the turn of the century and was almost demolished in the 1960s. Thanks to the Landmarks Preservation Commission and its current owners, however, the Haughwout Building remains standing and is being cleaned and restored to some of its original grandeur.

Jefferson Market Library—I've included this courthouse-turned-public library because it looks like a castle in a fairy tale and people are always wondering exactly what it is. Built in 1877 and modeled after Mad King Ludwig's *Neuschwanstein* in Bavaria, it was saved from years of neglect and abuse by community activists and is now one of the city's nicest (and most used) public libraries. A wonderful community garden grows on its south side during warmer months. A bit of trivia: the library's bell, thought to be the second largest in New York, was rung in 1995 for the first time in 97 years. The last time it was rung? To commemorate Admiral George Dewey's triumph in Manila Bay during the Spanish-American War. Thus the graffiti on the bell, which reads: "To hell with Spain—Remember the *Maine*—1898"! It's now rung every day on the hour. You'll find the library at 425 Avenue of the Americas (at 10th Street) in Greenwich Village. Call 212/243-4334 for more information.

Lincoln Center—This amazing complex sits along Columbus Avenue near Broadway between 62nd and 65th streets. Constructed between 1959 and 1969, Lincoln Center includes Avery Fisher Hall, the New York State Theater, Alice Tully Hall, a wonderful public library and museum devoted to the performing arts, the Julliard School of Music, the Guggenheim Bandshell, the Vivian Beaumont Theater, and the Metropolitan Opera House. An open plaza, complete with a fountain, sits in the center of the complex, and small parks and open spaces flank the opera houses. The entire complex is a pleasant place to wander or sit for awhile, and craft fairs and free concerts are often held in the outdoor spaces in warmer months. (For information about backstage tours, see the "Tours" section in this chapter.) Make sure to visit the specialty stores inside the Opera House and to dine in the delightful Paneviro Ristorante (212/874-7000) at Avery Fisher Hall. For a real treat, operagoers can also dine in great style at the Grand Tier Restaurant (212/799-3400), located in a balcony of the Opera House's lobby. Call the Lincoln Center information hotline at 212/546-2656.

Madison Square Garden—The only real sporting arena in Manhattan, Madison Square Garden plays host to everything from the International Cat Show and the circus to professional basketball's New York Knicks. There have been three Madison Square Gardens; the one at this location opened in 1968. It covers most of the blocks from 31st to 33rd streets between Seventh and Eighth avenues. Oddly enough, Penn Station—the terminal for Amtrak and New Jersey Transit, through which 750 trains pass every day—sits directly underneath "the Garden." You'll also find the Paramount Theater inside the complex. (For information about tours, see the "Tours" section of this chapter.) To find out what's going on at any given time, call 212/465-6741.

New Amsterdam Theater—Say what you will about the Disney Company and its takeover of Times Square, but the $36 million renovation of this historic theater on 42nd Street just west of Broadway is nothing short of amazing. Built for $1.5 million at the turn of the last century, this theater housed the Ziegfeld Follies from 1913 to 1927 and later presented performers like Bob Hope and

Jack Benny. Painted brown and used as a movie theater in the 1970s and early 1980s, the New Amsterdam finally shut its doors in 1983. Pigeons, cats, and mushrooms the size of dinner plates made it home for the next 15 years, until Disney started cleaning it out. The theater is now home to the enormously popular *The Lion King*. (If you're interested in touring the theater, see the "Tours" section of this chapter.)

New York Public Library — The main branch of the extraordinary New York Public Library is a treasure trove for researchers and architecture fans alike. This beautiful building sits on Fifth Avenue between 40th and 42nd streets, adjacent to Bryant Park. The marble stairs and open areas outside — a favorite brown-bag lunch spot for people who work in the area — are dominated by statues of two lions, Patience and Fortitude. You'll find a gallery with changing exhibits and a terrific gift shop on the first floor. But the greatest treat for tourists and even hard-to-impress New Yorkers is the stunning recent renovation of the Rose Main Reading Room (actually two connected rooms) on the library's third floor. This is where the Gilded Age meets the computer age, and the results are splendid. A nonprofit group, Friends of the New York Public Library, offers frequent tours of exhibits and the library itself. (For more information, stop by the desk in the lobby or see the "Tours" section of this chapter.) You're also free to wander alone and marvel at this glorious place. Call 212/869-8089 for recorded information about the library, current exhibits, and special events. For information on branch libraries in Manhattan, call 212/621-0626. **Hours:** Monday, Thursday, Friday, and Saturday from 10 to 6, Tuesday and Wednesday from 11 to 7:30.

New York Public Library for the Performing Arts — If you're interested in the performing arts, put this amazing place at the top of your list. While it's not a museum, you'll always find something interesting in its four galleries. An exhibit of material from the New York Philharmonic may be in one gallery, and the history of ballet in another. Not just a book library, its collection includes tens of thousands of recordings, videos, and printed materials from dance, theater, classical music, and other media. You can listen or watch whatever you choose without leaving the library! The library is located in Lincoln Center between the Metropolitan Opera House and the Vivian Beaumont Theater. Because the library is being completely renovated (including discarding all but a fraction of its aging LP collection!), however, its research collection is temporarily housed at 521 West 43rd Street (between Tenth and Eleventh avenues), and the circulating collection is stored at New York Public Library's midtown branch (40th Street at Fifth Avenue) as this goes to press. Call 212/870-1600 for event information. **Hours:** Monday and Thursday from noon to 8; Wednesday, Friday, and Saturday from noon to 6. **Admission:** free.

New York Stock Exchange — Although the elegant home of the New York Stock Exchange is on the corner of Broad and Wall streets, the visitors entrance is at 20 Broad Street, between Wall and Exchange streets. Tickets are distributed outside or immediately inside the door for entrance to the two-tiered visitors gallery on the third floor, overlooking the trading floor. You will be turned away at the elevators if you do not have one. When the place gets crowded they stagger the tickets, so there may be a short wait to get in. Once inside you can move around at your own pace. The visitors gallery sometimes closes for renovations and other reasons, so call (212/656-5167) before coming. **Hours:** weekdays (except federal holidays) between 9:15 and 2:45.

Plaza Hotel—On the south side of Central Park South, just west of Fifth Avenue, this elegant old hotel is a sentimental and architectural favorite. A stroll through the lobby is pure class. You might even catch a glimpse of Eloise (or at least her portrait)!

Radio City Music Hall—This 6,200-seat art deco wonder was the largest theater in the world when it was built in the early 1930s as part of the Rockefeller Center complex. Its murals and art alone are worth a visit, but Radio City is best known for its long-running Christmas and Easter shows, featuring the Rockettes. Now owned by Cablevision, this is yet another New York institution that has been renovated and refurbished in recent years. Call 212/247-4777 or drop by the lobby at the corner of Avenue of the Americas and 50th Street to find out what's scheduled. (If you're interested in taking a tour, see the "Tours" section of this chapter for more information.) **Hours:** weekdays and Saturday from 10 to 8, Sunday from 11 to 8.

Rockefeller Center—The 19 buildings in Rockefeller Center stretch from 47th to 52nd streets between Fifth and Seventh avenues, but the heart of it all is off Fifth Avenue, between 49th and 50th streets. All sorts of interesting shops, the famed statue of Prometheus, the ice-skating rink, the *Today Show*'s studios, and the beautiful Channel Gardens are all here in the shadow of 30 Rockefeller Plaza. "30 Rock" is the home of NBC's network studios. (For information about the NBC Studio Tour, see the "Tours" section of this chapter.) In December, Rockefeller Center is also the home of one of the nation's most photographed Christmas trees. Call 212/632-3975 for more information about the complex and special events.

Roosevelt Island—If you want an experience even most New Yorkers haven't had, along with amazing views of the city's skyline, take the tram to Roosevelt Island in the middle of the East River. It leaves regularly from its station on Second Avenue between 59th and 60th streets and costs $1.50 per person each way. Although they are only minutes away from midtown Manhattan, the 7,500 people who live over here might as well be on another planet. Their island—which was at various times home to a hog pasture, a debtor's prison, and an insane asylum—is quiet, unhurried, and almost crime-free. For 10¢ you can take one of the rather elderly red buses that traverse the island from the tram station through the small shopping area to Lighthouse Park on the island's northern end. Buy a map at the tram station and see the sights or just wander around. Be sure to walk along the island's west side to get a priceless view of the Manhattan skyline. Call 212/832-4555 for tram schedules and other information.

Schomburg Center for Research in Black Culture—This branch of the New York Public Library is a stunningly comprehensive resource for scholars and others interested in the Harlem Renaissance, enduring African traditions, the civil rights movement, and a wide variety of topics associated with the African-American experience in this country. It's also home to some 300,000 prints and photographs, 10,000 pieces of art and artifacts, and 5,000 hours of oral histories. While its two galleries are small and not in the best shape, you'll often find unique exhibits here. The Center's Langston Hughes Theater is used for performances and special programs. Call 212/491-2200 for more information or 212/491-2265 to schedule a tour. The Center is located at the corner of Malcolm X Boulevard and 135th Street, across from Harlem Hospital. To get here from midtown, take the M102 bus up Third Avenue to the corner of Malcolm X Boulevard and 135th Street. To return, catch the M102 bus from the opposite corner down to what becomes Lexington Avenue. **Hours:** Monday through Wednesday from noon to 8, Thursday through Saturday from 10 to 6. (Since hours for the galleries and collections vary, call ahead to confirm they are open.)

Science, Industry, and Business Library—Known around town as SIBL (as in the woman's name), this amazing library in the old B. Altman department store is among the most technologically advanced and user-friendly libraries in the world. Intended for use by the general public and business people, the library unites the New York Public Library system's enormous collections of scientific, technological, mathematical, and business-related materials. (How enormous? Try comprehending 1.2 million books, along with microfilm, microfiche, magazines, and journals!) Whether you're interested in patents and trademarks, labor history, advertising practices, or how the Small Business Administration works, this is the place to look for information. But don't expect to browse the stacks. With the exception of a circulating collection of 40,000 books on the first floor, everything is housed in electrically operated moving stacks at the core of the building. Each of the library's 500 seats is wired for laptop computer use, and 100 computer stations are available if you want to search electronic databases or go online. If you're interested in learning how to "surf the Net," sign up for one of the library's free classes, offered through its Electronic Training Center. Call 212/592-7000 for more information. The library is located at the corner of Madison Avenue and 34th Street. **Hours:** Monday and Friday from 10 to 6; Tuesday and Thursday from 11 to 8, Wednesday from 11 to 7, and Saturday from noon to 6.

Seventh Regiment Armory—Most New Yorkers know this as a giant exhibition space in a prime location, but the Seventh Regiment Armory at Park Avenue and 66th Street is also what the *New York Times* recently called "a bit of New York in a bottle." The Seventh Regiment was founded in 1806 as a volunteer militia. Its members were a Who's Who of New York throughout the 19th Century. They built this armory as their headquarters in 1879. It includes rooms designed by famed architect Stanford White and decorated by Louis Comfort Tiffany, as well as paintings by such artists as Thomas Nast. Though it is used for all sorts of exhibits, including the prestigious Winter Antiques Show, the building itself is in dreadful disrepair and most of it is closed to the public. If you're interested in a walk through history, however, call the Seventh Regiment Fund (212/744-2968) for information on periodic tours.

Sony Wonder Technology Lab—A brilliant public-relations and merchandising ploy, and a huge favorite among preteens and teenagers, this four-story interactive wonderland is housed inside the Sony Corporation's building on Madison Avenue and 56th Street. After checking in on the ground floor and getting a personal access card, you'll be whisked by elevator to the fourth floor, where you "log in" your voice, name, and photograph. You then wind through a good exhibit on the history of communication technologies before reaching a variety of interactive laboratories and stations. Whether you want to try your hand at surgery or making a music video, you'll definitely find something to do and explore. The lab is often very crowded, especially on weekends and in summer. Call 212/833-8100 for more information. **Hours:** Tuesday through Saturday from 10 to 6 (Thursday until 8), Sunday from noon to 6.

South Street Seaport—This is the only place I've included in both the "Museums" section and "Sights and Other Pleasant Places," because it's a little of both.

The main entrance to this popular area is on Water Street at Fulton Street, but the area stretches for several blocks between Water Street and the East River. If you've ever been to Boston's Quincy Market or Baltimore's Inner Harbor, you'll recognize the concept here immediately: upscale shops, food courts, restaurants, and history all wrapped into one. South Street was one of the city's most important ports for many years, and this district was created more than two decades ago to preserve that history. You can stroll cobblestone streets, look at the early 19th-century buildings along Schermerhorn Row, and gaze at the tall ships. Alternatively, you can buy a ticket to tour the ships and visit the seaport's galleries and children's center. (For a few extra dollars in warmer months, you also can take a cruise of New York Harbor.) Start your trek at the visitors center, a block and a half inside the main entrance on Fulton Street. Call 212/748-8600 for information about South Street Seaport and special events. **Hours:** South Street Seaport Museum is open daily from 10 to 6 (Thursday until 8) in summer and daily (except Tuesday from 10 to 5) in winter, although many shops and restaurants in the area stay open much later.

Statue of Liberty—This 151-foot gift to the United States from France was built on Liberty Island in New York Harbor in 1886 and has been among New York's most recognized sights ever since. (Before the statue was erected, the island was used as a fort, and later for hanging pirates!) Generations of immigrants remember seeing Lady Liberty and her raised torch when they arrived at nearby Ellis Island, and the Emma Lazarus poem ("Give me your tired . . .") still expresses the most noble instincts of our country. It's more than a little touristy these days, but the 22-story climb up to the crown or a stroll around the grounds can be fun for children and adults alike. (You may want to opt for the latter if contending with stairs, crowds, and tight spaces is a challenge.) A small exhibit tells you about the statue's construction. To reach the Statue of Liberty means taking a ferry from Castle Clinton in Battery Park. For more information about the ferry (which also goes to Ellis Island), call 212/269-5755. For recorded information about the Statue of Liberty, call 212/363-3200. Be forewarned: go early, particularly in warmer months, as lines here can grow very long indeed. **Hours:** 9:30 to 5 in winter, 9:30 to 5:30 in summer (although the last boat leaves Castle Clinton at about 3). **Admission:** $7 for adults, $6 for senior citizens and students, and $3 for children between 3 and 17. Admission to both Ellis Island and the Statue of Liberty is included in the price of a ferry ticket.

Times Square—When I first began writing this book, Times Square was among the most unpleasant places in Manhattan. It was synonymous with petty crime, pornography, and filth. Not anymore. In fact, it's increasingly hard to believe it's actually the same place. The Disney Company has remade life on 42nd Street with the stunning success of *The Lion King* in the lovingly restored New Amsterdam Theater. Virgin Records has a user-friendly superstore here, and a Planet Hollywood Hotel is going up as this book goes to press. Even the Times Square subway station, the city's busiest, is being redesigned, refurbished, and fitted for a 53-foot porcelain mural by Roy Lichtenstein! The Times Square Business Improvement District runs a great tourist information center on Seventh Avenue between 46th and 47th streets.

Trump Tower—This 66-floor building, named for flamboyant financier Donald Trump, sits on Fifth Avenue between 56th and 57th streets. Its six-story pink marble atrium—complete with galleries, shops, restaurants, outdoor gardens (on levels 4 and 5), and a dramatic waterfall—is open to the public and almost always crowded. Apartments begin on the 30th floor; tenants enter and leave via a separate entrance to avoid the perpetual crowds. **Hours:** daily between 8 a.m. and 10 p.m.

United Nations – The United Nations runs along First Avenue (called United Nations Plaza) between 42nd and 47th streets. The flags of member nations fly along the entire length of the complex, and you'll hear all sorts of languages spoken inside the UN and on surrounding streets. The main visitors entrance, between 45th and 46th streets, is well marked and manned by UN guards. The park and plaza inside the gate offer wonderful views of the East River and comfortable benches. Once you've passed through a security checkpoint inside the main building, you can wander the enormous lobby, eat in the Delegates Dining Room, take a formal tour, or head downstairs to visit the wonderful UN post office and a great assortment of shops. An information desk located in the middle of the main lobby provides daily schedules of meetings and events. Remember that those who work here are busy with world affairs, so look around and ask questions but be quiet and respectful. For information about UN tours and other programs, call 212/963-7713. **Hours:** weekdays from 9 to 5; Saturday, Sunday, and holidays from 9:15 to 5 (closed weekends in January and February).

Venetian Room – The building now houses the French Cultural Service's mission and is hardly ever noticed by tourists headed to the nearby Metropolitan Museum of Art. The grand townhouse at 972 Fifth Avenue (just south of 79th Street) was designed at the beginning of the 20th century for Payne and Helen Hay Whitney by famed architect Stanford White. While its rooms are now largely occupied by French bureaucrats, the home's almost indescribably elegant Venetian Room (just inside the main entrance) has been painstakingly rebuilt from the contents of 75 crates that were packed and stored in a stable when Helen Hay Whitney died in 1944. Furnished largely with items purchased by the Whitneys and White on a trip to Europe in 1905, the room was designed to allow visitors a chance to catch their breath before ascending the stairs to the townhouse's main living areas. Doing so now is indeed a challenge – particularly after seeing the Marble Boy in the main foyer, a sculpture White bought in 1905 that many experts believe to be the work of Michelangelo. Call 212/439-1400 for more information and to confirm hours. **Hours:** 12:30 and 2:30 on Fridays. **Admission:** free.

— Millennium Note —

The city's narrowest house stands at 75½ Bedford Street, in Greenwich Village; it is nine and a half feet wide, 30 feet long, and three stories high. Edna St. Vincent Millay and John Barrymore lived there at different times.

Vietnam Veterans Memorial – While certainly moving, this is somewhat of a disappointment if you've been to the unforgettable Vietnam Veterans Memorial in Washington, D.C. It's made of green glass etched with excerpts from speeches given during the war and letters written by soldiers during their tours. The plaza surrounding it is full of places to sit and offers terrific views of downtown Brooklyn and New York Harbor. The memorial and plaza lie between enormous office buildings on Water Street, just north of Broad Street. (The actual cross street is named Coenties Slip, but I defy you to find that on any map!)

Washington Arch—Thanks to scenes in movies like *When Harry Met Sally,* you probably know what this marble triumphal arch looks like. It was erected at the end of the 19th century at the foot of Fifth Avenue, just south of 8th Street in Washington Square Park. The marble arch replaced a wooden structure commemorating the inauguration of George Washington, who was sworn in as president in New York.

Woolworth Building—Constructed of 17 million bricks, 28,000 tons of tile, and 53,000 pounds of bronze and iron hardware, this national landmark is among the city's most impressive office buildings. The cathedral-like lobby has extraordinary mosaics on its vaulted ceilings; it is a definite "don't miss" if you're in the area. Dime-store king F.W. Woolworth paid $13.5 million in cash to have his namesake building erected in 1913, and it reigned as the world's tallest building for more than a decade. You'll find the Woolworth Building near City Hall at 233 Broadway (between Barclay Street and Park Place). **Hours:** The lobby is open to the public 24 hours a day.

World Financial Center—In the heart of Battery Park City, between Vesey and Albany streets at the Hudson River, the World Financial Center resides in the newer part of an area known as home to many of the nation's leading brokerage and financial firms. Often confused with its bigger neighbor, the World Trade Center, this complex of four buildings surrounding the exquisite Winter Garden does indeed have a life and character of its own. In general, the World Financial Center complex tends to be significantly cleaner and quieter than the World Trade Center complex. You'll find several dozen upscale stores and restaurants in the World Financial Center, great views of the Hudson River, and some very pleasant sitting areas both indoors and out. Call 212/945-0505 for information about events and programs.

World Trade Center—This complex of office buildings is dominated by the towering twin stories of 1 and 2 World Trade Center. (Believe it or not, thanks to a recent boom in the construction of tall buildings in Asia, they are no longer even close to being the world's tallest buildings!) You'll find eight acres of stores and restaurants on the lower levels, all sorts of outdoor markets and events around the complex during spring and summer, and stunning views and lots of touristy entertainment on the recently renovated observation deck on the 107th floor of 2 World Trade Center. The observation deck itself is entirely glass-enclosed, although you can venture one floor higher to an open-air roof deck on calm days. Those with a fear of heights may want to avoid this. The complex sits between West, Vesey, Liberty, and Church streets. A TKTS outlet, tourist information desk, and ticket desk for the observation deck can all be found on the mezzanine of 2 World Trade Center. For more information about the "Top of the World" observation deck, call 212/435-7377. For information about the World Trade Center itself, call 212/435-4170. **Hours:** The observation deck is open daily from 9:30 to 9:30 (11:30 in summer). **Admission:** $12.50 for adults, $10.75 for students with ID, $9.50 for senior citizens, $6.50 for children 6 to 12, and free for kids under 6.

Sports

Some people associate New York with fine food and expensive stores, while others link the city with the Yankees, the Mets, the Knicks, the Rangers, or one of the city's other professional sports teams. In fact, the New York area is home to more than half a dozen professional sports teams—although only two, basketball's Knicks and hockey's Rangers, actually play in Manhattan. (Home field for the city's two pro football teams is across the river in New Jersey!) Diagrams of all area stadiums appear near the front of the Manhattan Yellow Pages.

Tickets for most regular-season baseball games often can be purchased as late as game day. Tickets for football's Giants and Jets, however, are almost impossible to find unless you have a generous friend who's a season-ticket holder. Even Knicks tickets are hard to come by. If you're planning a trip to New York, it's worth finding out which team is in town and who they're playing.

A word of warning: New York sports fans are like no others. They are loud, rude, and typically very knowledgeable about their teams and the sport they're watching. I'm not sure which would be worse: being a referee or a fan of an opposing team at a New York sporting event. A friend from Oregon who goes to see the Knicks play the Portland Trail Blazers when they come to Madison Square Garden would argue the latter!

Belmont Park—Home to the Triple Crown's Belmont Stakes and some of this country's best thoroughbred racing in the late spring, summer, and early fall, this famous racetrack is out on Long Island. At other times of year, try Aqueduct in Jamaica, Queens. Both are run by the New York Racing Association. Call 718/641-4700 during regular business hours for information about either track.

New York Giants—The Giants (Super Bowl champions back in 1991) play in the National Football Conference of the National Football League. Here's how unlikely it is that you will get tickets for a Giants game: if you were to put your name on the waiting list for season tickets, you would wait roughly three decades! Individual tickets are sold at least a season in advance. If you're really planning ahead, write the New York Giants (The Meadowlands, East Rutherford, NJ 07073) or call their offices (201/935-8222). If you happen to get tickets, buses run between Port Authority Bus Terminal and the team's home stadium at New Jersey's Meadowlands.

New York Jets—The Jets play in the American Football Conference of the National Football League. Tickets for Jets games are easier to score than those for Giants games, but you still ought to plan well in advance. Like the Giants, they play their home games at New Jersey's Meadowlands. For information, write the Jets (1000 Fulton Avenue, Hempstead, Long Island, NY 11553) or call 516/560-8200. Buses run between Port Authority Bus Terminal and the Meadowlands.

New York Knickerbockers—The Knicks play at Madison Square Garden. The better the Knicks are doing, the harder it is to get tickets. (In the 1998-99 season, they went all the way to the NBA finals!) For information, call Ticketmaster at 212/307-7171 or Madison Square Garden at 212/465-6741. You might also try writing the Knicks (Madison Square Garden, 4 Penn Plaza, New York, NY 10001). Unlike the Meadowlands, Madison Square Garden is easily accessible by public transportation—it sits right above Penn Station!

New York Mets—The Mets play in Major League Baseball's National League. Their home (at least until they build a new one next door) is Shea Stadium in Queens, an easy subway ride from Manhattan. (Take the 7 line from 42nd Street to the Willets Point/Shea Stadium stop.) Tickets for Mets games are usually easy to get and, relative to their football and basketball counterparts, are not very expensive. Call Ticketmaster (212/307-7171) or the Shea Stadium box office (718/507-8499) for tickets and schedule information, or write the Mets (Shea Stadium, 126th Street at Roosevelt Avenue, Flushing, NY 11368).

New York Rangers—Like the Knicks, the National Hockey League's Rangers play at Madison Square Garden. The Rangers are very popular and tickets are often hard to get. Call Ticketmaster (212/307-7171) or the Garden (212/465-6741) to find out if tickets are available.

New York Yankees—The Yankees—the team America loves to hate—play in Major League Baseball's American League. Although there often is talk of moving to a new stadium (and it may happen when their lease expires in 2002), for now they play at Yankee Stadium in the Bronx. Known to many as the House that Ruth Built, because Babe Ruth played here in the early part of this century, it's a real sports landmark. It's also an easy subway ride from Manhattan. (Take the 4 line from the East Side or the C or D line from the West Side to the 161st Street/Yankee Stadium stop in the Bronx.) Call the Yankee Stadium ticket office (718/293-4300) or write the Yankees (Yankee Stadium, 800 Rupert Place, The Bronx, NY 10451) for ticket and schedule information.

U.S. Open—The U.S. Open, one of professional tennis' four Grand Slam tournaments, is held in late August and early September at the United States Tennis Center in Queens. The finals are held over Labor Day weekend. Tickets to the semifinals and finals sell out immediately, but tickets for earlier rounds can usually be purchased before the tournament. Call Ticketmaster (212/307-7171) for ticket information. For tournament information, write the U.S. Tennis Center (Flushing Park, Queens, NY 11365) or call 718/760-6200.

College basketball and boxing fans should call Madison Square Garden (212/465-6741) to find out about schedules and tickets. College basketball's **National Invitation Tournament** is played at the Garden every March, and boxing's **Golden Glove** series is held there in January and February.

Tickets

Nowhere else in the world will you find such a wealth of performing arts. And no trip to New York would be complete without going to see at least one play, musical, ballet, concert, or opera.

The trick, of course, is getting tickets. People have written entire books about how and where to get tickets, and others have made lucrative careers out of procuring them for out-of-towners. What I've tried to do is provide a variety of approaches for getting theater tickets and to help you find out about other performances. (If you want tickets to sporting events, see the "Recreation" section immediately preceding this one.) Keep your eye out for student and other discounts, but be forewarned that good deals for the best shows and performances are few and far between.

For reliable service and superb ticket availability (at a price, naturally), call **Continental Guest Services Golden Leblang** (212/944-8910 or 800/299-8587). Started in 1894, they can provide reserved theater tickets; set rates are charged. They are the largest broker in the city and have counters at many area hotels.

BROADWAY

Different people may have different things in mind when they say they want to see a show. Some have their hearts set on great seats at a Saturday night performance of the hottest show on Broadway, while others are willing to sit anywhere to see anything. A lot of people fall somewhere between those extremes. In addition, some are willing to pay whatever it takes to see the show they want, while others just won't go if they can't pay less than full price. If the whole reason for your trip is to see a particular show (or shows), call Theatre Direct International at 800/334-8457 or the League of American Theaters and Producers' Broadway Babies hotline at 888/411-2929 to find a travel agent near you who can put together a tour package that includes theater tickets. Here are some other approaches:

Box Offices and Phone Orders — Look in the Sunday Arts and Leisure section or the Friday Weekend section of the *New York Times,* the front of a current *New Yorker,* the "Theater" section of *Time Out New York,* or the back of a current *New York Magazine* to find out where the play or musical you want to see is being performed. The front section of the Manhattan Yellow Pages has a list of Broadway and off-Broadway theaters and a map of the Theater Districts; *Stubs* magazine contains detailed diagrams of seating in most theaters. The Theater Development Fund's NYC/Onstage line (212/768-1818) tells you what is playing and where and also gives a plot summary.

If you want to save a little money and pick your seat, go directly to the theater's box office with cash or a major credit card. Ask to see a diagram of the theater if it isn't posted, although most theaters are small enough to insure that everybody has a pretty good view. The best time to try is midweek.

If you're willing to spend a little extra and let a computer pick what is in theory the "best available" seat, call the number listed for phone orders and have your credit card ready. Most numbers will be for Telecharge (212/239-6200) or Ticketmaster's Broadway performance line (212/307-4100). Both services charge a per-ticket handling fee in addition to the ticket price. Other options include stopping by the Times Square Business Improvement District's Tourist Information Center (in the Embassy Theater, on Seventh Avenue between 46th and 47th streets). It's the only place in the city where you can get tickets to every Broadway show. You can also try the New York City Convention and Visitors Bureau's new information center on Seventh Avenue at 53rd Street.

Be forewarned: full-price tickets to Broadway shows typically cost between $50 and $70. Moreover, if the play or musical you want to see is really hot, it may be sold out the entire time you're in New York. In fact, a few — most notably *The Lion King* — may be sold out for months. If you still have your heart set on seeing it, ask the hotel concierge for help or look under "Ticket Sales — Entertainment & Sports" in the Manhattan Yellow Pages for the name and phone number of a ticket broker. Either way, this approach will cost extra.

TKTS Outlets — If you want to see a Broadway show but are willing to be a little flexible and have some free time, go to one of the TKTS outlets in Manhattan. Operated by the Theater Development Fund, these outlets sell whatever tickets happen to be left for various shows on the day of performance for half price or less (plus a $2.50 per-ticket charge). The most popular TKTS outlet is in Duffy Square, at 47th Street and Broadway. It's open from 3 to 8 daily, although matinee tickets are sold from 10 to 2 on Wednesday and Saturday and from 11 to 7 on Sunday. You can't miss the line. A less crowded TKTS outlet with better hours is on the mezzanine level of 2 World Trade Center, diagonally across from the ticket booth for the World Trade Center's Observation Deck. It's open from 11 to 5:30 on weekdays and from 11 to 3:30 on Saturday. They don't sell day-of tickets for evening performances past 1 p.m., but matinee and Sunday tickets go on sale here the day *before* a performance. You must pay with cash or traveler's checks at both places.

The Theater Development Fund also offers extremely good deals on tickets to theater and other performances to its members. If you're a student, member of the clergy, on active duty in the armed forces, teacher, union member, retired, or a performing artist and are planning well in advance, send a stamped, self-addressed envelope for an application to Theater Development Fund, Attention: Application, 1501 Broadway, New York, NY 10036. All Broadway theaters offer a small number of deeply discounted tickets to people in wheelchairs and their companion or attendant. Call the theater box office directly for more information. Finally, standing-room-only tickets are sometimes available for sold-out performances on the day of the performance for between $10 and $20. Again, call the theater box office for more information.

Twofers—If you just want to see *something* on Broadway and save money too, keep your eye open for twofers. This is one way theaters sell tickets to less-than-hot shows and old standbys that have been running for years. By exchanging them at the theater's box office, you can get two tickets for the price of one. (Actually, discounts run anywhere between 15% and 50%.) Twofers look like actual tickets and can be found in hotel lobbies, restaurants, and at the New York City Convention and Visitors Bureau's new information center on Seventh Avenue at 53rd Street. You can also get twofers by sending a self-addressed, stamped envelope to Hit Show Club, 630 Ninth Avenue, Room 808, New York, NY 10036 or going by the Hit Show Club offices in person between 9 and 4 on weekdays. Call 212/581-4211 for more information.

Off-Broadway and Off-Off Broadway—In part because staging a Broadway production has become almost prohibitively expensive in recent years, off-Broadway and off-off-Broadway theater have really taken *off*. Thanks to a glut of talented actors and actresses in New York, such theater is typically excellent and often quite innovative. The front section of the Manhattan Yellow Pages lists off-Broadway theaters, and descriptions of what's playing both off-Broadway and off-off-Broadway are published every Sunday in the *New York Times* Arts and Leisure section, in the back of *New York Magazine,* and in *Time Out New York.* Tickets for off-Broadway and off-off-Broadway productions tend to be significantly less expensive, and TKTS outlets and twofers sometimes offer discounts.

OPERA AND CLASSICAL MUSIC

I think it's safe to say that no other city in the world has as much music from which to choose as New York. Look in the "Annual Events" section of Chapter VII for information about some of the free concerts offered here or in the "Dancing and Other Clubs" section of Chapter VII for information about rock, big band, and jazz clubs. I also urge you to call the 92nd Street YMHA (212/996-1100) if you're interested in chamber music or recitals by top performers. The front section of the Manhattan Yellow Pages contains diagrams of the city's major music halls. If you're willing to pay for the service, ask the hotel concierge for help if you have a particular opera or concert in mind and tickets are sold out. *Time Out New York* has an excellent listing of classical and opera performances, including information on locations, times, and ticket prices. Otherwise, here's how to find schedule and ticket information:

Carnegie Hall—You'll find individual musicians, out-of-town orchestras, and chamber music ensembles performing in Carnegie Hall all year. If you're planning well in advance, write Carnegie Hall (881 Seventh Avenue, New York,

NY 10019) for a schedule and ticket information. You can also drop by the lobby or call CarnegieCharge (212/247-7800) between 11 and 6.

Lincoln Center Chamber Music Society — To get schedule and ticket information about the Lincoln Center Chamber Music Society and other performances, write Alice Tully Hall (1941 Broadway, New York, NY 10023), call CenterCharge (212/721-6500), or call the box office (212/875-5030). If you're a student or senior citizen, call around 11:30 on the morning of a performance to see if they have any inexpensive "rush" tickets available.

Metropolitan Opera — This internationally renowned opera's season runs from fall through spring, but ticket sales are broken into three periods. Write the Metropolitan Opera House (Lincoln Center, New York, NY 10023) for schedule and ticket information, drop by the Opera House lobby, or call the box office (212/362-6000). Be warned: orchestra seats can cost as much as $150 each! (For a real bargain, bring cash only to the Metropolitan's box office at 10 on Saturday morning, when standing-room-only tickets for upcoming performances are sold for $15 each.)

New York City Opera — This exceptional but often overlooked opera's season runs through the summer and early fall. Write the New York City Opera (New York State Theater, 20 Lincoln Center Plaza, New York, NY 10023) for schedule and ticket information or call the box office (212/870-5570). You can also try Ticketmaster (212/307-4100). Standing-room-only tickets are sometimes available for $8 on the morning of a performance from the New York State Theater's box office.

New York Philharmonic — The Philharmonic's season runs from September through June. Write the New York Philharmonic (Avery Fisher Hall, to Lincoln Center Plaza, New York, NY 10023) for schedule and ticket information or call CenterCharge (212/721-6500), the box office (212/721-6500), or the New York Philharmonic information line (212/875-5656). If you're a student, call around 10:30 on the morning of a performance to see if they have any $10 "rush" tickets available.

DANCE AND BALLET

Ballet and dance companies have experienced a tough time financially in recent years, but New York still is home to several world-class companies and a great many smaller ones. *Time Out New York* has a particularly good section on dance, including reviews and a day-by-day calendar of large and small performances by local and visiting companies. If you're interested in seeing one of the large dance companies, I suggest writing or calling the specific companies to get schedule and ticket information:

Alvin Ailey — 211 West 61st Street, New York, NY 10023 (212/767-0590)

American Ballet Theater — Metropolitan Opera House, Lincoln Center, New York, NY 10023 (212/362-6000)

Dance Theater of Harlem — 466 West 152nd Street, New York, NY 10031 (212/690-2800)

New York City Ballet — New York State Theater, 20 Lincoln Center Plaza, New York, NY 10023 (212/870-5570)

Paul Taylor Dance Company — 552 Broadway, New York, NY 10012 (212/431-5562)

TELEVISION SHOW TAPINGS

Fine arts aside, there is one other kind of ticket everybody wants to get in New York: those that allow you to become part of the television studio audience for one of the many talk shows filmed here. I've listed some of the most popular shows (in alphabetical order) and rules for getting tickets. Tickets are free

Late Nite with Conan O'Brien—Tickets can be obtained by sending a postcard to NBC Tickets/Late Nite, 30 Rockefeller Plaza, New York, NY 10112 or by calling 212/664-3056. You can specify the date you want (tapings are usually done on Tuesday through Friday evenings). There is a four- to five-month wait for tickets and children under 16 are not admitted. A limited number of standby tickets are distributed on taping days at 9 a.m. in the NBC lobby, on 50th Street between Fifth Avenue and Avenue of the Americas. Call 212/664-3056 or 212/664-3057 for more information.

Late Show with David Letterman—These are among the hottest tickets in town. Send a postcard to The Late Show Tickets, 1697 Broadway, New York, NY 10019. Include your name, address, and phone number. Two tickets are allotted per postcard. (Don't send more than one postcard, as duplicates are discarded.) Expect to wait at least six to eight months. And bring a jacket: Dave insists that the theater be kept at 52° all year! Call 212/975-1003 for more information.

Live with Regis and Kathie Lee—These tickets are pretty hot, too. Send a postcard to Live Tickets, P.O. Box 777, Ansonia Station, New York, NY 10023-0777. Include your name, address, phone number, and how many tickets you want (up to four). Expect to wait at least a year. A standby ticket line forms at the ABC Studio (67th Street at Columbus Avenue) early in the morning, and one standby ticket is distributed per person after regular ticket holders have been seated at about 8 a.m. Be forwarned that the studio where the show is taped is pretty chilly, and that nobody under ten will be admitted. Call 212/456-3537 for more information.

Rosie O'Donnell Show—These tickets are so hot they're now being distributed by lottery. If you're interested in trying for a pair, send a postcard to NBC Tickets, The Rosie O'Donnell Show, 30 Rockefeller Plaza, Suite 800E, New York, NY 10112. Include your name, address, and phone number. Tickets are distributed in pairs. Children under five are not allowed in the audience, and children 16 and younger must be accompanied by an adult. Standby tickets are available at 8:30 a.m. on the day of tapings (usually Monday, Tuesday, and Wednesday) outside the 49th Street side of 30 Rockefeller Center, between Fifth Avenue and Avenue of the Americas.

Saturday Night Live—Year in and year out, these are the hardest tickets of all to get. A lottery is held every August from postcards collected during the preceding 12 months, and every winner gets only two tickets. If you want to be included in the lottery, send a postcard to Saturday Night Live, NBC Tickets, 30 Rockefeller Plaza, New York, NY 10112. Standby tickets are available at 9:15 a.m. on the day of the show at the 49th Street entrance to 30 Rockefeller Plaza. They do not guarantee entrance, and only one ticket is distributed per person over 16.

Today Show—As anybody who watches this popular morning show knows, its broadcast studio has windows in front of which crowds gather to watch hosts Matt Lauer and Katie Couric. You don't need tickets to be part of that crowd.

Just show up on the sidewalk on 49th Street at Rockefeller Plaza (between Fifth Avenue and Avenue of the Americas), a little before 7 a.m. on any weekday.

Both **Good Morning America** (ABC) and **CBS This Morning** (CBS) are planning ground-floor, tourist-friendly studios as well, on Times Square and near the southeast corner of Central Park, respectively.

Tours

No matter what your interest, price range, or schedule, chances are that New York has a tour for you. I've divided "Tours" into four categories: tour organizers, tours of New York, tours of specific sights and neighborhoods, and individuals and organizations that put together walking tours of various areas. In general, the first category is for groups and corporate clients rather than individuals who want to tag along. Some of the tours in the other three categories simply require you to show up and pay a couple of dollars, while others require reservations in advance and can be costly. Some are well established and reliable, while others are either new or eccentric and may not be around by the time you read this. As with just about everything else, my advice is to call in advance. Speaking of calling, you can always get in touch with the Guides Association of New York (212/969-0666) for advice about the kind of tour or guide you're looking for, as well as a list of its members and their specialties.

TOUR ORGANIZERS

Art Horizons International — If your group is serious about art and would like to meet some gallery owners or museum curators, give Art Horizons International a call and they'll help arrange it. This well-regarded organization also puts together tours of the fashion industry and Broadway. Call 212/969-9410 for more information or a brochure.

Cover New York — This is a specialty tour operator that does "insider" visits for groups. They specialize in shopping, fashion, theater, art, architecture, and interior design visits. Corporations, school groups, and tourist organizations make use of their specialized service and find their multilingual guides to be a real advantage. Call 212/737-1726 for more information.

Daily-Thorp Cultural Tours — In addition to organizing tours for opera and music lovers around the world, Daily-Thorp teams up with the Metropolitan Opera Guild in New York to arrange spectacular "deluxe" and "Opera Express" tours to New York involving the Metropolitan Opera, the New York Philharmonic, and the New York City Opera, as well as Broadway shows. Guests on the deluxe tours usually stay at New York's best hotels and have just about every need and want taken care of by a staff of professionals. The Opera Express tours are a bit more downscale (and cheaper) but are run just as well. Call 212/307-1555 for more information or a brochure.

Doorway to Design — Sheila Sperber offers a personalized approach to educational and fun events in the Big Apple. For over 20 years she has created exclusively tailored itineraries for individuals and groups with an emphasis on entree to private homes and clubs, plus shopping and behind-the-scenes visits to Manhattan's creative community. You can tour auction houses, Soho studios, wholesale fashion outlets, private kitchens of top chefs, interior design showrooms closed to the general public, and even landmark townhouses and Victorian mansions! Call 212/221-1111 for more information.

Manhattan Passport—Run by Ina Lee Selden, this terrific company organizes customized trips and tours to New York and other places in the region for corporate clients and special-interest groups from the U.S. and other countries. Whether you're thinking ultimately elegant or more than a little offbeat, chances are Ina and her staff can make it happen. Call 212/861-2746 for a brochure and information.

New York Inside/Out—Groups interested in interior design, the fashion world, or arts and antiques ought to call these folks. Gaile Peters and her staff at New York Inside/Out are professionals who can organize daylong tours or weeklong trips. Call 212/861-4114 for more information or a brochure.

Unique New York—Chris Richie is a terrific resource for anyone who plans to visit New York but feels a little intimidated by it. For reasonable rates, he and partner Gina Burton will work with you to find a little slice of the Big Apple that's right for your tastes and appetites. They can show how New Yorkers really live or take you on a shopping tour or to Central Park. Unique New York handles individuals, families, and groups. Call 212/267-8374 for more information, and give some advance notice so they can design your unique itinerary.

Viewpoint International—Whether you're organizing a gala event for thousands or just want a first-class customized tour for a couple of people, these folks can help. Their extraordinary client list speaks volumes about the professional, reliable, and creative service you'll get here. While they're best known for corporate-event work, Viewpoint International offers lots of interesting tours, too. Call 212/355-1055 for more information or a brochure.

TOURS OF NEW YORK

Big Apple Greeter—A volunteer service, this outfit will hook you up with a personal guide to New York. If you're looking for a personalized introduction to this sometimes overwhelming city, Big Apple Greeters may be for you. Best of all, it's free! Just give a couple days notice and tell them what part of New York you would like to see. Call 212/669-8159 for more information.

Circle Line—Particularly on warm days, the three-hour boat trip around the entire island of Manhattan on one of Circle Line's boats is a real treat. In addition to some nice breezes, you'll get a good sense of how Manhattan is laid out and what neighborhoods are where. A guide offers commentary as the boat makes its way down the Hudson River, into New York Harbor, up the East River, across the top of the island in the Harlem River, and back down the Hudson. Trips depart Pier 83 (43rd Street at the Hudson River) daily (and far more frequently at the height of the season) between mid-March and December. In warmer months, tours also depart from Pier 16 at South Street Seaport. Tickets cost $22 for adults and $12 for senior citizens and children under 12. Shorter tours are also available. Call 212/563-3200 for more information or a brochure.

Gray Line—If you're feeling overwhelmed by New York and want to be completely anonymous as someone shows you the highlights, try a Gray Line tour. The company offers a wide range of partial and full-day bus tours to different parts of Manhattan, including a marathon eight-and-a-half-hour "Manhattan

Comprehensive" that goes from Harlem to Wall Street and even out to the Statue of Liberty and Ellis Island. Most tours run at least once a day, and some are offered in French, German, Italian, Portuguese, and Spanish, as well as English. Gray Line also offers package tours to places like West Point, factory outlets north of the city, Niagara Falls, and even Washington, D.C. Tickets are available at the Gray Line office in the Port Authority Bus Terminal (42nd Street at Eighth Avenue), the Times Square Business Improvement District's Tourist Information Center (Seventh Avenue between 46th and 47th streets), and from many hotel concierge desks. Call 212/397-2600 for more information or a brochure.

Gray Line Double-Decker Loop—This is a terrific way to see many of the city's major sights without having to pay for taxis or brave the public transportation system. Somewhat like the Tour Mobile in Washington, D.C., Gray Line's open-air double-decker buses and trolleys run every half hour between Battery Park, South Street Seaport, the Empire State Building, and three dozen other places. Tickets cost $33 for adults and $21 for kids, and they're good for two days and as many different stops as you want to make. Tickets for less extensive routes are less expensive. Like other Gray Line tickets, tickets are available at the Gray Line office in the Port Authority Bus Terminal (42nd Street at Eighth Avenue), the Times Square Business Improvement District's Tourist Information Center (on Seventh Avenue between 46th and 47th streets), and from many hotel concierge desks. Schedules change by season. Call 212/397-2600 for more information.

Island Helicopter—One of several outfits in Manhattan offering helicopter tours, this one is based at the heliport at the eastern end of 34th Street. Prices range from $49 to $129, depending on the flight pattern you choose. (Save $5 on tickets by purchasing them from a hotel concierge rather than at the heliport.) Island Helicopters operates from 9 a.m. to 9 p.m. seven days a week but requires at least two passengers per flight. Call 212/683-4575 for more information.

Liberty Helicopter Tours—This company's helicopters take off from the heliport at the west end of 30th Street and from the Wall Street Heliport on Pier 6, near the end of Whitehall Street. Prices begin at $46 and go up to $159, depending on the flight pattern and day you choose. Liberty Helicopter Tours also operates daily but requires at least three passengers per flight. Call 212/967-6464 for more information or a brochure.

New York Double-Decker Tours—Another one of the tour companies using double-decker buses and offering dozens of "hop on, hop off" stops all over Manhattan, this one also gives you two days to see the sights, but you also get up to ten days between them. You can do the "downtown" or "uptown" route for $20 ($12 for children under 12) or combine the two for $30 ($18 for children under 12). Call 800/692-2870 for more information.

TOURS OF SPECIFIC PLACES AND AREAS

ARTime—A relative newcomer to the tour scene, this outfit puts together "Saturday in the Galleries" tours of various Soho and Chelsea galleries. Tours are centered around particular themes and geared to elementary schoolchildren and their families. It's run by two art historians whose background includes working with children at the Brooklyn Museum. Ninety-minute tours cost $20 for each child-adult pair and $5 for each additional child (additional adults are free). Call 718/797-1573 for more information.

Carnegie Hall—Lincoln Center may have the Metropolitan Opera and the New York Philharmonic, but Carnegie Hall remains synonymous with classical music. If you want to take a look around during the day, one-hour tours are offered on weekdays (except Wednesday) at 11:30, 2 and, 3. The tour costs $6 for adults, $5 for students and senior citizens, and $3 for children under 12. Call 212/903-9790 for more information, or drop by the house manager's window inside the Carnegie Hall lobby at 153 West 57th Street, just off Seventh Avenue. The box office opens at 11 a.m.; advance reservations are not accepted. Tours meet inside the lobby.

Cathedral Church of St. John the Divine—If you're even remotely interested in Gothic architecture or just want to see one of the most amazing and beautiful places in all of New York, I urge you to take a tour of this cathedral-in-progress. Located on Amsterdam Avenue at 112th Street, this Episcopal church makes a real effort to welcome people of all faiths. Regular tours cost $2 and meet at a table in the back of the narthex, inside the main doors. They begin at 11 Tuesday through Saturday and after morning services at 1 p.m. on Sunday. The so-called "vertical tour" takes place on the first and third Saturday of every month and costs $10. Although definitely not something for small children, people with disabilities, or those afraid of heights (you must sign a waiver at the outset), this tour affords participants an absolutely fascinating view of the cathedral's spectacular stained-glass windows, architecture, and many hidden areas. Space is limited and reservations are required at least one week in advance. Also, if you can get ten people together, the folks here will organize a tour tailored to your particular interests. Call 212/316-7540 for general information and 212/932-7347 on weekday afternoons to make reservations.

Central Park—The Central Park Conservancy runs a wide array of free tours in Central Park. Call the visitors information center at The Dairy (212/794-6564) daily (except Monday) between 10 and 4 for more information. Another possibility is Tom Ahern's Central Park Bicycle Tour, a two-hour romp through "New York's front yard." For $30 per adult and $20 for children, you get a tour and a bicycle. For reservations or more information, call Bite of the Apple Tours at 212/541-8759. You might also check with the city's Urban Park Rangers (212/427-4040) to see if they have any free walking tours scheduled.

Downtown and Wall Street—With four well-marked trails to guide you throughout the areas now known as downtown and Wall Street, Heritage Trails New York will escort you on a wonderfully educational walking trip through early American history. Stop by the Heritage Trails information booth on the corner of Nassau and Wall streets before setting out to get a copy of their fascinating and well-written guide (which costs $5). If you would rather join a guide for a late morning walk, prices are $11 for adults, $9 for students and senior citizens, and $7 for children. Reservations are required. Call 212/269-1500 (ext. 207) or 888/487-2457 for more information.

Eldridge Street Synagogue—This stunning synagogue was built by Eastern European immigrants at 12 Eldridge Street (between Canal and Division streets) on the Lower East Side in 1887. Although the same congregation that built it still worships here, the building fell into disrepair in the middle of this century and is now being renovated. Fascinating tours are offered every Sunday on the hour between 11 and 3 and on Tuesday and Thursday at 11:30 and 2:30. Admission, which helps pay for the renovation, is $4 for adults and $2.50 for students, senior citizens, and children. They also have all sorts of specially designed tours and talks for student groups and children. Call 212/219-0888 for more information.

Federal Reserve Bank—Free tours of the gold vaults (which contain almost 11,000 tons of monetary gold) and other parts of this incredible institution are given twice in the morning and twice in the afternoon on weekdays (except major holidays). Call 212/720-7839 to find out whether they have space on a day that works for you. You'll find the Federal Reserve Bank on Liberty Street between Nassau and Williams streets.

Fulton Fish Market—This amazing operation on Pier 17 in the South Street Seaport complex supplies the city's restaurants with tons of fish every day. Business hours are from midnight to 8 a.m., and tours are offered at 6 a.m. on the first and third Thursday of every month from April through October. Reservations are required. The market seems to be in a constant state of upheaval, so call 212/669-9424 to be sure it's open and the tour is being offered.

Gracie Mansion—Thanks to Fiorello LaGuardia, New York is the only city in the U.S. with an official mayoral residence. This historic mansion, built in 1799 and one of the oldest continuously occupied homes in New York, is located in Carl Schurz Park, overlooking the East River (at about 88th Street and East End Avenue). Two morning and two afternoon tours are offered on Wednesday by appointment. Call 212/570-4751 for more information or a reservation. A contribution of $4 for adults and $3 for senior citizens is suggested.

Grand Central Station—In addition to excellent walking tours, the Municipal Art Society conducts a 90-minute free tour of this beautiful building every Wednesday at 12:30. I highly recommend this popular tour. Grand Central Station is one of the city's real landmarks, and the society's tour conveys a sense of its grandeur and history while allowing you to see a lot of features most commuters don't even know exist. The tour meets at the information booth on the main concourse directly across from the grand staircase. Call 212/935-3960 for more information. The Grand Central Partnership also offers a free tour of the neighborhood on Friday at 12:30 p.m. It meets at the Whitney Museum's gallery inside the Philip Morris Building, across 42nd Street from Grand Central Station.

Harlem—Whether you want to visit a jazz club, stop by historic buildings like the Morris-Jumel Mansion and the Apollo Theater, or go to church on Sunday morning to hear a gospel choir, Harlem Spirituals probably has a tour that's right for you. In addition to English, they offer tours in Italian, German, Spanish, French, and Portuguese when there's a demand. All tours are by bus, and prices depend on your itinerary. Stop by their offices at 690 Eighth Avenue (between 44th and 43rd streets) between 8:30 and 6 or call 212/757-0425 for more information. You can also try Harlem Your Way! (212/690-1687), a tour group specializing in customized tours for individuals and groups, family reunions, and other events. Finally, if you're interested in creating your own tour, get a copy of the New York Landmarks Conservancy's *Touring Historic Harlem: Four Walks in Northern Manhattan*. It's available for $18 from the Landmarks Conservancy located at 141 Fifth Avenue. Call 212/995-5260 for more information. City College's Architecture Center (138th Street at Covent Avenue; 212/650-6751) also sells a wonderfully detailed map of Harlem and its landmarks for $4.

Lincoln Center—If the Lincoln Center complex seems a little overwhelming but you are interested in seeing its magnificent auditoriums and concert halls, a minimum of four hour-long tours are given every day between 10 and 4:30. Because the center's schedule is put together only a day in advance, you must call on the day you want to take a tour to find out exactly when they will be offered. The tour costs $9.50 for adults, $8 for students and senior citizens, and $4.75 for children 6 to 12. (If that seems a little steep, check out the prices of opera and concert tickets!) Lincoln Center stretches from 62nd to 65th streets along Columbus Avenue. The tour office is on the lower level of the Metropolitan Opera House, directly in back of the main square. Call 212/875-5350 for more information or a brochure.

Lower East Side—This is really a shopper's tour put on by the Historic Orchard Street Shopping District (an association of its merchants). If you're interested in learning about this wonderful area's shops and its retailing history, the tour meets on Sunday at 11 at Katz's Delicatessen (East Houston at Ludlow streets) from April through December. It lasts about an hour and is free. Call 212/226-9010 for more information.

Lower East Side Tenement Museum—I can't say enough good things about this wonderful museum and its docents. In addition to tours of the restored apartments in the tenement at 97 Orchard Street, the museum offers fascinating tours exploring the surrounding area's rich and diverse ethnic heritage on weekends in warmer months. They aren't cheap but are well worth the price. Tours leave from the museum's offices at the corner of Orchard and Broome streets. Call 212/431-0233 for more information.

Madison Square Garden—If you've always wanted to go into the Knicks' locker room, this is the tour for you! It's offered every hour between 10 and 3 Monday through Saturday, and between 11 and 3 on Sunday (although schedules are frequently abbreviated because of events at the Garden). Tickets cost $14 for adults and $12 for children under 12, and are available at the Garden's box office. Call 212/465-5800 for more information.

Metropolitan Opera—The Metropolitan Opera Guild offers 90-minute tours of this extraordinary place between the start of the opera season, around the end of September, and the end of the ballet season, in or around June, on weekday afternoons and Saturday mornings. You should make reservations well in advance, but you can always call at the last minute to see if space is available or go on a standby basis. Tickets cost $8 for adults and $4 for full-time students. Call 212/769-7020 between 10 and 4 on weekdays for more information or a brochure.

NBC Studios—Children under six are not admitted, but anybody else can take an hour-long tour of the NBC's television studios for $10 per person. The quality of the tour varies dramatically, depending on both chance (what famous person happens to be getting off the elevator as you're getting on) and whether some big news event is breaking. The tour leaves every 15 minutes from 9:30 to 4:30 daily (Sunday from 10:30 to 4) from NBC's lobby on 50th Street between Fifth Avenue and Avenue of the Americas. Call 212/664-7174 for more information.

New Amsterdam Theater—Whether or not you've seen *The Lion King,* tours of this beautifully restored theater offer a glimpse into Broadway's past and present. They're offered hourly on Mondays and Tuesdays between 10 and 5.

Tickets are available at the theater's box office and cost $10 for adults, $5 for children under 12. Call 212/282-2907 for more information.

New York Harbor—Kayaking tours of New York Harbor and even a 30-mile circumnavigation of the island of Manhattan are available through Atlantic Kayak Tours. The company also offers lessons for students at all skill levels. The full-day tours typically run around $45, plus a $35 rental fee if you need to use their equipment. Call 914/246-2187 for more information.

New York Public Library—An informative tour of the grand New York Public Library is offered free of charge Monday through Saturday at 11 and again at 2. It leaves from the Friends of the Library desk, to the right of the library's main entrance on Fifth Avenue at 41st Street. Tours of the changing exhibits in the library's Gottesman Hall are also offered free Tuesday through Saturday at 12:30 and 2:30. Call the library's volunteer office at 212/930-0501 for more information or to schedule a tour for groups of ten or more.

Penn Station—If you want to soak up some of the great history of this railroad station, the 34th Street Partnership offers a free tour on the fourth Monday of each month at 12:30. The tour meets at the Partnership's visitors information center, off the main waiting area. Call 212/868-0521 for more information.

Radio City Music Hall—If you want to get inside this art deco treasure but don't want to go to a concert or other event, try one of the daily tours. Schedules vary depending on activities going on, and tours run about an hour. An extensive renovation is in progress as this book goes to press, and tours won't resume until late 1999. Call 212/247-4777 for more information. Radio City Music Hall is on the corner of Avenue of the Americas and 50th Street, and tours meet inside the main lobby.

Schomburg Center for Research in Black Culture—Tours of the collection and galleries in this rich cultural resource on the corner of Malcolm X Boulevard and 135th Street are offered by appointment only, Monday through Wednesday as well as Friday and Saturday between 10 and 2. Call 212/491-2207 for more information or reservations.

34th Street—The 34th Street Partnership sponsors a free 90-minute tour of the neighborhood around the Empire State Building on Thursdays at 12:30. The tour meets at the Fifth Avenue entrance of the Empire State Building, between 33rd and 34th streets. Call 212/868-0521 for more information.

Trinity Church—A guided tour of this historic church at Broadway and Wall streets leaves from the pulpit inside the sanctuary at 2 p.m. daily. It's free, although donations are accepted. Call 212/602-0800 for more information.

United Nations—If you want to peek inside the chambers of the United Nations General Assembly and learn a little about this incredible organization, tours begin about every half hour between 9:15 and 4:45 seven days a week (weekdays only in January and February). The tour costs $7.50 for adults, $5.50 for senior citizens, and $4.50 for students and children five and up. Children under five are not allowed on the tours, which last between 45 minutes and an hour and are offered in languages other than English. The visitors entrance to the United Nations is on First Avenue, between 45th and 46th streets, and the tour desk is directly across from the entrance, past the main lobby and down the hall. Call 212/963-7713 for more information.

Upper East Side — If you're interested in architectural history and want to take your own walking tour, get a copy of the New York Landmarks Conservancy's *Touring the Upper East Side: Walks in Five Historic Districts*. Written by Andrew Dolkart, an architectural historian at Columbia University, it's full of interesting stories about well-known and not-so-well-known parts of New York's most prestigious neighborhood. The $13 book is available from the Conservancy (141 Fifth Avenue, third floor, NY, NY 10010). Call 212/995-5260 for more information.

Wall Street — If you are interested in high finance, there's nowhere else in the world like Wall Street. Every Friday at 9:30, Heritage Trails New York leads a three-and-a-half tour of the New York Stock Exchange, the Federal Reserve Bank, and the many buildings and landmarks in this incredible area. Reservations are required. Tours cost $15 for adults, $10 for senior citizens and students 16 and up. For another $10 per person, you can kick off the morning with breakfast at the 14 Wall Street Restaurant (in financier J. P. Morgan's refurbished apartment). Call 212/269-1500 (ext. 207) or 888/487-2457 for details.

Yankee Stadium — Even in the off-season, baseball fans can tour the dugout, press box, and clubhouse of "the House that Ruth Built" (which is, by the way, in the Bronx). If you're alone or with a few other people, simply show up at the stadium's press gate at noon anyday except Sunday (or game days). If you're part of a group of 12 or more, advance reservations are required. Tours cost $8 for adults and $4 for children. Call 718/579-4531 for more information.

Most museums offer tours of particular galleries, special shows, or their entire collection. Look under specific entries in the section on "Museums" in this chapter, or call the museums for more information.

WALKING TOURS

Time Out New York lists scheduled walking tours in its "Around Town" section each week. Among the potential sources are:

Adventure on a Shoestring — The name pretty much sums up this marvelous organization. For a small annual membership fee, plus a nominal attendance fee for each event, you can go on any and all of the scores of interesting and often offbeat tours of the city and surrounding areas they put together. Call 212/265-2663 for more information.

Big Onion Walking Tours — Seth Kamil and his band of guides (most of whom have graduate degrees in American history from Columbia and NYU) share their vast knowledge of New York through a wide array of walking tours in different parts of the city. Governor's Island, George Washington's New York, Historic Catholic New York, and the Civil War and Draft Riots are just a few of their many topics. Most tours cost $10 for adults and $8 for senior citizens and students; some are a bit more expensive and all can be arranged for private parties. All last between two and two-and-a-half hours. Call 212/439-1090 for more information or to get on their mailing list.

Cooper-Hewitt National Museum of Design — One of New York's two branches of the Smithsonian, this museum offers unusual and sometimes rather expensive educational walking tours of areas in and around New York. The museum also offers periodic trips abroad. Reservations are required. Call 212/849-8389 for more information.

Municipal Art Society – This terrific advocacy group offers a wide array of thematic and area-specific walking tours for people interested in the city's architecture and history. Most tours are led by historians. The diverse topics include architectural oddities, immigrant New York, downtown skyscrapers, and subway art and design. Tours are offered on different days and meet at different places, but most last about 90 minutes and cost between $10 and $15 for adults (less for students and senior citizens). Call 212/439-1049 for general information or to get on the Society's mailing list. If you want a private tour, call 212/935-3960.

Museum of the City of New York – This museum makes a real effort to be part of the city rather than an aloof observer, and its walking tours are very much in keeping with that spirit. Typically held every other Sunday from April to October, tours are led by experts and cost $15. Registration is required. Call the museum's education department at 212/534-1672, ext. 206, for more information or to get on the museum's mailing list.

92nd Street Y – This amazing institution (the Young Men's Hebrew Association) often offers walking tours to complement its frequent lectures and other programs, as well as open houses in historic areas. Prices vary, but the guides are always knowledgeable and the tours are well run. They fill up quickly, and reservations are required. Call 212/415-5628 for more information or to get on the mailing list.

River-to-River Downtown Walking Tours – I don't know of a better guide for a "river to river" walk through lower Manhattan than Ruth Alscher-Green, a retired high-school teacher and lifelong New Yorker. A two-hour tour costs $35 for one person and $50 for two, and special rates are offered for groups and senior citizens. Call 212/321-2823 for more information or to get on her mailing list.

Urban Explorations – Landscape designer Patricia Olmstead offers thoughtful and informative walking tours of Battery Park City, Soho, Chinatown, the Flower District, the area around the 96th Street Mosque, and just about any other neighborhood or district you want to see. She specializes in garden tours throughout the city and will happily design an itinerary or private tour if nothing in her current repertoire suits you or your group. Most tours are held on weekends and cost $12 for adults and $10 for students, senior citizens, and repeat customers. Call 718/721-5254 for more information or to get on her mailing list.

Urban Park Rangers – No, you didn't misread that. The city's Department of Parks and Recreation employs Urban Park Rangers, and they give wonderful weekend walking tours and talks in Central Park and other parks throughout Manhattan and the city's four other boroughs. These tours are free, and many are designed for children or families. Call 212/427-4040 for more information or to get on their mailing list.

A Week in New York

You could spend an entire lifetime in New York and still never have time to see and do and eat everything this fabulous city has to offer. If you're here for a week or two, you obviously have a lot of choices to make.

The first thing you need to know when planning an itinerary is that some areas are best on certain days—Soho on Saturday and the Lower East Side on Sunday, for example. Others shut down on the weekend (the Financial District), Saturday (the Lower East Side), Sunday (Soho and most of midtown), or Monday (many major museums and theaters). If time is limited, I suggest picking a couple of things you really want to do or places you really want to see and build your days around them. Check the hours of the places you're planning to visit and plan your days accordingly so you can make the most of your time.

If you're at a loss—you want to see everything but don't know where to start—I've sketched an outline of possible itineraries for seven days in New York that will give you some ideas. In so doing, however, I do not mean to imply that the places I've included are necessarily better than others. Moreover, I do not recommend trying to do everything in every day. Part of the pleasure of New York is wandering and lingering and taking your time, and I don't want you to collapse from exhaustion.

MONDAY (Upper West Side)

- Breakfast to go from Fairway (2127 Broadway) or Zabar's (2245 Broadway)
- Cathedral Church of St. John the Divine (Amsterdam Ave at 112th St)
- Columbia University, main campus (entrance off 116th St, at Broadway and Amsterdam Ave)
- Riverside Church's bell tower (Riverside Dr bet 120th and 122nd St)
- American Museum of Natural History (Central Park W, bet 77th and 81st St)
- Late lunch at Tavern on the Green (inside the park near 67th St at Central Park W)
- Stroll through Central Park
- Lincoln Center (Columbus Ave bet 62nd and 65th St)
- Museum of American Folk Art (Columbus Ave bet 65th and 66th St)
- Dinner at Gabriel's (11 W 60th St)

TUESDAY (Midtown)

- Macy's (151 W 34th St)
- Morgan Library (29 E 36th St)
- New York Public Library (Fifth Ave bet 40th and 42nd St)
- International Center for Photography (1133 Ave of the Americas)
- Saks Fifth Avenue (611 Fifth Ave)
- Lunch at Grand Central Oyster Bar Restaurant (Grand Central Station)
- Rockefeller Center (49th to 51st St bet Fifth Ave and Ave of the Americas)
- Museum of Modern Art (11 W 53rd St)
- Carnegie Hall (153 W 57th St)
- Dinner at Docks Oyster Bar and Seafood Grill (633 Third Ave)
- Empire State Building observation deck (Fifth Ave bet 33rd and 34th St)

WEDNESDAY

- United Nations (First Ave bet 45th and 46th St)
- Ford Foundation Gardens (320 E 43rd St)
- Early lunch at Tropica (MetLife Building, 200 Park Ave)
- 12:30 tour of Grand Central Station (offered by the Metropolitan Art Society)
- The Cloisters (Fort Tryon Park)
- Dyckman Farmhouse (4881 Broadway)

- Dinner at Carnegie Delicatessen and Restaurant (Seventh Ave at 55th St)

THURSDAY (Museum Mile)

- Museum of the City of New York (1220 Fifth Ave)
- Jewish Museum (1109 Fifth Ave)
- Cooper-Hewitt National Museum of Design (2 E 91st St)
- Solomon R. Guggenheim Museum (1071 Fifth Ave)
- Lunch at the Museum Cafe in the Guggenheim
- Metropolitan Museum of Art (Fifth Ave bet 80th and 84th St)
- Whitney Museum of American Art (945 Madison Ave)
- Frick Collection (1 E 70th St)
- Bloomingdale's (1000 Third Ave)
- Dinner at Sette Mezzo (969 Lexington Ave)

FRIDAY (Financial District)

- Battery Park to Statue of Liberty and Ellis Island
- Museum of the American Indian (1 Bowling Green)
- Museum of Jewish Heritage (18 First Pl)
- Pick up half-price tickets for the theater (TKTS booth on the mezzanine of 2 World Trade Center)
- Lunch at Nobu (105 Hudson St)
- New York Stock Exchange (20 Broad St)
- Federal Hall National Monument (Wall at Nassau St)
- Trinity Church (Broadway at Wall St)
- Fraunces Tavern Museum (54 Pearl St)
- Pre-theater dinner at La Réserve (4 W 49th St)
- Theater

SATURDAY (Chelsea and Soho)

- Gallery hopping on and around 22nd Street in Chelsea
- Dia Center for the Arts (548 W 22nd St)
- Gallery hopping on and around West Broadway
- Alternative Museum (594 Broadway)
- Museum for African Art (593 Broadway)
- Contemporary Museum (583 Broadway)
- Guggenheim Museum Soho (575 Broadway)
- Dinner at Blue Ribbon (97 Sullivan St)

SUNDAY (Lower East Side)

- Lower East Side shopping
- Brunch at Katz's Delicatessen (205 East Houston St)
- Lower East Side Tenement Museum (97 Orchard St)
- Eldridge Street Synagogue (12 Eldridge St)
- Museum of Chinese in the Americas (70 Mulberry St)
- Dinner in Chinatown at the Golden Unicorn (18 East Broadway)

IV. Where to Find It: New York's Best Food Shops

Nobody knows and loves food like a New Yorker. That's true for restaurants, but it's also true for food shops. That's why the typical New Yorker doesn't do all his food shopping in one big, bland grocery store. He buys bread from one place, meat somewhere else, fruits and vegetables at another store, and pasta at yet another. He's looking for the best, the freshest, and the most interesting.

What I've tried to do here is give you the "best of the best." Whether you're eating your way through New York or looking for a place to get just the right food for a special occasion, the following pages are filled with lots of mouthwatering possibilities.

Bakery Goods

AMY'S BREAD
75 Ninth Ave   212/462-4338
Mon-Fri: 8-8; Sat: 8-7; Sun: 10-6

672 Ninth Ave   212/462-4323
Mon-Fri: 8-7; Sat: 8-6; Sun: 9-4

This is a tasty place to visit at any hour, but breakfast time is very special. There are handmade specialty breads, black olive twists, and wonderful French baguettes. Semolina with black sesame seeds or with golden raisins and fennel are justly famous. My favorites are the walnut apple raisin roll and the walnut stick. Amy's started in an old storefront on Ninth Avenue and evolved into a bakery that uses only organic whole grains and unbleached flour. All breads are low-fat or fat-free. Each location has a cozy cafe with sandwiches, sweets, and high-quality coffee. Each day different items are specially priced at the Chelsea Market location.

A. ORWASHER BAKERY
308 E 78th St (nr Second Ave)   212/288-6569
Mon-Sat: 7-7; Sun: 9-4

Orwasher has been in existence for over three quarters of a century at the same location, operated by the same family. Many of its breads are from recipes handed down from father to son. You'll find Old World breads that once existed in the local immigrant bakeries but have now become extremely rare. Over 30 varieties are always available. Hearth-baked in brick ovens and made with natural ingredients, the breads come in a marvelous array of shapes and sizes—

242

triple twists, cornucopias, and hearts, just to name a few. Be sure to sample the onion boards, rye, cinnamon raisin bread, and challah, available on Fridays. It's almost as good as the home-baked variety. Best of all is raisin pumpernickel, which comes in small rolls or loaves. When warm, it's especially sensational. The Irish soda bread is also special!

A. ZITO AND SON'S BAKERY
259 Bleecker St (bet Ave of the Americas and Seventh Ave)
212/929-6139
Mon-Sat: 6-7; Sun: 6-3

Those in the know, know Zito's. They flock here at sunrise to buy bread straight from the oven. Greenwich Village residents love Zito's because the bread crust is crunchy perfection—a sharp contrast to the soft, delicate inside. Two best sellers are the whole-wheat loaf and the Sicilian loaf. Anthony John Zito is proudest of the house specialties: Italian, whole-wheat, and white breads. The latter two come in sizes of 4, 7, and 13 ounces.

BREAD MARKET & CAFE
485 Fifth Ave (bet 41st and 42nd St)   212/370-7356
Mon-Fri: 7-6; Sat: 8-6

Freshness is the key here! The bread is baked fresh daily in their rotating oven. You'll find very good San Francisco sourdough, cinnamon raisin, Italian braid, Jewish rye, European corn rye, German pumpernickel, and much more. They make a wide variety of excellent sandwiches. Free delivery is offered. Leftovers go to City Harvest.

BREAD SHOP
3139 Broadway (at LaSalle St)   212/666-4343
Daily: 7 a.m.-11 p.m.

The Bread Shop is a tiny, out-of-the-way bakery under the tracks at 123rd Street. It supplies some of the best handmade, preservative-free bread in the city. Its customers are mostly local stores and New York's better food shops, but if you arrive between 10 and 3, one of the house specialties will be available fresh from the oven. They are big on healthy, natural ingredients, so the bread is delicious and good for you.

CAFE LALO
201 W 83rd St (at Amsterdam Ave)   212/496-6031
Mon-Thurs: 8 a.m.-2 a.m.; Fri: 8-4; Sat: 9-4;
Sun: 9 a.m-2 a.m.

In my opinion, this is the best dessert shop in town. You will be reminded of a fine European pastry shop as you enjoy cappuccino, espresso, cordials, and a large selection of delicious desserts. Cafe Lalo offers 63 kinds of cake, 24 cheesecakes, 20 tarts, and 20 pies! Yogurt and ice cream are also available, and soothing music makes every calorie go down sweetly. Breakfasts and brunches are all a treat.

CHARLES AND LAUREL DESSERTS
537 Greenwich St   212/229-9339
Mon-Fri: 9-5 (phone orders only; no drop-in sales)

You've found a real winner! Charles and Laurel Desserts, a mother and son operation since 1990, is essentially a wholesale business but will take phone orders from readers of this volume. What treats are in store here: the best semisweet chocolate brownies in town, blondies, innovative bar cookies (like raspberry truffle brownies, espresso caramel hazelnut bars, peanut butter and jelly bars, tortes, rugelach, mini bundt cakes, loaf cakes, and much more. Give them a call and tell them Gerry sent you!

Don't miss the pastries (from Guy Pascal) at the **Lexington Cafe** (200 Lexington Ave) in the New York Design Center (New York Chapter, American Society of Interior Designers).

COLUMBUS BAKERY
474 Columbus Ave (at 83rd St)   212/724-6880
Daily: 8 a.m.-10 p.m.

The Upper West Side has a quality bakery that it can call its own. Columbus Bakery sells great rosemary rolls, delicious onion rolls for burgers, multigrain breads, really crusty sourdoughs, wonderful cakes and pastries, and more. You can eat in or take out, but what a pleasure just to sit there and smell those fresh loaves. Gift baskets and catering are available.

CREATIVE CAKES
400 E 74th St (at First Ave)   212/794-9811
Mon-Fri: 8-4:30; Sat: 9-11

Being in the "creative cake" business myself, I know all about making special concoctions. Creative Cakes knows how to have fun using fine ingredients and ingenious patterns. Cake lovers are fans of the fudgy chocolate with frosted buttercream icing and the sensational designs. Bill Schutz, the boss, has done such things as make a replica of the U.S. Customs House for a Fourth of July celebration. Prices are reasonable, and the results are sure to be a conversation piece at any party.

DUFOUR PASTRY KITCHENS
25 Ninth Ave (at 13th St)   212/929-2800
Mon-Fri: 8-5; call for Sat hours

The location is not the handiest. The air is full of pastry dough, so don't wear your best black outfit. And all items are frozen, so you'll have to bake them yourself (instructions included). But these are the only drawbacks! You'll find delicious and sensibly priced pastry items of high quality at Dufour, which counts many fancy uptown restaurants among its customers. Chocolate and regular puff-pastry dough are available in sheets and in bulk. Try slice-and-bake savory puff pastry logs in such flavors as artichoke, black olive and tomato, asparagus, fontina, and three-cheese spinach *rustica*. Wonderful hors d'oeuvres can be ordered in quantity: bite-size, hand-filled "party lites" in flavors like fresh-mushroom paté, Swiss and spinach.

ECCE PANIS
1126 Third Ave (bet 65th and 66th St)   212/535-2099
Mon-Fri: 8-8; Sat, Sun: 8-7

1260 Madison Ave (off 90th St)   212/348-0040
Mon-Fri: 8-7; Sat, Sun: 8-5

282 Columbus Ave (at 73rd St)   212/362-7189
Daily: 8-8

434 Ave of the Americas (at 10th St)   212/460-5616
Daily: 8-9

5 World Trade Center   212/432-2820
Mon-Fri: 6:30 a.m.-8:30 p.m.; Sat: 8-6; Sun: 8-5

This is one of Manhattan's better bakeries. Their offerings are unique and of high quality. Breads include dark and light sourdough, neo-Tuscan, whole-wheat currant, double walnut, dried fruit focaccia, Sunday raisin, baguettes, olive bread, and more. The chocolate biscotti is superb! Unusual gift baskets are a specialty.

FERRARA PASTRIES
195 Grand St (bet Mulberry and Mott St)   212/226-6150
Daily: 7:30 a.m.-midnight (Sat to 1 a.m.)

This store in Little Italy is one of the largest little *pasticcerias* in the world. The business deals in wholesale imports and several other ventures, but the sheer perfection of their confections could support the whole business. Certainly, the atmosphere would never suggest that this is anything but a very efficiently run Italian bakery. Its Old World Caffe is famous for numerous varieties of pastry, gelati, and coffee.

GERTELS
53 Hester St   212/982-3250
1592 Second Ave (bet 82nd and 83rd St)   212/734-3238
Sun-Thurs: 7-5:30; Fri: 7-2

You must stop here and try their blackout cake! Customers who come here are almost evenly divided between those who call it Ger*tels* (accent on the last syllable) and those who call it *Ger*tels (as in girdles). Regardless, all agree that the cakes and breads here are among the best in New York. Locals prefer the traditional babkas, strudels, and kuchens, but I find the chocolate rolls and aforementioned blackout cake to be outstanding. For those who want to sample the wares, tables are available for enjoying baked goods, coffee, or a light lunch. From the regulars at these tables, one can glean the choicest shopping tidbits on the Lower East Side. A final tip: every Thursday and Friday, Gertels makes potato kugels. People claim to have come all the way from California for a Thursday kugel! During a slow week, you can occasionally find one left over on a Sunday. (Note: They will ship anywhere in the U.S.)

GLASER'S BAKE SHOP
1670 First Ave (bet 87th and 88th St)   212/289-2562
Tues-Fri: 7-7; Sat: 8-7; Sun: 8-3
Closed July and half of Aug

If it's Sunday, it won't be hard to find Glaser's. The line frequently spills outside as people queue up to buy the Glaser family's fresh cakes and baked goods. One isn't enough of anything here. Customers always walk out with arms bulging. The Glasers run their shop as a family business (since 1902 at this same location) and pride themselves on their breads, cakes, cookies (try the chocolate chip!), and wedding cakes.

H&H BAGELS
2239 Broadway (at 80th St)   212/595-8000
639 W 46th St (bet Eleventh and Twelfth Ave)   212/595-8000
Daily: 24 hours

If you find yourself out and about at 2 a.m., you can get a fresh, piping hot bagel without having to wait on H&H's long daytime line. Regardless of the hour, you can satisfy your hot bagel craving day or night at H&H. Another only-in-New-York special, H&H bakes the best bagels in Manhattan. They ship worldwide; call 800/NY-BAGEL for mail order.

KOSSAR'S BIALYSTOKER KUCHEN BAKERY
367 Grand St   212/473-4810
Daily: 24 hours (closed between 3 p.m. Fri and 8 p.m. Sat)

Tradition has it that the bialy derives its name from Bialystoker, where they were first made. Kossar's brought the recipe over from Europe almost a century ago, and their bialys, bagels, horns, and onion boards are fresh from the oven. The taste is Old World and authentic.

LITTLE PIE COMPANY
424 W 43rd St (at Ninth Ave)   212/736-4780
Mon-Fri: 8-8; Sat: 10-6; Sun: 12-6

Former actor Arnold Wilkerson started baking apple pastries for private orders in his own kitchen. Now he and Michael Deraney operate a unique shop that makes handmade pies and cakes using fresh seasonal fruits. Although they specialize in apple pie (available every season), they also make fresh peach, cherry, blueberry, and other all-American fruit-pie favorites, along with cream, meringue, and crumb pies. Stop by for a hot slice of pie a la mode and a cup of cider. Also available are delicious brownies, bars, and muffins, applesauce carrot cake, white coconut cakes, chocolate cream pies, and cheescakes with wild blueberry, cherry, and orange toppings. No preservatives used here!

MOISHE'S HOME MADE KOSHER BAKERY
181 E Houston St (bet Orchard and Allen St)   212/475-9624
Sun-Thurs: 7 a.m.-6 p.m.; Fri: 7-3

115 Second Ave   212/505-8555
Sun-Thurs: 7 a.m.-9 p.m.; Fri: 7-3

Jewish bakery specialties are legendary, and they are done to perfection at Moishe's. The cornbread is prepared exactly as it was in the old country (and as it should be now). The pumpernickel is dark and moist, and the ryes are simply scrumptious. The house specialty is black Russian pumpernickel, which probably cannot be bested in an old-fashioned bakery in Russia. But the cakes and pies are special, too! The owners, Mordechai and Hymie, are charming and eager to please, and they run one of the best bakeries in the city, with the usual complement of bagels, bialys, cakes, and pastries. By all means, try the challah; Moishe's produces the best. The chocolate layer cakes are also superb.

PATISSERIE LANCIANI
414 W 14th St   212/989-1213
Mon-Sat: 8-8; Sun: 9-8

For those who haven't yet observed the delicacies at Patisserie Lanciani, a quick review of Joseph Lanciani's extensive credentials is in order. For starters, you may have sampled Joseph's work while he was chief pastry chef at the Plaza (a major recommendation in itself). One of the best pastry chefs in the city, he is also a certified expert in spun-sugar creations. Lanciani's cakes, cookies, pastries, tortes, and mousses defy description.

PATISSERIE LES FRIANDISES
972 Lexington Ave (bet 70th and 71st St)   212/988-1616
Mon-Sat: 8-7: Sun: 10-6 (closed Sun in July and Aug)

Owner Jean Kahn offers breakfast goodies like really sticky buns and pear-and apple-tart tatins. Also available are excellent soups, salads, quiches, and sandwiches at noon for eat-in or takeout. The double-chocolate ruffle log cake is a winner!

POSEIDON GREEK BAKERY
629 Ninth Ave (bet 44th and 45th St)   212/757-6173
Tues-Sat: 9-7

Poseidon is a family-run bakery that endlessly and seemingly effortlessly produces Greek specialties. Tremendous pride is evident here. When a customer peers over the counter and asks what something is, the response is usually a long description and sometimes an invitation to taste. There is homemade baklava, strudel, *kataif, trigona, tiropita* (cheese pie), spanakopita, *saragli,* and phyllo. They have cocktail-size frozen spinach, cheese, vegetable, and meat pies for home or parties. Poseidon was founded in 1922 by Greek baker Demetrios Anagnostou. Today it is run by grandson Anthony Fable and his wife Lili to the same exacting standards. Poseidon's specialty is handmade phyllo, which is world-renowned.

At the **New York Cake and Baking Center** (56 W 22nd St, 212/675-2253), you'll find everything you could imagine for decorating cakes, making chocolate forms or whatever. It's a treasure house!

ST. FAMOUS BREAD
796 Ninth Ave (at 53rd St)   212/245-6695
Daily: 7-8

You can tell from the minute you enter this shop that everything is baked fresh in a kitchen that is busy all night. Customers get to choose from a real international selection: sourdough breads, homemade mini-muffins, cornbread (including jalapeno-cheese-onion), cookies, focaccia, banana-walnut bread, Irish soda bread, croissants, and many daily specials. The folks here seem genuinely happy to see you, and I guarantee you won't leave empty-handed!

STICKY FINGERS
121 First Ave (at 7th St)   212/529-2554
Mon-Sat: 6 a.m.-9 p.m.; Sun: 7 a.m.-8 p.m.

This is an old-fashioned bakery with one of the best reputations in town. The diverse ethnic makeup of the neighborhood is reflected in the variety of breads made here. The quality is endorsed by the neighborhood locals with roots in Italy, Poland, the Ukraine, and Russia, who claim the peasant bread tastes as good as grandma's (or even great-grandma's)! There is so much to recommend. The pumpernickel is dark and moist, and it tastes nothing like the commercial variety. The Italian breads are authentic. The Jewish contingent is represented by bagels and bialys. Each group thinks Sticky Fingers is their bakery. Could there be a higher compliment? There are also cakes, focaccia, muffins, scones, cookies, and wonderful turtle brownies.

STREIT MATZOTH COMPANY
150 Rivington St (bet Clinton and Suffolk St)   212/475-7000
Sun-Thurs: 9-5

Matzoth, for the uninitiated, is a thin, waferlike cracker. According to tradition, it came out of Egypt with Moses and the children of Israel when they had to flee so swiftly that there was no time to let the bread rise. Through the years, matzoth was restricted to the time around Passover, and even when matzoth production became automated, business shut down for a good deal of the year. But not today and not in New York. In a small building with a Puerto Rican mural stretching the length of one side, Streit's matzoth factory produces matzoth throughout the year, pausing only on Saturday, Jewish holidays, and to clean the machines. Streit's factory allows a peek at the actual production, which is both mechanized and extremely primitive. It also sells matzoth to the general public. Matzoth is baked in enormous thin sheets that are later broken up. If you ask for a batch that happens to be baking, they might break it right off the production line.

We try to provide all manner of information. If an erotic baker is what you are looking for, **Masturbakers** (Old Devil Moon Restaurant, 511 E 12th St) might be able to custom design your fantasy.

SULLIVAN STREET BAKERY
73 Sullivan St (bet Spring and Broome St)   212/334-9435
Daily: 7-7

If you savor really fresh authentic Italian country bread, this is the place to go. Their sourdough is used by a number of restaurants, so you know it is first-rate. Sullivan carries the only Pizza Bianca Romania (six feet long) in Manhattan. Raisin-walnut bread is one of their specialties.

SYLVIA WEINSTOCK CAKES
273 Church St (bet Franklin and White St)   212/925-6698
Mon-Fri: 9-4 (by appointment only)

Sylvia Weinstock has been in the cake business for over a decade, so she knows how to satisfy customers who want the very best. Her trademark is floral decorations, which are almost lifelike! Although weddings are a specialty (two months notice is required), she will produce a masterpiece for any occasion.

VESUVIO BAKERY
160 Prince St (bet West Broadway and Thompson St)   212/925-8248
Mon-Sat: 7-7

Tony Dapolito was born and bred (no pun intended) in his family's store in

Soho. Since that time, the family's expertise in baking has grown along with the bakery's claim to fame as Soho's common green. When he's not manning the ovens, Tony serves on the community planning board and disperses Soho lore to customers. Visitors unaware of Dapolito's status (it doesn't remain a secret long) come for the bread, biscuits, and rolls. They all have a reputation that reaches far beyond Soho. After all, it isn't every commercial bakery that eschews sugar, shortening, and preservatives and still manages to produce the tastiest Italian bread around. Try the biscotti, the pepper biscuits, or the whole-wheat brick-oven baked bread.

Wonderful Doughnuts

Some of the best doughnuts in New York are made by lately arrived franchises of the North Carolina-based **Krispy Kreme**: 265 W 23rd St, 280 W 125th St, 5 World Trade Center, 38 E 8th St, Penn Station, 1497 Third Ave; and Port Authority Bus Terminal. Also, don't forget **Georgie's Pastry Shop** (50 W 125th St).

More doughnuts!

ABC Carpet & Home (888 Broadway)
Campo (89 Greenwich Ave)
Dean & Deluca (560 Broadway)
Drovers Tap Room (9 Jones St)
Grace's Marketplace (1237 Third Ave)
Home Away from Home (270 Bleecker St)
Jefferson Market (450 Ave of the Americas)
Mitchel London (542 Ninth Ave and 22A E 65th St)
Osteria del Circo (120 W 55th St)

WHOLE EARTH BAKERY & KITCHEN
130 St. Mark's Pl (bet First Ave and Ave A)   212/677-7597
Daily: 9 a.m.-midnight

This is the only bakery in Manhattan that makes baked goods using exclusively organic flours. No animal products, honey, or egg whites are used here, and all of their products are sugar-free. For the health-conscious, this is a good bet.

YONAH SCHIMMEL
137 E Houston St   212/477-2858
Daily: 8-6

Yonah Schimmel has been selling perfect knishes for so long that his name is legendary. National magazines have written articles about him. Schimmel started out dispensing knishes among the pushcarts of the Lower East Side, and a Yonah Schimmel knish is still a unique experience. It doesn't look or taste anything like the mass-produced things sold at supermarkets, lunch stands, or New York ballgames. A Yonah Schimmel knish has a very thin, flaky crust— almost like strudel dough—surrounding hot, moist filling, and is kosher. The best-selling filling is potato, but kasha (buckwheat), spinach, and a half-dozen others are also terrific. No two knishes come out exactly alike, since each is handmade.

Beverages

B&E QUALITY
511 W 23rd Ave   212/243-6559
Mon-Thurs: 8-6:30; Fri, Sat: 8-7

If you are planning a party and want to make a quantity purchase of beer and soda, this is a good place to go. They are a wholesale distributor but will pass along savings to retail customers. Some 800 beers from around the world are available, as well as kegs in over 15 brands.

Confused About Ale and Lager?

- **Abbey ale:** strong, fruity beer
- **Pale ale:** English-style bitter
- **Porter ale:** dark-brown with chocolate malt flavor
- **Stout ale:** made with dark-roasted malts
- **Wheat beer:** ale brewed with raw wheat and barley
- **Bock lager:** malty sweet
- **Pilsener lager:** clean, floral aroma
- **Schwarzbier black beer:** chocolatey bitter lager

NEW YORK BEVERAGE WHOLESALERS
428 E 91st St (at York Ave)   212/831-4000
Mon: 10-7:30; Tues-Thurs: 10-8:30; Fri, Sat: 10-9; Sun: 12-7

The *buy*-words here: tremendous variety, great prices. This outfit has one of the largest retail beer selections in Manhattan, with over 500 brands available. Prices are good for beer, soda, mineral and natural waters, iced teas, and seltzers. They will deliver to your door, supply specialty imports, and work with you on any quantities needed.

RIVERSIDE BEER AND SODA DISTRIBUTORS
2331 Twelfth Ave (at 133rd St)   212/234-3884
Mon-Sat: 9-6

Run by Hector Borrero, this place mainly supplies wholesalers and large retail orders, but he's not averse to serving retail customers. Once you've shlepped up there, might as well take advantage of the discount and buy in quantity.

It's All in the Water . . .

Artesian water: underground well water
Distilled water: no minerals
Mineral water: between 250-1500 milligrams per liter of dissolved solids
Natural water: no processing
Still water: no natural or added effervescence
Sparkling water: carbonated naturally
Spring water: underground water that surfaces at springs

British

MYERS OF KESWICK
634 Hudson St (bet Horatio and Jane St)   212/691-4194
Mon-Fri: 10-7; Sat: 10-6; Sun: noon-5

Peter and Irene Myers are doing with English food what Burberry, Church, and Laura Ashley have done with English clothing. They've made it possible for you to visit "the village grocer" for imported staples and fresh, home-baked items you'd swear came from a kitchen in Soho—the London neighborhood, that is. Among the tins, a shopper can find Heinz treacle sponge pudding, trifle mix, ribena, mushy peas, steak and kidney pie, Smarties, Quality Street toffee, lemon barley water, chutneys, jams and preserves, and all the major English teas. The fresh goods include sausage rolls, kidney pie, Scotch eggs, and Aberdeen kippers. There are also cheeses (the double Gloucester is outstanding) and chocolates. For Anglophiles and expatriates alike, Myers of Keswick is a *luverly* treat.

Candy

Luxury Chocolates:

Burdick Chocolates: 800/229-2419 (mail order/delivery)
Christopher Norman Chocolates: 8 Rivington St (212/677-3722; call first). These chocolates are also available at Dean & Deluca and Balducci's.
Fifth Avenue Chocolatiere: 510 Madison Ave
L.A. Boss: 230 Park Ave (in the Helmsley Building)
Laderach Chocolatier Suisse: 800/231-8154. These chocolates are worth every expensive cent. They're also carried at Macy's, Bloomingdale's, and Dean & Deluca.
La Maison du Chocolat: 25 E 73rd St
Leonidas: 485 Madison Ave
Manhattan Fruitier: 105 E 29th St
Neuchatel Chocolates: 758 Fifth Ave (in the Plaza Hotel) and 60 Wall St
Richart Design et Chocolat: 7 E 55th St
Teuscher Chocolates: 25 E 61st St and 620 Fifth Ave

ECONOMY CANDY
108 Rivington St   212/254-1531, 800/352-4544 (outside New York)
Sun-Fri: 8:30-6; Sat: 10-5

The same family of owners has been selling everything from penny candies to beautiful gourmet gift baskets since 1937. What a selection of dried fruits, nuts, candies, coffees, teas, jams, spices, cookies, crackers, and chocolates! The best part is the price. You can get gourmet items like caviar and paté without exceeding your party budget. Mail orders are filled efficiently and promptly; a free catalog is available.

LA MAISON DU CHOCOLAT
1018 Madison Ave (bet 78th and 79th St)   212/744-7117
Mon-Fri: 10-7:30; Sat: 11-7; Sun: 12-6

What a place! Under one roof are about 40 delicious variations of light and dark chocolates. There are French truffles, plain and fancy champagnes, orangettes, coffee beans, chocolate-covered almonds, caramels, candied chestnuts, and fruit paste—even a tea salon that serves pastries and drinks. Everything is made in Paris, and La Maison du Chocolat is the first expansion store outside of France. Prices are a cut above the candy-counter norm, but then so are exotic flavors like September raspberries, freshly grated ginger root, raisins flamed in rum, marzipan with pistachio and kirsh, and caramel butter. What a way to go!

LEONIDAS
485 Madison Ave (bet 51st and 52nd St)   212/980-2608
Mon-Fri: 9-7; Sat: 10-7; Sun: 12-6

3 Hanover Sq (1 block south of Wall St)   212/422-9600
Mon-Fri: 7-6

This is a U.S. franchise of the famous Belgian confectionary company and a haven for those who appreciate good things. Over 80 varieties of confections— milk, white, and bittersweet chocolate pieces, chocolate orange peels, solid chocolate medallions, fabulous fresh cream fillings, truffle fillings, and marzipan—are flown in fresh every week. Leonidas' pralines are particularly sumptuous. Jacques Bergier, the genial owner, can make the mouth water just describing his treasure trove. Best of all, prices are reasonable. The new Hanover Square location features a European style espresso bar.

LI-LAC CANDY SHOP
120 Christopher St (bet Bleecker and Hudson St)   212/242-7374
Mon-Fri: 10-8; Sat: 12-8; Sun: 12-5

Since 1923, Li-Lac has been *the* source for fine chocolate in Greenwich Village. The most delicious creation is Li-Lac's own chocolate fudge, which is made fresh every day. If you tire of the chocolate, maple walnut fudge is every bit as good. Then there are pralines, mousses, French rolls, nuts, glacé fruits, hand-dipped chocolates, and more, all made on premises.

MONDEL CHOCOLATES
2913 Broadway (at 114th St)   212/864-2111
Mon-Sat: 11-7; Sun: 12-6

Mondel has been a tasty gem in the neighborhood for about a half-century. It was founded by the father of its present owner, Florence Mondel. The aroma here is fantastic! The chocolate-covered ginger, orange peel, nut barks, and turtles are special winners. They also offer a dietetic chocolate line.

NEUCHATEL CHOCOLATES
Plaza Hotel   212/751-7742   60 Wall St   212/480-3766
758 Fifth Ave   Mon-Fri: 10-5:30
Daily: 9 a.m.-10 p.m.

Neuchatel Chocolates is a class act—and you pay for it. Neuchatel offers a discount for orders of over $1,000, and it's not difficult to earn that savings. To create the finest Swiss chocolates from family recipes, they are prepared by hand with natural ingredients. The taste has been likened to velvety silk. There are 70 varieties of chocolate, with the house specialty being handmade truffles. The marzipan and pralines with fruit or nuts are also worth trying. Neuchatel's origins are Swiss, but the chocolates are created fresh in New York.

NEUHAUS CHOCOLATES
Saks Fifth Avenue
611 Fifth Ave (at 50th St), 8th floor   212/940-2891
Mon-Wed, Fri, Sat: 10-6; Thurs: 10-8; Sun: 12-6
Daily: 9 a.m.-10 p.m.

NEUHAUS CHOCOLATE BOUTIQUE
922 Madison Ave (bet 73rd and 74th St)   212/861-2800
Mon-Sat: 10-6:30

NEUHAUS CHOCOLATE BOUTIQUE
ABC Carpet & Home
888 Broadway   212/254-7400
Mon-Fri: 10-8; Sat: 10-7; Sun: 11-6:30

In 1857, the same year my great-grandfather started his one-man store on the riverfront in Portland, Jean Neuhaus settled in Belgium and established a pharmacy and confectionery shop. Succeeding generations have produced some of the finest handcrafted, enrobed, and molded-design bittersweet, dark, and milk chocolates in the world. They are still imported from Belgium. The showpiece is the Astrid Praline, named after the beloved late queen of Belgium; it is a sugar-glazed delight! Candy is sold in bulk, bars, pre-packs, and holiday and seasonal collections.

TEUSCHER CHOCOLATES OF SWITZERLAND
25 E 61st St (at Madison Ave)   212/751-8482
Mon-Sat: 10-6

620 Fifth Ave (Rockefeller Center)   212/246-4416
Mon-Sat: 10-6; Thurs: 10-7:30; Sun: 10-5:30

If there was an award for "most elegant chocolate shop," it would have to go to Teuscher. Theirs are not just chocolates; they're imported works of art. Bernard Bloom, who owns these Teuscher stores, imports chocolates once a week from Switzerland. The chocolates are packed into handmade boxes so stunning that they add to the decor of many a customer's home. The truffles are almost obscenely good. The superb champagne truffle has a tiny dot of champagne cream in the center. The cocoa, nougat, butter-crunch, muscat, orange, and almond truffles each have their own little surprise. Truffles are the stars here, but Teuscher's marzipan, praline chocolates, and mints (shaped like sea creatures) are of similar high quality.

Catering, Delis, Food to Go

AGATA & VALENTINA
1505 First Ave (at 79th St)   212/452-0690
Mon-Sat: 8 a.m.-8:30 p.m.; Sun: 8-8

This is a very classy, expanded gourmet shop with an ambience that will make you think you're in Sicily. There are all kinds of good things to eat, with one counter more tempting than the next. In summer they have a sidewalk cafe. You'll love the great selection of gourmet dishes, bakery items, seafood, magnificent fresh vegetables, meats, candies, and gelati. One specialty of the house is extra virgin olive oil. Don't expect bargain prices; come instead for quality!

AZURE
830 Third Ave (at 51st St)   212/486-8080
Daily: 24 hours

What a salad bar! Azure's 125 feet of hot and cold offerings is a sight. Of course, there is more: homemade soups, stuffed baked potatoes, pizzas, sushi, and great muffins. This place is tempting to the eyes and stomach.

For the first time, an upscale food market is available in Lower Manhattan, where the pickings had been rather slim. **Amish Market,** with other outlets at 731 Ninth Avenue and 240 E 45th Street, is now open for business at Washington and Cedar streets.

BALDUCCI'S
424 Ave of the Americas (at 9th St)   212/673-2600
Daily: 7 a.m.-8:30 p.m.

Most everyone who visits Greenwich Village wants to stop at Balducci's, one of the premier food emporiums in the city. When Balducci's opened as a greengrocer in 1946, Mom and Pop tended a single cast-iron register, answered questions, serviced customers, and kept pencil accounts for their neighbors. To this day, you will see members of the family in the store helping customers. Under one roof they sell nearly everything: coffee, pastries, fine cheese, smoked salmon, fresh pasta, aged beef, hearth-baked breads, prepared entrees, and the largest selection of quality produce in the city. They produce many traditional specialties like focaccia, fresh-cut pasta and ravioli, sauces, *taralli,* country breads, and fresh-fruit tarts. Special services include personal shopping, catering, gift baskets, and seasonal catalogs from which you can mail-order many Italian home-cooked specials. Free delivery is available between Broadway, Houston, 15th, and West streets. The crowded aisles and family atmosphere are half the fun of shopping here. Village residents and city-wide fans jostle for space in this yummy emporium.

Now you don't have to wait until you finish shopping at **Balducci's Cafe** to taste some of their tempting dishes. Just cross the street to 424 Avenue of the Americas, where you will find goodies like pizzas, sandwiches, salads, pastries, desserts, and pastas to eat in or bagged to take out. Prices are not in the bargain category, but the quality is excellent, as you would expect from an offspring of the mother store.

BARNEY GREENGRASS
541 Amsterdam Ave (bet 86th and 87th St)   212/724-4707
Tues-Sun: 8-6 (takeout)
Tues-Sun: 8:30-4 (restaurant)
closed first two weeks in Aug

Barney Greengrass is synonymous with sturgeon to New Yorkers. This family business has been located at the same place since 1929. Barney has been succeeded by his son Moe and grandson Gary, but the same quality gourmet smoked fish is still sold over the counter, just as it was in Barney's day. The Greengrasses lay claim to the title of "Sturgeon King," and few would dispute it. While sturgeon is king here, Barney Greengrass also has other smoked-fish delicacies:

Nova Scotia salmon, belly lox, white fish, caviar, and pickled herring. The dairy-deli line—including vegetable cream cheese, great homemade cheese blintzes, homemade salads and borscht, and a smashing Nova Scotia salmon with scrambled eggs and onions—is world-renowned. In fact, because so many customers couldn't wait to get home to unwrap their packages, Greengrass started a restaurant next door.

BARRAUD CATERERS
405 Broome St (nr Centre St)   212/925-1334
Mon-Fri: 10-6 (office)

Owner Rosemary Howe has an interesting background. She was born in India and is thus familiar with Indian and Anglo-Indian food. Her training in developing recipes was on the French side. Because she grew up in the tradition of afternoon tea, she knows finger sandwiches and all that goes with them. Her menus are unique. All breads are made menu-specific, every meal is customized from a lengthy list, a wine consultant is available, and even consultations on table etiquette are given. This is a real hands-on operation, with Rosemary taking care of every detail. No wonder Barraud has been mentioned numerous times as one of New York's best.

BROADWAY FARM
2339 Broadway (at 85th St)   212/787-8585
Open 24 hours

Upper West Side shoppers enjoy this quality food outlet, which features a full deli, fruits, vegetables, seafood, pasta, excellent coffee and cheese selections, smoked fish, specialty beers, and unusual imported items. Delivery is free from 75th to 95th streets between Central Park West and Riverside Drive.

CAVIARTERIA
502 Park Ave (at 59th St)   212/759-7410, 800/4-CAVIAR
Mon-Thurs: 9-7; Fri, Sat: 9-8; Sun: 11-4

Soho Grand Hotel
310 West Broadway (bet Canal and Grand St)   212/925-5515
Sun, Mon: noon-10; Tues, Thurs: noon-midnight; Fri, Sat: noon-2 a.m.

Kiosk in Grand Central Terminal (takeout)   212/682-5355

This is really a caviar department store! Caviarteria is the largest distributor of caviar in the U.S. It is known for high-quality products at reasonable prices. Much of the business is done by phone; shipments are packed with ice and handled responsibly. You will find paté de foie gras, Scotch and Swedish smoked salmon platters, sturgeon, homemade biscotti, and New Zealand smoked eel. There is an on-premises restaurant and a caviar- and champagne-tasting bar. Delivery and catering are special conveniences. Specialties include a Caspian caviar sampler, lobster-tail medallions, Caviarteria club *du roi* sandwiches, caviar crepes, and Caviarteria carpaccio. Owners Eric and Bruce Sobel are right on the job, accounting for the superior operation of these shops.

CHARLOTTE'S
146 Chambers St (bet Greenwich St and West Broadway)   212/732-7939
Mon-Fri: 10-6

Quality is Number One here! Charlotte's has developed an outstanding reputation for catering, with no detail too small for their careful attention. Their client list reads like a who's who, including Bankers Trust, New York Philharmonic, Tiffany's, and Walt Disney. Charlotte's is a full-service catering establishment, from menus and music to flowers and waiters' outfits. Come here when you want real experts to do the work for wedding receptions, dinner dances, teas, luncheons, business meetings or dinners, and so forth. Specialties include wonderful tapas, a spa buffet menu, and outrageous desserts.

CHELSEA MARKET
75 Ninth Ave (bet 15th and 16th St)   212/243-6005
Mon-Sat: 8-8; Sun: 10-6

Once again, there is no place like New York City! In a complex of 18 former industrial buildings, including the old Nabisco Cookie Factory of the late 1800s (where Oreo cookies first captured the stomachs of hungry kids), an 800-foot-long concourse houses one of the most unique marketplaces in the city. The space is innovative, including a waterfall supplied by an underground spring. Among the nearly two dozen shops, you'll find **Amy's Bread** (big choice, plus a cafe), **Bowery Kitchen Supplies** (kitchen buffs will go wild!), **Chelsea Wholesale Flower Market** (cut flowers that look really fresh), **Chelsea Wine Vault** (climate-controlled), **Cleaver Company** (catering/event planning), **Hale & Hearty Soups** (dozens of varieties), the **Lobster Place** (takeout seafood), **Sarabeth's Baker**, **Frank's Butcher**, **Manhattan Fruit Exchange** (bulk buying), plus bagels, ice creams, rugelach, meats, hospitality products, and more. **Ruthie's Cheesecake** (212/463-8800) is outstanding!

DEAN & DELUCA
560 Broadway (at Prince St)   212/431-1691
Mon-Sat: 10-8; Sun: 10-7

This is one of the great gourmet stores in the country. Long a tradition for smart food buyers, Dean & Deluca is now housed in a store four times as large as the original location. The temptations here are extraordinary: wonderfully fresh produce; a huge selection of cheeses; fresh bakery items; takeout dishes; all kinds of meat, poultry, and fish products; coffees; magnificent pastries and desserts; housewares; books; and much more. A very popular espresso and cappuccino bar greets customers at the door. This part of the operation has been expanded into convenient smaller locations at 75 University Place, the Paramount Hotel in midtown, and 50 Rockefeller Center. Professional kitchen equipment is available to both wholesale and retail customers, and a catering kitchen is located on-premises.

ELI'S MANHATTAN
1411 Third Ave (bet 80th and 81st St)   212/717-8100
Daily: 7 a.m.-9 p.m.

In the former Morgan Manhattan Warehouse, Eli Zabar (of the famous food family) has opened yet another upscale food emporium to take care of Upper East Siders. The new store features a fish department with an oyster and sushi bar, a butcher shop with a windowed aging-room, a large selection of organic produce, and an excellent cheese department. That is in addition to all the usual sections: bakery, prepared foods, appetizers, housewares, flowers, and so on. Home shopping is available, as is free delivery (with $50 purchase) between 61st and 110th streets. A cafe/restaurant serves breakfast and lunch daily.

FAIRWAY
2127 Broadway (at 74th St)   212/595-1888
Daily: 24 hours (closed Sun midnight to Mon 7 a.m.)

132nd St at Hudson River   212/234-3883
Daily: 8 a.m.-11 p.m.

The battle of the food shops continues unabated on both the Upper East Side and the Upper West Side. Right in the middle, much to the benefit of the customers, is the popular institution known as Fairway, which made its name with an incredible selection of fruits and vegetables. They offer produce in huge quantities at very reasonable prices. The Hudson River store is newer and larger, stocking a wonderful array of cheeses, meats, bakery items and more. Recent additions to the Broadway store include an on-premises bakery, a cafe, organically grown produce, expanded fish and meat departments, and a catering service. Fairway operates its own farm on Long Island and has developed a good relationship with area produce dealers. As you make your rounds on the Upper West Side, you can't go wrong by carrying a Fairway bag on one arm and a Zabar's bag on the other.

FINE & SCHAPIRO
138 W 72nd St   212/877-2874
Daily: 9 a.m.-10 p.m.

Ostensibly a kosher delicatessen and restaurant, Fine & Schapiro offers some of the best dinners for at-home consumption in the city. Because of the quality of their foods, they term themselves "the Rolls-Royce of delicatessens." That description is cited only because it is very apt. Fine & Schapiro dispenses a complete line of cold cuts, hot and cold hors d'oeuvres, Chinese delicacies, catering platters, and magnificent sandwiches. Everything that issues from Fine & Schapiro is perfectly cooked and artistically arranged. The sandwiches are masterpieces; the aroma and taste are irresistible. Chicken in the pot and stuffed cabbage are two of their best items.

FISHER & LEVY
875 Third Ave (at 53rd St, concourse level)   212/832-3880
Mon-Fri: 7:30-3:30 (call before 3 p.m. for dinner delivery)

Chip Fisher and his partner Thom Hamill have served the corporate catering needs of Manhattan with style and high-quality service for nearly two decades. They take care of big parties and solitary diners alike. Fisher & Levy begins the day with delicious breakfast items. How does a slice of coffee crumb cake sound? Or a fresh-baked blueberry scone? For lunch, dive into a juicy filet mignon sandwich with grilled red peppers or a roasted turkey breast with honey glaze. In addition to delicious pizza, their small retail store in the food court at 875 Third Avenue offers daily sandwiches, soups, interesting pastas and vegetable salads, Cobb salad, and desserts like homemade bread pudding. Desserts are all made in-house and include gooey brownies, raspberry rugelach, and fabulous all-butter cookies.

FLAVORS CATERING & CARRYOUT
8 W 18th St (at Fifth Ave)   212/647-1234
Mon-Fri: 8-6:30

Flavors' specialties range from "High French" custom catering to modern, healthy to-go (or eat-in) items from their retail shop to home and office delivery.

They can do it all: special vegetarian dishes, custom gift baskets, picnic outings, catered cruises, and even a full-scale wedding in a historic New York City mansion. The client list includes ABC, Condé Nast, Nike, Martha Stewart Living, Revlon, and Tiffany. The price is right!

GARDEN OF EDEN
162 W 23rd St   212/675-6300
310 Third Ave (bet 23rd and 24th St)   212/228-4681
7 E 14th St (bet University Pl and Fifth Ave)   212/254-4200
Mon-Sun: 7 a.m.-10 p.m.

These stores are a real farmer's market! Not only are all the food items fresh, appetizing, and priced to please, the stores are immaculate and well organized. To complete the pleasant shopping experience: the personnel are exceptionally helpful. You'll find breads and bakery items, cheeses, veggies, meat, seafood, pastas, desserts and whatever else your hungry tummy yearns for. All manner of catering services are available, including suggestions for locations, rentals, and service.

GLORIOUS FOOD
504 E 74th St   212/628-2320
Mon-Fri: 9-5

Glorious Food is at the top of many New Yorkers' list when it comes to catering. They are a full-service outfit, expertly taking care of every small detail of your event. Having been in business for over a quarter of a century, they have met most every challenge. Give 'em a try!

GOURMET GARAGE
451 Broome St (at Mercer St)   212/941-5850
301 E. 64th St   212/535-6271
2567 Broadway (at 96th St)   212/663-4927
117 Seventh Ave S (bet 10th and Christopher St)   212/229-2650
Daily: 7:30 a.m.-8:30 p.m.

A working-class gourmet food shop is the best way to describe Gourmet Garage. These stores carry a good selection of in-demand items, like fruits and veggies, cheeses, breads, pastries, coffees, meats, and olive oils, all at low prices. Organic foods are a specialty.

GRACE'S MARKETPLACE
1237 Third Ave (at 71st St)   212/737-0600
Mon-Sat: 7 a.m.-8:30 p.m.; Sun: 8-7

Founded by Grace Balducci Doria, Joe Doria, and their family, Grace's Marketplace is one of the city's most popular food emporiums for New Yorkers. Only the best of everything in products, service, and ambience is here. Many sections have been remodeled and expanded. You'll find smoked meats and fish, cheeses, fresh pastas, fresh homemade sauces, produce, a full range of baked goods, candy, coffee, tea, dried fruits, pastries, gourmet groceries, and prepared foods. Grace's now features prime meats and fresh seafood, and they are also well known for quality gift baskets and catering. Get a taste of Puglia at their restaurant, **Grace's Trattoria** (201 East 71st Street). No visit to New York is complete without an excursion to Grace's!

GREAT PERFORMANCES
287 Spring St   212/727-2424

Great Performances has been creating spectacular events in the New York area for 20 years with the help of folks from the city's artistic community. Each division of this full-service catering company has a team of experienced and expert staff. They take pride in recruiting and maintaining the best and brightest the industry has to offer. Their people bring creativity, personality, and technical expertise to each event. From intimate dinner parties to gala dinners for thousands, Great Performances is a complete event-planning resource.

H&H BAGELS EAST
1551 Second Ave (bet 80th and 81st St)   212/734-7441
Daily: 24 hours

The initials H&H have long been synonymous with the best bagels on New York's Upper West Side. Now Upper East Siders can feast upon this fresh, delicious New York specialty, along with a choice of homemade croissants, pastries, super sandwiches, tasty salads, salmon, lox, sturgeon, and pickled herring. Although this is mainly a takeout operation, there are a few tables for those who can't wait to start noshing. H&H bagels are so good they're served at some of New York's classiest hotels: the Pierre, the Plaza, the Four Seasons, the Drake, and Essex House.

INDIANA MARKET & CATERING
80 Second Ave (at 5th St)   212/505-7290
Mon-Sat: 8-6

Indiana Market offers a full-service catering and corporate food-service operation. They will take care of staffing, rentals, insurance, unique party sites, music, photography, flowers, and all the incidentals necessary for a successful event. Their fax menu is sent out daily to clients who want to know the specials. Menu items include food from the heartland: a wide choice of soups, salads, entrees (poultry, meat, seafood, and vegetarian), side dishes (like dried corn casserole and wild-rice pancakes), and great desserts. Ask to be put on their newsletter mailing list.

INTERNATIONAL GROCERIES AND MEAT MARKET
529 Ninth Ave (bet 39th and 40th St)   212/279-5514
543 Ninth Ave (at 40th St)   212/279-1000
Mon-Sat: 8-6

Ninth Avenue is one great wholesale market of international cookery. So what would an international market on Ninth Avenue be if not a retailer of exotic spices at wholesale prices? International Groceries and Meat Market is both a spice emporium and an excellent source for rudiments on which to sprinkle the spices. Here you will sacrifice frills for some of the best prices and freshest foodstuffs in town. Lamb and kid are available at the 543 Ninth Avenue location.

KELLEY & PING
127 Greene St (bet Houston and Prince St)   212/228-1212
Daily: 11:30-11 (closed 5-6)

One of the fastest growing categories in foreign flavors is in the exotic cuisine of Asia. Thai, Chinese, Vietnamese, Japanese, Malaysian, and Korean foods are popular in restaurants and on home diningroom tables. Kelley & Ping specializes in groceries and housewares from this part of the world. A restaurant is now a major part of the operation, and they do catering. If you have questions about how to prepare Asian dishes, these are the folks to ask.

LEE & ELLE
336 Madison Ave (bet 43rd and 44th St)   212/867-5322
Mon-Fri: 6 a.m.-7:30 p.m.; Sat: 7-5:30; Sun: 7-5

Located almost in the center of midtown activity, this place is a must-visit for the hungry shopper or office worker. Seldom have I seen a more appetizing display of prepared foods: salads, meats, veggies, fresh turkey, and a great variety of freshly made sandwiches (which you may customize). There is much more: burgers. light lunches, homemade soups, breakfasts (until 11 a.m.), cakes, bagels. homemade muffins, croissants, cookies . . . 150 items in all to choose from! Patrons can select from a raw bar with foods cooked on a hibachi during the noon hour, Monday through Friday. You can eat in or take out, and free delivery is available.

LUCKY DELI
138 Fifth Ave (bet 18th and 19th St)   212/675-0640
Daily: Open 24 hours

Manhattan has plenty of great delis and markets, many of which offer a good sandwich and salad selection. But few do any better than Lucky Deli. Fancy it is not. For quality, selection, and reasonable prices, it is among the best. Here you will find over two dozen classic sandwiches, a dozen grilled and hot sandwiches, seven different triple-decker jobs (with French fries), and 43 specialty combination sandwiches, all served on your choice of bread. In addition, there are a dozen salad platters, a sushi bar, and homemade soup. For a quick bite on the run or a meal at your desk, Lucky Deli should be your destination. Free delivery is available, and corporate catering is a specialty.

MANGIA
50 W 57th St (bet Fifth Ave and Ave of the Americas)   212/582-5882
Mon-Fri: 7 a.m.-8 p.m.; Sat: 8-7

16 E 48th St (bet Fifth and Madison Ave)   212/754-7600
Mon-Fri: 7-6

40 Wall St (bet Broad and William St)   212/425-4040
Mon-Fri: 7 a.m.-6 p.m.

At Mangia, the old European reverence for ripe tomatoes and brick-oven bread endures. This outfit offers four distinct services: corporate catering, with anything needed for an office breakfast or luncheon; a juice bar; a carryout shop with an antipasto bar, sandwiches, entrees, and cappuccino; and a restaurant with a full menu and pastas made to order. Prices are competitive, and delivery service is offered.

MIKE'S TAKE-AWAY
160 E 45th St (bet Lexington and Third Ave)   212/856-6453
Mon-Fri: 11-7:30

Grand Central Station
Open daily

Mike Bergen started right on the street—yes, outside the MetLife building. He served good stuff, and now he has become a popular purveyor for those who want to eat healthy. His menu changes every day, but you might find chicken stew, curried sweet potato bisque, or chopped chicken salad among the several dozen choices. In addition to the original cart, expanded services include lunch and dinner catering and delivery service, packaged dinner items, and special Friday afternoon prices.

PETAK'S
1246 Madison Ave (bet 89th and 90th St)   212/722-7711
Daily: 7:30 a.m.-8 p.m.; Sun: 9-8

Richard Petak, third-generation member of a family that has owned appetizing businesses in the South Bronx and New Jersey, made the leap to Manhattan, offering the first "appy shop" the Carnegie Hill neighborhood had seen in a long time. No neighborhood has truly *arrived* without having a gourmet shop, and Petak's fills that need. There are all the appy standbys, such as salads (60 of them!), corned beef, pastrami, smoked fish, and all sorts of takeout foods. The store offers full corporate catering, a sushi chef, picnic hampers, box lunches, and a full-service cafe/restaurant.

PRANZO
1500 Second Ave (at 78th St)   212/439-7777
Mon-Fri: 7 a.m-9 p.m.; Sat, Sun: 8-8

In addition to delicious food, there are two special reasons to shop at Pranzo: the extended hours and free delivery service (from 60th to 96th streets between Fifth Avenue and East River). Prices are not inexpensive, but the quality is apparent in the wide selection of appetizers and entrees. Their custom-made sandwiches, served on a variety of specialty breads, are excellent. Table service in the retail store and a very good catering service are available.

RUSS & DAUGHTERS
179 E Houston St   212/475-4880, 800/RUSS-229
Mon-Sat: 9-7; Sun: 8-5:30

A family business in its third generation, Russ & Daughters has been a renowned New York shop since it first opened its doors. They carry nuts, dried fruits, lake sturgeon, salmon, sable, and herring. Russ & Daughters has a reputation for serving only the very best. Five varieties of caviar are sold at low prices. Their chocolates are premium quality. They sell wholesale and over the counter, and will ship anywhere. Many a Lower East Side shopping trip ends with a stop at Russ & Daughters. It is clean, first-rate, friendly—what more could you ask?

SABLE'S SMOKED FISH
1489 Second Ave (bet 77th and 78th St)   212/249-6177
Mon-Fri: 8:30-7:30; Sat: 8-7:30; Sun: 8-5

Kenny Sze was the appetizers manager at Zabar's for many years, and he learned the trade well at that famous gourmet store. Now out on his own, he has brought that knowledge to the Upper East Side, where he offers wonderful smoked salmon, sturgeon, caviar (good prices), cold cuts, cheeses, salads, fresh breads, and prepared foods. Sable's catering service can provide platters (smoked fish, cold cuts, and cheese), jumbo sandwiches, whole hams, cured meat, and more. Free delivery is offered in the immediate area, and they ship anywhere in the U.S. Cold cuts and chicken dishes are specialties. Tables for eat-in are available.

SALUMERIA BIELLESE
376-378 Eighth Ave (at 29th St)   212/736-7376
Mon-Fri: 6:30-6; Sat: 9-5

This Italian-owned grocery store (with a restaurant in back) is also the only French *charcuterie* in the city. If that isn't contradiction enough, ponder that the loyal lunchtime crowd thinks it's dining at a hero shop when it's really enjoying the fruits of a kitchen that serves many fine restaurants in the city. To understand how all this came about, a lesson in New York City geography is necessary. In 1945, when Ugo Buzzio and Joseph Nello came to this country from the Piedmontese city of Biella, they opened a shop a block away from the current one in the immigrant neighborhood called Hell's Kitchen. (Today, it's gentrified and known as Clinton.) The two partners almost immediately began producing French *charcuterie*. Word spread rapidly among the chefs of the city's restaurants that Salumeria Biellese was producing a quality product that could not be duplicated anywhere. Buzzio's son Marc is one of four partners who run the business today.

— Millennium Note —

The only people ever to walk through the Holland Tunnel for pleasure were members of the throngs that attended the dedication ceremonies on November 12, 1927, at the Broome Street entrance plaza in Manhattan and the 12th Street entrance plaza in Jersey City.

SARGE'S
548 Third Ave (bet 36th and 37th St)   212/679-0442
Daily: 24 hours

It isn't fancy, but Sarge's could feed an army, and there's much to be said for the taste, quality, and price. Sarge's will cater everything from hot dogs to hot or cold buffets for almost any size crowd. Prices are gauged by the number of people and type of food, but there are several package deals, and all are remarkably reasonable. Sarge's also caters deli items and has an excellent selection of cold hors d'oeuvre platters, offering everything from canapes of caviar, sturgeon, and Nova Scotia salmon to shrimp cocktail. To make the party complete, Sarge's can supply serving pieces, condiments, and staff.

SONNIER & CASTLE FOOD
532 W 46th St   212/957-6481
Hours by appointment

These folks are full-service caterers who can provide assistance in finding locations, designer flowers, entertainment, and anything else a customer might need for a special gathering. Russ Sonnier and David Castle are young enough to be inventive and aggressive, yet mature enough to do a first-class job. They will do presentations that show a French, Italian, Asian, or Mediterranean influence.

TAYLOR'S PREPARED FOODS AND BAKE SHOPS
523 Hudson St (bet 10th and Charles St)   212/645-8200
Daily: 7 a.m.-10 p.m.

175 Second Ave (bet 11th and 12th St)   212/674-9501
Mon-Fri: 7 a.m.-11 p.m.; Sat, Sun: 8 a.m.-11 p.m.

228 W 18th St (bet Seventh and Eighth Ave)   212/378-2895
Mon-Fri: 6 a.m.-7:30 p.m.; Sat, Sun: 9-6

156 Chambers St (bet West Broadway and West Side Hwy)
Daily: 7-6   212/328-0092

These stores sell delicious pies and cakes; specialty baked items like scones, muffins, and bagels; assorted salads; and hot takeout entrees. Breakfasts are a treat. A catering service for both informal and elegant affairs is available. Production companies may pick up their items as early as needed.

TODARO BROTHERS
555 Second Ave (bet 30th and 31st St)   212/532-0633
Mon-Sat: 7 a.m.-9 p.m.; Sun: 7 a.m.-8 p.m.

This is food heaven! Great lunch sandwiches, fresh homemade mozzarella, and authentic *panettone* are offered daily. Todaro carries the very best in imported and domestic gourmet food. Just about everything here is irresistible: imported stuffed pasta, fresh fish, rare cheeses, olive oils, patés, jams, coffees, homemade sausages, and more. Todaro even stocks fresh truffles, a delicacy seldom seen this side of a haughty restaurant. To top it off, Lucian Todaro imports the very best chocolates from Europe.

VINEGAR FACTORY
431 E 91st St (near York Ave)   212/987-0885
Daily: 7 a.m.-9 p.m.
Brunch: Sat, Sun: 8-4

It's not exactly in a great location: the site of what used to be a working vinegar factory. But this operation of Eli Zabar's has bearable prices on fresh produce, pizzas, fish, flowers, meats, wines, liquors, desserts, seafood, cheeses, baked goods (including Eli's great bread), coffee, deli items, paper goods, books, and housewares. Breakfast and brunch (on weekends) are available on the balcony. This is one of the most intriguing food factories around! Catering is also offered.

WORD OF MOUTH
1012 Lexington Ave (bet 72nd and 73rd St)
212/734-9483 (store); 212/249-5351 (cafe)
Store: Mon-Fri: 10:30-7; Sat, Sun: 10:30-5
Cafe: Mon-Fri: 8-7; Sat: 9-5; Sun: 10-5 (closed Sun in Aug)

The history of Word of Mouth is actually the gastronomic history of Manhattan—or at least the Upper East Side. When Christi Finch (an Oregonian— we pop up everywhere!) opened her tiny shop in 1976, it was one of the first to offer home-style prepared foods for home or picnic use. Success was almost instantaneous, and by 1979 she had incorporated and moved her shop around the corner. Today she enjoys a reputation as one of the finest sources for pasta, soups, vegetable and chicken salads, quiches, baked goods, and specialty meat dishes. The aim is still the same, however. Full-service home catering is offered. There is no ethnic orientation, though there are worldwide influences. The philosophy is basically home-style cooking that makes use of the finest ingredients. A wonderful brunch menu is offered on weekends.

ZABAR'S
2245 Broadway (at 80th St)   212/787-2000
Mon-Fri: 8-7:30; Sat: 8-8; Sun: 9-6
Mezzanine (housewares): Mon-Fri, Sun: 9-6; Sat: 9-7

When people ask about special places to visit in Manhattan, my answer always includes Zabar's. This New York institution is one unique operation! No fancy fixtures, carpets, or expensive decor. You come to Zabar's for quality, bargain prices, and an immense selection. You will find a huge array of bakery goods at excellent prices, every kind of cheese imaginable, an appetizer counter so busy you must take a number, a coffee selection that is world-renowned (they do one of the largest coffee businesses in the world), and prepared food items that taste as good as they look. There's much more: sushi, great gift baskets, organic produce, candy, and a cafe next door that features many of the in-store goodies at comfortable prices. Upstairs is one of the best housewares departments in America, with every conceivable item represented at low prices. For native New Yorkers, visiting Zabar's is part of daily life. For visitors, it can only be described as a special experience. Besides, Saul Zabar (of the founding family) and managers Scott Goldshine and David Tait are all superior, hands-on merchants.

All in the Family!

No city in the world has as many great gourmet shops as New York. Perhaps one of the reasons is that several families are intertwined in their ownership. **Zabar's** (2245 Broadway) is a Manhattan institution and a must for visitors. Saul and Stanley Zabar preside here. Their brother, Eli, has opened **Eli's Manhattan** (1411 Third Ave), famous for great bread among other things. He also owns the **Vinegar Factory** (431 E 91st St), a comfortable and satisfying place to shop.

Nearby is **Grace's Marketplace** (1237 Third Ave), where Grace Balducci Doria and husband Joe operate one of the classiest gourmet shops in the country. Next door, the meat and fish sections have been expanded, a cafe has opened, and wonderful pastries are served. Grace is the daughter of the founder of **Balducci's in the Village** (424 Ave of the Americas), known for its excellent selection of fruits and vegetables. To complete the picture, Grace is the aunt of Louis Balducci, one of the owners of **Agata & Valentina** (1505 First Ave). This store is known for top-grade service.

That just leaves **Dean & Deluca** (560 Broadway), which offers great edibles in an atmosphere of mouth-watering goodness. They're not involved with the Zabar or Balducci clans, however!

Cheese

ALLEVA DAIRY
188 Grand St (at Mulberry St)   212/226-7990, 800/4-ALLEVA
Mon-Sat: 8:30-6; Sun: 8:30-3

Alleva, founded in 1892, is the oldest Italian cheese store in America. The

Alleva family has operated the business from the start, always maintaining meticulous high standards. Robert Alleva is the current boss, overseeing the production of over 4,000 pounds of fresh cheese a week: *parmigiano, fraschi, manteche, scamoize,* and *provole affumicale.* The ricotta is superb, and the mozzarella tastes like it was made on some little side street in Florence. A mail-order catalog is available.

Craving cheese but afraid of the calories?

Here are some of the best low-fat cheeses:

- Alpine Lace cheddar or grated cheese
- Alpine Lace Swiss
- Coach goat milk low-fat cheese
- Fat-free farmer cheese
- French *fromage blanc*
- Fresh goat-milk quark from Brier Run
- Light *crème havarti* (plain or dill)
- Lite Jarlsberg
- Natural cream cheese
- Simpless cheddar

EAST VILLAGE CHEESE
40 Third Ave (bet 9th and 10th St)   212/477-2601
Mon-Fri: 8:30-6:30; Sat, Sun: 8:30-6

Value is the name of the game here. For years this store has prided itself on selling cheese at some of the lowest prices in town. Now relocated to larger quarters, they claim the same for bean coffee, fresh pasta, extra virgin olive oil, quiche, paté, and a wide selection of fresh bread. An added reason to shop here: this is not a self-service operation.

IDEAL CHEESE SHOP
1205 Second Ave (bet 63rd and 64th St)   212/688-7579,
                                             800/382-0109
Mon-Fri: 9-6:30; Sat: 9-6 (summer: Mon-Fri: 9-6; Sat: 9-5)

Hundreds of cheeses from all over the world are sold here. As a matter of fact, the owners are constantly looking around for new items, just like in the fashion business. This store has been in operation since 1954, and many Upper East Siders swear by its quality and service. Members of the founding family are on hand to answer your questions or to prepare special platters and baskets. A catalog is available.

JOE'S DAIRY
156 Sullivan St (bet Houston and Prince St)   212/677-8780
Tues-Fri: 9-6; Sat: 8-6

This is the best spot in town for fresh mozzarella. Joe Campanelli makes it all ways: smoked, with prosciutto, and more.

Wonderful ricotta and ravioli are found at **DiPalo Dairy** (206 Grand St, 212/226-1033).

MURRAY'S CHEESE SHOP
257 Bleecker St (at Cornelia St)   212/243-3289
Mon-Sat: 8:30-7:30; Sun: 9-5

This is one of the very best cheese shops in Manhattan, and has been so rated by any number of polls. Murray's was founded in 1940; they offer both wholesale and retail international and domestic cheeses of every description. Frank Meilak is the man to talk to behind the counter. Boy, does this place smell good! But that isn't all. There is also a fine selection of cold cuts, pasta, antipasti, bread, sandwiches, and specialty grocery items. Owner Rob Kaufelt has built on the traditions of the city's oldest cheese shop. Special attractions include great cheese platters, gift baskets, and wholesale charge accounts for locals. Mail-order is big; a catalog is available.

Chinese

CHINESE AMERICAN TRADING COMPANY
91 Mulberry St (at Canal St)   212/267-5224
Daily: 9-8

If a homecooked authentic Chinese dinner is on your itinerary, there may be no better source than this store in Chinatown. Chinese American Trading Company boasts that 95% of its business is conducted with the Chinese community. They have an open and friendly attitude here, and great care is taken to introduce customers to the wide variety of imported Oriental foodstuffs, including Japanese, Thai, and Filipino products.

FUNG WONG BAKERY
30 Mott St   212/267-4037
Daily: 7 a.m.-8:30 p.m.

Fung Wong is the real thing. Everyone from local Chinatown residents to the city's gourmands extol its virtues. The pastries, cookies, and baked goods are traditional, authentic, and delicious. Flavor is not compromised to appeal to Western tastes. The bakery features a tremendous variety, and it has the distinction of being New York's oldest and largest "real" Chinese bakery. Fung Wong is rated number one, and a visit is the surest way to see why.

KAM MAN FOOD PRODUCTS
200 Canal St (bet Mott and Mulberry St)   212/571-0330
Daily: 9-9

Kam Man is the largest Oriental grocery store on the East Coast. They also carry Japanese, Vietnamese, Philippine, Thai, and Singapore products. Even native Chinese will feel at home in this shop, where every possible ingredient for a Chinese meal is sold. Speaking Chinese is not a requirement for shopping at Kam Man. Some of the best English in Chinatown is spoken by the staff here, and the amenities will be totally familiar to those who patronize the city's other gourmet delis and supermarkets. The difference is that at Kam Man the shopping carts wheel past produce displays of water chestnuts, bok choy, winter melon, and tofu; 50 types of Oriental delicacies (like shark's fin); and butcher and fish counters offering duck, sausages, pork dumplings, and shrimp. Desserts and teas round out the selection, and the prices—even for American tangerines and oranges—are inexpensive.

Coffee, Tea

BELL-BATES HEALTH FOOD CENTER
97 Reade St (bet Church St and West Broadway)   212/267-4300
Mon-Fri: 9-8; Sat: 10-6

Bell-Bates is a hot-beverage emporium, specializing in all manner of teas and coffees for the retail customer. Their selection is extensive and prices are competitive. Bell-Bates considers itself a complete food center, stocking health food, vitamins, nuts, dried fruit, spices, herbs, and gourmet food, along with freshly ground coffees and teas. Ask for the marvelous Mrs. Sayage.

COFFEE GRINDER
348 E 66th St (bet First and Second Ave)   212/737-3490
Mon-Fri: 7-7

All you have to do is smell the aroma when you walk into this tiny spot. The coffee appeal is overwhelming! For honest-to-goodness fine coffees, teas, and cookies, look no further.

EMPIRE COFFEE AND TEA COMPANY
592 Ninth Ave (bet 42nd and 43rd St)   212/586-1717
Mon-Fri: 8-7; Sat: 9-6:30; Sun: 11-5

Midtown java lovers have all wandered in here at one time or another. There is an enormous selection of coffee (75 different types of beans), tea, and herbs. Because of the aroma and array of the bins, choosing is almost impossible. Empire's personnel are very helpful, but perhaps most helpful of all is a perusal of their free mail-order catalog before entering the shop. Fresh coffee beans and tea leaves are available in bulk, along with gourmet gift baskets. Everything is sold loose and can be ground. Empire also carries a wide selection of teapots and coffee and cappuccino machines.

MCNULTY'S TEA AND COFFEE COMPANY
109 Christopher St (bet Bleecker and Hudson St)   212/242-5351
Mon-Sat: 10-9; Sun: 1-7

McNulty's has been supplying choosy New Yorkers with coffee and tea since 1895. Over the years they have developed a complete line that includes spice and herb teas, coffee blends ground to order, and coffee and tea accessories. They have a reputation for personalized gourmet coffee blends and work hard to maintain it. That reputation will take its toll on the pocketbook, but the blends are unique and the personal service is highly valued. McNulty's maintains an extensive file on customers' special blends.

M. ROHRS HOUSE OF FINE TEAS AND COFFEES
303 E 85th St (off Second Ave)   212/396-4456
Mon-Sat: 7-8; Sun: 10-6

In 1996, M. Rohrs' 100th year, Donald Wright became the new owner. He has expanded the lines of tea and coffee, and honey, jam, cookies, and chocolate are also offered in the store. Rohrs now has a bar for espresso and ten types of brewed coffees. This is truly a village store in the big city. Wright, himself a great lover of coffee, claims to drink ten cups a day. He vows to carry on Rohr's tradition of Old World charm in the new century. They will ship coffee and gift baskets anywhere.

Types of Coffee Drinks:

Americano: A two-ounce shot of espresso with hot water. This drink substitutes for drip coffee.

Caffe Latte: A popular version of espresso, combining a two-ounce shot of espresso with steamed milk and a spoonful of milk froth on top.

Caffe Mocha: A latte with an ounce of chocolate flavoring (either powder or syrup).

Cappuccino: A two-ounce shot of espresso with equal parts steamed milk and milk froth.

Espresso: A coffee beverage produced by using pressure to rapidly infuse ground coffee beans with boiling water. A "tall" is any 12-ounce espresso drink, while a "grande" is any 16-ounce espresso drink. A "double" is any espresso drink with a second shot added. Finally, a "skinny" is any drink that uses nonfat milk. Here are some additional variations:

Flavored Caffe Latte: A latte with an ounce of Italian syrup. Almond, hazelnut, and vanilla are a few of the more common flavors. Some like their espresso flavored with liqueurs.

Granita: Made with a granita machine, or *granitore,* these frozen Italian drinks can be made with espresso and milk, or with fresh fruits and juices.

PORTO RICO IMPORTING COMPANY

201 Bleecker St (main store)   212/477-5421
Mon-Sat: 9-9; Sun: 12-7

40½ St. Marks Pl (coffee bar)   212/533-1982
Mon-Fri: 8-8; Sat: 9-8; Sun: 12-7

107 Thompson St (coffee bar)   212/966-5758
Mon-Thurs: 8-6; Fri: 8-7; Sat: 10-7; Sun:10-6

50 Grove St   212/633-9453
Mon-Sat: 9-9; Sun: 12-7

In 1907, Peter Longo's family started a small coffee business in the Village. Primarily importers and wholesalers, they were soon pressured to serve the local community, so they opened a small storefront as well. As that storefront gained a reputation for having the best and freshest coffee available, it developed a loyal corps of customers. Since much of the surrounding neighborhood consisted of Italians, the Longo family reciprocated their loyalty by specializing in Italian espressos and cappuccinos, as well as "health" and medicinal teas. Dispensed along with such teas are folk remedies and advice to mend whatever ails you. Today, the store remains true to its tradition. Peter has added coffee bars, so now it is possible to sit and sip from a selection of 150 coffees and 225 loose teas while listening to the folklore or trying to select the best from the bins. All coffees are roasted daily. (Hint: The inexpensive house blends are every bit as good as some of the more expensive coffees.)

SENSUOUS BEAN OF COLUMBUS AVENUE

66 W 70th St (at Columbus Ave)   212/724-7725
Mon, Tues, Fri: 8:30-7; Wed, Sat: 8:30-6; Thurs: 8:30-9; Sun: 9:30-6

In business long before the coffee craze started, this legendary coffee and tea house carries 72 varieties of coffee and 52 teas. A coffee-of-the-month club is offered, and after customers purchase ten pounds of coffee they receive one pound free! The bulk bean coffees and loose teas come from all around the world. Teas from England, France, Germany, Ireland, and Taiwan are featured.

TIMOTHY'S COFFEES OF THE WORLD
1295 Ave of the Americas (near 51st St)   212/956-0690
Mon-Fri: 7-6

Freshness is the byword here! Timothy's purchases its own coffee crops to insure that their customers get the very best-tasting beans. All of their coffees are fresh-roasted and shipped directly to the store. Loose coffees and teas are all self-service; however, there is a full-service cappuccino and espresso bar. They carry a reasonably priced selection of accessory items like mugs, pitchers, teapots, and coffee makers.

A cup of tea and . . .
- **Black tea:** deep, hearty taste
- **Ceylon:** crisp, black, tasty
- **Chai:** homemade blends of tea leaves, spices, milk
- **Darjeeling:** dark, dry, and full with a muscatlike bouquet
- **First flush:** April harvest of Darjeeling tea
- **Green tea:** healthy, light, grassy
- **Oolong:** smooth, semi-fermented

Foreign Foodstuffs (the best)

Chinese, Thai, Malaysian, Philippine, Vietnamese:
Asia Market (71½ Mulberry St)
Bangkok Center Market (104 Mosco St, at Mott St)
Chinese American Trading Company* (91 Mulberry St)
East Broadway Meat Market (36 East Broadway)
Fong Inn Too (46 Mott St)
Fung Wong Bakery* (30 Mott St)
Hong Keung Seafood & Meat Market (75 Mulberry St)
Kam Kuo Foods (7 Mott St)
Kam Man Food Products* (200 Canal St)
Thuan-Nguyen Market (84 Mulberry St)

Complete ethnic market:
Soho Provisions (518 Broadway)

English:
Myers of Keswick (634 Hudson St)

German:
Schaller & Weber (1654 Second Ave)

Indian:
Foods of India (121 Lexington Ave)

Italian:
DiPalo Fine Foods (206 Grand St)
Todaro Brothers (555 Second Ave)

Japanese:
Katagiri* (224 E 59th St)

Korean:
Han Arum (25 W 32nd St)

Mexican:
Azteca Deli Grocery (698 Amsterdam Ave)

Middle Eastern:
Kalustyan's (123 Lexington Ave)

Polish:
East Village Meat Market (139 Second Ave)

West African:
West African Grocery (535 Ninth Ave)

*Detailed writeups can be found in this chapter

Fruits, Vegetables

GREENMARKET
130 E 16th St (office)   212/477-3220

Bowling Green (Broadway at Battery Park Pl)
World Trade Center (Church at Fulton St)
City Hall (Chambers at Centre St)
Washington Market Park (Greenwich at Chambers St)
P.S. 234 (Greenwich at Chambers St)
Federal Plaza (Broadway at Thomas St)
Lafayette Street (Lafayette at Spring St)
Tompkins Square (7th St at Ave A)
St. Mark's Church (10th St at Second Ave)
Abingdon Square (12th St at Eighth Ave)
Union Square (17th St at Broadway)
Sheffield Plaza (5th St at Ninth Ave)
Verdi Square (72nd St at Broadway)
P.S. 44 (77th St at Columbus Ave)
97th Street (97th St bet Amsterdam and Columbus Ave)
Harlem (144th St at Lenox Ave)
175th St (175th St at Broadway)
Soho (Ave of the Americas at Spring St)

Starting in 1976 with just one location, these unique open-air markets have been springing up in various neighborhoods. They are sponsored and overseen by a nonprofit organization. No middle man means prices are significantly less than at supermarkets. Another great advantage is that all produce (over 600 varieties), baked goods, flowers, and fish are straight from the source. When the supply is gone, the stand closes for the day. Come early for the best selection. Call the above number to find out the address of the nearest Greenmarket and when it will be open. Most are seasonal, operating from 8 to 3, although some stay open all year. Hours also may vary.

Gift and Picnic Baskets

MANHATTAN FRUITIER
210 E 6th St (at Third Ave)   212/686-0404
Mon-Fri: 9-5; Sat: deliveries only

Most fruit baskets are pretty bad, but this outfit makes some great-looking and great-tasting masterpieces using fresh seasonal and exotic fruits. You can add such comestibles as hand-rolled cheddar-cheese sticks, biscotti, and individually wrapped chocolates. Locally handmade truffles and fresh flowers are also available. Delivery charges in Manhattan are very reasonable.

SANDLER'S
530 Cherry Ln, Floral Park, NY   212/279-9779, 800/75-FRUIT
Mon-Fri: 9-5:30

Sandler's is a key source for scumptious candies, delicacies, and some of the best chocolate-chip cookies in New York. Yet they are best known for gift baskets filled with fancy fresh fruit, natural cheeses, and gourmet delicacies. No one does it better!

Caviar

We aim to please all palates and pocketbooks in this volume, including sophisticated tastes:

Bubble Room (228 West Broadway): the real stuff, plus hundreds of champagnes and wines

Caviar Russe (538 Madison Ave): a new luxury spot

Caviarteria (502 Park Ave and 310 West Broadway): I like everything about this place, especially the friendly attitudes of Eric and Bruce Sobol.

Firebird (365 W 46th St): re-creation of a pre-Revolutionary Russian mansion

Petrossian (182 W 58th St): Stepping inside here provides ambience befitting the caviar set. It's a spectacular place to dine.

Zabar's (2245 Broadway): If price is important, make this your first stop.

Caviar selection

Beluga: roe is large, firm, and well-defined, with a smooth, creamy texture

Osetra: strong, with a sweet, fruity flavor

Sevruga: subtle, clean taste with crunchy texture

WEST SIDE FRUITIER
145 W 20th St (bet Ave of the Americas and Seventh Ave)
212/727-2045, 888/BASKET8, 800/289-2106
Mon-Fri: 10-6

If you are looking for an upscale fresh-fruit gift basket, this is the place. West Side Fruitier uses both domestic and exotic fruits (like passion fruit, star fruit, papayas, and persimmons) and mixes them with a fine selection of cheese, crackers, truffles, coffee, and the like. The baskets all have great eye appeal; they are custom-designed with attractive flowers, ferns, and wrappings. Deliveries can be made to homes, hotels, hospitals, or offices. Ask for manager Dylan Wallace, who puts his seal of approval on every basket.

Greek

LIKITSAKOS
1174 Lexington Ave (bet 80th and 81st St)   212/535-4300
Daily: 8 a.m.-9 p.m.

Likitsakos is one of the better places in New York to find all kinds of Greek and international specialties, including salads, fruits, vegetables, grains, dips, and appetizers.

Health Foods

BENNIE'S
321½ Amsterdam Ave (at 75th St)   212/874-3032
Daily: 11-10:30

Bennie's specializes in vegetarian foods, and they're among the best anywhere. Homage is paid to their Lebanese roots with the best tabbouleh in the city and a plate that speaks with a definite Middle Eastern and European accent. The health aspect is not ignored, either. In addition to three sensational chicken salads, Bennie's boasts the biggest selection of health foods in the neighborhood. A prime example is the *muda-data* (a salad of rice, onions, and lentils). It, too, is reasonably priced and excellent. English is not spoken fluently here, but with all these goodies, who cares?

COMMODITIES
117 Hudson St (at Moore St)   212/334-8330
Daily: 10-8

Commodities is the largest natural-foods store within a hundred-mile radius, according to the store's staff. Their produce is of excellent quality, and prices are comparable to those of local supermarkets. They've earned that "largest" reputation with a well-rounded stock of canned and processed health foods, including vegetable and meat substitutes and a full line of health-food products. They are able to serve everyone from macrobiotics to those who are only marginally interested in chemically free food. The staff is helpful, and the store is large.

GOOD EARTH FOODS
1330 First Ave (bet 71st and 72nd St)   212/472-9055
Mon-Fri: 9-7:30; Sat: 9-6; Sun: 12-6

167 Amsterdam Ave (at 68th St)   212/496-1616
Mon-Fri: 9:30-7:30; Sat: 9:30-6:30; Sun: 12-6

Good Earth has the reputation of being one of the best-stocked health-food stores in New York. The helpful and knowledgeable sales personnel will vehemently deny they are overpriced, but a quick comparison of prices shows otherwise. Just as surely, a quick visit will confirm their reputation for having one of the largest and freshest stocks. In addition to their enormous selection, Good Earth offers delivery anywhere within the city.

HEALTHY PLEASURES
93 University Pl (bet 11th and 12th St)   212/353-FOOD
Daily: 7:30 a.m.-11:30 p.m.

You feel healthy just walking in this place—and what a selection! Healthy Pleasures is a full-scale deli/health-products emporium and then some, with entree items (like roasted chicken, lasagna, and fish) for takeout, healthy platters (like organic steamed vegetables, salads, and soups), and delicious sandwiches. The soups have no added fat or dairy products and are full of organic veggies. Pies and cakes are baked on the premises. Delivery is free on all menu items, an all-natural catering service is available, and a daily breakfast-to-go menu features fresh juice, all-natural muffins and bagels, organic and decaf coffees, and herbal teas.

INTEGRAL YOGA NATURAL FOODS
229 W 13th St (bet Seventh and Eighth Ave)   212/243-2642
Mon-Fri: 10-9:30; Sat: 10-8:30; Sun: 12-6:30

Selection, quality, and health are the order of the day in this clean, attractive shop, which features a complete assortment of natural foods. Vegetarian items, packaged groceries, organic produce, bulk foods, juice bar, salad bar, deli, and baked items are all available at reasonable prices for the health-conscious shopper. They are located in the same building as a center that offers classes in yoga, meditation, and philosophy. A vitamin and health-food store is across the street.

LIFETHYME NATURAL MARKET
408-410 Ave of the Americas (bet 8th and 9th St)   212/420-9099
Mon-Fri: 8 a.m.-10 p.m.; Sat, Sun: 9 a.m.-10 p.m.

You'll find one of the largest selections of organic produce in the area at this complete natural supermarket. In addition there is an organic salad table, over 5,000 titles of health-related books, a deli serving natural foods, a "natural cosmetics" boutique, complete vegan bakery, and an organic juice bar. Located in two renovated 1839 brownstones in the heart of the Village, this busy shop also discounts vitamins, does catering, offers custom-baked goods for dietary needs, and will custom cook foods on premises.

WHOLE FOOD MARKETS
117 Prince St (bet Greene and Wooster St)   212/982-1000
Mon-Fri: 8 a.m.-10 p.m.; Sat, Sun: 9 a.m.-10 p.m.

2421 Broadway (at 89th St)   212/874-4000
Daily: 8 a.m.-11 p.m.

These are Manhattan's premier health-food supermarkets. Featured are organic produce, fresh juices, vitamins at up to 25% discount, and a full line of healthy supermarket products. They will deliver in the metro area and ship anywhere in the world. The deli and salad bar are organic and kosher.

Ice Cream

CONES, ICE CREAM ARTISANS
272 Bleecker St (at Seventh Ave)   212/414-1795
Mon-Thurs, Sun: 2-11 p.m.; Fri, Sat: 2 p.m.-1 a.m.

The D'Aloisio family brought their original Italian ice cream recipes to

Manhattan . . . and boy, are they good! Cones specializes in creamy gelato made with all-natural ingredients. Over 36 flavors (try the coffee mocha chocolate chip) are carried, and fat-free fruit flavors are available. All are made daily on the premises, insuring freshness and creamy goodness.

Manhattan Ice Cream Guide

Ceci-Cela (55 Spring St): fruit flavors
Chinatown Ice Cream Factory (65 Bayard St): a longtime favorite
Ciao Bella Gelato Co. (262 Mott St): exciting flavors of gelati and sorbets at good prices
Cones (272 Bleecker St): ice cream and gelati: 36 flavors
Custard Beach (33 E 8th St, Winter Garden at World Financial Center, and Grand Central Station): unique taste; will make any flavor of frozen custard
Emack and Bolio (389 Amsterdam Ave): vanilla-bean ice cream
La Maison du Chocolat (1018 Madison): chocolate
Moondog (378 Bleecker St): super hot fudge concoctions
Payard Patisserie (1032 Lexington Ave): top grade
Peppermint Park (1225 First Ave): a brand new look, and again dishing up ice creams, sodas, floats, shakes
Rocco Pastry Shop (243 Bleecker St): creamy Italian ices
Ronnybrook (75 9th St): ice cream lover's dream
Sant Ambroeus (1000 Madison Ave): great upscale selection

Indian

K. KALUSTYAN
123 Lexington Ave (bet 28th and 29th St)   212/685-3451
Mon-Sat: 10-8; Sun: 11-7

In 1944, Kalustyan opened as an Indian spice store at its present location. After all this time, Kalustyan is still a great spot. Many items are sold in bins or bales rather than prepackaged containers and are available in bulk or wholesale sizes for retail customers. The difference in cost, flavor, and freshness compared to regular grocery stores is extraordinary. The best indication of freshness and flavor is a simple whiff of the store's aroma! Kalustyan is not strictly an Indian store but also an Orient export trading corporation with a specialty in Middle Eastern and Indian items.

Italian

MELAMPO
105 Sullivan St (bet Spring and Prince St)   212/334-9530
Mon-Sat: 11:30-5

In a tiny store not much larger than an oversized closet, Melampo displays a sizable variety of the best Italian food items. The specialty, however, is their sandwiches. This is the place to go for super combinations like Marina (salami, provolone), Cristina (mozzarella, artichoke), and Alessandro (tuna, peppers, bel paese). All sandwiches are served on individual-sized white or whole-wheat bread loaves. For a treat you'll never forget in the summer, try the Bombolo Tricolore, consisting of fresh mozzarella, Jersey tomato, basil, and special dressing, served on focaccia.

RAFFETTO'S CORPORATION
144 W Houston St (bet Sullivan and MacDougal St)   212/777-1261
Tues-Fri: 9-6:30; Sat: 9-6

You could go to a gourmet market for pasta, or you could go straight to the source. Raffetto's has been the source for all kinds of pasta and stuffing since 1906. Though most of the business is wholesale, Raffetto's will sell anyone 12 flavors of noodles, ravioli, mini-ravioli, tortellini, manicotti, gnocchi, and fettuccine with no minimum order. Variations include Genoa-style ravioli with meat and spinach, and Naples-style ravioli with cheese. Featured are over ten kinds of homemade sauces prepared by Mrs. Raffetto herself, as well as daily bread, dry pasta, and bargain-priced olive oils and vinegars.

RAVIOLI STORE
75 Sullivan St (bet Spring and Broome St)   212/925-1737
Mon-Sat: 10-7; Sun: 11-5

The Ravioli Store was among the first to launch the pasta craze, stuffing gourmet fillings inside ravioli. Their products are all-natural. Custom shapes and fillings are available, and healthy (cholesterol- and wheat-free) items are in their product line.

Japanese
KATAGIRI & COMPANY
224 E 59th St (bet Second and Third Ave)   212/755-3566
Mon-Sat: 10-7; Sun: 11-6

Are you planning a Japanese dinner? Do you have some important clients from across the Pacific that you would like to impress with a sushi party? Katagiri features all kinds of Japanese food, sushi ingredients, and utensils. You can get some great party ideas from the helpful personnel here. They also provide wholesale items for major hotels and restaurants.

Kosher
SIEGEL'S KOSHER DELI AND RESTAURANT
1646 Second Ave (bet 85th and 86th St)   212/288-3632, 212/288-2094
Mon-Thurs: 11-10; Fri-Sun: 10-10

If you are looking for a top kosher deli and gourmet appetizer store on the Upper East Side, you can't do better than Siegel's. Not only do they keep long hours (Sundays, too), but they also deliver from 10 to 9. Featured are fresh, decorated turkey dishes; overstuffed sandwich platters; barbecued, roasted, and fried chicken platters; hors d'oeuvre selections; smoked fish platters; fresh baked breads and salad trays; and a large selection of cakes, cookies, and fruit platters. The number of selections on the menu is awesome, with nearly two dozen sandwiches, ten kinds of soups, dozens of salads, and side dishes ranging from potato and meat knishes to kugel and kishka.

Liquor, Wine
ACKER, MERRALL & CONDIT
160 W 72nd St (bet Broadway and Columbus Ave)   212/787-1700
Mon-Sat: 8:30 a.m.-10 p.m.

AMC is the oldest operating wine and liquor store in America, having opened its doors in 1820. And what a place it continues to be! There are in-store wine tastings Friday evenings and Saturday afternoons. Wine seminars are offered to companies. Wine parties can be arranged in homes for special occasions. Free delivery is available in Manhattan. This service-oriented firm carries an especially good inventory of American wines and specializes in purchases from Bordeaux and the Rhine. The Wine Workshop, Acker, Merrall & Condit's special-events affiliate, offers wine-tasting classes and dinners that range in price from $40 to $1,295.

BURGUNDY WINE COMPANY
323 W 11th St   212/691-9092
Mon-Sat: 10-7

One of the great pleasures of shopping in New York is that there is a store for just about every specialty. The customer is the winner, because the selection is huge and the price range broad. Such is the case with the Burgundy Wine Company, a compact and attractive store in the Village. These folks are specialists in fine Burgundies and Rhones, with over 1,500 labels to choose from. There are some great treasures in their cellars; ask the knowledgeable personnel.

CROSSROADS WINES AND LIQUORS
55 W 14th St (at Ave of the Americas)   212/924-3060
Mon-Sat: 9-9

Crossroads carries 3,000 wines from all the great wine-producing countries. They stock rare, unique, and exotic liquors as well. Crossroads will special-order items, deliver, and help with party and menu planning. Finally, they are not in a snobby neighborhood, and their prices are as low as their attitude is low-key.

GARNET WINES & LIQUORS
929 Lexington Ave (bet 68th and 69th St)
212/772-3211, 800/USA-VINO (out of state)
Mon-Sat: 9-9

You'll love Garnet's prices, which are among the most inexpensive in the city for specialty wines. If you're in the market for champagne, Bordeaux, Burgundy, or other imported wine, check here first. Prices are good on other wines and liquors, too.

K&D FINE WINES AND SPIRITS
1366 Madison Ave (bet 95th and 96th St)   212/289-1818
Mon-Sat: 9-9

K&D is an excellent wine and spirits market on the Upper East Side. Hundreds of top brands and top wines are sold at more than competitive prices. Major ads in local newspapers occasionally highlight special bargains, but even on a regular basis K&D's values are outstanding.

MORRELL & COMPANY
One Rockefeller Plaza
14 W 49th St
Mon-Fri: 9-6:45; Sat: 9:30-6:30

Charming and well informed, Peter Morrell is the wine expert at this small, jam-packed store, which carries all kinds of wine and liquor. The stock is overwhelming; since there isn't room to display everything, a good portion is kept in the wine cellar. All of it is easily accessible, however, and the Morrell staff is amenable to helping you find the right bottle. The stock consists of spirits, including brandy liqueurs, and wine vintages ranging from rare and old to young and inexpensive.

QUALITY HOUSE
2 Park Ave (bet 32nd and 33rd St)   212/532-2944
Mon-Fri: 9-6:30; Sat: 9-5:30; closed Sat in July, August

Quality House boasts one of the most extensive assortments of French wine in the city; an equally fine offering of domestic and Italian wines; and selections from Germany, Spain, and Portugal. Oenologist Willie Gluckstern claims that Bernie Fradin (Quality House's owner) and his son Gary have the best wine palates in the city. This is a quality house, not a bargain spot. Delivery is available and almost always free.

SOHO WINES AND SPIRITS
461 West Broadway (bet Prince and Houston St)   212/777-4332
Mon-Sat: 10-8

Stephen Masullo's father ran a neighborhood liquor store on Spring Street for over 25 years. When his local neighborhood evolved into the Soho of today, his sons expanded the business and opened a stylish Soho establishment for wine. The shop is lofty. In fact, it looks more like an art gallery than a wine shop. The various bottles are tastefully displayed, and classical music plays in the background. Stephen boasts that Soho Wines also has one of the largest selections of single malt Scotch whiskeys in New York. Again, in keeping with the neighborhood, Soho Wines and Spirits offers several unique services. Among them are party planning, wine-cellar advice, and specialty items of interest to the neighborhood.

Want to Send the Best of New York?

Great for gifts or for you if you're housebound.
Appetizers from **Russ & Daughters** (212/475-4880
Bagels from **H&H Bagels** (800/NY-BAGEL)
Basket from **Zabar's** (800/697-6301)
Beef from **Lobel's** (800/5-LOBELS)
Cheesecake from **Junior's** (800/9-JUNIOR)
Coffee from **Porto Rico Importing Company** (800/453-5908)
Country bread from **Ecce Panis** (212/517-4219)
Knishes from **Yonah Schimmel** (212/477-2858)
Mozzarella from **Alleva Dairy** (800/4-ALLEVA)
Pickles from **Guss Pickles** (800/252-GUSS)
Ricotta from **Alleva Dairy** (800/4-ALLEVA)
Salami from **Katz's Delicatessen** (800/4-HOTDOG)
Steak sauce from **Peter Luger Steak House** (718/387-0500)
Sturgeon from **Barney Greengrass** (212/724-4707)

Meat, Poultry

FAICCO'S PORK STORE
260 Bleecker St (at Ave of the Americas)   212/243-1974
Tues-Thurs: 8:30-6; Fri: 8:30-7; Sat: 8-6; Sun: 9-2:30

An Italian institution, Faicco's carries delectable dried sausage, cuts of pork, and sweet and hot sausage. They also sell an equally good cut for barbecue and an oven-ready rolled leg of stuffed pork. The latter, a house specialty, is locally famous. Note Faicco's full name: the shop really specializes in pork sausage and cold cuts rather than meats. There is no veal or lamb. But if you're into Italian-style deli, try Faicco's first. And if you're pressed for time to cook, take home some heat-and-eat chicken rollettes: breasts of chicken rolled around cheese and then dipped in a crunchy coating. It's the perfect introduction to Faicco's specialties. Prepared hot foods to take home, like eggplant parmesan, are also available.

A word about sausages

Bratwurst: smooth sausage, made from pork
Chorizo: fiery, coarsely ground pork sausage
Hot links ("red hots"): combination of turkey, beef, and pork, with
   spices
Italian: Italian pork sausage, either sweet or hot
Kielbasa: robust Polish pork sausage
Kolbasz: Hungarian sausage with spicy paprika
Linguica: pork, garlic, dried chilies, and cayenne
Merguez: coarsely ground lamb or beef, spiked with dried herbs
Saucisson à l'ail: two-inch-thick weiner that is a deluxe bologna
Weisswurst: German veal link made with cream and eggs

JEFFERSON MARKET
450 Ave of the Americas (at 10th St)   212/533-3377
Mon-Sat: 8 a.m-9 p.m.; Sun: 9-8

Quality and personal service are the bywords here. Originally a prime-meat and poultry market, Jefferson has grown into an outstanding full-line store. Second-generation family management insures hands-on attention to service. Prime meats, fresh seafood, select produce, fancy groceries, Bell and Evans chicken, and fresh salads are all tempting. There are expanded deli, cheese, produce, and fish sections. Delivery service is available. If you don't feel like cooking dinner, let Louis Montuori send you home with some delicious hot or cold prepared foods.

KUROWYCKY MEAT PRODUCTS
124 First Ave (bet 7th and 8th St)   212/477-0344
Mon-Sat: 8-6; closed Mon in July, Aug

Erast Kurowycky came to New York from Ukraine in 1954 and opened this tiny shop the same year. Almost immediately it became a mecca and bargain spot for the city's Poles, Germans, Hungarians, Russians, Lithuanians, and Ukrainians. Many of these nationalities still harbor centuries-old grudges, but they all come to Kurowycky's, where they agree on at least two things: the meats are the finest and the prices are the best available. A third-generation family member, Jaroslaw, Jr., now runs the shop. Hams, sausages, meat loaves, and breads are sold. There are also condiments, including homemade imported or reproduced Polish mustard, honey imported from Poland, sauerkraut, and a half-dozen other Ukrainian specialties.

M. LOBEL AND SONS
1096 Madison Ave (bet 82nd and 83rd St)   212/737-1373
Mon-Sat: 9-6: closed Sat in summer

Lobel's runs periodic sales on some of the best cuts of meat in town (poultry and veal, too). Because of their excellent service and reasonable prices, few carnivores in Manhattan haven't heard of the shop. The staff has published four meat cookbooks, and they are always willing to explain the best use for each cut. It's hard to go wrong, since Lobel carries only the best. They will ship all over the country. Great hamburgers, too!

OPPENHEIMER PRIME MEATS
2606 Broadway (bet 98th and 99th St)   212/662-0246, 212/662-0690
Mon-Fri: 9-7; Sat: 8-6

Reliable and trustworthy, Oppenheimer is one of the first names mentioned for prime meats in New York. Under the ownership of Robert Pence, an experienced chef, the traditions of Harry Oppenheimer are continued. It's an old-fashioned butcher shop offering the kind of service that used to be expected (and that supermarkets have never had). Supermarkets have never had this quality, either. There's prime dry-aged beef, milk-fed veal, free-range poultry, and game, all sold at competitive prices.

OTTOMANELLI'S MEAT MARKET
285 Bleecker St (bet Seventh Ave and Jones St)
212/675-4217
Mon-Fri: 8-6:30; Sat: 7-6

Looking for the unique? The stock-in-trade here is rare gourmet fare. Among the regular weekly offerings are such meats as boar's head, whole baby lambs, game rabbits, and pheasant. They also stock buffalo, ostrich, rattlesnake, and alligator meat. Quality is high, but service from the right person can make the difference between a good and an excellent cut. Other family members run similar operations in other sections of town, but this is the original store, and it's noteworthy. They gained their reputation by offering full butcher services and a top-notch selection of prime meats, game, prime-aged steaks, and milk-fed veal. The latter is available as prepared Italian roast, chops, and steaks, and its preparation by Ottomanelli's is unique. Best of all, they will sell it by the piece for a quick meal at home.

A West Village must: **Florence Meat Market** (5 Jones St, 212/242-6531).

PREMIER VEAL
555 West St (off West Side Hwy, two blocks south of 14th St)
212/243-3170
Mon-Fri: 4 a.m.-1 p.m.

Mark Hirschorn worked various business jobs from Albany to Aspen before deciding to join the family's wholesale veal distribution center. As he says, he's been on both sides of the counter. This translates as a wholesaler who has a good eye for what sells in restaurants while running a business that is friendlier than most to small, individual customers. Premier Veal offers veal and lamb stew, Italian cutlets, shoulder or leg roasts, and veal pockets for stuffing, all at wholesale prices with no minimum order. Of course, if you're trekking to West Street, it might be economical to make the order as large as possible. Hirschorn suggests that three or four customers get together and order a few loins. Less than that leaves too much waste and is not profitable for him or the customer. A loin weighing 26 pounds breaks down to 16 or 24 steaks and chops, and the price is a fraction of that at a butcher shop.

ROYALE PRIME MEATS
833 Washington St (at Little W 12th St)   212/243-3161
Mon-Fri: 5 a.m.-1 p.m.

Chances are good that delicious meat entree at your favorite Manhattan restaurant came from Royale Prime Meats. Although they have operated for years as a wholesaler, the public can now enjoy the same quality meats at excellent prices. They deliver and ship all over the world. Royale Prime is located in the oldest meat market in the United States; ask Eddie or Michael to fill you in on the history of the area. In addition to steaks, this firm offers other beef cuts, veal, lamb, pork, poultry, and game (including rabbit, squab, duck, goose, and guinea hens).

SCHALLER & WEBER
1654 Second Ave (bet 85th and 86th St)   212/879-3047
Mon-Fri: 9-6; Sat: 8:30-6

Once you've been in this store, the image will stay with you because of the sheer magnitude of cold cuts on display. Schaller & Weber is a *Babes in Toyland* for delicatessen lovers, and there is not a wall or nook that is not covered with deli meats. Besides offering a complete line of delicatessen items, Schaller & Weber also stocks game and poultry, and they claim to be a butcher shop as well. Try the sausage and pork. They will bake, prepare, smoke, or roll it for you, and that's just the beginning.

For the best burger, choose the cut called the chuck, which is the forequarter of the cow. It will provide the juiciest and most flavorful burger, as it contains about 20% fat.

YORKVILLE PACKING HOUSE
1560 Second Ave (at 81st St)   212/628-5147
Mon-Fri: 8:30-6:30; Sat: 8-7; Sun: 11-5:30

Yorkville used to be a bastion of Eastern European ethnicity and culture before becoming the Upper East Side's swinging singles playground. Here and there, remnants of Old World society remain. Yorkville Packing House is patronized by Hungarian-speaking little old ladies in black, as well as some of the city's greatest gourmands. And the reason is simple: except for its neighbors, these prepared meats are available nowhere else in the city and possibly nowhere else on the continent. The shop offers a vast variety of sausages and salami. Smoked meats include pork shoulder and tenderloin. Goose is a mainstay of Hungarian cuisine, so there is goose liverwurst, smoked goose, and goose liver.

Fried bacon bits and bacon fried with paprika (another Hungarian staple) are other offerings. Ready for on-the-spot consumption is a selection of preserves, jams, spices, ground nuts, jellies, prepared delicacies, head cheese, and breads, as well as takeout meals. All of it is authentic.

Nuts

KADOURI IMPORT
51 Hester St (at Essex St)   212/677-5441
Sun-Thurs: 8-6; Fri: 8-3

Kadouri is a wholesale-retail store where everything sold is natural and healthful. The main staples are nuts and dried fruits. The almonds and their derivatives are especially good. Kadouri also carries candies, beans, canned items, and spices. Prices are wholesale, no matter how small the purchase. Specialty items from Israel—like pickles, jams, and soups—are available.

Pickles

GUSS PICKLES
35 Essex St (bet Grand and Hester St)   212/254-4477, 800/252-GUSS
Sun-Thurs: 9-6; Fri: 9-3

This enterprise is the best place in the world for fresh-from-the-barrel pickles. Pickles come sour or half sour, with a half-dozen gradations in between, and business is still conducted out on the street, with the stock taking up the store's interior. Customers can glimpse a semblance of order and even a refrigerator inside. That refrigerator is stocked with such items as watermelon rind (in season), hot peppers, freshly ground horseradish, sauerkraut, and whole pickled melons. Pickled celery and carrots are a welcome new addition.

Seafood

Oyster Guide

Remember that oysters must be alive when eaten (test by touching with knife point), can be kept in the refrigerator for two or three days if covered with a damp towel, and should only be eaten raw between September and April. Best places to buy them in Manhattan:

Agata & Valentina (1505 First Ave)
Catalano's Fresh Fish Market (80th St at Third Ave and at the Vinegar Factory, 431 E 91st St)
Citarella (2135 Broadway and 1313 Third Ave)
Pisacane Midtown (940 First Ave)
Rosedale Fish and Oyster Market (1129 Lexington Ave)
Wild Edibles (255 Elizabeth St)

CATALANO'S FRESH FISH MARKET
Vinegar Factory
431 E 91st St (bet York and First Ave)   212/987-0885
Fish Market: Daily: 7 a.m.-8 p.m.; Vinegar Factory: Mon-Sun: 7 a.m.-9 p.m.

Joe Catalano is that rare blend of knowledge and helpfulness. He feels that the only way to attract new customers is to educate them. His customers, including many local restaurants, rely on him to select the best items for their dinner menus. This he does with a careful eye toward health, price, and cookery.

Catalano's at the Vinegar Factory also has a good selection of poached fish and fish cakes, plus crawfish and soft-shell crabs in season. On cold winter days, don't miss the Manhattan clam chowder.

CENTRAL FISH COMPANY
527 Ninth Ave (bet 39th and 40th St)   212/279-2317
Mon-Fri: 7:30-6:30; Sat: 7:30-5:30

Central doesn't look like much from the outside, but the stock is so vast that it's easier to list what is *not* available than what is. They have 35 fish species in stock at any given time, including fresh imported sardines from Portugal and live carp. Conducting customers through this whale of a selection are some of the friendliest and most knowledgeable salespeople I've encountered. Louis and Anthony Riccoborno and Calogero Olivri are skillful guides who stock all manner of fresh and frozen fish and seafood products. That includes fish that even the most devoted seafood lover would have trouble identifying. Prices are among the most reasonable in town.

CITARELLA
2135 Broadway (at 75th St)
1313 Third Ave (at 75th St)   212/874-0383
Mon-Sat: 7 a.m.-9 p.m.; Sun: 9-7

Citarella now has both the Upper West Side and the Upper East Side covered . . . and with expanded offerings! Originally a place for all kinds of fish (fresh and smoked), selections have increased to include prepared foods, prime meats, appetizers, cheeses, pastries, bread, and pastas. Delivery service and house accounts are offered.

DOWN EAST SEAFOOD
402 W 13th St   212/243-5639
Mon-Fri: 6:30-4:30; Sat: 8-2
Cash only

Two excellent reasons to shop here: they have just about anything in seafood you could possibly want, and their prices are usually about 30% to 40% below retail. Also, there is free delivery in Manhattan with orders of $100 or more. A good catch!

JAKE'S FISH MARKET
2425 Broadway (bet 89th and 90th St)   212/580-5253
Daily: 8-8

The menu at Jake's: catering (including raw bar) and delivery; fresh fish, cut kosher upon request; prepared foods, including a seven-course weekend dinner with a menu that changes weekly; steamed lobsters; and clams and oysters on the half shell. The owner also operates several first-class restaurants (Docks, Carmine's, EJ's Luncheonette). Phone customers get special attention. They ship anywhere in the country.

LEONARD'S SEAFOOD AND PRIME MEATS
1385 Third Ave (bet 78th and 79th St)   212/744-2600
Mon-Fri: 8-7; Sat: 8-6; Sun: 11-6

In new quarters, Leonard's, a family-owned business since 1910, has expanded its inventory. You'll find sea trout, oysters, crabs, haddock, scampi, striped bass, halibut, salmon, live lobsters, and squid. In addition, there are farm-fresh vegetables and organic dairy products. Their takeout seafood department sells codfish cakes, deviled crab and lobsters, and some of the best Manhattan clam chowder in town. Barbecued poultry, cooked and prepared foods, and prime meats round out Leonard's complete selection. This service-oriented establishment provides fast, free delivery.

If you can put up with the service, this wholesale/retail seafood operation is worth a visit: **Pisacane Midtown Seafood** (940 First Ave, 212/752-7560).

MURRAY'S STURGEON SHOP
2429 Broadway (bet 89th and 90th St)   212/724-2650
Sun-Fri; 8-7; Sat: 8-8

Murray's is the definitive place to buy fancy and smoked fish, dispensing the finest in appetizing products. There is sturgeon, Eastern and Norwegian salmon, whitefish, kippered salmon, sable butterfish, pickled herring, schmaltz herring, and caviar. The quality is magnificent, and prices are fair. Murray's also offers kosher cold cuts and dried fruits and nuts.

ROSEDALE FISH AND OYSTER MARKET
1129 Lexington Ave (at 79th St)   212/861-4323
Mon-Fri: 8-7; Sat: 8-6

Rosedale, started in 1906, has a new owner who used to work in the store! Quality seafood is in good supply at all times. Takeout fish dishes and salads are tasty, unusual, and noteworthy. All are individually prepared. They are not inexpensive; their high quality is accompanied by equally high prices. But according to many of the city's restaurants and caterers, they are the best fish source in New York. Free delivery is offered in most areas.

Spices

ANGELICA'S TRADITIONAL HERBS & FOODS
147 First Ave (at 9th St)   212/677-1549
Mon-Wed, Fri, Sat: 12:30-7:15; Sun: 1-6

The scent of Angelica's is heavily organic and home-remedy medicinal. This East Village shop caters to folks who want fresh, high-grade spices, essential oils, teas, and coffees. The bulk of the business is in medicinal herbs, dried fruits and nuts, and related books. They claim to be the largest and best-stocked herb retailer in the country.

APHRODISIA
264 Bleecker St (bet Ave of the Americas and Seventh Ave)
212/989-6440
Mon-Fri: 11-7; Sat: 11-7; Sun: 12-5:30

Aphrodisia is stocked from floor to ceiling with nearly every herb and spice that exists. Eight hundred of them are neatly displayed in glass jars. Some of the teas, potpourri, dried flowers, and oils (200 of them!) are really not what one might expect. The general accent is on folk remedies, but most every ingredient for ethnic cooking can be found here as well. Aphrodisia also conducts a mail-order business.

V. Where to Find It: New York's Best Services

One of the many reasons I love New York is that you can find someone — and usually several someones — for every need imaginable. Whether you need a chair re-caned, a typewriter (remember those?) repaired, or stained glass restored, I can find you an expert who will take care of you with great skill and quality service. I can also find you a place to rent formal wear, televisions, and even a personal assistant. On top of it all, I can find you just the right hotel at just the right price.

Air Conditioning

AIR-WAVE AIR CONDITIONING COMPANY
212/545-1122
Mon-Fri: 9-5 (Sat in Spring)

Is there anything more miserable than a humid, sticky summer day in Manhattan? Well, if the dog days are getting you down or you want to take advance precautions so that they don't, give these folks a call. Air-Wave has been in business for half a century and comes highly recommended. They have sold tens of thousands of units over the years — top brands like Friedrich, Carrier, Westinghouse, and Panasonic. They will deliver and install the same day!

Animal Adoptions

AMERICAN SOCIETY FOR THE PREVENTION OF CRUELTY TO ANIMALS
424 E 92nd St   212/876-7700
Mon-Sat: 11-7; Sun: 11-5

This is one of the oldest animal protection organizations in the world, and the folks here take pet adoptions very seriously. You'll need to fill out an application, go through an interview, bring two pieces of identification (at least one with a photograph), provide a reference that the ASPCA folks can call, and show a utility bill to prove that you do indeed live where you say. The whole process sometimes takes longer than you might wish — but then *they're* sure you're serious, and *you* can go home with a good pet who needs a home. Dogs and puppies cost $50; cats and kittens, $45. The fee includes a veterinarian's exam, vaccinations, and spaying or neutering. Animal cruelty law enforcement and an on-site animal hospital are also offered.

BIDE-A-WEE HOME ASSOCIATION
410 E 38th St   212/532-4455
Mon-Sat: 10-6; Sun: 10-4

Bide-a-wee means "stay awhile" in Gaelic. This is a warm, friendly place complete with volunteers who will match you up with the perfect pet. Puppies and kittens under six months require a $55 donation, while dogs and cats over that age will set you back $30. The fee includes age-appropriate shots and spaying or neutering.

Animal Services

ANIMAL MEDICAL CENTER
510 E 62nd St (bet FDR Dr and York Ave)   212/838-8100
Daily: 24 hours

If your pet becomes ill in New York, try the Animal Medical Center first. This nonprofit organization handles all kinds of veterinary work reasonably and competently with board-certified specialists. They see over 60,000 cases a year and have over 80 veterinarians on staff. The care here is among the best offered anywhere in the city. They suggest calling for an appointment first, unless it is an emergency. Emergency care costs more.

CAROLE WILBOURN
299 W 12th St   212/741-0397
Mon-Sat: 9-6

Want to talk to the author of *Cats on the Couch* and *Cat Talk?* Need a fascinating speaker? Carole Wilbourn is an internationally known cat therapist who has the answer to most of your cat problems. She writes a monthly column for *Cat Fancy* magazine and has a special way with her furry patients. Carole makes house calls from coast to coast and can take care of many cat problems with just one session and a follow-up phone call. She does international consultations, sees appointments at Westside Veterinary Center and the Animal Clinic of New York, and is available for speaking engagements.

CAT GROOMING IN YOUR HOME BY HOWARD
240 E 35th St, #5A   212/889-1449
Daily: 8 a.m.—whenever

Grooming can be a traumatic experience for your cat, so why not do it where your cat is happiest—in his or her own home. If your cat wants regal treatment, give grooming professional Howard Bedor (the official groomer for the New York City Cat Show) a call. He gets the job done with patience and understanding. The familiar surroundings of home are less stressful for cats and convenient for owners. No tranquilizers are used—just tender loving care.

DOGGIE DO AND PUSSYCATS, TOO!
567 Third Ave (bet 37th and 38th St)   212/661-9111
Mon-Fri: 8-7; Sat: 9-7

How to describe this place? Someone has called it "the Georgette Klinger for dogs and cats." In any case, you will find top-notch grooming facilities, an exclusive collection of custom-tailored coats and sweaters, European-designed collars, and much more. Doggie measurements are kept on file, of course, and your companion could even sport a Burberry's of London label. But there is more: a great day-care facility and exercise room. Hand-painted food and water dishes are sold here as well. In 1999 they opened their ultra-posh new boarding facility: a Ritz-Carlton style hotel for pets!

EAST VILLAGE VETERINARIAN
241 Eldridge St (at Houston St)   212/674-8640

This is the only practicing homeopathic veterinary in New York City. It features one of the most complete homeopathic dispensaries in New York, with over a thousand remedies in stock. It is also a full-service hospital with an emphasis on prevention.

FIELDSTON PETS   718/796-4541
Mon-Sat: 9-7

Bash Dibra is a warm, friendly man who speaks dog language. Known as the "dog trainer to the stars" (clients include Mariah Carey, Martin Scorsese, Henry Kissinger, and Matthew Broderick), Bash is an animal behaviorist. If your dog has bad manners, Bash will teach it to behave. He believes in "tandem training"—training owners to train their dogs—because it's the owner who'll be in charge. Bash's experience in training a pet wolf gave him unique insight into the minds of dogs (the wolf's direct descendants), and his success in bringing the most difficult pets to heel has made him a regular on the talk-show circuit. In addition to training sessions, dog and cat grooming is available.

LE CHIEN
Trump Plaza
1044 Third Ave (bet 61st and 62nd St)   212/861-8100
Mon-Fri: 8:30-7; Sat: 9-7

Here is a place to drop off your little beauty while you shop in the Big Apple! Le Chien is known for their tiny AKC (American Kennel Club) puppies, all bearing very distinguished credentials! All dogs and cats at this establishment drink and are bathed in chlorine- and bacteria-free water. It is a veritable canine Saks and finishing school rolled into one. Le Chien carries doggie dresses, coats, sweaters, collars and leashes, 14-karat gold ID tags, travel bags, cultured pearls, and special fragrances in French crystal bottles. Lisa Gilford runs this establishment as an elegant spa for small and large breeds. A separate business grooms and trains cats and dogs. Day care, pickup, and delivery are offered, and boarding is provided for some breeds.

PET CARE NETWORK
Daily: 9-6 and by appointment   212/580-6004

Pet Care Network is a kennel alternative with 35 pet vacation homes where your animal companion can receive individual, exclusive care. There are no cages! You might inquire about their pet lovers' singles club, which arranges dinners and provides up-to-date pet information. Discounts and wholesale prices are also available. The person to contact is Evelyn McCabe, who has a fine crew of pet sitters and trainers to work with your prized possession!

Sometimes it is very handy to have a vet make a house call. One of the best is **Dr. Amy Attas** (212/581-7387).

Antiques Repair

MICHAEL J. DOTZEL AND SON
402 E 63rd St (at York Ave)   212/838-2890
Mon-Fri: 8-4:30

Do you want a chandelier wired or assembled? Dotzel specializes in the repair and maintenance of antiques and precious heirlooms. Dotzel won't touch modern pieces or inferior antiques, but if your older piece is made out of metal and needs repair, this is the place for the job. They pay close attention to detail and will hand-forge or personally hammer metal work, including brass. If an item has lost a part or if you want a duplication of an antique, it can be re-created. Dotzel also does stripping and replating but since it isn't always good for an antique, they may try talking you out of it.

SANO STUDIO
767 Lexington Ave (at 60th St), Room 403   212/759-6131
Mon-Fri: 10-5 (by appointment); closed Aug

Mrs. J. Baran presides over this fourth-floor antiques repair shop, and she has an eye for excellence. That eye is focused on the quality of the workmanship and goods to be repaired. Both must be the best. Baran is a specialist who limits herself to repairing porcelain, pottery, ivory, and tortoise-shell works and antiques. She has many loyal adherents.

Appliance Repair

AUDIOVISION
1221 Second Ave (at 64th St)   212/593-3326
Mon-Fri: 10-7; Sat: 10-5

Few things are more annoying than unkept promises from a repair outfit, particularly when it comes to radio and TV repairs. Audiovision has been in business for nearly two decades, providing top-quality work (guaranteed for six months) on all major brands. Pickup and delivery, installation, and hookup are also provided.

Appraisals

ABIGAIL HARTMANN ASSOCIATES
415 Central Park W (at 101st St)   212/316-5406
Mon-Fri: 9-6 (by appointment); weekends also available

This firm specializes in personal property (fine and decorative art) appraisals for insurance, donation, or other reasons. Theirs is a highly principled and experienced staff that does not buy, sell, or receive kickbacks. (This can be a common practice with some auction houses, insurance companies, and galleries.) Fees are by the hour, consultations are available, and the friendly personnel can provide restoration, framing, shipping, and storage contacts.

Art Services

A. I. FRIEDMAN
44 W 18th St   212/243-9000
Mon-Fri: 9-6:30; Sat: 10-5; Sun: 11-5

Those who want to frame it themselves can take advantage of one of the largest stocks of ready-made frames in the city at A.I. Friedman. Nearly all are sold at discount. In addition to fully assembled frames, they sell do-it-yourself frames that come equipped with glass and/or mats. Custom framing is also available.

ELI WILNER & COMPANY
1525 York Ave (bet 80th and 81st St)   212/744-6521
Mon-Fri: 9:30-5:30; Sat: by appointment

Eli Wilner's primary business is period frames and mirrors. He keeps over 3,300 19th- and early 20th-century American and European frames in stock and can locate any size or style. Wilner can create an exact replica of a frame in his inventory to your unique specifications. With a staff of over 25 skilled craftsmen, Wilner also does expert restoration of frames. With such clients as the Metropolitan Museum of Art and the White House, Wilner's expertise speaks for itself.

GUTTMANN PICTURE FRAME ASSOCIATES
180 E 73rd St (bet Lexington and Third Ave)   212/744-8600
Mon-Thurs: 9-5

Though the Guttmanns have worked on frames for some of the nation's finest museums, including the Metropolitan, they stand apart from other first-class artisans in that they are not snobby or picky about the work they will accept. They will restore, regild, or replace any type of picture frame. They are masters at working with masterpieces but are equally at home restoring or framing a Polaroid snapshot. Even better, they are among the few experts who don't price themselves out of the market. Bring a worn-out frame, and they will graciously tell you exactly what it will cost to fix it.

J. POCKER & SON
135 E 63rd St (bet Park and Lexington Ave)   212/838-5488
Mon-Fri: 9-5:30; Sat: 10-5:30 (closed Sat in summer)

Three generations of this family have been in the custom framing business since 1926, so rest assured they know what they are doing. Pickup and delivery are offered, plus expert advice from a superbly trained staff. As a sidelight, Pocker offers a gallery specializing in English sporting and botanical prints.

JULIUS LOWY FRAME AND RESTORING COMPANY
223 E 80th St (bet Second and Third Ave)   212/861-8585
Mon-Fri: 9-5:30

Serving New York City since 1907, Lowy is the definitive firm for the conservation and framing of fine works of art. Being the oldest and largest such firm in the nation, Lowy's comprehensive services include painting and paper conservation, professional photography, conservation framing, and curatorial services. They sell antique frames (Lowy has the largest inventory in the U.S.) and authentic reproduction frames (the broadest selection anywhere). In addition. Lowy provides complete conservation, mat-making, and fitting services. Their client base includes art dealers, private collectors, auction houses, corporate collections, institutions, and museums.

LEITH RUTHERFURD TALAMO
212/396-0399 (by appointment only)

Does your treasured painting have a dent? Did your movers handle a painting like a ping-pong table? Has the masterpiece that hung over the fireplace darkened with age? Do you need help hanging or lighting a collection? All of these services—plus cleaning, relining, and polishing paintings and frames —are done here with expert class.

Babysitters

BABYSITTERS GUILD
60 E 42nd St, Suite 912   212/682-0227
Daily: 9-9

Established in 1940, the Babysitters Guild charges high rates, but their professional reputation commends them. All of their sitters have passed rigorous scrutiny, and only the most capable are sent out on jobs. They enforce a four-hour minimum.

Call Kathleen Lewis at **Pinch Sitters** (212/260-6005). Your youngster(s) will love their babysitter and you will relax, appreciating this firm's reliability.

BARNARD COLLEGE BABYSITTING SERVICE
3009 Broadway (Milbank Hall), Room 11   212/854-2035
Mon, Thurs, Fri: 10-4; Tues, Wed: 10-8

Barnard College Babysitting Service is a nonprofit organization run entirely by students of Barnard College, the undergraduate women's college affiliated with Columbia University. The service provides affordable child care for parents in the New York metropolitan area. At the same time, it allows students to seek convenient employment. Live-in help is also available. A minimum registration fee is required.

Nannies (all highly recommended):

Basic Trust (212/222-6602): day care
Fox (212/753-2686): good record
Innovative Learning Center (212/523-7461): day care
Pavillion (212/889-6609): very reliable

Beauty Services

Cosmetic Surgery Consultant

Denise Thomas (212/734-0233)

Day Spas

Anushka Institute (241 E 60th St, 212/355-6404)
Away Spa (W Hotel, 541 Lexington Ave, 4th floor, 212/407-2970)
Bliss Spa (568 Broadway, 212/219-8970)
Carapan (5 W 16th St, 212/633-6220)
Catharine Atzen Day Spa (856 Lexington Ave, 212/517-2400)
Christiana & Carmen Beauty Center (128 Central Park S, Suite 1A, 212/757-5811)
Dorit Baxter Skin Care, Beauty & Health Spa (47 W 57th St, 212/371-4542)
Elizabeth Arden Red Door Salon (691 Fifth Ave, 212/546-0200)
Estée Lauder Spa/Lancome's Institut de Beauté (Bloomingdale's, 1000 Third Ave, 212/705-2318)
Frederic Fekkai Beauté de Provence (15 E 57th St, 212/753-9500): the ultimate
Ilona (629 Park Ave, 212/288-5155): very relaxing

Lia Schorr (680 Lexington Ave, 212/486-9670): efficient, reasonable
Origins (Sports Center, Chelsea Piers, 60 Twelfth Ave, 2nd floor, 212/336-6780)
Paul Labrecque Salon (150 Columbus Ave, 212/362-6800)
Peninsula New York Spa (700 Fifth Ave, 212/247-2200)
Soho Sanctuary (19 Mercer St, 212/334-5550)
Spa at Equinox (140 W 63rd St, lower level, 212/750-4671)
Spa 227 (227 E 56th St, 212/754-0227)
Susan Ciminelli Day Spa (Bergdorf Goodman, 754 Fifth Ave, 9th floor, 212/872-2650): highly recommended
Yasmine Djerradine (30 E 60th St, 212/588-1711): personable and technically advanced; one of the city's best-kept secrets
Yi Pak (10 W 32nd St, 2nd floor, 212/594-1025)

Hair Blowout

Jean Louis David (locations throughout the city): good work at reasonable prices

Hair Care (best in Manhattan)

A.K.S. Salon (694 Madison Ave, 212/888-0707): former stylists from Frederic Fekkai
Astor Place Hair Stylists (2 Astor Pl, at Broadway, 212/475-9854): one of the world's largest barber shops, very inexpensive
Frederic Fekkai (15 E 57th St, 212/753-9500): elegant, with a staff of 150
Garren New York (Henri Bendel, 712 Fifth Ave, 3rd floor atrium, 212/841-9400): personally customized services
John Barrett Salon (Bergdorf Goodman, 754 Fifth Ave, 212/872-2700): top cut
John Frieda (30 E 76th St, 2nd floor, 212/879-1000): very "in"
Kenneth (Waldorf-Astoria Hotel, 301 Park Ave, lobby floor, 212/752-1800): full service and an able staff, but a long wait for Kenneth himself
La Beauté (142 E 49th St, 212/754-0048): reasonably priced
La Coupe (22 E 66th St, 212/371-9230): popular
Nardi Salon (143 E 57th St, 212/421-4810): long-hair specialists
Oribe (Elizabeth Arden, 691 Fifth Ave, 212/546-0200): world-renowned
Ouidad Hair Salon (846 Seventh Ave, 212/333-7577): curly- and frizzy-hair specialists
Peter Coppola (746 Madison Ave, 212/988-9404): reliable
Private World of Leslie Blanchard (680 Fifth Ave, 2nd floor, 212/421-4564): excellent value
Privé (Soho Grand Hotel, 310 West Broadway, 212/274-888): all hair services, trendy
Saks Fifth Avenue Beauty Salon (Saks Fifth Ave, 611 Fifth Ave, 9th floor, 212/940-4000): top grade, full service
Stephen Knoll (625 Madison Ave, 212/421-0100): highly recommended
Vidal Sassoon (767 Fifth Ave, 212/535-9200): popular with men and women

Hair Coloring

Brad Johns (693 Fifth Ave, 212/583-0034): If it's good enough for Carolyn Bessette-Kennedy . . .

Linda Tam Beauty Salon (680 Fifth Ave, 2nd floor, 212/757-2555)
Louis Licari Salon (797 Madison Ave, 212/517-8084)
Oribe (691 Fifth Ave, 212/319-3910)
Warren Tricomi (16 W 57th St, 212/262-8899)

Haircut/shampoo/shiatsu massage

Hair Kuwayama (210 E 10th St, 212/529-6977)
Hair Mates (13 Third Ave, 212/777-4612)

Hair Removal

Allana of New York (160 E 56th St, 212/980-0216)
J. Sisters Salon (35 W 57th St, 212/750-2485)
Vanishing Point (4 W 16th St, 212/255-3474 and 102 W 73rd St,
212/362-1327)

Home Services

Eastside Massage Therapy Center (212/249-2927)
John Sahag Workshop (212/750-7772): styling
Joseph Martin (212/838-3150): hair coloring, nails, pedicure, makeup
Lia Schorr Skin Care (212/486-9670): haircuts, makeup, massage
Lori Klein (212/996-9390): makeup
Makeup Shop (212/807-0447)
Trish McEvoy (212/758-7790): makeup

Makeup

Kimara Ahnert Makeup Studio (1113 Madison Ave, 212/452-4252)
Makeup Center (150 W 55th St, 212/977-9494): good value
Makeup Shop (131 W 21st St, 212/807-0447)

Nails

Christine Valmy (437 Fifth Ave, 2nd floor, 212/779-7800): inexpensive
Cornelia's Nail Design (151 E 71st St, 212/535-5333): nail-wrapping,
facials, massage, body-waxing, eyelash-tinting
John Allan's Men's Club (95 Trinity Pl, at Thames St, 212/406-3000):
for men, full-service
Rescue (21 Cleveland Pl, 212/431-3805)
Sirene (1044 Madison Ave, 212/737-3545)

Pedicures

Paul Labrecque Salon & Spa (160 Columbus Ave, 212/595-0099)
Sirene (1044 Madison Ave, 2nd floor, 212/737-3545 and 1377 Third Ave,
212/585-2044)

Skin Care

Alla Katkov (Miano Viel, 16 E 52nd St, 2nd floor, 212/980-3222): great
facials
Anushka (241 E 60th St, 212/355-6404)
Bloomingdale's (1000 Third Ave): Check the Chanel and Estée Lauder
counters.
Georgette Klinger (501 Madison Ave, 212/838-3200 and 978 Madison
Ave, 212/744-6900)
Lia Schorr (686 Lexington Ave, 212/486-9670)

Toupees

Bob Kelly (151 W 46th St, 212/819-0030)
Ira Senz (13 E 47th St, 212/752-6800)

Bookbinding

TALAS
568 Broadway (at Prince St)   212/219-0770
Mon-Fri: 9-5; call for Sat hours

Jake and Marjorie Salik preside over this outlet, which offers tools, supplies, and books for artists, restorers, collectors, bookbinders, museums, archives, libraries, calligraphers, and retail customers. Expanded inventories feature custom boxes and portfolios, a wide variety of photo-storage and display items, and archival papers. They are also distributors of conservation supplies.

WEITZ, WEITZ & COLEMAN
1377 Lexington Ave (bet 90th and 91st St)   212/831-2213
Mon-Thurs: 9-7; Fri: 9-5; Sat: 12-5 (Sun and evenings by appointment)

Weitz is a highly respected name in the rare-book field. Leo Weitz began a rare-book business in New York in 1909, becoming so well known that he did work for the Rockefellers, DuPonts, Firestones, and other famous families. Today, Herbert Weitz (his son) and partner Elspeth Coleman continue the tradition of fine bookbinding. Weitz and Coleman restore and rebind books and family heirlooms. They also design and create leather photo albums, guest books, archival boxes, presentation folders, and special gift books. Coleman's specialty is custom-designing to clients' specifications. Weitz and Coleman buy and sell rare books, too!

Cabinetry

HARMONY WOODWORKING
153 W 27th St, Room 1001   212/366-7221
Daily: by appointment

Jerry Gerber ran a cabinetry business and woodworking school until the demolition of his old location forced him to move. Instead of merely relocating, Gerber reassessed the entire operation. When he went back into business, he stressed aspects of the craft that most appealed to him. Nowadays Gerber devotes his time to making custom cabinetry, particularly bookcases, wall units, tables, turnings, and carvings.

Calligraphy

CALLIGRAPHY STUDIOS, INC
100 Reade St (bet Church St and West Broadway)   212/964-6007
By appointment

Nothing sets off a card or a letter like calligraphy. Many claim to be experts, but if you really want first-class work, let Linda Stein and her crew customize your order. They are able to do work in any language you desire. Moreover, they create 3-D memory boxes, custom monograms and logos, leatherbound books, and party accessories. This studio is considered tops in protocol.

Camping Equipment

DOWN EAST
50 Spring St   212/925-2632
Mon-Fri: 11-6

Owner Leon Greenman provides a phenomenal range of services to outdoors enthusiasts. He started Down East as a service center for hiking, camping, and outdoor equipment. He has excellent credentials, having owned another camping equipment store and long been a veteran hiker, camper, and trailblazer. From his own experience he came to recognize the lack of service centers for camping equipment. When he was ready to run a store again, he made Down East a godsend for campers. It offers guidebooks, hiking maps, and USGS (U.S. Geological Survey) topographic maps. Outdoor gear can be modified, repaired, and customized.

Carriages

CHATEAU STABLES/CHATEAU THEATRICAL ANIMALS
608 W 48th St   212/246-0520
Daily: 9-6

How would you like to arrive at your next dinner party in a horse-drawn carriage? Chateau is the place to call. They have the largest working collection of horse-drawn vehicles in the United States. Although they prefer advance notice, requests for weddings, group rides, tours, movies, and overseas visitors can be handled at any time. There is nothing quite as romantic as a ride in an authentic hansom cab.

Cars for Hire

AAMCAR CAR RENTALS
315 W 96th St (bet West End Ave and Riverside Dr)   212/222-8500
Mon-Fri: 7:30-7:30; Sat, Sun: 9-5

506 W 181st St (at Amsterdam Ave)   212/927-7000
Mon-Fri: 9-7; Sat: 9-1

This independent car rental company specializes in renting to customers who do not have credit cards—a rarity in this business! They have a full line of cars, vans, and sport utility vehicles. This owner-operated business has been around for several decades and offers a selection of over 200 cars.

Driving around Manhattan is never easy, but when your wheels are not doing what they should, try the master mechanics at **Cooper Classics** (132 Perry St, 212/929-3909). Besides doing good work, they are honest. What more could you ask for?

CAREY LIMOUSINE NY
212/599-1122 (reservations)   718/898-1000 (office)   800/336-4646
24 hours

Carey is considered the grandfather of car-for-hire services. They provide chauffeur-driven limousines and sedans at any time and will take clients anywhere in almost any kind of weather. Last-minute reservations are accepted on an as-available basis. Discuss rates before making a commitment.

COMPANY II LIMOUSINE SERVICE
24 hours   718/430-6482

Steve Betancourt provides a responsible, efficient, and confidential service at reasonable prices. His reputation for reliability is well earned.

ROSA'S INTERNATIONAL LIMOUSINE
11-01 43rd Ave   212/989-5400
24 hours

Rosa's claim they can get a car to you within minutes of your call. Their garage includes everything from 12-passenger super stretch limos to luxury sedans and 14-passenger executive transports. Ask for a Bentley, Rolls-Royce, Mercedes, Jaguar, or BMW, and they can probably fill the order. They also have executive jets!

Stretch limos are big these days (in more ways than one!). If you want to make a big impression or take a carload of friends or kids out for a fun time, try **Dav El Chauffered Transportation Network** (800/922-0343). The company uses standard indexed hourly prices.

Casting

SCULPTURE HOUSE CASTING
155 W 26th St (bet Ave of the Americas and Seventh Ave)
212/645-9430, 888/374-8665
Mon-Fri: 8-6; Sat: 10-4

Sculpture House has been a family-owned business since 1918, making it one of the city's oldest casting firms. A full-service casting foundry, it specializes in classical plaster reproductions, mold-making, and casting in all mediums and sizes. Sculpting tools and supplies and ornamental plastering are also available.

Chair Caning

VETERAN'S CHAIR CANING AND REPAIR SHOP
442 Tenth Ave   212/564-4560
Mon-Fri: 8-4:30; Sat: 9:30-12:30
closed Sat in summer

John Bausert, a third-generation chair caner, has written a book about his craft. Certainly, the prices and craftsmanship are among the best in town, and Bausert believes in passing along his knowledge. His wife Nancy is store owner and sales manager. Customers are encouraged to repair their own chairs. The procedure is outlined in Bausert's book, and necessary materials are sold in the shop. If you don't want to try or have had disastrous results on your own, Veteran's will repair the chair. For a slight charge, they'll even pick it up from your home. In addition to caning, Veteran's also stocks materials for chair and furniture repair, does wicker repair, and repairs and reglues wooden chairs.

WESTSIDE CHAIR CANING AND REPAIR
371 Amsterdam Ave (bet 77th and 78th St), 2nd floor   212/724-4408
Wed-Sat: 11-7; Sun: 1-5

Jeffrey Weiss has assembled a talented crew that does hand- and machine-caning, rush- and splint-seating, wicker restoration, and the regluing and repairing of furniture. They also have a substantial stock of unclaimed chairs for sale.

China and Glassware Repair

CENTER ART STUDIO
250 W 54th St, Room 901   212/247-3550
Mon-Thurs: 9-6; Fri: 9-5 (by appointment only)

"Fine art restoration and display since 1919" is the motto here. The word *fine* should be emphasized, for owners of really good crystal, porcelain, china, or bronze art should make Center Art Studio *the* place to go for repairs. The house specialty is antique restoration. They will restore or repair scagliola, lacquer, porcelain, terra cotta, shells, and precious stones. They will also restore antique furniture and decorative objects, using original materials whenever possible. They'll even design and install display bases and cases. Finally, they can pack and crate articles for shipment. Among the oldest and most diverse art restoration studios in the city, Center Art offers a multitude of special services, like designs and sketches by fax and multilingual personnel for overseas shoppers. The owner, Lansing Moore, has a superbly talented staff that has worked on furniture designed by the likes of Frank Lloyd Wright.

GLASS RESTORATIONS
1597 York Ave (bet 84th and 85th St)   212/517-3287
Mon-Fri: 9:30-5

Chip your prize Lalique glass treasure? No worry! Glass Restorations restores all manner of crystal, including pieces by Steuben, Baccarat, Daum, and Waterford, as well as antique art glass. This place is a find, as too few quality restorers are left in the country. Ask for Gus!

HESS RESTORATIONS
200 Park Ave S (at 17th St)   212/260-2255, 212/979-1143
Mon-Fri: 10:30-4; by appointment for later times

Hess has been in business since 1945, providing a restoration service so professional that previous damage is usually unnoticeable. Repairing and restoring silver and crystal are available. Their emphasis is on restoration of fine European porcelains, ivory, tortoise shell, sculptures, and *objets d'art*. They are recommended by leading museums, auction houses, and galleries in Manhattan. The replacement of blue glass liners for antique silver salt dishes is unique. Hess accepts insured shipments of items to be repaired and will send an estimate for restoration work.

Clock and Watch Repair

FANELLI ANTIQUE TIMEPIECES
790 Madison Ave (bet 66th and 67th St), Suite 202   212/517-2300
Mon-Fri: 10-6; Sat: 11-5

In a beautiful clock gallery, Cindy Fanelli specializes in the care of high-quality "investment-type" timepieces, especially carriage clocks. They have one of the nation's largest collections of rare and unusual early-American grandfather clocks and vintage wristwatches. They do both sales and restorations, make house calls, give free estimates, rent out timepieces for special assignments, and purchase single pieces or entire collections. Granddad would be proud to see his prize in the hands of these exceptionally able folks.

FOSSNER TIMEPIECES CLOCK SHOP
1057 Second Ave (at 56th St)   212/980-1099
Mon-Fri: 10-6; Sat: 11-4

In Europe, fine-watch repairing is a family tradition, but this craft is slowly being forgotten in our country. Fortunately, Manhattan has a four-generation family, the Fossners, who have passed along this talent from father to son. You can have complete confidence in their work on any kind of watch. They guarantee repairs for six months and will generally get a job done within a week.

TIME PIECES
115 Greenwich Ave (at 13th St)   212/929-8011
Tues-Fri: 11-6:30; Sat: 9-5

Grace Szuwala services, restores, repairs, and sells antique timepieces. Szuwala's European training makes her an expert on antique watches and clocks. She has a strong sensitivity for pieces that have more sentimental than real value. This amazing Grace can really do wonders with keepsakes from another time!

Clothing Repair
FRENCH-AMERICAN REWEAVING COMPANY
119 W 57th St (bet Ave of the Americas and Seventh Ave), Room 1406
212/765-4670
Mon-Fri: 10:30-5:30; Sat: 11-2

Has a tear, burn, or other catastrophe ruined your favorite outfit? These folks can be a godsend. They will work on most any garment for men or women in nearly every fabric. In most cases, the item will look just like new!

Suppose you got off a plane, have an important dinner engagement, and notice a tear in your jacket. What to do? Go straight to **Ban's Custom Tailor Shop** (1544 First Ave, 212/570-0444), and they will take care of you.

Computer Service and Instruction

For rentals—Try **Business Equipment Rental** (250 W 49th St, 212/582-2020). Prices are reasonable; pickup and delivery are available.

For repair—these are the best:

Datavision (445 Fifth Ave, 212/689-1111)
Machattan (145 Ave of the Americas, 212/242-9393): Macintosh only
RCS Computer Experience (261 Madison Ave, 212/949-6935)
Tekserve (155 W 23rd St, 4th floor, 212/929-3645): Macintosh only

ABC COMPUTER SERVICES
375 Fifth Ave (bet 35th and 6th St), 2nd floor   212/725-3511
Mon-Fri: 9-6

These folks provide sales, service, and supplies for desktop and notebook computers, as well as all kinds of printers. They have been in the game for over ten years, which is a good recommendation.

Craft Instruction

CRAFT STUDENTS LEAGUE
YWCA of the City of New York
610 Lexington Ave   212/735-9731

For over 65 years, the Craft Students League has offered programs in crafts and fine arts. The curriculum is wide ranging and includes bookbinding, jewelry, pottery, woodworking, drawing, painting, and decorative finishes. For anyone yearning for a creative outlet, this school—with its convenient midtown location and professional teaching staff—is a winner. It's easy on the pocketbook, too!

Delivery, Courier, Messenger Services

AIRLINE DELIVERY SERVICES
60 E 42nd St (bet Park and Madison Ave)   212/687-5145
24-hour service, 7 days a week

Before the big guys got in the business, this outfit was doing round-the-clock local and long-distance deliveries. If you have some time-sensitive material, give them a call. They'll promptly pick up your item, even in the middle of the night or a snowstorm. They boast a 97% on-time delivery rate for the more than 60 years they have been in operation.

JIMINY SPLIT DELIVERY SERVICES
147 W 46th St   212/354-7373
Mon-Fri: 7-7

Jiminy Split can hand-deliver a package from New York to Washington, D.C., in less than five hours. Federal Express can't match that, and the U.S. mail is not even in the running. If you want fast, reliable, and personal service, call Jiminy Split. They'll deliver anywhere within the continental U.S. as fast as a plane or train can deliver a messenger. Rates include travel fare, plus delivery expense. Within the city, rates depend upon distance traveled (the city is divided into zones) and time. There are several branches.

KANGAROO COURIER
120 E 32nd St   212/684-2233
Mon-Fri: 8-6 (scheduled services all the time)

Kangaroo's philosophy is that *all* shipping is in-house, and they are therefore set up to provide any and all courier services. Kangaroo boasts they can handle everything from a cross-town rush letter (delivery completed within an hour) to a 10,000-pound cross-country shipment, tracking the entire job all the way.

NOW VOYAGER
74 Varick St, Suite 307   212/431-1616
Mon-Fri: 10-5:30; Sat: 12-4:30

Now Voyager runs an international courier service, and you can be a part of it. The firm has a schedule of flights to various areas, mostly Europe, South America, and the Far East. You can go at a fraction of the regular fare if you're willing to take only carry-on luggage. They now have great deals on domestic flights and are starting to get into cruise discounts. Usually flights are booked some weeks ahead, so it is a good idea to call or write as early as possible. Discounted domestic and international non-courier flights are also available. Who knows—you might be able to take an exciting trip for next to nothing!

Detectives

DECISION STRATEGIES INTERNATIONAL
505 Park Ave (at 59th St)   212/599-9400
Mon-Fri: 8:30-7

Need a corporate investigation? Someone cheating on you? Want assistance with fraud prevention? Bart Schwartz and his staff of more than a dozen top-notch investigators are the ones to call. Their experience in nearly every field can save you headaches—and maybe a lot of cash.

Doll Repair

NEW YORK DOLL HOSPITAL
787 Lexington Ave (bet 61st and 62nd St), 2nd floor   212/838-7527
Mon-Sat: 10-6

New York Doll Hospital has been fixing, mending, and restoring dolls to health since 1900. Owner Irving Chais has operated in this cramped two-room "hospital" since 1947. That was the year he took over from his father, who had begun fixing the dolls of his clients' children in his hair salon. Chais came into the business one Christmas season when his father was ailing and needed help. He has replaced antique fingers, reconstructed china heads and German rag dolls, and authentically restored antique dolls. Additional services include appraisals, made-to-order dolls, and buying and selling antique dolls and toys. He will also work on teddy bears and other stuffed animals, as well as talking dolls with computer chips.

Dry Cleaners, Laundries

CLEANTEX
2335 Twelfth Ave (at 133rd St)   212/283-1200
Mon-Fri: 8-4

Cleantex specializes in cleaning draperies, furniture, balloon and Roman shades, vertical blinds, and Oriental and area rugs. They provide free pickup and delivery service. Museums, churches, and rug dealers are all among Cleantex's satisfied clients.

HALLAK CLEANERS
1232 Second Ave (at 65th St)   212/879-4694
Mon-Fri: 7-6:30; Sat: 8-3; closed Sat in July, August

Hallak has been a family-operated business for nearly 40 years. Joseph, Sr., a native of France, instilled his work ethic and dedication to detail into sons John-Claude and Joseph, Jr. This no doubt accounts for the pride and personal service they offer customers. Much of their work comes from referrals by boutiques such as Armani, Celine, Hermes, Ferragamo, and St. John, to name a few. Hallak does all work in their state-of-the-art plant. They will clean shirts, linens, suede, leather, and draperies. Their specialty is museum-quality cleaning and preservation of wedding gowns. For those (like your author) who have trouble with stains on ties, Hallak is the place to go for help. Their skilled work takes time, but rush service is available at no additional cost.

LEATHERCRAFT PROCESS OF AMERICA
Call for locations   212/564-8980
Mon-Fri: 7:30-6:30

Leathercraft is all things to all suedes, sheepskins, and leathers. They will clean, re-dye, re-line, repair, and lengthen or shorten any suede or leather garment. That includes boots, gloves, clothing, and handbags, as well as odd leather items. Because leather is extremely difficult to clean, the process can be painfully expensive. However, Leathercraft has a reputation dating back to 1938, and their prices remain competitive.

MEURICE GARMENT CARE
31 University Pl (bet 8th and 9th St)   212/475-2778
Mon-Fri: 7:30-7; Sat: 7:30-5

245 E 57th St (bet Second and Third Ave)   212/759-9057
Mon-Fri: 8-6; Sat: 7:30-5

Meurice specializes in cleaning and restoring fine garments. They handle each piece individually, taking care of details like loose buttons and tears. Special services: exquisite hand-finishing, expert stain removal and dyeing, museum-quality preservation, cleaning and restoration of wedding gowns, and on-site leather cleaning and repairs. Delivery and shipping are available.

MIDNIGHT EXPRESS CLEANERS
212/921-0111, 800/7MIDNITE
Mon-Fri: 9 a.m-11 p.m.; Sat: 9-3

What a handy place to know about! Midnight does dry cleaning, shirt laundering, leather and suede cleaning and repair, and bulk laundering. Best of all, they will pick up and deliver, day or night, for a small charge. Prompt return is assured. They specialize in dry-cleaning restoration of smoke, fire, and water-damaged goods. This is Manhattan's only OSHA (Occupational Safety & Health Administration)-compliant laundry service. Be sure to keep their number near your phone!

MME. PAULETTE DRY CLEANERS
1255 Second Ave (bet 65th and 66th St)
877/COUTURE   212/838-6827
Mon-Fri: 7:30-6:30; Sat: 8-5

160 Columbus Ave (Reebok Sports Club NY)   212/501-1408
Mon-Fri: 5 a.m.-11 p.m.; Sat: 8 a.m.-9 p.m.

What a clientele: Versace, Christian Dior, Romeo Gigli, Geoffrey Beene, Saks, Bloomingdale's, and Henri Bendel. This full-service establishment has been in business for nearly 40 years. They do dry cleaning (including knits, suedes, and leathers), tailoring (including reweaving and alterations), laundry, and household and rug cleaning. They provide fur and box storage. Taking care of wedding dresses is a specialty. In addition, they can repair water-, bleach- and fire-damaged garments, do wet cleaning, and clean upholstery and tapestry by hand. Mme. Paulette offers free pickup and delivery service throughout Manhattan, has charge accounts, and will provide one-day service upon request.

NEW YORK'S FINEST FRENCH CLEANERS
144 Reade St (bet Hudson and Greenwich St)   212/431-4010
Mon-Fri: 7:30-6:30; Sat: 8:30-6

Three generations of the same family have operated this quality business, featuring pickup, delivery, and one-day service. Tailoring and storage are available, as is care for fine silks and leathers.

TIECRAFTERS
252 W 29th St   212/629-5800
Mon-Fri: 9-5

This place is particularly handy for out-of-town customers. Old ties never die or even fade away here. Instead, they're dyed, widened, straightened, and cleaned. Tiecrafters believe that a well-made tie can live forever, and they provide services to make that possible. In addition to converting tie widths, they restore soiled or spotted ties and clean and repair all kinds of neckwear. Perhaps most impressive is Andy Tarshis' willingness to discuss tie maintenance. (Hint: if you roll your tie at night, wrinkles will be gone by morning.) Tiecrafters offers several pamphlets on the subject, including one that tells how to take out spots at home. They accept business via any carrier, and their charge for cleaning a tie is reasonable. They also make custom neckwear.

Best Upholstery Cleaners:

Buff-Away of Manhattan (212/477-7100)
Clean Bright (212/283-6400)
Cohen Carpet, Upholstery and Drapery Cleaning (212/663-6902)

Electricians

ALTMAN ELECTRIC
283 W 11th St   212/741-7372, 800/287-7774
Daily: 24 hours

There is hardly anything as upsetting as an electrical emergency, especially in the middle of the night or just before a party. Don't fret. The licensed crew at this reliable outfit (all 18 of them) is available day and night. They will do small or large jobs at home or office, and rates are reasonable. They must be first-class, since they have been in business for over half a century.

Exterminators

ACME EXTERMINATING
460 Ninth Ave (bet 35th and 36th St)   212/594-9230
Mon-Fri: 7-5

Are you bugged? I'm referring to the type of bugs that crawl around. Acme is expert at debugging private homes, offices, stores, museums, and hospitals. They are state of the art in pest control, employing integrated pest management.

Eyeglass Repair

E.B. MEYROWYTZ AND DELL
19 W 44th St (at Fifth Ave)   212/575-1686
Mon-Fri: 9-6; Sat: 9-1
July, Aug: Mon-Fri: 9-5:30; closed Sat

If you desperately need E.B. Meyrowytz and Dell, you probably can't read this. No need to worry, as they do on-the-spot emergency repair on glasses. This is *the* place to go for eyeglass emergencies in the city. They also repair binoculars. Of course, you're welcome to stop by for regular optical needs, too.

Fashion Schools

FASHION INSTITUTE OF TECHNOLOGY
Seventh Ave at 27th St
212/217-7675 (admission), 212/217-7999 (general information)

The Fashion Institute of Technology (FIT), a branch of the State University of New York, is the world's premier educational facility serving the fashion industry. The school was founded more than 50 years ago. It includes a graduate roster that reads like a "who's who" of the fashion world. Jhane Barnes, Calvin Klein, and Norma Kamali are just a few. The school offers a multitude of majors: accessories, advertising, display and exhibit, toy, jewelry, interior, textile and fashion design, illustration, photography, fine arts, fashion buying and merchandising, apparel production management, pattern making, and marketing. FIT also maintains a student-placement service. All students are top-caliber. The museum at FIT is the world's largest repository of fashion, with over a million articles of clothing. It is frequently open to the public. Call 212/217-5800 for information about exhibits and shows before planning a visit.

Formal Wear Rental and Sales

A. T. HARRIS FORMALWEAR
11 E 44th St (bet Madison and Fifth Ave), 2nd floor   212/682-6325
Mon, Tues, Wed, Fri: 9-5:45; Thurs: 9-6:45
Sat: 10-3:45 by appointment

Ten U.S. presidents have been fitted for formal attire at this store, so it must be the place to go! A. T. Harris has been in business since 1892, selling and renting formal wear of the highest quality. You will find cutaways, tails, tuxedos, shoes, top coats, stud and cuff-link sets, and kid and suede gloves.

BALDWIN FORMALS
52 W 56th St (bet Fifth Ave and Ave of the Americas)   212/245-8190
Mon, Thurs: 8:30-7; Tues, Wed, Fri: 8:30-6; Sat: 10-4

If you are suddenly called to a state dinner at the White House or some similarly spiffy function, Baldwin will take care of all the dressing details. They rent and sell all types of formal attire: suits, overcoats, top hats, shoes, and more. They will pick up and deliver for free to many midtown addresses and for a slight charge to other addresses. Same-day service is guaranteed for rental orders received by early afternoon. Rapid alteration service (two or three days) is available on sale merchandise.

Funeral Service

FRANK E. CAMPBELL FUNERAL HOME
1076 Madison Ave (at 81st St)   212/288-3500
Daily: 24 hours

In time of need, it is good to know of a highly reliable funeral home. These folks have been in business since 1898, providing superior professional service.

Furniture Rental

CHURCHILL-WINCHESTER FURNITURE RENTALS
6 E 32nd St (bet Fifth and Madison Ave), 2nd floor   212/686-0444
Mon-Thurs: 9-6; Fri: 9:30-4; Sun: 11-5

Mention Churchill, and you think of staid old England, right? Well, *this* Churchill is starkly contemporary, as well as traditional. They can fill any size order for a business or residence, and they offer free interior-decorating advice and a lease-purchase plan. A customer simply selects what is needed from stock or borrows from the loaner program until special orders are processed. Churchill also offers a comprehensive package, including housewares and appliances.

They specialize in executive locations, both corporate and personal. They will rent out anything from a single chair to an entire home. Their clients include team-sports managers, executives on temporary assignment, and actors on short-term contracts.

CORT FURNITURE RENTAL
711 Third Ave (bet 44th and 45th St)   212/867-2800
Mon-Sat: 9-6

Cort rents furnishings for a single room, entire apartment, or office. They show accessories as well, and all furnishings (including electronics and housewares) are available for rental with an option to purchase. An apartment-locator service is offered, free professional decorating is available, and a multi-lingual staff is at your service. A specialty is working with Japanese clients. The stock is large, delivery and setup can often be done within 48 hours, and all styles of furniture and accessories are shown in their 12,000-square-foot showroom, conveniently located near Grand Central Station.

INTERNATIONAL FURNITURE RENTALS
345 Park Ave (at 51st St)   212/421-0340
Mon-Thurs: 9-6; Fri: 9-5:30; Sat: 10-2

International Furniture Rentals is the largest home and office furniture-rental firm in the metropolitan area. A decorating and design specialist is available for free consultation. The firm carries accessories to coordinate with furnishings, and all items are of executive quality. Quick delivery from their warehouse is a plus.

Furniture Repair and Restoration

ANTIQUE FURNITURE WORKROOM
210 Eleventh Ave (bet 24th and 25th St), 9th floor   212/683-0551
Mon-Fri: 8-4

For years, Antique Furniture Workroom was the traditional place of choice for French polishing, chair repair, and woodwork restoration. William Olsen added antique furniture restoration (especially American, English, Oriental, and continental originals), gold-leafing, furniture-making, and caning. Re-creation of classic French art deco furniture is a new specialty. If a piece of furniture needs special attention, this is a reliable place to go. Estimates are given in the home.

Gardening

COUNCIL ON THE ENVIRONMENT OF NEW YORK CITY
51 Chambers St, Room 228   212/788-7900
Mon-Fri: 9-5

It's a little-known fact that the city will loan tools to groups involved in community-sponsored open-space greening projects. Loans are limited to one week, but the waiting period is not long and the price (nothing!) is right. You can borrow the same tools several times a season. A group can be as few as four people. The council will also design office-waste prevention and recycling programs for commercial businesses. They carry a number of interesting free publications.

PROFESSIONAL PLANT SERVICES
516/797-6923
Daily

The best part of this service is that Anita Cheikin-Heiser will come right to your apartment or home to give expert advice. She specializes in using low-maintenance plants to create exterior gardens with year-round interest at both residential and commercial sites. This very talented lady, who makes sure her work has "kid appeal," will also install drip irrigation systems.

General Services

TOP SERVICE
845 Seventh Ave (bet 54th and 55th St)   212/765-3190
Mon-Fri: 8-6; Sat: 9-1

Shoe repair is the main business here, but there is much more. Dance shoes are a specialty, and Top Service is used by many Broadway theater groups. In addition, Top Service will make rubber stamps, cut keys, engrave anything, do luggage and handbag repair, and dye and clean shoes. They are good people to know about in case of last-minute emergencies.

— Millennium Note —

The Washington Square Memorial Arch, which has towered over the southern end of Fifth Avenue since 1889, was first constructed of wood and was later re-created in marble by popular demand.

Gift Wrapping and Packaging

THE PADDED WAGON
1569 Second Ave (bet 81st and 82nd St)   212/570-5500
Mon-Sat: 9-7; Sun: 12-5

For gift-wrapping help, this is *the* place to visit. The Padded Wagon carries all sizes of boxes and paper, and they can provide UPS and Federal Express service.

UNITED SHIPPING & PACKAGING
200 E 10th St (at Second Ave)   212/475-2214
Mon-Fri: 9-8; Sat: 11-6

United Shipping will send anything anywhere in the world. They also sell packaging supplies and boxes. Additional services include faxing, mailboxes, office supplies, messenger services, and small moves in the city.

Haircuts

Children

COZY'S CUTS FOR KIDS
1125 Madison Ave (at 84th St)   212/744-1716

448 Amsterdam Ave (at 81st St)   212/579-2600
Mon-Sat: 10-6

Cozy's really takes care of kids of all ages, including the offspring of many famous personalities. What an experience here: videos and videogames, special theme barber chairs, Polaroid pictures, balloons, candy, and free toys. They issue a "first-time" diploma with a keepsake lock of hair! Besides providing professional styling services, Cozy's is a toy boutique.

MICHAEL'S CHILDREN'S HAIRCUTTING SALON
1263 Madison Ave (at 90th St)   212/289-9612
Mon-Sat: 9-5; closed Sat in July, Aug

This place is totally dedicated to children. Since 1910, Michael's drawing card has been rapport with kids and consistency of personnel and style. Nick Di Sisto, the salon's owner, is living proof of this. He worked for Michael for years, and when Michael retired, he bought him out. Many of the hairstylists have worked under both owners. Appointments are unheard of, and lollipops, seats shaped like toy cars, and comic books make the experience fun for kids.

Family

ASTOR PLACE HAIR STYLISTS
2 Astor Pl (at Broadway)   212/475-9854
Mon-Sat: 8-8; Sun: 9-6

Does your hairstylist shop have a deejay on staff? They do here! Getting a haircut at Astor Place is not unlike being admitted to the hallowed halls of the latest "in" nightspot. The personnel inside what was once a modest neighborhood barbershop give the trendiest, wildest, and most unusual haircuts on the scene. How did this all get started? It seems that the Vezza brothers inherited a barbershop from their father in the East Village at a time "when not even cops were getting haircuts." Enrico took note of the newly gentrified neighborhood's young trendies and their sleek haircuts and changed the name of the shop to "Astor Place Hair Stylists." Now, the shop is staffed with a resident manager, a doorman, a loft, and an ever-increasing number of barbers.

ATLAS BARBER SCHOOL
32 Third Ave   212/475-1360
Mon-Fri: 9-8; Sat: 9-5

This school offers students (and customers) general barbering and shaving techniques. They've been at it for half a century. High style it ain't; good value it is!

PAUL MOLE FAMILY BARBERSHOP
1031 Lexington Ave (at 74th St)   212/535-8461
Mon-Sat: 7:30-6:30; Sun: 9-4

This shop is just what it says: a family business. They will trim the heads of both dad and the kids, with customer-friendly hours and pocketbook-friendly prices. The place is packed after school and on weekends, so appointments are suggested.

Shaves for gentlemen:
Art of Shaving (373 Madison Ave, 212/986-2905)
Chelsea Barbers (465 W 23rd St, 212/741-2254)
Harrison James (5 W 54th St, 212/541-6870): play billiards while waiting
Jerry's Men's Hair Styling Salon (Rockefeller Center, 212/246-3151)

FEATURE TRIM
1108 Lexington Ave (bet 77th and 78th St)   212/650-9746
Tues-Fri: 11-7; Sat: 10-6

This neighborhood establishment maintains its standard of basic hair care for men, women, and children. Low maintenance is the key to Feature Trim's haircuts. Easy care, reasonable prices, friendly faces, and over 50 years combined experience keep an impressive clientele asking for proprietors Victor and Joe. Appointments are encouraged, but walk-ins are welcome.

PEPPE AND BILL
Plaza Hotel
Fifth Ave at Central Park S, mezzanine   212/751-8380
Mon-Fri: 9-6; Sat: 9-2

When you pay the kind of prices charged here, you expect the best. That is exactly what you get with highly professional hairstyling by Jacques and first-rate manicure work by his wife, Marie. You can also be confident of the other personnel here.

Hardware Installation
F&J HARDWARE
15 Ave A (bet 1st and 2nd St)   212/473-6977
Mon-Fri: 8-7; Sat: 9-6

This store is a general housewares emporium with an emphasis on bathroom fixtures. Ceramic tile, medicine cabinets, shower doors, and hardware are specialties, and F&J can install all of them. They also have a good stock of gates and locks. This store really shines in service. Mirrors and shower doors are hung with ease. Locksmith emergencies are answered routinely. They even stock and hang drapery hardware. Customers can get almost any kind of handiwork done. In this city, that kind of service is rare indeed.

Health and Fitness

What's new at Manhattan fitness centers?

Chelsea Piers (Pier 60, West Side Hwy at 23rd St): huge spinning room and sun deck
Club La Raquette (Parker Meridien Hotel, 119 W 56th St): new type of tanning equipment
Crunch Fitness (404 Lafayette St): Netplus cardiovascular equipment
David Barton Gym (626 Broadway): body-sculpting classes and high-impact aerobics
Equinox (Barbizon Hotel, 140 E 63rd St): detox programs
New York Health & Racquet Club (various locations): day spas and belly dancing at the 56th St branch
New York Sports Club (various locations): new family programs, babysitting services
Reebok Sports Club NY (160 Columbus Ave): karate
World Gym (232 Mercer St): great Pilate class boxing ring, kick boxing

---

With all the interest in keeping fit, health clubs have sprung up all over Manhattan. Some do not last long, so it is wise to be careful about making long-term financial arrangements with any but the largest and most secure operations. Prices and facilities vary. For those who live in the city, watch newspaper and television ads for special introductory offers. For visitors, many clubs honor reciprocal memberships or allow one- or two-day guest memberships. A number of hotels have excellent facilities, including the Peninsula, Holiday Inn Crowne Plaza, Four Seasons, Intercontinental, Vista, Parker Meridien, United Nations Plaza, St. Regis, Trump International and RIHGA Royal. For chains, New York Health and Racquet Club and New York Sports Club are recommended. Following are some of the better clubs, by district.

Downtown

Adolphus Fitness (5 E 17th St, 212/206-1504)
Bally Sports Club (25 Broadway, 212/425-8127)
Carmine Recreation Center (1 Clarkson St, 212/242-5228)
Crunch Fitness (404 Lafayette St, 212/614-0120; 54 E 13th St, 212/475-2018; and 152 Christopher St, 212/366-3725)
David Barton Gym (552 Ave of the Americas, 212/727-0004 and 623 Broadway, 212/420-0507)
Dolphin Gym (155 E 3rd St, 212/533-0090; 242 E 14th St, 212/614-0390; and 22 W 19th St, 212/929-6789)
Equinox Fitness Club (897 Broadway, 212/780-9300)
Executive Fitness Center (3 World Trade Center, 22nd floor, 212/466-9266)
Johnny Lat's Gym (7 E 17th St, 212/366-4426)
Lucille Roberts Health Club (80 Fifth Ave, 212/255-3999)
New York Health and Racquet Club (39 Whitehall St, 212/269-9800 and 24 E 13th St, 212/924-4600)
New York Sports Club (30 Cliff St, 212/349-7700; 151 Reade St, 212/571-1000; and Sheridan Square, 125 Seventh Ave S, 212/206-1500)
Plus One Fitness (106 Crosby St, 212-334-1116), 1 World Financial Ctr, 200 Liberty St, 212/945-2525; and Waldorf-Astoria Hotel, 301 Park Ave, 212/872-4970)
World Gym (232 Mercer St, 212/780-7407)

Midtown

Asser Levy (23rd St at Asser Levy Pl, 212/447-2020)
Atrium Club (115 E 57th St, 212/826-9640)
Bally Sports Club (335 Madison Ave, 212/983-5320; 139 W 32nd St, 212/465-1750; and 350 W 50th St, 212/265-9400)
Club La Raquette, Parker Meridien Hotel (119 W 56th St, 212/245-1144)
Dolphin Gym (201 E 23rd St, 212/679-7300)
Equinox (895 Broadway, 212/780-9300 and 250 E 54th St, 212/277-5400)
Manhattan Plaza Health Club (482 W 43rd St, 212/563-7001)
New York Health and Racquet Club (132 E 45th St, 212/986-3100; 20 E 50th St, 212/593-1500; 110 W 56th St, 212/541-7200; and 115 E 57th St, 212/826-9650)
New York Sports Club (50 W 34th St, 212/868-0820; 380 Madison Ave, 212/983-0303; Holiday Inn Crowne Plaza, 49th St at Broadway, 212/977-8880; 59th St at Park Ave, 212/308-1010; 614 Second Ave, 212/213-5999; 541 Lexington Ave, 212/838-2102; and 404 Fifth Ave, 212/594-3120)
Prescriptive Fitness Gym (250 W 54th St, 212/307-7760)

Sports Center at Chelsea Piers (Pier 60, West Side Hwy at 23rd St, 212/336-6000)
Sports Training Institute (575 Lexington Ave, 212/752-7111)
YMCA (215 W 23rd St, 212/741-9210)
YWCA (610 Lexington Ave, 212/735-9755)

Upper East Side

Asphalt Green (555 E 90th St, 212/451-0004)
Crunch Fitness (1109 Second Ave, 212/758-3434)
David Barton Gym (30 E 85th St, 212/517-7577)
Equinox Fitness Club (205 E 85th St, 212/987-8500 and Barbizon Hotel, 140 E 63rd St, 212/750-4900)
New York Health and Racquet Club (1433 York Ave, 212/737-6666)
New York Sports Club (151 E 86th St, 212/860-8630; 1470 First Ave, 212/744-7050; 349 E 76th St, 212/288-5700; and 1635 Third Ave, 212/987-7200)
92nd Street Y Health and Fitness Center (1395 Lexington Ave, 212/415-5700)
Tower Tennis Courts (1725 York Ave, 212/860-2464): all-year indoor tennis club

Upper West Side

Crunch Fitness (160 W 83rd St, 212/875-1902)
Dolphin Gym (700 Columbus Ave, 212/865-5454)
Equinox (344 Amsterdam Ave, 212/721-4200 and 2465 Broadway, 212/799-1818)
New York Sports Club (248 W 80th St, 212/873-1500 and 61 W 62nd St, 212/265-0995)
Paris Health Club (752 West End Ave, 212/749-3500)
Reebok Sports Club NY (67th St at Columbus Ave, 212/362-6800): big, excellent
Riverbank State Park (679 Riverside Dr, 212/694-3600)
West Side YMCA (5 W 63rd St, 212/787-4400)
World Gym (1926 Broadway, 212/874-0942)

EXUDE
16 E 52nd St   212/644-9559
Mon-Sun: 6 a.m.-10 p.m.

Edward Jackowski is the founder of Exude, the largest motivational and one-on-one fitness-consulting organization in the country. In addition to consulting, Exude offers a weight loss and control program, nutritional counseling, exercise therapy, cardiac rehabilitation, sports training (golf, tennis, and skiing), children's fitness programs, pre- and post-natal exercise, boxing, self-defense, home-gym design, and massage therapy. Services and seminars, including classes and training programs, are available for groups and corporate clients. Exude's fitness consultants can also come to your home, office, gym, or hotel room. All programs are arranged on an appointment basis. Prices are reasonable, and they work with men, women, and children.

Personal trainers

Art Clyde (212/262-4040)
Bob Shaw (212/755-3550)

Bodysmith (212/249-1824: women only
Casa Specialized Private Fitness (212/717-1998)
Jonathan Urla (212/996-7088)
Mike Creamer (212/353-8834)
Rich Lettau (212/945-2525)
Timothy Callaghan (212/585-4245)

Massage

Cynthia Bernardi (80 E 11th St, Room 625, 212/473-0760): Shiatsu
Eastside Massage Therapy Center (351 E 78th St, 212/249-2927): 13 massage
    therapists; daily, by appointment; Swedish, sports, and deep muscle therapy
Healing Hands (849 Lexington Ave, 212/486-1122): house and hotel calls,
    and corporate services
John Wehr (Reebok Sports Club NY, 160 Columbus Ave, 212/362-6800)
Lewis Harrison (40 W 72nd St, 212/724-8782): hotel and house calls; stress
    management
Robert Lane (ESP Vitamins & Bodywork Center, 1727 Second Ave, 212/534-
    8970): house calls and Saturdays available

Specialized massages

Acupuncture: Stephanie Tyiska (500/445-1452)
Chinese back rub: (212/334-3909)
Hot rocks: Spa at Equinox (212/439-8500)
Reflexology: Providence Hogan (718/638-0097)
Reiki: Maxine Gaudio (212/645-3210)
Russian/Turkish: (212/674-9250)
Thai: Rachel Perkoff (917/857-6035)

Help for Hire

A.E. JOHNSON EMPLOYMENT AGENCY
686 Lexington Ave (bet 56th and 57th St)   212/644-0990
Mon-Fri: 8:30-4:30

Dating from 1890, Johnson's is the oldest employment agency in the world
dealing exclusively with household help. They specialize in providing affluent
clients with highly qualified butlers, cooks, housekeepers, chauffeurs, valets,
maids, and couples. Both temporary and permanent workers are available, many
on a moment's notice. All employment references, criminal records, and driver's
licenses are checked.

COLUMBIA BARTENDING AGENCY
212/854-4537
Mon-Fri: 9-5

Columbia Bartending Agency uses students so expert at bartending that one
wonders what profession they could possibly do as well after college. The service has been around a long time, and there is none better. Columbia also supplies waiters, waitresses, and coat checkers.

DIRTBURSTERS
111 W 16th St, #5K   212/721-4357
Daily: anytime

Boy, are these handy folks! They will clean apartments, residences, and small offices at hourly rates. Their staff, hours, and rates are flexible, and they are bonded. Dirtbursters can arrange for upholstery and window cleaning, walk your dog, wax your floors, serve as party waiters, and paint your rooms.

Walls need attention? For decorative finishing, painting, murals, or hanging wallpaper, call **Silver Lining** (212/496-7800).

FLATIRON SERVICES
230 E 93rd St (at Second Ave)　　212/876-1000
Mon-Fri: 7-4:30

Can you imagine how many homes and apartments these people have cleaned since opening for business in 1893? They certainly know what they are doing! Expert services include residential house and window cleaning, installation and refinishing of wood floors, and maid service. You might call the Rockefellers for references!

LYNN AGENCY
250 W 57th St　　212/582-3030
Mon-Fri: 8-4

If you need home care for a private patient, give Lynn a call. They have a good reputation for highly qualified personnel at reasonable rates.

NEW YORK LITTLE ELVES
143 First Ave (at 9th St), Suite 2　　212/673-5507
Daily: 7-7

Just finish a construction or remodeling job? Is the place a mess? You need some elves to help clean up, and this is the outfit to call. They provide estimates, employ screened personnel, carry liability insurance, and are fully bonded. The "elves" will also help set up for a party and return afterwards to put your home or apartment back in shape.

PAVILLION AGENCY
15 E 40th St, Suite 900　　212/889-6609
Daily: 9-5

Pavillion has been a family-owned and -operated business for nearly 40 years. If you are in need of nannies, housekeepers, laundresses, couples, butlers, housemen, major-domos, chefs, chauffeurs, security personnel, caretakers, gardeners, property managers, or personal assistants, these are the folks to call. Ask for Keith or Clifford Greenhouse.

RED BALL, INC.
221 E 85th St (bet Second and Third Ave)　　212/861-7686
Mon-Sat: 7-5

These people have cleaned a lot of windows since their establishment opened in 1928! Still a family business, they specialize in residential and commercial window cleaning. The higher the windows, the more they like it!

WHITE GLOVE ELITE
1265 Broadway (bet 31st and 32nd St), Room 801　　212/684-4460
Mon-Fri: 9-6 (cleaners available anytime)

Actors Sarah and Jim Ireland started this business as an adjunct to their stage careers. They specialize in providing trained cleaners for apartments in Manhattan, Bronx, Brooklyn, and Queens. About half of their cleaners are also actors between jobs.

Hotels

Hotel Tips

- Hotlines for New York hotel rooms: **Hotel Reservations** (800/846-7666) and **Central Reservation Service** (800/548-3311)
- Last-minute rooms: Many times guests cancel the same day or just don't show up. Check hotel desks between 4 and 6 p.m.
- Package deals: Check carefully what individual items cost; these are not always the best deals.
- Half-price promotions: These are not always as good as they sound, as discounts are figured from "rack rates" (the highest published rates).
- Try a hotel consolidator: **Quikbook** (800/789-9887), **Hotel Reservations Network** (800/964-6835), **RMC Travel** (800/782-2674) and **priceline.com**. They buy up excess rooms and pass along the savings.
- Call a hotel directly: Hotel-chain 800 numbers are convenient, but you will *not* get the best prices this way.
- Bargain for a special rate: Ask for American Automobile Association (AAA) and AARP (American Association of Retired People) discounts, and inquire about weekend, frequent flyer, corporate, and seasonal specials.
- Check out your room: Insist on air conditioning and heating that works and good reading lights. Inquire about parking rates, non-smoking rooms, health club, free continental breakfasts, happy hour, and evening turndown service.
- No-no's: Remember that in-room telephone charges are grossly excessive and that prices on in-room mini-bars are similarly outrageous. Keep your jewelry at home or in the hotel safe. Don't give out your room number to strangers.

Special Hotel Classifications

B&B

Abingdon Guest House (13 Eighth Ave, 212/243-5384): charming!

Extended Stays

If you are planning to stay awhile in Manhattan, check out these extended stay facilities. All require 30-day minimum stays. Washers and dryers are conveniently available.

Bristol Plaza (200 E 65th St, 212/753-7900): kitchens, daily maid service, health club, concierge

Phillips Club (1965 Broadway, 212/835-8800): kitchens, daily maid service, computer friendly, business center, concierge

Sutton Hotel (330 E 56th St, 212/752-8888): kitchens, daily maid service, health club, concierge

Hip (run-down buildings converted to trendy hotels)

Ameritania (230 W 54th St, 212/247-5000)
Bentley (500 E 62nd St, 212/644-6000)
East Side Inn (201 E 24th St, 212/696-3800)

Inexpensive

Carlton Arms (160 E 25th St, 212/679-0680)

Chelsea Inn (46 W 17th St, 212/645-8989)
Edison (228 W 47th St, 212/840-5000)
Excelsior (45 W 81st St, 212/362-9200)
59th Street Bridge Apartments (351 E 60th St, 212/754-9388)
Habitat Hotel (130 E 57th St, 212/755-8841)
Hostelling International New York (891 Amsterdam Ave, 212/932-2300)
Hotel 31 (120 E 31st St, 212/685-3060)
Larchmont (27 W 11th St, 212/989-9333)
Manhattan (273 W 38th St, 212/921-9791)
Martha Washington (29 E 29th St, 212/689-1908): women only
Milburn (242 W 76th St, 212/362-1006)
Off-Soho Suites (11 Rivington St, 212/353-0860)
Washington Square (103 Waverly Pl, 212/777-9515)
Webster Apartments (419 W 34th St, 212/967-9000): women only
Wellington (871 Seventh Ave, 212/247-3900)
Wolcott (4 W 31st St, 212/268-2900)

Moderate-priced charmers

Beacon (2130 Broadway, 212/787-1100)
Franklin (164 W 87th St, 212/369-1000)
Lucerne (201 W 79th St, 212/875-1000)
Mansfield (12 W 44th St, 212/944-6050)
Paramount (235 W 46th St, 212/764-5500)
Roger Smith (501 Lexington Ave, 212/755-1400)
Roger Williams (131 Madison Ave, 212/448-7000)
Wales (1295 Madison Ave, 212/876-6000)

Small luxury hotels

Elysee (60 E 54th St, 212/753-1066)
Fitzpatrick (687 Lexington Ave, 212/355-0100)
Inn at Irving Place (56 Irving Pl, 212/533-4600)
Lowell (28 E 63rd St, 212/838-1400)
Mark (25 E 77th St, 212/744-4300)
Stanhope (995 Fifth Ave, 212/288-5800)

Time Shares

Manhattan Club (200 W 56th St, 212/489-8488)

Manhattan has everything, as you know. For those distressed folk whose relationships have gone asunder, the extended-stay **Envoy Club** (587 First Ave, 212/481-4600) provides a list of divorce lawyers, marriage counselors, and psychics. There are one- and two-bedroom suites (you could bring along a sympathetic friend) that rent for $4,800 to $11,500 a a month.

Hotel Bars

For decades, New York hotel bars have been popular places to see and be seen, knock back hefty drinks, and overhear big shots making big deals. Hotel bars are also known to be pretty good pickup spots! You can order food at some of them. Here are the best of them:

Bemelman's Bar, at the Carlyle (35 E 76th St): classic
Cafe Pierre, at the Pierre (2 E 61st St): dull

Fifty-seven Fifty-seven, at the Four Seasons (57 E 57th St): crowded
Hudson's Sports Bar & Grill, at the Sheraton New York (790 Seventh Ave): fun
King Cole Bar, at the St. Regis (2 E 55th St): top-notch
Library, at the Regency (540 Park Ave): charming
Mark's Bar, at the Mark (225 E 77th St): cozy
Mercer Kitchen, at the Mercer (147 Mercer St): fashionable
Morgan's Bar, at Morgan's (237 Madison Ave): for the young at heart
Oak Bar, at the Plaza (Fifth Ave at Central Park S): civilized
Oasis Bar, at the Peninsula New York (700 Fifth Ave): great views

Hotels Allowing Pets

Not all Manhattan hotels are dog-friendly, but the following will let your canine friend share a room: Stanhope, Soho Grand, Pierre, Parker Meridien, Morgan's, Marriott Marquis, Four Seasons, and Essex House Westin.

If you want to exercise your pet, try these parks: DeWitt Clinton Park (Eleventh Ave at 52nd St), Madison Square Park (Madison Ave at 25th St), Theodore Roosevelt Park (Central Park W at 81st St), Robert Moses Park (First Ave at 41st St), and Carl Schurz Park (York Ave at 86th St).

Hotel Concierges

A concierge is the handiest person in a hotel if you want special services or advice. There is no charge for this help, but tipping is expected. Ten dollars is about right for the average service, more if a request takes an unusual amount of time. For requests above and beyond the call of duty, 15% of the value of the service is a good guideline. If you are a regular guest, it is wise to keep on the good side of these helpful folks.

A few services a concierge can help with: babysitting, business cars, couriers, emergency medical services, escorts, flowers, gifts, health and beauty care, kennels, massage, notary public, party venues, pet services, photographers, restaurants, secretarial services, tickets for events, shows, transportation, tours, translators, and videos. In other words, concierges are *almost* as helpful as this book!

Hotel Lingo

All-suite hotels: lodging units are suites, often with free breakfast and evening cocktails
American plan: room rate includes breakfast, lunch, and dinner
Corporate rate: room price for employees of corporations
Double occupancy rate: price per person, two to a room
Double room rate: full price of a room shared by two
Economy hotels: good beds, basic rooms, and often a free continental breakfast for about half the price of traditional hotel rooms
European plan: breakfast included
Extended-stay hotels: fully equipped apartments in townhouse-style developments for longer stays
Full-service hotels: top-of-the-line amenities for when you want to be pampered
Half-board/demi-pension: room rate includes breakfast and either lunch or dinner
Hotel broker: a service provider that finds out what's available, quotes prices and makes confirmed reservations; fee paid by hotels
Hotel consolidator: acts as a clearinghouse for unsold hotel accommodations
Limited-service hotels: oversized guest rooms with work spaces at prices about one-third below traditional hotel rates

Modified American Plan: room rate includes breakfast and dinner
Rack rate: retail price of a room as listed on rate cards or brochures
Service charge: fixed percentage automatically added to a room and meal bills

Hotels Near Airports

All of the following are conveniently located, provide airport transportation, have restaurants, and are reasonably priced (ask for corporate rates). Some have recreation facilities, such as fitness gyms and pools.

John F. Kennedy International: Hilton (328 rooms, Jamaica, Queens, 718/322-8700), Holiday Inn (359 rooms, Jamaica, Queens, 718/659-0200), Radisson (386 rooms, Jamaica, Queens, 718/322-2300), Four Points by Sheraton (185 rooms, Jamaica, Queens, 718/489-1000)
LaGuardia: Holiday Inn Crowne Plaza (358 rooms, East Elmhurst, Queens, 718-457-6300), Marriott (437 rooms, East Elmhurst, Queens, 718/565-8900), Sheraton (173 rooms, Flushing, Queens, 718/460-6666)
Newark International: Courtyard by Marriott (146 rooms, Newark, NJ, 201/643-8500), Sheraton (258 rooms, Elizabeth, NJ, 908/527-1600), Hilton Gateway (253 rooms, Newark, NJ, 973/622-5000)

Hotels with Swimming Pools

Holiday Inn Crowne Plaza (1605 Broadway): for exercise buffs
Millenium Hilton (55 Church St): gorgeous
Parker Meridien (119 W 56th St): visibly exciting
Peninsula New York (700 Fifth Ave): very classy
Sheraton Manhattan (790 Seventh Ave): kid-friendly
Trump International Hotel and Tower (1 Central Park W): magnificent

Hotels: New York's Best

ALGONQUIN
59 W 44th St (bet Fifth Ave and Ave of the Americas)   212/840-6800
Moderately expensive

The Algonquin is truly legendary; it was designated a historic landmark by the city of New York in 1996. This home of the famous Round Table—where Dorothy Parker, Harold Ross, Robert Benchley, and other literary wits sparred and dined regularly—now reflects the same charm and character as it did in the Roaring Twenties! There are 165 rooms, including 23 suites (some named after well-known personalities), and the atmosphere is intimate and friendly. The remodeled lobby is the best place in the city for people-watching, and the Oak Room still features renowned cabaret artists.

CASABLANCA
147 W 43rd St (bet Broadway and Ave of the Americas)
Moderate   212/869-1212

Now that the Times Square area has been cleaned up, you might consider staying at this attractive, safe, and clean European-style boutique hotel with a Moroccan flavor. It's small (48 rooms and suites) and offers complimentary amenities, along with comfortable rates. Best of all, the atmosphere is friendly. Special attractions: free beer, wine, and snacks on weekday evenings; passes to the New York Sports Club; free Internet-browsing on the lounge computers;

free bottled water, iced tea, and chocolates in the rooms. Besides, you are right in the center of the action!

CHELSEA INN
46 W 17th St (bet Fifth Ave and Ave of the Americas)
Moderate   212/645-8989, 800/640-6469

In the true sense of the word *inn*, the Chelsea is a small, informal, European-style operation. Most rooms have kitchenettes. The two attached, refurbished townhouses offer studio rooms, guest rooms (with shared bath at a very modest price), and one and two-bedroom suites. For those with business in the Flatiron District, this is a handy destination.

DELMONICO
502 Park Ave (at 59th St)   212/355-2500
Moderately expensive

This all-suites hotel offers one- and two-bedroom suites with terraces, walk-in closets, and dining rooms. The location is right in the heart of things. A triplex health club and fitness center is at your disposal. The Delmonico Lounge is a popular bistro.

DRAKE SWISSOTEL
440 Park Ave (at 56th St)   212/421-0900
Moderate

A $33 million facelift—including the addition of a business and conference center, state-of-the-art fitness center, and complete renovation of all 485 guest rooms and suites—underscores the commitment of the Swissotel group to their superbly located Manhattan property. Special features include a multilingual concierge staff, valet parking, limousine service to the Wall Street area, and guest rooms equipped with all the latest electronics (computer outlets, fax/modem units). The Drake Bar serves fine wine and champagne by the glass. This is a class operation!

ELYSEE
60 E 54th St   212/753-1066
Moderate

The Elysee is a comfortable 99-room European-style hotel in a very good neighborhood. Located within walking distance of Manhattan's best shopping, it is very popular with business travelers, has a multilingual staff, and offers kitchenettes in some rooms and suites. Rooms are filled with attractive antique pieces, marble baths invite the visitor to take a relaxing soak after a tough day, and rates include continental breakfast. Complimentary wine and cheese are offered on weeknights. The refurbished Monkey Bar downstairs is one of New York's hottest sipping and dining spots.

EMPIRE HOTEL
44 W 63rd St (bet Broadway and Columbus Ave)   212/265-7400
Moderate

A $30 million renovation injected new life into this 1923 building, located across from Lincoln Center. Special features include CD players, VCRs, two-line phones, room service, and a voice-mail messaging service. West 63rd Street

Steakhouse serves breakfast and dinner, and a four-story health club is adjacent to the hotel.

ESSEX HOUSE WESTIN
160 Central Park S   212/247-0300
Moderately expensive to expensive

This 65-year-old architectural treasure, now operated by Westin, has been completely restored to its original art deco grandeur. The restaurants (see "Restaurants" section) offer fine dining. The rooms feature classic Louis XVI and Chippendale decor, and many have spectacular views of Central Park. All offer two-line speaker phones, voice mail and message retrieval, in-room fax, VCR, minibar, and safe. The all-marble baths come with robes, scale, hairdryer, and toiletries. A business center and health spa are added features.

FOUR SEASONS
57 E 57th St (bet Madison and Park Ave)   212/758-5700
Expensive

In the hotel world, fewer names elicit higher praise or win more awards than Four Seasons. They are considered one of the best in the business. Now visitors to the Big Apple have an elegant 52-story limestone building to call their home away from home. The Four Seasons (designed by I.M. Pei and Frank Williams) provides 367 rooms and suites; several fine eating places, including the top-notch Fifty-seven Fifty-seven and a lobby lounge for light snacks and tea; a fully equipped business center, complete with freestanding computer terminals and modem hookups; a 5,000-square-foot fitness center with all the latest equipment; and numerous meeting rooms. The principal appeal, however, is the size of the guest rooms. They average 600 square feet, offer spectacular views of the city, and feature huge, luxurious marble bathrooms with separate dressing areas. A classy staff is determined to make this another award-winning property for the the world's largest operator of luxury hotels and resorts.

HILTON NEW YORK
1335 Ave of the Americas   212/586-7000
Moderate to moderately expensive

A $100 million renovation and redesign of this large (over 2,000 guest rooms and suites) hotel at Rockefeller Center is expected to be completed in December, 1999; some features will be open sooner. Two new restaurants have been added in the lobby: New York Marketplace, an all-day dining facility, and Etrusca, an intimate Italian room featuring Tuscan foods and wines. Special features of this busy hotel include an outstanding art collection; upscale executive floors with a private lounge and large luxury suites; dozens of rooms specially equipped for the disabled; a highly trained international staff; and a state-of-the-art fitness center. As a popular business and convention hotel, the Hilton equips its rooms with data ports and other modern communications equipment. For those interested in shopping, the theater, Radio City Music Hall, and other midtown attractions, this location is highly desirable.

IROQUOIS
49th W 44th St   212/840-3080
Moderate

A multimillion-dollar facelift has transformed this 1923 hotel into a comfortable, modern, privately owned facility that has always been a favorite of tourists and overseas tour groups. Round-the-clock room service, a multilingual staff, marble bathrooms, a roof garden, and an on-premises restaurant are among the amenities at the Iroquois.

KIMBERLY
145 E 50th St   212/755-0400
Moderate

If big hotels turn you off, then the Kimberly may be just what you are looking for. This charming and hospitable boutique suites hotel and spa located in the center of Manhattan offers guests the kind of personal attention that is a rarity in today's commercial world. There are deluxe guest rooms, marble bathrooms, one- and two-bedroom suites with fully equipped kitchens, and private terraces with some of the suites. Room service is available, as well as the urbane supper club Tatou (where Desi Arnez once presided as the house bandleader in a room that was once a speakeasy). The Tam-Tam bar provides three meals daily in an Indochinese atmosphere. Complimentary membership at the New York Health and Racquet Club is offered.

> **— Millennium Note —**
> The biggest real estate bargain since the purchase of Manhattan from the Indians involved the sale of the site of St. Patrick's Cathedral. The city turned it over to the church in 1857 for $1.00.

LOWELL
28 E 63rd St   212/838-1400
Moderately expensive

This classy, well-located hotel features 44 suites and 21 deluxe rooms. Amenities include a 24-hour multilingual concierge service, at least two phones per room, fax machine with a dedicated line, VCRs and outlets for personal computers, marble bathrooms, complimentary shoeshine service, fitness center, and all the rest that goes with a top operation. Thirty-three suites have wood-burning fireplaces, ten have private terraces, and one has a separate gym room and stereo. Oh, the latter also has *seven* telephones! The Hollywood suite has all the latest entertainment facilities, plus a fully equipped kitchen.

LUCERNE
201 W 79th St   212/875-1000, 800/492-8122
Moderate

With Manhattan hotel rates moving out of price range for many visitors, it is reassuring to know that there is still a property offering fine accommodations in a safe, convenient neighborhood at tariffs that won't break the bank. The Lucerne has 250 deluxe rooms and suites, room service, a fitness center, and exceptionally friendly and hospitable personnel. A full-service restaurant and jazz bar are located next door. Best of all, manager Anthony Melchiorri, who was brought up in the service industry, is committed to keeping his treasured landmark hotel a prime destination.

MANHATTAN EAST SUITES HOTELS

Beekman Tower, 3 Mitchell Pl (49th St at First Ave)	212/320-8018
Benjamin, 125 E 50th St	212/715-2500
Dumont Plaza, 150 E 34th St	212/320-8019
Eastgate Tower, 222 E 39th St	212/320-8021
Lyden Gardens, 215 E 64th St	212/320-8022
Lyden House, 320 E 53rd St	212/320-8023
Plaza Fifty, 155 E 50th St	212/320-8024
Shelburne Murray Hill, 303 Lexington Ave	212/320-8025
Southgate Tower, 371 Seventh Ave	212/320-8026
Surrey Hotel, 20 E 76th St	212/320-8027

Moderate

Looking for style and value? These all-suites hotels are among the most reasonably priced and conveniently located in New York. Each features 24-hour attendants and modern kitchens. Nearly 2,000 suites in all—studio suites, junior suites, and one- or two-bedroom suites—are available at very attractive daily, weekly, or monthly rates. These are particularly convenient accommodations for long-term corporate visitors and traveling families. Families can economize by having the kids sleep on the pull-out couches and by using the fully equipped kitchens. Additional attractions: fitness centers at most properties, recent renovations at Shelburne and Southgate Tower. Food facilities vary. The famous Cafe Boulud can be found at the Surrey. Women especially like these accommodations when they must travel and dine alone. A great buy!

MARK
25 E 77th St   212/744-4300
Moderately expensive

An older residency building (the Hyde Park, built in 1926) has been converted into one of the most charming hotels in New York. There are 125 guest rooms, 26 junior suites, and 34 one- and two-bedroom suites, all decorated in exquisite taste. Every room has cable TV, fax capability, and two-line phones, and most have pantries. The suites (which I strongly recommend) have separate vanities and marble baths. Some even have libraries, wet bars, and terraces with views of Central Park. The location is terrific, and the personnel extremely nice. Mark's, an excellent restaurant just off the lobby, serves all meals, plus tea and brunch. Everyone gets Frette linens, heated towel racks, down pillows, umbrellas, and Molton Brown of London soaps. The bar is sensational!

MARRIOTT MARQUIS
1535 Broadway   212/398-1900
Moderate to moderately expensive

The opening in 1985 of this 50-story showplace in Times Square represented a major step in the rejuvenation of the area. The Marriott Marquis boasts over 1,900 rooms, huge meeting and convention facilities, and the largest hotel atrium in the world. In addition, guests can enjoy a 700-seat, three-story revolving restaurant and lounge at the top of the hotel; a revolving lounge overlooking Broadway on the eighth floor; a legitimate Broadway theater on the premises; a fully equipped health club; suites with walk-in wet bars and refrigerators; oversized rooms; and a sky lounge. There are eight restaurants and lounges in all! A concierge level offers special amenities, including 24-hour room service.

MAYFLOWER
15 Central Park W (at 61st St)   212/265-0060, 800/223-4164
Moderate

If you are coming to New York for cultural events at Lincoln Center or Carnegie Hall, this is an ideal place to stay. Overlooking Central Park, this is a safe, comfortable hotel with spacious rooms and suites. Renovated bathrooms offer hairdryers. There are a number of two- and three-bedroom suites and several terraced penthouses, all with refrigerators. A fitness center and restaurant are on the property. Room service is available until midnight.

MERCER
147 Mercer St   212/966-6060
Expensive

Not to include the Mercer in this edition would be to ignore one of the city's newest happenings, made famous mainly because it is the location of Jean-Georges Vongerichten's much-heralded Mercer Kitchen restaurant. The rooms are relatively less spacious than the bathrooms, the decor is already showing signs of wear, and many rooms can be quite noisy. A plus: good location in Soho. A minus: no room service. My rating: not worth the exorbitant prices.

MILLENIUM HILTON
55 Church St (bet Fulton and Dey St)   212/693-2001
Moderate to moderately expensive

For the traveler who has business appointments downtown, the 55-story Millenium is a good bet. Most rooms are king-size. Nonsmoking accommodations are available, each room has two telephone lines, and amenities like robes and umbrellas are standard. The Taliesin restaurant features New American cuisine in an elegant atmosphere. Weekend packages, with reasonable parking fees, are featured. Additional attractions include a business center and an up-to-date fitness center with a swimming pool. Various facilities have been upgraded in recent years.

Given the astronomical rents charged for apartments in Manhattan, you might want a roommate to share costs. These outfits may be of some help: **Roommate Finders** (212/489-6860) and **Roommates NYC** (212/982-6265).

NEW YORK MARRIOTT WORLD TRADE CENTER
3 World Trade Center   212/938-9100 or 800/228-9290
Moderate to moderately expensive

This is a big place, as befits the neighborhood. The 818-room hotel features a handy location, large meeting facilities, a first-rate rooftop fitness center with a pool, spacious rooms, and several eating facilities.

NEW YORK PALACE
455 Madison Ave (between 50th and 51st St)   212/888-7000
Expensive

Located close to Saks Fifth Avenue, the New York Palace (900 rooms) offers commanding views of the city skyline, which is particularly enchanting in the evening. The public rooms encompass the 115-year-old Villard Houses, a legendary New York landmark. The hotel has undergone a comprehensive renovation. New facilities include an expansive fitness center; an executive lounge; the two-floor Villard Center, with its selection of meeting and function rooms; and a casually elegant Mediterranean restaurant called Istana. The famous Manhattan restaurant Le Cirque has new quarters in the Villard Houses.

PENINSULA NEW YORK
700 Fifth Ave (at 55th St)   212/956-2888
Expensive

Throughout the world, when the name Peninsula is mentioned in hotel service, the words *quality* and *class* immediately come to mind. This is surely true in Manhattan, where, after a $45 million facelift, the property is even more luxurious than before. The building is a 1902 landmark with 186 rooms and 55 suites, including the palatial Peninsula Suite (more than 3,000 square feet at $5,500 per night!). Room features include oversized marble bathrooms, in-room fax machines, large work desks, audio-visual systems with cable/satellite, and numerous bathroom amenities (including TVs in the bathrooms of the deluxe rooms and suites). General manager Niklaus Leuenberger, one of the most able hoteliers in the nation, has personally supervised the modernization program. An outstanding amenity is the Peninsula Spa and Health Club on the 21st floor. Facilities include an indoor pool, jacuzzi, sun decks, modern fitness equipment, and spa service (spa menu, too). Sophisticated dining is available in Adrienne, with the Gotham Bar & Lounge on the lobby level serving cocktails, afternoon tea, and light refreshments. On the roof, the Pen-Top Bar and Terrace are seasonally available for private parties.

— **Millennium Note** —

The first World Series ever to be broadcast was in 1921, in which the New York Giants faced the New York Yankees. Radio Station WJZ, based in Newark, provided a play-by-play account of the eight games. The Giants snatched the series.

PIERRE
2 E 61st St (at Fifth Ave)   212/838-8000
Expensive

Combine the Pierre's name with the Four Seasons' reputation, and you're bound to get top quality. Overlooking Central Park, the Pierre provides 202 elegant rooms and suites, a magnificent lobby, the Rotunda (famous for afternoon tea and light meals), and Cafe Pierre (for fine dining). Function rooms are the site of many of Manhattan's glitziest events. A new fitness center, outfitted with Italian marble, provides the latest in cardiovascular equipment. With a staff of over 650, you can be assured of highly personalized service.

PLAZA
768 Fifth Ave (at Central Park South)   212/759-3000
Expensive

Every great city has a legendary hotel, and in New York it is the Plaza. With a fabulous location, this grande dame of Manhattan exudes the physical charm and grace that has made it the home of distinguished guests and New York visitors for decades. The public rooms host some of Manhattan's most chichi affairs. The lobby Palm Court is as romantic a setting as you will find in the city; the Sunday brunch is outstanding. Guest rooms and suites vary in size. Magnificent floral arrangements, priceless chandeliers, and gilded ceilings adorn the foyers. Super-polite and efficient bellmen and doormen, some of whom have been at the hotel since I first visited as a child, provide friendly greetings. Horse-drawn carriages wait at the front door to take you on a never-to-be-forgotten Central Park experience. Under construction is a new health facility in a downstairs area formerly occupied by a theater and restaurant.

PLAZA ATHENEE
37 E 64th St (bet Park and Madison Ave)   212/734-9100
Expensive

This hotel is among the tops in New York in several categories, including service. A renovation has spruced up most of the rooms; all have marble bathrooms. Some of the suites on the higher floors feature solariums and roof terraces. Additional amenities include a workout facility, 24-hour room service, and an outstanding restaurant, Le Régence.

RAMADA MILFORD PLAZA
270 W 45th St (at Eighth Ave)   212/869-3600, 800/221-2690
Moderate

Value is the key word here. The Milford Plaza, a Ramada operation located at the edge of the Theater District in midtown Manhattan, offers reasonable rates that are partially offset by its location. But the hotel has extremely tight security (electronic door locks), which lessens the need to be concerned. Rooms are small yet clean, and late-night dining is available. Very attractive rates are available on weekends and for groups. The Milford has been totally refurbished, with new bathrooms, furniture, carpeting, and wall coverings.

REGENCY
540 Park Ave (at 61st St)   212/759-4100
Moderately expensive to expensive

With an outstanding location on Park Avenue and a recently completed room renovation that has created a more contemporary and relaxed feeling, this hotel now offers 350 spacious guest rooms and 86 outstanding suites, including 12 grand suites that have housed many of the entertainment world's greats. The one-bedroom suites feature two bathrooms. Rooms contain all modern business conveniences, including fax machines, printers, two-line phones, and data ports. Use of the fitness center and overnight shoeshine service is free. Two excellent restaurants—the classy, renovated 540 Park and the Library, an intimate residential-style lounge—offer daily meal service. Power breakfasts at the Regency are legendary. More than 70% of the hotel's guests are repeat visitors! One of the rising stars in the hotel world, Christopher Knable, is the very able general manager.

RIHGA ROYAL
151 W 54th St (bet Ave of the Americas and Seventh Ave)
212/307-5000
Moderately expensive

This is one special New York find! The RIHGA Royal is a residential-style all-suites hotel that is great for international travelers. The staff speaks 54 languages among them! The hotel, located handy to New York's business and cultural institutions, offers a fully equipped 24-hour business center, fitness center, complimentary newspapers, and Wall Street-area limo shuttle. Their Pinnacle suites offer guests Town Car service from New York area airports, personalized business cards, cell phones, and more. The hotel restaurant, Halcyon, is a casual, elegantly appointed room serving contemporary American cuisine. The spectacular Sunday "Marketplace in the Sky Brunch" (served on the 53rd and 54th floors) is sensational. The RIHGA is one of Manhattan's best deals!

ST. REGIS
2 E 55th St (at Fifth Ave)   212/753-4500
Expensive

The St. Regis, a historic landmark in the heart of Manhattan, is the crown jewel of Starwood Hotels, and for good reason. With 314 oversized deluxe rooms and 91 suites, the hotel provides luxurious accommodations. Each room has marble baths; in addition, round-the-clock butler service is provided (including free pressing of two garments upon arrival), and 24-hour room service is available. Outstanding restaurants are a feature here: Lespinasse for superb French cuisine; the Astor Court for breakfast, lunch, and dinner; and the King Cole bar, which serves great Bloody Marys. The St. Regis roof—the only hotel-roof ballroom in the city—is available for private functions.

SALISBURY
123 W 57th St   212/246-1300
Moderate

I highly recommend this place to the price-savvy traveler. The Salisbury has just over 300 rooms and suites, most of which have been redecorated. Many are outfitted with butler's pantries and refrigerators. Suites are large, comfortable, and reasonably priced. The thick walls are really soundproof! If you want to be in the vicinity of Carnegie Hall and other midtown attractions, this hotel is for you. If you've waited until the last minute for reservations, the Salisbury is a good place to call. Since it is not very well-known among out-of-towners, rooms are usually available.

SHERATON MANHATTAN
790 Seventh Ave (at 52nd St)   212/581-3300, 800/325-3535
Moderate

With a convenient location and recently upgraded rooms, this hotel is ideal for both family travelers and business types. It is within easy walking distance of Manhattan's best stores, theaters, and restaurants. The Sheraton Manhattan is a "Corporate Club Room" hotel, meaning each guest room is outfitted as both an office and a place to sleep. A 50-foot indoor swimming pool (a rarity in midtown), a first-rate health club, and an excellent on-property restaurant combine to make this an attractive 650-room property.

SHERATON NEW YORK HOTEL AND TOWERS
811 Seventh Ave (at 52nd St)   212/581-1000, 800/325-3535
Moderate to moderately expensive

Try one of New York's best, where value is guaranteed! Now a part of Starwood Hotels, the largest hotel operator in the world, this property is even more attractive. Frequent guests can take advantage of the worldwide hotels and resorts operated by this superior chain. The outstanding location in central Manhattan and a wide selection of restaurants and lounges make this an excellent choice for tourists and business travelers alike. Sheraton Towers, the more luxurious upper floors, offer exclusive digs that include butler service. "Corporate Club Rooms" come equipped with office amenities. This property offers a wide selection of package deals and seasonal specials.

SHERATON RUSSELL
45 Park Ave (at 37th St)   212/685-7676
Moderately expensive

Following an extensive renovation and refurbishment, this 146-room boutique hotel, formerly the Sheraton Park Avenue, reopened as the Sheraton Russell. It is ITT Sheraton's first all-business hotel in New York City. Designed in the traditional style of a 19th-century English club, each of the "Corporate Club Rooms" provides a "virtual office," with an oversized desk, ergonomic swivel chair, task lighting, in-room data ports, battery chargers, dual telephone lines, and a Hewlett-Packard OfficeJet printer/fax/copier. Complimentary continental breakfast buffet and evening hors d'oeuvres are served in the new club lounge.

SOHO GRAND
310 West Broadway (at Grand St)   212/965-3000
Moderately expensive

If business or pleasure takes you to Soho, this new facility may be your bag . . . but at a price. The custom-designed rooms will not appeal to traditionalists, though yuppies will love them. Four penthouse suites with outdoor terraces are special. A fitness center, business amenities, 24-hour room service, and valet parking are available. The on-premises Canal House restaurant is convenient but not memorable.

STANHOPE
995 Fifth Ave (at 81st St)   212/288-5800
Moderately expensive

The Stanhope is a quiet and refined hotel just right for those who are touring museums or wish to be away from the throngs. The hotel has 180 rooms (50 of which are spacious and attractive suites), a health club, and a wonderful park view from many rooms. The Terrace, an outside garden for tea and snacks, is pleasant.

TRUMP INTERNATIONAL HOTEL AND TOWER
1 Central Park West (at 60th St)   212/299-1000
Expensive

This place is everything you would expect with the name Trump attached. There are special amenities, complete office facilities, entertainment centers in every room, state-of-the-art fitness center, swimming pool, marble bathrooms, and complimentary cellular phones. One of Manhattan's best (and most expensive) restaurants, Jean-Georges, will pamper your taste buds.

W
541 Lexington Ave (bet 49th and 50th St)   212/755-1200
Moderately expensive

The former Doral Inn has been reborn as a hotel with a single letter for a name. A Starwood property, W has 720 rooms, a large ballroom, full-service health club, 24-hour room service, and two-line telephones with data ports in every room. The look is strictly modern, right down to the funereal black staff uniforms. Health addicts will love the place. There's a juice bar near the front entrance and Heartbeat, a Drew Nieporent restaurant (everything he does is special), is also on the premises.

WALDORF-ASTORIA
301 Park Ave (at 50th St)   212/355-3000
Moderately expensive

The Waldorf is once more a symbol of class in Manhattan. Hilton has invested more than $200 million in restoring their flagship—and the work shows! The lobby, bedecked with magnificent mahogany wall panels, hand-woven carpets, and a 148,000-tile mosaic floor, is rich and impressive. Responding to complaints about the size of some guest rooms, the management oversaw renovations that have created larger spaces by reducing the number of rooms. Oversize executive business rooms are available. All-marble bathrooms have been installed in some suites. There is a fitness center, a number of restaurants, and special deluxe rooms and suites in the Waldorf Towers. An event at the Waldorf is sure to be something special. Junior League members have access to rooms at very substantial savings. Sign up for a behind-the-scenes tour of the Waldorf on Friday and Sunday (call 212/872-4790).

WALES
1295 Madison Ave (bet 92nd and 93rd St)   212/876-6000
Moderate

The Wales is a small European boutique hotel that has been restored to its original condition. It was built in 1901 as the Chastaigneray, and it is personally operated, which is unusual in this day of corporate chains. A complimentary European breakfast, complimentary video and CD library, and room service are provided. The uptown Madison Avenue address is safe for shoppers. Every Sunday night there is a chamber music concert. Busby's (a bistro) and Sarabeth's Kitchen (an excellent restaurant) are on the ground floor.

WOLCOTT
4 W 31st St (bet Fifth Ave and Broadway)   212/268-2900
Inexpensive

This is one of Manhattan's better-kept hotel-bargain secrets. Here you will find a good location (just south of midtown), refurbished clean rooms with private baths, good security, direct-dial phones, color TV, new fitness and business centers, and individual air conditioners. It is no wonder that students, foreign travelers, and savvy businessmen and -women are regular patrons.

WYNDHAM
42 W 58th St (at Fifth Ave)   212/753-3500
Moderate

John Mados has created a winner! This charming hotel is more like a large home in which rooms are rented out. Many guests regularly make the Wyndham their Manhattan headquarters. The advantages are numerous: great location, uniquely decorated rooms and suites, complete privacy, individual attention, and no business conventions. On the other hand, the hotel is always busy, and reservations may be difficult for newcomers. No room service is available; however, there is a restaurant, and suites have pantries with refrigerators.

Housing Alternatives

. . . AAAH! BED & BREAKFAST #1
P.O. Box 2093, New York, NY 10108   212/246-4000

This outfit mainly serves the business person who is more interested in the comforts of home than a fancy address. They also have a following among tourists who like to have a host clue them in about what to do and what not to do in the big city. Will Salisbury, the manager, was a butler for many years, and he knows the hospitality business. Hosted or unhosted apartments are available. It is desirable to contact the firm two to four weeks in advance of your stay.

ABODE
P.O. Box 20022, New York, NY 10021
212/472-2000, 800/835-8880 (outside tri-state area)
Mon-Fri: 9–5

Do you have your heart set on staying in a delightful old brownstone? How about a contemporary luxury apartment in the heart of Manhattan? Abode selects apartments with great care, and all homes are personally inspected to insure the highest standards of cleanliness, attractiveness, and hospitality. All are nicely furnished. Nightly rates begin at $135 for a studio and rise to $400 for a three-bedroom apartment. Extended stays of one month or longer are available at a discounted rate. There is a minimum stay of four nights.

BED AND BREAKFAST NETWORK OF N.Y.
134 W 32nd St, Suite 602   212/645-8134, 800/900-8134
Mon-Fri: 8-6

Would you like to stay in a million-dollar high-rise condo? Or are you more comfortable in an artist's loft? This outfit can fix you up with either for one night or several months. They offer over 300 accommodations, mostly in Manhattan. Guests can choose to stay with a host or have their own furnished apartment. Leslie Goldberg has been in business since 1986 and is sensitive to the needs and desires of guests.

BROADWAY BED & BREAKFAST INN
264 W 46th St (at Eighth Ave)   212/997-9200, 800/826-6300

This is the only European country-style inn in New York City. The 41 rooms are immaculate, the price is right, the atmosphere is homey, the location is safe, and the operation is family-owned. Additional features include continental breakfast and a library with newspapers. The facility, built as a hotel in 1907, has been fully restored!

A HOSPITALITY COMPANY
580 Broadway (bet Houston and Prince St), Suite 1009   212/965-1102
Moderate

If you are looking for a reasonably priced, full-service, short-term furnished apartment in Soho, Midtown East, Upper West Side, Greenwich Village, Chelsea, or the Theater District, this is a good number to call. They have over a hundred apartments in their inventory, offer free local phone calls, and feature discounts for extended stays.

HOSTELLING INTERNATIONAL NEW YORK
891 Amsterdam Ave (at 103rd St)   212/932-2300
Inexpensive

This facility is available to visitors of all ages (under 18 must be accompanied by an adult). The hostel provides over 624 beds in a newly renovated century-old landmark. They offer meeting spaces, cafeteria, coffee bar, airport shuttle, catering, tours, self-service kitchens, and laundry facilities to individuals and groups. Best of all, the price is right! The neighborhood can be rough, however.

INN NEW YORK CITY
266 W 71st St   212/580-1900
Moderately expensive

Inn New York City is a brownstone that has been tastefully transformed into a comfortable four-suite guest residence. A two-night minimum stay is mandated. Extended-stay facilities are available, room refrigerators are stocked with delicacies, robes are provided, and the living room and bedrooms have cable TV. Daily newspaper and maid service are offered, and on-site copy and fax machines are available.

INTERNATIONAL HOUSE
500 Riverside Dr   212/316-8436 (single rooms)
Moderate   212/316-8473 (guest rooms and suites)

This is a community of over 700 graduate students, interns, trainees, and visiting scholars from nearly 100 countries. Occupants spend anywhere from a day to a few years in New York City. It is located on the Upper West Side near Columbia University and the Manhattan School of Music. There are all sorts of special features, including a low-budget cafeteria, a pub with dancing, a gymnasium, and a self-service laundry. Free programs include ballroom dancing, lectures, films, recitals, and organized sports. During the summer, single-room occupancy, with a shared bath on the floor, runs $45 per night and drops to $40 per night for a stay of 10-29 days. Rates are less still by the semester. Reasonably priced guest suites ($105-130 per night) are also available with private bath, air conditioning, daily maid service, and cable television.

LEO HOUSE
332 W 23rd St   212/929-1010, 800/732-2438
Inexpensive

This is the answer to one of the major questions asked about New York: Where can a visitor find an inexpensive, safe, and clean place to stay in the city? You should have no qualms about the Leo House, a Catholic guest house. A secure, refined, and quiet place, it is still run by the Sisters of St. Agnes. Reservations are required and may be made as much as a year in advance. A small deposit must be placed; it is refundable if cancellation is made 24 hours prior to scheduled arrival. The maximum length of stay is two weeks. No smoking is allowed in guest and meeting rooms. Although outside doors are locked at midnight, registered guests may still get in after that hour. Breakfast, featuring homemade bread, is available for a moderate price. It is a great place for the single student!

92ND ST Y (DE HIRSCH RESIDENCE)
1395 Lexington Ave
212/415-5650, 800/858-4692 (toll-free in the U.S. and Canada)
Mon-Thurs: 9-7; Fri: 9-5; Sun: 10-5
Inexpensive

This facility offers convenient, inexpensive, and secure housing for men and women between the ages of 18 and 30. There are special discounts for Y health-club memberships, and both single and double rooms are available. Lengths of stay can range from three days to one year. Admission is by application.

PHILLIPS CLUB
Lincoln Square, 1965 Broadway (at 67th St)   212/835-8800
Moderate to moderately expensive

This 96-unit residential hotel near Lincoln Center is designed for long-term visitors. Minimum stay is 30 days. There is no room service, but suites come with fully equipped kitchens, individually assigned telephone numbers, and stereo systems in all living areas. Other impressive features include a 24-hour business center and concierge, laundry and valet service, a handy conference room, and preferential membership at the nearby Reebok Sports Club. There are 22 deluxe rooms and 74 one- and two-bedroom suites available.

SHORT TERM MANAGEMENT
862 Lexington Ave (at 64th St)   212/570-2288
Mon-Fri: 10-6; Sun: 1-5
Summer: Mon-Fri: 10-8; Sat, Sun: noon-5

While Short Term Management (formerly Short Term Housing) caters to the needs of business execs and well-heeled New York City visitors, it remains a good source for others who need help finding lodging when a hotel is not the answer. Short Term can sometimes find an apartment for as little as one month, but the usual stay is two months to one year. (The shorter the stay, the harder it is to find suitable space.) Property owners contact Short Term when their apartment is available, but it is the lessee whom they represent.

SOLDIERS', SAILORS', MARINES', AND AIRMEN'S CLUB
283 Lexington Ave (bet 36th and 37th St)   212/683-4354
Inexpensive

Here is a great find for American servicemen and women—active, retired, veterans, reservists, military cadets, and Coast Guard personnel alike! Rates are extremely low (with no tax), and the facility has 29 comfortable rooms with club-style facilities to enjoy. There are several lounges with fireplaces, a grand piano, and even a jukebox to bring back pleasant memories. Free and reduced-price tickets for Broadway shows and sports events are also available.

URBAN VENTURES
P.O. Box 426, New York, NY 10024   212/594-5650
Mon-Fri: 8-5

Mary McAulay founded this service in 1979, modeling it after Britain's famous bed-and-breakfast rooms, because she felt something needed to be done about Manhattan's lack of reasonably priced lodging. After being carefully screened, 650 hosts—who live in apartments, townhouses, brownstones, and lofts—signed up with Urban Ventures. Hosts range from older people living in big apartments to young artists. Both groups need a little help with the rent, and they are friendly and interested in their guests. The spare bedrooms are found on the Upper West Side, in the Village, in midtown, on the East Side, in Soho and Tribeca, and even in Brooklyn. Security is good—after all, this is someone's home—and these B&B's are especially convenient for visiting parents, since their child's apartment may not be large enough to house them. Accommodations without hosts, ranging from studios to three-bedroom apartments, are available from four nights to two months or more. The price is right, and this is a first-rate chance to get a sense of what it's really like to live in Manhattan, Queens, Brooklyn, and Staten Island.

WEBSTER APARTMENTS
419 W 34th St (at Ninth Ave)   212/967-9000
Inexpensive

This has to be one of the best deals in the city for working women with moderate incomes. It is *not* a transient hotel but operates on a policy developed by Charles B. Webster, a first cousin of Rowland Macy (of the department-store family). Webster left the bulk of his estate to found these apartments, which opened in 1923. Residents include college students, designers, actresses, secretaries, and other business and professional women. Facilities include dining rooms, recreation areas, a library, and lounges. The Webster also has private gardens for its guests, and meals can be taken outdoors in nice weather. Rates at press time were $162-$199 per week, which includes two meals a day, plus maid service. Visitors must be sponsored by a current guest. The Webster is a secret find, known mainly to residents and readers of this book.

Interior Designers

AERO STUDIOS
132 Spring St (bet Wooster St and Greene St)   212/966-4700

Whether it is a design project for a major commercial space or just a little one at home, the Aero Studio staff is well equipped to handle the task. Be sure to visit their store, and you'll no doubt come away with some special ideas.

ALEX CHANNING
250 W 19th St (bet Seventh and Eighth Ave), Suite 11C
By appointment   212/366-4800

Alex Channing, a licensed interior designer, is building a reputation as one of the area's young up-and-comers. He does furniture design and custom-made furnishings, and he'll help with site selection, move-ins, and installations. Channing does commercial and residential work.

DESIGNER PREVIEWS
212/777-2966

Having problems finding the right decorator? Designer Previews keeps tabs on over a hundred of Manhattan's most trustworthy and talented designers, architects, and landscaping experts. They will present the decorators' work to you by way of slides and photographs. They will also discuss designers' fees. Karen Fisher, the genius behind this handy service, was formerly the decorating editor at *Cosmopolitan* and the style editor at *Esquire*. She charges $100 for her services.

MARTIN ALBERT INTERIORS
9 E 19th St (bet Broadway and Fifth Ave)
212/673-8000, 800/525-4637
Mon-Fri: 9-6; Sat: 10-6; Sun: 12-4

Martin Albert specializes in window treatments, and they really know their business. They measure and install their products at prices that are considerably lower than most decorators. Any store has to be good to survive in this highly competitive field. Martin Albert offers 125,000 fabric samples, ranging from $8 to $400 a yard. Services include custom upholstery and slipcovers, a furniture shop, and at-home service. A large selection of drapery hardware is also available, and they'll deliver to all 50 states.

A Touch-Up Here . . . A Touch-Up There . . .

It is sometimes difficult, expensive, and exasperating to get even the smallest painting job done. Expect to wait longer than you want, and always get estimates. The really good people in the business will take special care in your home and bring their own supplies. Here are some outfits that have been especially recommended to me:

Robert Star Painting (212/737-8855)
Roth Painting (212/758-2170)

PARSONS SCHOOL OF DESIGN
66 Fifth Ave (at 13th St)   212/229-8940
Mon-Fri: 9-5

Parsons, a division of the New School for Social Research, is one of the two top schools in the city for interior design. Those who call will get their request posted on the school's board, and every effort is made to match clients with prospective decorators. Individual negotiations determine the price and length of a job, but it will be considerably less than what a not-so-recent student charges. The disadvantage is that most of these students don't yet have a decorator's card. (One can always be borrowed.) This is a good place to contact if you just want a consultation.

RICHARD'S INTERIOR DESIGN
1390 Lexington Ave (bet 91st and 92nd St)   212/831-9000
Mon-Wed, Fri, Sat: 10-6; Thurs: 10-7; Sun: 11-5

Here you will find over 10,000 decorator fabrics, including tapestries, damasks, stripes, plaids, silks, velvets, and floral chintzes. These are all first-quality goods at competitive prices. They will do upholstery, furniture, reupholstery, slipcovers, draperies, top treatments, shades, bedroom ensembles, and wall coverings. Design services, in-home consultation, and installation are available.

Jewelry Services
GEM APPRAISERS LABORATORY
608 Fifth Ave (at 49th St), Suite 403   212/333-3122
Mon-Fri: 9-5 by appointment

Robert C. Aretz, who owns Gem Appraisers Laboratory, is a graduate gemologist and a certified member of the Appraisers Association of America. He is a past officer and director who currently sits on the membership committee.

He is entrusted with appraisals for major insurance companies, banks, and retail jewelry stores. His specialty is antique jewelry, precious colored stones, diamonds, and natural pearls. Appraisals and/or consultations can be done for many purposes, including estate, insurance, tax, and equitable distribution.

RISSIN'S JEWELRY CLINIC
4 W 47th St (at Fifth Ave)   212/575-1098
Mon, Tues, Thurs: 9:30-5; closed first two weeks of July

This is indeed a clinic! The assortment of services is staggering: jewelry repair and design, antiques repair, museum restorations, supplying diamonds and other stones, eyeglass repair, pearl and bead stringing, redoing of old necklaces, stone identification, and appraisals. Joe Rissin and his wife, Toby, run the place. Joe's father was a master engraver, so the family tradition has been passed along for decades. *Honesty* and *quality* are bywords here, and customers can rest assured that merchandise will be returned in excellent condition. Estimates are gladly given, and all work is guaranteed.

ZDK COMPANY
48 W 48th St (bet Fifth Ave and Ave of the Americas), Suite 1410
Mon-Thurs: 10:30-4:30   212/575-1262

Most of his work has been the creation of rare and original pieces for neighbors in the Diamond District, but Zohrab David Krikorian will do professional work for you, too, in his free time. In addition to making jewelry, ZDK mends and fixes broken jewelry as only a professional craftsman and artist can. He makes complicated repairs look easy and has yet to encounter a job he can't handle. If he can't exactly match the stones in an antique earring, he'll redo the whole piece so it looks even better than before. He loves creating the latest designs from traditional materials, and his prices are reasonable.

Leather Repair

ARTBAG CREATIONS
735 Madison Ave (at 64th St)   212/744-2720
Mon-Fri: 9:30-5:45; Sat: 10-5:30

Artbag will make, sell, or repair any type of handbag. The range of services goes from mounting needlepoint bags to relining heirloom bridal bags, as well as making leather, reptile, and beaded evening bags. The Moores, a father-and-son team, are highly trained craftsmen who modestly advertise themselves as "understanding, genteel, and good listeners who know their business." Any one of their customers could have said the same thing! Artbag is also known for its sense of style. They carry the latest designs and frequently refashion old handbags into chic trendsetters. It isn't every day you come across men who know more about handbags than women, but these gentlemen certainly keep up with the latest styles.

CARNEGIE LUGGAGE
1392 Ave of the Americas (bet 56th and 57th St)   212/586-8210
Mon-Sat: 9-6; Sun: 11-6

It's a pleasure to do business with these people. Carnegie is handy to most major midtown and Central Park hotels. Service can be fast, if you let them know you're in a hurry. They are responsible and offer reliable work at competitive prices that run just 10% over wholesale. A complete line of luggage and travel accessories includes Delsey and Samsonite.

JOHN R. GERARDO
30 W 31st St (bet Broadway and Fifth Ave)   212/695-6955
Mon-Fri: 9-5; Sat: 10-2 (closed Sat, April-Aug)

John Gerardo dispenses luggage and carries out luggage repairs that rival Crouch and Fitzgerald's (minus the glamour). Gerardo carries the standard brands in almost all sizes and shapes. There are sample cases, overnighters, two-suiters, and drawers with seemingly endless spare parts. Zippers, handles, locks, and patches of fiber and material are available for emergencies. Gerardo does quick, professional repair work. They will also pick up and deliver for a nominal fee.

SUPERIOR REPAIR CENTER
133 Lexington Ave   212/889-7211
138 W 72nd St   212/769-2099
Mon-Thurs: 10-7; Sat: 10-3

Do you own a fine leather garment that's been damaged? Leather repair is the highlight of the service at Superior. Many major stores in the city use them for luggage and handbag work. They are experts in cleaning leather (suede and shirling are their specialties) and in the repair or replacement of zippers on leather items, and they will work on sporting equipment, such as tents and backpacks. If there is a leather problem, Superior has the answer. At least Gucci, Calvin Klein, Bergdorf, and Prada think so!

Locksmiths

AAA LOCKSMITHS
44 W 46th St (at Ave of the Americas)   212/840-3939
Mon-Thurs: 8-5:30; Fri: 8-5

You can learn a lot from trying to find a locksmith in New York. For one thing, as a profession it probably has the most full-page ads in the Manhattan Yellow Pages. For another, this particular "AAA" is *not* the place to call about an automobile emergency. However, in an industry that has little company loyalty or recommendations, AAA Locksmiths has been in the business for over a half-century, and that says a lot right there.

LOCKWORKS
By appointment   212/736-3740

Lock problems? Give Joel at Lockworks a call; he has been at the locksmith game for two decades, and there isn't anything he can't do. This gentleman does not put a lot of A's in front of his name and does not even advertise, but he is highly regarded by some of the top businesses in Manhattan.

NIGHT AND DAY LOCKSMITH
1335 Lexington Ave (at 89th St)   212/722-1017
Mon-Sat: 8-7 (24 hours for emergencies)

You should carry Night and Day's number in case you're ever locked out. New Yorkers, even those who are in residence for a short time, become experts on locks and cylinders. Cocktail-party conversation is frequently peppered with references to dead bolts, and locksmiths are revered professionals. They've got to stay ahead of the local burglar's latest expertise and must offer fast, on-the-spot service for a variety of devices designed to keep criminals out. (After all, no apartment has just *one* lock.) Mena Sofer, Night and Day's owner, fulfills these rigid requirements. The company answers its phone 24 hours a day; posted hours are for the sale of locks, window gates, intercoms, car alarms, safes, and keys. Inside and outside welding is a specialty.

Marble Works

PUCCIO MARBLE AND ONYX
661 Driggs Ave, Brooklyn (factory warehouse showroom)
718/387-9778, 800/7-PUCCIO

Work of the highest quality is a tradition with Puccio. The sculpture and furniture designs range from traditional to sleekly modern. John and Paul Puccio show dining and cocktail tables, chairs, chests of drawers, buffets, desks, consoles, and pedestals. Custom-designed installations include foyer floors, complete bathrooms, kitchens, bars, staircases, fountains, and fireplaces. Retail orders are accepted. Work of the highest quality is a tradition with Puccio.

Matchmaking

FIELD'S EXCLUSIVE SERVICE
317 Madison Ave, Suite 1600   212/391-2233, 800/264-7539
Daily

The motto "New York lives by this book!" is a big challenge. I can't let anyone down, so this edition even includes a hint on matchmaking. Dan Field's company has been playing Cupid for three quarters of a century. If Dan is successful for you, how about a testimonial for *Where to Find It, Buy It, Eat It in New York*—the Romance Edition, of course!

Medical Services

AMERICAN PREFERRED PRESCRIPTION
197 Eighth Ave (at 20th St)   212/691-9050
Mon-Fri: 9 a.m.-10 p.m.; Sat: 9-7:30; Sun: 10-5:30

APP provides home delivery of prescription medications, comprehensive claims management, and linkages to community resources and national support networks. Their specialties include HIV and transplantation prescriptions. All pharmaceuticals are available, as is an extensive line of vitamins, nutritionals, and homeopathic and holistic products. Many rare items can be provided with one-day service. They will bill insurance companies directly so that customers need not pay cash up front. Nationwide shipping is available.

PHYSICIAN'S HEALTH CARE
718/238-2100

This service answers a real need in the city. In the past, hotels always had staff doctors on call. Medical and dental associations would arrange for doctors to cover the city during off hours, and, of course, hospital emergency rooms are open 24 hours a day. But private doctors have stopped making house calls, even to regular patients. Physician's Health Care was created to take care of that problem. Most calls are to residents who need in-home care, but visitors may use this service as well. The fee in Manhattan is $80–$125, which also covers the cost of transportation and parking. Most visits are made within two hours of your phone call. All members here are licensed, and further tests or treatments can be arranged, if necessary.

UNION SQUARE DRUGS
859 Broadway (bet 17th and 18th St)   212/242-2725
Mon-Fri: 7:30-7; Sat: 9-4

This store consistently offers the best prices on prescription drugs, industrial first-aid supplies, and vitamins. It is equally well-known for its reliability. The service is so conscientious that the pharmacist on duty will call—long-distance, if necessary—to verify prescriptions. Union Square also fills union prescriptions.

Metal Work

RETINNING AND COPPER REPAIR
525 W 26th St (at Tenth Ave)   212/244-4896
Mon-Fri: 9-6

Jamie Gibbons has taken over a long-established Manhattan business whose specialty is retinning (which is basically tin plating). Gibbons, who has over a decade of experience in the field, restores brass and copper antiques; designs and creates new copperware (almost all copper pots in use today are heirlooms); restores lamps, chandeliers, and brass beds; and sells restored copper pieces.

Movers

BIG APPLE MOVING & STORAGE
83 Third Ave (bet Bergen and Dean St), Brooklyn   718/625-1424
Mon-Sat: 9-5   212/505-1861

This is a handy number to have. Even though Big Apple is not located in Manhattan, 80% of their local moving business is in the city. They do all kinds of packing jobs, using special containers for valuable and hard-to-handle items. Also on hand are packing supplies, including wooden crates, and custom paper for wrapping antiques and fine furniture. Local, interstate, and international moving service is provided. Furniture is fully wrapped and padded before removal from your residence. A high-security heated warehouse is available for storage. These folks get commendations from previous customers.

BROWNSTONE BROS. MOVING
426 E 91st St (bet First and York Ave)   212/289-1511
Mon-Fri: 9-5; Sat: 9-12

The best kind of recommendation for a moving company is the words of customers who have used their services. Brownstone Bros. gets high marks in this regard. The firm has been offering moving and storage services since 1977, with a very personal touch by head man Bill Gross.

IKE BANKS
718/527-7505

Ike Banks breaks just about every rule for inclusion in this book. He's not bonded or licensed, nor is he a resident of Manhattan (he lives in Queens). But he never breaks anything, and I trust him more than anyone else. He was first recommended to me by an appliance store when a delicate and temperamental washing machine needed to be delivered. Since then, he has moved pianos, households, and dining rooms for friends of mine. Ike will travel anywhere in the city, sometimes farther, and will work odd hours.

MOISHE'S MOVING & STORAGE
449 W 14th St (at Tenth Ave)   800/266-8387

Moishe's grew from one man and a van to the largest independent moving and storage business in the New York area in just ten years. They handle over 8,000 relocations annually, ranging from around the block to around the world. Moishe's storage facilities meet most any need.

MOVING STORE
644 Amsterdam Ave (bet 91st and 92nd St)   212/874-3800
Mon-Fri: 8-6; Sat: 9-4; Sun: 9-3

Steve Fiore started West Side Movers in the kitchen of his studio apartment more than 20 years ago. Business was so good that he soon moved into a store-front. He was happy there until he realized the magnitude of requests he was getting from people who wanted dollies and boxes of all sizes. Fiore then moved into a brownstone storefront on Amsterdam Avenue in order to sell nothing but moving aids and paraphernalia. The main stock-in-trade is boxes. They come in a multitude of sizes, including three different ones just for mirrors. He rents and sells dollies and moving pads. Since all items are built to the specifications of professional movers, they are durable.

WEST SIDE MOVERS
644 Amsterdam Ave (bet 91st and 92nd St)   212/874-3800
Mon-Fri: 8-6; Sat: 9-4; Sun: 9-3

We came to West Side Movers via their Moving Store (see preceding entry). West Side Movers pays close attention to efficiency, promptness, care, and courtesy. Customer after customer has called their staff the most courteous they've dealt with—and they don't nick the furniture, either!

Music Services

W K STUDIO
611 Broadway (bet Bleecker and Houston St), Room 721
212/473-1203
Mon-Fri (and alternate Sats): 9:30-6

This family-owned business has been servicing the music and recording industry since 1985, and they enjoy a very reliable reputation. Services include CD, cassette, and video duplication; use of a recording studio; and on-site recording.

Office Services

PURGATORY PIE PRESS
19 Hudson St (bet Duane and Reade St), Room 403
212/274-8228
Mon-Fri: 10-2:30, by appointment only

Purgatory Pie is ideal for a small printing job! They do typography designs, hand letter-press printing, and hand bookbinding. They'll also craft handmade envelopes, do logos and other identity designs, and provide handmade paper with uniquely designed watermarks. Specialties include the full range of printings for weddings and parties, plus limited-edition post cards. They say that working with this firm is an adventure, and part of the fun is learning how they came up with such a name for their business!

SEEFORD ORGANIZATION
75 Varick St (bet Canal and Watts St)   212/431-4000
Mon-Fri: 8:30-5

Seeford does quality general commercial printing and advertising specialties of all kinds. They can handle jobs from concept and design right through printing, binding, and delivery. The boss, Sam Goldstein, is on the job, and the quality of the work and service shows his personal concern. Besides, he is one of the nicest individuals in New York.

WORLD-WIDE BUSINESS CENTRES
212/605-0200
Mon-Fri: 9-5:30; Sat, Sun: by request

Alan Bain, a transplanted English lawyer, has created a business that caters to executives who need more than a hotel room and companies that need a fully equipped, furnished, and staffed office in New York on short notice. The operation grew out of Bain's own frustrations in trying to put together a makeshift office. On-premises, administrative, word-processing, clerical, and mail-room staff services are available, as is a full range of high-quality voice and data communications capabilities, including high-speed Internet access. Desk space, private offices, and conference rooms may be rented on a daily, weekly, monthly, or quarterly basis. The daily rate includes a private office, telephone answering, and receptionists. The company also operates a full-service travel agency that specializes in travel and travel-management services to small and medium-sized companies, as well as meeting planning.

Parenting Resources

EARLY CHILDHOOD DEVELOPMENT CENTER
163 E 97th St (at Third Ave)   212/360-7803
Mon-Fri: (call for class schedule)

If you're a new parent in New York who's feeling a bit overwhelmed, this place will be a godsend. Becky Thomas and her team offer classes for parents of children from newborn to age three. Whether you're looking for something during the day or a class at night, the Early Childhood Development Center can accommodate your needs. Prices are reasonable, admission is rolling, and they offer groups for siblings. The Early Childhood Development Center has been working with Manhattan parents for almost 30 years, so they must be doing something right!

PARENTING CENTER AT THE 92ND STREET Y
1395 Lexington Ave (at 92nd St)   212/415-5609

Just about everything the 92nd Street Y does is impressive, and its Parenting Center is no exception. It offers every kind of class you can imagine: a newborn-care class for expectant parents, a baby massage and exercise class for new parents and their infants, a cooking class for preschoolers, and so on. As this Y is a Jewish institution, Shabbat Get-Togethers and a Jewish heritage class for preschoolers are offered, along with workshops and seminars on a wide range of topics, from potty training to raising an only child. They also host new-parent get-togethers and, perhaps most important, act as a resource and support center for members. Membership costs $175 a year, and benefits include priority in signing up for classes, as well as discounts. Non-members are welcome to take classes, too.

PARENTS LEAGUE
115 E 82nd St   212/737-7385
Mon-Thurs: 9-4; Fri: 9-12

This nonprofit organization is a goldmine for parents in New York. In addition to putting together a calendar of events for children of all ages, the Parents League maintains extensive files on such topics as babysitters, birthday party places, tutors, summer camps, early childhood programs, and private schools throughout the city. For a $50 annual membership fee, you can access those files, as well as attend workshops and other events throughout the year. If you are the parent of a small child, you also get a copy of *The Toddler Book,* an invaluable list of more than 200 activities in New York for little ones.

— Millennium Note —

The city's first ferry, which ran between Dover and Pearl streets in Manhattan and Fulton Street in Brooklyn, began operating in 1638.

Party Services

BALOOMS
147 Sullivan St   212/673-4007
Mon-Fri: 10-6; Sat: 12-6; Sun: available for parties

Balooms is a small balloon store that encourages browsing and spur-of-the-moment sales. In addition to balloon bouquets, they offer party decorating and custom-designed bouquets with names and logos on each balloon. Balooms will deliver in Manhattan and the boroughs, and will ship anywhere. The store also rents helium tanks. As befits this lighthearted business, owners Marlyne Berger and Raymond Baglietto are delightful.

For the absolute most unique ideas and help for a party, call **Marcy Blum Associates** (251 E 51st St, Suite 2N, 212/688-3057).

BLAIR McMILLEN
212/579-6010
24-hour phone service

If you are looking for top-notch piano entertainment, look no further. Blair McMillen is an extremely talented and ultra-personable concert pianist, having performed on some of the world's classiest cruise ships and at top events in Manhattan. McMillen is a Julliard School graduate (he still teaches there on weekends) and will work with other musicians in the area. Flexible in style, he is equally adept at Broadway, pop, New Age, Latin, and jazz standards, although classical piano is his first love.

ECLECTIC ENCORE
620 W 26th St (at Eleventh Ave)   212/645-8880
Mon-Fri: 9-5

Do you need to rent an armoire, a zebra, or anything in-between? If so, this outfit specializes in extremely hard-to-find props for a party at home, a set for motion pictures or television, or some novel product announcement. They have been in business since 1986 and are known for an extensive collection of 18th-, 19th- and 20th-century furniture and accessories. If you're looking for unusual items, how about the front half of a rhino or one of those cakes from which a scantily clad lady pops out?

HIGHLY EVENTFUL
11 Fifth Ave (bet 8th and 9th St), Suite 7C   212/777-3565
Daily: 10-6

Since 1994, Highly Eventful has been arranging events in New York and locations throughout the world. These folks take charge of everything, including food, liquor, equipment rentals, tents, flowers, lighting, music, and trained personnel. They offer prime locations, such as grand ballrooms, churches (like the Cathedral of St. John the Divine), museums (like the Metropolitan), and spacious yachts.

LINDA KAYE'S BIRTHDAYBAKERS, PARTYMAKERS
195 E 76th St (bet Lexington and Third Ave)   212/288-7112
Parties seven days a week

Linda Kaye offers children's birthday parties at one of the most unique locations in Manhattan: the Central Park Wildlife Center. These safari-themed birthday parties are for children from one to ten. Some of the themes offered are Breakfast with the Penguins, Animal Alphabet Party, and a Mystery Movie Making theme. In addition to safari parties at the zoo, Linda specializes in creative corporate family events. She also offers a wide variety of custom-made cakes, a pop-out cake for special occasions, and themed party paper goods.

PARTY POOPERS
104 Reade St (bet West Broadway and Church St)
212/587-9030, 212/941-1990
Call ahead

Party Poopers are really entertainers who make sure they never throw the same party twice. Offering some of the best private party rooms in New York, Party Poopers handle all the setup, clean-up, and entertainment, allowing parents to sit back and relax. Themes include fairytales, superheroes, game shows, dance parties, murder mysteries, or anything you can dream up. They also have an array of costume characters, magicians, and other party entertainers. There's even an on-line store, the Pooper Cavern, which carries favors, theme paper goods, balloons, and gift items.

PROPS FOR TODAY
330 W 34th St (bet Eighth and Ninth Ave)   212/244-9600
Mon-Fri: 8:30-5; Sat: 9-1

This is the handiest place in town when you are planning a party. Props for Today has the largest rental inventory of home decorations in New York. Whether you want everyday china and silver or unique antiques going back a hundred years, they have the goods in stock. There are platters, vases, tablecloths, and more. There is a Christmas section, children's items, books, fireplace equipment, artwork, garden furniture, foreign items, and ordinary kitchenware. Over a million items are available! Phone orders are taken, but it is a good idea to call for an appointment and check things out for yourself.

Pen and Lighter Repair

AUTHORIZED REPAIR SERVICE
30 W 57th St (bet Fifth Ave and Ave of the Americas), 2nd floor
212/586-0947
Mon, Tues, Thurs, Fri: 9-5; Wed: 9-6; Sat: 10-3:30

This outfit remains incredibly busy after over four decades in business, perhaps because it is almost without competition. Those who use fountain pens or are interested in vintage pens or lighters are devoted customers. Authorized Repair sells and services nearly every brand, and the shop can refill all kinds of ball point, cartridge, and fountain pens and lighters. Authorized also sells (at a discount), repairs, and services electric shavers. Tourists can pick up 220-volt appliances and adapter plugs. The polite and helpful staff is well versed in the fine points of each brand.

FOUNTAIN PEN HOSPITAL
10 Warren St (across from City Hall)   212/964-0580
Mon-Fri: 8-6   800/253-7367

This experienced establishment is one of the few in town that repairs fountain pens. The Fountain Pen Hospital sells and repairs pens of all types, as well as what is perhaps the largest selection of fine modern and vintage writing tools in the world.

Personal Services

BIG APPLE GREETER
1 Centre St (at Chambers St)   212/669-8159
Office: Mon-Fri: 10-5
Greeter appointments, daily, daytime (2-3 days prior notice)

More than 400 volunteers from all five boroughs will meet individuals and small groups and give them tours of various New York City neighborhoods. Notice is requested for those who need greeters in languages other than English. Greeters will come to a visitor's hotel and arrange a special itinerary of sights that will be of interest. This is a wonderful way to get an insider's view of the city. Tipping, home visits, and use of private transportation are considered inappropriate. Visitors are provided with transportation maps, site and attraction information, and arts and entertainment options. It is like having a new friend show you the wonders of the city!

Are you planning a move?
   One of the best calls you can make is to Linda Rothschild at **Cross It Off Your List** (212/725-0122). She will help with all those time-consuming details.

DIAL A SECRETARY
126 E 83rd St (bet Lexington and Park Ave)
521 Fifth Ave (bet 43rd and 44th St)   212/348-9575
Open every day

If you need a resume written or reproduced, a book or screenplay processed, or an audio tape transcribed, these folks will do it in a hurry—and do it well. Given notice, they will even send an assistant to your office. Their list of clients includes several movie stars. The business started in owner Natalie Parnass' apartment a quarter of a century ago with one electric typewriter. Now they have a staff of super-talented people, some of whom can type 160 words a minute.

DOMESTICITY
137 Thompson St (bet Houston and Prince St)   212/529-2373
Daily: 9-9

You will want to become friends with partners Katherine Hammond and Kathejo Bohlman. Technically, they are a design and organizing team (both have art and design backgrounds) who will help improve your home environment. In reality, they will do just about anything, including such chores as putting up a Christmas tree, wrapping gifts, and baking cookies. Need to find some odd object? Give 'em a call!

EMILY CHO
212/289-7807, 201/816-8530
By appointment

Emily Cho's job is to make her clients "look and feel terrific!" She is a clothing psychologist who has been in this line of work for a quarter of a century. The process begins with an in-depth interview at your home or hotel, where your wardrobe is reviewed. She will organize and update your clothes, then escort you on a personal shopping tour. Emily finds new resources every year, and she promises to stay within a client's budget. Corporate services and an intensive two-day course in personal image consulting are also available. This talented professional has had prior experience at Bloomingdale's, *Seventeen* magazine, and the Ford Model Agency.

In the market for a tattoo? They *are* all the rage! Try **New York Adorned** (47 Second Ave, 212/473-0007).

FASHION UPDATE
718/377-8873
Mon-Fri: 9-5

Sara Gardner is a mother of three who naturally wants to make sure she gets the best value out of every clothing dollar spent. Gardner found she could get apparel for her family at wholesale prices from some manufacturers, so she decided to share her discovery. Thus she started *Fashion Update,* a quarterly publication that uncovers over 360 bargains per season in women's, men's, and children's designer clothing and accessories, plus furniture and home accessories. She conducts special shopping expeditions to designer showrooms at $175 for three hours.

FLOOD'S CLOSET
212/348-7257
By appointment

Want to be pampered? Barbara Flood will shop for or with you. She can even bring items to consider in your own home. She will help with clothes, jewelry, organizing closets, decor, and all those other time-consuming chores.

G. BRUCE BOYER
212/581-9003
Consultations available

Finding a gentleman who does personal and corporate image consulting is not easy! All paths lead to Mr. Boyer, who was men's fashion editor of *Town and Country* magazine for 15 years and has written three books on the subject. You can't do better, so if you want to spruce up your look, give this expert a call.

GLENN BRISTOW, CFP
218 W 10th St (at Bleecker St)   212/243-0571
Hours: by appointment

Glenn Bristow is a certified financial planner who claims she can demystify the process of managing money and paperwork, especially for the critically ill. Her clients include homemakers, dentists, designers, restaurant operators, and horticulturists. She has had over 25 years of experience in business administration, is computer literate, and comes highly recommended for bookkeeping and budgeting advice.

INTREPID NEW YORKER
1230 Park Ave (bet 95th and 96th St)   212/534-5071
Daily: 24 hours

Kathy Braddock, founder and owner of this service, is indeed "the Intrepid New Yorker." She was born, bred, and educated in the Big Apple. Like your author, she delights in helping folks unravel the hassles and confusion of this great city. She provides one of the most complete personal-service businesses in the area and is available at any time. A corporate relocation service for people moving into the tri-state area (especially New York City) is available. Kathy can take you on private guided tours and shopping expeditions, help you find a place to live, and take care of your decorating or refurbishing needs.

IT'S EASY
30 Rockefeller Plaza   212/586-8880
Mon-Fri: 9-6

Some time ago, David Alwadish found himself trying to keep cool amid an angry crowd at the passport office in Rockefeller Center. When someone told him they would pay anything to get off that line, Alwadish took him at his word, and a new business was born. Over the next decade Alwadish did so well as a stand-in and go-fer that he went national and branched out into doing research for attorneys and businesses, auto leasing, and even motor-vehicle inspection. His company can help with passports, visas, and bureaucratic transactions of all kinds.

LET MILLIE DO IT!
212/535-1539
Daily: 10 a.m.

Millie Emory has been in business for two decades as a professional organizer, saving people time, money, and stress. She especially likes working for theatrical folks but can help anyone with a broad variety of tasks. She will organize and unclutter apartments, desks, files, closets, libraries, attics, basements, garages, and storage rooms. She will also pay bills, reconcile checkbooks, and get papers in order for a tax accountant or IRS audit. She can help with paper flow, time management, and space problems. Millie is also good at finding things like antiques and out-of-print books and records. She assists seniors in dismantling their homes before entering nursing facilities. When loss of a loved one strikes, she will handle estate liquidations, selling, donating, and leaving the space "broom clean." Millie is a real problem solver!

LIGHTEN UP! FREE YOURSELF FROM CLUTTER!
254 W 98th St, Suite 3F   212/222-2488
By appointment

Michelle Passoff, the genius behind this operation, calls New York City "the clutter capital of the world." Lighten Up is a service for people who want to free themselves from all the clutter in their lives and develop some new habits. Being very much of an "unclutterer" myself, I think Michelle offers a real service in handling trash flow and all that goes with it. She offers private consultations, classes, workshops, training, lectures for organizations and corporations, and an audio-cassette instructional program. Right on, Michelle!

LSA & ASSOCIATES
220 E 65th St, Suite 14K   212/935-5041

LSA & Associates has a unique specialty: they assist in acquiring artwork for personal and corporate clients, as well as advice on updating and appraising art at its current market value. They also arrange tours of New York galleries and artists' studios.

Find room on your refrigerator door for this name: Linda Siegal at **New York Concierge** (304 Park Ave S, 11th floor, 212/590-2530). She can do anything to make your day easier. All you have to do is ask. How about breakfast in bed?

SAVED BY THE BELL
11 Riverside Dr   212/874-5457
Mon-Fri: 9-7 (or by appointment)

Susan Bell's goal is to take the worry out of planning virtually any type of job for people who are too busy or disorganized to do it themselves. Bell says "doing the impossible is our specialty," and you can believe her. Specialties include weddings, fundraising and charity benefits, party planning, tag sales, relocations, shopping, delivery arrangements, and service referrals.

SMARTSTART
334 W 86th St   212/580-7365

There is always someone in New York alert enough to fill a special niche or need. Such a person is Susan Weinberg. By her own experience, she learned that many expectant mothers and fathers are too busy to plan for the arrival of their little bundle of joy. So she started Smartstart, a consulting service to aid folks in pulling everything together. Her service provides the basics of what a newborn will need, as well as room design, birth announcements, thank-you cards, gifts, and personal shopping. In addition, Susan sells hand-painted children's furniture, from table and chair sets to coat hooks and toy chests. Custom cabinet work is a specialty. She is truly the stork's number one assistant.

TALKPOWER
333 E 23rd St (bet First and Second Ave)   212/684-1711
Mon-Fri: 9:30-5:30

Do you know that speaking in front of a group is the single most feared experience? If you suffer from this problem, give these folks a call. They are true professionals, training clients to make public appearances. Personal or group sessions are available for intensive weekends.

VIP AIRPORT SERVICE
516/431-6938, 800/225-0256 (PIN 80053)
24 hours a day; 7 days a week

VIP provides professional, personalized airport service for arriving or departing passengers. They are facilitators and troubleshooters. Handling tedious chores like tracking lost luggage and assisting with delayed flights is a specialty. As they belong to a number of airline clubs, they can make these members-only lounges available to their customers.

Is Your Closet a Mess?

If it is—and whose isn't?—you might want to call **Creative Closets** (364 Amsterdam Ave, 212/496-2473) or the **Closet Lady** (212/362-0428). Both do specialized work and come highly recommended. Their prices are reasonable compared to others in the field.

Photographic Services

A. IDENTIFICATION SERVICE
698 Third Ave (bet 43rd and 44th St)   212/682-5045
Mon-Fri: 8-6

A.A.'s main virtue is the ability to expedite the taking and processing of passport and identification photos. This is no small matter, as some photo shops near passport offices can be very unreliable. A.A. has a good reputation for one-day business portraits, one-hour photo-lab services, and laminating.

DEVEREUX PHOTOGRAPHIC SERVICES
45 W 57th St, 7th floor   212/688-4555
Mon-Fri: 9-6

These folks were trained as commercial photographers and have now parlayed their expertise into digital imaging and restoration of old and damaged photographs. It's amazing what they can do. They are pros at retouching, making a copy negative when the original is missing, and doing quantity work at special prices. Some work is hand-done, and some is done on the computer.

GALOWITZ PHOTOGRAPHICS
18900 Main Rd, Mattituck, NY 11952   516/298-3537
Mon-Fri: 8:15-5:30; Sat: 10-4

In a city that has two button shops, two seashell shops, and a dozen pet groomers, you would think there would be a number of photographic restoration establishments. No sir. This very exacting art is a rare bird, but I am happy to recommend Galowitz as a fine practitioner whose specialty is making old photos look presentable. Galowitz is a quality, full-service photo lab. They do conservation work, can preserve family photos on CD, and can restore or copy an old photo. Mail orders are accepted.

HAND HELD FILMS
118 W 22nd St (at Ave of the Americas)   212/691-4898
Mon-Fri: 9-6

This is one of the largest independent rental houses for motion-picture camera equipment for feature films, commercials, music videos, and documentaries. You can be assured of the very latest equipment and "toys" here, including sound equipment.

LIQUID IMAGE
390 West Broadway (bet Spring and Broome St)   212/334-4443
Mon-Thurs: 10-10; Fri, Sat: 10 a.m.-midnight; Sun: 11-10

Liquid Image offers over 70,000 backgrounds of all kinds and descriptions into which people (or animals) can be seamlessly inserted. The only fully digital portrait studio around, they can make highly unusual and personal greeting or business cards. Looking for a unique invitation? This is the place to visit. They can also work from personal snapshots.

PHOTOGRAPHICS UNLIMITED/DIAL-A-DARKROOM
17 W 17th St (bet Fifth Ave and Ave of the Americas), 4th floor
212/255-9678
Mon-Fri: 9 a.m.-11 p.m.; Sat: 10-7; Sun: noon-7

Here's another only-in-New York idea. Photographics Unlimited offers photographers a full range of darkroom equipment and rental workspace. The shop has everything from the simplest equipment to an 8x10 Saltzman enlarger, including all manner of printing paper and film supplies, as well as a lab for on-the-spot developing of black-and-white and color photography. They also do custom processing and printing. Ed Lee claims his center is equipped to meet the needs of amateurs and advanced professional photographers alike. A hotline is available to answer technical questions.

PROFESSIONAL CAMERA REPAIR SERVICE
37 W 47th St (bet Fifth Ave and Ave of the Americas)   212/382-0550
Mon-Fri: 8:30-5

Rush jobs are the specialty here, so there's no need to spoil your vacation because your camera is on the blink. Professionals work on still cameras from 35mm on up. They can also perform modifications and adaptations for special camera equipment.

VISKO HATFIELD
212/979-9322
Mon-Fri: 9-5

A rising star! Here is an opportunity to have a truly one-of-a-kind portrait done by a young photographer whose name you will be seeing in lights very soon. He possesses great talent and magnetic personality. He has captured images of dozens of celebrities in the book, magazine, fashion, and art scenes around the world. You could be next!

> One of the best deals in town for color copying is at **Clicks** (49 W 23rd St, 212/645-1971). You can do the work yourself at any hour of the day or night for 75¢ per copy.

Plumbing and Heating
JACK LICHTENBERGER & COMPANY
304 Spring St (bet Renwich and Hudson St)   212/807-8811
Daily: 7:30-4:30 (24-hour emergency service available)

Plumbing problems should not be left to novices. Four generations of this family have run the business, so you know they have the credentials to do luxury alterations, repairs, and maintenance in all kinds of situations. The average staffer has over 15 years experience.

KAPNAG HEATING AND PLUMBING
212/289-8847

When a reliable plumber and/or heating expert is needed, you can't do better than this outfit. They do plumbing renovations for kitchens and bathrooms, replacement of toilets, repair of pipes and heating equipment, and much more. Kapnag's two dozen highly qualified workers have kept this firm at the top of the list since 1935.

Postal Services

MAIL BOXES ETC. USA
212/642-5000 (information on nearest facility)

Mail Boxes Etc. has over 30 locations in New York. They represent all major carriers and can handle professional packaging and shipping jobs. Handy services (not all of them available at every location) include faxing, private mail boxes, mail forwarding, business cards, office stationery, notary and secretarial work, passport photos, laminating, key duplication, and computer letters. They also sell stamps, envelopes, boxes, and packing supplies.

Rug Cleaning

BESHAR'S
1513 First Ave (at 79th St)
212/288-1998 (gallery), 718/292-3301 (cleaning plant)
Mon-Wed, Fri: 10-5; Thurs: 10-8; Sat: 10-4

The Beshar family has run this rug and antiques business for three generations. Their expertise and experience are the basis of the "Besharizing" cleaning process, developed by grandfather Arteen Beshar. This treatment makes fine rugs last longer and cuts down on costly repairs. Beshar's will pick up and deliver. All rugs are cleaned by hand at the company's warehouse. Beshar's also stocks a broad range of new and antique rugs.

Scissors and Knife Sharpening

HENRY WESTPFAL AND COMPANY
105 W 30th St   212/563-5990
Mon-Fri: 9-6

Henry Westpfal has been in business since 1874, and the same family has been in charge all that time. They do all kinds of sharpening and repair, from barber scissors and pruning shears to cuticle scissors. They'll also work on light tools. Tools for leather workers, cutlery, shears, and scissors are all sold here. They also sell those hard-to-find left-handed scissors!

Shoe Repair

B. NELSON SHOE CORPORATION
1221 Ave of the Americas (McGraw-Hill Bldg), Level C-2
212/869-3552
Mon-Fri: 7:30–5:15

When several luggage dealers recommend the same shoe repair outfit, you know it must be pretty good. This is how I heard about B. Nelson. They are very good at repairing dress, leisure, and athletic shoes.

JIM'S SHOE REPAIR
50 E 59th St (bet Madison and Park Ave)   212/355-8259
Mon-Fri: 8-5:45; Sat: 9-3:45; closed Sat in summer

This operation offers first-rate shoe repair, shoeshine, and shoe supplies. The shoe repair field is rapidly losing its craftsmen, and this is one of the few shops that upholds the tradition. Owner Joseph A. Rocco specializes in orthopedic work-shoe and boot alterations.

Silver Repair

BRANDT & OPIS
46 W 46th St, 5th floor   212/302-0294
Mon-Thurs: 8-5; Fri: 8-2

If it has anything to do with silver, Roland Markowitz can fix it. This includes silver repair and polishing, buying and selling estate silver, repairing and replating silver-plated items, and fixing silver tea and coffee services. They restore combs, brushes (dresser sets), and replace old knife blades. Gold-plating, lamp restoration, and plating antique bath and door hardware are other services. Brandt & Opis are, in short, complete specialists in metal restoration.

THOME SILVERSMITHS
49 W 37th St (bet Fifth Ave and Ave of the Americas), Room 605
212/764-5426
Mon-Fri: 8:30-5:30

Thome cleans, repairs, and replates silver, in addition to buying and selling some magnificent pieces. They have a real appreciation for the material, and it shows in everything they do. They will repair and polish brass and copper, as well as restoring antique silver and *objets d'art,* silver and gold plating, pewter repair and cleaning, restoring the velvet backs of picture frames and velvet box linings, lacquering, and refining. Thome also specializes in brasswork and is, in fact, one of the very few still engaged in that business.

Stained-Glass Restoration

VICTOR ROTHMAN FOR STAINED GLASS
212/255-2551, 914/776-1617

With over 25 years experience, this studio specializes in museum-quality stained-glass restoration, from residences to churches and public buildings. Consultation is provided, and specification reports are prepared for professional and private use. New stained-glass windows can be designed and fabricated.

Tailors

BHAMBI'S CUSTOM TAILORS
14 E 60th St (bet Fifth and Madison Ave)   212/935-5379
Mon-Fri: 10-7; Sat: 10-5

With notice, this firm can cut suits in as little as two weeks. They have been in business for over a quarter of a century and have developed an excellent reputation. Next-day alterations are a specialty, as is hand-stitching on suits. Most of their fabrics come from England and Italy, so you can be assured that quality materials are used.

For those who demand the very best in alterations, try former dressmaker **Nelson Ferri** (766 Madison Ave, 4th floor, 212/988-5085).

CLAUDIA BRUCE
140 E 28th St (bet Lexington and Third Ave)   212/685-2810
By appointment

Suppose you just can't part with that beautiful but outdated dress you got on your honeymoon in Paris. Or perhaps you don't trust a dry cleaner to give that gown you wore to your daughter's wedding a new look. Just call Claudia Bruce, a talented lady who has been taking care of such problems with finesse for over a decade. She will repair and rejuvenate garments from the simplest to the most difficult with high standards. Home-fitting appointments and wardrobe consultations are also available.

MARSAN TAILORS
162 Fifth Ave (bet 21st and 22nd St), 7th floor   212/475-2727
Mon, Tues, Wed, Fri: 9:30-6:30; Thurs: 9:30-7:30;
Sat, Sun: 9:30-5:30

Before Moe Ginsburg—one of the biggest men's clothing emporiums in Manhattan—established its own tailor shop, all of its alterations were done by Marsan. Any tailor who survives in the middle of the men's wholesale garment area must be good, and Marsan is among the best. All work is done by hand.

PEPPINO TAILORS
780 Lexington Ave (at 60th St)   212/832-3844
Mon-Fri: 8:30-6:30; Sat: 9-4

Here you get the services of Mr. Peppino himself, a fine craftsman who has been in the tailoring field for over a quarter of a century. He will do custom tailoring for men and women at home, office, or hotel. All types of garments, including evening wear, receive his expert attention.

SEBASTIAN TAILORS
767 Lexington Ave (at 60th St), Room 404   212/688-1244
Mon-Fri: 8:30-5:30; Sat 9-4:30

Tailors are a peculiar breed in New York. In a city that is the home of the garment industry, most professionals who repair garments bill their trade as "custom alteration and design specialists," or else they're dry cleaners who mend whatever bedraggled outfits have been brought in for cleaning. Sebastian Tailors is one of the few true tailor shops in the city. Custom alterations for men and women are quick, neat, and reasonable. Sebastian also does reweaving. Best of all, everything is accomplished without the usual ballyhoo most such establishments seem to regard as their due.

Television Rental

TELEVISION RENTAL COMPANY
386 Park Ave S, 15th floor   212/683-2850
Mon-Fri: 9-5

Ted Pappas runs a rental service that is fast and efficient. He will rent televisions for long- or short-term periods and will happily deliver and pick up the sets. He also rents big-screen TVs, karaoke machines, beepers, fax machines, VCRs, camcorders, and other audio-visual aids. Prices are among the best in the city, and in a business like this, Pappas' solid reputation is a formidable recommendation in itself.

Translations

BERLITZ GLOBALNET
132 W 31st St, 12th floor   917/339-4700
Mon-Fri: 9-6

For translating technical data, Berlitz Globalnet is the place. Nontechnical translation services are available at Berlitz's 12 other centers in Manhattan. Call the above number to find the best location for the particular service you require.

Travel Services

MOMENT'S NOTICE
718/234-6295, 212/873-0908 (hotline)
Daily: 9-5:30

Moment's Notice is the place to call for last-minute travel arrangements. A reputable operation that has been in the travel business for over 30 years, they are a clearinghouse for leading tour operators, airlines, and cruise lines that are often faced with undersold or canceled bookings. This outfit provides sizable discounts on all types of vacation destinations, including European air tickets, Caribbean packages, and international cruises. Discounts are offered for travel 30 days or less prior to departure. Membership is required. A hotline for members announces last-minute travel bargains.

Saving travel money and time:

- Online bidding for airline tickets: www.priceline.com. If you want to do this by phone, call 800/774-2354.
- Most major airlines offer special weekly fares over the Internet. The catch is that they are usually restricted to the next weekend. Prices are much lower than the cheapest advance-purchase tickets, but the list of destinations is quite limited.
- Passport expediters: **It's Easy** (30 Rockefeller Plaza, concourse level, 212/586-8880), **Passport Plus** (20 E 49th St, 212/759-5540), and **Travco Services** (1265 Broadway, 800/987-2826).
- Reliable airline coupon broker: **Air Coupon Exchange** (800/558-0053).

PASSPORT PLUS
20 E 49th St, 3rd floor   212/759-5540, 800/367-1818
Mon-Fri: 9:30-5

Sometimes getting a passport and the proper visas can be a real pain in the neck. Passport Plus takes care of these tedious chores by securing business and tourist visas; renewing and amending U.S. passports; obtaining duplicate birth, death, and marriage certificates; and obtaining international driver's licenses. Their airline ticket pickup service is available to those requiring prepaid tickets from midtown Manhattan ticket offices. A photo service for passport, visa, and ID photos is also available. These folks serve customers all over the country.

TRAVEL COMPANION EXCHANGE
P.O. Box 833, Amityville, NY 11701   516/454-0880
Mon-Fri: 8:30-4:30

Tired of traveling alone? These folks can help you find a compatible travel companion or partner. They are a nationwide outfit that has been serving individuals from 20 to 80 years of age for two decades. A newsletter gives tips for solos, so you can make contacts in other cities. One of the nicest services is the opportunity to have company for a meal in New York. Although there are a number of good solo-dining places listed in the "Manhattan a la Carte" section at the front of this book, having someone to share the dining experience is a lot more fun. But do plan ahead.

Typewriter Repair

TYTELL TYPEWRITER COMPANY
116 Fulton St (bet William and Nassau St), 2nd floor   212/233-5333
Tues, Fri, Sat: 10-3 and by appointment

Martin K. Tytell is a legend. Now in his 80s, he signed a new ten-year lease! This is the definitive place for any kind of typewriter service or repair, with antique restorations a specialty. Tytell claims to have the largest collection of type in the world: over 2 million pieces, in many languages. He is the United Nations of the typewriter business! Tytell has also become a center for old and antique typewriters. With a 68-year-old collection of typewriters and parts, Tytell can restore virtually any machine. They'll give free estimates, too!

Uniform and Costume Rental

ALLAN UNIFORM RENTAL SERVICE
121 E 24th St (bet Lexington and Park Ave), 7th floor   212/529-4655
Mon-Fri: 9-5; open Sat in Oct

Because you will probably use a costume only once, it is far less expensive to rent than buy. At this establishment you can rent any number of costumes: contemporary, period, animal, Santa, and more. They also provide a uniform rental service.

Upholstering

RAY MURRAY, INC.
121 E 24th St (bet Park and Lexington Ave), 2nd floor   212/838-3752
Mon-Thurs: 8:30-5; Fri: 8:30-3:30

This is definitely an Old World shop that does things the old-fashioned way. It is a very fine and expensive drapery workroom that also does upholstery. Their specialty is creating classic custom-made furniture, and they can copy any design you want, including heirloom pieces.

If you wake up one day, look around and feel like you don't want to spend another minute with the same surroundings, give **XYZ Total Home** a call (212/388-1942). They are experts in giving tired homes or offices new looks. Or you can always visit their store (15 E 18th St). Here "personal styling" has been brought to new heights!

VI. Where to Buy It: New York's Best Stores

In recent years, many of the superstore chains that have overtaken the rest of the country have invaded New York as well. But look beyond the giant operations and prepare to discover what makes shopping in New York *special*. In the following pages, you'll find writeups of hundreds of stores that just can't be found anywhere else. There are two that sell bones and fossils, one that just sells light bulbs, and a resale store devoted exclusively to large sizes. There's a UNICEF store that sells cards and other items otherwise available only overseas, a bookstore devoted entirely to biographies, and a store that sells nothing but zippers. Amazing! You can even find the East Coast's only retail gift gallery dedicated to the native cultures and art of Hawaii and the South Pacific.

Just as with the other chapters of this book, I urge you to call *first* before setting out on your shopping adventure. It's always possible that some of these "where to" gems may close between now and the next edition. And don't be afraid to venture out on your own; you never know what you'll discover!

Gerry's Tips For Saving When Shopping

- **Comparison shop:** There can be wide price differences.
- **Read ads carefully:** Sometimes the fine print can be misleading.
- **Look beyond brand names:** Many items without fancy labels are just as good.
- **Color coordinate:** Buy outfits that can be mixed and matched.
- **Budget your dollars:** Know exactly what you can afford to spend.
- **Follow monthly sales:** Study the following section on best times to buy given types of merchandise.
- **Frequent thrift shops:** Some excellent values can be found at secondhand stores.
- **Beware of garage sales:** Be very selective, as there can be lots of junk here.
- **Shop alone:** Don't let peer pressure influence you.
- **Approach price tags warily:** Be careful of a series of markdown prices; the merchandise might be undesirable.
- **Keep receipts:** Returns are much easier.
- **Avoid seasonal buying:** Buy in the off-season, when items are less expensive.
- **Avoid impulse buying:** You may regret it later.

- **Use coupons:** They can save you big bucks.
- **Look into store shopping programs:** Good discounts for regular customers can be had.

Best Times For Bargains

January: coats, white sales, jewelry, cosmetics, electronics. luggage
February: furniture, kitchen appliances, hosiery, winter clothes
March: washers and dryers, silver, china, glassware
April: jewelry, lingerie, sleepwear, air conditioners
May: home furnishings, housewares, luggage
June: furniture
July: garden and patio supplies, swimwear
August: garden furniture, fashion accessories, back-to-school items
October: coats
November: furniture (Note: the day after Thanksgiving is *the* major shopping day!)
December: Christmas gifts for next year at after-Christmas sales

Bargain Outlet Lingo

As is: what you see is what you get, regardless of condition
Cancellation: item refused by major retailer
Closeout: no longer in fashion
Discontinued: no longer made
First-quality: could be sold in retail store
Irregular: minor imperfections
Open stock: pieces can be purchased separately at any time
Overrun: excess due to manufacturer's error
Overstocked: surplus first-quality items
Past season: last year's style
Sample: items made for showing to retailers
Seconds: easily detected flaws

Manhattan Malls

- **Trump Tower**, with a selection of high-end specialty stores
- **Herald Center**, a disaster from the start, now featuring Toys 'R' Us and Kids 'R' Us (and little more)
- **Manhattan Mall**, with **Stern's** as the major tenant and a number of nationally known shops, plus a food fair
- The mall at the **World Financial Center** (Battery Park City), where the open-space Winter Garden is a magnificent setting for events and trendy stores add to the excitement
- **South Street Seaport**, a fun place to visit for sightseers and young folks, though the shopping is not that great
- **Grand Central** will be truly grand when (and if) they get finished with the promised restaurants and stores. Among the present and expected occupants: Banana Republic, Discovery Channel Store, El Fogoncito, Joon Stationery, Kenneth Cole, Papyrus, Posman Books, Starbucks, Train Tunes, Vermont Candle Company, Watch Station, Zaro's Bread Basket, and Zocalo.

The Best Places to Shop for Specific Items in New York: An Exclusive List

Things for the Person (Men, Women, Children)

Albert Nippon apparel, discounted: **Lea's Designer Fashion** (119 Orchard St)

Baby gift ensemble: **Ovations** (World Financial Center)

Backpacks: **Bag House** (797 Broadway)

Bags, antique: **Sylvia Pines Uniquities** (1102-B Lexington Ave)

Boots, Western: **Lord John's Bootery** (428 Third Ave)

Boots and shoes, men's, handmade: **E. Vogel Boots and Shoes** (19 Howard St)

Bridal gowns and accessories, expensive: **Vera Wang** (991 Madison Ave, by appointment)

Bridal gowns, used: **Michael's** (1041 Madison Ave)

Bridal wear, non-traditional: **Jane Wilson-Marquis** (30 E 82nd St and 155 Prince St; appointments preferred, call 212/452-5335 and 212/477-4408)

Briefcases: **Per Tutti** (37 Greenwich Ave) and **Jobson's Luggage** (666 Lexington Ave)

Buttons: **Tender Buttons** (143 E 62nd St)

Clothing, antique: **Antique Boutique** (712-714 Broadway) and **Alice Underground** (481 Broadway)

Clothing, cancer survivors': **Underneath It All** (444 E 75th St)

Clothing, children's basics: **Morris Bros.** (2322 Broadway)

Clothing, children's French: **Jacadi** (787 Madison Ave and 1281 Madison Ave)

Clothing, children's French and Italian: **Prince and Princess** (33 E 68th St)

Clothing, children's funky and fun: **Chocolate Soup** (946 Madison Ave) and **Peanutbutter & Jane** (617 Hudson St)

Clothing, children's party dresses: **Spring Flowers** (1050 Third Ave and 905 Madison Ave)

Clothing, children's resale: **Second Act Children's Wear** (1046 Madison Ave)

Clothing, custom-made men's clothing, shirts, and ties: **Ascot Chang** (7 W 57th St)

Clothing, designer, men's and women's: **Showroom Seven** (498 Seventh Ave, 24th floor)

Clothing, designer resale: **Ina** (101 Thompson St)

Clothing, high-priced infants': **Wicker Garden's Baby** (1327 Madison Ave)

Clothing, imported designer: **India Cottage Emporium** (1150 Broadway)

Clothing, maternity, discounted: **Maternity Works** (16-18 W 57th St)

Clothing, men's brand-name, discounted: **L.S. Men's Clothing** (19 W 44th St, Room 403) and **Century 21** (22 Cortlandt St)

Clothing, men's classic: **Peter Elliot** (1070 Madison Ave)

Clothing, men's custom-made: **Alan Flusser** (Saks Fifth Ave, 611 Fifth Ave, 6th floor)

Clothing, men's good value: **Saint Laurie** (350 Park Ave) and **Gorsart** (9 Murray St)

Clothing, men's resale: **Exchange Unlimited** (563 Second Ave)

Clothing, men's ridiculously high prices: **Bijan** (699 Fifth Ave)

Clothing, party and wedding dresses: **Mary Adams** (159 Ludlow St)

Clothing, unusual: **Gallery of Wearable Art** (34 E 67th St)

Clothing, vintage: **Gene London's The Fan Club** (22 W 19th St)

Clothing, women's (be careful of pricing): **S&W** (165 W 26th St)

Clothing, women's hip designer: **Red Tape by Rebecca Danenberg** (333 E 9th St)

Clothing, women's designer sportswear, discounted: **Giselle** (143 Orchard St)

Clothing, women's discounted: **Irving Katz** (209 W 38th St, 5th floor)

Clothing, women's, good prices: **Miriam Rigler** (14 W 55th St)

Clothing, women's trendy: **Betsey Johnson** (248 Columbus Ave, 251 E 60th St, 1060 Madison Ave, and 138 Wooster St)

Clothing, youth: **TG-170** (170 Ludlow St)

Condoms: **Condomania** (351 Bleecker St)

Cosmetics, discounted: **Kris Cosmetics** (1170 Broadway)

Diamonds: **Rennie Ellen** (15 W 47th St; by appointment only, 212/869-5525)

Dresses, evening and wedding, made-to-order: **Jane Wilson-Marquis** (155 Prince St and 130 E 82nd St)

Dresses, knit sets and suits: **Sam's Knitwear** (93 Orchard St)

Earrings, custom-designed: **Sheri Miller** (578 Fifth Ave)

Eyelashes: **Eastside Fashion Center** (110 E 58th St)

Eyewear, discounted: **Quality Optical** (1333 Broadway, lower level of Conway Store)

Eyewear, elegant: **Vision Fashion Eyewear** (34 W 46th St) and **Morgenthal-Frederics Opticians** (944 Madison Ave, 399 West Broadway, and 685 Madison Ave)

Fabrics, couture and designer: **Beckenstein Home Fabrics** (4 W 20th St)

Fabrics, decorator, discounted: **Harry Zarin** (72 Allen St)

Fabrics, designer, discounted: **B&J Fabrics** (263 W 40th St)

Fabrics, discounted: **A&N Fabrics** (268 W 39th St)

Fabrics, Oriental: **Oriental Dress Company** (38 Mott St)

Footwear, women's small sizes: **Giordano's** (1150 Second Ave)

Furs: **G. Michael Hennessy** (333 Seventh Ave, 5th floor)

Gloves, fabric and leather: **LaCrasia Gloves** (304 Fifth Ave)

Gowns, couture, secondhand: **Irvington Institute Thrift Shop** (1534 Second Ave)

Handbags: **Fine and Klein** (119 Orchard St)

Handbags, magnificent (very expensive): **Judith Leiber on Madison** (987 Madison Ave)

Hats, custom fur: **Lenore Marshall** (235 W 29th St)

Hats, men's: **Arnold Hatter** (620 Eighth Ave), **J.J. Hat Center** (310 5th St), **P. Chanin** (152 Eighth Ave and 89 Christopher St), and **Young's Hat Store** (139 Nassau St)

Hats, men's discounted: **Makin's Hats** (212 W 35th St; call ahead, 212/594-6666)

Jackets, leather: **Arizona** (91 Spring St)

Jeans, antique 501: **Antique Boutique** (712-714 Broadway)

Jeans, discounted: **O.M.G., Inc** (546 Broadway, 476 Broadway, 55 Third Ave, 217 Seventh Ave, and 850 Second Ave)

Jeans, vintage: **What Comes Around Goes Around** (351 West Broadway)

Jewelry: **Fortunoff** (681 Fifth Ave) and **Antique Source** (271 Madison Ave)

Jewelry, fine: **Stuart Moore** (128 Prince St)

Jewelry, Indian: **David Saity** (450 Park Ave)

Jewelry, vintage: **Antique Addiction** (436 West Broadway)

Jewels, rare and historic: **Edith Weber & Associates** (994 Madison Ave)

Kimonos: **Kimono House** (93 E 7th St)

Knit suits, sportswear: **Sam's Knitwear** (93 Orchard St)

Leather, jackets and wallets, men's and women's: **Rugby North America** (115 Mercer St)

Leather goods: **Il Bisonte** (72 Thompson St)

Lingerie, discounted: **Orchard Corset** (157 Orchard St) and **Howard Sportswear** (85 Orchard St)

Lingerie, fine: **The Bra Smyth** (905 Madison Ave)

Lingerie, sexy: **Victoria's Secret** (34 E 57th St, 1240 Third Ave, 115 Fifth Ave, and 565 Broadway)

Massage oils: **Fragrance Shoppe** (21 E 7th St)

⦿ Millinery, one-of-a-kind: **Kelly Christy** (235 Elizabeth St)

Outdoor wear: **Eastern Mountain Sports** (20 W 61st St and 611 Broadway)

Pearls: **Sanko Cultured Pearls** (45 W 47th St; by appointment, Mon-Fri: 11-3, 212/819-0585)

Perfume: **Warwick Chemists** (1348 Ave of the Americas)

Perfume copies: **Essential Products** (90 Water St)

Perfume, discounted: **R.S.V. Trading** (49 W 27th St), **Kris Cosmetics** (1170 Broadway), **Jay's Perfume Bar** (14 E 17th St), and **Hema Cosmetics** (313 Church St)

Piece goods, men's: **Beckenstein** (121 Orchard St)

Police uniforms and equipment: **Frielich Police Equipment** (211 E 21st St)

Prescriptions: **J. Leon Lascoff & Sons** (1209 Lexington Ave)

Resale, women's designer: **Kavanagh's** (146 E 49th St) and **New & Almost New** (65 Mercer St)

Sandals: **Barbara Shaum** (60 E 4th St)

Sewing patterns: **P&S Fabrics** (355 Broadway)

Shaving products: **The Art of Shaving** (141 E 62nd St and 373 Madison Ave)

Shawls: **Patricia Pastor** (by appointment only, 212/734-4673)

Shirts, custom-made: **Arthur Gluck Shirtmaker** (47 W 57th St) and **Seewaldt and Bauman** (17 E 45th St)

Shirts, men's, great prices: **Acorn Shirts** (54 W 21st St, 4th floor; call ahead, 212/366-1185)

Shirts, sport: **Sosinsky's** (143 Orchard St)

Shoes, big sizes: **Tall Size Shoes** (3 W 35th St)

Shoes, bridal: **Peter Fox Shoes** (105 Thompson St and 806 Madison Ave)

Shoes, children's party, discounted: **Trevi Shoes** (141 Orchard St)

Shoes, children's upscale: **Harry's** (2299 Broadway) and **Shoofly** (465 Amsterdam Ave)

Shoes, comfort, adult and children's: **David Z** (655 Ave of the Americas)

Shoes, discounted: **Stapleton Shoe Company** (68 Trinity Pl)

Shoes, men's discounted: **Statesman Shoes** (6 E 46th St)

Shoes, men's and women's custom-made: **Oberle Custom Shoes/Mathias Bootmaker** (17 E 45th St; by appointment: 12-4, 212/737-3984)

Sneakers, men's and women's discounted: **Shoe City** (133 Nassau St)

Sportswear, name-brand discounted: **Atrium** (644 Broadway)

Sportswear, women's, good prices: **Giselle** (143 Orchard St)

Suits and dresses: **Blue** (125 St. Marks Pl)

Suits, European men's: **Jodamo International** (321 Grand St)

Sweaters, cashmere, men's: **Alberene** (435 Fifth Ave)

Sweaters, cashmere, men's and women's: **David Berk** (781 Madison Ave)

Sweaters, Coogi, discounted: **Penn Garden Shirt** (63 Orchard St)

Swimwear, women's: **Malia Mills Swimwear** (199 Mulberry St) and **Wolford** (122 Greene St)

T-shirts, baby doll: **Eisner Bros.** (75 Essex St)

T-shirts, custom printing: **Marcoart** (186 Orchard St)

Ties, discounted: **Goidel** (138 Allen St)

Tuxedo shirts and accessories, discounted: **Ted's** (83 Orchard St) and **Allen Tie & Shirt Center** (146 Allen St)

Umbrellas, wind-proof: **Uncle Sam** (161 W 57th St)

Uniforms: **Dornan** (653 Eleventh Ave) and **Ja-Mil Uniforms** (92 Orchard St)

Used items, unusual: **Out of the Closet Thrift Shop** (220 E 81st St)

Vest, kimonos: **Nicolina of New York** (247 W 46th St)

Watchbands: **George Paul Jewelers** (1023 Third Ave)

Watches: **Mostly Watches** (200 W 57th St) and **G. Wrublin Co.** (134 W 25th St)

Watches, discount: **Yaeger Watch** (578 Fifth Ave) and **Foto Electric Supply Co.** (31 Essex St)

Watches, vintage: **Galleria Per Tutti** (50 Central Park S), **Aaron Faber** (666 Fifth Ave), **Time Will Tell** (962 Madison Ave), and **Fanelli Antique Timepieces** (790 Madison Ave, Suite 202)

Wigs: **Theresa's Wigs** (217 E 60th St) and **Jacques Darcel International** (1034 Third Ave)

Wigs, fashion, men's and women's: **Eastside Fashion Center** (110 E 58th St)

Yard goods: **P&S Fabrics** (355 Broadway)

Zippers: **A. Feibusch** (27 Allen St)

Things for the Home

Accents, bath and home: **Collectania** (1194 Lexington Ave)

Air conditioners: **Elgot Sales** (937 Lexington Ave)

Appliances, discount: **LVT Price Quote Hotline** (516/234-8884), **Dembitzer Bros.** (5 Essex St), **Kaufman Electrical Appliances** (365 Grand St), **Price Watchers** (800/336-6694), and **Bloom and Krup** (504 E 14th St)

Appliances, kitchen: **Gringer & Sons** (29 First Ave) and **Zabar's** (2245 Broadway)

Appliances for overseas: **Appliances Overseas** (276 Fifth Ave, Suite 407)

Art, ancient European, Oriental, and pre-Columbian: **Royal Athenia Galleries** (153 E 57th St)

Art, antique Oriental: **Imperial Fine Oriental Art** (790 Madison Ave)

Art deco, French: **Maison Gerard** (53 E 10th St)

Art, decorative: **Susan Meisel Decorative Arts** (135 Prince St)

Art, erotic: **Erotics Gallery** (41 Union Sq W, Suite 1011; by appointment only, 212/633-2241)

Art, North American Indian: **Common Ground** (113 W 10th St)

Art, pop: **Pop Shop** (292 Lafayette St)

Art, primitive: **Lands Beyond** (1218 Lexington Ave) and **Eastern Arts** (365 Bleecker St and 107 Spring St)

Art, 20th century, American and European: **Timothy Baum** (212/879-4512)

Art, Western, 19th and 20th century: **J.N. Bartfield Galleries** (30 W 57th St)

Artifacts: **Jacques Carcanagues** (106 Spring St)

Bakeware, discounted: **Broadway Panhandler** (477 Broome St)

Baking supplies: **N.Y. Cake & Baking Distributor** (56 W 22nd St)

Baskets: **Bill's Flower Market** (816 Ave of the Americas)

Baskets, custom scented: **Bath Island** (469 Amsterdam Ave)

Baskets, fruit: **Macres** (173 W 57th St)

Beds, Murphy: **Murphy Bed Center** (20 W 23rd St, 2nd floor)

Beds, sofa: **Avery-Boardman** (979 Third Ave)

Bird cages: **Lexington Gardens** (1011 Lexington Ave)

Bonsai: **Living Sculture Bonsai** (127 W 24th St)

Boxes, wooden: **An American Craftsman Galleries** (317 Bleecker St and other locations)

Cabinets, old lawyer: **On Lafayette** (325 Lafayette St)
Candles: **Candleshtick** (181 Seventh Ave and 2444 Broadway), **Candle Shop** (118 Christopher St), and **Terra Verde Trading Company** (120 Wooster St)
Candles, discount: **Empire Restaurant Supply** (114 Bowery)
Candles, illuminating: **Imprescia** (1407 Broadway)
Carpets, antique: **Ghiordian Knot** (by appointment, 212/722-1235)
Chairs, folding, inexpensive: **Crate & Barrel** (650 Madison Ave)
Chairs, folding, quality: **Coconut Company** (131 Greene St)
China, Amari: **Bardith** (901 Madison Ave)
China and glass, discounted: **Lanac Sales** (500 Driggs Ave, Brooklyn)
China, bargain odds and ends: **Fishs Eddy** (889 Broadway and 2176 Broadway)
China, French hand-painted: **Solanee** (866 Lexington Ave)
Christmas decorations, discounted (mid-November through Christmas): **Kurt Adler's Santa's World** (1107 Broadway)
Christmas ornaments: **Matt McGhee** (22 Christopher St)
Clocks, cuckoo: **Alfry** (48 W 46th St, 5th floor) and **Time Pieces** (115 Greenwich Ave)
Closet fixtures: **Hold Everything** (1311 Second Ave, 104 Seventh Ave, 2109 Broadway, and 250 W 57th St)
Coca-Cola merchandise: **Coca-Cola** (711 Fifth Ave)
Crafts, handmade American: **Eclectic Energy** (102 Christopher St)
Dinnerware, Fiesta (individual pieces): **Mood Indigo** (181 Prince St)
Dinnerware, porcelain: **Bernardaud** (499 Park Ave)
Displays, jewelry: **Premier** (33 W 46th St)
Domestics: **Harris Levy** (278 Grand St)
Doorknobs: **Simon's Hardware** (421 Third Ave)
Electronics, good values: **The Wiz** (726 Broadway and other locations) and **Vicmarr** (88 Delancey St)
Electronics, vintage: **Waves** (110 W 25th St, 10th floor)
Environmental products: **Terra Verde Trading Company** (120 Wooster St)
Fixtures, impossible-to-find vintage: **Carpe Diem Antiques** (187 Ave of the Americas)
Floor coverings: **ABC Carpet & Home** (888 Broadway)
Floral arrangements, imported dried flower: **Melonie de France** (41 E 60th St)
Floral designs: **Spring Street Garden** (186 Spring St)
Flowers, silk: **Pany Silk Flowers** (146 W 28th St)
Frames, picture: **Ready Frames** (44 W 18th St) and **Framed on Madison** (740 Madison Ave)
Furnishings, traditional hand-carved: **Devon Shops** (111 E 27th St)
Furniture, antique: **H.M. Luther Antiques** (35 E 76th St)
Furniture, children's, high quality: **Kids' Supply Company** (1325 Madison Ave)
Furniture, contemporary: **Totem Design Group** (71 Franklin St) and **Furniture Co.** (818 Greenwich St)
Furniture, custom-made: **Navedo Woodcraft** (179 E 119th St)
Furniture, department store: **Bloomingdale's** (1000 Third Ave)
Furniture, discounted: **Knoll** (105 Wooster St)
Furniture, fine mica: **Room Plus** (1555 Third Ave)
Furniture, foam, and mattresses: **Dixie Foam** (104 W 17th St)
Furniture, French Country: **Pierre Deux Antiques** (870 Madison Ave)
Furniture, handcrafted, 18th-century American reproductions: **Barton-Sharpe** (66 Crosby St)
Furniture, hardwood: **Pompanoosuc** (470 Broome St)

Furniture, leather: **Sofa So Good** (106 Wooster St)
Furniture, modular: **Room Plus Furniture** (1555 Third Ave)
Furniture, one-of-a-kind: **Props for Today** (330 W 34th St)
Furniture, pine: **Better Times Antiques** (201 W 84th St) and **Evergreen Antiques** (1249 Third Ave)
Furniture reproductions: **Foremost Furniture** (8 W 30th St, 5th floor)
Furniture, summer: **Smith & Hawken** (394 West Broadway)
Furniture, Swedish antique: **Eileen Lane** (150 Thompson St)
Furniture, unusual children's: **Wynken, Blynken & Nod's** (306 E 55th St)
Furniture, vintage: **Full House** (133 Wooster St)
Gadgets: **Brookstone** (18 Fulton St)
Garden items: **Lexington Gardens** (1011 Lexington Ave)
Glass: **Simon Pearce** (120 Wooster St and 500 Park Ave)
Glass, Venetian: **Gardner & Barr** (213 E 60th St)
Glass and tableware: **Avventura** (463 Amsterdam Ave)
Glassware, Steuben, used: **Lillian Nassau** (220 E 57th St)
Hardware: **Barson Hardware** (35 W 44th St)
Home accessories: **Carole Stupell** (29 E 22nd St)
Lamp finials: **Grand Brass** (221 Grand St)
Lampshades: **Just Shades** (21 Spring St)
Lightbulbs: **Just Bulbs** (936 Broadway)
Lightbulbs, discounted: **Wiedenbach-Brown** (mail order only, 800/243-0030)
Lighting fixtures: **City Knickerbocker** (781 Eighth Ave) and **New York Gas Lighting Company** (195 Bowery)
Linens, antique: **Jean Hoffman** (207 E 66th St) and **Jana Starr** (236 E 80th St)
Linens, Indian: **Pondicherri** (454 Columbus Ave)
Linoleum, vintage: **Second Hand Rose** (138 Duane St)
Locks: **Lacka Lock** (253 W 46th St)
Mattresses, good values: **Town Bedding & Upholstery** (205 Eighth Ave)
Movie-star photos: **Movie Star News** (134 W 18th St)
Perfume bottles, vintage: **Gallery 47** (1050 Second Ave)
Pianos, grand, decorative: **Maximiliaan's House of Grand Pianos** (200 Lexington Ave)
Plants, cactus: **Grass Roots Garden** (131 Spring St)
Plumbing parts: **George Taylor Specialties** (100 Hudson St)
Poster originals, 1880-1940: **Philip Williams** (60 Grand St)
Posters, best selection: **Paris Images** (170 Bleecker St) and **Poster America** (138 W 18th St)
Posters, international movie: **Triton Gallery** (323 W 45th St) and **Jerry Ohlinger Movie Material Store** (242 W 14th St)
Posters, vintage: **La Belle Epoque Vintage Posters** (280 Columbus Ave)
Prints, botanical: **W. Graham Arader** (29 E 72nd St)
Prints, contemporary wildlife and sporting: **Holland & Holland** (50 E 57th St)
Quilt fabric: **City Quilter** (157 W 24th St)
Quilts: **Down Quilt Shop** (1225 Madison Ave and 518 Columbus Ave) and **J. Schachter's** (5 Cook St, Brooklyn)
Quilts, antique: **Kelter/Malce** (74 Jane St; by appointment, 212/989-6760), and **Susan Parrish** (390 Bleecker St)
Rugs, old: **Doris Leslie Blau** (724 Fifth Ave, 6th floor; by appointment, 212/586-5511)
Screens, shoji: **Miya Shoji** (109 W 17th St)
Shelves: **Shelf Shop II** (1295 First Ave)

Signs, interior: **De-Sign Letters of New York** (135 W 20th St)
Silver and wedding gifts: **Rogers and Rosenthal** (2337 Lemoine Ave, Fort Lee, NJ 07024)
Silver, unusual: **Jean's Silversmiths** (16 W 45th St)
Silverware and Holloware, good values: **Eastern Silver** (54 Canal St)
Sofas: **J. Mabley Custom Furniture** (355 West Broadway)
Sofas, vintage: **Regeneration Modern Furniture** (38 Renwick St)
Software: **Electronics Boutique** (Manhattan Mall, Third Ave and 71st St, and 687 Broadway)
Stairs and rails, replacement: **Stairbuilders by B&A** (516/432-1201)
Stationery, personalized: **Jamie Ostrow** (876 Madison Ave)
Stone pieces: **Modern Stone Age** (111 Greene St)
Strollers and other baby equipment: **Schneider's** (20 Ave A)
Tableware: **Fishs Eddy** (889 Broadway, 551 Hudson St, and 2176 Broadway)
Tapestries: **Lovelia Enterprises** (356 E 41st St; by appointment, 212/490-0930) and **Saint-Remy** (818 Lexington Ave)
Tiles, ceramic, and marble and wall coverings: **Quarry Tiles, Marble & Granite** (128 E 32nd St) and **Tiles** (42 W 15th St)
Vacuum cleaners: **Desco** (1236 Lexington Ave and 131 W 14th St)
Venetian glass: **End of History** (548½ Hudson)
Wallpaper, discounted: **Janovic** (1555 Third Ave and other locations)
Wrought iron items: **Morgik Company** (20 W 22nd St)

Things for Leisure Time

Albums, out-of-print: **Bleecker Street Records** (239 Bleecker St)
Art supplies: **Pearl Paint Company** (308 Canal St)
Athletic gear: **Modell's** (1535 Third Ave and 51 E 42nd St)
Athletic gear, team: **Yankee Clubhouse** (110 E 59th St and 393 Fifth Ave) and **New York Mets Clubhouse** (143 E 54th St)
Baseball cards, best selection: **Card Collectors** (mail order, 212/787-1863)
Bicycles: **Bicycle Habitat** (244 Lafayette St)
Binoculars: **Clairmont-Nichols** (1016 First Ave)
Books, academic: **Labyrinth Books** (536 W 112th St)
Books, African-American history: **Liberation Bookstore** (421 Lenox Ave)
Books, art: **Hacker Art Books** (45 W 57th St, 5th floor)
Books, astrology: **New York Astrology Center** (124 E 40th St, Suite 402)
Books, children's: **Barnes & Noble, Jr.** (120 E 86th St)
Books, children's and parents': **Bank Street Book Store** (610 W 112th St)
Books, decorative arts: **Archivia** (944 Madison Ave)
Books, discounted, new and used: **Soho Books** (351 West Broadway) and **Bleecker Street Books** (350 Bleecker St)
Books, exam-study and science-fiction: **Civil Service Book Shop** (89 Worth St)
Books, fashion design: **Fashion Design Bookstore** (234 W 27th St)
Books, gay and lesbian: **A Different Light** (151 W 19th St)
Books, Japanese: **Zakka** (147 Grand St)
Books, mystery: **Murder Ink** (2486 Broadway) and **Partners & Crime** (44 Greenwich Ave)
Books, mystical and religious: **Quest Bookshop** (240 E 53rd St)
Books, old and rare: **Imperial Fine Books** (790 Madison Ave, 2nd floor)
Books, plate: **George D. Glazer** (28 E 72nd St)
Books, rare: **Martayan Lan** (48 E 57th St) and **J.N. Bartfield Galleries** (30 W 57th St)

Books, readings: **Shakespeare** (1 Whitehall St, 939 Lexington Ave, 716 Broadway, and 137 E 23rd St)
Books, religious: **Paraclete Book Center** (146 E 74th St)
Books, tribal art: **Oan-Oceanie-Afrique Noire** (15 W 39th St, 2nd floor)
Books, used and review copies: **Strand Book Store** (828 Broadway)
Cameras: **Grand Central Camera** (420 Lexington Ave)
Camera and professional movie supplies: **Cine 60** (630 Ninth Ave)
Cigarettes, luxury: **Nat Sherman** (500 Fifth Ave)
Cigars: **Arnold's Tobacco Shop** (323 Madison Ave)
Comic books: **Village Comics** (214 Sullivan St)
Compact discs, records, tapes, laser discs, discounted: **Disc-O-Rama** (40 Union Sq E and 146 W 4th St)
Compact discs, rock and roll: **Smash Compact Discs** (33 St. Marks Pl)
Compact discs, used: **NYCD** (426 Amsterdam Ave) and **St. Mark's Sounds** (20 St. Marks Pl)
Compact discs, wholesale: **Every CD** (music club, 800/EVERY-CD)
Computer printers, discounted: **TriState Computer** (650 Ave of the Americas)
Computers: **Computrs** (7 Great Jones St)
Computers, hand-held: **RCS Computer Experience** (575 Madison Ave, 1230 Ave of the Americas, and 425 Lexington Ave)
Costumes, makeup, and accoutrements: **Halloween Adventure** (104 Fourth Ave)
Dance-related items: **World Tone Music** (230 Seventh Ave)
Diving equipment: **Pan Aqua Diving** (460 W 43rd St) and **Sea Horse Divers** (1416 Second Ave)
Dogs, exotic breeds: **International Kennel Club** (1032 Second Ave)
Dolls: **Bear Hugs & Baby Dolls** (311 E 81st St)
Dolls, vintage: **Manhattan Doll House** (236-A Third Ave)
Dollhouses: **Tiny Doll House** (1146 Lexington Ave)
Drums: **Drummers World** (151 W 46th St, 3rd floor)
Films, videotape (classics): **Evergreen Video** (37 Carmine St)
Filofax, discounted: **Altman Luggage** (135 Orchard St)
Fishing tackle: **Orvis** (355 Madison Ave)
Fly-fishing equipment: **Hunting World** (16 E 53rd St)
Games, war: **Compleat Strategist** (11 E 33rd St and 342 W 57th St)
Gifts: **Mxyplyzyk** (125 Greenwich Ave)
Globes, antique world and celestial: **George D. Glazer** (28 E 72nd St)
Golf equipment, best selection: **New York Golf Center** (131 W 35th St)
Guitars: **Carmine Street Guitars** (42 Carmine St), **Rogue Music** (251 W 30th St, 10th floor), and the **Guitar Salon** (45 Grove St; by appointment, 212/675-3236)
Guns: **Beretta Gallery** (718 Madison Ave)
Handicrafts and art, imported: **Sam's Souk** (979 Lexington Ave)
Holographs: **Holographic Studio** (240 E 26th St)
Home Entertainment: **J&R Music & Computer World** (23 Park Row)
Horseback-riding equipment: **Miller Harness Co.** (117 E 24th St)
Jazz albums and compact discs: **Jazz Record Center** (236 W 26th St, 8th floor)
Jukeboxes: **Back Pages Antiques** (125 Greene St; by appointment, 212/460-5998)
Kaleidoscopes: **After the Rain** (149 Mercer St)
Kites: **Big City Kite Company** (1210 Lexington Ave)
Knitting supplies: **Yarn Company** (2274 Broadway)
Luggage, soft: **Bag House** (797 Broadway)

Magazines: **DINA Magazines** (270 Park Ave S), **Eastern Newsstand** (MetLife Building, 200 Park Ave, and many other locations), **Magazine Store** (30 Lincoln Plaza), and **Universal News** (977 Eighth Ave and 676 Lexington Ave)

Magic tricks: **Tannen's** (24 W 25th St)

Maps: **Hagstrom Map and Travel Center** (57 W 43rd St)

Maps, prints, and books of Old New York: **Pageant Book & Print Shop** (114 W Houston St)

Maps, rare, vintage: **Richard B. Arkway** (59 E 54th St, 6th floor)

Maps and prints, antiquarian: **Argosy Book Store** (116 E 59th St)

Marine supplies: **E&B Goldberg's Discount Marine** (12 W 37th St)

Microscope and science-related kits: **Unique Science** (410 Columbus Ave)

Movie memorabilia: **Warner Bros. Studio Store** (1 E 57th St)

Movie-star photos: **Movie Star News** (134 W 18th St)

Musical instruments: **Music Inn** (169 W 4th St) and **Sam Ash Music Store** (160 W 48th St)

Needlecraft: **Yarn Company** (2274 Broadway)

Newspapers, out-of-town: **Hotalings News Agency**

New York history: **Museum of the City of New York** (1220 Fifth Ave)

Novelties (5,000 types): **Gordon Novelty** (933 Broadway)

Outdoor gear: **Tent & Trails** (21 Park Pl)

Papers, elegant: **Il Papiro** (1021 Lexington Ave)

Paper, sheet: **Kate's Paperie** (561 Broadway, 1282 Third Ave, and 8 W 13th St)

Pens, antique: **Arthur Brown & Brother** (2 W 46th St)

Pens, discounted: **Altman Luggage** (135 Orchard St)

Photo supplies: **Ben Ness Camera & Studio** (114 University Pl)

Pipes: **Connoisseur Pipe Shop** (PaineWebber Bldg, 1285 Ave of the Americas, concourse level)

Postcards: **Art Market** (75 Grand St)

Records: **Tower Records** (692 Broadway and 1961 Broadway)

Records, Broadway shows: **Footlight Records** (113 E 12th St)

Records (singles): **Downstairs Records** (1026 Ave of the Americas, one flight up)

Records, old rock and roll: **Strider Records** (22 Jones St)

Science fiction: **Forbidden Planet** (840 Broadway)

Sci-fi and New Age gifts: **Star Magic** (745 Broadway and 1256 Lexington Ave)

Skateboards, offbeat: **Supreme** (274 Lafayette St)

Skating equipment: **Blades Board & Skate** (120 W 72nd St, 160 E 86th St, 1414 Second Ave, 659 Broadway, and other locations)

Snorkeling equipment: **Scuba Network** (124 E 57th St and 655 Ave of the Americas)

Soccer supplies: **Soccer Sport Supply** (1745 First Ave)

Software, computer: **J&R Music & Computer World** (15 Park Row)

Soldiers, lead: **Second Childhood** (283 Bleecker St)

Soldiers, toy: **Classic Toys** (218 Sullivan St)

Sports cards: **Alex's MVP Cards** (256 E 89th St)

Sports photos, autographed: **Future Sports & Memorabilia** (659 Lexington Ave)

Sports video: **Famous Sports Video** (32 W 39th St)

Teddy bears: **Bear Hugs & Baby Dolls** (311 E 81st St)

Theater items: **One Shubert Alley** (1 Shubert Alley)

Tobacco: **J.R. Tobacco** (11 E 45th St and 1 Wall St)

Toys, handmade: **Dinosaur Hill** (306 E 9th St) and **Geppetto's Toy Box** (161 Seventh Ave S)

Toys, high-quality imports: **Geppetto's Toy Box** (161 Seventh Ave S)
Toys, museum quality (1900-1940): **Bizarre Bazaar** (130¼ E 65th St; by appointment, 212/517-2100)
Toys, vintage: **Alphaville** (226 W Houston St), **Classic Toys** (218 Sullivan St), and **Darrow's Fun Antiques** (1101 First Ave)
VCRs, discounted: **Sound City** (58 W 45th St)
Videos, foreign-film: **Evergreen Video** (37 Carmine St)
Videotapes, hard-to-find (for sale or rent): **Evergreen Video** (37 Carmine St)
Writing instruments, great selection: **Rebecca Moss** (510 Madison Ave)

Things from Far Away

African art: **Boca Grande Arts & Crafts** (66 Greene St) and **York's** (319½ Bleecker St)
African handicrafts: **Craft Caravan** (63 Greene St)
Australian outfitter: **Kangaroo and Ewe Too** (46 E 59th St)
British imports: **99X** (84 E 10th St)
Buddhas: **Leekan Design** (93 Mercer St)
Chinese antiques: **Chinese Arts & Antiques** (825 Broadway) and **John Chen Chinese Antiques** (238 E 60th St)
Chinese dinnerware: **Wing On Wo & Co.** (26 Mott St)
Chinese goods: **Pearl River Emporium** (277 Canal St) and **Chinese American Trading Company** (91 Mulberry St)
Chinese patent medicines, herbal tinctures, and incense: **Flynn's School of Herbology** (60 E 4th St)
Chinese sandals: **Phoenix Import Corporation** (96 Bayard St)
Egyptian and Near Eastern antiquities: **Royal-Athena Galleries** (153 E 57th St)
European pottery: **La Terrine** (1024 Lexington Ave)
Himalayan craft items: **Himalayan Crafts and Tours** (2007 Broadway)
Indian imports: **Sarajo** (130 Greene St)
Indian rugs, shawls, and other fine exports: **Kashmir** (157 E 64th St)
Indonesian art: **Eastern Arts** (107 Spring St and 365 Bleecker St)
Irish gifts: **Grafton Gifts & Baskets** (830 Third Ave)
Irish imports: **Shamrock Imports** (Manhattan Mall, Ave of the Americas and 33rd St, 4th level)
Italian clothing and shoes: **Cellini Uomo** (59 Orchard St)
Japanese gift items: **Katagiri** (224 E 59th St)
Japanese prints: **Japan Gallery** (1210 Lexington Ave)
Leather items, imported: **Il Bisonte** (72 Thompson St and 22 E 65th St)
Middle Eastern caftans: **Paracelso** (414 West Broadway)
Oriental lampshades: **Oriental Lamp Shade Co.** (223 W 79th St)
Scottish kilts and tartans: **Scottish Products** (60 E 42nd St, Suite 1544)
Swedish paper-goods store: **Ordning & Reda** (253 Columbus Ave)
Tibetan rugs, handicrafts: **Potala** (9 E 36th St)
Tibetan treasures: **Do Kham** (51 Prince St), **Tibetan Handicrafts** (144 Sullivan St), and **Vision of Tibet** (167 Thompson St)
Turkish carpets: **Beyond the Bosphorus** (79 Sullivan St)

Miscellaneous Other Things

Bottles, perfume: **Gallery 47** (1050 Second Ave)
Butterflies: **Mariposa, the Butterfly Gallery** (South Street Seaport, Pier 17, 2nd floor)
Calendars: **Calendar Club** (888/422-5637)
Cat memorabilia: **Just Cats** (244 E 60th St)

Fire memorabilia: **New York Firefighters Friend** (263 Lafayette St)

Fish, tropical: **New World** (5 W 8th St)

Flags and banners: **Art Flag Co.** (8 Jay St)

Gardening supplies: **Chelsea Garden Center** (205 Ninth Ave)

Globes: **George D. Glazer** (28 E 72nd St)

Holographs: **Holographic Studio** (240 E 26th St)

Office furniture, discounted: **Frank Eastern Company** (599 Broadway, 6th floor) and **Discount Office Furniture** (132 W 24th St)

Office supplies: **MoMA Design Store** (44 W 53rd St) and **Seventh Avenue Stationers** (470 Seventh Ave)

Optical instruments: **Clairmont-Nichols** (1016 First Ave)

Parrots: **Urban Bird** (177 West Broadway)

Pet supplies, discounted: **Petland Discounts** (numerous locations)

Pharmacy, complete: **Windsor Pharmacy** (1419 Ave of the Americas)

Plexiglas & Lucite: **Plexi-Craft Quality Products** (514 W 24th St)

Stone items: **Modern Stone Age** (111 Greene St)

Store fixtures: **Liberty Display & Supply** (37 W 26th St)

Surveillance equipment, covert: **Counter Spy Shop** (444 Madison Ave)

Travel items: **Civilized Traveller** (864 Lexington Ave, 2003 Broadway, and 1 E 59th St)

Typewriter ribbons: **Abalon Office Equipment** (60 E 42nd St)

Factory Outlet Centers in the Tri-State Area

Connecticut

Clinton Crossing Premium Outlets (20 Killingworth Turnpike, Clinton, CT; 860/664-0700): 70 outlets, including Anne Klein, Barney's New York, Bass, Brooks Brothers, The Gap, Liz Claiborne, Nautica, Off 5th (Saks Fifth Avenue Outlet), Polo/Ralph Lauren, Waterford, Wedgewood, and more.

Factory Outlets at Norwalk (230 East Ave, Norwalk, CT; 203/838-1349): Bed Bath & Beyond, Carter's Childrenswear, Famous Footwear, Tanner's, and more.

New Jersey

Flemington Area

Circle Outlet Center (Route 202, at Route 31, Flemington, NJ; 908/782-4100): Bed Bath & Beyond, Bugle Boy, Carter's Childrenswear, Dress Barn, Dress Barn Woman, Famous Brands Housewares, Toy Liquidators, and more.

Flemington Cut Glass (156 Main St, Flemington, NJ; 908/782-3017): Asta Cookware, Bill Healy Crystal, Flemington Cut Glass, Flemington Mill Fabric Outlet, Le Cruset, and Main Street Antiques.

Heritage Place (Route 31 at Church St, Flemington, NJ; 908/782-3414): Flemington's Coat World, Jockey, Levi's, Reebok, and Wamsutta.

Liberty Village Premium Outlets (1 Church St, Flemington, NJ; 908/782-8550): Over 60 outlets, including Anne Klein, Brooks Brothers, Calvin Klein, Capezio, Donna Karan, Geoffrey Beene, Izod, Joan & David, Polo/Ralph Lauren, Sunglass World, Totes, Villeroy & Boch, and more.

Secaucus Area

Castle Road Outlet Center (600 Meadowlands Parkway, Secaucus, NJ): Fragrance & Accessories, Male Ego Fashion Outlet, Marty's Wholesale Shoe Outlet, and Prato Menswear Outlet.

Designer Outlet Gallery (55 Hartz Way, Secaucus, NJ): Adolfo II, Donna Karan, Evan Picone, Joan & David, Jones New York, Jones NY Dress, Jones NY Woman, Maternity Works, OshKosh B'gosh, and The Executive Suite.

Harmon Cove Outlet Center (20 Enterprise Ave N, Secaucus, NJ; 877/OUTLET2): Carter's Childrenswear, Geoffrey Beene, G.H. Bass Company Store, London Fog, Olga/Warner, Oneida Factory Store, Panasonic/Technics, Perry Eilis, Welcome Home, and more.

Outlets at the Cove (45 Meadowlands Parkway, Secaucus, NJ; 877/OUTLET2): Calvin Klein Company Store, Evan Picone, Maidenform, National Luggage, Nine West & Co., Van Heusen Direct, and more.

For a free comprehensive directory of all Secaucus outlet stores, send $4.00 to Hudson Reporter, 1400 Washington Street, Hoboken, NJ 07030, or call 201/798-7800. Request *The Secaucus Guidebook.*

Circle Factory Outlets (Route 35 at Manasquan Circle, Wall Township, NJ: 732/223-2300): Bass, Brass Outlet, Bugle Boy, Carter's Childrenswear, Corning Revere, Geoffrey Beene, Harry & David, Izod, Jones NY, Jones NY Sport, Nautica, and more.

Marketplace I (Route 34, Matawan, NJ): Dress Barn, Bannister Shoe Outlet, Calico Corners, Bernina Sewing Center, Christmas Warehouse, Cinderella Bridal, Lighting for Less, Van Heusen, Wholesale for Kids, and more.

Marketplace II (Route 34, Matawan, NJ): Bon Worth, Carter's Childrenswear, L'eggs/Hanes/Bali, New Vision, and more.**Olde Lafayette Village** (Route 15 at Route 94, Lafayette, NJ; 973/383-8323): Bass Shoe, Bugle Boy, Capacity, Izod, Sneaker Factory, and Van Heusen.

Princeton Forrestal Village Factory Outlet Stores (Route 1 at College Road West, Princeton, NJ; 609/799-7400): Casual Corner Outlet, Charter Club Outlet, Corning Revere, Famous Brands Housewares, Geoffrey Beene, Van Heusen, Welcome Home, West Point Pepperell, and more.

Six Flags Factory Outlets (537 Monmouth Road, Jackson, NJ: 732/833-0680): Brooks Brothers, Bugle Boy, Claire's Accessories, Donna Karan, Dress Barn, London Fog, OshKosh B'Gosh, Sunglass Hut, Timberland, and more.

Pennsylvania

Franklin Mills (1455 Franklin Mills Circle, Philadelphia, PA: 800/336-MALL): Over 200 stores, including Baby Guess, Guess, Nordstrom Rack, Off 4th (Saks Fifth Avenue Outlet), Neiman Marcus Last Call, and more.

New York

Apollo Plaza Outlet Center (855 E Broadway, Monticello, NY: 914/794-2010): Bass, Carter's Childrenswear, Fieldcrest/Cannon, Hush Puppies, Kay Bee Toy Outlet, Pfaltzgraff, Toy Liquidators, and more.

Bellport Outlet Center (Sunrise Highway, Bellport, NY: 516/286-3872): Bass, Claire's Accessories, Corning Revere, The Gap, Harry & David, Liz Claiborne, Maidenform, Naturalizer, Nautica, Nine West, Van Heusen, and more.

Manufacturers Outlet Center (195 N Bedford Rd, Mt. Kisco, NY: 914/241-8503): Bass, Casual Corner, Corning Revere, Farberware, Leather Loft, Levi's by Designs, Mikasa, Socks & More, Welcome Home, and more.

Woodbury Common Premium Outlets (Route 32, Central Valley, NY: 914/928-4000): More than 220 outlets, including Adidas, Ann Taylor Loft, Betsey Johnson, Brooks Brothers, Danskin, Donna Karan, Escada, Espirit,

Etienne Aigner, Giorgio Armani General Store, Jones NY, Joan & David, Kenneth Cole, Neiman Marcus Last Call, Rodier Paris, Williams Sonoma, and more.

Looking for **famous** brands? Here is where to find them:

A. Testoni (665 Fifth Ave)
Armani (760 Madison Ave, 568 Broadway)
Asprey (725 Fifth Ave)
Brioni (55 E 52nd St, 57 E 57th St)
Bruno Magli (677 Fifth Ave)
Burberry's (9 E 57th St)
Cartier (653 Fifth Ave, 725 Fifth Ave)
Chanel (15 E 57th St)
Charles Jourdan (777 Madison Ave)
Christian Dior (703 Fifth Ave)
Coach (342 Madison Ave)
Disney (711 Fifth Ave)
Dolce & Gabbana (660 Madison Ave, showroom; 825 Madison Ave, boutique)
Emanuel Ungaro (792 Madison Ave)
Emilio Pucci (24 E 64th St)
Escada (7 E 57th St)
Etro (720 Madison Ave)
Fendi (720 Fifth Ave)
Ferragamo (661 Fifth Ave, 725 Fifth Ave)
Georg Jensen (683 Madison Ave)
Gianfranco Ferre (845 Madison Ave)
Givenchy (954 Madison Ave)
Harry Winston (718 Fifth Ave)
Hermés (11 E 57th St)
Iceberg (772 Madison Ave)
Kenzo (805 Madison Ave)
Laura Biagiotti (4 W 57th St)
Liz Claiborne (650 Fifth Ave)
Louis Vuitton (49 E 57th St)
Mikimoto (730 Fifth Ave)
Missoni (1009 Madison Ave)
Nicole Miller (780 Madison Ave)
Niketown (6 E 57th St)
Piaget (730 Fifth Ave)
Polo Ralph Lauren (867 Madison Ave)
Prada (57th St & Fifth Ave, 45 E 57th St)
Rodier (610 Fifth Ave)
Romeo Gigli (1310 Third Ave)
St. John (665 Fifth Ave)
Tiffany (727 Fifth Ave)
Valentino (747 Madison Ave)
Van Cleef & Arpels (744 Fifth Ave)
Versace (647 Fifth Ave)
Yves St. Laurent (855 Madison Ave)
Zegna (743 Fifth Ave)

Anatomical Supplies

EVOLUTION
120 Spring St. (bet Greene and Mercer St)   212/343-1114
Daily: 11-7

Evolution is one of the most unique stores in Manhattan. This Soho emporium offers mounted butterflies and beetles, seashells, fossils, skulls and skeletons, horns, feathers, jewelry, books, and more. You've gotta see it to believe it!

MAXILLA & MANDIBLE, LTD.
451 Columbus Ave (bet 81st and 82nd St)   212/724-6173
Mon-Sat: 11-7; Sun: 1-5

Henry Galiano grew up in Spanish Harlem. On the days his parents weren't running their beauty parlor, the family often went to the American Museum of Natural History. His interest in things skeletal increased when Galiano got a job at the museum as a curator's assistant. He soon started his own collection of skeletons and bones. That, in turn, led to his opening Maxilla & Mandible (the scientific names for upper and lower jaw, respectively), which is the first and only such store in the world. That's understandable. How many people need complete skeletons—or even a single maxilla? Apparently more than you might think. The shop started by supplying museum-quality preparations of skulls, skeletons, bones, teeth, horns, skins, butterflies, beetles, seashells, fossils, taxidermy mounts, and anatomical charts and models to artists, sculptors, painters, interior decorators, jewelry manufacturers, propmasters, medical personnel, scientists, and educators. They also carry natural-history books, African art, Papua New Guinea art, bronze skeletal models, and scientific equipment.

Animals, Fish, and Accessories

PACIFIC AQUARIUM & PET
46 Delancey St (bet Forsyth and Eldridge St)   212/995-5895
Daily: 10-8

Goldfish are the specialty of the house, but Pacific Aquarium & Pet also carries all types of freshwater and saltwater fish, parakeets and other exotic birds, and every kind of aquarium and supply you could imagine. With advance notice they will even come to your home and maintain an aquarium.

PETCO
147-149 E 86th St (at Lexington Ave)   212/831-8001
Mon-Sat: 9-9; Sun: 10-6

With a selection of over 10,000 items, including food, toys, treats, and pet-care products, this store is a pet owner's treasure trove. There are sections for cats, dogs, birds, fish, and other animals. If reptiles turn you on, there is a section devoted to them!

PETLAND DISCOUNTS
85 Delancey St	212/477-6293
132 Nassau St	212/964-1821
7 E 14th St	212/675-4102
530 E 14th St	212/228-1363
312 W 23rd St	212/366-0512
137 W 72nd St	212/875-9785
404 Third Ave	212/447-0739

976 Second Ave	212/755-7228
389 Ave of the Americas	212/744-1913
734 Ninth Ave	212/459-9562
2708 Broadway	212/222-8851
304 E 86th St	212/472-1655

Hours vary from store to store

The folks at the New York Aquarium recommend this chain for fish and accessories. Petland also carries birds and discount food and accessories for dogs, cats, and other pets.

Animation

ANIMAZING GALLERY—SOHO
415 West Broadway (bet Spring and Prince St, 2nd floor)
212/226-7374
Mon-Sat: 11-7; Sun: 12-6

No one is better at showing animation than Animazing Gallery. They are New York City's largest authorized Disney Art Gallery. They also showcase the *Peanuts* pop art of Tom Everhart. Vintage and contemporary cels and drawings from all major studios are featured. Specialties include appraisals, consignments, searches, and autographed books; there are also monthly gala events, shows and sales.

Antiques

Bleecker Street Area

Pierre Deux Antiques (369 Bleecker St): French Country
Susan Parrish (390 Bleecker St): quilts

Chelsea

Chelsea Antiques Building (110 W 25th St): 150 dealers
John Koch Antiques (514 W 24th St): furniture
Poster America (138 W 18th St): vintage advertising posters
Royal de Paris Antiques and Furniture (600 W 27th St): furniture
Showplace (40 W 25th St): 100 dealers
Upstairs Downtown Antiques (12 W 19th St): eclectic

East 60th Street Area

A. Smith Antiques (235 E 60th St): European furniture
Antiques on 60th (207 E 60th St): Renaissance religious art
Darrow's Fun Antiques (1101 First Ave): lighthearted pieces
Luxor Gallery (238 E 60th St): 18th- and 19th-century Chinese
Paris to Province (207 E 60th St): French and English furniture
Roy Anderson (212 E 47th St): American paintings
Stubbs Books & Prints (330 E 59th St, 6th floor): books
Victor Antiques (223 E 60th St): European furniture

Greenwich Village Area

Agostino Antiques, Ltd. (808 Broadway): English and French 17th- to 19th-century furniture
Charterhouse Antiques (115 Greenwich Ave): porcelain
Donzella (90 E 10th St): 1930s, 1940s, and 1950s furnishings

End of History (548½ Hudson St): vintage hand-blown glass
George N. Antiques (67 E 11th St): mirrors
Howard Kaplan Antiques (827 Broadway): *belle époque*
Hyde Park Antiques (836 Broadway): English antique furniture
Karl Kemp & Associates (34 E 10th St): furniture
Kensington Place Antiques (80 E 11th St): furniture
Kentshire Galleries (37 E 12th St): English antiques
L'Epoque (30 E 10th St): armoires
Little Antique Shop (44 E 11th St): formal antiques
Maison Gerard (36 E 10th St): French art deco
Nesle (151 E 5th St): antique gallery; all styles and periods
Philip Colleck (830 Broadway): diverse
Proctor Galleries (824 Broadway): European antiques
Ritter-Antik (35 E 10th St): Beidermeier (early first period)

Lexington Avenue Area

Akdeniz & Hayko (857 Lexington Ave): kilims
Antiques Salon (870 Lexington Ave): clothing
Bob Pryor Antiques (1023 Lexington Ave): English brass and crystal paper-
    weights
Evergreen Antiques (1249 Third Ave): furniture
James Hepner Antiques (130 E 82nd St): 17th-, 18th-, and 19th-century pieces
L'Art de Viere (978 Lexington Ave): early 20th-century
Nancy Brous Antiques (1008 Lexington Ave): furniture
S. Wyler (941 Lexington Ave): silver, china
Sam's Souk (979 Lexington Ave): chests
Sara (952 Lexington Ave): Japanese pottery and porcelain
Sylvia Pines Uniquities (1102 Lexington Ave): diverse

Madison Avenue Area

Alie McAdams (942 Madison Ave): English 18th- and 19th-century furniture
Art of the Past (1242 Madison Ave): East Asian
Barry Friedman (32 E 67th St): art deco
Bernard & S. Dean Levy (24 E 84th St): American furniture and silver
Cora Ginsburg (19 E 74th St): antique textiles
DeLorenzo (958 Madison Ave): art deco
Didier Aaron (32 E 67th St): 18th- and 19th-century pieces
Eagles Antiques (1097 Madison Ave): English Country
Edith Weber & Associates (994 Madison Ave): rare and historic jewels
Fanelli Antique Timepieces (790 Madison Ave, Suite 202): antique timepieces
Florian Papp (962 Madison Ave): furniture
Gorevic & Gorevic (635 Madison Ave): jewelry
Guild Antiques II (1089 Madison Ave): English Country
J.J. Lally (41 E 57th St): Chinese art
L'Antiquaire & the Connoisseur (36 E 73rd St): French and Italian furniture
Leigh Keno American Antiques (980 Madison Ave, 2nd floor): 18th-century
    American furniture
Leo Kaplan, Ltd. (967 Madison Ave): ceramics and glass
Linda Horn Antiques (1015 Madison Ave): eclectic
Macklowe Gallery & Modernism (667 Madison Ave): Tiffany
Marco Polo (1135 Madison Ave): silver
Navin Kumar Gallery (212/734-4075, by appointment): Asian art

Orientation Gallery (802 Madison Ave): Japanese antiques
Time Will Tell (962 Madison Ave): watches
Ursus Books and Prints (981 Madison Ave): books
W. Graham Arader (29 E 72nd St): rare prints

Midtown Area

A La Vieille Russie (781 Fifth Ave): Russian art
Ares Rare (608 Fifth Ave, 6th floor): jewelry
Dalva Brothers (44 E 57th St): French furniture
Doris Leslie Blau (724 Fifth Ave, 6th floor): rugs
Fanelli Antique Timepieces (790 Madison Ave, Suite 202): clocks, watches
Gotta Have It! (153 E 57th St): celebrity memorabilia
I. Freeman & Son (60 E 56th St): silver
James Robinson (480 Park Ave): silver flatware
Martayan Lan (48 E 57th St): 16th- and 17th-century maps and prints
Newel Art Galleries (426 E 53rd St): antique gallery; all styles and periods
Ralph M. Chait Galleries (12 E 56th St): Chinese art
S.J. Shrubsole (104 E 57th St): English silver

Soho

Alan Moss (436 Lafayette St): furniture
Alice's of Soho (72 Greene St): iron beds
Antiquarian Traders (399 Lafayette St): desks, dining suites
Antique Addiction (436 West Broadway): eclectic
Art & Industrial Design Shop (399 Lafayette St): 1950s items
Back Pages Antiques (125 Greene St): classic Americana
Beyond the Bosphorus (79 Sullivan St): Turkish kilims and pillows
Chameleon (231 Lafayette St): lighting
City Barn Antiques (269 Lafayette St): Heyword-Wakefield
CMR (192 Ave of the Americas): artworks and furniture
Cobweb (116 W Houston St): imported furniture
Cranberry Hole Road (252 Lafayette St): furniture
Crosby Studio Decorative Arts (117 Crosby St): Venetian glass
David Stypmann (190 Ave of the Americas): eclectic
Eileen Lane Antiques (150 Thompson St): refurbished art deco
Form and Function (95 Vandam St): 1940s to 1960s furniture
Greene Street Antiques (65 Greene St): 19th and early 20th-century furniture
Historical Materialism (125 Crosby St): 19th-century collectibles
Lost City Arts (275 Lafayette St): architectural items
Penine and Hart (457 Broome St): lighting, garden furniture, accessories
Portobello Antiques (190 Ave of the Americas): eclectic
Rhubarb Home (26 Bond St): furniture
T&K French Antiques (200 Lexington Ave, Room 702): French furniture
Urban Archaeology (285 Lafayette St): architectural antiques

Tribeca

Gill & Lagodich (108 Reade St; by appointment only): frames
J.H. Antiques and Design (174 Duane St): furnishings
Oser (148 Duane St): Hawaiian vintage, including surfboards
Second Hand Rose (138 Duane St): eclectic
Wyeth (151 Franklin St): furniture

Upper East Side

Antiquarium (948 Madison Ave): jewelry
Bizarre Bazaar (130¼ E 65th St): antique toys
Galleria Hugo (304 E 76th St): 19th-century lighting
Gardner & Barr (213 E 60th St): vintage Venetian glass
George D. Glazer (28 E 72nd St): prints
Hugo, Ltd. (233 E 59th St): 19th-century lighting and decorative arts
Jean Hoffman Antiques (207 E 66th St): vintage wedding gowns and veils
Manhattan Art & Antiques Center (1050 Second Ave): 100 galleries
Naga Antiques (145 E 61st St): antique Japanese screens

Upper West Side

La Belle Epoque Vintage Posters (282 Columbus Ave): advertising posters

---

— Millennium Note —

The biggest crowd ever to attend a baseball game in New York jammed Yankee Stadium on opening day of its first season, April 18, 1923. The game drew 74,217 fans, and another 25,000 were turned away.

Art Supplies

LEE'S ART SHOP
220 W 57th St (nr Broadway)   212/247-0110
Mon-Fri: 9-7; Sat: 9:30-6:30; Sun: 12-5:30

Ricky, the very able boss, offers an expanded stock of materials for amateur and professional artists. There are architectural and drafting supplies; lamps, silk screens, and art brushes; paper goods, stationery, pens, cards, gifts, and much more. Same-day on-premises framing is available, along with catalog ordering and free delivery. Designer lighting equipment and good-looking furniture are available at Lee's other stores (1755 Broadway and Third Ave at 63rd St). This place is a must-visit!

NEW YORK CENTRAL ART SUPPLY
62 Third Ave (at 11th St)   212/473-7705; 800/950-6111
Mon-Sat: 8:30-6:30

Since 1905, artists have looked to this firm for fine-art materials, especially unique and custom-made items. There are two floors of fine-art papers, including one-of-a-kind decorative papers and over a hundred Oriental papers from Bhutan, China, India, Japan, Thailand, Taiwan, and Nepal. Amateur and skilled artisans will find a full range of decorative paints and painting materials. This firm specializes in custom priming and custom stretching. Their collection of brushes is outstanding.

PEARL PAINT COMPANY
308 Canal St (bet Broadway and Church St)
212/431-7932, 800/221-6845
Mon-Sat: 9-6; Sun: 10-5:30

Thirteen retail selling floors contain a vast selection of arts, graphics, and crafts merchandise. Selections and services include fabric paint, silk-screening and gold-leaf items, drafting and architectural goods, a fine-writing department, and custom framing. They provide fine-art supplies at some of the best prices in town and can ship overseas. The furniture and lighting sections have been expanded, and the Custom Frame Factory sells wall, photo, and custom frames at discount prices. A fine gift section carries items from all over the world.

SAM FLAX
425 Park Ave (at 55th St)   212/620-3060
12 W 20th St   212/620-3038
Mon-Wed: 8:30-6:30; Thurs: 8:30-6:30; Fri: 8:30-6:30;
Sat: 10-6; Sun (downtown only): 12-5 (except July and Aug)

Sam Flax is one of the biggest and best art supply houses in the business. The stock is enormous, the service special, and the prices competitive. They carry a full range of art and drafting supplies, gifts, pens, drawing-studio furniture, and photographic products. Framing services are offered at both stores, and one-day framing is available. The 20th Street store is primarily devoted to furniture but also carries a full line of art supplies.

UTRECHT ART AND DRAFTING SUPPLIES
111 Fourth Ave (at 11th St)   212/777-5353
Mon-Sat: 9-7; Sun: 12-5

Utrecht is a major manufacturer of paint, art, and drafting supplies with a large factory in Brooklyn. At this retail store, factory-fresh supplies are sold at discount, and the Utrecht name stands behind every purchase. Quality and prices are superb. Utrecht also carries other manufacturers' lines at impressive discounts.

Autographs

ANNA SOSENKO
25 Central Park West (bet 62nd and 63rd St)   212/247-4816
By appointment

This lady is in love with the showbiz, music, and literary worlds, and it shows. She has assembled a fine collection of letters, photos, and autographs of leading figures in these fields, offering them for sale from her home. There are plenty of stories to go with the collection.

JAMES LOWE AUTOGRAPHS
30 E 60th St (bet Madison and Park Ave, Suite 304)
212/759-0775
Mon-Fri: 9-5

James Lowe is one of the nation's most established autograph houses. Regularly updated catalogs make visiting the gallery unnecessary, but in-person inspections are fascinating and invariably whet the appetite of autograph collectors. The gallery shows whatever superior items are in stock, including historic, literary, and musical autographs, manuscripts, documents, and 19th-century photographs. The offerings range from autographed pictures of Buffalo Bill to three bars of an operatic score by Puccini.

KENNETH W. RENDELL GALLERY
989 Madison Ave (at 77th St)   212/717-1776
Mon-Sat: 10-6 or by appointment

Kenneth Rendell has been in the business for over 30 years. He offers a fine collection of pieces from famous figures in literature, arts, politics, and science. Rendell shows autographed letters, manuscripts, documents, books, and photographs. All are authenticated, attractively presented, and priced according to rarity. Rendell evaluates collections for possible purchase.

TOLLETT AND HARMAN AUTOGRAPHS, LLC
175 W 76th St   212/877-1566
By appointment only

Autographs used to be a big business in New York, perhaps because of the number of celebrities in the city. Lately, however, there are less than a handful of reliable dealers. Tollett and Harman is one of the best. They carry or will try to obtain original autographs, manuscripts, signed books, maps, and vintage photographs. Collectors of specific items can leave requests. (I collect U.S. presidents and members of the Continental Congress.) When they come across an item, they will notify you. Each item is carefully authenticated. Ask for a catalog!

Baskets

BASKETFULL
1123 Broadway (at 25th St)   212/255-6800, 800/645-GIFT
Mon-Fri: 9-5:30

If you want a basket designed with unique and innovative ideas, this is the place to call. These designers custom-create gift collections for special events and holidays. For example, you could send an "Indulgence" basket containing Belgian chocolate truffles and chocolate pralines! Or a New York-style basket that includes a genuine New York cheesecake, deli salami, bagel chips, and an egg cream! Other options are Bakeshop, Tex-Mex, Get Well, Sympathy, and various personalized and hand-painted baby baskets. Same-day hand delivery is available in Manhattan, and arrangements can be made for shipment anywhere in the world.

Bathroom Accessories

A. F. SUPPLY CORPORATION
22 W 21st St (bet Fifth Ave and Ave of the Americas)   212/243-5400
Mon-Fri: 8-5 and by appointment

A. F. Supply offers a great selection of luxury bath fixtures, whirlpools, faucets, bath accessories, door and cabinet hardware, saunas, steam showers, shower doors, medicine cabinets, and spas from top suppliers.

HOWARD KAPLAN BATH SHOP
831 Broadway (bet 12th and 13th St)   212/674-1000
Mon-Fri: 9-5

Howard Kaplan presents the largest assortment of top-quality antique bath items (1890-1920) in the country. Even the setting—an 1870 Napoleon III building—is special. You will definitely want to inspect the unusual French, English, and American merchandise.

SHERLE WAGNER INTERNATIONAL
60 E 57th St (at Park Ave)   212/758-3300
Mon-Fri: 9-5; Sat: 10-6; closed Sat in summer (bed and bath shop only)

Sherle Wagner takes the often-skirted topic of the bathroom and places it in the most elegant location in the city, where it rubs elbows with silversmiths, art galleries, and exclusive antique shops. The luxurious bathroom fixtures and bed and bath items are deserving of their 57th Street location. Fixtures come in a variety of materials, some so striking that they warrant being exhibited in a glass display case. Prices are high, as might be expected. One warning! The displays are in the basement, and what seems like the world's slowest elevator may make you feel claustrophobic.

Beads

GAMPEL SUPPLY
11 W 37th St (bet Fifth Ave and Ave of the Americas)
212/398-9222
Mon-Fri: 9-5

This is the kind of esoteric business New York does best. Request a particular kind of bead, and Gampel will invariably have it—at a cheap price, too. While single beads go for a dollar each at a department store one block away, Gampel sells them in bulk for a fraction of that price. Though they prefer to deal with wholesalers, individual customers are treated as courteously as institutions, and wholesale prices are offered to all. As for the stock—well, a visit to Gampel is an education. Pearlized beads alone come in over 20 different guises and are used for everything from bathroom curtains to earrings and flowers. Since many of its customers are craftspeople, Gampel also sells supplies for bead-related crafts. They stock needles, cartwheels, cord (in enough colors to match each bead), threads, glues, jewelry tools, jewelry findings, and costume-jewelry parts and pieces.

Bed and Bath

BED BATH & BEYOND
620 Ave of the Americas (bet 18th and 19th St)   212/255-3550
Mon-Sat: 9:30-9; Sun: 10-6

I've been in the business for a long time, and I have never seen an operation like this! It is an absolute must if you are in the market for anything for the apartment or home. In a huge store of over 80,000 square feet on lower Avenue of the Americas, these home-furnishings experts show stocks as far as the eye can see. There are sheets, blankets, rugs, kitchen gadgets, hangers, towels, dinnerware, hampers, cookware, kiddie items, pillows, and much more, with hundreds of choices in each category. Best of all, prices are discounted, the personnel are friendly and helpful, checkout is well organized, and carts are available so you can pile up purchases.

Books

The book business has changed drastically over the past decade. Superstores are now the name of the game. Unless a small dealer has a special location or niche in book marketing times are not easy.

Antiquarian

COMPLETE TRAVELLER ANTIQUARIAN BOOKSTORE
199 Madison Ave (at 35th St)   212/685-9007
Mon-Fri: 9-7; Sat: 10-6; Sun: 11-5

The largest collection of Baedeker Handbooks is but one feature of this store, which deals exclusively in rare, antiquarian, and out-of-print books pertaining to travel. The 8,000-book collection includes volumes on polar expeditions, adventure travel, and 18th- and 19th-century maps.

Architecture

URBAN CENTER BOOKS
457 Madison Ave (bet 50th and 51st St)   212/935-3595
Mon-Thurs: 10-7; Fri: 10-6; Sat: 10-5:30

The Municipal Art Society is a nonprofit organization dedicated to urban planning and historic preservation. Although best known for exceptionally diverse and well-conceived walking tours, the organization also runs a gallery and bookstore in its headquarters at the north end of the elegant Villard Houses. The bookstore is among the best sources in the country for books, magazines, and journals on such topics as urban and land-use planning, architecture, and interior design. It also carries a wide selection of guidebooks to New York City.

Art

HACKER ART BOOKS
45 W 57th St   212/688-7600
Mon-Sat: 9:30-6

There can only be one "largest" in any field, and Hacker is it in art books. You'll find books on fine arts, decorative arts, architecture, and much more. They have been in business for half a century. If Hacker doesn't have it, it probably doesn't exist!

PRINTED MATTER
77 Wooster St   212/925-0325
Tues-Sat: 10-6

The name Printed Matter is a misnomer, since this store is the only one in the world devoted exclusively to artists' books—a trade term for a portfolio of artwork in book form. They stock 9,000 titles by over 3,500 artists. The result is inexpensive, accessible art that can span an entire artist's career or focus in on a particular period or theme. The idea is carried further with a selection of periodicals and audio tapes in a similar vein. Nearly all featured artists are contemporary, so just browsing through the store will bring you up-to-date on what is happening in the art world. They sell wholesale and retail; a catalog is available.

Biography

BIOGRAPHY BOOKSHOP
400 Bleecker St (at 11th St)   212/807-8655
Mon-Thurs: 12-8; Fri: 12-10; Sat: 11-11; Sun: 11-7

This shop specializes in books of a biographical nature. If you are researching a particular person or have an interest in someone's life story, this is the place to find it. There are biographies, books of letters, autobiographies, diaries, journals, current fiction and nonfiction, and biographies for children.

Children's

BANK STREET BOOKSTORE
2879 Broadway (at 112th St)
212/678-1654, 800/724-1486 (outside New York State)
Mon-Thurs: 10-8; Fri-Sat: 10-6; Sun: 12-5

Adjacent to the Bank Street College of Education—a progressive graduate school for teachers—this store is a marvelous source of books for children, as well as books *about* children, education, and parenting. It also has a great selection of tapes, videos, and CDs, plus a small section of educational toys. While the store is a little cramped and not conducive to snuggling up with a good book, the sales staff really knows its stock and cares enormously about quality children's literature. Make sure to ask about readings and other special events for children. A free monthly newsletter is available.

BARNES & NOBLE, JR.
86th St and Lexington Ave   212/427-0686
Mon-Sat: 9-9; Sun: 11-7

Although there are Barnes & Noble, Jr. locations in Barnes & Noble bookstores throughout the city (including a particularly friendly one on the second floor of the Broadway at 82nd Street location), this store is devoted entirely to kids. In addition to being a good source for children's books and book-related items, Barnes & Noble, Jr. is a great place to bring young children on a cold day to browse books and sit in on story hour.

BOOKS OF WONDER
16 W 18th St   212/989-3270, 800/345-6665
Mon-Sat: 10-7; Sun: 12-6

Owner Peter Glassman has moved his wonderful children's book store several times, most recently to this good-sized space in the bustling used and antiquarian book district. In addition to the largest selection of Oz (as in the *Wizard of*) books in the world, the store is known for frequent "Meet the Author" events, a newsletter, and a story hour for young children on Sunday mornings. Books of Wonder remains an enchanting place.

TOOTSIE'S
555 Hudson Street (bet Perry and 11th St)   212/242-0182
Mon-Fri: 9-6; Sat: 11-6; Sun: 11-5

Kathleen Murphy has created a special place for kids and parents alike. This fascinating shop specializes in books for young ones, but there is more: toys, games, puppets, and videos. Tootsie's provides play areas for toddlers, birthday parties, space for instructive classes, and meeting areas for moms and dads.

Comics

ACTION COMICS
337 E 81st St (bet First and Second Ave)   212/639-1976
Mon-Sat: 12-8; Sun: 12-6

Here you will find the best selection of comic books and more in the city. There are new comics from all publishers, collector's comics from the 1930s to the present, new and collector's sports (and non-sports) cards, new and collector's action figures, magic cards, posters, T-shirts, and collecting supplies.

ST. MARK'S COMICS
11 St. Mark's Pl (bet Second and Third Ave)   212/598-9439
Mon: 10 a.m.-11 p.m.; Tues-Sat: 10 a.m.-1 a.m.; Sun: 11-11

This unique store carries mainstream and licensed products, as well as smallpress and underground comics that are difficult to find elsewhere. They have a large selection of back issues and claim, "If it's published, we carry it." The folks here are very service-oriented and will hold selections for you. Comic-related toys, T-shirts, posters, and cards are also stocked.

SUPERSNIPE COMIC BOOK EUPHORIUM
P.O. Box 502-S, Plantarium Station, New York, NY 10024
212/580-8843
by appointment and mail order
Call Fri, Sat: 10-4:30

The ultimate comic-book emporium, Supersnipe deals only by phone and mail order. It is worth your time and trouble, however, because their stock is unequaled.

VILLAGE COMICS
214 Sullivan St (bet Bleecker and 3rd St)   212/777-2770
Mon, Tues: 10:30-7; Wed: 10:30-9; Thurs: 10:30-8:30; Fri, Sat: 10-9; Sun: 11-7

You will find just about everything for all tastes and age groups at Village Comics. There are collector's items, a large selection of videos, old and new books, limited editions, collector's cards, a large and varied adult section, a large selection of videos, model kits of comic and horror figures in resin, vinyl, and plastic, hard-to-find items, and built-up display models. Check the stores for personal appearances by authors of comics, as well as rock and film stars!

Cookbooks

CHARLOTTE F. SAFIR
1349 Lexington Ave, Apt 9B   212/534-7933
phone anytime

If you want to add to a book collection or find out more about a particular author, this lady can save you a lot of time and effort. Charlotte Safir provides a search service for out-of-print books by mail or phone only. She has a fantastic network of contacts and can locate any kind of book, although she specializes in cookbooks and children's books. There is no charge for the search. Charlotte is efficient, persistent, and a pleasure to deal with.

KITCHEN ARTS & LETTERS
1435 Lexington Ave (at 94th St)   212/876-5550
Mon: 1-6; Tues-Fri: 10-6:30; Sat: 11-6;
closed Sat in July and Aug

Cookbooks traditionally are best sellers, and with renewed interest in health, fitness, and natural foods, they are selling better than ever. It should come as no surprise that Nachum Waxman's Kitchen Arts & Letters found immediate success as a store specializing in books, literature, photography, and original art about food and its preparation. Imported books are a specialty. Waxman claims his store is the only one like it in the city and one of less than ten in the entire country. Waxman is a former editor at Harper & Row and Crown publishers, where he supervised several cookbook projects. Bitten with the urge to start a specialty bookshop, he identified a huge demand for out-of-print and original cookbooks. So while the tiny shop stocks more than 10,000 titles, as well as a gallery of photography and original art, much of the business consists of finding out-of-print and want-listed books.

Foreign

LIBRAIRIE DE FRANCE/LIBRERIA HISPANICA
Dictionary Store/Learn-a-Language Store
Rockefeller Center Promenade
610 Fifth Ave (bet 49th and 50th St)   212/581-8810
Mon-Sat: 10-6:15 (sometimes Sun)

A short stroll through Rockefeller Center Promenade takes you to this unique foreign-language bookstore, which has occupied the same location since 1934. Inside you will find an interesting collection of French magazines and newspapers, children's books, cookbooks, best sellers, greeting cards, and recorded French music. It is on the lower level, however, where most of the treasures are found. French books are available on seemingly almost every topic. There is a Spanish bookstore, as well as French and Spanish films on video, books on cassettes, a multimedia section, books and recordings for learning more than a hundred foreign languages, and a specialized foreign-language dictionary section covering engineering, medicine, business, law, and dozens of other fields. You can even arrange to rent a car for your next European trip.

NEW YORK KINOKUNIYA BOOKSTORE
10 W 49th St (at Fifth Ave)   212/765-7766
Daily: 10-7:30

Kinokuniya is Japan's largest and most esteemed bookstore chain. An American branch, located in Rockefeller Plaza, has two floors of books about Japan. The atmosphere is the closest thing to Tokyo in New York. On the first floor are 20,000 English-language books on all aspects of Japanese culture: art, cooking, travel, language, literature, history, business, economics, management techniques, martial arts, and more. The rest of the floor is rounded out with books on the same subjects written in Japanese. Comic books and Japanese stationery are sold on the second floor. Kinokuniya has the largest collection of Japanese books in the city and possibly anywhere outside of Japan.

General

BARNES & NOBLE
branches throughout Manhattan   212/807-0099
hours vary by store

For value and selection, you can't beat these folks! Barnes & Noble stores offer unexcelled opportunities for book buyers and browsers, no matter what area of the city. Generations of New York students have bought textbooks at the main store (105 Fifth Ave). Barnes & Noble has lately opened a number of magnificent superstores with enormous stocks of books (including bargain-priced remainders), comfortable shopping conveniences (including cafes), and a large selection of discounted magazines. Best of all, they continue to offer discounts on best sellers and other popular titles. Barnes and Noble, Jr. stores are targeted to children with stocks that are similarly exciting and complete.

BORDERS BOOKS AND MUSIC
5 World Trade Center (bet Church and Vesey St)   212/839-8049
Mon-Fri: 7 a.m.-8:30 p.m.; Sat: 10-8:30; Sun: 11-8:30

461 Park Ave (at 57th St)   212/980-6785
Mon-Fri: 7 a.m.-10 p.m.; Sat: 10-8; Sun: 11-8

Borders is one of the major chains in Manhattan, offering books, CDs, periodicals, places to read, and a coffee bar. The stock at Borders is wide and deep. There is plenty of well-informed help, and in-person author events draw crowds to their downtown location.

GOTHAM BOOK MART
41 W 47th St   212/719-4448
Mon-Fri: 9:30-6:30; Sat: 9:30-6

The Gotham is a New York institution founded in 1920 by the late Frances Steloff. In the early days, as is true today, there was a heavy emphasis on poetry, arts, and the theater, because those were Steloff's passions. Steloff, who could never understand how a book could be banned, once smuggled 25 first editions of Henry Miller's *Tropic of Cancer* into the country from Paris via Mexico. She developed a deep personal interest in authors and clients alike. Even as she grew older, Steloff would always make one daily visit downstairs to the shop around 2 p.m. Steloff lived to reach the century mark; her influence on this charming store will probably live on for another century. An exceptional search service is a special attraction.

MADISON AVENUE BOOKSHOP
833 Madison Ave (bet 69th and 70th St)   212/535-6130
Mon-Sat: 10-6 (closed Sat in summer)

Though smaller independent bookstores continue to disappear at an alarming rate, Madison Avenue Bookshop endures by providing highly personalized service. Knowledgeable personnel guide readers to books they might enjoy, secure out-of-print volumes, and offer the convenience of house charge accounts.

McGRAW-HILL BOOKSTORE
1221 Ave of the Americas (bet 48th and 49th St)   212/512-4100
Mon-Sat: 10-5:45

This is a well-run store that carries professional books by all publishers. Located downstairs in the McGraw-Hill Plaza (at Rockefeller Center), this huge shop is limited in fiction and general titles, but for anything published by McGraw-Hill or written with a business, technical, or scientific bent, it is excellent. One-third of their books are about computers.

RIZZOLI
31 W 57th St (bet Fifth Ave and Ave of the Americas)   212/759-2424
454 West Broadway   212/674-1616
3 World Financial Center (at Wintergarden)   212/385-1400
Mon-Sat: 9-8; Sun: 11-7

When you talk about class in the book business, Rizzoli tops the list. They have maintained an elegant atmosphere that makes a patron feel as if he or she is browsing a European library rather than a midtown Manhattan bookstore. The emphasis is on art, architecture, literature, photography, music, dance (particularly ballet), and foreign languages. There is also a good selection of paperbacks. Upstairs you will find Italian books, a music department, and children's books. Art objects are shown throughout the store.

STRAND BOOK STORE
828 Broadway (at 12th St)   212/473-1452
Mon-Sat: 9:30-10:30; Sun: 11-10:30;

Strand Book Annex
95 Fulton St (at Gold St)   212/732-6070
Mon-Fri: 9:30-9; Sat, Sun: 11-8

For book lovers, no trip to New York is complete without a visit to the Strand. This fabulous institution is the largest used bookstore (over 2.5 million volumes) in the world. For New Yorkers, the Strand is the place to start looking for that volume you must have. Outside, there are carts full of bargains. Inside, according to George Will, "the only eight miles worth saving in New York are the shelves at the Strand Book Store." These miles of books are tagged at up to 85% off list price. This enormous bookstore houses secondhand, out-of-print, and rare books at heavily discounted prices. In addition, the Strand offers thousands of new books at 50% off publisher's list price, plus a huge stock of quality remainders. In the rare book rooms, indivdual titles are priced from $10 to $100,000. There is also a fine selection of more moderately priced books, including 20th-century first editions, limited signed editions, fine bindings, and art books. The store imports English remainders, sells to libraries, sells books by the foot (supplying decorators, TV networks, and hotels), and does a booming mail-order business. Strand Book Annex, located three blocks east of Broadway, has 15,000 square feet of books, features 20-foot ceilings, and is surprisingly sunny and organized. There's even a children's reading room. Owner Fred Bass is one of the nicest and brightest individuals in the book business.

Checkmate . . .
   Chess is king here! In addition to being a chess cafe and studio, **Chess Forum** (219 Thompson St, 212/475-2369) offers the biggest selection of chess sets in the city, for both the player and collector.

TOWER BOOKS
383 Lafayette St (at 4th St)   212/228-5100
Daily: 9 a.m.-midnight

The highly successful Tower chain has lately entered the book business in a big way. Their first bookstore on the East Coast houses over 100,000 books and 1,200 periodicals, including national and international magazines. They specialize in hard-to-find literature, art, music, and pop culture. Best sellers are 30% off, while current hardcover releases are 20% off.

If you are bargain hunting or just browsing in the Chelsea area, and you feel in the need for some good food to help you with energy for *more* shopping, you might try:

Antique Cafe (101 W 25th St): good breakfasts; excellent sandwiches and salads; kid friendly

Milanes (162 W 25th St): a coffeehouse for tripe soup or try meatballs from a menu that is heavy on the esoteric

Johny's (124 W 25th St): breakfasts and lunches in a cubby-hole place; delicious pizza pita

Irish

IRISH BOOKSHOP
580 Broadway (bet Prince and Houston St, Room 1103)   212/274-1923
Mon-Fri: 11-5; Sat: 1-4

The written word has an Irish accent at this shop, which sells only new and used Irish books. They are offered in both Gaelic and English.

Military

MILITARY BOOKMAN
29 E 93rd St   212/348-1280
Tues-Sat: 10:30-5:30

The inventory here is limited to books of a military nature. Proprietors Harris and Margaretta Colt specialize in out-of-print and rare books on military, naval, and aviation history. At any given time there are 10,000 titles in stock. Topics run the gamut from Attila the Hun to atomic warfare. The Military Bookman also has a large mail-order business and a subscription mail-order catalog.

Music

JUILLIARD MUSIC ADVENTURE
60 Lincoln Center Plaza (65th St and Broadway, plaza level)
212/799-5000, ext 237
Mon-Thurs: 9:30-7:30; Fri, Sat: 10-6

With over 20,000 sheet music titles and scores in stock, this bookstore claims to carry *every* classical music book in print! But there is more: imprinted stationery and apparel, such things as conductor's batons, metronomes. historic recordings, and Juilliard music adventure software.

Mystery

MURDER INK®
2486 Broadway (bet 92nd and 93rd St)   212/362-8905
Mon-Sat: 10-7:30; Sun: 11-6

For the diehard Sherlock Holmes fan, this is the place! They have a great selection of rare mystery books, as well as signed first editions of current mysteries.

MYSTERIOUS BOOKSHOP
129 W 56th St   212/765-0900
Mon-Sat: 11-7

Otto Penzler is a Baker Street Irregular, a Sherlock Holmes fan extraordinaire (an elementary deduction!), and the Mysterious Bookshop's owner. As you might expect, the shop is friendly, and spontaneous conversation among customers is the norm. Mysterious stocks new hardcover and paperback books that deal with all types of mystery. ("But not science fiction," says the store manager. "Science fiction is not mystery.") Upstairs, via a winding circular staircase, the store branches out to the width of two buildings and is stocked floor-to-ceiling with out-of-print, used, and rare books. Amazingly, they seem to know exactly what is in stock. If it is not on the shelves, they will order it. There is as much talk as business conducted here, and you can continue the conversation with authors who sign their works from time to time in the back room. Mysterious carries *thousands* of autographed books, and several book clubs provide autographed first editions to members.

New York

CITYSTORE
1 Centre St (Municipal Bldg), north lobby   212/669-8246
Mon-Fri: 9:30-4:30

This city government bookstore has access to more than 120 official publications, all of which are dedicated to helping New Yorkers cope with their complex lives. *The Green Book* is the official directory of the city of New York, listing phone numbers and addresses of more than 900 government agencies and 6,000 officials. It includes state, federal, and international listings, as well as courts and a section on licenses. There is also a unique collection of New York memorabilia: city-seal ties, pins, and more.

Out-of-Print

ACADEMY BOOK STORE
10 W 18th St (nr Fifth Ave)   212/242-4848
Daily: 11-7

Academy Book Store houses one of New York's largest selections of used, rare, and out-of-print books. Its stock is carefully selected, and new collections are acquired weekly. Academy has been in business since 1977, offering secondhand and discounted scholarly books in all subject areas. Its stock is particularly strong in art, photography, decorative arts, architecture, philosophy, psychology, history, and music. The store also maintains a selection of antiquarian books and modern first editions. The quality and diversity of the stock make a visit to Academy a rewarding experience for the casual browser, scholar, or collector.

ARGOSY BOOK STORE
116 E 59th St   212/753-4455
Mon-Fri: 9-6; Sat: 10-5 (closed May-Sept)

Argosy is the largest out-of-print, secondhand, and rare-volume bookstore in New York. The six-story building houses a stock of books from the 16th through the 20th centuries, including modern first editions and regional American-history volumes, as well as others on art, science, and medicine. A separate autograph section includes items from a number of well-known personalities. Their print department is famous for its large collection of antique maps from all over the world, prints of every conceivable subject, and vintage posters. The stock is undeniably great, but their personnel could stand to lower their noses a little.

Photography

A PHOTOGRAPHER'S PLACE
133 Mercer St (at Prince St)   212/431-9358
Mon-Sat: 11-8; Sun: 12-6
Mail-order address: P.O. Box 274, Prince Street Station,
New York, NY 10012

Photography is an art form to Harvey Zucker and the staff of A Photographer's Place. It is not a supply shop. Rather, it pays homage to great pictures of various eras and the photographers who took them. It is claimed to be "the only all-photographic book shop in the city and, perhaps, the country." The shop excels at offering advice, inspiration, and the latest technological advances. A super catalog is free for the asking.

Rare

ALABASTER BOOKSHOP
122 Fourth Ave (bet 12th and 13th St)   212/982-3550
Mon-Sat: 10-8; Sun: 11-8

There was a time when Fourth Avenue was known as "Bookshop Row." Back then, it was *the* place for used books in Manhattan. All that has changed with the advent of superstores and the demise of smaller entrepreneurs. Well, Steve Crowley has bucked the trend, offering a great selection of used and rare books in all categories, ranging from a $2 paperback to a $1,000 first edition. Specialties include New York City, photography, and modern first editions.

BAUMAN RARE BOOKS
Waldorf-Astoria Hotel
301 Park Ave (at 50th St), lobby level   212/759-8300
Mon-Sat: 10-7

Bauman offers a fine collection of books and autographs dating from the 15th through the 20th centuries. Included are works of literature, history, economics, law, science, medicine, nature, travel, and exploration. They also provide services from designing and furnishing libraries to locating books for customers.

IMPERIAL FINE BOOKS
790 Madison Ave (bet 66th and 67th St), 2nd floor   212/861-6620
Mon-Sat: 10:30-6

If you are in the market for books that look as great as they read, Imperial is the place to visit. You will find fine leather bindings, illustrated books, vintage children's books, unique first editions, and magnificent sets of prized volumes. Their inventory includes literary giants like Twain, Dickens, Bronte, Churchill, and Shakespeare. There is also an outstanding Oriental art gallery, featuring Chinese, Japanese, and Korean ceramics and antiques. (They will purchase fine pieces.) Services include complete restoration and binding of damaged or aged books. A search office will locate titles and make appraisals.

J.N. BARTFIELD GALLERIES AND FINE BOOKS
30 W 57th St, 3rd floor   212/245-8890
Mon-Fri: 10-4; Sat: 10-3 (summer hours by appointment)

This shop is a spectacular hunting ground for lovers of fine paintings and rare books. Since 1937 they have specialized in masters of the American West and 19th- and 20th-century American paintings and sculptures. I have purchased outstanding collections of leatherbound books from them and can vouch for their expertise. First editions, sporting books, and high-quality antiquarian books are featured. Who wouldn't be excited to browse elegantly bound volumes that once graced the shelves of old family libraries?

PAGEANT PRINT AND BOOK SHOP
114 W Houston St (bet Thompson and Sullivan St)   212/674-5296
Mon-Sat: 12-8

A holdover from the days when this area was the rare- and old-book capital of the world, this shop displays and sells antiquarian books, maps, prints, and first editions from the 15th to the 20th centuries. I doubt that anyone inside could readily tell you what year it is, but the shop is as timeless as its antiquarian attitude. Pageant carries virtually every kind of printed matter. There are etchings and early printed items; it would require several days just to admire the prints. But this is a print and book shop, and the emphasis is on the latter. In the old days, this would have been one of a dozen such shops. Today, it is one of the few places left where bibliophiles can have an authentic rare book-buying experience.

Religious

CHRISTIAN PUBLICATIONS BOOK STORE
315 W 43rd St (bet Eighth and Ninth Ave)   212/582-4311
Mon-Wed: 9:30-6:45; Thurs, Fri: 9:30-7:45; Sat: 9:30-6:45

This is the largest Christian bookstore in the metropolitan area. It has over 20,000 titles in stock, along with religious CDs, tapes, videos, and church and school supplies. A large number of these items are available in Spanish, as befits the Latino neighborhood.

J. LEVINE BOOKS & JUDAICA
5 W 30th St
212/695-6888, 800/5-JEWISH (outside New York City)
Mon-Wed: 9-6; Thurs: 9-7; Fri: 9-2; Sun: 10-5 (except July)

The history of the Lower East Side is reflected in this store. Started back in 1902 on Eldridge Street, it was a fixture in the area for many years. Now J. Levine operates out of uptown, just off Fifth Avenue. Being one of the oldest Jewish bookstores in the city, Levine is a leader in the Jewish-book marketplace. They have added a second floor with many gift items, tapes, coffee-table books, and thousands of items of Judaica, though the emphasis is still on the written word. A 100-page catalog is available.

ST. PATRICK'S CATHEDRAL GIFT STORE
15 E 51st St (bet Fifth and Madison Ave)   212/753-2261
Daily: 8:30-8

Located at the rear of the grand cathedral, this store is an oasis of calm in midtown. Lovely music plays in the background as you browse displays of rosary beads, books on Catholicism, statues of saints, and related items. Proceeds of every sale benefit the cathedral. A catalog is available.

Science Fiction

FORBIDDEN PLANET
840 Broadway (at 13th St)   212/473-1576
Mon-Sat: 10-10; Sun: 10-8:30

When Mike Luckman started a science-fiction bookstore and toy shop in his native London, he quickly discovered that a good number of his customers were Americans clamoring for a similar shop at home. He thereupon designed an even more unique shop that is a shrine of science-fiction literature and artifacts. While most stock is devoted to sci-fi comic books and publications, there are also videos, posters, T-shirts, cards, toys, and games. There is seemingly at least one copy of every science-fiction title ever published.

VILLAGE COMICS & SCIENCE FICTION, HORROR, AND FANTASY SHOP
214 Sullivan St   212/777-2770
Mon-Fri: 10-7:30; Sat: 10-8; Sun: 11-7

Hardcover and softcover editions of newly published horror, sci-fi, and fantasy are carried here. They specialize in small-press releases, signed and limited editions, and out-of-print and hard-to-find books. You will also find collector's cards and display models.

Theater

APPLAUSE THEATER & CINEMA BOOKS
212 W 71st St (at Broadway)   212/496-7511
Mon-Sat: 10-8; Sun: 12-6

Quite simply, this store offers the best selection of theater and cinema books in the world. There is great interest in theater literature, and these folks are on the cutting edge. They specialize in new and out-of-print plays, film scripts, videos, and vocal scores.

DRAMA BOOK SHOP
723 Seventh Ave (bet 48th and 49th St), 2nd floor
212/944-0595, 800/322-0595
Mon-Fri: 9:30-7 (Wed: 9:30-8); Sat: 10:30-5:30; Sun: 12-5

This shop has been providing a valuable service to the performing arts community since 1923. Its stock includes a wide variety of publications dealing with theater, film, dance, music, puppetry, magic, and more. The Drama Book Shop is known for courteous and knowledgeable service, in-store and by mail.

RICHARD STODDARD—PERFORMING ARTS BOOKS
18 E 16th St (bet Fifth Ave and Union Sq), Room 305
212/645-9576
Mon, Tues, Thurs-Sat: 11-6

Richard Stoddard runs a one-man operation dedicated to rare, out-of-print, and used books, and to memorabilia relating to the performing arts. Equipped with a Ph.D. from Yale in theater history and more than 20 years of experience as a dealer and appraiser of performing arts materials, Stoddard offers a broad range of items. So while there is an extensive collection of rare books, playbills, souvenir programs, and back issues of performing-arts magazines, Stoddard also stocks a case of paperback plays within the financial reach of the most impoverished actor. There is a similar table of bargain books. Stoddard's pride is his collection of original scenic and costume designs. The sole agent for the estate of Jo Mielziner, an esteemed Broadway designer, Stoddard is also in possession of the drawings of a half-dozen other set designers. In fact, this is the only shop in the country that regularly sells such designs.

Travel

COMPLETE TRAVELLER BOOKSTORE
199 Madison Ave (at 35th St)   212/685-9007
Mon-Fri: 9-7; Sat: 10-6; Sun: 11-5

Planning to travel? Harriet Greenberg offers contemporary guides, maps, and language aids, plus the kind of personal service not often found in bookstores anymore.

Butterflies

MARIPOSA, THE BUTTERFLY GALLERY
South Street Seaport, Pier 17   212/233-3221
Daily: 10-9

At Mariposa, butterflies are regarded as art. Marshall Hill is a renowned designer in this unusual medium. Butterflies are unique, and Mariposa (the Spanish word for butterfly) displays them separately, in panels, and in groups. There are even butterfly farms, which breed and raise butterflies. They live their full one-month life spans under ideal conditions for creating this art.

Buttons

GORDON BUTTON COMPANY
222 W 38th St (near Seventh Ave)   212/921-1684
Mon-Fri: 9-5

Peter Gordon's extensive collection of elegant, unusual, and antique buttons is fascinating, but I would mainly come to Gordon for new buttons. The enormous stock is of such high quality that Gordon's is patronized by neighboring garment manufacturers. Belt buckles, chains, and brass rings are also sold at excellent discounts. Mail orders are accepted. Courtesy is the byword. Most garment-center manufacturers cannot be bothered with small retail customers, and their attention tends to vary in direct proportion to the size of an order. But at Gordon, the size of the order is irrelevant.

TENDER BUTTONS
143 E 62nd St   212/758-7004
Mon-Fri: 11-6; Sat: 11-5:30

Owner Millicent Safro has assembled a retail button store that is complete in variety as well as size. One antique wooden display cabinet shows off Tender Buttons' selection of original buttons, many imported or made exclusively for them. There are buttons of pearl, wood, horn, Navajo silver, leather, ceramics, bone, ivory, pewter, and precious stones. Many are antiques. Some are as highly valued as artwork; a French enamel button, for instance, can cost almost as much as a painting! Unique pieces can be made into special cuff links—real conversation pieces for the lucky owner. They also have a fine collection of antique and period cuff links and men's stud sets. A cuff-links buff, I have purchased some of my best pieces from this shop.

Candles

CANDLE SHOP
118 Christopher St (bet Bleecker and Hudson St)   212/989-0148
                                                    888/823-4823

Mon-Thurs: 12-8; Fri, Sat: 12-9; Sun: 1-7

Thomas Alva Edison's inventions haven't made a flicker of an imprint on the folks at the Candle Shop. They have assembled a collection of beeswax, paraffin, and stearin candles in an assortment of sizes and colors. It's positively illuminating to learn that candles are available in so many configurations! The shop also carries candle holders and accessories, oil lamps, and incense.

CANDLE THERAPY
213 W 80th St (bet Amsterdam Ave and Broadway)   212/799-3000
Tues-Sun: 2-8

OTHER WORLDLY WAXES
131 E 7th St (bet Ave A and First Ave)   212/260-9188
Tues-Sun: 2-10

These two interesting stores are sister outfits, owned by the same people. You'll find scented candles, aromatherapy products, handmade incense, and blended oils. They also offer spiritual advice, promising that their candles "merge psychological goals with whatever spiritual framework you have." Here's a sampling of the properties associated with their oils and incense: "Cleopatra" (balm of Gilead) is a secret weapon of seduction, while "Vavoom" (coconut) promises big-time sex appeal and flair. Who knows? A visit here might change your whole life! Ask for Catherine Riggs-Bergesen, who is a practicing clinical psychologist.

China, Glassware

Big Names in Tabletop

Baccarat (625 Madison Ave)
Buccellati (46 E 57th St)
Cartier (653 Fifth Ave)
Christofle (680 Madison Ave)
Daum Boutique (694 Madison Ave)
Lalique Boutique (680 Madison Ave)
Orrefors and **Kosta Boda** (58 E 57th St)
Royal Copenhagen/Georg Jensen (683 Madison Ave)
Villeroy & Boch (974 Madison Ave)

CRATE & BARREL
650 Madison Ave (at 59th St)   212/308-0011
Mon-Fri: 10-8; Sat: 10-7; Sun: 12-6

Even if you aren't in the market for china, glassware, bedroom furnishings, or casual furniture, the displays here will make shopping hard to resist. First, the place is loaded with attractive, quality merchandise at sensible prices. Second, it is fixtured magnificently, with every item shown to best advantage. Third, the lighting and signing are masterfully done. Finally, the store layout and number of check-out stands make for quick work in completing a sale. These folks are professional merchants in the best sense of the word.

FISHS EDDY
889 Broadway   212/420-9020
2176 Broadway   212/873-8819
Mon-Sat: 10-9; Sun: 11-8

Besides being treasure troves for bargain hunters, these shops are fun to browse for some of the most unusual china and glassware items available anywhere. Everything is made in America, and the stock changes on a regular basis. For young people setting up a new residence or a business looking for unique pieces, try Fishs Eddy first.

LANAC SALES
500 Driggs Ave, Brooklyn   718/782-7200, 800/522-0047
Mon-Thurs: 9-6; Fri: 9-2; Sun: 10-5

Lanac is a great source for chinaware, jewelry, paintings, cut glass, silverware, and gifts at discount prices. They offer excellent discounts on everything in stock, including some of the finest domestic and imported tableware and crystal in the city. A computerized bridal registry is available.

MIKASA HOME STORE
30 W 23rd St (bet Fifth Ave and Ave of the Americas)   212/206-3766
Mon-Wed: 10-7; Thurs-Sat: 10-8; Sun: 12-6

The name Mikasa means real quality china, crystal, and other types of giftware. This outlet is company owned, and prices on Mikasa products are up to 60% less than elsewhere. They also carry an assortment of linens, flatware, and furniture accessory pieces. This is a special place for Christmas shopping!

Clothing and Accessories

Antique/Vintage

ANTIQUE BOUTIQUE
712-714 Broadway (at Washington Pl)   212/460-8830
Mon-Sat: 11-9; Sun: 12-8

Both vintage and new clothing are featured at this hip boutique. This is the place to find recently recycled clothing, as opposed to something from the Victorian period. You will see wedding dresses from the 1940s, a big selection of used Levi jeans, suede jackets, and incredible sweaters. Prices reflect the fact that these clothes are not one-of-a-kind antiques.

FAN CLUB
22 W 19th St (bet Fifth Ave and Ave of the Americas)   212/929-3349
Tues-Sat: 12-6 (Sun and Mon by appointment)

You won't find a more exciting collection of vintage clothing, film and opera costumes, and bridal gowns than at Fan Club. Broadway theater addicts will discover some great glamour gowns here for rent or re-sale.

HARRIET LOVE
126 Prince St   212/966-2280
Daily: 11-7

Harriet Love is on the front line in the field of "new with retrofeel" apparel and accessories. Her shop overflows with beautiful purses, sweaters, jackets, and jewelry. Harriet also buys from vendors who interpret vintage pieces to create new treasures that have a classic feeling.

JEAN HOFFMAN ANTIQUES
207 E 66th St   212/535-6930
Tues-Fri: 12-6; Sat: 12-5; also by special appointment

Jean Hoffman offers one of the best selections of quality vintage items in the city. She has an extensive collection of fine lace, trims, parasols, shawls, linens, jewelry, evening bags, paisleys, and textiles, plus antique gifts of silver and brass for dressing table, dining room, and desk. All kinds of vintage clothing is available, too. For the bride-to-be who wants something special, the stock of antique wedding gowns, veils, and accessories is unequaled.

REMINISCENCE
50 W 23rd St (bet Fifth Ave and Ave of the Americas)   212/243-2292
Mon-Sat: 10:30-7:30; Sun: 12-7

It's fun to revisit the 1960s and 1970s at this hip emporium, created by Stewart Richer on lower Fifth Avenue. Although he is a child of this era, most of Richer's customers are between the ages of 13 and 30. The finds here are unusual and wearable, with large selections of colorful vintage clothing and attractive displays of jewelry, hats, gifts, and accessories. Richer's goods, although vintage in style, are mostly new, and the company has become a manufacturer that sells to outlets all over the world. Because of its vast distribution, Richer is able to produce large quantities and sell at low prices.

SCREAMING MIMI'S
382 Lafayette St   212/677-6464
Mon-Fri: 12-8; Sat: 12-8; Sun: 12-6

Laura Wills presides over this shop, which features styles for men and women from the 1940s through the 1970s, as well as more contemporary merchandise. There are vintage housewares; an excellent showing of handbags, shoes, and lingerie; and a good selection of sportswear. A gift department offers new and vintage items, including a great selection of unique New York souvenirs. Everyone agrees this is a fun place to shop!

TRASH AND VAUDEVILLE
4 St. Mark's Pl (bet Second and Third Ave)   212/982-3590
Mon-Thurs: 12-8; Fri: 11:30-8:30; Sat: 11:30-9; Sun: 1-7:30

This place is hard to pin down, since the stock changes constantly and seems to have no boundaries. Trash & Vaudeville describes its stock as punk clothing, accessories, and original designs. "Punk clothing" means rock and roll styles from the 1950s to the 1990s, including outrageous footwear. They also carry new clothing from Europe.

WHAT COMES AROUND GOES AROUND
351 West Broadway (bet Broome and Grand St)   212/343-9303
Daily: 11-8 (summer 11-11)

This store sold a pair of 1890 Levi's for $25,000! If you are looking for vintage clothing, here is a good place to start. This shop with the clever name offers one of the nation's largest collections of vintage clothing, with Levis, denim, and leather its specialties. They are also in the market to buy at all times.

For one of the best selections of 1960s and 1970s designer vintage clothing, try **Resurrection Vintage Clothing** at 217 Mott Street and 123 E 7th Street.

Bridal

HERE COMES THE BRIDESMAID . . .
326 E 11th St (bet First and Second Ave)   212/674-3231
Tues-Thurs: 2-8; Sat, Sun: 11-5, by appointment only

After walking down the aisle as a bridesmaid in 13 weddings, Stephanie

Harper decided it was time that bridesmaids had a store of their own offering a decent selection. Her establishment carries gowns from Vera Wang, Nicole Miller, Jim Hjelm, and others. She also features gowns that can be hemmed and worn again to occasions other than weddings. Weekend hours make "Here Comes the Bridesmaid" especially convenient for working women, but be sure to call ahead for an appointment.

SIZE COMPARISON CHART FOR CLOTHES

Children's clothing

American	3	4	5	6	6x
Continental	98	104	110	116	122
British	18	20	22	24	26

Children's shoes

American	8	9	10	11	12	13	1	2	3
Continental	24	25	27	28	29	30	32	33	34
British	7	8	9	10	11	12	13	1	2

Women's dresses, coats and skirts

American	3	5	7	9	11	12	13	14	15	16	18
Continental	36	38	38	40	40	42	42	44	44	46	48
British	8	10	11	12	13	14	15	16	17	18	20

Women's blouses and sweaters

American	10	12	14	16	18	20
Continental	38	40	42	44	46	48
British	32	34	36	38	40	42

Women's stockings

American	8	8½	9	9½	10	10½
Continental	1	2	3	4	5	6
British	8	8½	9	9½	10	10½

Women's shoes

American	5	6	7	8	9	10
Continental	36	37	38	39	40	41
British	3½	4½	5½	6½	7½	8½

Men's suits

American	34	36	38	40	42	44	46	48
Continental	44	46	48	50	52	54	56	58
British	34	36	38	40	42	44	46	48

Men's shirts

American	14	15	15½	16	16½	17	17½	18
Continental	37	38	39	41	42	43	44	45
British	14	15	15½	16	16	17	17½	18

Men's shoes

American	7	8	9	10	11	12	13
Continental	39½	41	42	43	44½	46	47
British	6	7	8	9	10	11	12

KLEINFELD
8202 Fifth Ave, Brooklyn   718/833-1100
Tues, Thurs: 11-9; Wed, Fri: 10-6; Sat: 9-6
(call for an appointment or Sun hours)

The bridal business has changed a great deal. Today there are very limited collections at some specialty stores (like Bergdorf and Saks), but there is only one true bridal complex. I use the word *complex* because there are seven separate buildings here. The bridal gown collection has 800 to 1,000 styles in stock at all times. Yes, I know this is a book about Manhattan, but no store can match Kleinfeld. The mother of the bride will find a special section called Kleinfeld's P.M., which specializes in evening wear. Kleinfeld carries every major name in bridal wear and accessories, including Amsale, Caroline Herara, and Scassi. One-fifth of the collection is of international origin. The store operates by appointment and can handle over a hundred customers a day with their specialized personnel. This is the place to come when wedding bells will soon be ringing.

TATI
475 Fifth Ave (bet 40th and 41st St)   212/481-TATI, 800/839-TATI
Mon-Wed, Fri: 10-6; Thurs: 10-8; Sat: 10-6; Sun: 11-6

Aptly called the "bridal superstore from France," Tati provides one-stop shopping for brides. Here you will find gowns for all members of the wedding party, as well as accessories, lingerie, and shoes. All merchandise is off the rack, with no waiting for gowns. Nothing is priced over $600. In-house alterations are offered for an extra charge. It is easy to see why this 50-year-old outfit dresses one-fifth of the brides in France!

VERA WANG
991 Madison Ave (at 77th St)   212/628-3400
Mon-Sat: 9-6

Vera Wang is considered one of the top bridal designers in the nation, and this is her only salon. Be prepared for beautiful styles that are priced accordingly. Wedding gowns start at about $2,500, and most are priced in the $3,000-$5,000 range. Exclusive evening-wear designs may be purchased off the rack.

Children's—General

Before I describe what I consider to be the best selection of children's clothing stores in New York, let me be clear about what I'm not including: big chains and haughty boutiques. That is not to say some of the national chains don't have great stores here. **Baby Gap** (341 Columbus Ave), **Gymboree** (1120 Madison Ave and other locations), **Oshkosh B'Gosh** (586 Fifth Ave), and **Oilily** (870 Madison Ave) are all fine outlets. But unlike the stores listed below, they sell very little that you can't buy in any other city in America. As for the haughty boutiques, I see no reason to patronize these wildly overpriced and unwelcoming places, which line Madison Avenue and are sprouting up in other parts of town.

AIDA'S & JIMI'S MERCHANDISING COMPANY
41 W 28th St (bet Broadway and Ave of the Americas)
212/689-2415
Mon-Fri: 9:30-6; Sat: 10-3

Young ladies will love this place, and so will their mothers: Aida and Jimi feature better girls' dresses from infant to preteen. You may also find boys' wear from toddler to size 7 and ladies' samples in sizes 5/6, 7/8, and 9/10. All merchandise is discounted.

BOMBALULU'S
101 W 10th St (at Ave of the Americas)   212/463-0897
Daily: 11-7

332 Columbus Ave (bet 75th and 76th St)   212/501-8248
Daily: 11-7

Owned by the same people who make much of the cheerful and durable clothing sold here, these little stores are packed with wonderful, one-of-a-kind designs for infants and children (although both the service and the selection at the 10th St location is consistently better). If batik rompers, colorful hand-knit sweaters, great hats, fun T-shirts, and snowsuits from Bali (yes, Bali) are to your taste, look around or talk to the owners about placing a special order. Bombalulu's also has a good selection of well-made toys and puzzles.

BU AND THE DUCK
106 Franklin St (bet Church St and West Broadway)
212/431-9226
Mon-Sat: 10-7

If money is no object and style is a priority for your young child, this new children's clothing store on a quiet street in Tribeca ought to be near the top of your list. The owner, clothing designer Susan Lang, is on a mission to replace pink and blue with darker colors and interesting textures. Many of the items in this spacious store are unisex, and none is mass produced. Unlike many of the chic new children's boutiques opening up all over downtown these days, Bu and the Duck happens to be a pleasant, kid-friendly place to shop.

CHOCOLATE SOUP
946 Madison Ave (bet 74th and 75th St)   212/861-2210
Mon-Sat: 10-6

Chocolate Soup features a special infant department for newborns to two years, an expanded children's sweater collection for infants to size 14, and also some adult sizes. An uncommon collection of handmade toys, dolls, quilts, pillows, and rugs are on display, along with special hats, T-shirts and leggings.

CO2
284 Columbus Ave (near 74th St)   212/721-4966
Daily: 12:30-6

You can see them coming from inside the store: hip pre-teen and early teenage girls making a beeline for their favorite West Side clothing store. Sizes run from 6 to 16. Stretchy and sleek are the watchwords here, with (at least while they're hot) lots of black, gray, and faux animal-skin designs.

G.C. WILLIAMS
1137 Madison Ave (near 84th St)   212/396-3400
Mon-Sat: 10-6:30; Sun: 12-5

If your preteen or teenager wants to be hip, but you want him or her to dress a bit more classic and conservative, this is the perfect compromise. The clothes—from size 6 to 16 for girls, 6 to 20 for boys—are mostly European, the fabrics are beautiful, and the designs are stylish but not over-the-top. Another plus: unlike other popular stores for kids this age, G.C. Williams is well organized, spacious, and inviting to moms.

JACADI
1281 Madison Avenue (at 91st St)   212/369-1616
787 Madison Ave (at 67th St)   212/535-3200
Mon-Sat: 10-6 (Thurs to 7); Sun: 12-5

If you're in the market for upscale French clothing for infants and children, this is the most pleasant and welcoming of the many Madison Avenue boutiques. They carry beautiful, almost doll-like clothing for infants through size 12 (14 in some cases) and are especially known for coordinated outfits that include everything down to hats and tights. They also carry shoes and a full line of baby furniture. Look for particularly good sales in January and June.

KIDS ARE MAGIC
2293 Broadway (bet 82nd and 83rd St)   212/875-9240
Mon-Wed: 10-7:45; Thurs-Sat: 10-8:45; Sun: 10-6:45

Some New York parents think that prices on baby, toddler, and preschooler (newborn through size 6) "basics"—onesies, T-shirts, pants, sweatshirts, and the like—are better here than anywhere else in the city. The prices on diapers and some toys for small children are also excellent. The displays aren't exciting, the service is disinterested, and the size selection—which goes up to 20 for boys and 14 for girls—is sometimes spotty. But if you're stocking up and don't care about designer labels, Kids Are Magic is definitely worth a stop.

LILLIPUT
265 Lafayette St (bet Spring and Prince St)   212/965-9567
Tues-Sat: 11-7; Sun-Mon: 12-6

Children's clothing stores in New York's hot shopping neighborhoods have multiplied in recent years, and a lot of them start to look alike after awhile. Sometimes a good buyer with a sharp eye can set a store apart, however. Lilliput does have the feel of a lot of other relatively upscale children's stores, and some of what you'll find here is neither unusual nor well-priced. But look a little closer and you'll see certain items that make a trip here worthwhile. In addition to a wide and varied selection of infant clothes, Lilliput has a great shoe selection, unusual accessories, and a diverse range of clothes for young children (through size 16).

MARSHA D.D.
1324 Lexington Ave (bet 88th and 89th St)   212/534-8700 (girls)
Mon-Sat: 10-6 (Thurs to 7)   212/876-9922 (boys)

At Marsha D.D., boys and girls now have separate stores in the same building. Owner Marsha Drogin Dayan has "in" clothing for the younger set. The girls' store has clothing and accessories appropriate for ages 7 to 15, including items for hard-to-fit youngsters. The boys' emporium carries items for pre-teens aged 7 to 13 in sizes from 8 to 20. You'll find yo-yos, trading cards, novelties, watches, and popular clothing lines, along with logo'ed Knicks and Yankees apparel.

MORRIS BROS.
2322 Broadway (at 84th St)   212/724-9000
Mon-Sat: 9:30-6:30; Sun: 12-5:30

You can't be a parent or kid on the Upper West Side and not know about Morris Bros. Whether you're looking for a backpack, hat, umbrella, tights, pajamas, jeans, underwear, or clothes for gym class, this is the place to go. This is a good source for basic kids' clothing and accessories at decent prices.

PEANUTBUTTER & JANE
617 Hudson St (at 12th St)   212/620-7952
Mon-Sat: 10:30-7; Sun: 12-6

A friend describes this store as "very Village." In addition to a varied and fun selection of clothing, it carries funky things like ruby slippers for children, leather jackets for toddlers, and wonderfully imaginative dress-up clothes. Indeed, almost everything here is unique to the store. Unlike a lot of children's clothing stores in which older children wouldn't be caught dead, Peanutbutter & Jane appeals both to teenagers and their younger siblings.

Children's — Used

GOOD-BYES
230 E 78th St   212/794-2301
Mon-Fri: 12-5; Tues-Fri: 11:30-5:30; Sat: 11-5

This comfortable, inviting little place on a largely residential street is still a relative newcomer to the children's consignment scene. In addition to clothing (up to size 8, although the focus is on younger ones), Good-Byes carries strollers, car seats, bassinets, toys, and the whole range of things that go along with having a baby or small children. Everything is in good condition, the service is very personal and attentive, and the prices are a fraction of those at retail stores. If you're interested in selling clothing or equipment, call first for an appointment. Good-Byes gives 40% of the selling price on clothing and 50% on equipment that's accepted.

SECOND ACT CHILDREN'S WEAR
1046 Madison Ave (bet 79th and 80th St)   212/988-2440
Tues-Sat: 9-5

This is the dean of children's consignment shops! Don't be put off by the hard time you may have finding this store (it's on the second floor, and you must be buzzed in), the dingy walk up to it, or the disinterested greeting that's extended when you arrive, because the selection and bargains are well worth the effort. Every square inch of the mazelike rooms of Second Act are jammed with everything imaginable: shirts, pants, belts, suits, party dresses, shoes, boots, skates, sweaters, jackets, ballet slippers, cowboy boots, and even videos, toys, and books. Take time to look around, and take cash. Do not, however, take kids. Everything is at least a third to half off its original price. If you're interested in selling clothes (they offer 40% of the selling price), call first for an appointment.

Costumes

ABRACADABRA
19 W 21st St   212/627-5194
Mon-Sat: 11-7; Sun: 12-5 (extended hours in Oct)

Here they can transform you into almost anything! They rent and sell costumes, provide theme-oriented needs, offer costume accessories, magician's supplies, theatrical makeup, and stock props for magic tricks. It is a gagster's heaven! Free magic shows are given on Saturday and Sunday afternoons.

HALLOWEEN ADVENTURE
104 Fourth Ave (bet 11th and 12th St)   212/673-4546
Mon-Sat: 11-8; Sun: 12-7 (extended hours at Halloween time)

Your kids will be the talk of the neighborhood after a visit here. You'll find wigs, costumes for adults and kids, hats, gags, magic items, props, and all manner of games and novelties. In addition, a professional makeup artist is available most of the time.

Dance Wear

CAPEZIO
1650 Broadway (at 51st St)   212/245-2130

CAPEZIO EAST
136 E 61st St (at Lexington Ave)   212/758-8833

CAPEZIO (CHILDREN'S)
1651 Third Ave (bet 92nd and 93rd St)   212/348-7210

Open seven days a week

Capezio stores are definitive outlets for dance, theater, and fitness paraphernalia. The shop on Broadway is the largest dance-theater retail store in the world. There is a special section for men, in addition to departments for ballet companies and theatrical shows. Capezio East reflects the East Side neighborhood.

FREED OF LONDON
922 Seventh Ave (at 58th St)   212/489-1055, 800/835-1701
Mon-Sat: 10-6 (phone orders: 10-4)

The venerable English establishment Freed of London has exported a tradition of supplying the best and finest dance supplies to its New York franchise. There is virtually no piece of dance gear Freed does not stock or cannot order. The store has leotards, skirts, dresses, tutus, and leg warmers, as well as ballet, jazz, tap, ballroom, character, and flamenco shoes. A list of the shop's clientele reads like a "who's who" of internationally known dance stars. The store carries the complete line of regulation wear for the Royal Academy of Dancing. For those who can't stop by, a measuring chart and mail-order catalog are available. For dancers, this store is a must.

Furs

FURS BY DIMITRIOS
130 W 30th St (bet Ave of the Americas and Seventh Ave)
212/695-8469
Mon-Fri: 9-6; Sat, Sun: 10-4

This store is the best source for men's fur coats at wholesale prices. The racks are shaggy with furs of all descriptions and sizes for both genders. Prices are wholesale but go up slightly if the garment has to be specially ordered. This shouldn't be necessary, though, since the high quality off-the-rack selection is the most extensive in the city.

G. MICHAEL HENNESSY FURS
345 Seventh Ave (bet 29th and 30th St), 5th floor   212/695-7991
Mon-Fri: 9:30-5; Sat: by appointment

When you buy a fur, you need to be sure of the people from whom you are buying. They must be reliable, honest, knowledgeable, and have the proper stock. This firm strongly fits the mold. Michael Hennessy started as an international fur trader, ran a salon in Beverly Hills, and later became fur director of Bonwit Teller and president of Maximilian Furs. His talented and charming wife Rubye is a former fashion editor. These folks manufacture high-quality designer furs for women that are sold to stores around the world. These items are available direct to the public at great values. Best prices are for in-stock furs, particularly the house specialty mink. Wonderful buys are available for ladies who want a made-to-order mink coat or fur-lined raincoat. Hennessy has the only license in the world for Givenchy furs. European ladies on the best-dressed list come to this showroom for their Givenchys. If you are in the market for a sable, Hennessy is also one of the world's top sable specialists. Large-size furs and cashmere-with-fur coats, exclusive shearlings for men and women, more classy men's furs, and fabulous lightweight mink coats and jackets are other specialties. Hundreds of my readers have been well taken care of by Rubye and Michael.

GUS GOODMAN
345 Seventh Ave (bet 29th and 30th St), 16th floor   212/244-7422
Mon-Fri: 10-6; Sat: 10-2 (Sat by appointment in summer)

Since 1918, the Goodmans have been creating fine fur styles. Now father Gus and sons David and Mark are carrying on the family tradition, offering a quality collection of fur-lined and reversible fur coats and jackets for both men and women. An unusually complete selection of outerwear fabrics is available: silk, poplin, microfiber, ultrasuede, leather, and cashmere. The cashmere collection, some trimmed with fur, is special. If you have a musty old fur coat in the closet, these folks can bring it back to life with a trendy design. Goodman has a full-time designer on staff and specializes in custom designs.

HARRIS FURS
333 Seventh Ave (at 29th St), 2nd floor   212/563-0079, 212/563-0080
210 W 29th St (bet Seventh and Eighth Ave)
Mon-Fri: 9-5:30; Sat: 9-4; Sun: 9-3 (closed July)

To have been in business for nearly a century means you must be doing something right. Harris furs, leathers, and shearlings are all excellent quality items at very acceptable prices. One of the best reasons to shop here is that most every frame—large or small, thin or plump—can be fitted. Harris also provides free alterations.

HARRY KIRSHNER AND SON
307 Seventh Ave (bet 27th and 28th St)   212/243-4847
Mon-Fri: 9-6; Sat: 10-5

Kirshner should be one of your first stops for any kind of fur product, from throw pillows to full-length mink coats. They re-line, clean, alter, and store any fur at rock-bottom prices. They are neither pushy nor snobbish. Harry Kirshner offers tours of the factory, and if nothing appeals to a customer, a staff member will design a coat to specifications. Often, however, the factory offers a collection of secondhand furs that have been restored to perfect and fashionable condition. Many customers come in for a new fur and walk out with a slightly worn one for a fraction of what they expected to spend.

RITZ FURS
107 W 57th St (bet Ave of the Americas and Seventh Ave)
212/265-4559
Mon-Sat: 9-6 (closed Sat in July); Sun: 11-5 (Nov-Jan only)

For luxurious furs at affordable prices, no one beats the Ritz! Famous for great prices for over half a century, the Ritz is New York's department store for fur. They offer an ever-changing variety of one-of-a-kind designer furs, luxurious shearlings, and fur-lined and fur-trimmed outerwear. In addition, the Ritz has one of New York's largest selections of previously owned luxury furs at good savings. Styles run from contemporary to classic, fun to funky, and include mink, sable, fox, lynx, and more. The Ritz takes gently used furs on consignment and occasionally buys them outright. The experienced, multilingual sales staff offers personal service.

Hosiery

FOGAL
680 Madison Ave (bet 61st and 62nd St)   212/759-9782

510 Madison Ave (at 53rd St)   212/355-3254
Mon-Wed, Fri, Sat: 10-6:30; Thurs: 10-8

Before Fogal came to New York from Switzerland, the thought of a Madison Avenue boutique devoted to hosiery was, well, foreign. But since opening in 1982, it's hard to imagine Manhattan without it. If it's fashionable and different leg wear you're after, Fogal has it. Plain hosiery comes in over 82 hues, at last count; the designs and patterns make the number of choices almost incalculable. You might say that Fogal has a leg up on the competition! Also carried at Fogal are lingerie, bodywear, swimwear, and men's hose.

LOUIS CHOCK
74 Orchard St   212/473-1929
Sun-Thurs: 9-5; Fri: 9-1

It's hard to find a classification for this store. It seems to stock a little of everything, but perhaps the old-fashioned term "dry goods" sums up the stock sold here. Louis Chock sells dry goods for the home, school, and entire family from some of the nation's best: Berkshire, Burlington, Carter's, Calvin Klein, Hanes, Duofold, and Munsingwear. They specialize in hosiery and underwear. Children's nightwear is available in a large choice of colors and sizes, and there is something in the hosiery section for every member of the family. Furthermore, everything in the store is sold at a discount that begins at 25%. An even larger discount is given on items bought in quantity. Louis Chock also has a mail-order department, offering a 25% to 30% discount on everything in stock. A catalog can be obtained for $2 (refundable with first order).

M. STEUER HOSIERY COMPANY
31 W 32nd St (nr Fifth Ave)   212/563-0052
Mon-Fri: 7:45-5:20

By walking one block from Herald Square, hosiery buyers can save a bundle.

STORES

M. Steuer is a wholesale operation that treats each retail customer as a wholesaler, no matter how small the order. They even speak a half-dozen languages—the better to welcome visitors to New York. They stock a huge inventory of name-brand hosiery, socks, pantyhose, and dance wear, and will fill unusual requests with aplomb.

Jeans

CANAL JEAN COMPANY
504 Broadway (off Spring St)   212/226-1130
Daily: 9:30-9

From the moment you walk past the exciting window displays, you know this is no ordinary store. Canal Jean buys and sells the latest Soho styles and has made itself a popular place. The looks are certainly casual. Even their best new clothing stretches the meaning of sportswear, but if it's motorcycle jackets and brightly colored pants, tops, and outfits you want, this is the place to shop. A large number of customers are Europeans and Japanese who stock up on as many pairs of jeans as they can hoard in their suitcases and backpacks. Other clothing items include outdoor outfits, beautiful new clothing done in vintage styles, and military surplus—all at low prices.

Leather

BARBARA SHAUM
60 E 4th St   212/254-4250
Wed-Fri: 1-8; Sat: 1-6

Barbara Shaum does magical things with leather. She's a wonder with sandals, bags, sterling-silver buckles, belts (with handmade brass, nickel-silver, inlaid wood, and copper buckles), jewelry, attaché cases, and briefcases. Everything is designed in the shop, and Shaum meticulously crafts each item using only the finest materials. She is regularly featured in leading fashion magazines.

Men's and Women's—General

Jeffrey Kalinsky, who received his retail training at Barneys' and operates a store in the south (Jeffrey-Atlanta), is now in lower Manhattan. In the former headquarters of the National Biscuit Company, Kalinsky is treating folks in the Meatpacking District to top fashion names at **Jeffrey-New York** (449 W 14th St). The store offers men's and women's clothing and accessories (with an emphasis on shoes), showcasing top labels like Gucci, Manolo Blahnik, Ferragamo, Helmut Lang, Jill Sander, Balenciaga, and many more. This entrepreneur's specialty is personal service, with Kalinsky serving both as buyer and personal salesman.

AVIREX, THE COCKPIT
595 Broadway (bet Houston and Prince St)   212/925-5455
Mon-Sat: 11-7; Sun: 12:30-6

This is a fascinating store for anyone interested in flying. A fabulous collection of flight jackets, varsity leather jackets, motorcycle jackets, T-shirts, coveralls, sweaters, insignias, watches, bags, flight suits, and gift items are displayed to create an attractive aviational atmosphere.

CASHMERE-CASHMERE
969 Madison Ave (bet 75th and 76th St)   212/988-5252
Mon-Sat: 10-6

At this shop, every possible type of cashmere clothing from all over the world is available. Weights vary, making it possible to wear cashmere year-round. The styles vary as well, reflecting different lifestyles. There's clothing for men and women, as well as cashmere accessories for the home. A visit here will make cashmere a necessity in one's life!

Cashmere is in!

Berk (781 Madison Ave)
Best of Scotland (581 Fifth Ave)
Cashmere-Cashmere (595 Madison Ave and 840 Madison Ave)
Loro Piana (46 E 61st St)
Malo (791 Madison Ave)
Tse (827 Madison Ave)

DAFFY'S
111 Fifth Ave (at 18th St)   212/529-4477
Mon-Sat: 10-9; Sun: 12-7

335 Madison Ave (at 44th St)   212/557-4422
Mon-Fri: 8-8; Sat, Sun: 10-6:30

1311 Broadway (at 34th St)   212/736-4477
Mon-Fri: 10-9; Sat: 10-8; Sun: 11-6

135 E 57th St (bet Lexington and Park Ave)   212/376-4477
Mon-Fri: 10-8; Sat: 10-7; Sun: 12-6

Daffy's describes itself as a bargain clothing outlet for millionaires. Since a lot of folks got to be millionaires by saving money, perhaps they have something going for them. Great bargains can be found here in better clothing (including unusual European imports) for men, women, and children. Fine leather items are a specialty. This is not your usual "off-price" store, as they have done things with a bit of flair.

FILENE'S BASEMENT
2220-26 Broadway (at 79th St)   212/873-8000
Mon-Sat: 10-9; Sun: 11-6
18th St and Ave of the Americas   212/620-3100
Mon-Sat: 9:30-9; Sun: 11-6

Anyone who has shopped in Boston knows the name Filene's Basement, recognized for many years for outstanding bargains. Well, Filene's is also in New York, offering great bargains in brand-name goods for misses and men. The store claims 30% to 60% savings. Sometimes it's more and sometimes less, but you can always depend on the quality. The store is easy to shop in, and there are huge stocks of merchandise in every category.

OTTO PERL HOUSE OF MAURIZIO
18 E 53rd St, 5th floor   212/759-3230
Mon-Fri: 9-5

Tony Maurizio caters to men and women who like the functional and fashionable tailored look of suits. Although they can copy almost any kind of garment, this house is known for coats, two- to four-piece suits, and mix-and-match combinations. This look is favored by busy executives, artists, and journalists who have to look well-dressed but don't have hours to spend dressing. They create blazers or suits in a range of 2,000 fabrics, and those in silk, linen, cotton, and solid virgin wool are sensational. In addition to women's garments, Tony can design and create coats and suits for men in the same broad range of fabrics. He promises fast service, expert tailoring, and moderate prices.

OUT OF OUR CLOSET
136 W 18th St (bet Ave of the Americas and Seventh Ave)
Mon-Sat:12-7; Sun: 12-6   212/633-6965

If you have your heart set on some designer outfit a favorite TV star wore, head down to Out of Our Closet and see if they have it hanging on their racks. If they do, the price will be about a third of what the star paid. This goes for men, too! A tailor is on the premises. A nice feature: all leftover goods go to the Housingworks Thrift Shop.

POLO RALPH LAUREN
867 Madison Ave (at 72nd St)   212/606-2100
Mon-Sat: 10-6; Thurs: 10-8

Ralph Lauren has captured the mood of the times, and I admit to being a fan. He has probably done as much as anyone to bring a classic look to American fashion and furnishings. His showcase store in Manhattan, housed in the magnificent remodeled Rhinelander mansion, is fabulous. Four floors of merchandise for men, women, and the home are beautifully displayed and expertly accessorized. You will see a much larger selection here than in the many specialty Polo boutiques in department stores. There are several things to be aware of, however. One is the above-it-all way some of the staff greet customers who don't look like they have big bucks to spend. Moreover, although the clothes and furnishings are stylish and classy, one can find items of equal or better quality elsewhere at considerably lower price. But shopping elsewhere is not nearly as stylish as carrying your item out in one of those popular green bags. That little monogrammed horse says something about your taste and lifestyle! Polo Sport, also done with class and flair, is across the street.

Good Deals!

Discount clothes shopping for men and women has recently gotten better in Manhattan! Wise shoppers can now roam the aisles of **Sym's** (400 Park Ave and 42 Trinity Pl), **Loehmann's** (101 W 17th St), and **Old Navy Clothing** (610 Ave of the Americas), where there are bargains galore! **Loehmann's** carries top labels at great prices, has a return policy, and takes credit cards. There is a huge selection (particularly for men) at **Sym's**, and fantastic stocks of casual wear for the whole family (including kids) at **Old Navy**. It pays to visit these stores often, as the merchandise moves rapidly and new labels and styles are constantly being shown.

REPLAY COUNTRY STORE
109 Prince St   212/673-6300
Mon-Sat: 11-7; Sun: 11-6

How about 25 different washings and fits in jeans? Or over 45 different shirt styles? You can find all that and more at this very attractive Soho store, which features outdoor clothing. There are stacks of jackets and overalls, too, and everything you might need for a Western party! Downstairs, a cafe will take care of any hunger pangs while you shop. This is one of the better-stocked stores in the area, and prices are as comfortable as the merchandise.

Men's Formal Wear

JACK AND COMPANY FORMAL WEAR
128 E 86th St   212/722-4609
Mon-Fri: 10-7; Sat: 10-4

Jack and Company rents and sells men's ready-to-wear formal wear. They carry an excellent selection of sizes and names (After Six, Lord West), and they've had a good reputation for service since 1925. In sales or rentals, Jack's can supply head-to-toe formal wear. The staff here is excellent at matching outfits to customers, as well as knowing exactly what is socially required for any occasion. Same-day service is available, and the full rental price will be applied toward purchase!

ZELLER TUXEDOS
Locations throughout Manhattan:
204 Broadway (at Fulton St), 2nd floor
201 E 23rd St (at Third Ave), 2nd floor
421 Seventh Ave (at 33rd St), 2nd floor
459 Lexington Ave (at 45th St), 3rd floor
201 E 56th St (at Third Ave)
1010 Third Ave (at 60th St)
212/355-0707 (store hours and information)

Zeller, with locations throughout the city, provides sales and rentals of ladies' and gentlemen's formal wear. In stock are tuxedos, formal shirts, dresses, and accessories for big-time occasions. Top names are featured: Canali, Bill Kaiserman, Bally, Valentino, Hugo Boss, Versace, and Giorgio Armani. A special made-to-order service is available.

If You Are Going Formal . . .

Here are a few fashion tips:
- Wear a black tie.
- Do not wear a white dinner jacket except on warm summer nights.
- Remember that cummerbund vents should face upward.
- Always show a little white shirt cuff and wear sensational cuff links.
- Forget the banded-collar formal shirts.
- Tux pants should not have cuffs.
- Wear a pair of classy suspenders with your tux.

Tuxedos

Moe Ginsburg (162 Fifth Ave; moderate prices), **Paul Smith** (108 Fifth Ave; fashionable), **J. Press** (16 E 44th St; traditional), and **Saks Fifth Avenue** (611 Fifth Ave, 6th floor; best selection in all price ranges).

Cuff Links

Berdorf Goodman Men (745 Fifth Ave), **Polo Ralph Lauren** (867 Madison Ave), and **Tender Buttons** (143 E. 62nd St; have them custom-made from unusual buttons).

Tuxedo Shirts

Paris Custom Shirt Makers (38 W 32nd St), **Nino Corvato** (510 Madison Ave), **Bergdorf Goodman Men** (745 Fifth Ave), **Saks Fifth Avenue** (611 Fifth Ave), **Macy's** (1621 W 34th St), and **Bloomingdale's** (1000 Third Ave). Barney's also carries formal wear, but why put up with their haughty attitude?

Shoes

Your polished black shoes are perfectly acceptable, but if you must splurge, the above-mentioned department stores carry patent-leather shoes in their shoe departments.

Tuxedo Rental

For those with bulging wallets, the Italian-made tuxedos offered by **Brioni** (57 E 57th St) are fabulous. They're available at their own store or **Saks Fifth Avenue** (611 Fifth Ave, 6th floor).

Men's — General

CAMOUFLAGE
141 Eighth Ave (at 17th St)   212/741-9118
Mon-Fri: 12-7; Sat: 11:30-6:30; Sun: 1-6

At Camouflage you'll find men's branded clothing, plus private-label trousers, shirts, ties, and accessories. Prices range from reasonable (their chinos are one of the best buys in the city) to good, considering some of the pricey designer names. Camouflage has the ability to dress customers with a dignified but unique look. Clothing from Camouflage definitely won't blend into the wallpaper!

EISENBERG AND EISENBERG
16 W 17th St (bet Fifth Ave and Ave of the Americas)   212/627-1290
Mon-Wed, Fri: 9-6; Thurs: 9-7; Sat: 9-5; Sun: 10-4

The Eisenberg and Eisenberg style is a classic one that dates from 1898, the year they opened. E&E consistently offers top quality and good prices on suits, tuxedos, coats, and sportswear. They also stock outerwear, slacks, name-brand raincoats, cashmere sport jackets, and 100% silk jackets. All are sold at considerable discounts, and alterations are available. London Fog coats are featured, and no label is better known for wet-weather needs.

FACONNABLE OF NEW YORK
689 Fifth Ave (at 54th St)   212/319-0111
Mon-Wed, Fri, Sat: 10-7; Thurs: 10-8; Sun: 12-6

Faconnable (a French outfit) has made a name for itself in the fashion world with clothes that appeal to conservative dressers. Their New York store — which is admittedly not up to the class or selection of the Beverly Hills shop — carries a good selection of men's sportswear, furnishings, tailored clothing, and suits.

GILCREST CLOTHES COMPANY
900 Broadway (at 20th St)   212/254-8933
Mon-Sat: 7:30-5:30; Sun: 9:30-4:30

Buying a suit usually means laying out a lot of money, so it is a good idea to shop around. Gilcrest provides savings on quality brands like Perry Ellis, Hugo Boss, Zegna, Mani, Jhane, Barnes, Ungaro, Andrew Fezza, Louis Feraud, and Baumler of Germany. Their own line is available at sensible prices. The sport-coat stock is worthy of inspection, and if you are in the market for a tux, the selection is enormous, including Cornelioni rental tuxedos. No charge for alterations!

GORSART
9 Murray St   212/962-0024
Mon, Wed, Fri: 9-6; Tues, Thurs: 9-7; Sat: 9-5:30

If you find the style and quality of Brooks Brothers or Paul Staurt appealing but the prices appalling, head to this little-known jewel. In 1921, two brothers started catering to the financial community with what was then a new twist: quality merchandise at a discount. Moe Davidson and Neil Roberts purchased the store from its founders in 1975, and they've carried on the same tradition. They offer classy suits made at prices that will make you smile. These are not seconds or markdowns. In addition to suits, you'll find a nice selection of sports-wear and furnishings, all discounted. The reason for the great prices? Simple: low overhead. You can pick up a tux for about half the department-store price, and you don't pay for tailoring unless it's a complete restructuring. They have 35 in-house tailors on the job all the time. This is a special store, fellows. No high-pressure selling or gimmicks, just value and service.

J. PRESS
7 E 44th St (bet Fifth and Madison Ave)   212/687-7642
Mon-Sat: 9-6

As one of New York's classic conservative men's stores, J. Press prides itself on its sense of timelessness. Its salespeople, customers, and attitude have changed little from the time of the founder. Styles are impeccable and distinguished. Blazers are blue, and shirts are button-down and straight. Even in the days when button-down collars were out, they never went away at J. Press.

L.S. MEN'S CLOTHING
19 W 44th St, Room 403   212/575-0933
Mon-Thurs: 9-7; Fri: 9-4; Sun: 10-5

L.S. Men's Clothing bills itself as "the executive discount shop," but I would go further and call them a must for fashion-minded businessmen. For one thing, the midtown location means one needn't go down to Fifth Avenue in the teens, which is the main area for men's discount clothing. Better still, as owner Israel Zuber puts it, "There are many stores selling $200 suits at discount, but we are one of the few in mid-Manhattan that discount the $475 to $975 range of suits." The main attraction, though, is the tremendous selection of executive-class styles. Within that category a man could outfit himself almost entirely at L.S. Natural. Soft-shoulder designer suits are available in all sizes. A custom-order department is available with over 2,500 bolts of Italian and English goods in stock. Custom-made suits take four to six weeks and sell for around $525; sport coats are priced at $415. This is one of the very best spots for top-drawer names. I would make it number one on my midtown shopping itinerary.

MOE GINSBURG
162 Fifth Ave (at 21st St)   212/242-3482
Mon-Fri: 9:30-7 (Thurs until 8); Sat, Sun: 9:30-6

Yes, there once was a Moe Ginsburg. Now that he is history, the family carries on the tradition of providing brand-name men's clothing from American and European designers. You have to go upstairs, but the bargains are worth it! Alterations are available at a modest cost.

NAPOLEON
Trump Tower
Fifth Ave at 57th St   212/759-1110
Mon-Sat: 10-6

Trump Plaza
1048 Third Ave (at 62nd St)   212/308-3000
Mon-Fri: 10-7; Sat: 10-6:30

Plaza Hotel
768 Fifth Ave, lobby   212/759-8000
Mon-Sat: 10-6:30

Napoleon carries clothes fit for a king—at kingly prices, too! You will find an extensive selection of handmade suits and jackets with high-fashion Italian tailoring in luxurious fabrics of cashmere and wool. Many are exclusive to this house. Great-looking shirts (they should be at those prices!) are cut from the finest Egyptian cottons. Leather goods by Zilli, handmade shoes of exotic skins and leathers, and a good showing of evening wear and accessories round out the appeal of this shop, where informed, professional service is the byword.

PAN AM SPORTSWEAR AND MENSWEAR
50 Orchard St (bet Grand and Hester St)   212/925-7032
Sun-Wed: 9-6; Thurs: 9-8; Fri: 9:30-3 (winter); 9-5 (summer)

With more stores like this, the Lower East Side could become synonymous with class as well as bargains. From the shiny glass windows (as opposed to the clutter of hangers that usually denotes an entrance) to the extremely fine stock (a large selection of Italian suits), Pan Am is distinctive enough to be on Madison Avenue, except for its prices. They are nothing short of super! Perry Ellis, Mani by Giorgio Armani, Polo by Ralph Lauren, and Andrew Fezza are but a few of the names that adorn the racks. Prices are at least a third below that of the uptown shops. What's more, styles are *au courant;* they often preview here first, and they're in classic good taste. Finally, the prompt and courteous sales help is a major exception to the Lower East Side norm.

PAUL STUART
Madison Ave at 45th St   212/682-0320
Mon, Tues, Wed, Fri: 8-6:30; Thurs: 8-7; Sat: 9-6; Sun: 12-5

This is the store for shoppers who don't really know what they want, have trouble putting things together to make a "look," and worry about quality. You would be hard-pressed to find a better selection of men's and women's fine apparel and accessories. One drawback: there is little excitement here, either in the presentation or merchandise. The men's suits, ties, and sport jackets are first-class, as is the collection of handmade English shoes.

ROTHMAN'S
200 Park Ave S (at Union Sq)   212/777-7400
Mon-Wed, Fri: 10-7; Thurs: 10-8; Sat: 9-6; Sun: 12-5
(closed Sun in summer)

Forget your image of the old Harry Rothman operation. Harry's grandson, Ken Giddon, runs this classy men's store, which offers a huge selection of quality clothes at discounts of up to 40% in a contemporary and comfortable atmosphere. He carries top names like Canali, Hickey-Freeman, Corneliani, Joseph Abboud, Calvin Klein, and Valentino. Sizes at Rothman's range from 36 to 50 in regular, short, long, and extra long. Raincoats, slacks, sport jackets, and accessories are stocked at the same attractive prices, as are Kenneth Cole and Cable and Co. shoes.

SAINT LAURIE MERCHANT TAILORS
350 Park Ave (bet 51st and 52nd St)   212/317-8700
Mon-Fri: 9:39-6:30; Thurs: 9:30-8; Sat: 9:30-6

Saint Laurie, one of the better-priced clothing outlets in the city, is located in a space just as unique as their former store on Broadway. They offer good-looking made-to-measure clothing for men and women at rack prices. An original tailoring system supposedly eliminates much of the trial and error typical of most custom clothiers. Saint Laurie buys directly from the weavers, thereby eliminating the markup of a fabric jobber. Shirts, haberdashery, and accessories are also available.

SOSINSKY'S
143 Orchard St (bet Delancey and Rivington St)   212/254-2307
Mon-Thurs: 10-5; Fri: 10-3; Sun: 9-5
(closed Fri in July and Aug)

Three generations of the Sosinsky family have been in business at this same location for over eight decades. This says something for the bargains offered on men's dress and sport shirts, sweaters, and robes by such famous names as Arrow and Alexander Julian. Unlike many of their neighbors, these folks are polite and helpful and will provide first-quality or irregular (always marked) merchandise at 25% to 50% or more off uptown prices. Ties by Zanara are offered at one-third of the list price. The Alexander Julian sport-shirt selection is especially deep, both in variety and value.

Men's Hats

J.J. HAT CENTER
310 Fifth Ave (at 32nd St)   212/239-4368, 800/622-1911
Mon-Sat: 8:45-5:45

If you can't find the hat you want here, it probably doesn't exist. This outfit stocks over 15,000 pieces of major-brand merchandise from all over the world. Founded in 1911, it is New York's oldest hat shop. Special services include free brush-up, hat-stretching or tightening, custom orders, and a free catalog. Hats and caps to size 8 are available.

Men's Shirts

MARK CHRISTOPHER
26 Broadway (at Wall St)   212/509-2355
Mon-Fri: 10-6; Sat by appointment

When it comes to custom shirts for well-dressed executives or upwardly mobile types aspiring to the big time, manager Mark Lingley is the guy to see. The classy shirts at Mark Christopher are made of fine cotton and hand-cut with superb tailoring. You pay for such special merchandise, but the service (they will make office calls) and the care (the typical shirt requires about 20 measurements for a fitting) are worth the extra bucks. Shirts are the foundation of the operation, but suits and ties are also available.

PENN GARDEN SHIRT CORP.
63 Orchard St (at Grand St)   212/431-8464
Sun-Wed, Fri: 9-6; Thurs: 9-8

Penn Garden is the accessory store affiliated with G&G International, which handles the men's clothing field. You'll find quality accessories sold here at 30% to 40% below normal retail.

SHIRT STORE
51 E 44th St (bet Vanderbilt and Madison Ave)   212/557-8040
Mon-Fri: 8-6:30; Sat: 10-5

71 Broadway (next to Trinity Church)   212/797-8040
Mon-Fri: 7:30-6:30

The attraction here is that you buy directly from the manufacturer, with no middle man to increase the price. The Shirt Store offers all-cotton shirts for men, from the smallest (14x32) to the largest (18½x37). Although the ready-made stock is great, they will also do custom work and even come to your office with swatches. Additional services include mail-order, alterations, and monogramming.

STATS
1776 Broadway, Suite 701   212/262-5844
Mon-Fri: 8-7; weekends with advance notice

And what does STATS stand for? Shirts, ties and terrific service, of course! Julie Manis sells custom shirts and neckwear in the private convenience of one's office or home. She carries tailoring tools and fabrics, and can do special orders for fabrics not in stock. Appointments can be made at any time to suit your busy schedule; she also takes the extra step of a sample shirt fitting.

VICTORY, THE SHIRT EXPERTS
125 Maiden Lane   212/480-1366, 800/841-3424
Mon-Fri: 8:30-6

Victory manufactures and retails all-cotton ready-to-wear and made-to-measure shirts. In their new facilities they will taper, shorten, alter, or monogram any shirt to individual specifications. Sizes run from 14x32 to 18½x36. They also carry a good assortment of ties, cuff links, and belts. Periodic sales make their already reasonable prices even more attractive.

Men's Ties

GOIDEL NECKWEAR
138 Allen St (bet Rivington and Delancey St)   212/475-7332
Sun-Fri: 9-5 (9-3 on Fri)

Since 1935 this has been *the* place for bargains on ties, cummerbunds, men's jewelry, and accessories. They triple as manufacturers, wholesalers, and retailers, so savings are passed on to customers. Special note to groups: these folks will match most items brought in, usually within a week or two.

Men's Underwear

UNDER WARES
210 E 58th St (bet Second and Third Ave)
212/838-1200, 800/237-8641
Mon-Fri: 10-7; Sat: 10-6; Sun: 12-5

It used to be that the average fellow couldn't tell you what kind of underwear he wore and probably didn't buy it himself. All that changed when ads began featuring celebrity jocks. These days men's underwear makes a fashion statement. Under Wares sells over a hundred styles of briefs and boxer shorts. They stock the largest selection of men's undergarments in the world, carrying many top labels. There are also T-shirts, hosiery, robes, pajamas, workout wear, swimwear, and gift items. If you are shy about browsing all the sexy styles, call for a free catalog.

Men's Western Wear

BILLY MARTIN'S
810 Madison Ave (at 68th St)   212/861-3100
Mon-Fri: 10-7; Sat: 10-6; Sun: 12-5 (Oct-Dec)

If Western wear is on your shopping list, Billy Martin's has a great selection of deerskin jackets, shirts, riding pants, skirts, hats, and parkas. They also boast one of the best collections of cowboy boots in the city for men and women. Great accessory items like bandannas, jewelry, buckles, and belt straps complete the outfit. The items are well-tooled, well-designed, and priced accordingly.

Resale Clothing

East 20s:

City Opera Thrift Shop (222 E 23rd St; 212/684-5344)
Goodwill Superstore (220 E 23rd St; 212/447-7270)
Help Line Thrift Shop (382 Third Ave; 212/532-5136)
Salvation Army Thrift Store (212 E 23rd St; 212/532-8115)
St. George's Thrift Shop (61 Gramercy Park N; 212/475-2674)

Upper East Side:

Arthritis Foundation Thrift Shop (121 E 77th St; 212/772-8816)
Bis Designer Resale (1134 Madison Ave; 212/396-2760)
Bryn Mawr Book Shop (502 E 79th St; 212/744-7682)
Call Again Thrift Shop (1711 First Ave; 212/831-0845)
Cancer Care Thrift Shop (1480 Third Ave; 212/879-9868)
Council Thrift Shop (246 E 84th St; 212/439-8373)
Housing Works Thrift Shop (202 E 77th St; 212/772-8461)
Irvington Institute for Immunological Research Thrift Shop (1534 Second Ave; 212/879-4555)
Kavanagh's (146 E 49th St; 212/702-0152)
Memorial Sloan-Kettering Thrift Shop (1440 Third Ave; 212/535-1250)
Michael's (1041 Madison Ave; 212/737-7273)
Out of the Closet Thrift Shop (220 E 81st St; 212/472-3573)
Spence-Chapin Thrift Shop (1473 Third Ave; 212/737-8448)
Stuyvesant Square Thrift Shop (1704 Second Ave; 212/831-1830)
Thrift & Things (1871 Second Ave; 212/876-7223)

ALLAN & SUZI
416 Amsterdam Ave (at 80th St)   (212/724-7445
Mon-Sun: 12-8

Now this is quite a store! Under one roof you'll find current designer and vintage clothing for men and women, old and new shoes, and accessories in what is called a "retro clothing store." There are big names (like Galliano, Lacroix, Ungaro, and Versace) and new ones you haven't heard of. Some outfits are discounted. They are proud of the fact that they dress a number of Hollywood and TV personalities. Ask for Allan Pollack or Suzi Kandel.

DESIGNER RESALE
324 E 81st St (bet First and Second Ave)   212/734-3639
Mon-Wed, Fri: 11-7; Thurs: 11-8; Sat: 10-6; Sun: 12-5

"Gently worn" is the byword here! Designer Resale offers previously owned ladies' designer clothing and accessories at moderate prices. Most major fashion names are represented; you might find Chanel, Armani, Hermes, or Valentino garments on the racks. If items do not sell, prices are further marked down. Call to ask about the latest bargains.

ENCORE
1132 Madison Ave (bet 84th and 85th St, upstairs)   212/879-2850
Mon-Wed, Fri: 10:30-6:30; Thurs: 10:30-7:30; Sat: 10:30-6; Sun: 12-6 (closed Sun from July to mid-Aug)

Because it is so chic and select, Encore can honestly be billed as a "resale shop of gently worn clothing of designer/couture quality." When one sees the merchandise and clientele at this shop, you'll see why. For one thing, it is a consignment boutique, not a charity thrift shop. Its donors receive a portion of the sales price, and according to owner Carole Selig, many of the donors are socialites and other luminaries who don't want to be seen in the same outfit twice. Selig can afford to be picky, and so can you. The fashions are up-to-date and are sold at 50% to 70% off original retail prices. There are over 6,000 items in stock. Prices range from reasonable to astronomical, but just think how much they sold for originally!

GENTLEMEN'S RESALE
322 E 81st St (bet First and Second Ave)   212/734-2739
Mon-Fri: 11-7; Sat: 10-6; Sun: 12-5

Gentlemen who are interested in top-quality designer suits, jackets, and sportswear now have a place where they can save a bundle. Shopping here is like a treasure hunt, and that is half the fun. Imagine picking up an Armani suit that originally sold for $1,000 and is now tagged at $200! You might also earn a few extra bucks by consigning some of your own merchandise here.

KAVANAGH'S
146 E 49th St (bet Third and Lexington Ave)   212/702-0152
Mon-Fri: 11-7; Sat: 11-5

Here is a designer resale shop for which I can vouch highly! It is owned by Mary Kavanagh, whom I had the pleasure of knowing and working with at Bergdorf. She has superb taste! As former director of personal shopping, she had access to the finest labels in the world. At Kavanagh's she carries many of those same labels: Chanel, Versace, Valentino, Ungaro, Armani, Galanos,

Beene, Bill Blass, Oscar de la Renta, and many more. Chanel clothes and accessories are a specialty. Mary describes her store as a sunny, happy spot filled with attractive antiques. It is a classy shopping haven where customers come first. Moreover, she will open early, stay late, or open on Sunday for special groups.

TATIANA
860 Lexington Ave (bet 64th and 65th St), 2nd floor   212/717-7684
Mon-Fri: 11-7; Sat: 11-6; Sun: 12-5

This is a unique designer consignment boutique outlet. For consignors, Tatiana offers free estimates and pickup service. For retail customers, she will try to find whatever outfit the customer may want. The stock here is top-grade, with clothing, jewelry, bags, shoes, hats, and furs bearing some of the best names: Chanel, Gucci, Valentino, Armani, YSL, Versace, and Bill Blass.

Shoes—Children's

EAST SIDE KIDS
1298 Madison Ave (bet 92nd and 93rd St)   212/360-5000
Mon-Fri: 9:30-6; Sat: 9-6

East Side Kids stocks footwear items up to a woman's size ten and a man's size nine. They can accommodate older children and juniors, plus all the adults with small feet. Of course, there is also a great selection of children's shoes in both domestic and imported styles. Frequent-buyer cards are kept on file for special discounts. The store is known for helpful service.

LITTLE ERIC SHOES
1331 Third Ave (at 76th St)   212/288-8987
Mon-Fri: 10-7; Sat: 10-6; Sun: 12-6

1118 Madison Ave (at 83rd St)   212/717-1513
Mon-Sat: 10-6; Sun: 12-5

This is the place to find shoes for your small fry. They are comfy, with many lined in soft leather. You'll note that most of the "in" styles are made in Italy. The staff here are just as colorful as the shoes they sell!

RICHIE'S DISCOUNT CHILDREN'S SHOES
183 Ave B (bet 11th and 12th St)   212/228-5442
Mon, Tues, Thurs-Sat: 10-5:30; Sun: 10-5

Richie's offers your children's feet a one-of-a-kind experience. The decor is old, but the stock includes the latest shoes at a fraction of the prices found elsewhere. Brands include Stride Rite, Jonathan Bennett, Babybotte, Blue Star, Jumping Jacks, and Skechers. You can rest assured that the fit will be extraordinary. Considerable time is spent with each customer. For each pair of shoes sold, another sale is forfeited for reasons that include telling a customer that a child's old shoes are still good! The one drawback is the neighborhood.

SHOOFLY
465 Amsterdam Ave (bet 82nd and 83rd St)   212/580-4390
42 Hudson St (bet Duane and Thomas St)   212/406-3270
Mon-Sat: 11-7; Sun: 12-6

Shoofly carries attractive and reasonably priced imported shoes for infants to 14-year-olds. Lots of women with tiny feet will appreciate Shoofly's chic selection of footwear as well. Shoofly will take care of your foot needs with styles both funky and classic.

Shoes—Family

BUFFALO CHIPS BOOTERY SOHO
131 Thompson St (bet Houston and Prince St)   212/253-2228
Mon-Sat: 11-7; Sun: 12-6

The best of the West comes East! You'll enjoy the Western ambience of the wall art, Indian and contemporary Western jewelry, leather items, artifacts, pottery, rugs, and blankets from this attractive outlet. Best of all are the unique Western boots, all designed by store personnel. Buffalo Chips can produce custom-made boots in about 6 to 8 weeks.

E. VOGEL BOOTS AND SHOES
19 Howard St (one block north of Canal St, bet Broadway and
Lafayette St)   212/925-2460
Mon-Fri: 8-4:30; Sat: 8-2
(closed Sat in summer and first two weeks of July)

Hank and Dean Vogel and Jack Lynch are the third and fourth generations to join this family business since 1879. They will happily fit and supply made-to-measure boots and shoes for any adult who can find the store. Howard is one of those streets that even native New Yorkers don't know exists. Many beat a path to Vogel for top-quality shoes and boots, personal advice, excellent fittings, and prices that, while not inexpensive, are reasonable for the service involved. Made-to-measure shoes do not always fit properly, but they do at Vogel. Once your shoe pattern is on record, they can make new shoes without a personal visit and will ship anywhere. For craftsmanship, this spot is top-drawer. There are more than 600 Vogel dealers throughout the world, but this is the grandfather store and the people here are super.

KENNETH COLE
597 Broadway (at Houston St)   212/965-0283
353 Columbus Ave (bet 76th and 77th St)   212/873-2061
95 Fifth Ave (at 17th St)   212/675-2550
107 E 42nd St (bet Vanderbilt and Park Ave)   212/949-8079
Mon-Sat: 11-8; Sun: 12-7

In addition to inducing a hearty laugh at the expense of some well-known personalities (by signs), Kenneth Cole offers quality shoes, belts, scarves, watches, outerwear, and accessories, all at sensible prices.

LEACH-KALE
1261 Broadway (at 31st St), Suite 815-816   212/683-0571
Mon-Fri: 9-5

While some custom-shoe craftsmen are determined to prove that their footwear can and should be owned by every man, Andre S. Feuerman of Leach-Kale is not among them. Perhaps he has been burned by too many bargain hunters who thought the gap between a high-class shoe salon and Leach-Kale couldn't be as great as it is, or by customers who think that at these prices a pair of shoes should cure all of their orthopedic problems for life. The business has customers who have been loyal patrons for 40 years, and these are the people Feuerman would rather court. They have neither unrealistic expectations nor impossible dreams but appreciate the quality items that Leach-Kale produces. They specialize in orthopedic work, which is why many customers pay the price without batting an eye. Shoes start at about $1,200 for the first pair, but some first orders and all subsequent orders can be substantially less.

LORD JOHN'S BOOTERY
428 Third Ave (bet 29th and 30th St)   212/532-2579
Mon-Fri: 9-8; Sat: 10-7

Lord John's Bootery has been family-owned and operated for three generations, spanning almost 50 years. Lord John's has been recently renovated and expanded and now carries one of the largest selection of dress, casual, and comfort shoes in midtown Manhattan. They offer footwear for men and women from such manufacturers as Ecco, Mephisto, Paul Green, Rockport, Sebago, Birkenstock, Clark's, Kenneth Cole, Santana, Bostonian, and Dansko.

T.O. DEY CUSTOM SHOE MAKERS
9 E 38th St   212/683-6300
Mon-Fri: 9-5; Sat: 9-1

T.O. Dey is a good jack-of-all-trades operation. Though their specialty is custom-made shoes, they also repair any kind of shoe. These folks will create both men's and women's shoes based on a plaster mold of a customer's feet; their styles are limited only by a client's imagination. They make arch supports and cover shoes to match a garment. They also sell athletic shoes for football, basketball, cross-country, hockey, boxing, and running. Downhill ski boots, too!

If you have large feet, these outfits have shoes that will fit them.

Johnston & Murphy: men's to size 15 (115 Broadway and 351 Madison Ave)

Kenneth Cole: men's to size 16, women's to 11 (95 Fifth Ave, 597 Broadway, and 353 Columbus Ave)

Stapleton Shoe Co.: men's to size 18 (68 Trinity Pl)

Shoes—Men's

CHURCH ENGLISH SHOES
428 Madison Ave (at 49th St)   212/755-4313, 800/221-4540
Mon-Fri: 9-6:30; Sat: 9-6; Sun: 12-5

Anglophiles have a ball here, not only because of the *veddy* English atmosphere but for the pure artistry and "Englishness" of the shoes. Church has been selling English shoes for men since 1873 and is known for classic styles, superior workmanship, and fine leathers. The styles basically remain unchanged year after year, although new designs are occasionally added as a concession to fashion. All are custom-fitted by shoe salesmen. If a style or size does not feel right, Church's will special-order a pair that does.

MCCREEDY AND SCHREIBER
213 E 59th St (bet Second and Third Ave)   212/759-9241
Mon-Sat: 9-7; Sun: 12-6

37 W 46th St (bet Fifth Ave and Ave of the Americas)   212/719-1552
Mon-Sat: 9-7; Sun: 11-5

How about a department store for shoes and boots? McCreedy and Schreiber features Lucchese, Tony Lama, Frye, Justin, and Timberland boots, as well as Bass and Alden shoes. Boots come in sizes up to 15, and prices are competitive.

STAPLETON SHOE COMPANY
68 Trinity Pl (at Rector St)   212/964-6329
Mon-Thurs: 8-6; Fri: 8-5

Their motto is "better shoes for less," but that doesn't begin to suggest the superlatives that Stapleton deserves. Gentlemen, this is *the* place to get Bally, Alden, Allen-Edmonds, Cole-Haan, Timberland, Rockport, Johnston Murphy, and a slew of other top names at a discount. Stapleton is located on the same block as the American Stock Exchange, near the World Trade Center. There probably isn't a better source for quality shoes anywhere. They are size specialists, carrying men's sizes 5-18 in widths A-EEE.

Shoes — Women's

ANBAR SHOES
60 Reade St (bet Church St and Broadway)   212/227-0253
Mon-Fri: 9-6:30; Sat: 11-6

Bargain hunters rejoice! Anbar customers can find great bargains on brand-name styles at discounts as high as 80%. This is a good place to save money.

GIORDANO'S PETITE SHOES
1150 Second Ave (at 60th St)   212/688-7195
Mon-Fri: 11-7; Sat: 11-6

Susan Giordano has a very special clientele. Her store stocks a fine selection of women's designer shoes in small sizes (a range that is nonexistent in regular shoe stores). If you're a woman who wears shoes in the 4 to 6 medium range, you are probably used to shopping in children's shoe departments or having shoes custom-made, either of which can cramp your style. For these women, Giordano's is a godsend. Brands carried include Anne Klein, Charles Jourdan, Fendi, Stuart Weitzman, Donald Pliner, and Nickels.

PETER FOX SHOES
105 Thompson St (bet Prince and Spring St)   212/431-6359
Mon-Sat: 11-7; Sun: 12-6

806 Madison Ave (at 68th St)   212/744-8340
Mon-Sat: 10-6; Thurs: 10-7; Sun: 12-5

Peter Fox was the downtown trailblazer for women's shoes. Everything sold in his two shops is exclusive, limited-edition designer footwear. Perhaps because of the original Soho location, Fox's designs seem more adventurous than those of its competitors; the look is younger and more casual than those of other designers. If you're looking for shoes to be seen in, ask for Lorraine (Upper

East Side) and Helga (downtown). Bridal and special-occasion shoes are available at both stores.

TALL SIZE SHOES
3 W 35th St (at Fifth Ave)   212/736-2060
Mon-Wed, Fri, Sat: 9:30-6; Thurs: 9:30-7

Finding comfortable shoes if you are a "tall size" is not easy. This store can solve the problem, as they carry a broad selection of shoes to size 15 in widths from 4A to extra-wide. There are custom-made shoes and designer names to choose from: Nickels, Via Spiga Vanelli, Sesto Meucci, Bandolino, Glacee, Evan Picone, and many more. They also have a Cinderella department with a wide selection of shoes in sizes 1 to 4½. They will take phone orders and ship anywhere.

Sportswear

GERRY COSBY AND COMPANY
2 Pennsylvania Plaza (32nd St at Seventh Ave)   212/563-6464
Mon-Fri: 9:30-7:30; Sat: 9:30-6; Sun: 12-5

There's a lot to like about this company. Located in the famous Madison Square Garden lobby, they are a professional business in an appropriate venue for "team sportswear"—as in what athletes wear. Gerry Cosby designs and markets protective equipment and is a top supplier to shoppers of professional licensed products. The protective equipment and bags are designed for professional use but are available to the general public as well. They accept mail and phone orders for all, including personalized jerseys and jackets.

HOWARD SPORTSWEAR
295 Grand St (bet Eldridge and Allen St)   212/226-4307
Sun-Fri: 9-5

Howard was transformed from a typical Lower East Side shop into a fashionable boutique without sacrificing the bargain prices. They carry an excellent selection of men's sportswear and women's wear, including top names like Sansabelt, Countess Mara, Members Only, and Pierre Cardin. For women, choose from Hanes, Bali, Vanity Fair, Warners, Maidenform, and Jockey.

NIKETOWN
6 E 57th St (bet Fifth and Madison Ave)   212/891-6453
Mon-Fri 10-8; Sat: 10-7; Sun: 11-6

Nike has created a mystique second to none in the athletic shoe and clothing business, and head honcho Phil Knight is a promotional genius. His new store in the heart of the high-rent district is different, to say the least; the effect is spectacular. In a building inspired by old school gyms, these folks show an extensive line of shoes, numbering 1,200 in all, and hundreds of Nike clothing and accessory items on five selling floors. It's an experience!

Surplus

KAUFMAN SURPLUS
319 W 42nd St (bet Eighth and Ninth Ave)   212/757-5670
Mon-Wed, Fri: 11-6; Thurs: 11-7; Sat: 12-6

Kaufman's has long been a favorite among New Yorkers and visitors alike for its extensive selection of genuine military surplus from around the globe.

Over the last half-century, Kaufman's has outfitted dozens of Broadway and TV shows and supplied a number of major motion pictures with military garb. The store is a treasure trove of military collectibles, hats, helmets, dummy grenades, uniforms, and insignias. Over a thousand military pins, patches, and medals from armies the world over are on display.

Sweaters

BEST OF SCOTLAND
581 Fifth Ave (bet 47th and 48th St, penthouse)   212/644-0403
Mon-Sat: 10-6

Two real pluses here: one of the largest collections of cashmere sweaters in the world and competitive prices. There is a big difference between cashmere from Scotland and the Far East. Best of Scotland carries only the Scottish best in sweaters, baby blankets, ladies' capes, scarves, mufflers, and blankets for both men and women. Ladies can find sizes up to 48; large gentlemen (those in the 6'6", 300-pound range) will find sweaters up to size 62! A variety of cableknit sweaters is an added attraction.

GRANNY-MADE
381 Amsterdam Ave (bet 78th and 79th St)   212/496-1222
Mon-Fri: 11-7:30; Sat: 10-6; Sun: 12-5

Bert Levy's grandson, Michael Rosenberg, has assembled an extensive collection of sweaters for young people, infants, and adults. Handmade sweaters from all over the world sit beside ones hand-loomed right here at home. The selection of women's sweaters, knitwear, suits, dresses, skirts, slacks, and accessories is unique, as are the men's sweaters and T-shirts. Granny-Made has an extremely service-oriented, knowledgeable staff. A new plus: moon and star cookies, from a recipe passed down through three generations!

T-shirts

EISNER BROS.
75 Essex St (bet Grand and Delancey St)
212/475-6868, 800/426-7700
Mon-Thurs: 9-6:30; Fri: 9-3; Sun: 9-5

Here you will find a full line of licensed NBA, NFL, NHL, MLB, collegiate, and other character and novelty products in T-shirts and sweat shirts. Major quantity discounts are offered; single pieces are also available. You will also find police, fire, emergency, and sanitation department logos, as well as Disney and Harley-Davidson. Personalizing is featured on all items. They are the largest source in the area for blank, printable corporate sportswear.

Umbrellas

UNCLE SAM
161 W 57th St (bet Ave of the Americas and Seventh Ave)
212/582-1976
Mon-Fri: 9:30-6:15; Sat: 10-5

This is a New York specialty store at its very best. Uncle Sam sells canes and services, re-covers, and customizes umbrellas. There are umbrellas for children, golfers, photographers, fashion models, travelers, chauffeurs, doormen, and beachgoers. All are carved, sewn, and assembled by hand. Uncle Sam also sells umbrella accessories and remakes old umbrellas and canes.

Uniforms

DORNAN
653 Eleventh Ave (bet 47th and 48th St)
212/247-0937; outside New York State: 800/223-0363
Mon-Wed, Fri. 8:30-4; Thurs: 8:30-6

Dornan is the largest supplier of chauffeur uniforms in the country, and they carry many other lines of work uniforms as well. This includes outfits for butlers, maids, beauticians, doormen, hospital workers, bellboys, bartenders, chefs, flight attendants, pilots, firemen, police, doctors, nurses, and . . . you get the picture. They have been in the business for over seven decades. Dornan is capable of setting up a uniform program, screen-printing, designing, customizing, and distributing outfits anywhere. A complete line of specialty advertising products is carried.

JA-MIL UNIFORMS
92 Orchard St (at Delancey St)   212/677-8190
Mon-Fri, Sun: 10-5

This is *the* bargain spot for those who wear uniforms and do not want to spend a fortune on work clothes. There are outfits for doctors, nurses, and technicians, as well as the finest domestic uniforms and chef's apparel. Dansks clogs and SAS shoes are available in white and colors. Mail orders are accepted.

Housekeeper uniforms: **House of Uniforms** (853 Lexington Ave, 212/355-7381)

Women's Accessories

FINE AND KLEIN
119 Orchard St (at Delancey St)   212/674-6720
Sun-Fri: 9-5

The finest handbag store for value and selection is not in Rome, Paris, or London. It is not even on Fifth Avenue in New York. It is on the Lower East Side, and the name is Fine and Klein. What a selection! There is a bag for every purpose, any time of day, in every fabric. Top labels are sold for a fraction of what you would pay uptown. Besides, shopping at Fine and Klein is fun. The crowds, especially on Sundays and holidays, are so great that the number allowed to enter must be controlled! My good friends Julius Fine and Murray Klein are the epitome of old-time merchants, and you will be delighted with their service. Tell them I sent you!

HYUK BAGS
39 W 29th St   212/685-5226
Mon-Fri: 7:30-6; Sat: 7-1; Sun: 9-3

Hyuk K. Kim runs an importing company exclusively devoted to handbags. Importing and wholesaling companies are common in this area. What is uncommon is the courtesy and selection Kim gives individual retail customers. She has a knack for making everyone feel like a valued customer and does not take offense when a finicky lady picks through the entire stock in search of the right handbag. Besides, it shouldn't be too hard to find, within certain guidelines. "Imported" here usually refers to origins from points west rather than east. Hyuk seems to import every type of handbag—leather, vinyl, canvas, and nylon. Most of this is average, serviceable stuff. But there are a few stars in the line, and prices border on magnificent. Minimum purchase is 12 pieces.

J.S. SUAREZ
450 Park Ave (bet 56th and 57th St)   212/753-3758
Mon-Fri: 9:30-6; Sat: 10-5:30

J.S. Suarez has been in business for nearly half a century (three generations). In that time, he has made his reputation by selling name-brand bags at discounts of 30% to 50%. Copies of name-brand bags go for even better prices. For years, Suarez was *the* source for unlabeled Gucci bags that sold for less than half price and were identical to the real thing (naturally, since they came from the same factory). There is also a great selection of exotic skins. Suarez delivers top quality, great service, good selection, and excellent prices.

P. CHANIN
152 Eighth Ave (bet 17th and 18th St)   212/924-5359, 800/P CHANIN
Mon: 12-8; Tues-Sat: 12-11; Sun: 12-6

Just one word describes this place: eclectic! There is a fascinating collection of unusual accessory items for men and women: fashion watches, Hypnotic hats (the largest selection in the country), jewelry, and attractive handmade items from local artisans. If you want raves from guests at a weekend party in the Hamptons, stop here first.

ST. REGIS DESIGNS
58 E 7th St (bet First and Second Ave)   212/533-7313
Daily: 9-7

From this unlikely spot in the East Village, Andrew Pelensky—who used to work for a top handbag designer—turns out handmade original custom-designed handbags and belts from the finest leathers, including snake and alligator skins. The workmanship is magnificent, and items can be custom-ordered. For the quality, prices are downright cheap. It's the personal touch, like a final fitting before a belt leaves the premises, that makes St. Regis special.

Women's—General

> Although the East Village is an unlikely place for designer boutiques, here are three good ones:
> **Eileen Fisher** (314 E 9th St)
> **Kenar at Friedlich** (196 Orchard St)
> **Steven Alan Outlet Store** (330 E 11th St)

BETSEY JOHNSON
248 Columbus Ave (bet 71st and 72nd St)   212/362-3364
138 Wooster St (bet Prince and Houston St)   212/995-5048
251 E 60th St (at Second Ave)   212/319-7699
1060 Madison Ave (at 80th St)   212/734-1257
Hours vary by store

In the 1960s and 1970s, Betsey Johnson was *the* fashion designer. Her designs appeared everywhere, as did Betsey herself. As an outlet for those designs not sold to exclusive boutiques, Betsey cofounded Betsey Bunky Nini, but her own pursuits led to more designing and ultimately a store in Soho. The Soho store proved so successful that Betsey moved first to larger quarters and then up and across town, as well as into such department stores as Bloomingdale's. While her style has always managed to be avant-garde, it has never been way-out. Johnson believes in making her own statement, and each store seems unique, despite the fact that she has over 20 of them across the country. Prices, particularly at the Soho store (which started as an outlet), are bearable. Incidentally, it's hard to overlook the shops: pink, with neon accents and great windows.

BEVERLY M.
By appointment only   212/744-3726

The special edge here is that Beverly Madden will make and design clothing just for you, from skirts and blouses to jackets and evening pants. Delivery usually takes two to three weeks, depending on fabric availability. Personal interest and patience are the rules of the house.

CHELSEA ATELIER
128 W 23rd St (bet Ave of the Americas and Seventh Ave)
212/255-8803
Mon-Sat: 12-7; Sun: 12-5

This unusual store sells comfort in a big way. They design, make, and sell one-size-fits-all clothing for women. Best of all, their items have no buttons, zippers, or any other kind of closures. Everything is made in natural fabrics, like crepe de chine silk, raw silk, silk velvet, linen, cotton, rayon, and wool. You have to try on their clothes to grasp the appeal.

— **Millennium Note** —

New York's first subway ran on wind power. Built in secret in 1870 by a virtually forgotten genius, it boasted an elegant, 120-foot-long underground waiting room adorned with paintings and frescoes, a fountain, settees, a grand piano, and a huge aquarium full of goldfish. The line ran under Broadway from Warren Street to Murray Street—a distance of 312 feet. Its one car, a fancily appointed tubular affair, seated 22 people and was propelled at ten miles an hour by a blast of air from a gigantic, stationary, steam-driven fan.

EILEEN FISHER
314 E 9th St   212/529-5715
521 Madison Ave (bet 53rd and 54th St)   212/759-9888
341 Columbus Ave (bet 76th and 77th St)   212/362-3000
103 Fifth Ave (at 18th St)   212/924-4777
1039 Madison Ave (at 79th St)   212/879-7799
395 West Broadway (bet Spring and Broome St)   212/431-4567
Open every day; hours vary by store

For the lady who likes her clothes cool, loose, and casual, look no further than Eileen Fisher. This talented designer has put together a collection of easy-care, natural-fiber outfits that travel well and will be admired for their simple and attractive lines. The colors are earthy. From a small start in the East Village to six units all over Manhattan and space in some of the top stores, Eileen has produced a winner. The East Village store features discounted merchandise, plus first-quality goods.

FORMAN'S
82 Orchard St (regular sizes)
94 Orchard St (petite sizes)
84 Orchard St (plus sizes)   212/228-2500
Sun-Wed: 9-6; Thurs: 9-8; Fri: 9-4

59 John St (all sizes)   212/791-4100
Mon-Wed: 7:30-6:45; Thurs: 7:30 a.m.-7:45 p.m.; Fri: 7:30-5;
Sun: 11:30-5:30

145 E 42nd St (bet Lexington and Third Ave) (all sizes)   212/681-9800
Mon-Thurs: 8-9; Fri: 8-4:30; Sun: 10-6

Forman's has a well-deserved reputation for being the "fashion oasis of the Lower East Side." You'll find trendy discounted sportswear, separates, and outerwear from such famous houses as Evan Piccone, Jones NY, Kasper, and Liz Claiborne in sizes that will satisfy petites, normal figures, and plus-size women alike. The stock changes rapidly, so periodic visits are in order.

GALLERY OF WEARABLE ART
34 E 67th St   212/425-5379
Tues-Sat: 10-6 (call first in summer)

The best phrase to describe this innovative business is "anti-trendy." The Gallery of Wearable Art carries New York's largest collection of unusual clothing, jewelry, and accessories from all over the world. It is primarily a cottage industry, with a specialty in creating and designing special-occasion and bridal wear, plus all the accessories. If you are looking for unusual evening gowns, cocktail suits, bridal alternatives for nonclassic weddings, attractive jewelry, one-of-a-kind art jackets in antique textiles, and lace collage ensembles, make this your destination. You can even create your own gown. One thing is guaranteed: you won't see similar apparel on a friend or relative!

GISELLE SPORTSWEAR
143 Orchard St (bet Delancey and Rivington St)   212/673-1900
Sun-Thurs: 9-6; Fri: 9-3

Women's designer sportswear, current-season goods, large selection, discount prices. These are the reasons Giselle is one of the more popular shopping spots on the Lower East Side. All merchandise is first quality only. Factor in excellent service, and it's certainly worth the trip.

LAURA ASHLEY
398 Columbus Ave (at 79th St)   212/496-5110
Mon-Wed: 10-7: Thurs, Fri: 10-8; Sat: 10-7; Sun: 12-6

Laura Ashley has a contemporary new look, mixed with the classic theme that has been so popular over the years. In trying to target a younger audience, she's designed some exciting new fashions. Dresses for infants and children are sure grandma-pleasers. There are also home furnishings, fabrics for wallpaper and curtains, and bolt fabrics.

LEA'S DESIGNER FASHION
119 Orchard St   212/677-2043
Mon-Fri: 9:30-5; Sun: 9-5

You don't have to pay full price for your Louis Feraud, Albert Nipon, or other famous designer dresses and suits if you head to this popular Lower East Side outlet. Lea discounts her merchandise up to 30% and sells the previous season's styles for 50% to 60% off. Don't expect much in the way of amenities, but you'll save enough here to afford a special dinner to show off your new outfit!

MIRIAM RIGLER
14 W 55th St   212/581-5519
Mon-Sat: 10-6 (Thurs: 10-7)

Miriam Rigler is the quintessential ladies' dress shop. They have it all: personal attention, expert alterations, wardrobe coordination, custom designing (including bridal), and a large selection of everything from sportswear to knits to evening gowns, in sizes from 4 to 20. Also featured: custom headpieces, traditional and nontraditional bridal gowns, and mother-of-the-bride ensembles. Despite the location, all items are discounted, including special orders. Don't miss the costume jewelry!

NICOLINA OF NEW YORK
247 W 46th St   212/302-NICO
Daily: 10-8

Theater people love this unique store, located in the midst of the Theater District, which features modern copies of old pieces crafted with charm and imagination. Vests and ties made of old kimonos and designed by the owner are a special feature of a stock that includes all manner of accessories and novelty ready-to-wear. An added incentive is the staff, who are as friendly and fun as the clothes.

PALMA
521 Broome St (at Thompson St)   212/966-1722
Tues-Sat: 12-7: Sun: 1-5

To have been in business in Soho for over two decades is a tribute to sound retailing. And that is exactly what you get at Palma, a store whose personnel design women's clothing from a large selection of styles and fabrics. Once your measurements are on file, you can easily order new items of clothing.

S&W
Coats:
287 Seventh Ave (at 26th St)

Bags, shoes, accessories:
283 Seventh Ave (at 26th St)

Dresses, sportswear:
165 W 26th St (at Seventh Ave)

212/924-6656
Mon-Thurs: 10-6:30; Fri: 10-3; Sun: 10-6

Each location of S&W features a specialty, as indicated above. While the source of supply isn't entirely clear, S&W is one of the best places in the city for ladies' designer clothing. Unlike so many other discount boutiques, S&W maintains a consistent level of quality. On the down side, they would hardly win my "service with a smile" award.

SPITZER'S CORNER STORE
101 Rivington St   212/477-4088
Sun-Thurs: 9:30-5:30; Fri: 9:30-3:30

Spitzer's on Rivington is a Lower East Side landmark. There are two good reasons for shopping here: excellent selection and terrific prices. On the down side, you have to put up with less than helpful salespeople, unmarked merchandise, and three rooms jammed with goods. A bit of "bargaining" may be necessary, but you should be able to get some great bargains and have a memorable shopping experience to boot. Good luck.

TG-170
170 Ludlow St (bet Houston and Stanton St)   212/995-8660
Mon-Sun: 12-8

You won't see the clothes carried here in any other store. That is because most of the merchandise is from individuals who make small quantities especially for this store. TG-170 started as a studio to make baseball hats and T-shirts but has graduated into a retail showroom that displays unique garments from young and emerging designers.

Women's Large Sizes

> **For Large-Size Fashions**
> You have finally come into your own with large-size clothing lines from some of the top names in the fashion world, including Ellen Tracy, Carole Little, Jones NY, Liz Claiborne, and Eileen Fisher. Special departments can now be found at **Macy's, Bloomingdale's,** and **Saks.**

ASHANTI
872 Lexington Ave (bet 65th and 66th St)   212/535-0740
Mon-Wed, Fri, Sat: 10-6; Thurs: 10-8; Sun: 12-5

Its name is a throwback to the days when ethnic boutiques were popular in Manhattan, but Ashanti's current image couldn't be more in vogue. Today, Ashanti carries better dresses, clothing, and accessories solely for the larger woman. What they can't buy, they will have made to order. In fact, says Bill Michael, 75% of his merchandise is of Ashanti's own design and manufacturing. Operating on the belief that large ladies deserve a positive, stylish fashion image, Ashanti may be the only place that carries classic, quality clothing to size 28. They will perform alterations and ship anywhere. There is even a bargain basement.

> For information on special sales in New York, dial 212/55-SALES.

Women's—Maternity

MADISON AVENUE MATERNITY AND BABY BOUTIQUE
1043 Madison Ave (bet 79th and 80th St), 2nd floor   212/988-8686
Mon-Fri: 10-7: Sat 10-6; Sun 12-5

The atmosphere here is unfortunately what is found all too often at expensive Madison Avenue boutiques, which is to say, chilly bordering on rude, unless you look like you have lots of money to spend. But the clothing, mostly a French line with lots of muted colors and luxurious fabrics that is exclusive to the boutique, is absolutely beautiful. If you're expecting and are willing to drop a bundle on your wardrobe, you can't find a better place to shop. Look for relatively good sale prices on whatever is going out of season.

MIMI MATERNITY
2005 Broadway (at 69th St)   212/721-1999
Other locations throughout Manhattan
Mon-Thurs: 10-8; Fri-Sat: 10-7 Sun: 12-5

This national chain is well-stocked with reasonably priced, good-quality maternity clothing for home and office. If you're shopping for maternity clothes for the first time, rest assured that the salespeople know what you should be looking at and how to think about sizing. There's nothing particularly exciting at Mimi Maternity, but it's a good source for fashionable basics.

MOM'S NIGHT OUT/ONE NIGHT OUT
147 E 72nd St (bet Lexington and Third Ave)
Mom's Night Out: 212/744-6667
One Night Out: 212/988-1122
Mon-Fri: 10:30-6 (Thurs until 8); Sat: 11-5; Sun: 12-4 (appointments appreciated)

There's no need to stay home from some big event just because the stork is on the way. Mom's Night Out specializes in the rental, sale, and custommaking of elegant formal maternity wear. Its partner store, One Night Out, rents fine dresses and gowns (Halston, Vera Wang, Oscar de la Renta, Prada, Gucci, etc.) to all women, expecting or not. Jewelry, wraps, handbags, hosiery, and other accessories are also sold or rented. A hair and makeup artist is available by appointment.

Women's Millinery

CARLOS NEW YORK HATS
By appointment   212/564-6825

Ladies will find unique handmade hats in this establishment, which is open by appointment only. Bridal party millinery is a specialty, and Carlos Lewis personally guarantees all work.

HAT SHOP
120 Thompson St (bet Prince and Spring St)   212/219-1445
Tues-Sun: 12-7 (special hours by appointment)

Hats are still very much in vogue. Why? First, they are stylish. Second, with all the concern about skin cancer, women want to keep their heads covered. The Hat Shop has capitalized on the trend, offering custom sizing, a wide selection of colors and styles, and prices from $9-$375. If you are looking for a full-service millinery outlet, this is it!

MANNY'S MILLINERY SUPPLY COMPANY
26 W 38th St   212/840-2235
Mon-Fri: 9:30-5:30; Sat: 10-4

Manny's is another New York institution. They carry millinery supplies, and that's an understatement. Row after row of drawers are dedicated to particular aspects of head adornment. The section for ladies' hatbands alone takes up almost a hundred boxes and runs the gamut from thin pearl lines to wide leather Western-style belts. They have rhinestone banding and an enormous selection of artificial flowers and feathers. The center of the store is lined with tables displaying odds and ends, as well as several bins bulging with larger items that don't fit in the wall drawers. At the front, hat forms can be found on hat-tree stands and sample hats are displayed in no particular order. Manny's will help fix up any hat with interchangeable decorations. They also sell completed hats, close-outs, and samples, and will even re-create an old hat.

PAUL'S VEIL AND NET
42 W 38th St (bet Fifth Ave and Ave of the Americas)
212/391-3822
Mon-Fri: 8:30-4; Sat: 8:30-2

The mob scene here is repeated up and down the block, and even that is a mere fraction of the bridal business nationwide. Unbelieveable! Despite the competition from its neighbors (or perhaps because of it), Paul's gets my top recommendation for any bride-to-be searching for a bridal headpiece. Although they deal in illusion (lace, that is), they are one of the few stores on the block that does not maintain the illusion that they are a wholesale-only outfit, doing the lowly retail customer a big favor by unbarring the doors. The staff at Paul's seems genuinely glad to share your joy and help create a truly unique bridal veil or crown. The store stocks all that's needed by the rest of the bridal party, as well as unusual accessories, bridal supplies, and a great collection of imported floral headpieces. The lucky bride-to-be will find both the selection and savings extraordinary.

Women's Undergarments

A. W. KAUFMAN
73 Orchard St (bet Broome and Grand St)   212/226-1629
Sun-Thurs: 10:30-5; Fri: 10:30-2

Trying to find that special someone a gift? A.W. Kaufman offers high-quality lingerie at good values: elegant European and domestic lingerie, fine cotton underwear, bra and panties, and stunning bridal sets. For three generations, Kaufman has combined excellent merchandise with quality customer service. Among the many outstanding labels found here are Hanro, Lejaby, Christian Dior, Diamond Tea, Chantelle, Pluto, Valentino, and Natori.

IMKAR COMPANY (M. KARFIOL AND SON)
294 Grand St (bet Allen and Eldridge St)   212/925-2459
Sun-Thurs: 10-5; Fri: 9:30-2; Sun (summer): 10-3

Imkar carries pajamas, underwear, and shifts for women at about 33% off retail prices. A full line of Carter's infants' and children's wear is also available at good prices. The store has a fine line of women's lingerie, including dusters and gowns. Featured names include Model's Coat, Barbizon, Vanity Fair, Arrow, Jockey, Lollipop, and Munsingwear. Gold Toe Hosiery and Arrow shirts for men are also stocked.

LA PETITE COQUETTE
51 University Pl (bet Ninth and Tenth Ave)   212/473-2478
Mon-Wed, Fri, Sat: 11-7; Thurs: 11-8; Sun: 12-6

Interested in a men-friendly lingerie store that will take care of your gift needs? La Petite Coquette offers a large, eclectic mix of lingerie from around the world. I like their description of the atmosphere: "flirtatious!" If you are interested in high-end hosiery and bodywear imported from Austria, visit Wolford located just across the street.

SCHACHNER FASHIONS
95 Delancey St (bet Orchard and Ludlow St)   212/677-0700
Sun-Fri: 9-5:30

Schachner is a Lower East Side institution, selling brand-name robes, sleepwear, underwear, and lounge wear at discount prices. More than 35 years later, they are still doing what they do best!

UNDERNEATH IT ALL
444 E 75th St (at York Ave)   212/717-1976
Mon-Thurs: 10-6

Underneath It All is a one-stop shopping service for women who have had breast cancer or are undergoing chemotherapy. You can be assured of attentive, informed, and personal service, as all the staff are breast-cancer survivors. The store carries a large selection of breast forms in light and dark skin tones and in a variety of shapes, sizes, and contours. There is also a complete line of mastectomy bras and name-brand bras; mastectomy and designer swimwear; sleepwear, loungewear, and body suits; and wigs and fashionable head accessories.

VICTORIA'S SECRET
34 E 57th St (bet Park and Madison Ave)   212/758-5592
Mon-Sat: 10-8; Sun: 12-7

This has to be one of the sexiest stores in the world, in terms of ambience. The beautiful lingerie and bedroom garb, bridal peignoirs, exclusive silks, and accessories are displayed against the most alluring backdrops. The personnel are absolutely charming as well.

Don't miss the luxurious leg-, body-, and swimwear imported from Austria at **Wolford** (122 Greene St, 212/343-0808; 619 Madison Ave, 212/688-4850; and 996 Madison Ave, 212/327-1000).

Coins, Stamps
STACKS RARE COINS
123 W 57th St (at Ave of the Americas)   212/582-2580
Mon-Fri: 10-5

Stacks, established in 1858, is the country's oldest and largest rare-coin dealer. Specializing in coins, medals, and paper money of interest to collectors, Stacks has a solid reputation for individual service, integrity, and knowledge of the field. In addition to walk-in business, Stacks conducts ten public auctions a year. Both neophytes and experienced numismatists will do well at Stacks.

Computers
(See also "Electronics")

COMPUSA
420 Fifth Ave (bet 37th and 38th St)   212/764-6224
Mon-Fri: 8:30-8; Sat: 10-7; Sun: 11-6

1775 Broadway (at 57th St)   212/262-9711
Mon-Fri: 9-8; Sat: 10-7; Sun: 11-6

There are over 5,000 computer products in stock at these computer superstores, from modern desktop models to sophisticated software. The best part of the operation, besides the selection and competitive pricing, is the service. Even though the places are incredibly big and busy, the uniformly courteous sales staff will take time to answer the simplest questions.

COMPUTRS
7 Great Jones St (3rd St bet Broadway and Lafayette St)
212/254-9000
Mon-Fri: 10-6:30 (Thurs till 7); Sat: 11-6

This outfit has been in business since 1978 — long before computers had become a way of life. Computrs is now an authorized Apple/Macintosh dealer, in addition to carrying a full line of IBM-compatible systems. They are expert in film industry software, software for learning and translating foreign languages, Professional Astrologer's software suites, and CAD systems, as well as entry-level systems. A good selection of desktop publishing systems, software, and audiovisual systems is offered. A large selection of computer books and magazines is available. Prices are competitive (games are discounted 30%), and computer upgrades and repairs are a specialty.

SOFTWARE, ETC.
Locations throughout Manhattan
Hours vary by store

Software, Etc. is the largest resource in the area for computer accessories, books, and software, with highly competitive prices and informed service. They will special-order any item not in stock.

Cosmetics, Drugs, Perfumes

BATH ISLAND
469 Amsterdam Ave (bet 82nd and 83rd St)   212/787-9415
Sun-Fri: noon-8; Sat: 10-8

The customer is queen here. Custom scenting of products and custom gift packages are offered at this shop, which offers highly personal service. Over a hundred essential perfume oils are available, plus a great variety of creams, cleansers, lotions, and hair and shaving products.

BOYD'S MADISON AVENUE DEPARTMENT STORE
655 Madison Ave (at 60th St)   212/838-6558
Mon-Fri: 8:30-7:30; Sat: 9:30-7; Sun: 12-6

Boyd's is a drugstore in a city full of drugstores, so it has to have something special to be worthy of mention. In addition to a drug and prescription service, Boyd's carries a complete line of cosmetics, magnifying mirrors, soaps, jewelry, and brushes. The latter range from the common to the esoteric: i.e., nail brushes and mustache combs in a variety of sizes and shapes. Boyd's has one of the city's most complete selections of over-the-counter drugs, cosmetics, and sundries. A boutique department carries handbags, lingerie, hats, scarves, gloves, jackets, and hair accessories.

ESSENTIAL PRODUCTS
90 Water St (bet Wall St and Hanover Sq)   212/344-4288
Mon-Fri: 9-6

Essential Products has been manufacturing flavors and fragrances for over a century. They know that advertising and packaging drives up the price of name-brand colognes and perfumes, so they set out to see how closely they could duplicate expensive scents at cheap prices. They describe their fragrances as "elegant interpretations" of designer names, sold at a fraction of the original's price. Essential features 49 sensual perfumes and 23 men's colognes, and they offer a money-back guarantee. If you send a self-addressed stamped envelope, they will send scented cards and ordering information.

JAY'S PERFUME BAR
14 E 17th St   212/243-7743
Mon-Fri: 9-6; Sat: 9-4; Sun: 10-3:30

Bargains, bargains, bargains! Perfumes, cosmetic bags, colognes, soaps, powders, and other great smells all sell for 10% to 95% off list prices. Most are recognizable brand names.

KIEHL'S
109 Third Ave (bet 13th and 14th St)
212/677-3171, 800/543-4571
Mon-Wed, Fri: 10-6:30; Thurs: 10-7:30; Sat: 10-6

Kiehl's has been a New York institution since 1851. It is a third-generation, family-owned company unlike any you have ever visited. Their special treatments and preparations are made by hand and distributed internationally. Natural ingredients are used in the full lines of cleansers, scrubs, toners, moisturizers, eye-area preparations, men's creams, masks, body moisturizers, bath and shower products, sports items, ladies' leg-grooming formulations, shampoos, conditioners, and treatments. Customers will also enjoy the unusual collection of memorabilia related to aviation and motorcycles—interests of the Aaron Morse family, which runs this famous shop.

Here are several excellent beauty boutiques:
Alcone (235 W 19th St; 212/633-0551)
Ricky's (718 Broadway; 212/979-5232)
Sephora (555 Broadway; 212/625-1309): highly recommended
Shu Uemura (121 Green St; 212/979-5600)

Crafts

ALLCRAFT JEWELRY & ENAMELING CENTER
45 W 46th St, 3rd floor   212/840-1860
Mon-Fri: 9-4:45

If there is a definitive jewelry-making supply store, Allcraft is it. Their all-inclusive catalog includes a complete line of tools and supplies for jewelry making, silversmithing, metal smithing, lost-wax casting, and much more. Out-of-towners usually order from their catalog, but New Yorkers shouldn't miss an opportunity to visit this gleaming cornucopia. (For a catalog, write Allcraft Jewelry & Enameling Center, 666 Pacific Street, Brooklyn, NY 11217.)

CLAYWORKS
332 E 9th St (bet First and Second Ave)   212/677-8311
Tues-Wed: 3-7; Thurs, Fri: 3-8; Sat: 12:30-8; Sun: 2:30-8

For over a quarter of a century, talented Helaine Sorgen has been at work here! If you are interested in stoneware and porcelain, Clayworks is the place to come. All of Clayworks' pottery is lead-free and dishwasher- and microwave-safe. Small classes in wheel-throwing are given for adults. Everything here is individually produced, from teapots to casseroles, mugs, and sake sets. Decorative pieces include unique vases, goblets, platters, and bowls.

ERICA WILSON
717 Madison Ave (at 63rd St), 2nd floor   212/832-7290
Mon-Wed, Fri, Sat: 10-6; Thurs: 10-7

Erica Wilson is a lady of many talents. This British émigré not only writes books and newspaper columns about needlework but also finds time to design needlepoint kits for the Metropolitan Museum of Art. You'll find the city's finest selection of hand-painted needlepoint patterns from London and elsewhere. You can select finished pillows, hand-painted canvases, gifts, needlepoint and velvet shoes or slippers, and beautiful accessories from Erica's stock. Her chintz bags are very special. Blocking, padding, mounting, finishing—as well as classes in these skills—are available.

LOVELIA ENTERPRISES
356 E 41st St (in Tudor City Place)   212/490-0930
Mon-Fri: 9:30-5 (by appointment only)

Lovelia F. Albright's establishment is one of New York's great finds. From a shop in Tudor City Place, overlooking the United Nations, she dispenses the finest European Gobelin, Aubusson, and Beauvais machine-woven tapestries at prices that are often one-third that of any other place. The tapestries are exquisite. Some depict the ubiquitous unicorns cavorting in a medieval scene; others are more modern. They come in all sizes. The latest additions include tapestries for upholstery, wool-pile miniature rugs for use as mats under objets d'art, and an extensive line of tapestry-woven borders. They're designed by Albright and made exclusively for her in Austria and France. Send $5 for Lovelia's impressive mail-order catalog.

RADIO HULA
105 Mercer St (bet Houston and Prince St)   212/226-4467
Tues-Sat: By appointment only

This is the only retail gift gallery on the East Coast dedicated to the native culture of Hawaii and the South Pacific. They carry traditional and contemporary arts and crafts, woodcarvings, weavings, clothing, gourmet foods, jewelry, and books, including vintage Hawaiiana and other unusual items.

WOMAN'S EXCHANGE
149 E 60th St (bet Lexington and Third Ave)   212/753-2330
Mon-Sat: 10-6

The Women's Exchange was started over a hundred years ago to provide a marketplace for the crafts of women widowed by the Civil War. Over the years it evolved into a source of income for women and men in need. In recent years it has regrouped and moved, but the tradition as a showcase for crafts continues. They are particularly known for hand-smocking on children's clothing. Every item is one-of-a-kind. There are handmade sweaters, toys, dresses, quilts, whittled animals, paintings, decoupage, watering cans, flower pots, delicious homemade jams, and chocolates. While prices are not cheap, they are certainly competitive. The consignors receive 60% of the sale, so you are supporting them while giving a special gift.

WOOLGATHERING
318 E 84th St (bet First and Second Ave)   212/734-4747
Tues-Fri: 10:30-6; Sat: 10:30-5

What is the Woolgathering? It is a unique oasis dedicated to the fine art of knitting! Featured here is a big selection of quality European woolen, cotton, and novelty yarns. There's free instruction for those of all skill levels. They carry many exclusive classic and contemporary designs, a complete library of knitting magazines and books, and European-made knitting implements and gadgets. Finally, they provide very professional finishing services.

Dance Items

BALLET COMPANY
1887 Broadway (bet 62nd and 63rd St)   212/246-6893, 800/219-7335
Mon-Sat: 10-7 (Thurs: 10-9); Sun: 11-6

This one-stop is a mecca for ballet fans. Half the display area is devoted to books, records, and other memorabilia, while the other half is devoted to wardrobing the dancer. There are leotards, tights, tutus, skirts, knitwear, and shoes for children and adults. Also available are gift and novelty items, T-shirts, rare and out-of-print books, limited editions, new books, albums, programs, posters, art, collector's items, ballet videotapes, and autographs of stars.

Department Stores

BARNEY'S
600 Madison Ave (bet 60th and 61st St)   212/826-8900
Mon-Fri: 10-8; Sat: 10-7; Sun: 12-6

World Financial Center (225 Liberty St)   212/945-1600
Mon-Fri: 9-7; Sat: 11-5; Sun: 12-5

Founder Barney Pressman would be distressed to see what has happened to his store, which once was *the* place to buy clothing and accessories for men and boys. Third-generation family members borrowed money to expand rapidly throughout this country and overseas, and the results spelled financial and merchandising disaster. The flagship store on Madison Avenue is a combination women's and men's operation. Merchandise is, in many cases, on the cutting edge of fashion; however, prices are high and service can be less than accommodating. There is a good food operation (Fred's) in the downstairs area at the Madison Avenue store. Still, with so many fine department stores in New York, seasoned shoppers no longer make this their first choice.

BERGDORF GOODMAN
754 Fifth Ave (at 58th St)   212/753-7300

BERGDORF GOODMAN MEN
745 Fifth Ave (at 58th St)   212/753-7300
Mon-Wed, Fri, Sat: 10-7; Thurs: 10-8

Occupying a prime location on Fifth Avenue, just off the southwest corner of Central Park, Bergdorf is the epitome of class. The operation has broadened its appeal, reaching out to young and affluent customers. Many sections of the store have been redone into smaller boutiques. Lines have been expanded, and practically every major fashion name in the world is represented here. Dollar sales per square foot are among the highest in the nation. Bergdorf emphasizes top fashion names in all departments, and many of the styles are found exclusively in this store. Their windows usually display a fine selection of this apparel. The top floor presents an exciting array of home-accessory merchandise, carefully selected and beautifully displayed. Personnel here are great if they know you; if not, don't appear in your grubbies. A very high-class men's store is located across the street, where you'll find top names, along with prices to match. If you're looking for a special men's gift or are intent on attiring yourself in the best-of-the-best, Bergdorf Goodman Men is the place to go.

BLOOMINGDALE'S
1000 Third Ave (at 59th St)   212/355-5900
Mon-Fri: 10-8:30; Sat: 10-7; Sun: 11-7

No trip to Manhattan is complete without a visit to the flagship Bloomingdale's store on the Upper East Side. Under one roof, in a building that has been added to and changed many times since 1879, you will find one of America's greatest showings of top brand names in clothing, accessories, and home furnishings. The fashion floors are filled with labels from top American and foreign designers. The children's floors display a great selection. The recently remodeled men's furnishings section is complete, but the men's clothing department leaves a bit to be desired. Don't miss the great "Main Course" on six; it is a treasure trove for the home. The first-floor cosmetics department has to be seen to be believed; every major name in the industry is represented. Most every service imaginable is available; Bloomies will store packages, wrap gifts, and provide personal shopping companions. If you get hungry, Le Train Bleu is unique.

CENTURY 21 DEPARTMENT STORE
22 Cortlandt St (bet Broadway and Church St)   212/227-9092
Mon-Wed: 7:45-7:30; Thurs: 7:45-8:30; Fri: 7:45-8; Sat: 10-7:30; Sun: 11-6

Ask anyone who works in the Wall Street area where they best like to shop, and the answer you will get most often is Century 21. Why? Because the 16 departments in this bargain palace carry an amazing selection of quality merchandise for men, women, children, and the home at discounts that run from 25% to 75%. Outstanding departments include housewares, women's shoes, and children's apparel, where the brand names are tops and prices comfortable. Don't expect fancy fitting rooms and special amenities. But the service is informed and courteous, and you will not be disappointed.

HENRI BENDEL
712 Fifth Ave (bet 55th and 56th St)   212/247-1100
Mon-Sat: 10-7 (Thurs: 10-8); Sun: 12-6

The Henri Bendel store on Fifth Avenue is one of the classiest stores around. Founded in 1896 as a millinery store, Bendel's was a fixture on 57th Street for years. In a boutique setting, the store catered to high-fashion women's apparel for the upwardly mobile New Yorker. The present store, in the former Coty Building, keeps the same boutique atmosphere but expands it into a series of shops that exude fashion, quality, and excitement. You will want to buy something in every section you visit; it is that colorful and attractive! Wood is used prominently throughout, and the magnificent original windows by Rene Lalique have been incorporated into the store design in a most appealing manner. The store re-creates the ambience of Paris in the 1920s. Don't miss the Gilded Cage (makeup), the Garren Hair Salon, and Salon de Thé (sandwiches, salads, pastries, and more by Les Delices Guy Pascal). Bendel's "stylists" can take you from boutique to boutique by oval staircases. (There are, happily, no escalators in the building!) Top billing is given to up-and-coming designers, and shoppers will find a spectacular setting for wardrobe selections, and new and antique gifts.

LORD & TAYLOR
424 Fifth Ave (at 39th St)   212/391-3344
Mon, Tues: 10-7; Wed, Thurs, Fri: 10-8:30; Sat: 10-7; Sun: 11-6

America's oldest specialty store, Lord & Taylor is a retailing institution on New York's fashion front. The late Dorothy Shaver made it that way. The "L" and "T" could easily refer to Luxury and Tradition, because the store has been recognized for quality, service, and value since 1826. Now owned by the May company, Lord & Taylor on Fifth Avenue is the flagship of 73 stores nation- wide (with more to come) that display their allegiance to American designers in merchandise and advertising that touts "the Signature of American Style." Shoppers will find ten floors of famous-name options for everyone—from fashions to gifts for the home, plus special-size shops for petites and the larger woman. There are three popular restaurants, including the traditional Soup Bar. During December, Lord & Taylor becomes one of New York's most popular family attractions with its award-winning Christmas windows. On the down side, service is uneven, the men's sections leave much to be desired, the decor of the main floor is uninviting, and the store's phone system is abysmal.

MACY'S
151 W 34th St (at Herald Square)   212/695-4400
Mon-Sat: 10-8:30; Sun: 11-7

Macy's is billed as "the world's largest department store," and I doubt anyone would dispute that! Changes in the retail field have had a profound impact on this store. The retail giant is now owned by Federated (who would have ever thought that Bloomie's and Macy's would be brothers?), and the new owner- ship shows. The store has renewed sparkle, more inventory, better service, and an increased showing of top names in clothing and accessories. The downstairs housewares are a highlight. However, I consider the food section— which is now operated by Eatzi's—a disaster. Even though they have a hun- dred chefs and bakers, it is singularly unappealing, and is an extremely dif- ficult section in which to shop. You'll find a great selection of items for kids, an outstanding home furnishings section, and several fun places to rest and grab a snack. At Easter time, the flower show is magnificent.

SAKS FIFTH AVENUE
611 Fifth Ave (at 50th St)   212/753-4000
Mon-Wed, Fri, Sat: 10-7; Thurs: 10-8; Sun: 12-6

Synonymous with the very best of New York, Saks Fifth Avenue is a retail institution that continually shows it is committed to quality and excellence in fashion merchandising and service. In a prime location on Fifth Avenue at Rockefeller Center, this store continues to be a favorite shopping place for overseas visitors, tourists, and local residents. The Evening Boutique on the third floor is the first shopping place for women who want to be dressed with flair for a special occasion. The street and sixth-floor men's sections offer the top names in the country, including the legendary Alan Flusser and Brioni. The professional woman will find timeless fashions in clothing and accessories. The award-winning Cafe SFA, with gourmet lunches and light fare, is a delightful eighth-floor resting place with a great view to recharge batteries during a shopping expedition. There is much more: outstanding departments for infants and young people, a sparkling gift section, a beauty salon, complimentary "One to One" shopping service, and linguists for foreign visitors. Saks' premium credit-card program, SaksFirst, rewards loyal shoppers for their yearly spending with a plethora of bonuses and perks. Saks is the only place in Manhattan where the limited hardcover edition of this book is available!

TAKASHIMAYA
693 Fifth Ave (bet 54th and 55th St)   212/350-0100
Mon-Wed, Fri, Sat: 10-6; Thurs: 10-8

Located on prestigious Fifth Avenue, right in the middle of the Tiffanys and Guccis, this store is as much a museum and gallery as it is a retail establishment. Upstairs are beautiful Japanese-made clothing and accessory items, home furnishings, and gifts. Gorgeous flowers arrangements are featured on the first floor. Downstairs is a Japanese cafe for rest and meditation.

Department Store Clearance Centers

Bloomingdale's: 155 Glencove Rd, Carleplace, Long Island, NY (516/294-3410): furniture

Lord & Taylor: 3601 Hempstead Turnpike, Levittown, Long Island, NY (516/731-5031) and 839-60 New York Ave, Huntington, NY (516/673-0009): clothing

Macy's: 155 Glencove Rd, Carleplace, Long Island, NY (516/742-8500): furniture and electronics

---

Domestics
AD HOC SOFTWARES
410 West Broadway (at Spring St)   212/925-2652
Mon-Sat: 11-7; Sun: 11:30-6

The name of this store means just what it says: soft textures for modern living. There are sheets and towels, blankets, table linens, robes, dressing gowns, and pajamas. You will also see luggage, table-top items (china, glassware), gifts, shower curtains, bathroom hardware, and furniture. After visiting you'll have a soft spot in your heart for this unusual establishment.

D. PORTHAULT
18 E 69th St   212/688-1660
Mon-Fri: 10-5:30; Sat: 10-5

Porthault, the French queen of linens, needs no introduction. Custom-made linens are available in a range of 600 designs, scores of colors, and weaves of luxurious density. Wherever the name Porthault appears—e.g., some fancy hotels—you know you're at a top-notch operation. Their printed sheets seem to last forever and are passed along from one generation to another. Porthault can handle custom work of an intricate nature for odd-sized beds, baths, and showers. Specialties include signature prints, printed terry towels, unusual gift items, and decorative accessories like trays, wastebaskets, tissue-box covers, and room sprays.

HARRIS LEVY
278 Grand St (at Forsyth St)   212/226-3102
Sun-Fri: 9-5

Harris Levy is the dominant store on the Lower East Side for bed and table linens, pillows, comforters, bath and closet accessories, and towels. They have been in business since 1894 and offer good values and custom services, such as monogramming on sheets and towels and special embroideries for tablecloths. Customers will find dozens of patterns from leading American and European manufacturers at a fraction of the prices paid in uptown stores. This is a true family operation, with fourth-generation family members right on the job.

J. SCHACHTER'S
5 Cook St, Brooklyn 718/384-2732, 800/INTOBED
Mon-Thurs: 10-5; Fri: 10-1:30

J. Schachter's is the foremost purveyor of quilts in the New York area and perhaps on the entire continent. Schachter's is the oldest quilting firm in New York, and they make them in white goose down, polyester, lamb's wool, and cotton. The talented staff can make a quilt in any size and in 20 different quilting patterns from any fabric given to them. Baby ensembles are a specialty. Schachter's has a complete line of linens as well. Some of their bed linens come from Europe and are offered at discounts ranging from 20% to 40%. Custom pillows can be made while you wait. Entire bedrooms and bathrooms—from rugs to ceiling and wall coverings—can be coordinated. The experts at Schachter's refurbish down pillows and comforters, as well as sofa cushions.

PONDICHERRI
454 Columbus Ave (at 82nd St)   212/875-1609
Daily: 11-7

The beautiful window displays might make you think you could never afford anything inside Pondicherri. However, if you like exotic cotton prints and are looking for pillows, pillowcases, bags, trays (from Hong Kong), handicrafts and furniture (from Indonesia), tablecloths, quilts, clothing, and the like, by all means go in. Both the selection and prices are excellent! You'll find items from Tibet, India, Africa, and other exotic spots. Keep an eye out for unusual pottery and interesting knickknacks, too. Because the selection is large and most things are folded on shelves, you might want to ask for help.

PORTICO BED & BATH
139 Spring St (at Wooster St)   212/941-7722
Mon-Sat: 10-7; Sun: 12-6

Portico is located in a turn-of-the-century factory loft—a suitable background for their highly unusual collection of bath and body-care products, cast- and wrought-iron beds, and fine domestic and imported linens. This is not a store for bargain hunters; rather, Portico is for discerning shoppers who take pride in making their home a very special place.

PRATESI LINENS
829 Madison Ave (at 69th St)   212/288-2315
Mon-Sat: 10-6

Pratesi says it carries the best linens the world has to offer, and they're right. Families hand them down for generations. Customers who don't have affluent ancestors will wish to avail themselves of the new collections that come out in spring and fall. The Pratesi staff is unsurpassed in coordinating linens to decor or creating a custom look. Nearly all of the linens are of natural fibers, although some easy-care versions are carried. The three-story store boasts a garden which sets the mood for perusing the luxurious linens. Towels are made in Italy exclusively for Pratesi and are of a quality and thickness that must be felt to be believed. Bathrobes are magnificent, plush, and quietly understated. (So are the price tags.) There is also a baby boutique.

Electronics, Appliances, Fax Machines

> If visiting the numerous electronics, camera, and office-supply stores along Fifth Avenue and in the 50s along Avenue of the Americas, don't be misled by the discounts quoted off the marked retail figure. In many cases, those prices are grossly inflated. It is a wise idea to shop around at reputable stores before deciding on a purchase. Don't say I didn't warn you!

BERNIE'S DISCOUNT CENTER
821 Ave of the Americas (bet 28th and 29th St)   212/564-9431
Mon-Fri: 9:30-6; Sat: 11-4; closed in July, Aug

Bernie's stocks appliances, TVs, video games, answering machines, refrigerators, washers, dryers, radios, tape recorders, and air conditioners from the finest names in the business (e.g., Mitsubishi, Sony, Panasonic, and Norelco). The discount may be better at other stores mentioned in this section, but Bernie's is more conveniently located. Besides, Bernie's also services what it sells. If you want first-class treatment, ask for George Vargas.

DEMBITZER BROS.
5 Essex St (at Canal St)   212/254-1310
Mon-Thurs: 10-5; Fri: 10-2; Sun: 10-5

Dembitzer was one of the first discount appliance stores on the Lower East Side, and it was so successful that it spawned many imitators. This is good for the consumer. With a host of competitors nearby, Dembitzer works to keep the business it has garnered so far. They specialize in appliances that operate in 220-volt, 50-cycle applications for overseas use. However, they also have appliances for domestic use. Dembitzer's motto is, "If it plugs in, we have it," but even that doesn't do justice to the stock. Left out of that description are pens, luggage, soda makers, cameras, film, ad infinitum. Dembitzer also breaks the Lower East Side rudeness code. Between them, the brothers speak 8 or 11 languages (depending on whom you ask). While they clearly don't have time to traffic with people who are "just looking" or comparing prices, they can be charming to real customers.

HARVEY ELECTRONICS
2 W 45th St (at Fifth Ave)   212/575-5000
Mon-Fri: 9:30-6 (Thurs: 9:30-8); Sat: 10-6; Sun: 12-5

Not everyone understands all the fine points of the new technologies flooding the markets these days. For those who need professional advice and individual attention, Harvey's is the place to shop for state-of-the-art consumer electronics. They offer the whole spectrum of quality audio/video components, with home theater and high-definition television being their specialty. Harvey has an in-home design and installation division that will integrate studio and video systems into new and existing residences.

For special home service for high-end audio and visual equipment, call **Sound by Singer** (18 E 16th St, 212/924-8600).

J&R MUSIC & COMPUTER WORLD
15 Park Row (one block south of City Hall)
212/238-9000, 800/221-8180
Mon-Sat: 9-7; Thurs: 9-7:30; Sun: 10:30-6:30

These folks pride themselves on being one of the nation's most complete computer, electronics, and home-entertainment department stores. They carry cameras, radios, televisions, speaker systems, VCRs, DVDs, cassette and CD players, personal electronics, records, tapes, compact discs, computer systems, telephone answering machines, telephones, typewriters, microwave ovens, and breadmakers. The place is well organized but gets rather hectic at times. Prices are competitive, and merchandise is guaranteed.

LYRIC HIGH FIDELITY
1221 Lexington Ave (bet 82nd and 83rd St)   212/439-1900
Mon, Wed, Fri, Sat: 10-6; Tues, Thurs: 10-7

Lyric is a favorite among audiophiles. As owner Michael Kay says, Lyric caters to those with a passion for recorded music and the cash to indulge their wildest audio fantasies. You can buy a basic music system at Lyric for under $1,000, but you can also part with a six-figure sum for an exotic component ensemble. Kay has owned Lyric since 1959, seling audio equipment to people who want the best, and he's very particular about the lines he carries.

P.C. RICHARD & SON
120 E 14th St (bet Third and Fourth Ave)   212/979-2600
Third Ave at 86th St   212/289-1700
Mon-Fri: 9 a.m.-9:30 p.m.; Sat: 9-9; Sun: 10-7

For nearly a century, this family-owned and -operated appliance, electronics, and computer store has been providing superior service to customers. They offer a large inventory, good prices, delivery seven days a week, and their own service center. The store started as a hardware outfit, and unlike so many other family operations, the genius of personalized service has been successfully passed from one generation to the next.

PHONE BOUTIQUE
828 Lexington Ave (at 63rd St)   212/319-9650
Mon-Fri: 10:30-6:30; Sat: 11-6

Here you can buy or rent new and antique-style phones, have them repaired, and purchase answering machines, fax machines, and telephone-related accessories. You can even have your phone painted. They also rent cellular phones and beepers to New York visitors.

RCS COMPUTER EXPERIENCE
575 Fifth Ave (at 47th St)   212/687-3773
Mon-Fri: 9-8; Sat: 10-7; Sun: 11-6

261 Madison Ave   212/949-6935
Mon-Fri: 9-7; Sun: 10-6

575 Madison Ave   212/949-6935
Mon-Sat: 9-9; Sun: 10-6

I would not recommend these mobile computing stores if it weren't for the fact that they have a good selection of the newest and best computers, organizers, and accessories. However, their service is among the poorest in Manhattan: disinterested salespeople, poor follow-through on orders, terrible handling at point-of-sale. Hopefully they're improving!

SHARPER IMAGE
4 W 57th St (at Fifth Ave)   212/265-2550
900 Madison Ave (at 73rd St)   212/794-4974
Mon-Fri: 10-7; Sat: 10-6; Sun: 12-5

Pier 17, South Street Seaport   212/693-0477
Mon-Sat: 10-9; Sun: 11-8

If you are a gadget freak like me, you'll go wild at the Sharper Image. This is truly a grown-up's toy store! The very latest electronic gadgets, household helpers, sports items, games, novelties, and clothing make browsing this fascinating emporium a unique experience.

SONY PLAZA
550 Madison Ave (bet 55th and 56th St)   212/833-8830
Mon-Sat: 10-7; Sun: 12-6

You'll delight at this mixture of two Sony retail stores and a consumer-friendly atrium. Sony is often at the cutting-edge of new developments in consumer electronics, so periodic visits here will reveal the latest in radios, televisions, audio equipment, home theater systems, cameras, clocks, and more. You'll find most of the sales personnel to be patient and knowledgeable, despite a somewhat overbearing security atmosphere.

SPECTRA AUDIO RESEARCH
903 Madison Ave (bet 72nd and 73rd St)
212/744-2255, 800/342-0456
Mon-Sat: 10-6

It's always best to deal with experts, and Spectra definitely fits that description. Spectra has a one-price policy and offers state-of-the-art items. If you want to phone someone in the middle of an African rain forest, these guys even sell and rent satellite phones!

STEREO EXCHANGE
627 Broadway (at Houston St)   212/505-1111
Mon-Fri: 11-7:30; Sat: 10:30-7; Sun: 12-7

You can't do better for high-end audio-video products than this outfit! They carry top names, have an on-site service department, and can handle customer installation. The personnel here really seem to care about their products.

VICMARR STEREO AND TV
88 Delancey St   212/505-0380
Sun-Fri: 9-6

In the middle of famed Delancey Street on the Lower East Side, Mal Cohen presides over a treasure house of electronics, including stereo and hi-fi equipment, multi-voltage items, telephones, answering machines, and camcorders, as well as microwave ovens, organs, sunglasses, and fans. Unlike many electronics outfits, everything here is well organized, marked, and displayed, with no high-pressure selling. Best of all, the prices are right, and you can be assured of not getting secondhand merchandise. Vicmarr is one of the largest JVC outlets in the area; they also carry Sony, Alpine, Kenwood, and Panasonic. Save yourself some time by calling ahead for prices.

WAVES
110 W 25th St, Suite 1005   212/989-9284
Mon-Fri: 12-6; Sat, Sun: 10-6

The past lives on at Waves, and Bruce and Charlotte Mager are trying to make it last forever with their collection of vintage record players, radios, receivers, and televisions. They have scorned the electronics age in favor of the age of radio. Their shop is a virtual shrine to the 1930s and before. Here you'll find the earliest radios (still operative!) and artifacts. There are radio promotion pieces, such as a radio-shaped cigarette lighter. Gramophones and anything dealing with the radio age are available. Waves is capable of repairing musical instruments and rents phonographs, telephones, and neon clocks. They make appraisals and will answer any questions on repair, sales, or rental.

THE WIZ
Locations throughout Manhattan
212/964-5196
Hours vary by store

There is a tendency to think twice about shopping at chain electronics stores. Service can be irregular. Prices may not be the lowest. Fortunately, this chain can be depended on for excellent customer relations, huge inventories, and a real concern for your satisfaction. I would recommend a stop at any of the Wiz stores. They claim "Nobody Beats the Wiz," and their prices are indeed extremely competitive.

Fabrics, Trimmings

A.A. FEATHER COMPANY
(GETTINGER FEATHER CORPORATION)
16 W 36th St (bet Fifth Ave and Ave of the Americas), 8th floor
212/695-9470
Mon-Thurs: 9-6; Fri: 9-3

Suppose you've made a quilt and want to stuff it with feathers? What if your latest outfit simply has to have an ostrich plume, feather fan, or feather boa? Well, you're in luck with A.A. Feather (a.k.a. Gettinger Feather Corporation). The Gettingers have been in the business since 1915 and have passed the trade down to Dan Gettinger, who is the first grandson. There aren't many family businesses around now, and there are even fewer sources for really fine-quality feathers. This is a find!

A. FEIBUSCH—ZIPPERS & THREADS
27 Allen St   212/226-3964
Mon-Fri: 9-5; Sun: 9-4 (closed Sun in summer)

Would you believe a large store dedicated entirely to zippers? Well, in New York, nothing is impossible. A. Feibusch boast of having "one of the biggest selections of zippers in the U.S.A," as if they really believe there are zipper stores throughout the country! They do stock zippers in every size, style, and color (hundreds of them), and can make zippers to order. I saw one woman purchasing tiny zippers for doll clothes! Feibusch carries matching threads to sew in a zipper as well. Eddie Feibusch assured me that no purchase is too small or large, and he gives each customer prompt, personal service.

ART MAX FABRICS
250 W 40th St   212/398-0755
Mon-Fri: 8:30-6; Sat: 9-5

The Fabric Wholesale District is conveniently adjacent to the Garment District, and the usual retail-shopper traditions of that area apply here. Some stores welcome retail customers, some don't, and others fluctuate with the market. Art Max is dedicated to the retail customer. Many languages are expertly spoken. Three floors are filled to overflowing with outstanding fabrics for clothing. They now carry full lines of fabric for everyday wear: linens, English all-wool suitings, domestic and imported wools, cotton prints, solids, wool and cashmere coatings, and silks. The really striking brocades, metallics, and laces require an experienced touch; it would be a shame for a novice to ruin such beautiful fabrics. The real specialty here is bridal fabrics. When the fabrics mentioned above are made into gowns, the wedding party could rival a *Vogue* layout. There are a dozen different types of nets for bridal veils and infinite combinations of heavier materials.

B&J FABRICS
263 W 40th St (bet Seventh and Eighth Ave)   212/354-8150
Mon-Fri: 8-5:45; Sat: 9-4:45

Martha Stewart likes this place! B&J started in the fabric business in 1940 and is now run by the second and third generations of the Cohen family. There are three complete floors of fashion fabrics, many imported directly from Europe. Specialties of the house: natural fibers, designer fabrics, bridal fabrics, and silk prints. There are over a thousand of the latter in stock! Swatches are sent free of charge, upon request. You will find a wonderful selection of hand-dyed batiks in a corner of the basement.

BECKENSTEIN MEN'S FABRICS—FABRIC CZAR USA, INC.
133 Orchard St   212/475-6666, 800/221-2727
Sun-Fri: 9-6

Simply put, this is the finest men's fabric store in the nation. Proprietor Neal Boyarsky and his son Jonathan have been called "the fabric czars of the U.S." These folks sell to a majority of all custom tailors in the country and to many top manufacturers of men's clothing, so you know the goods are best quality. Their customer list reads like a who's who: Warren Beatty, Al Pacino, all three *Godfather* movies, Robert DeNiro, diplomats and politicians like the Kennedys and Rockefellers, Magic Johnson, Wayne Gretsky, and on and on. You will find every kind of fabric, from goods selling for $10 a yard to fabulous pieces at $1,000 a yard. There are pure cashmeres, fine English suitings, pure silks, camel hair, and more. This professional operation is not typical of most Lower East Side stores. Don't miss it!

BUTTONHOLE FASHIONS
580 Eighth Ave (bet 38th and 39th St)   212/354-1420
Mon-Fri: 8-5:30

For nearly half a century these folks have been offering bound buttonholes and buttonhole eyelets, plus straight and curved pockets with cords in all lengths and sizes.

CINDERELLA FLOWER AND FEATHER CO.
48 W 37th St (bet Fifth Ave and Ave of the Americas)   212/840-0644
Mon-Fri: 9-5:30; Sat: 10-4

In the midst of a particularly cold and dreary winter not so long ago, Seventh Avenue fashions began to blossom with artificial flowers as the "in" look for spring. The department stores quickly got the message, and in just a few weeks, people were removing their fur-lined gloves to hand over $10 for a single flower for their lapel. Many such transactions were made along 34th Street or Fifth Avenue, and only a few wise New Yorkers walked an extra two blocks to the "trimmings district," where they could buy an identical flower for 75 cents. There were even buyers of the $10 variety who knew of the district and assumed they couldn't get in! Cinderella Flower and Feather Company is for them. They have the country's largest selection of feather trimmings, decorations, craft supplies, and conversation pieces. You can also find silk and other artificial flowers, ribbons, shoulder pads, veiling, netting, and feather boas in many colors.

HANDLOOM BATIK
214 Mulberry St (at Spring St)   212/925-9542
Wed-Sat: 12-7; Sun: 1-6

At Handloom you'll find one of the largest and best collections of batik outside a crafts museum. Carol Berlin runs Handloom Batik with near reverence for her merchandise. All of the fabrics are handmade, and she is quick to show how each can be set off to best advantage. Imported hand-woven and hand-batiked fabrics (primarily from India and Indonesia) are sold by the yard as fabric or are made up as clothing, napkins, tablecloths, and handiwork. Handloom Batik will also use its own fabrics for custom-made shirts and other garments. In addition, a gift selection features handicrafts of wood, stone, brass, and paper from the aforementioned countries. Pillows, bed covers, curtains, and napkins can be custom-made from the store's cotton ikat and batik.

HARRY ZARIN CO.
318 Grand St   212/925-6112
Daily: 9-5:30

Harry Zarin is one of the largest and oldest (since 1936) fabric warehouse/ showrooms in New York. Many of Manhattan's top decorators use this source. It was here that the trend of direct selling in the fabric industry began. They ship anywhere. A custom workroom is on the premises, along with a bargain basement where they sell remnants. Another Zarin operation worthy of mention is BZI Distributors (105 Eldridge St), which sells drapery and upholstery hardware.

HYMAN HENDLER AND SONS
67 W 38th St (bet Fifth Ave and Ave of the Americas)   212/840-8393
Mon-Fri: 9-5:30; Sat: 10-3 (closed Sat in July and Aug)

Although Hyman Hendler has passed away, the store that proudly bears his name is in the capable hands of his sons and niece. In the middle of the trimmings center of the world, Hyman Hendler is one of the oldest businesses (established in 1900) and the crown head of the ribbon field. This organization manufactures, wholesales, imports, and acts as a jobber for every kind of ribbon. It's hard to believe as many variations exist as are jammed into this store.

LONG ISLAND FABRIC WAREHOUSE
406 Broadway (bet Canal and Walker St)   212/431-9510
Daily: 9-6

Island Fabric Warehouse has one huge floor of every imaginable kind of fabric and trimming. Since it is all sold at discount prices, it's one of the best places to buy fabrics. Some of the attractions include an extensive wool collection and such dressy fabrics as chiffon, crepe, silk, and satin. Most amazing are the bargain spots, where remnant and odd pieces go for so little it's laughable. They sell an excellent selection of patterns, notions, and trimmings at the same low prices so that customers won't have to make several stops. Dollar-a-yard fabrics are also available.

MAISON DECOR
1094 Madison Ave (at 82nd St)   212/744-7079
Mon: 1-6; Tues-Fri: 10-6; Sat: 11-5

If you want to jazz up your surroundings with a bit of color, make this one of your first stops. Maison Decor features a great fabric selection that combines the Spanish tradition of textile manufacturing with the hospitable colors of the Mediterranean. The prices are moderate and quality superb. Best of all, a number of fabrics are available immediately.

M&J TRIMMING CO.
1008 and 1014 Ave of the Americas (bet 37th and 38th St)
212/391-9072
Mon-Fri: 9-6; Sat: 10-5

These folks say they have the largest selection of trims at one location in the entire country. After visiting the store, I'm inclined to believe them! You will find imported trims, buttons, decorator trims, and various fashion accessories. One store specializes in clothing and fashion trims; the other features interior decor trim. They have over a half century of experience in this business.

PARON FABRICS/PARON II
56 W 57th St (bet Fifth Ave and Ave of the Americas), 2nd floor
212/247-6451
Mon-Sat: 9-5:45

PARON EAST
855 Lexington Ave (bet 64th and 65th St)   212/772-7353
Mon-Sat: 9-5:45 (Thurs until 7)

PARON WEST
206 W 40th St (at Seventh Ave)   212/768-3266
Mon-Sat: 9-5:45

At Paron, you will find an excellent selection of designer fabrics uptown at discount prices. Paron carries the very latest, and many of the goods are available only in their stores. This is a family operation, so personal attention is assured. Paron West is their 50% off outlet.

PIERRE DEUX-FRENCH COUNTRY
870 Madison Ave (at 71st St)   212/570-9343
Mon-Sat: 10-6

Pierre Deux, the French Country home-furnishings company, specializes in authentic handcrafted products from the provinces of France. Everything from 18th-century antique and reproduction furniture to fabrics, brightly colored pillows, faience, pewter, lighting, table linens, and glassware can be found here. A personalized bridal registry and custom orders are also available.

SILK SURPLUS/BARANZELLI HOME
1127 Second Ave   212/753-6511
Mon-Fri: 10-6; Sat: 10-5:30

Silk Surplus is the exclusive outlet for Scalamandre close-outs of fine fabrics, trimmings, and wallpaper, as well as Baranzelli's own line of imported and domestic informal fabrics and trimmings. Scalamandre is sold for half off retail, and a choice selection of other equally luxurious fabrics is offered at similar savings. There are periodic sales, even on fabrics already discounted, at this elegantly run fabric store. They have added custom workrooms to complete window treatments and upholstery slipcovers, and custom furniture is a specialty.

TINSEL TRADING
47 W 38th St   212/730-1030
Mon-Fri: 10-5:30; Sat: call for hours

The personnel at Tinsel Trading claim it is the only firm in the United States specializing in antique gold and silver metallics from the 1900s. They have everything from gold thread to lamé fabrics. Tinsel Trading offers an amazing array of tinsel threads, braids, fringes, cords, tassels, gimps, medallions, edging, banding, gauze lamés, bullions, tinsel, fabrics, ribbons, soutache, trims, and galloons. All are genuine antiques, though many customers buy them for accenting modern clothing. The collection of military gold braids, sword knots, and epaulets is unsurpassed.

TOHO SHOJI (NEW YORK)
990 Ave of the Americas (at 36th St)   212/868-7466
Mon-Fri: 9-6; Sat: 10-5

Ever hear of a trimmings supermarket? Only in New York will you find an establishment like this. Toho Shoji stocks all manner of items that allow customers to design and make custom jewelry: earring parts, metal findings, chains, and every kind of jewelry component. Items are well displayed for easy selection.

Fireplace Accessories

DANNY ALESSANDRO
223 E 59th St (bet Second and Third Ave)   212/421-1928
Mon-Fri: 9-5 (open weekends seasonally)

New Yorkers have a thing for fireplaces, and Danny Alessandro caters to that infatuation. Just as New York fireplaces run the gamut from antique brownstone to ultramodern blackstone, Danny Alessandro's fireplaces and accessories range from antique pieces to a shiny new set of chrome tools. The shop also stocks antique marble and sandstone mantelpieces, andirons, and an incredible display of screens and tool kits. In the Victorian era, paper fans and screens were popular for blocking fireplaces when not in use. Alessandro's collection of surviving pieces is great for modern decorating. Danny Alessandro will also custom-order mantels, mantelpieces, and accessories. Bear in mind that this is primarily a fireplace accessory source, so neither advice nor information is given on how to put a fireplace in working order. Alessandro has been in business for over 40 years, and they assume every New Yorker who has a fireplace knows how to use it.

For the Best Barbecues!

Northeast Consolidated Charcoal (630 Supor Boulevard, Harrison, New Jersey; 718/456-8876) has been servicing the New York metropolitan area since 1905 with 100% natural wood charcoal and packaged firewood that is kiln-dried and insect-free. They are located ten minutes outside the Lincoln and Holland tunnels in Harrison, New Jersey and are open Monday through Friday from 6-5.

WILLIAM H. JACKSON
210 E 58th St   212/753-9400
Mon-Fri: 9:30-5

"WBFP" in the real-estate ads stands for "wood-burning fireplace," and they are the rage in New York. In business since 1827, William H. Jackson is familiar with the various types of fireplaces in the city. In fact, many of the fireplaces were originally installed by the company. Jackson has hundreds of mantels on display in its showroom. The variety ranges from antiques and antique reproductions (in wood or marble combinations) to starkly modern pieces. There are also andirons, fire sets, screens, and excellent advice on enjoying your fireplace. Jackson does some repair work (removing and installing mantels is a specialty), but they're better known for selling fireplace paraphernalia. Handy item: a reversible hanging sign that reads "Damper is open"/"Damper is closed."

Flags

ACE BANNER AND FLAG COMPANY
107 W 27th St   212/620-9111
Mon-Fri: 7:30-4

If you need a flag, Ace is the place. Established in 1916, Ace prides itself on carrying the flags of every nation in the world. Other kinds of flags can be ordered. They range in size from 4" by 6" desk flags to bridge-spanning banners. Ace also sells custom banners, buttons, pins, patches, and pennants. If you're running for any kind of office, campaign paraphernalia can be ordered with a promise of quick delivery. Carl Calo, Ace's owner, claims that a large part of his business consists of outfitting grand openings and personalizing equipment with such items as boat flags.

Floor Coverings

BEYOND THE BOSPHORUS
79 Sullivan St (bet Spring and Broome St)   212/219-8257
Tues-Sun: 12-6

Ismail Basbag, the owner of this establishment, was a kilim dealer for 12 years in Istanbul's grand bazaar before opening his shop in Soho in 1985. Anyone who can survive at that colorful, crowded, and noisy marketplace can certainly do business in Manhattan! Here you will find hand-woven Turkish kilim rugs and pillows in a variety of sizes, patterns, and colors. The owner travels to Turkey several times a year and will try to unearth customers' special requests. Rug cleaning and repair is also available.

CENTRAL CARPET
81 Eighth Ave (at 14th St)   212/741-3700
Mon-Fri: 10-7 (Thurs: 10-8); Sat: 10-6; Sun: 11-6

Imagine over 20,000 rugs in stock! Central Carpet carries new, antique, and handmade semi-antique Oriental rugs from Persia, China, India, and Tibet; machine-made rugs from Belgium and Egypt; and hand-hooked rugs from China. Also featured are needlepoints, kilims, area rugs, and items suitable for children's rooms. A large selection of broadloom, as well as sisal carpeting and rug padding, is shown. Everything is sold at discount prices, and all rugs are displayed on racks for easy viewing.

COUNTRY FLOORS
15 E 16th St   212/627-8300
Mon-Fri: 9-6 (Thurs: 9-8); Sat: 9-5 (closed Sat in summer)

Country Floors is one of New York's biggest success stories, probably because they offer a magnificent product. Begun in 1964 in the tiny, cramped basement under the owner's photography studio, Country Floors has grown to include huge stores in New York, Philadelphia, Miami, and Los Angeles, with nearly 60 other affiliates nationwide. Customers from across the country have learned that Country Floors carries the finest in floor and wall tiles and stone. Their sources include a variety of styles and artisans from all over the world. All are unique, and a visit—or at least a look at their catalog—is necessary to appreciate the fineness and intricacy of each design. Even the simplest solid-color tiles are beautiful.

ELIZABETH EAKINS
21 E 65th St   212/628-1950
Mon-Fri: 10-5:30

If you are looking for a first-class source for hand-woven wool and cotton rugs, look no further. Elizabeth Eakins custom-designs and makes hand-woven and hand-hooked rugs in standard and hand-dyed colors. She also offers beautiful pillows made of antique fabrics.

I.J. PEISER'S SONS
475 Tenth Ave (bet 36th and 37th St)   212/279-6900
Mon-Fri: 9-5

In business for nearly a century, these folks specialize in furnishing and installing new hardwood flooring. They work with top-end architects, designers, and general contractors. A large showroom displays various types of wood that may be installed in both residential and commercial spaces.

MOMENI INTERNATIONAL
36 E 31st St, 2nd floor   212/532-9577
Mon-Fri: 9-5

The people here will tell you they are wholesale only, but don't let that scare you away. Those who do visit will be rewarded by what may be the single best source for Oriental rugs in the city, because Momeni is a direct importer. Since they don't officially suffer individual retail customers, their prices reflect wholesale rather than retail business. That doesn't make them cheap (good Oriental rugs never are), but it does assure top quality at a fair price.

NEMATI COLLECTION
Art and Design Building
1059 Third Ave (bet 62nd and 63rd St), 3rd floor
212/486-6900
Mon-Fri: 9-6; Sat: 10-4 (or by appointment)

Parviz Nemati has been in the business for nearly four decades, and his store offers an extensive collection of antique Oriental rugs, period European tapestries, and a full-service restoration department. Additional services include consultations, insurance appraisals, and professional cleaning and conservation.

PASARGAD CARPETS
105 Madison Ave (at 30th St)   212/684-4477
Mon-Fri: 9-6; Sat: 10-6; Sun: 11-5

Pasargad is a fifth-generation family business, established in 1904. They know what they are talking about when it comes to antique, semi-antique, and new Persian and Oriental rugs. They have one of the largest collections in the country, and they provide decorating advice, repair and cleaning, and a pickup and delivery service. Pasargad will also buy or trade quality antique rugs.

PILLOWRY
P.O. Box 6902, New York, NY 10128-0016   212/308-1630
By appointment only

Although she has given up the store temporarily, Marjorie Lawrence still has a superior collection of antique and semi-antique pillows that she has assembled since 1971. She has set up several rooms at a warehouse in midtown Manhattan, where she gives personal attention to her clients and those interested in individually created pillows from over a thousand fragments in her possession: tapestry, needlepoint, silk, knotted rug, Aubusson, and more.

RUG WAREHOUSE
220 W 80th St (nr Broadway)   212/787-6665
Mon-Sat: 10-6 (Thurs: 10-8); Sun: 11-5

One of the largest collections of antique and semi-antique Oriental rugs in the city is available at the Rug Warehouse. The current owners come from a family tradition of five decades in the rug business. A huge inventory of over 5,000 antique and contemporary rugs includes creations from 13 countries. Modern premises provide an attractive setting for rugs that are often offered at good discounts.

SAFAVIEH CARPETS
153 Madison Ave (at 32nd St)   212/683-8399
238 E 59th St (at Second Ave)   212/888-0626
Mon-Fri: 9-6; Sat: 10-6; Sun: 11-5

902 Broadway   212/477-1234
Mon, Thurs: 10-8; Tues, Wed, Fri: 10-7; Sat, 10-6; Sun: 11-6

There was a time when it was possible to visit the teeming markets of Tehran and find some real bargains in rugs. No more. One is still able to see a vast selection of these beautiful works of art at Safavieh, even if the setting is a little less glamorous. Safavieh has one of the finest collections of Persian, Indian, Pakistani, and Chinese rugs in this country. They're displayed in a showroom spacious enough for you to visualize how the prized pieces would look in your own home or place of business. These rugs are truly heirlooms, and you will want to spend time hearing about their exotic origins. Prices, although certainly not inexpensive, are competitive for the superior quality represented. It doesn't hurt to do a little haggling.

Flowers, Plants, Gardening

CHELSEA GARDEN CENTER NURSERY
205 Ninth Ave (at 22nd St)   212/929-2477
Daily: 9-6:45

There's no shortage of stock here. That is one of the big advantages of Chelsea Garden Center Nursery, as you will be able to compare dozens of plant varieties. There are big selections of plants, shrubs, trees, and pots, and prices are competitive. The sales personnel are reasonably helpful. Be sure to get on their mailing list.

GARDEN CRAFTERS (THE SOHO GARDEN)
37 Grand St   212/966-6030
Tues-Fri. 10-7; Sat, Sun. 11-8
Hours vary by season; call ahead

A garden oasis amid the cast-iron columns of Soho? Everything for the garden can be found at Garden Crafters, from the finest plants to the largest selection of planters, garden furniture, and ornaments. Here you'll find the leading edge in planters: lightweight fiberglass in metallic antique finishes, bronze verdigris, and rusted cast iron. All of the fiberglass and distinctive gift items can be shipped anywhere in the country.

GRASS ROOTS GARDEN
131 Spring St (bet Wooster and Greene St)   212/226-2662
Tues-Sat: 9-6; Sun: 12-6

Larry Nathanson's grassroots movement began more than a quarter of a century ago when he turned his hobby into a full-time vocation. The genuine possessor of a green thumb, Nathanson couldn't understand why city pavement had to be an inhibiting factor for would-be urban farmers. So he blithely set up his Grass Roots Garden, paying no mind to the boutique atmosphere or cutesy merchandising that marked the shops of his peers. Every square inch in Nathanson's shop is crammed with sprouting green plants. In addition to selling plants, they also design, install, and maintain outdoor rooftop, backyard, and terrace gardens. Grass Roots makes house calls all over town and runs a plant-maintenance and consulting service. They also show one of the largest stocks of pottery in Manhattan.

SIMPSON & COMPANY FLORISTS
852 Tenth Ave (at 56th St)   212/772-6670
Mon-Fri: 9-6: Sat: 10-5

Simpson offers unusual flowers, plants, and beautiful freeze-dried arrangements of flowers, fruits, and vegetables done on premises. These are very lifelike; you can only tell the difference from fresh flowers by touching them. The fourth floor houses an orchid greenhouse, which is the only one of its kind in the city. These folks can decorate for gatherings of all sizes, and their prices are very competitive.

SPRING STREET GARDEN
186½ Spring St (bet Thompson and Sullivan St)   212/966-2015
Mon-Sat: 11:30-7 (closed Sat in July and Aug)

You'd never know you were in the bowels of Manhattan in this store. The service is highly personalized, and there is a great selection of cut flowers and plants. They arrange everything to order and will deliver all over Manhattan. You'll also enjoy the picturesque 19th-century building.

TREILLAGE
418 E 75th St (at York Ave)   212/535-2288
Mon-Fri: 10-6; Sat: 10-5 (closed weekends in July, Aug)

People forget that New Yorkers have gardens, too, although they are small. Many times they are just patios, but still they add a special dimension of charm to city living. Along comes Treillage to help make an ordinary plot of outside living into something special. There are all sorts of garden items, including furniture and accessories for indoors and outdoors, with a great selection of unusual pieces that will set your place apart. They sell everything except plants and flowers! Prices are not inexpensive, but why not splurge to enhance your little corner of the great outdoors?

VSF
204 W 10th St (bet 4th and Bleecker St)   212/206-7236
Mon-Fri: 10-6; Sat: 11-5 (summer: Mon-Fri: 10-5)

Those who want a special look when it comes to fresh-cut flowers or dried creations know that you can't do better than this outfit. They have a top-drawer list of clients who take advantage of their talents for weddings and other special events. Ask for owners Jack Follmer or Spruce Rodens.

ZEZÉ FLOWERS
398 E 52nd St (bet First Ave and East River)   212/753-7767
Mon-Fri: 8-6 (and holiday weekends)

Zezé came to New York several decades ago from Rio de Janeiro, a city known for its dramatic setting, and he brought a bit of that drama to the flower business in Manhattan. Zezé's windows reflect his unique talent. The exotic orchid selection is outstanding. Here you will find the ultimate in personalized service, including same-day deliveries, and filling special requests.

Furniture, Mattresses

General

CHARLES P. ROGERS BRASS & IRON BED COMPANY
55 W 17th St (bet Fifth Ave and Ave of the Americas)
212/675-4400
Mon-Fri: 10-7; Sat: 10-6; Sun: 12-6

Are you hunting for a real antique piece? Rogers has been in the bed business for a century and a half and knows everything about good looks and comfort. Rogers shows over 50 models in four-poster, contemporary, canopied, and hand-painted styles. There are replicas of original designs and old-time beds, and all sizes are available in stock or on order. These folks sell factory-direct, so prices are competitive.

DEUTSCH WICKER
200 Lexington Ave, Suite 1101   212/683-8746, 800/223-4550
Mon-Fri: 9-5:30; Sat: by appointment

Wicker and rattan became popular in the mid-1970s, but Deutsch had been in the business for 20 years by that time. What an inventory! Over 600 pieces of furniture are carried here. They originally sold only to interior designers, furniture stores, and large businesses, but now the public can directly purchase this high-quality merchandise from Deutsch. All of it is imported. Roger Deutsch is rightfully proud of his standing in the field, and you should seek him out for advice when shopping here. Also available are leather and rattan chairs.

FOREMOST FURNITURE SHOWROOMS
8 W 30th St (at Fifth Ave), 5th floor   212/889-6347
Mon-Fri: 10-6; Sat: 10-5; Sun: 11-5

Decorators recommend Foremost to friends who want to avoid decorator commissions. It's a good place to get quality furniture at a 20% to 50% discount. Foremost has five full floors of furniture. The personnel are friendly and helpful, making this an excellent source. The values are indeed very good, so shop around and then make this one of your last stops.

FRANK EASTERN COMPANY
599 Broadway (at Houston St)   212/219-0007
Mon-Fri: 9-5; Sat: 11-3:30 (closed Sat in summer)

For business and computer furniture, Frank Eastern Company should be a first choice. They are capable of completely furnishing a business or home office with tables, desks, chairs, files, bookcases, partitions, and a full line of computer work stations. Frank Eastern Company specializes in advanced ergonomic chairs that prevent backache and premature fatigue. The company president has conducted years of extensive research in this field. He has personally tested over

2,370 different chairs from all over the world in an ongoing attempt to find the ultimate chair for the person who works at a desk or a computer. All of it is sold at discount, and a free catalog is available on request.

GRANGE
200 Lexington Ave (at 32nd St), 2nd floor   212/685-9057
Mon-Fri: 9-6 or by appointment

Superb French furniture and accessories dominate the selling floor of this very attractive showroom. The goods are all French-inspired, and the furniture is clean-lined, functional, and in great taste. What the Italians have contributed to the classy look in ready-to-wear, the French have achieved in home collections. Note, however, that this is not a place for bargain hunters.

J. MABLEY CUSTOM FURNITURE
355 West Broadway (bet Grand and Broome St)   212/966-3930
Tues-Fri: 10-6; Sat: 11-6; Sun: 12-5

If you are looking for handcrafted fine-quality upholstered sofas, chairs and ottomans at reasonable prices, this is a good place to start. Fabrics range from high-end printed linens from England to simple cottons. Each frame is hand-assembled from fine California hardwoods; most deliveries are made within eight weeks.

KENTSHIRE GALLERIES
37 E 12th St (bet University Pl and Broadway)   212/673-6644
Mon-Fri: 9-5; Sat: 10:30-3 (Oct-April)

Kentshire presents eight floors of English furniture and accessories, circa 1690-1870, with a particular emphasis on the Georgian and Regency periods. This gallery has an excellent international reputation, and the displays are a delight to see, even if the price tags are a bit high. There is also a collection of 18th- and 19th-century English jewelry. A Kentshire boutique at Bergdorf Goodman features antiques, accessories, and antique jewelry.

KLEINSLEEP
962 Third Ave (at 58th St)   212/755-8210
874 Broadway (at 18th St)   212/995-0044
2330 Broadway (at 84th St)   212/501-8077
Mon-Fri: 10-9; Sat: 10-8; Sun: 11-7

Kleinsleep is a chain of stores specializing in bedding needs for less than department-store prices. At each store, the byword is discount, and at their three New York locations, prices are reduced even further. Kleinsleep showrooms feature mattresses from Stearns & Foster, Sealy Posturepedic, Simmons Beautyrest, Serta Perfect Sleeper, Kingsdown Sleeping Beauty, and their newest handcrafted line of Aireloom products. The Aireloom models feature an eight-way hand-tied box spring at prices you'd normally pay for a regular mattress and box spring. At Kleinsleep, customers get advice, expertise, and discounts up to 65% off department-store prices.

NORTH CAROLINA FURNITURE SHOWROOM
12 W 21st St (at Fifth Ave), 5th floor   212/645-2524
Mon-Sat: 10-6 (Thurs 10-8); Sun: 12-5

You'll find 409 famous name brands in furniture here, and most everything is discounted. There are items for livingrooms and bedrooms, dinettes and dining-room tables and chairs, sofa beds, recliners, platform beds and bedding, and things for children's rooms. For New Yorkers, who must make every square inch of apartment space count, this place is a must-visit.

OAK-SMITH & JONES
1510 Second Ave (bet 78th and 79th St)   212/327-3462
Mon-Sat: 10-8; Sun: 11-7

A distinct foreign accent can be detected in the furniture and accessories carried here. Unique original and reproduction antiques and accessories from all over the world are shown next to an outstanding collection of antique pine items and brass and iron beds. Upholstery and decorating services are available.

OFFICE FURNITURE HEAVEN
22 W 19th St, 7th floor   212 989-8600
Mon-Fri: 9-6

Have you nearly exhausted your budget opening a new office? Relax. This place has bargains in first-quality contemporary pieces. Some are manufacturer's close-outs, others are discontinued items. You'll find the big boys of the industry represented: Knoll, Herman Miller, and Steelcase. There are conference tables, chairs, bookcases, file cabinets, accessories, and much more.

Good Places to Shop for Bargains!

The 17th-floor clearance center at the **New York Design Center** (200 Lexington Ave; 212/213-8911) has furniture and gift items. There are exceptional values on showroom samples, available for immediate delivery. Hours: Mon-Fri: 9-5 p.m.

For furniture overstocks, canceled orders, and slow-moving items, try **Macy's Clearance Center** (155 Glen Cove Rd, Carleplace, Long Island, 516/742-8500) and **Bloomingdale's Clearance Center** (same building, different entrance, same phone). These clearance centers are open seven days a week.

OSBORNE & OSBORNE
508 Canal St   212/431-7075
Sat-Sun: 1-6 or by appointment

Since 1975, Kipp and Margot Osborne have been building custom-made hardwood furniture for private and corporate clients. Each of their pieces is signed, dated, and numbered, marking both the continuing evolution of their work and the unique nature of each piece. They are shown in an 1827 landmark rowhouse in Tribeca. Traditional, time-proven cabinetmaking techniques and joinery provide the quality basis for Osborne furniture. Using these methods in conjunction with a careful process of wood selection and matching of wood grain, the Osbornes have created a body of work that numbers more than 2,000 pieces.

PHILIP ENGEL
220 E 54th St (at Third Ave)   212/759-9595
Mon: 10-8; Tues-Sat: 10-6; Sun: 12-5

They like to call themselves the "world's greatest leather store," and indeed they do feature outstanding pieces of furniture in leather: sofas, dining-room tables and chairs, sectionals, sofa beds, and reclining chairs from all over the world. The company has been in business since 1967 and has five stores throughout the metropolitan area. Prices are reasonable, delivery is quick, pieces may be custom-ordered, and free in-store design service is available.

Infants and Children

ABC CARPET & HOME
888 Broadway (at 19th St)   212/473-3000
Mon-Fri: 10-8; Sat: 10-7; Sun: 11-6:30

ABC has a baby department filled with whimsical, unusual, and well-designed furniture and other items. Cribs and bassinets, handmade quilts, bumper sets, infant clothing, chairs that Goldilocks would no doubt find "just right," and lots of wood toys are among the highlights here. From an iron bassinet that carries a $795 price tag to a line of high-quality terrycloth bathrobes for toddlers and children, nothing in this department is a bargain. But if you're looking for good-quality furnishings for infants and small children, ABC is worth a look.

ALBEE'S
715 Amsterdam (at 95th St)   212/662-5740
Mon-Sat: 9-5:30 (Thurs to 7:30)

This place makes me crazy. It's got one of the city's best selections of basics for infants and toddlers—everything from strollers and car seats to cribs and rocking chairs—and the staff can be very helpful. But the place is a disaster area, and it's hard to get anyone's attention in the chaos, particularly on weekends. That said, Albee's is very popular with Manhattan parents (and grandparents!), and it's worth a visit if you're expecting. For the record, prices aren't the best in town, but they *are* the best north of 23rd Street.

BABY DEPOT
707 Ave of the Americas (at 23rd St), 3rd floor   212/229-2247
Mon-Sat: 9-9; Sun: 10-6

As part of Burlington Coat Factory, this is exactly the kind of place that has some New Yorkers bemoaning the "malling" of their city. The service stinks, the stock is poorly presented, and the selection is spotty . . . but prices on baby furniture and accessories are great. If you know what you want and are willing to put up with shabby retailing to save a couple bucks, I regretfully recommend this perpetually crowded place.

BEN'S FOR KIDS
1380 Third Avenue (bet 78th and 79th St)   212/794-2330
Mon-Fri: 9:30-5 (Thurs to 8); Sat: 10:30-5

If you aren't willing to leave the East Side and yet want a good selection of basic baby and toddler furniture, clothing, toys, and accessories at relatively reasonable prices, this is the place to go. One real price-saver: Ben's doesn't charge for delivery or setup. The store's good organization and helpful staff make it easy to look around and try out different options.

CHILDREN'S ROOM
140 Varick St (at Spring St)   212/627-2006
Mon-Fri: 10-5:30; Sat 10-5

The name says it all. While there is absolutely nothing fun or fancy about this long-lived children's furniture store, it does have all the basics at good prices. If you're looking for beds (particularly bunk beds, which are quite popular in this space-starved city), bookcases, dressers, desks, and the like but don't want to spend their college tuition, take a trip down here.

KID'S SUPPLY COMPANY
1325 Madison Ave (bet 93rd and 94th St), 2nd floor   212/426-1200
Mon-Fri: 10-6; Sat: 10-5

This relative newcomer to the children's-furniture scene advertises itself as an "elegant but reasonable resource for antique and contemporary furuishings." (Read: You have really good taste and a lot of money to spend on your child's room.) I highly recommend visiting these talented folks in their beautiful but crowded showroom. From bunk beds and desks to rugs and other accessories, the owners of Kid's Supply Company have really put together a classy operation. A worthwhile extra: they'll visit your home and work up a floor plan for $150.

PLAIN JANE, INC.
525 Amsterdam Ave (bet 85th and 86th St)   212/595-6916
Mon-Sat: 11-6

What a pleasure it is to discover a store brimming with quality merchandise and a friendly, knowledgeable staff! This relative newcomer to the New York baby and small child home-furnishing scene offers unique furniture, bedding, and accessories. Prices are certainly higher than you'd pay straight off the shelf, but you're purchasing excellent personal service and terrific style at Plain Jane. If you're having a baby or know somebody who is, stop in and look around. You'll be glad you did.

SCHNEIDER'S
20 Ave A (at 2nd St)   212/228-3540
Mon-Sat: 10-6

If you are in the market for baby furniture and accessories, this little-known store (at least to "uptown" people) often has the best prices in Manhattan. On top of that, the staff knows its stock, and there's enough space in the store to take a stroller for a test drive. Whether you're looking for cribs, car seats, strollers, backpacks, or other items for little ones, Schneider's is well worth a visit. They carry juvenile furniture as well.

WICKER GARDEN'S BABY
1327 Madison Avenue (at 93rd St)   212/348-1166
Mon-Sat: 10-6 (call for special hours in July and Aug)

There are no two ways about it: Pam Scurry has a great sense of style. If you like wicker furniture, handpainted detail and unusual, often whimsical designs, you'll love the baby and juvenile furniture on the second floor of this store. You'll also no doubt be quite taken with the extensive selection of almost quaintly formal infant and children's clothing on the first floor. (The infant clothing is heavy on pink, blue, and white.) That's the good news. The bad news is that everything at Wicker Garden is incredibly expensive, and the staff are among the haughtiest I've encountered in New York.

Games—Adult

COMPLEAT STRATEGIST
11 E 33rd St (at Fifth Ave)   212/685-3880
Mon-Wed, Fri, Sat: 10:30-6; Thurs: 10:30-9

342 W 57th St (bet Eighth and Ninth Ave)   212/582-1272
Mon-Sat: 11-8; Sun: 12-5

The Compleat Strategist was established as an armory of sorts for military games and equipment. As the only such place in the city, it was soon overrun with military strategists. As time went on, the store branched into science fiction, fantasy, and murder-mystery games, as well as adventure games and books. When this, too, captured the imagination of the public, the Compleat Strategist opened two more outposts. Today people who are fighting the Civil War all over again can browse alongside Dragon Masters at three locations in the city! The stock is more than ample, and the personnel are knowledgeable and friendly. For more cerebral sorts, they have chess and backgammon sets—even good old Monopoly!

GAME SHOW
474 Ave of the Americas (bet 11th and 12th St)   212/633-6328
Mon-Sat: 12-7 (Thurs: 12-8); Sun: 12-5

If you can't find a kid's or adult's game or puzzle at Game Show, it probably doesn't exist. This store is crammed with the best of the lot, and the folks here love to talk to customers about their stock.

VILLAGE CHESS SHOP
230 Thompson St (bet Bleecker and 3rd St)   212/475-9580
Daily: noon-midnight

People who enjoy chess can play at the Village Chess Shop for about a dollar an hour. Those searching for really unique chess pieces should patronize this shop as well. Chess sets are available in pewter, brass, ebony, onyx, and more. Village Chess has outstanding backgammon sets, too. In short, this should be the first stop when you're moving chess pieces—either from one square to another or from their store to your home!

Gifts, Accessories

ADRIEN LINFORD
927 Madison Ave (bet 73rd and 74th St)   212/628-4500
1339 Madison Ave (at 93rd St)   212/426-1500
Daily: 11-7

Here you will find an eclectic mixture of gifts, decorative accessories for the home, occasional furniture, lighting, jewelry, and whatever else Gary Yee finds interesting and exciting. The atmosphere and price tags are definitely upscale; you'll be suitably impressed with the tasteful stock.

À LA MAISON
1078 Madison Ave (bet 81st and 82nd St)   212/396-1080
Mon-Sat: 10-7; Sun: 11-6

What a wonderful shop this place is for those who want to present a really spectacular table! There are tabletop items, gifts for the home, some furniture items, and a bridal registry. Most of the merchandise is European in origin.

BERTABRASIL
151 W 46th St (bet Ave of the Americas and Seventh Ave), 7th floor
212/354-9616
Mon-Fri: 9-5:30; Sat: 9-2

This is a loft discount boutique featuring a number of well-known names in watches, sunglasses, electronics, cosmetics, and some clothing items. Don't expect to find depth in any classification, but good bargains exist if you don't mind disinterested salespeople.

BE-SPECKLED TROUT
422 Hudson St (at St. Luke's Pl) 212/255-1421
Mon-Sat: 10-9; Sun: 10-7

Here is a turn-of-the-century general store that features unique items for fishermen and anyone else with good taste. There is folk art, tea-related antiques, English bone china from the 1920s and 1930s, and handmade chocolates, plus the owner's collection of angling antiquities and eccentricities. An old-fashioned soda fountain of 1860s vintage now serves egg creams, lemonade, and more. Craig and Charlotte Bero's grandfather owned the shop's original fixtures. You can try homemade American pies on what used to be a real fishing ground. Yes, Be-Speckled Trout occupies the former site of Minetta Creek, which still flows under the Village.

BIZARRE BAZAAR
130¼ E 65th St (bet Lexington and Park Ave)   212/517-2100
Gallery hours by appointment

Some people collect baseball cards, others find political buttons fascinating. I collect "Do Not Disturb" signs from hotels I have stayed at! For the discerning and serious collector, Bizarre Bazaar offers antique toys, aviation and automobilia, vintage Louis Vuitton luggage, enamel glassware, French perfume bottles, Lalique pieces, artist's mannequins, architectural miniatures, and much more of good quality. This is a place for browsing and buying!

CAROLE STUPELL
29 E 22nd St   212/260-3100
Mon-Sat: 10-6

wow!

Are you planning a party? Imagine the fun of setting a table with the most beautiful accessories available. The first place that anyone who has such a yen should visit is Carole Stupell. In my opinion, this is the finest home-accessory store in the country. The taste and thought that has gone into the selection of merchandise is simply unmatched. Keith Stupell, a second-generation chip-off-the-old-block, has assembled a fabulous array of china, glassware, silver, and gift treasures, and he displays them in spectacular settings. In addition, the store offers a large selection of china and glassware replacement patterns that date back over 30 years. The prices are not in the bargain range, but the quality is unequaled.

CERAMICA GIFT GALLERY
1009 Ave of the Americas (bet 37th and 38th St)
212/354-9216, 800/666-9956
Mon-Fri: 9:30-6; Sun: 12-5

We've been looking for a place that has good bridal-registry giftware at discount prices, as it's been one of the most frequent requests from readers. We've found just the place, and the convenient midtown location is a bonus. At Ceramica Gift Gallery, you'll find all major brands of china, crystal, tableware, and collectibles, including Waterford, Royal Doulton, Gorham, Minton, Wedgwood, and Lenox. In addition, they ship anywhere in the country and will accept mail and phone orders. Discounts can go as high as 50%, and they will quote prices over the phone.

CURACAO
20 W 57th St, 4th floor   212/581-6970
Mon-Fri: 9-6; Sat, Sun: 10-3

This is a special find, but only for those with non-U.S. passports. There is a great selection of pens, electronics, perfumes, gifts, and some clothing at considerable savings. For visitors from overseas, Curacao is a bonanza. New York residents should go with someone who has a foreign passport and share in the savings.

EVERYTHING ANGELS
112 Mulberry St (at Canal St)   212/334-7230
Sun-Thurs: noon-10; Fri, Sat: noon-midnight

Everything Angels' new store is a little piece of heaven in the heart of Little Italy, brimming with heavenly gifts from all over the world. There is jewelry, artwork, clothing, books, and much more. The sky is the limit! They also work with groups and conduct a corporate, bridal, and wholesale gift business.

FELISSIMO
10 W 56th St   212/247-5656
Mon-Wed, Fri-Sat: 10-6; Thurs: 10-8

Felissimo is a highly unique gift store with an emphasis on tabletop merchandise. The five-story building, a turn-of-the-century townhouse, has eight rooms displaying beautiful merchandise, including jewelry, scarves, cashmeres, outdoor living items, and plants and flowers, as well as things to make your dining table extra special. They are known for their *furoshiki* gift wrap: beautiful fabric squares that are a longstanding Japanese tradition. On the fourth floor are bimonthly exhibits featuring the work of renowned and up-and-coming artists. Afternoon haiku tea (sandwiches, scones, sweet bits, and other goodies) are served in the store's fourth-floor tearoom.

FLIGHTS OF FANCY
1502 First Ave (bet 78th and 79th St)   212/772-1302
Mon-Fri: 12-7 (Wed until 8); Sat: 10-6; Sun: 12-6

Flights of Fancy exudes charm, presenting soft music and an array of American treasures in a Victorian parlor setting beckoning passers-by. Many of the gifts are handmade and exclusive to the shop, and the window display (which changes weekly) often showcases only one item in a line. That item is often so unusual and special that orders pour in from around the country. Prices range from $2 to $2,000, so there is something for every gift-giving budget. Suggestions? It's hard to be specific, but a handmade American theme runs through the ever-changing stock.

GOLDMAN'S TREASURES
655 Ave of the Americas (at 20th St)   212/924-4900
Mon-Thurs: 10-9; Fri: 10-3; Sun: 11-3

Goldman's Treasures offers a unique shopping experience. Here you will find an attractively priced selection of things for the home, including furniture, decorative accessories, lighting, mirrors, pictures, china, crystal, and silver. Goldman's also stocks a huge selection of gifts. In business since 1907, they moved to this location from the Lower East Side in 1994.

L. S. COLLECTION
494 Broome St   212/334-1194
Mon-Sat: 11-7; Sun: 12-6

Even if you have no intention of buying a thing, you'll get a thrill out of this superb collection. Seldom have I seen home- and office-accessory items done in such superb taste. Each piece is almost museum-quality. You'll find furniture, art glass, vases, tea and coffee sets, desk pieces, and leather goods that would be just the thing for your dream home. Prices are not low, but neither are they out of line for the quality represented.

MAYA SCHAPER CHEESE & ANTIQUES
106 W 69th St (at Columbus Ave)   212/873-2100
Daily: 10-8

Maya Schaper is one of those special personalities who knows what she likes and wants to share her interest, which pertains to cheese and food-related antiques. Granted, this is an unusual combination. But Maya is an unusual person. You'll find interesting gifts, gift baskets, imported dried flower arrangements from France, country antiques, and painted furniture. Schaper is willing to locate special items for customers.

MICHAEL C. FINA
545 Fifth Ave (at 45th St)   212/557-2500, 800/BUY-FINA
Mon-Fri: 9:30-6 (Thurs: 9:30-7); Sat: 10:30-6

A New York tradition for over 60 years, Michael C. Fina is a popular bridal-registry firm with an extensive selection of sterling silver, china, crystal, and housewares. Prices are attractive, quality is top-notch, and the store is well organized.

ONLY HEARTS
386 Columbus Ave (at 79th St)   212/724-5608
Mon-Sat: 11-8; Sun: 12-7

This is one of the most fun places to shop in New York! Helena Stuart offers the romantic in the family a fascinating array of intimate apparel and lingerie, heart-shaped or printed jewelry, balloons, boudoir pillows, soaps, tissues, and even heart-shaped candles and pasta.

SUSAN P. MEISEL DECORATIVE ARTS
133 Prince St (bet West Broadway and Wooster St)   212/254-0137
Tues-Sat: 10-6

Meisel is really a toy store for nostalgic adults. You will find the area's largest selection in certain specialized categories: pond sailboats, pinup originals, and airplanes of all sorts. It strikes me as a rather unusual combination, but if the mentioned items are on your want list, this is the place to visit!

WORKS GALLERY
1250 Madison Ave (bet 89th and 90th St)   212/996-0300
Mon-Wed, Fri: 10-6; Thurs: 10-7; Sat: 10-6; Sun: 12-5

Sometimes we all need a unique gift for a special person or occasion. If so, this is a place to visit. At Works Gallery you will find one-of-a-kind jewelry and art-glass items handmade by talented artists. You can even have a personal piece made from your own stones. They have been in business for over 20 years.

YELLOW DOOR
1308 Avenue M, Brooklyn   718/998-7382
Mon-Fri: 10-5:45; Sun: 11-5

One of the best things about Brooklyn is a discount gift store on Avenue M in Flatbush, off the promenade of Ocean Parkway. It is run by native-born entrepreneur Sallee Bijou. For over 30 years the Yellow Door has been providing "Madison Avenue style at Brooklyn prices." The store carries an unparalleled selection of the finest name brands (Lalique, MacKenzie-Childs, Waterford, Lenox, Orrefors, Alessi, Towle) in 14- and 18-carat gold jewelry, gifts, china, table accessories, and bath items. Many prices are at least 20% to 30% below suggested retail. Services include free local delivery, a bridal registry, and phone orders. One service they do *not* provide: pleasant telephone manners.

Greeting Cards

UNICEF CARD & GIFT SHOP
3 United Nations Plaza (44th St bet First and Second Ave)
212/326-7054
Mon-Fri: 10-6; Sat: 10-2

For half a century the United Nations Children's Emergency Fund (UNICEF) has been improving the lives of the world's children. One way this tremendous organization raises money for its life-saving projects and programs is through the sale of cards and gifts. If you've never seen UNICEF products before, you're in for a treat at this well-planned and friendly store. In addition to greeting cards, stationery, books and games for children, and a fascinating assortment of Nepalese paper products, this store sells cards chosen for sale in Asia, Africa, Europe, and South America. In fact, it's the only store in the U.S. that sells these exotic cards.

UNTITLED
159 Prince St (at West Broadway)   212/982-2088
Mon-Sat: 10-10; Sun: 11-7

The Metropolitan Museum and the Louvre each have approximately 1,500 art cards for sale. Untitled, by contrast, has 4,000-plus cards in stock at any given moment. Those cards include modern-art postcards, greeting cards, and note cards. The postcards are filed either as pre- or post-1945, and they're further ordered within those classifications by artist. There are also postcards featuring famous photos and depictions of every possible type of art. Some of these items are good for gags, while others are suitable for framing. Untitled also sells art magazines, boxed cards, and books on art, design, typography, architecture, and photography.

Hearing Aids
EMPIRE STATE HEARING AID BUREAU
31 W 43rd St 212/921-1666
Mon-Fri: 9-5:30 (Wed until 6)

If President Reagan has left no other legacy, he's set a shining example by not being ashamed to wear a hearing aid. The latest generation of hearing aids are so small that most people cannot even tell they're being used. Empire State has been in the business for over 40 years and carries the top names in the field: Siemens, Starkey, Bosch, Danavox, and the lastest in digital hearing aids by Widex. Skilled personnel will test and fit quality hearing aids in a quiet, unhurried atmosphere.

— Millennium Note —
The first private telephone in the city was installed in May 1877 at 89 Fifth Avenue by order of a Mr. Charles Cheever, acting on behalf of a friend whose name he did not give.

Hobbies
AMERICA'S HOBBY CENTER
146 W 22nd St 212/675-8922
Mon-Fri: 8:45-5:30; Sat: 8:30-3:30

While hobbies and models are serious business here, there's also a lighthearted touch evident in the shop. Marshall Winston introduces himself as the "known authority on vehicular hobbies," which include model airplanes, boats, ships, trains, cars, radio-controlled items, model books, helicopters, model rocketry, tools, and everything for model builders. They also sell wholesale to dealers and by mail order to retail customers, as well as conducting an export business. Ask for a catalog to see what they have in your field of interest.

JAN'S HOBBY SHOP
1557 York Ave (bet 82nd and 83rd St) 212/861-5075
Mon-Sat: 10-7; Sun: 12-5

Jan is one of my favorite examples of New York retailing! When Fred Hutchins was young (he's now in his 40s), he was obsessed with building models and dioramas, particularly on historical themes. Eventually, it became economically viable for his parents to buy his favorite source of supply. Now he runs the shop, keeping Jan's stocked with everything a serious model builder could possibly want. The store has a superb stock of plastic scale models, model war games, paints, books, brushes and other paraphernalia, like toys, trains, planes, ships, and tank models. It also carries remote-controlled planes, sailboats, ships, and tanks. Fred himself creates models and dioramas to order for television, advertising, and private customers. In addition to his craft skills, he is noted for accurate historical detail and can provide information from his vast library of military subjects. There is yet a third business: showcase building. Because any hobbyist likes to show his wares, Fred builds custom-made wood, plexiglass, glass, and mahogany showcases.

Home Furnishings — General

It used to be that only those with designers' cards were admitted to some trade buildings. Now, however, a number of design outfits will take care of individual customers even if the signs on their doors say "trade only." Don't be put off by that sign. Here are some of the buildings in New York to check out; each has a multitude of shops where you can find just about anything you want to fix up an apartment or home.

Architects & Designers Building: 150 E 58th St; Mon-Fri: 9-5
Decoration & Design Building: 979 Third Ave; Mon-Fri: 9-5
(It's a good idea to bring a decorator along with you.)
Decorative Arts Center: 305 E 63rd St; Mon-Fri: 9-5
Decorators Center Building: 315 E 62nd St; Mon-Fri: 9-5
Fine Arts Building: 232 E 59th St; Mon-Fri: 9-5
56th Street Art and Antiques Center: 160 E 56th St; Mon-Sat: 10-6 (public welcome)
Interior Design Building: 306 E 61st St; Mon-Fri: 9-5
Manhattan Art & Antiques Center: 1050 Second Ave; Mon-Sat: 10:30-6; Sun: 12-6 (Dozens of shops here are open to the public.)
New York Design Center: 200 Lexington Ave; Mon-Fri: 9-5

ABC CARPET & HOME
888 Broadway (at 19th St)   212/473-3000
Mon-Fri: 10-8; Sat: 10-7; Sun: 11-6:30

ABC CARPET & HOME OUTLET
1055 Bronx River Ave (corner of Bruckner Blvd), The Bronx
718/842-8772
Mon-Fri: 10-7; Sat: 9-7; Sun: 11-6

If you had time to visit just one store in Manhattan, this should be it! What started in 1897 as a pushcart business has grown and expanded into one of the city's most unique, exciting, and well-merchandised emporiums. (It's actually two buildings, which are across the street from each other.) ABC is the Bergdorf Goodman of home furnishings. There are floors of great-looking furniture, dinnerware, linens, gifts, accessories, antiques and everything in between. You will see many one-of-a-kind pieces as you explore corner after corner. There is an entire floor of fabrics by the yard and an extensive carpet and rug selection at great prices. The Parlor Cafe on the main floor helps out hungry shoppers, or one may shop the expanded and attractive Food Halls. It's almost like Harrod's in London!

Colina, a new restaurant on the main floor at **ABC Carpet & Home,** features a rustic Italian menu. My advice: stick to the home furnishings; the restaurant is a real disappointment.

Home Furnishings in Soho

These stores, with goods ranging from the generic to the unique, help make Soho a home-furnishings mecca:

Ad Hoc Softwares (410 West Broadway; 212/925-2652)
Broadway Panhandler (477 Broome St; 212/966-3434)
Dialogica (484 Broome St; 212/966-1934)
Interieurs (114 Wooster St; 212/343-0800)
Knoll (105 Wooster St; 212/343-4000)
Lechter's Housewares and Gifts (536 Broadway; 212/274-0890)
Moss (146 Greene St; 212/226-2190)
Platypus (126 Spring St; 212/219-3919)
Poltrona Frau (145 Wooster St; 212/777-7592)
Portico Bed & Bath (139 Spring St; 212/941-7722)
Portico Home (72 Spring St; 212/941-7800)
Terra Verde Trading Co. (120 Wooster St; 212/925-4533)
Zona (97 Greene St; 212/925-6750)

Housewares, Hardware

AMERICAN STEEL WINDOW SERVICE
108 W 17th St (bet Ave of the Americas and Seventh Ave)
212/242-8131
Mon-Fri: 7:30-4:30

Peter Weinberger runs one of the most esoteric businesses in the city, and one that his family has been in for over 75 years. What he does is sell window hardware. If you need a lock, latch, handle, or bracket, American undoubtedly has it. The store is actually a tiny office, but the warehouse, which resembles a garage crammed full of window hardware, is right next door. How he stays in business is beyond comprehension.

APPLIANCES OVERSEAS
276 Fifth Ave (at 30th St), 4th floor   212/545-8001
Mon-Fri: 8:30-5

For 41 years Appliances Overseas has been a valuable resource for folks traveling or living overseas, or relocating to the U.S. from overseas. This firm offers a full range of large and small appliances and electronics for use in every country of the world (100-240 volt). If purchased overseas, these same items are significantly more expensive. Besides, all appliances sold here have American features, are larger in capacity, and most are dual voltage and multisystem. Between them, Allen, Manny, Tony, Anna, and Koby average over 20 years experience, and they are known for their technical knowledge and excellent service. They distribute over 4,000 international appliances and electronics. Mention this book and they will give a 5% discount on orders over $250.

BARSON HARDWARE
35 W 44th St (bet Fifth Ave and Ave of the Americas)   212/944-8181
Mon-Fri: 8:30-6; Sat: 10-5

Can you imagine a hardware store in the middle of Manhattan that is well organized and competitively priced? Founder Barney Rubin's daughter Anita and David Schneiderman operate a store that carries everything from first-aid kits to drill bits, 29 sizes of scissors, hair curlers, and fire extinguishers. They specialize in travel needs, unique kitchen and housewares items, tools, and plumbing needs. The personnel know their stock and can come up with the right item to fix a broken "whatjamagig." The staff is fluent in Hebrew, Yiddish, Italian, Spanish, and English.

BRIDGE KITCHENWARE
214 E 52nd St   212/688-4220
Mon-Fri: 9-5:30; Sat: 10-4:30

Bridge Kitchenware is a unique-to-New York store that supplies almost every restaurant within 500 miles. Bridge carries bar equipment, cutlery, pastry equipment, molds, copperware, cast-iron ware, woodenware, stoneware, and kitchen gadgets. All goods are professional quality and excellent for home gourmets. Be sure to see the line of imported copperware from France, as well as the professional knives and baking pans. After trying them, people use no other. A catalog is available. By the way, Bridge takes its name from founder Fred Bridge, not from the nearby 59th Street Bridge.

BROADWAY PANHANDLER
477 Broome St (at Wooster St)   212/966-3434
Mon-Fri: 10:30-7; Sat: 11-7; Sun: 11-6

In new and expanded quarters, thousands of cutlery, bakeware, tabletop items, and cookware pieces are available at sizable savings. Guest chefs make periodic appearances here, and a fine selection of professional items is offered to both walk-in customers and restaurant and hotel buyers.

CK&L SURPLUS
307 Canal St (at Broadway)   212/966-1745
Mon-Sat: 8:30-5:45; Sun: 9:30-5:30

In New York, a shopping trip for hardware wouldn't be complete without a trip to Canal Street. On Canal Street, CK&L is the oldest and best hardware store down here. Years ago, these stores dealt in industrial and war surplus. With the passing demand for such goods and an influx of electronics, the Canal Street surplus stores turned to what is best described as "hardware and whatever." All of the stores do business the same way. Sawed-off cardboard boxes containing an assortment of junk are "displayed" in front. The real merchandise is sold inside. There are power tools, simple tools, plumbing and electrical goods, accessories, and supplies. Prices are much lower than retail stores uptown. When you see the place, you'll understand why the overhead is so low.

CLOSET KING
415 E 72nd St (bet First and York Ave)   212/717-6110
Mon-Sat: 10-6

Living quarters in the city have always been notoriously tight, but people tend to stay put and small apartments are measured for every inch of usable space. Frequently, closets—if they exist at all—are the first to go. They are reincarnated as nurseries, bars, bathrooms, eating areas, and even at-home offices. It was inevitable that experts would specialize in organizing closet space, and Don Constable and his Closet King staff do just that. The overall aim is to provide maximum storage space, tailored to a customer's needs. Since the store exists to sell components, they encourage do-it-yourselfers. A customized system can be planned and purchased here, then self-installed at a fraction of the cost a professional would charge.

GARBER HARDWARE
49 Eighth Ave (bet Horatio and Jane St)   212/929-3030
Mon-Fri: 8-5; Sat: 8-3

This is another unique family business that has become a New York institution. The Garbers have been operating for over 116 years at the same location with the appealing motto "Either we have it or we can get it for you." You will find a complete inventory of paints, hardware, plumbing and electrical supplies, housewares, locks, tools, and building materials. Same-day or next-day free delivery, locksmith service, custom window shades, instant lamp repair, and pipe cut to size are just a few of the many handy services offered here.

GARRETT WADE
161 Ave of the Americas (at Spring St)   212/807-1155
Mon-Fri: 9-5:30; Sat: 10-3

The Garrett Wade customer appreciates fine woodworking tools, as the store prides itself on offering only the highest-quality tools from all over the world. The main business is mail-order, and the catalog is all-encompassing. It lists every imaginable woodworking aid, explaining each piece's function and advantage over its peers. It reads like a how-to guide! Garrett Wade assumes that anyone can put together a rocker or, at the very least, appreciate the function of a lightweight spokeshave. After a visit here, you may become a believer, too!

GEORGE TAYLOR SPECIALTIES
100 Hudson St (bet Franklin and Leonard St)   212/226-5369
Mon-Wed: 7:30-5; Thurs: 7:30-6; Fri: 7:30-4

Taylor stocks plumbing replacement parts to fit all faucets, and custom faucets can be fabricated via special order. They also offer reproduction faucets and custom designs of fittings for unique installations. Antique towel bars, bath accessories, and pedestal sinks are a specialty. Founded in 1869, Taylor remains a family-run operation. Ask for father Chris, daughter Valerie, or son John.

Now here is a special find . . . a store that does not like to be listed in books like this one! If you are in need of professional kitchen supplies, small housewares, books on cooking, and the like, trot up 11 floors to **J.B. Prince** (36 E 31st St; 212/683-3553). You'll like the prices!

GRACIOUS HOME
1217 and 1220 Third Ave (bet 70th and 71st St)
212/988-8990, 212/517-6300
Mon-Fri: 8-7; Sat: 9-7; Sun: 10-6

1992 Broadway (at 67th St)   212/231-7800
Mon-Thurs: 9-8; Fri, Sat: 9-9; Sun: 10-7

For over three decades Gracious Home has been a local New York-style hardware store. Run with personal style, it gears its products and services for New York life. They sell appliances, wall coverings, brass hardware, decorative bath accessories, lighting, china, casual furniture, bedding, shelving, pots and pans . . . you get the picture. Services include cooking demonstrations and tool rentals and repairs. They will special-order items and deliver in Manhattan.

LEESAM KITCHEN AND BATH CENTER
124 Seventh Ave (at 17th St)   212/243-6482
Daily: 9:30-6 (Thurs: 9:30-8); Sat: 11-5

There is a new look here! For over a half-century these folks have been fixing up kitchens and bathrooms. Whether it is medicine cabinets, kitchen cabinets, faucets, shower enclosures, or counters, you will see one of the largest selections of top brands from domestic and foreign suppliers. There's no excuse not to remodel your cluttered, dysfunctional old kitchen using one of their computer-designed plans.

NEW CATHAY HARDWARE CORPORATION
49 Mott St (nr Canal St)   212/962-6648
Daily: 10-7

In the heart of Chinatown, this gem of a shop has been dispensing Chinese cooking items, utensils, knives, hardware, small appliances, and restaurant equipment since 1928. There's no more authentic place to get your woks, chopsticks, steamers, or eggroll rollers. Prices and quality are geared toward professionals. This is also a great place to find an unusual housewarming or shower gift.

P.E. GUERIN
23 Jane St (bet Greenwich and Eighth Ave)   212/243-5270
Mon-Fri: 9:30-4:30 by appointment only

Andrew Ward, P.E. Guerin's current president, is the fourth generation of the oldest decorative hardware firm in the country and the only foundry in the city. What's more, they've been on Jane Street for nearly 110 years of the firm's existence. In that time, the firm has grown into a worldwide operation. The main foundry is now in Valencia, Spain (although work is still done at the Village location), and there are branches and showrooms across the country and in Puerto Rico. The Jane Street location is still headquarters for manufacturing and importing decorative hardware and bath accessories. Much of it is done in brass or bronze, and the foundry can make virtually anything in those materials, including copies and reproductions. The Guerin table has garnered design and production awards and enjoys a worldwide reputation. No job is too small for this firm, which operates like the hometown industry it thinks it is. They offer free estimates and help with such hardware problems as locks. Their work is impressive!

SIMON'S HARDWARE & BATH
421 Third Ave (bet 29th and 30th St)   212/532-9220
Mon-Fri: 8-5:30 (Thurs until 7); Sat: 10-6

This is really a hardware supermarket. Customers take numbers just as they would at a bakery counter. No one minds waiting, because Simon's offers one of the city's finest selections of quality decorative hardware items, bath and kitchen fixtures and accessories, plus marble, stone, and tile. The personnel are patient, even if you just need something to fix a broken handle on a chest of drawers.

WILLIAMS-SONOMA
1175 Madison Ave (at 86th St)   212/289-6832
110 Seventh Ave (at 17th St)   212/633-2203
20 E 60th St (bet Madison and Park Ave)   212/980-5155
1309 Second Ave (at 69th St)   212/288-8408
Hours vary by store

From humble beginnings in the wine country of Sonoma County, California, these stores have expanded over the nation and now are referred to as the "Tiffany of cookware stores." The serious cook will find a vast display of quality cookware, bakeware, cutlery, kitchen linens, specialty foods, cookbooks, small appliances, kitchen furniture, glassware, and tableware. The stores also offer a gift- and bridal-registry service, cooking demonstrations, free recipes, gift baskets, and shopping assistance for corporations or individuals. Ask for their very attractive catalog, which includes a number of excellent recipes.

Imports

Afghan

NUSRATY AFGHAN IMPORTS
215 W 10th St (at Bleecker St)   212/691-1012
Sun-Fri: 1-9; Sat: 1-11

Abdul Nusraty has transformed a corner of the Village into a corner of Afghanistan that is fascinating (and thankfully free of political strife). Nusraty is probably the best source of Afghan goods on the continent. There are magnificently embroidered native dresses and shirts displayed alongside semiprecious stones mounted in jewelry or shown individually. One part of the store features carpets and rugs, while another displays antique silver and jewelry. Nusraty has an unerring eye; all of his stock is of the highest quality and often is unique as well. The business operates on both a wholesale and retail level.

Central American

BAZAAR SABADO
54 Greene St (bet Broome and Grand St)   212/941-6152
Mon-Sat: 11:30-6:30; Sun: 12-5:30

How about some Mexican or Central American artwork and furnishings to jazz up your abode? Assembled in one spot is a great collection of silver jewelry, religious pieces, textiles, pottery, frames, wood carvings, glassware, and furniture from the 1940s to the present. Suzanne Rubin, the owner, travels extensively throughout the world, selecting unique pieces.

Chinese

CHINESE PORCELAIN COMPANY
475 Park Ave (at 58th St)   212/838-7744
Mon-Fri: 10-6; Sat: 11-5 (closed Sat in summer)

Khalil Rizk and his partners opened this store in 1985 as a source for Chinese decorative arts, with a particular emphasis on porcelain and furniture. They show Chinese export porcelain, ancient Asian sculptures, Chinese scholars' works of art, snuff bottles, and European furniture and accessories. You will also find a good selection of lacquer furniture, cloisonné, woodcarvings, paintings, and watercolors.

— Millennium Note —
The first of the apple orchards for which New York became famous was planted by Governor Peter Stuyvesant in 1647 on his Bowery Farm.

WING-ON TRADING
145 Essex St   212/477-1450
Mon-Sat: 9-6

No need to go to Hong Kong to get your Chinese porcelain or earthenware. Even though it is located on the disorganized Lower East Side, Wing-On has a complete and well-organized stock of household goods. One of their specialties is Chinese teas, sold at low prices.

Eskimo/Native American

ALASKA ON MADISON
937 Madison Ave   212/879-1782
Tues-Sat: 11:30-6 or by appointment

This store and gallery is New York's most complete source for Eskimo art. Rare antiquities and artifacts of centuries-old Arctic cultures are displayed next to sculptures of Indians of the Northwest. Periodic shows highlight different aspects of Northern culture. A number of contemporary artists whose works have been shown here have gained international acclaim.

General

BACK FROM GUATEMALA
306 E 6th St (bet First and Second Ave)   212/260-7010
Daily: 12-11:30

Back from Guatemala celebrates the tribal arts by presenting a unique collection of clothing, jewelry, artifacts, music, and musical instruments from over 30 countries. Also included are masks, hats, scarves, deities, puppets, wall hangings, ornaments, and much more.

JACQUES CARCANAGUES
106 Spring St (at Mercer St)   212/925-8110
Daily: 11:30-7

After a stint in the diplomatic service, Frenchman Jacques Carcanagues decided to assemble and sell the best artifacts he had run across in his world travels. So while the store is mostly Southeast Asian, it is, in Jacques own words, "a complete ethnic department store, not a museum." Yet the stock is all of museum quality. Textiles and *tansus* (dressers) are everywhere, as are jewelry and lacquerware. It is also very appealing to Soho shoppers who can choose among Indian, Burmese, and Thai sculptures of many periods and unusual household objects not likely seen elsewhere in New York. The overall effect is like an Eastern marketplace; all that is lacking are water pipes and music.

KATINKA
303 E 9th St (at Second Ave)   212/677-7897
Tues-Sat: 4-7 (call first as hours may vary)

This is an import paradise, with jewelry, natural-fiber clothing, shoes, scarves, belts, hats, musical instruments, incense, and artifacts from India, Thailand, Pakistan, Afghanistan, and South America. The most popular items are colorful shoes and embroidered silk skirts from India. The place is small, and prices are reasonable. Jane Williams and Billy Lyles make customers feel like they have embarked on a worldwide shopping expedition!

PIER 1 IMPORTS
461 Fifth Ave (at 40th St)   212/447-1610
Mon-Fri: 9-8; Sat: 10-7; Sun: 11-7

71 Fifth Ave (at 15th St)   212/206-1911
Mon-Fri: 9-9; Sat: 10-7; Sun: 11-7

1551 Third Ave (at 87th St)   212/987-1746
Mon-Sat: 10-9; Sun: 12-7

No need to spend your time or money running off to distant places; just come to Pier 1. Here you will find imported dining-room sets, occasional furniture, bathroom accessories, picture frames, brassware, china and glassware, floor coverings, bedding, pillows, and much more. The goods come from exotic lands throughout Asia and the rest of the world. The selections are inviting, the prices are right, and the places are fun to visit. Besides, the chain's head honcho, Marvin Girouard, is one of the best merchants in the business!

PUTUMAYO
147 Spring St   212/966-4458
Mon-Sat: 11-7; Sun: 12-6

The merchandise carried here is mostly designed by Putumayo and imported from India and Indonesia. The emphasis is on fashions and accessories, but there are also music and crafts from around the world. In the fall, Putumayo displays a variety of hand-knit virgin-wool sweaters and jackets inspired by tradtional cultures. For summer, there are sun dresses, skirts, and loose-fitting pants—all of them cool, comfortable, and practical.

Indian

HIND INDIA COTTAGE EMPORIUM
1150 Broadway (at 27th St)   212/685-6943
Mon-Fri: 9:30-6:30; Sat: 10-5

Hind India Cottage Emporium features clothing, jewelry, handicrafts, and gifts imported directly from India. Moti R. Chani has a sharp eye for the finest details, and the saris and other Indian clothing he sells reflect his good taste and expertise. The clothing is prized by Indian nationals and neighborhood residents for its sheer beauty. The garments are made of cotton and feature unique madras patterns. Pay particular attention to the leather bags and jewelry.

Irish

GRAFTON GIFTS & BASKETS
830 Third Ave (entrance on 51st St, bet Lexington and Third Ave)
212/489-7029
Mon-Fri: 8-8; Sat: 10-8; Sun: 12-5

Grafton Gifts & Baskets is a delightful touch of Ireland in the middle of the hustle and bustle of New York. Stop by in the afternoon for a cup of tea with Bernadette Ryan in this Irish cottage setting (complete with fireplace, wooden floors, and pine furniture). On the way out, pick up some beautiful Irish imports, including sweaters, capes, blouses, hats, scarves, jewelry, crystal, and china. They also make gift baskets for all occasions and carry a full line of Irish teas and foodstuffs.

MATTIE HASKINS SHAMROCK IMPORTS
Manhattan Mall
901 Ave of the Americas (at 32nd St), 4th floor
212/564-7474
Mon-Sat: 10-8; Sun: 11-6

This delightful bit of Old Ireland is famous for hospitality and Irish goods like tapes, candies, tweed caps, Irish china, glassware, and pewter and brass gifts. Every day is St. Patrick's Day at this spot!

Italian

CAROSELLO MUSICALE COMPANY (PENTAGRAMMA)
119 Mulberry St (nr Canal St)   212/925-7253
Mon-Sun: 11-11

Every section of New York with a concentrated ethnic population has a group of stores that serve its specific needs. Usually the group will include a bakery, coffee shop, bookstore, and import shop featuring various items of the homeland. There is often one shop devoted to a distinctive characteristic of that nationality. What could be more natural than a shop in Little Italy dedicated to recordings and music? Carosello is primarily a music shop specializing in Italian recordings and operas, but it is also a bookstore, import store, and gift shop. One can find perfumes, Italian newspapers, magazines, and gifts, as well as Caruso recordings. The atmosphere is informal, and frequently customers can be heard humming an aria while checking record jackets.

FORZANO ITALIAN IMPORTS
128 Mulberry St (at Hester St)   212/925-2525
Daily: 10 a.m.-midnight

If you are looking for something Italian, Forzano is the place. You will find imported Italian CDs and cassettes; espresso, cappucino and pasta machines; soccer-team shirts; and all kinds of novelties. Forzano is a landmark in Little Italy, having been run by the same family since 1958.

Japanese

SARA
952 Lexington Ave (bet 69th and 70th St)   212/772-3243
Mon-Fri: 11-7; Sat: 12-6

Looking for something unusual with a Japanese flair? Sara is the place to go for modern Japanese functional ceramics, glassware, tableware, and gifts.

THINGS JAPANESE
127 E 60th St, 2nd floor   212/371-4661
Mon-Sat: 11-5 (Tues: 11-6)

Things Japanese believes that the Japanese "things" most in demand are prints. So while there are all sorts of Japanese artworks and crafts, prints highlight the selection. They know the field well and recognize that the market, while almost exhausted for high-priced established artists, is just beginning for less well-known artists. The store will help would-be collectors establish a grouping or assist decorators in finding pieces to round out the decor. There are also original 18th- to 20th-century Japanese woodblock prints, porcelains, baskets, chests, lacquers, and books. Prices range from ten dollars to several thousand, and every piece is accompanied by a certificate of authenticity. Things Japanese claims that you need to appreciate both the subject matter and the artistry in the works it sells, and that's not a difficult or unpleasant task at all.

Middle Eastern

PERSIAN SHOP
534 Madison Ave (bet 54th and 55th St)   212/355-4643
Mon-Sat: 10-7

This outfit has been in business since 1940, featuring unusual Middle Eastern items including end tables, chairs, frames, mirrors, and brocades sold by the yard or made up into magnificent neckties for men. There are also Chinese vases, garden stools, Russian and Greek icons, and planters that will add a special air of interest to any setting. The jewelry selection is especially noteworthy. You'll find precious and semiprecious items, silver and gold cuff links, rings, earrings, bracelets, necklaces, belts, and heirloom pieces.

Russian

RUSSIAN WORLD
18 W 55th St (bet Fifth Ave and Ave of the Americas)
212/399-6500
Mon-Sat: 12-9

It's fun to look around Russian World, especially if you are in the market for some nifty gift ideas. You'll see top-quality traditional Russian art; nesting dolls (*matrioshka*); lacquered boxes of *paleich, fedoskino, mstiora,* and *kholui;* enamel imperial eggs; antique icons; collectible toy soldiers and miniatures; and much more. Everything in the store is handmade and hand-painted in the home country.

VICTOR KAMKIN
925 Broadway (at 21st St)   212/673-0776
Mon-Fri: 9:30-5:30; Sat: 10-5

Fluency in the Russian language is increasingly prized in business and government, and Victor Kamkin can be of great help in this area. His store features books in and translations from Russian, guidebooks, art albums and reproductions, textbooks, and dictionaries. There is also an excellent stock of Russian recordings and souvenirs like lacquer boxes and dolls. An added feature is a subscription service for Russian magazines and newspapers.

Swedish

ORDNING & REDA
253 Columbus Ave (bet 71st and 72nd St)   212/799-0828
Mon-Sat: 11:30-8; Sun: 11:30-6

1035 Third Ave (at 61st St)   212/421-8199
Mon-Fri: 11-8; Sat: 11-7; Sun: 12-5

Everything here is designed and made in Sweden, including stationery, archive boxes, photo albums, and ring binders of the highest quality. Practically everything here is manufactured with environmentally friendly materials, and most are hand-finished.

Ukrainian

SURMA (THE UKRAINIAN SHOP)
11 E 7th St (nr Third Ave)   212/477-0729
Mon-Sat: 11-6

Since 1918, Surma has conducted business as the "general store of the Slavic community in New York City." My only quarrel with the description is that it should not be limited to the city, since it seems capable of serving the entire hemisphere. More than a store, Surma is a bastion of Ukrainianism. Once inside, it is difficult to believe you're still in New York. The clothing here is ethnic opulence. There are dresses, vests, shirts, blouses, hand-tooled and soft-soled leather dancing shoes, and accessories. All are hand-embroidered with authentic detailing. For the home, there are accent pieces (including an entire section devoted to Ukrainian Easter-egg decorating), brocaded linens, and Surma's own Ukrainian-style honey (very different and very good). Above all, Surma is known for its educational tapes (learn conversational Ukrainian for your next travels to Kiev), stationery, and books. Not surprisingly, the business is also known as the Surma Book and Music Company. Pay particular attention to the paintings and stationery, which feature modern-day depictions of ancient Ukrainian glass painting.

Jewelry

When you purchase pearls, fully understand what you are getting. Practically all pearls on the market these days are cultured, which means that a mother-of-pearl bead is implanted in an oyster to start the pearl-coating process.

Akoya pearls: These come from Japan. The best ones are round and white, with high luster and a slight rose tint.
South Sea pearls: very large, from the South Pacific
Black pearls: grown in black-lipped oysters in Tahiti
Baroque pearls: less expensive, unusual shapes
Mabe pearls: Grown as a blister on the inside of an oyster shell, these can be brittle and break easily. Prices have become inflated.
Dome pearl: Grown in Tennessee, these are more durable.

Freshwater pearls: Inexpensive and attractive, these are grown by a type of mollusk that produces many pearls simultaneously.

Gems of the Month

January: garnet
February: amethyst
March: aquamarine
April: diamond
May: emerald
June: pearl, moonstone
July: ruby
August: peridot, sardonyx
September: sapphire
October: opal
November: topaz
December: turquoise, zircon

BILL SCHIFRIN
National Jewelers Exchange
4 W 47th St (Booth 86)   212/221-1873, 212/944-1713
Mon-Fri: 10-5

From a booth in the National Jewelers Exchange—better known for its diamond engagement rings than its plain wedding bands—Bill Schifrin and son-in-law Herman Rotenberg preside over a collection of nearly 2,000 unusual wedding bands. Prices range from a few dollars to several thousand, depending upon the complexity of the work and the stones used, and there's a story behind each ring. Bill's been doing this for over 40 years. After all this time you might think he'd be cynical, but he's just "cautious," and his stories, prices, and selection draw customers from all over the world.

DAVID SAITY/SAITY JEWELRY
450 Park Ave (bet 56th and 57th St)   212/308-6570
Mon-Sat: 10-6

David Saity's magnificent store creates a great showcase for his renowned collection of authentic Native American jewelry. In this collection are numerous rare and breathtaking turn-of-the-century collector's items, such as watchbands, belt buckles, bolo ties, squash-blossom necklaces, chokers, bracelets, rings, hair accessories, cuff links, earrings, and concha belts. Over 10,000 original masterpieces, handcrafted by artisans of the Zuni, Navajo, Hopi, and Santa Domingo tribes, are shown here. They have recently received a large quantity of rare and antique artware and jewelry from isolated reservations. The collection spans over 50 years, featuring sterling silver, turquoise, coral, jet, and mother-of-pearl gemstones.

FORTUNOFF
681 Fifth Ave (at 54th St)   212/758-6660
Mon-Wed, Fri, Sat: 10-6; Thurs: 10-8

This is one of the best stores in Manhattan devoted to quality merchandise. Prices on all items are very competitive, and the store has a reputation for meeting or beating any legitimately quoted price in town. There is a crystal and clock department, but it is in the jewelry area (especially antique silver) that the store really shines. There is a jeweler in residence at all times. Fortunoff shows one of the largest and finest collections of 14-, 18-, and 24-karat gold jewelry in the city, as well as a fine selection of precious and semiprecious stones and brand-name watches.

GALERIA CANO
Trump Tower
725 Fifth Ave (at 57th St), Level 4   212/832-8172
Mon-Sat: 10-6

Galeria Cano is a third-generation jewelry and accessory business with items made from 24K gold-plated brass. If you want to attract some attention at the next big party, put on one of their dramatic, handcrafted reproductions of original pre-Columbian artifacts. Mention this book to receive some special prices on 18K jewelry!

MAX NASS
118 E 28th St (bet Park Ave S and Lexington Ave)   212/679-8154
Mon-Fri: 9:30-6; Sat: 9:30-4

The Shah family members are jewelry artisans; Arati is the designer and Parimal ("Perry") is the company president. Together they make and sell handmade jewelry; service, repair clocks and watches; and restore antique jewelry. At Max Nass, they deal in virtually any type of jewelry: antique (or merely old), silver, an expanded gold selection, and semiprecious stones. Two special sales each year bring their already low prices down even further. One occurs during the last three weeks in January (33% discount), and the other runs for two weeks in July (25% discount). In between, Arati will design pieces on a whim or commission. Necklaces are particularly impressive; his work is often one-of-a-kind. The store also restores, restrings, and redesigns necklaces.

MURREY'S JEWELERS
1395 Third Ave (bet 79th and 80th St)   212/879-3690
Mon-Sat: 9:30-6

I heartily recommend this one! Murrey's, family jewelers since 1936, sells fine jewelry and giftware. In the service area, they do fine-jewelry repair, European clock repair, engraving, pearl stringing, and watch repair. They have three talented goldsmiths for custom-designed pieces and three talented watch- and clockmakers.

MYRON TOBACK
25 W 47th St (bet Fifth Ave and Ave of the Americas)   212/398-8300
Mon-Fri: 8-4 (closed first two weeks in July and Dec 25-Jan 1)

Myron Toback is ostensibly a refiner of precious metals with a specialty in findings, plate, and wire. Not very useful to the average customer, you might think. But note the address. Toback is not only in the heart of the Diamond District, but he is a bonafide landlord of a new arcade crammed full of wholesale artisans of the jewelry trade. Taking their cue from Toback, they are open and friendly to individual retail customers. So note Toback as a source of gold, gold-filled, and silver chains sold by the foot at wholesale prices. And don't overlook the gold and silver earrings, beads, and other jewelry items sold at prices that are laughably less than those at establishments around the corner on Fifth Avenue. Moreover, tools and other materials with which to string beads and pearls are now carried. Even though most customers are professional jewelers or wholesale organizations, Toback is simply charming to do-it-yourselfers, schools, and hobbyists.

PEDRO BOREGAARD
18 E 53rd St, 15th floor   212/826-3660
Mon-Fri: 10-5:30 (call for appointment)

Unusual rings, earrings, and bracelets—all handmade and each a true work of art—are hallmarks of this very talented designer, who features items for men and women. Boregaard's credentials are impressive: apprenticeship and professional work in Germany, a jewelry workshop in England, and work with Tiffany for designers such as Angela Cummings, Elsa Peretti, and Paloma Picasso.

RENNIE ELLEN
15 W 47th St, Room 401   212/869-5525
Mon-Fri: 10-4:30 by appointment only

Rennie Ellen is a wholesaler offering the sort of discounts the city's wholesale businesses is famous for. She was the first woman diamond dealer in the male-dominated Diamond District. Ellen personally spent so much time and effort to keep the district straight and honest that she earned the title "Mayor of 47th Street." Ellen's reputation is impeccable. Her diamond-cutting factory deals exclusively in diamond jewelry. There are pendants, wedding bands, engagement rings, and diamonds to fit all sizes, shapes, and budgets. All sales are made under Ellen's personal supervision and are strictly confidential. There is a $3 catalog for mail orders.

Ladders

PUTNAM ROLLING LADDER COMPANY
32 Howard St (bet Lafayette St and Broadway)   212/226-5147
Mon-Fri: 8-4:30

Putnam is a great, esoteric shop on an esoteric street! Why, you might ask, would anyone in New York need those magnificent rolling ladders used in traditional formal libraries? Could there possibly be enough business to keep a place like this going since 1905? The answer is that clever New Yorkers turn to Putnam for designing access to their lofts (especially sleeping lofts). Here's a partial list of ladders, which come in many different hardwoods: rolling ladders (custom-made, if you want), rolling work platforms, telephone ladders, portable automatic ladders, scaffold ladders, pulpit ladders, folding library ladders, library stools, aerial platforms, library carts with steps, steel warehouse ladders, safety ladders, electric stepladders for industrial use, and mechanics' stepladders.

Leather Goods, Luggage

JOBSON'S LUGGAGE
666 Lexington Ave (bet 55th and 56th St)
212/355-6846, 800/221-5238
Mon-Sat: 9-6; Sun: 11-5

The key to a successful luggage store in New York is to offer a vast selection at discount prices. With the exception of a store such as T. Anthony, which depends on quality and service to offset its high prices, most of the stores I've listed offer good variety and discounts. At Jobson's, they stock the largest selection of brand-name luggage, attaché cases, and small leather goods in the metropolitan area. Their sales volume enables them to sell at prices that are close to wholesale. While other stores make similar claims, Jobson's sales staff and personal attention set it apart. They also offer free monogramming, a complete repair department, and free delivery in Manhattan.

ORIGINAL LEATHER STORE
176 Spring St (bet Thompson St and West Broadway)   212/219-8210
Mon-Fri: 11-8; Sat: 10-8; Sun: 12-8

171 W 4th St (bet Ave of the Americas and Seventh Ave)
212/675-2303
Mon-Wed: 11-8; Thurs-Sat: 11 a.m.-12 a.m.; Sun: 12-8

1100 Madison Ave   212/585-4200
256 Columbus Ave (at 72nd St)   212/595-7051
552 LaGuardia Pl   212/777-4362

This is one of those special smaller stores where craftspeople make all the products shown. There are beautiful leather jackets, pants, belts, classy briefcases, bags, and luggage. The styles are current, fun, and functional, and prices are competitive. If you enjoy the aroma of a good leather store, you'll love these outlets.

T. ANTHONY
445 Park Ave (at 56th St)   212/750-9797, 800/722-2406
Mon-Fri: 9:30-6; Sat: 10-6

T. Anthony handles luxurious luggage of distinction. Anything purchased here will stand out in a crowd, and that is what T. Anthony customers expect and receive. Luggage ranges in size from small overnight bags to massive pieces that just fall short of being steamer trunks. The wallets, key cases, and billfolds make terrific gifts, individually or in matched sets. Don't come looking for discount prices, but the high quality and courteous service are well-established New York traditions. Exclusive T. Anthony products are also available through the store's catalog.

> You'll find some great travel items at **Flight 101** (96 Greenwich Ave, 212/691-1001).

Lighting Fixtures and Accessories
CITY KNICKERBOCKER
781 Eighth Ave (bet 47th and 48th St)   212/586-3939
Mon-Fri: 8-5

The fourth generation of the Liroff family operates this outfit, which has been in business since 1906. If it has anything to do with lighting—including quality antique reproductions, glassware, and first-rate repair—rest assured these folks are completely reliable. In addition to a large sales inventory, there is a rental service. Not all of the inventory is vintage; their art-glass lamps, for instance, are new.

JUST BULBS
936 Broadway (bet 21st and 22nd St)   212/228-7820
Mon-Fri: 9-6 (Thurs until 7); Sat: 10-6; Sun: 12-6

This is probably the only shop in the world that can supply certain types of bulbs. In addition to all the standard sizes, Just Bulbs has lightbulbs for use in old fixtures. The staff boasts that the store stocks almost 25,000 types of bulbs. The shop looks like an oversized backstage dressing-room mirror, and everywhere you turn there are bulbs connected to switches that customers are invited to flick on and off.

JUST SHADES
21 Spring St   212/966-2757
Thurs-Tues: 9:30-4

This store specializes in lampshades. They are experts on matching shades to lamps, and they willingly share their expertise with retail customers. They have lampshades of silk, hide, parchment, and just about any other material imaginable. Interestingly, they say their biggest peeve is customers who neglect to remove the protective cellophane from their shades. When left on, the shade actually collects ruinous dust.

LIGHTING BY GREGORY
158 Bowery (bet Delancey and Broome St)   212/226-1276
Daily: 9-5:30

No false modesty here. This full-service discount lighting store claims to be the most technically knowledgeable such outfit in the country. I'll take them at their word and pass on that they are major dealers of Lightolier, Tech Lighting, and Casablanca ceiling fans, as well as being experts in track lighting.

LIGHTING PLUS
676 Broadway (bet 2nd and 3rd St)   212/979-2000
Mon-Sat: 10-7; Sun: 11-7

Few things are more annoying than not having the electrical gadget you need to fix a lamp, hair dryer, or whatever. Save yourself a lot of running around and go straight to Lighting Plus. In this well-organized store, you can find just about anything connected with electricity, and the personnel are eager to help.

TUDOR ELECTRICAL SUPPLY
222-226 E 46th St (bet Second and Third Ave)   212/867-7550
Mon-Thurs: 8:30-5; Fri: 8:30-4:30

Although you may feel like you need an engineering degree to enter Tudor Electrical, the staff is trained to explain everything in stock. Light bulbs are the store's forte. They are cataloged by wattage, color, and application by a staff who can quickly locate the right bulb for your needs. For instance, quartz, tungsten, and halogen bulbs offer undistorted light, while incandescent and fluorescent lamps are best for desk work. Tudor discounts by at least 20%.

UPLIFT
506 Hudson St (bet Christopher and 10th St)   212/929-3632
Daily: 12-8

This uplifting store mainly sells art-deco and Victorian lighting fixtures. Uplift has one of the largest collections of original American art-deco chandeliers in the country. They also carry less expensive reproductions and a full line of fantasy figures, like wizards and dragons made of pewter. Uplift has accessories for lighting fixtures: lamps, wiring, bases, glass bowls, and shades.

Magic

FLOSSO AND HORNMANN MAGIC
45 W 34th St, Room 607   212/279-6079
Mon-Fri: 10:30-5:30; Sat: 10:30-4

Harry Houdini is one of a score of professional magicians who have owned this shop at one time or another since its creation in 1856. Flosso and Hornmann is proof that magic is timeless. Its clientele spans all ages, and the store seems unchanged since Houdini's day. In part, that's due to the dim light and dust, but mostly it's because the stock is so complete. It's hard to think of a trick prop that's *not* stocked here. The staff will gladly show you what's new. In addition to magic acts, Flosso and Hornmann carries books, manuals, historical treatises, and photographs. They'll even create stage sets. Ask for a catalog which explains many of the tricks in detail.

LOUIS TANNEN/TANNEN MAGICAL
DEVELOPMENT COMPANY
24 W 25th St, 2nd floor   212/929-4500
Mon-Fri: 10-5:30; Sat: 10-4

This is a magical place! Tony Spina or one of his helpful associates will spend time with both amateur and professional magicians. A fabulous catalog is available for a modest price, and classes are offered each week. The quality is first-rate, as they produce many pieces in their own machine and wood shops. There are over 8,000 individual items and 350 books in Tannen's inventory. Tannen runs the only summer magic camp for boys and girls (ages 12 to 18).

Maps

HAGSTROM MAP AND TRAVEL CENTER
57 W 43rd St (at Ave of the Americas)   212/398-1222
Mon-Wed, Fri: 8:30-6; Thurs: 8:30-7; Sat: 10:30-4:30

125 Maiden Ln (nr Water St)   212/785-5343
Mon-Fri: 8:30-6:30

The staff are experts when it comes to maps and travel information. Hagstrom is the only complete map and chart dealer in the city, highlighting the maps of major manufacturers and five branches of government. There are also nautical, hiking, global, and travel guides, as well as globes and world atlases.

Memorabilia

GOTTA HAVE IT! COLLECTIBLES
153 E 57th St (bet Lexington and Third Ave)   212/750-7900
Mon-Fri: 10-7; Sat: 11-6

Do you have a favorite sports star? Hollywood personality? Musical entertainer? Political figure? If you are a collector or are looking for a gift for someone who is, this store features original and unique products in these categories. There are signed photos, musical instruments, baseball bats, used sports uniforms, documents, and movie props.

LOST CITY ARTS
275 Lafayette St (bet Prince and Houston St)   212/941-8025
Mon-Fri: 10-6; Sat, Sun: 12-6

Surgical lamps? An Eames lounge chair? Penny banks from the 1920s? You'll find them all at this amazing place. Lost City specializes in architectural antiques, vintage New York souvenirs, and classic mid-century American and European furniture and lighting.

MOTION PICTURE ARTS GALLERY
133 E 58th St, Suite 1001   212/223-1009
Tues-Fri: 12-5

The Motion Picture Arts Gallery displays and sells original posters and lobby cards from motion pictures. Ira Resnick's customers include film buffs and vintage poster collectors and investors. A *Casablanca* poster that could be had for a couple of dollars in the early 1960s fetches upward of $4,500 today! There are over 15,000 items in stock here.

MOVIE STAR NEWS
134 W 18th St (bet Ave of the Americas and Seventh Ave)
212/620-8160
Mon-Fri: 10-6; Sat: 11-6

Movie Star News claims to have the world's largest collection of movie photos. Stars past and present shine brightly in this shop, which offers posters and other movie memorabilia. The store is laid out like a library. The Kramers, who run Movie Star News, do a lot of research for magazines, newspapers, and the media. This store may be the closest thing to Hollywood on the East Coast!

NEW YORK FIREFIGHTERS FRIEND
265 Lafayette St (bet Prince and Spring St)   212/226-3142
Mon-Sat: 10-6

Firemen and fire-fighting buffs from all over the world will no doubt find this the most fascinating store in Manhattan! They carry alarms, boots, bumper stickers, door knockers, earrings, extinguishers, fire engines, hydrants, nozzles, patches, posters, T-shirts, toys, turnout coats, work shirts, and related items. Firefighters' jackets for kids are a big hit!

ONE SHUBERT ALLEY
1 Shubert Alley (bet Broadway and Eighth Ave)
212/944-4133, 800/223-1320 (mail order only)
Mon-Thurs: 12-8; Fri, Sat: 9 a.m.-11:30 p.m.; Sun: 12-6:30

Shubert Alley is a narrow alleyway in the Broadway Theater District that is often used as a shortcut between theaters. One Shubert Alley is the only retail establishment in the alley, and it's a fascinating place to browse for T-shirts, posters, recordings, buttons, and other paraphernalia from current shows on and off-Broadway. They have a mail-order catalog and a special number for telephone orders.

Mirrors
SUNDIAL-SCHWARTZ
1582 First Ave   212/289-4969
Mon, Thurs: 10-6; Tues, Wed, Fri: 10-5; Sat 10-3

The people at Sundial supply "decorative treatments of distinction." Anyone who has ever seen a cramped New York apartment suddenly appear to expand with the strategic placement of mirrors will understand that claim. Sundial deals with professional decorators and do-it-yourselfers, and both benefit from the staff's years of experience. They carry mirrors for the home, office, and showroom. In addition, Sundial will remodel, re-silver, and antique mirrors. Sundial also custom-designs window treatments, blinds, shades, and draperies.

Museum and Library Shops

As anybody on a mailing list knows, scores of museums across the country now produce catalogs that allow people to browse their gift shops from a great distance. In New York, however, you can browse in person at more than four dozen museums. Even at museums that charge an admission fee, you need not pay it if you're only there to shop. Rather than simply list all the museum gift shops in New York, I've chosen particularly large or unique ones. Indeed, whether you're looking for a one-of-a-kind gift or unusual books and posters, I highly recommend shopping in the following places. Instead of Empire State Building salt-and-pepper shakers, expect to find classy, well-made items. In most cases, at least some of the wares directly relate to current and past exhibits or the museum's permanent collection. You might save money by becoming a member and taking advantage of discounts as you buy gifts throughout the year.

AMERICAN CRAFT MUSEUM
40 W 53rd St (bet Fifth Ave and Ave of the Americas)
212/956-3535
Tues-Sun: 10-6 (Thurs until 8)

Although quite small, this sales desk in the lobby of the American Craft Museum is worth a visit if you're interested in contemporary crafts. Much of the selection changes with the exhibits, but you will always find exhibition catalogs and postcards, as well as interesting jewelry and other original work by contemporary artists.

AMERICAN MUSEUM OF NATURAL HISTORY
Central Park West (bet 77th and 81st St)   212/769-5100
Sun-Thurs: 10-5:45; Fri, Sat: 10-8:45
Junior Shop: Mon-Fri: 10-4:45; Sat, Sun: 10-5:45

The main store for adults on the first floor of this grand institution has always been a great source for interesting jewelry, minerals, books and videos on natural history, and beautifully made items from around the world. But thanks to renovations in recent years, it's now also a pleasant place to browse. The various shops throughout the museum, including one set in a turret and the "Dinostore" on the fourth floor, all have a specialty and are well worth a visit. If your child cannot leave without a souvenir but you don't want to break the bank, check out the Junior Shop on the lower level. Be forewarned that it closes much earlier than the museum itself, especially on weekends.

ASIA SOCIETY
725 Park Ave (bet 70th and 71st St)   212/288-6400
Mon-Fri: 10-6 (Thurs until 8); Sat: 11-6; Sun: noon-5

Off the Asia Society's main lobby is an exceptional book and gift store that's a little-known treat for anyone interested in Asiana. Its collection of books on Asian religions, philosophy, art, culture, history, and other topics is among the largest in the nation. The store also carries a wide range of children's, language, and coffee-table books. Inside the bookstore to the left is a rather small but wonderful gift store full of games, dolls, prints and posters, jewelry, scarves, wrapping paper, T-shirts, stationery, and other Asian imports.

BROOKLYN MUSEUM
787 Seventh Ave (bet 51st and 52nd St)   212/554-4888
Mon-Fri: 11-6

This tiny shop in a corner of the Equitable Center's soaring atrium specializes in Egyptian art and artifacts, for which the Brooklyn Museum is best known. Whether you're looking for jewelry, picture frames, textiles, cards, or books, this is a great place.

CATHEDRAL CHURCH OF ST. JOHN THE DIVINE
Amsterdam Ave (at 112th St)   212/222-7200
Daily: 9-5

Known as the Cathedral Shop, this pleasant gift shop and bookstore is tucked off the left side of the main sanctuary. It specializes in stained glass and antique crosses. They also carry Christian books, creches, and Christmas tree ornaments from all over the world. Pressed flowers in glass, wrapping paper, wind chimes, mobiles, jewelry, Ghanaian *kente* cloth, note cards and stationery, jams, spices, and children's books are just a sampling of the eclectic selection. Make sure to ask about "adopting" an organ pipe if you're looking for a unique gift for a music lover.

THE CLOISTERS
Fort Tryon Park   212/650-2277
Tues-Sun: 9:30-4:30 (summer); Tues-Sun: 9:30-4:15 (winter)

The Cloisters gift shop is stocked mostly with items related to the museum's medieval collection. It closes half an hour earlier than the museum.

COOPER-HEWITT NATIONAL MUSEUM OF DESIGN
2 E 91st St (bet Fifth and Madison Ave)   212/849-8400
Tues: 10-8:45; Wed-Sat: 10-4:45; Sun: noon-4:45

Housed in what was once the music room of the elegant Carnegie Mansion, this terrific store offers an eclectic mix of items that relate to the museum's extensive collection or reflect its dedication to design excellence and innovation. Whether you're looking for pens or other office items, tea cups, silverware, plates, or an unusual wedding present, this is a good place to start. The store also sells books relating to the museum's collection. Be aware that it closes 15 minutes earlier than the museum.

EL MUSEO DEL BARRIO
1230 Fifth Ave (near 105th St)   212/831-7272
Wed-Sun: 11-5

This unique museum gift shop was added to the museum during its 1994 renovation. In addition to housing a small collection of Latin American art books and books about such topics as Caribbean culture and the Puerto Rican experience in New York, the shop sells children's books in both English and Spanish. It also sells carnival masks made in Puerto Rico and a variety of crafts from throughout the Caribbean and Latin America.

FRICK COLLECTION
1 E 70th St (bet Fifth and Madison Ave)   212/288-0700
Tues-Sat: 10-5:45; Sun: 1-5:45

The Frick's gift shop makes the most of its small space by concentrating on exquisite cards, stationery, maps, guidebooks, and art books. Be forewarned that it closes 15 minutes earlier than the museum.

GUGGENHEIM MUSEUM STORES
1071 Fifth Ave (bet 88th and 89th St)   212/423-3615
Fri, Sat: 10-8; Sun-Thurs: 10-6

575 Broadway (at Prince St)   212/423-3867
Mon-Sat: 10-7; Sun: 11-6

Although much that's for sale in these stores is ordinary—including scarves, T-shirts, prints and posters, tote bags, umbrellas, note cards and stationery, jewelry, and children's toys—the designs and craftsmanship are anything but. If you're looking for an unusual clock, a great wedding present, or the right pair of earrings to set you apart from the crowd, look here. Prices, however, are often through the roof. Both shops also carry books on modern art and exhibition catalogs. Note that the Fifth Avenue location is open on Thursday, but the museum itself is not. Also note that the Soho location is open during the remodeling going on at the Guggenheim Soho.

INTERNATIONAL CENTER OF PHOTOGRAPHY
1130 Fifth Ave (at 94th St)   212/860-1777
1133 Ave of the Americas (at 43rd St) 212/768-4684
Tues-Thurs: 10-5; Fri: 10-8; Sat, Sun: 10-6

These two shops—which are really museums with a museum store—are definitely worth a look if you're shopping for a photography buff with high-quality gifts in mind. They are both relatively small but have excellent collections of books about the history and technology of photography and photojournalism. You can also find coffee-table books of collected works by photographers, as well as prints, picture frames, and unusual postcards.

INTREPID SEA-AIR-SPACE MUSEUM
Pier 86 (at 46th St and the Hudson River)   212/245-0072
Daily: 10-5 (summer)

This museum's gift shop has all sorts of junk, but it's also a great source for books on military history, space exploration, and aircraft and weapon systems. This is a good place to look for model airplanes and ships, as is the Intrepid Museum itself. Although the museum is open only Wednesday through Sunday in the winter, the gift shop is open daily all year.

JEWISH MUSEUM
1109 Fifth Ave (at 92nd St)   212/423-3200
Sun: 10-5:45; Mon, Wed, Thurs: 11-5:45; Tues: 11-8; Fri: 11-3

This relatively large store is an excellent source for both Jewish literature and decorative art. Its selection of menorahs, for example, is among the classiest in the city. The store also sells cards, coffee-table books, and a wide selection of children's books with Jewish themes and characters. The Jewish Museum Design Shop, housed in a brownstone next to the museum, is also worth a look if you're interested in ceremonial objects, jewelry, and things for the home. Although the museum is closed on Friday, the stores are open abbreviated hours on that day.

METROPOLITAN MUSEUM OF ART
Fifth Ave (bet 80th and 84th St)   212/570-3894
Sun, Tues-Thurs: 9:30-5:15; Fri, Sat, 9:30-8:45

Macy's Herald Square (34th St and Ave of the Americas, mezzanine) 212/268-7266

Rockefeller Center (15 W 49th St, bet Fifth Ave and Ave of the Americas) 212/332-1360

Soho (113 Prince St, bet Wooster and Greene St)   212/614-3000

The Cloisters (Fort Tryon Park)   212/923-3700

The two-floor store inside the Metropolitan Museum of Art is the grandfather of all museum gift shops. It specializes in reproductions of paintings and other pieces in the Met's incredible collection, as well as museum collections around the world. You can find jewelry, statues, vases, scarves, ties, porcelains, prints, rugs, napkins, silver serving dishes, and scores of other beautiful gift ideas. They also carry books relating to special exhibits and the museum's extensive holdings, as well as umbrellas, tote bags, and other things with the Metropolitan's name emblazoned on them. There's even a bridal-registry department! Prices range from reasonable to wildly expensive, and the salespeople are usually patient and helpful. Satellite gift shops are located inside the museum itself (there's a beautiful one specializing in jewelry across the main entrance hall to your right) and throughout Manhattan. The hours of the satellite shops vary. The second floor of the main store in the Met and the second floor of the satellite shop in Rockefeller Center have particularly good children's sections.

METROPOLITAN OPERA SHOP
Metropolitan Opera House (at Lincoln Center)   212/580-4090
Mon-Sat: 10 a.m. through second intermission; Sun: noon-6

This is an opera lover's heaven. In addition to operas on video, compact discs, and other media, you'll find books, mugs, umbrellas, stationery, T-shirts, and pillows for the opera buff. It even has opera-buff hours: the store does not close on weekdays and Saturday until the second intermission of the evening's performance. Be sure to check out the Performing Arts Shop on the lower concourse, too. And if you're looking for posters and prints from various seasons, visit the Gallery, also on the lower concourse.

MORGAN LIBRARY SHOP
29 E 36th St (at Madison Ave)   212/685-0008, ext. 358
Tues-Fri: 10:30-4:45; Sat: 10:30-5:45; Sun: noon-5:45

This elegant shop is housed in a beautiful room once used by J.P. Morgan as a dining room. You'll find all sorts of books about medieval and Renaissance art, master drawings, current and past exhibitions, and related subjects. There's also unusual china, clocks, painted trays, boxes, and other gifts. The shop sells cards and postcards with pictures of paintings and other pieces from the library's remarkable collection. The shop closes 15 minutes before the museum.

MUSEUM FOR AFRICAN ART
593 Broadway (bet Houston and Prince St)
212/966-1313, ext 115
Tues-Fri: 10:30-5:30; Sat, Sun: noon-6

Anybody interested in African art ought to make a stop at this relatively small but unusual gift shop. The shop begins just inside the door and runs around the right side of the main desk. In addition to beautiful coffee-table books and a wonderful collection of children's books, the shop carries African art and artifacts from throughout the continent.

MUSEUM OF AMERICAN FOLK ART
2 Lincoln Sq (Columbus Ave bet 65th and 66th St)   212/496-2966
Mon: 11-6; Tues-Sat: 11-7:30; Sun: noon-6

Like the small galleries at the museum's Lincoln Square location, this shop offers a wide range of Americana—innovative toys and books for children, quilts, cookbooks, picture frames, and lots of unusual handcrafted knicknacks you would expect to find in an upscale country cottage. It's also an excellent source for books on folk and decorative arts. The shop is adjacent to the museum.

MUSEUM OF THE CITY OF NEW YORK
1220 Fifth Ave (bet 103rd and 104th St)   212/534-1672, ext 227
Wed-Sat: 10-5; Sun: 12-5

What a pleasure it is to find someone who cares so passionately about her store as manager Ann Goldsmith, who has transformed this little gem into a wondrous reflection of the city and its history. Whether you're looking for black-and-white prints from the museum's extensive archives, videos on such subjects as the construction of the subway system, books on the so-called outer boroughs, thoughtful and imaginative children's toys and books, or selections relating to the museum's permanent and changing exhibitions, this is a really exciting place to shop. (One caveat: the museum itself is in the process of an enormous expansion and may temporarily move from this location in the near future, so call before going.)

MUSEUM OF JEWISH HERITAGE
18 First Pl (adjacent to Battery Park)   212/968-1800
Sun-Fri: 9-5 (Thurs until 8; closed on all Jewish holidays and after noon on Fri in winter)

Tucked off to the right of the museum's main entrance, this store is a fitting companion to the museum in its celebration of Jewish art, crafts, and culture. The selection of items, many of which are related to the museum's collection, is diverse. Everything here is high-quality and much is quite unusual. A small but carefully chosen section includes books and gifts for children of various ages. The prices are remarkably good.

MUSEUM OF MODERN ART BOOKSTORE
11 W 43rd St (bet Fifth Ave and Ave of the Americas)   212/708-9700
Sat-Thurs: 10-6:30; Fri: 10-9

Most of the items in this two-story shop relate to the museum's incredible modern-art collection and exhibitions. Its selection of books on the subject is second to none, but you'll also find stationery, prints, wrapping paper, children's books, toys, CD-ROMs, videos, and calendars.

MUSEUM OF MODERN ART DESIGN STORE
44 W 53rd St (bet Fifth Ave and Ave of the Americas)   212/767-1050
Sat-Thurs: 10-6:30; Fri: 10-9

Across the street from the museum, this magnificent store is dedicated to what the curators consider the very best in modern design. Furniture, vases, ties, kitchen gadgets, silverware, frames, watches, lamps, and toys and books for children are just a few things you'll find here. These items are not cheap (keep your eye out for a great summer sale), but they are of the highest quality.

NATIONAL MUSEUM OF THE AMERICAN INDIAN
1 Bowling Green (at the foot of Broadway)
Museum Shop   212/825-8093
The Gallery   212/825-8094
Daily: 10-4:45 (Thurs until 7:45)

Like everything else about the museum, its two gift shops are classy operations. The Gallery, on the main floor to the right of the entrance, has a wide selection of books and high-quality Native American weavings, jewelry, and other handicrafts. The Museum Shop, down the grand marble staircase from the main entrance, is more focused on kids and families. Children's books, videos, toys, craft kits, and the obligatory arrowheads are for sale, along with T-shirts and some moderately priced jewelry. Both stores close 15 minutes before the museum. Because the museum is part of the Smithsonian Institution, both stores offer discounts to Smithsonian Associates.

NEW YORK PUBLIC LIBRARY SHOPS
New York Public Library
Fifth Ave bet 41st and 42nd St   212/930-0641
Mon-Sat: 11-6

New York Public Library Midtown Branch
Fifth Ave and 40th St   212/340-0849
Mon-Fri: 10-7; Sat: 10-6; Sun: noon-5

If ever there were a perfect gift shop for intellectuals (and those who fancy themselves as such), this is it. The original one is located just off the main lobby of the New York Public Library's main branch, while the other is across the street, where one of the Metropolitan Museum's satellite shops used to be. They feature everything from magnets with sayings like "I Think, Therefore I'm Dangerous" and "Think for Yourself, Not for Me" to books about the library's history. The one in the midtown branch has a particularly good selection of gifts and books for children and families. In addition to stocking an unusual, high-quality selection of merchandise, the staff in both places are particularly pleasant and helpful.

NEW YORK TRANSIT MUSEUM
Boerum Pl and Schermerhorn St, Brooklyn   718/243-8601
Tues-Fri: 10-4 (Wed until 6); Sat, Sun: noon-5

Grand Central Station   212/878-0106
Mon-Fri: 8-8; Sat: 10-4

Run by the Metropolitan Transit Authority, these three shops are enough to make train and subway buffs downright giddy. Items for sale include books, conductor's caps, clever T-shirts, replicas of old station signs, banks for children in the shape of city buses, giant chocolate subway tokens, jewelry made from old tokens, and even old token boxes. Bus and subway maps, as well as other MTA information, are also available.

PERFORMING ARTS SHOP
Metropolitan Opera House
Lincoln Center, lower concourse   212/580-4356
Mon-Sat: 10 until second intermission; Sun: noon-6

This store is lots of fun for anyone interested in opera, classical music, and the performing arts. Much like the Metropolitan Opera Shop on the floor above it, the Performing Arts Shop also has a wide selection of music, books, instruments, and toys for children, plus an even wider selection of recordings. It stays open weekdays and Saturdays until the end of the second intermission. If you're interested in prints and posters from past seasons, walk a little further down the hall and visit the Gallery.

STUDIO MUSEUM
144 W 125th St (bet Malcolm X and
Adam Clayton Powell, Jr Blvd)   212/864-4500, ext 237
Wed-Fri: 10-4:45; Sat, Sun: 1-5:45

Located just inside the museum's entrance on the right, this store sells a wide and generally high-quality selection of jewelry, textiles, crafts, notecards, and calendars created by African and African-American artists. It also sells an unusually broad selection of cookbooks, fiction, biographies, and children's books by and about Africans and African-Americans. The store closes 15 minutes before the museum.

UKRAINIAN MUSEUM
203 Second Ave (bet 12th and 13th St), 5th floor   212/228-0110
Wed-Sun: 1-5

This unique little place is not exactly on any tourist routes, but it's a real goldmine for anyone interested in Ukrainian eggs (already made and kits for do-it-yourselfers), embroidery, and other crafts.

UNITED NATIONS
First Ave bet 45th and 46th St   212/963-4465
Mon-Sun: 9-5:15 (March-Dec);
Mon-Fri: 9-5:15 (January and February)

On the lower level of the main UN building is a bookstore, post office (a real treat for stamp collectors), small UNICEF shop, and an even smaller shop run by the UN Women's Guild. That's in addition to the main gift shop, also on the lower level. The bookstore features calendars, postcards with the flags of member nations, holiday cards in dozens of different languages, and a wide variety of books about the UN and related subjects. The main gift shop features a wonderful array of carvings, jewelry, scarves, dolls, and other items from all over the world. The better imports can get pricy, but it's definitely going to a good cause! One final thought: if you are interested in UNICEF cards and gifts but find the selection at the UN itself rather thin, then visit the store in the lobby of the nearby UNICEF House (331 E 38th St). Note that the UN stores are closed on weekends in January and February.

WHITNEY MUSEUM'S STORE NEXT DOOR
943 Madison Ave (bet 74th and 75th St)   212/606-0200
Tues-Sun: 11-6 (Thurs: until 8)

Although there is a small and rather perfunctory book shop in the lobby of the Whitney Museum itself, any fan of modern art looking for unusual gifts ought to stop by the Store Next Door. In addition to creative toys and games for children, you'll find a changing collection of jewelry, T-shirts, scarves, ties, and offbeat things created for the museum's exhibitions. Some items are pricy and the staff can be a bit haughty, but the store is a hit with area residents and visitors alike. It is quite narrow, and its street entrance—to the right of the Whitney itself—is easy to miss, though you can now get to the store through the museum as well.

Music

ACADEMY RECORDS & CDs
12 W 18th St (at Fifth Ave)   212/242-3000
Mon-Sat: 9:30-9; Sun: 11-9

Academy Records & CDs has Manhattan's largest stock of used, out-of-print, and rare classical LPs and CDs. Emphasizing opera, contemporary classical, and early music, Academy has an international reputation. Prices are fair, and a catalog of rarer records (both popular and classical) is issued occasionally. Academy has built one of the finest secondhand selections of CDs. The rock and jazz holdings, while less extensive, are steadily growing.

BLEECKER BOB'S GOLDEN OLDIES RECORD SHOP
118 W 3rd St (bet MacDougal St and Ave of the Americas)
212/475-9677
Sun-Thurs: noon-1 a.m.; Fri, Sat: noon-3 a.m.

Let us sing the praises of Bleecker Bob, who is nothing if not perverse. (Name another store that's open till 3 a.m. on Christmas Day!) For one thing, although there is a real Bob (Plotnik, the owner), the store isn't on Bleecker Street. For another, Bleecker Bob is an institution to generations of New Yorkers who have sifted through his selection of virtually every rock record ever recorded. With a stock that includes old rock and soul records (plus some rare jazz), autograph parties for rock stars, and a boast that they can fill any wish list from their stock, Bleecker Bob's is much more than a punk-rock store. It is also *the* gathering place in the wee hours of the morning in the Village. But above all, it's a great source for out-of-print, obscure, and imported compact discs.

FOOTLIGHT RECORDS
113 E 12th St (bet Third and Fourth Ave)   212/533-1572
Mon-Fri: 11-7; Sat: 10-6; Sun: 11-5

In keeping with this outfit's passion for rare and unusual records, the emphasis is on show tunes, film soundtracks, and jazz. Their prices are among the best around, and many of their records just aren't available anywhere else. If there's an original cast album of a Broadway show, you can bet Footlight has it. They have one of the most comprehensive collections of film scores in the country, whole collections of artists from the 1920s through the 1960s, an impressive showing of European and Japanese imports in related fields, and a large selection of big-band and early jazz.

FRANK MUSIC
244 W 54th St, 10th floor   212/582-1999
Mon-Fri: 10-6

Founded in 1938, this professional business has never advertised, relying instead on word of mouth. They sell classical sheet music from European and American publishers. There is an aisle for voice and violin, another for piano, and so on. Frank Music gladly fills mail orders. Ask for Heidi Rogers, the helpful owner, or Dean Streit, her assistant.

GRYPHON RECORD SHOP
233 W 72nd St, 2nd floor   212/874-1588
Mon-Sat: 11-7; Sun: 12:30-6:30

Gryphon is one of a handful of stores specializing in rare and out-of-print
LPs. Raymond Donnell will help customers search out the most elusive LP,
be it classical (the main area of emphasis), jazz, Broadway, pop, or spoken
word. Books on music are also available.

> The largest retail music and entertainment complex in the world is
> **Virgin Megastore** (1540 Broadway, 212/921-1020), a $15 million com-
> plex in Times Square. There are over one million CDs in stock, more
> than a thousand listening and viewing stations, a huge selection of CD-
> ROMS, a 12,000-square-foot classical-music section, and the broadest
> selection of laserdisc, DVD, and video titles in the world. When you
> decide to buy, 45 cash registers are ready to ring up your sale!

HMV U.S.A.
1280 Lexington Ave (at 86th St)   212/348-0800
57 W 34th St (at Herald Square)   212/629-0900
2081 Broadway (at 72nd St)   212/721-5900
565 Fifth Ave (at 46th St)   212/681-6700
Call individual stores for hours; all open Sun

This is truly a musical supermarket! There are separate departments for rock
and pop, classical, dance, jazz, and video. Listening booths are available. This
outfit is nearly a century old, with outlets all over the world. If you are looking for CDs, DVDs, cassettes, VHS tapes, or accessories, HMV is a good place
to visit.

JAZZ RECORD CENTER
236 W 26th St, Room 804   212/675-4480
Tues-Sat: 10-6 (Sept-May); Mon-Fri: 10-6 (June-Aug)

This is the only jazz specialty store in the city. They deal primarily in out-
of-print jazz records, but there are also CDs, videos, books, posters, photos,
periodicals, postcards, and T-shirts on the topic. The center buys collections,
runs a search service, fills mail orders, and offers appraisals. Every two years
a jazz rarities auction is held. The operation is run by Frederick Cohen, a world-
famous specialist in jazz records. Cohen is a charming guy who really knows
his business.

JOSEPH PATELSON MUSIC HOUSE
160 W 56th St   212/582-5840
Mon-Sat: 9-6 (closed Sat in summer)

Located behind Carnegie Hall, Joseph Patelson is a shop known to every
student of music in the city. From little first-graders to artists from Carnegie
Hall, everyone stops here first because of the fabulous selection and excellent
prices. The stock includes music scores, sheet music, music books, and orchestral and opera scores. All are neatly cataloged and displayed in open cabinets.
One can easily browse his or her section of interest—be it piano music, chamber
music, orchestral scores, opera scores, concerts, ethnic scores, or instrumen-
tal solos. Sheet music is filed in bins the way records are elsewhere. There

are also musical accessories, like metronomes and pitch pipes. Patelson is an unofficial meeting place for the city's young musicians. Word goes out that "we're looking for a violinist," and meetings are often arranged in the store. Mail and phone orders are accepted.

MULTI KULTI
218 Thompson St (bet Bleecker and 3rd St)   212/979-1872
Mon-Thur: 1:30-10; Fri, Sat: 1:30-midnight; Sun: 12-8

From humble beginnings in a flea market stall, this outfit has become a first-class resource for international music compact discs. Another specialty are the underground dance and ethnic-influenced new-age CDs. A knowledgeable staff, a special order service, and listening stations make visits here fun and rewarding.

Where to find some of the best stocks of prerecorded music, by category:

Classical/Opera: **A Classical Record** (547 W 27th St)
Dance music: **Satellite Records** (342 Bowery)
Jazz: **Jazz Record Center** (236 W 26th St)
Latin: **Record Mart/Times Square** (BMT mezzanine, Times Square subway station)
Popular music and collectibles: **Norman's Sound & Vision** (67 Cooper Sq, bet St. Mark's Pl and 7th St)
Vintage music: **Footlight Records** (113 E 12th St)

NOSTALGIA . . . AND ALL THAT JAZZ
217 Thompson St (bet Bleecker and 3rd St)   212/420-1940
Mon-Thurs: 1-8; Fri: 1-9; Sat: 1-10; Sun: 1-7:30

Recorded nostalgia—especially jazz, original cast, and soundtrack recordings—is sold here. All are very reasonably priced. The shop has a sideline in photography, with Kim Deuel and Mort Alavi doing a healthy business producing, cataloging, and reproducing photos. Nostalgia will reproduce any photograph, in any size or quantity, up to 30" x 40". They also have a good collection of posters, sports photos, movie and jazz stills, and large (16"x 20") showbiz photos in black-and-white and color.

TOWER RECORDS AND VIDEO
Locations throughout Manhattan (see below)
Hours vary by store

692 Broadway (212/505-1500): records, tapes, CDs
Trump Tower, 75 Fifth Ave (212/838-8110): records, video
383 Lafayette St (212/228-5100): books and video sales and rentals
20 E 4th St (212/228-7317): clearance outlet

These stores are well-stocked and busy.

VENUS RECORDS
13 St. Mark's Pl (bet Second and Third Ave)   212/598-4459
Sun-Thurs: 12-8; Fri, Sat: 12-11

For the rock and roll enthusiast, Venus offers one of New York's finest selections of 1950s and 1960s reissues and original editions, plus punk, alternative, and other new and used rock records not usually found in the Top Forty. They also carry imported and independent releases, many out-of-print items, and a large selection of 45s. You can bring in used LPs, CDs, and cassettes for cash or trade. A mail-order service is available.

VINYL MANIA RECORDS
60 Carmine St   212/924-7223
Mon-Fri: 11-9; Sat, Sun: 11-7

Vinyl Mania Records is New York's specialty shop for DJs. Its business is 80% vinyl, as they cater to the dance, hip-hop, and rap community. They also carry a choice selection of imported and domestic CDs and CD singles.

Looking for hard-to-find vinyl records? These shops stock used LPs and more:

Housing Works Used Book Cafe (126 Crosby St, 212/334-3324)
Salvation Army Warehouse (536 W 46th St, 212/664-8563)
Thrift & New Shoppe (602 Ninth Ave, 212/265-3087)
Tower Records Clearance Outlet (20 E 4th St, 212/228-7317)

Musical Instruments

DETRICH PIANOS
211 W 58th St (nr Broadway)   212/245-1234
Mon-Fri: 10-6; Sat: 10-4

Kalman Detrich fled Hungary for the United States many years ago, bringing his love and knowledge of pianos with him. His shop, within earshot of Carnegie Hall, ministers to any of the myriad needs a piano player might have. Detrich will tune, repair, polish, rent, buy, sell, and even buy back a piano with all the finesse of his Old World training. His specialty is antique and Steinway pianos. He lovingly restores them, and the few he can't bring back to life are polished to a gloss and sold as furniture. The small shop is jammed with the cream of whatever is being refurbished at the moment, and passers-by cannot help but understand Detrich's pride when viewing the finished results. The Museum of the American Piano is also housed at this location.

DRUMMERS WORLD
151 W 46th St   212/840-3057
Mon-Fri: 10-6; Sat: 10-4

This is a great place unless the patron is your teenager or an upstairs neighbor! Barry Greenspon and his staff take pride in guiding students and professionals through one of the best and well-rounded percussion stores in the country. Inside this drummer's paradise is everything from commonplace equipment to one-of-a-kind antiques and imports. All of the instruments are high-quality symphonic percussion items, and customers receive the same attention whether they are members of an orchestra, rock band, or rap act. The store also offers instructors and how-to books. There are esoteric ethnic instruments for virtuosos who want to experiment. Drummers World has a catalog and will ship anywhere in the country.

GUITAR SALON
45 Grove St (at Sheridan Sq)
212/675-3236
By appointment only

Beverly Maher's Guitar Salon is a unique one-person operation located in a historic brownstone in Greenwich Village. Here you will find handmade classical and flamenco guitars for serious students and professionals priced from $2,500. The shop buys and sells fine instruments, giving outstanding personal service from a talented guitarist and guitar teacher. The salon specializes in 19th- and 20th-century vintage instruments. Appraisals are available, and lessons are given on all styles of guitars. Maher appraised Segovia's guitars, which he donated in 1987 to the Metropolitan Museum. Even the Rolling Stones shop here!

MANNY'S MUSIC
156 W 48th St (bet Ave of the Americas and Seventh Ave)
212/819-0576
Mon-Fri: 10-6:30; Sat: 10-6

Manny's is a huge discount department store for musical instruments. "Everything for the musician" is their motto, and it is borne out by a collection of musical equipment so extensive that each department has its own salespeople. There is an emphasis on modern music, as evidenced by the hundreds of autographed pictures of contemporary musicians on the walls and the huge collection of electronic instruments. There is a good collection of classical instruments as well. All of the instruments, keyboards, electronic equipment, accessories, and supplies are sold at discount. They also have a large computer department for musical software needs.

RITA FORD
19 E 65th St (at Madison Ave)   212/535-6717
Mon-Sat: 9-5

Gerry and Nancy Wright and Joseph and Diane Tenore collect antique music boxes and have become experts in all aspects of the business. Stock consists of valuable antique music boxes, as well as some not-so-valuable old pieces in various states of disrepair. The main stock-in-trade is expertise; having been in business for half a century, these folks know all there is to know about music boxes. They are acknowledged experts on music box scores, workings, and outer casings. Some pieces are rare antiques and are priced accordingly. Somewhat more reasonable are contemporary reproductions. The store also does repairs.

If you're looking for musical instruments, the best overall store in Manhattan is **Manny's Music** (156 W 48th St), on a block of 48th Street that's crowded with them. Here are some others, arranged alphabetically by their musical instrument specialty.

Accordions: **Main Squeeze** (19 Essex St, 212/614-3109)
Drums: **Drummers World** (151 W 46th St, 212/840-3057)
Guitars: **Guitar Salon** (45 Grove St, at Sheridan Square) and **Matt Umanov** (273 Bleecker St, 212/675-2157)
Violins: **Universal Music** (732 Broadway, 212/254-6917)

Newspapers, Magazines

HOTALINGS NEWS AGENCY
1560 Broadway (at Times Square Visitors Center)   212/730-4772
Daily: 8-8

As every homesick out-of-towner should know, hometown newspapers can be picked up at Hotalings for the cover price, plus the cost of shipping. Domestic and foreign newspapers are sold on the day of issue (or soon thereafter). Many non-natives keep in daily contact with their hometowns through these papers. Hotalings also carries a full line of dometic magazines

Optical

THE EYE MAN
2264 Broadway (bet 81st and 82nd St)   212/873-4114
Mon, Wed: 10-7; Tues, Thurs: 10-7:30; Fri, Sat: 10-6;
Sun: 12-5 (closed Sun in summer)

There are dozens of stores in Manhattan that carry eyeglasses, but few that take special time and care with children. The Eye Man carries a great selection of frames for young people, as well as specialty eyewear for grownups.

GRUEN OPTIKA
1225 Lexington Ave (bet 82nd and 83rd St)   212/628-2493
599 Lexington Ave (bet 52nd and 53rd St)   212/688-3580
1076 Third Ave (bet 63rd and 64th St)   212/751-6177
740 Madison Ave (at 64th St)   212/988-5832
2383 Broadway (at 87th St)   212/724-0850
2009 Broadway (at 69th St)   212/874-8749
Mon-Fri: 9:30-6:30; Sat: 10-5; Sun: 12-5 at Third Ave,
Madison Ave and Broadway locations only

Gruen Optika boasts the same faces and personal quality care year after year. The firm enjoys a reputation for excellent service, be it emergency fittings or one-day turnaround, and there's a super selection of specialty eyewear. Their sunglasses, theater glasses, sport spectacles, and party eyewear are noteworthy.

JOEL NAME OPTIQUE DE PARIS
65 W Houston St (at Wooster St)   212/777-5888
Mon-Fri: 11-7; Sat: 11-6; Sun: 12-5

Service is the name of the game here. Owner Joel Nommick and his crew are true professionals, and they stock some of the most fashionable specs in town.

MORGENTHAL-FREDERICS OPTICIANS
685 Madison Ave (bet 61st and 62nd St)   212/838-3090
Mon-Fri: 9-7; Sat: 10-5:30; Sun: 12-6
944 Madison Ave (bet 74th and 75th St)   212/744-9444
Mon-Fri: 10-7; Sat: 10-5:30; Sun: 12-6 (Oct-May)
399 West Broadway (at Spring St)   212/966-0099
Mon-Fri: 11-8; Sat: 11-7; Sun: 12-6
at Bergdorf Goodman (754 Fifth Ave)   212/753-7300
Mon-Sat: 10-7

If you are looking for state-of-the-art creative and elegant eyewear, Morgenthal-Frederics is the place. Owner Richard Morgenthal is a knowledgeable and helpful gentleman. He features his own designs, manufactured in Europe and created in-house. As an added service they will make appointments with some of New York's best-known ophthalmologists. The fact that they have been in business for eight decades says something about the caliber of products and service.

20/20
150 E 86th St (bet Third and Lexington Ave)   212/876-7676
956 Third Ave (at 57th St)   212/228-2192
57 E 8th St (bet Broadway and University St)   212/228-2192
Mon-Fri: 10-7:30; Sat: 10-6; Sun: varies

The folks at 20/20 offer the hippest eyewear in the city. For over two decades they have been offering trendsetting eyewear along with convenient services like overnight delivery, eye exams, and prescription fulfillment.

Photographic Equipment and Supplies

ADORAMA CAMERA
42 W 18th St (bet Fifth Ave and Ave of the Americas)   212/741-0052
Mon-Thurs: 9-6:45; Fri: 9-1:45; Sun: 9:30-6

These people operate one of the largest photographic mail-order houses in the country. They carry a huge stock of photographic equipment and supplies, telescopes, video paraphernalia, and digital equipment. All is sold at discount.

ALKIT PRO CAMERAS
820 Third Ave (at 50th St)   212/832-2101
222 Park Ave S (at 18th St)   212/674-1515
466 Lexington Ave (at 46th St)   212/286-8700
830 Seventh Ave (at 53rd St)   212/262-2424
Mon-Fri: 7:30-6:30; Sat: 9-5

If you want to shop where the photographers of the Elite and Ford modeling agencies go, Alkit is the place. Don't feel like you have to be a professional to come here, however. While most establishments that deal with the real pros have little time for amateurs, nothing gives Edward Buchbinder (the store's president) more pleasure than introducing the world of photography to neophytes. Alkit maintains a full line of cameras, film, and equipment, as well as stereos, TVs, VCRs, and electronics, and they have a one-hour professional processing lab on-premises. The shop repairs and rents photographic equipment, and it also publishes an informative catalog full of praise and gripes about particular models. Very rude telephone service is the one downside.

B&H PHOTO-VIDEO-PRO AUDIO
420 Ninth Ave (bet 33rd and 34th St)   212/444-6600
Mon-Thurs: 9-7; Fri: 9-1; Sun: 10-5

This is quite a store! You'll find professional and nonprofessional departments for video, pro audio, photo, pro lighting, darkroom, film and film processing, books, used equipment, and more. The store has been in operation since 1974 and is staffed by knowledgeable personnel. Inventory levels are high, prices are reasonable, and hands-on demo areas make browsing easy.

KEN HANSEN PHOTOGRAPHIC
509 Madison Ave (at 53rd St)   212/317-0923
Mon-Fri: 9-6

This is a classy, upscale outlet for photographic equipment. There is a vast selection of merchandise and a great showing of cameras not found elsewhere. Equipment is available for rent. You will find Ken Hansen and his crew to be professional and well-informed.

LAUMONT PHOTOGRAPHICS
333 W 52nd St   212/245-2113
Mon-Fri: 9-5:30 (evenings and weekends by appointment)

Whether you're a professional or amateur, Laumont can take care of your photographic needs. They do excellent work producing Cibachrome and Iris prints, all of them exhibition-quality. They are patient and understanding with those who need counseling and advice. Laumont's staff are also experienced digital retouchers and duplicators, and they can repair damaged originals or create brand-new images on state-of-the-art computers. Lamination and print-mounting are done on-premises.

NEW YORK FILM WORKS
928 Broadway (at 21st St)   212/475-5700
Mon-Fri: 8-8; Sat: 10-4

Specialties here include computer slides and prints and photo business cards. These folks can produce a color photograph in one hour at prices that are extremely competitive.

WILLOUGHBY'S KONICA IMAGING CENTER
136 W 32nd St (bet Ave of the Americas and Seventh Ave)
212/564-1600, 800/378-1898
50 E 42nd St (bet Park and Madison Ave)   212/681-7844
Mon-Fri: 8:30-8; Sat, Sun: 10-7

Established in 1898, this is the largest camera shop in the world, boasting a huge stock, an extensive clientele, and a solid reputation. It is now a high-tech camera shop as well. Willoughby's can handle almost any kind of camera order, either in person or by mail order. Willoughby's also services cameras, supplies photographic equipment, and recycles used cameras. Moreover, they sell computers, video cameras, and cellular phones.

Pictures, Posters, Prints

JERRY OHLINGER'S MOVIE MATERIAL STORE
242 W 14th St   212/989-0869
Daily: 1-7:45 p.m.

Jerry Ohlinger has a huge selection of movie posters, plus photographs from film and TV, and he will gladly provide a catalog. He also does research for these kinds of items.

OLD PRINT SHOP
150 Lexington Ave (bet 29th and 30th St)   212/683-3950
Winter: Tues-Fri: 9-5; Sat: 9-4
Summer: Mon-Thurs: 9-5; Fri: 9-4

Established in 1898, the Old Print Shop exudes an old-fashioned charm, and its stock only reinforces the impression of timelessness. Kenneth M. Newman specializes in Americana, including original prints, town views, Currier and Ives prints, and original maps that reflect America as it used to be. Most of the nostalgic bicentennial pictures that adorned calendars and stationery were copies of prints found here. Amateur and professional historians have a field day in this shop. Newman also does "correct period framing," and prints housed in his custom frames are striking. Everything bought and sold here is original, and Newman purchases estates and single items.

POSTER AMERICA
138 W 18th St (bet Ave of the Americas and Seventh Ave)
212/206-0499
Tues-Sat: 11-6; Sun: 12-5 (except summer)

You've never seen a poster gallery like this one! Poster America features original posters from 1905 to 1965, nearly all of which are lithographs. Poster America, one of the oldest galleries in the country devoted to vintage poster art, is set in a former stable and carriage house that used to serve the department stores on Ladies' Mile in the 1880s. The magnificent mahogany-and-glass storefront still catches the eyes of passers-by, luring them into a huge, well-appointed gallery. Poster America is known for brilliant graphics and the magnitude of its rare and unusual posters.

TRITON GALLERY
323 W 45th St (bet Eighth and Ninth Ave)   212/765-2472
Mon-Sat: 10-6; Sun: 1-6

Theater posters are presented at Triton like nowhere else. The posters of current Broadway shows are but a small part of what's available. There's also a broad range of older show posters from here and abroad. Show cards, the most readily available items, are the standard 14"x22" size. Posters range in size from 23"x46" to 42"x84" and are priced according to rarity, age, and demand. The collection is not limited to Broadway or even American plays, and some of the more interesting pieces are of plays from other times. Triton also does custom framing. Much of the business is conducted via mail and phone orders.

Plastics

INDUSTRIAL PLASTICS
309 Canal St (bet Mercer St and Broadway)   212/226-2010
Mon-Sat: 9-5:30

Industrial Plastics is dedicated to hard and soft plastics. Their line includes waterproofing material, Lucite cubes, and plastic sheets. They are particularly accommodating to do-it-yourselfers.

PLEXI-CRAFT QUALITY PRODUCTS
514 W 24th St   212/924-3244
Mon-Fri: 9:30-5

Plexi-Craft offers anything made of Lucite and Plexiglas at wholesale prices. If you can't find what you want among the pedestals, tables, chairs, shelves, computer tables, and cubes, they will make it for you. The helpful personnel will point out various styles of cocktail tables, shelves, magazine racks, television stands, and chairs. A catalog is available for $2.

Religious Arts

GRAND STERLING SILVER COMPANY
345 Grand St (bet Essex and Ludlow St)   212/674-6450
Sun-Thurs: 10:30-5:30

Ring the bell and you will be admitted to a stunning collection of silver religious art pieces. You'll also find almost anything from silver toothpick holders to baroque candelabras over six feet tall. Grand Sterling will repair and re-silver any item, be it religious or secular. They are manufacturers and importers of fine sterling holloware. Silver is revered with unmatched dedication here!

Rubber Goods

CANAL RUBBER SUPPLY COMPANY
329 Canal St (at Greene St)   212/226-7339
Mon-Fri: 9-5; Sat: 9-4

"If it's made of rubber, we have it" is this company's motto, and that sums up this wholesale-retail operation. There are foam mattresses, bolsters, cushions, pillow foam, pads cut to size, hydraulic hoses, rubber tubing, vacuum hoses, floor matting, tiles, stair treads, sheet-rubber products, and much more.

Security Devices

CCS COUNTER SPY SHOP
444 Madison Ave (at 49th St)   212/688-8500

Waldorf Astoria Hotel, 301 Park Ave   212/750-6645
Mon: 9-6; Tues-Fri: 9-7; Sat: 11-4; Sun: 11-3

With security and surveillance high on many people's minds these days, the CCS Counter Spy Shop provides relief for worriers. These folks supply all manner of security items for business and private use. There is bulletproof clothing—everything from T-shirts to safari outfits. Other items include covert video systems, night-vision equipment, debugging devices, phone or fax scramblers, voice-stress analyzers, and lie detectors. There are even bulletproof cars! It's all here, and confidential consultations can be arranged.

EMPIRE SAFE COMPANY
6 E 39th St (bet Fifth and Madison Ave)
212/684-2255, 800/543-5412
Mon-Fri: 9-6:30; Sat: 10-3

Empire shows one of the largest and most complete selection of safes available anywhere. Their products are used in residences and businesses, with delivery and installation offered. Also on display are rare antique and art-deco safes, memorabilia, old photos, and historical documents. Whether you want to protect documents in a small apartment or huge office building, these folks are able to help.

QÜARK SPY CENTRE
537 Third Ave (at 36th St)   212/889-1808, 800/343-6443
Mon-Fri: 9-6; Sat: by appointment

Qüark is Manhattan's most extensive countersurveillance showroom. With more than 400 items on display, Qüark is able to service all personal and professional security needs, no matter how unique. Products offered include night-vision equipment, bug detection and telephone security items, body armor, voice scramblers, long-play recording devices, and alarm briefcases.

Sexual Paraphernalia

COME AGAIN
353 E 53rd St (at First Ave)   212/308-9394
Mon-Fri: 11-7:30

Come Again is a large one-stop shopping center for sexual paraphernalia. There's exotic lingerie for men and women, adult books and magazines, oils and lotions, gift baskets, party gifts, and toys and equipment of a decidedly prurient nature. They boast an X-rated shop-at-home catalog.

CONDOMANIA
351 Bleecker St   212/691-9442
Sun-Thurs: 11-11; Fri, Sat: 11 a.m.-midnight

Yes, this store specializes in condoms: all shapes, sizes, and colors. Mixed in are suggestive postcards and the like. Reflecting the liberated times, Condomania is as popular with ladies as gentlemen.

EVE'S GARDEN INTERNATIONAL
119 W 57th St, Suite 1201   212/757-8651
Mon-Sat: 11-7

This is a pleasure chest of games, books, and videos to seduce your mind and a vast array of sensuous massage oils, candles, and incense to help realize your wildest fantasies.

Signs

LET THERE BE NEON
38 White St   212/226-4883
Mon-Fri: 8:30-5:30; Sat by appointment

Though the image of neon is modern, it harks back to Georges Claudes' capturing of it from oxygen in 1915. While the flashing neon sign has perhaps become the ultimate urban cliché, Rudi Stern has turned neon into a modern art form. Let There Be Neon operates as a gallery with an assemblage of sizes, shapes, functions, and designs to entice the browser. Almost all of Let There Be Neon's sales are commissioned pieces. Stern claims that even a rough sketch is enough for them to create a literal or abstract neon sculpture.

Silver

EASTERN SILVER COMPANY
54 Canal St, 2nd floor   212/226-5708
Mon-Thurs: 9-5; Fri: 9-12:30; Sun: 10:30-4

Prepare to enter a floor-to-ceiling wonderland of top-quality silver. Not all of it is cleaned and polished, but each piece has the potential of becoming as beautiful as only silver can be. The stock includes virtually any product made of silver, and Robert Gelbstein can put his hand on just about any desired item almost immediately. Eastern has a large collection of Jewish ceremonial silver and secular silver items, such as candlesticks and wine decanters. However, most of the collection would look perfect gracing any home. Prices are extremely reasonable.

JEAN'S SILVERSMITHS
16 W 45th St (at Fifth Ave)   212/575-0723
Mon-Thurs: 9-4:30; Fri: 9-3:30

Having a problem replacing a fork that went down the garbage disposal? Proceed directly to Jean's, where you will find over a thousand discontinued, obsolete, and current flatware patterns. They specialize in antique and second-hand silver, gold, and diamond jewelry, and they also sell watches.

ROGERS AND ROSENTHAL
201/346-1862 (mail order)
Mon-Fri: 10-4

Rogers and Rosenthal is one of the very best places for silver, china, and crystal. Nearly all of their business is done by mail. They feature major brand names and offer a 25% or more discount on every piece by mail. They will send price lists upon request, and what isn't in stock will be ordered.

TIFFANY AND COMPANY
727 Fifth Ave (at 57th St)   212/755-8000
Mon-Wed, Fri, Sat: 10-6; Thurs: 10-7

Despite the fact that Tiffany has appeared in plays, movies, books, and songs, this legendary store really isn't that formidable or forbidding, and it can be an exciting place to shop. Yes, there really is a Tiffany diamond, and it can be viewed on the first floor. That floor also houses the watch and jewelry departments. While browsing is welcome, salespeople are quick to approach loitering customers. The second floor has clocks, silver jewelry, sterling silver, bar accessories, centerpieces, leather accessories, scarves, and knickknacks. The third floor highlights china, crystal, flatware, and engraved stationery. The real surprise is that Tiffany carries an excellent selection of reasonably priced items. Many come emblazoned with the Tiffany name and are wrapped in the famed blue box—all at prices less than some neighborhood variety stores.

Sporting Goods

Bicycles and Accessories

BICYCLE RENAISSANCE
430 Columbus Ave (at 81st St)   212/724-2350
Mon-Fri: 10-7:30; Sat: 10-6; Sun: 10-5; summer: 10-7:30 daily

Biking is a way of life at Bicycle Renaissance. Services include custom-building bikes and bicycle repair, with the mechanics aiming for same-day service on all makes and models. They carry all manner of racing and mountain bikes, including Trek, Cannondale, and Specialized, as well as custom frames for Campagnolo, Shimano, and many others. Prices are on par with so-called discount shops.

LARRY & JEFF'S SECOND AVENUE BICYCLES PLUS
1690 Second Ave (at 87th St)   212/722-2201
Daily: 10-7; (summer: 10-8:30)

Larry started fixing bicycles at age 15, so you can bet he knows all about them. He then taught the art to Jeff, and together they have been operating this unique shop since 1977. You can find bikes ranging from $200 to $5,000, with parts and accessories to boot. Lots of special services: a lifetime of free tune-ups with the purchase of a new bicycle, bike rentals for rides through Central Park, and free delivery.

Billiards

BLATT BILLIARD
809 Broadway (bet 11th and 12th St)   212/674-8855
Mon-Fri: 9-6; Sat: 10-4 (closed Sat in summer)

Blatt's six floors are outfitted from top to bottom with everything for billiards. You can also get friendly pointers from a staff that seems, at first glance, to be all business.

Darts

DART SHOPPE
30 E 20th St (bet Park Ave S and Broadway)   212/533-8684
Mon-Fri: 12-6; Sat: 11-5

Most towns have sporting goods shops, but few have a department or even a display for darts. In New York, of course, things are different. Dart Shoppe is dedicated solely to darts and darting equipment. Their collection of darts, dartboards, accessories, and English darting equipment is impressive.

Exercise Equipment

GYM SOURCE
40 E 52nd St (bet Park and Madison Ave)   212/688-4222
Mon-Fri: 9-6; Sat: 10-5

This is the largest exercise-equipment dealer in the Northeast. They carry treadmills, bikes, stair and weight machines, rowers, and more. Over 300 top brands at good prices are available, and Gym Source's skilled technicians provide competent service. They will rent equipment and can even provide items for use in a Manhattan hotel room.

Fishing

CAPITOL FISHING TACKLE COMPANY
Chelsea Hotel
218 W 23rd St (at Seventh Ave)
212/929-6132
Mon-Fri: 9-6; (Thurs until 7); Sat: 10-5

Where else but in New York could one find a fishing store so totally landlocked that a subway roars beneath it, yet one that offers bargains unmatched at seaport fishing stores? Amid the hustle and bustle of Chelsea, Capitol features a complete range of fishing tackle with such brand names as Penn, Shimano, Tycoon Finnor, Garcia, and Daiwa at low prices. There is a constantly changing selection of specials and close-outs. Capitol buys up surplus inventories, bankrupt dealers, and liquidations, and the savings are passed on to customers.

General

EASTERN MOUNTAIN SPORTS (EMS)
20 W 61st St (bet Broadway and Columbus Ave)   212/397-4860
Mon-Fri: 10-9; Sat: 10-6; Sun: 12-6

611 Broadway (at Houston St)   212/505-9860
Mon-Fri: 10-9; Sat: 10-8; Sun: 12-6

This is the place to go for outdoor clothing and gear. Although prices can be bettered elsewhere, it's an excellent source for one-stop shopping and the merchandise is of better quality than that found in department stores. EMS covers virtually all outdoor sports, including mountain climbing, backpacking, skiing, hiking, tenting, kayaking, and camping.

G&S SPORTING GOODS
43 Essex St   212/777-7590
Mon-Fri, Sun: 9:30-6

If you are looking for a place to buy a birthday or Christmas gift for a sports buff, I'd recommend G&S. They have a large selection of brand-name sneakers, in-line skates, boxing equipment, balls, gloves, toys, games, sports clothing, and accessory items. Prices reflect a 20% to 25% discount.

MODELL'S
280 Broadway   212/962-6200
200 Broadway   212/964-4007
91 Ave of the Americas   212/594-1830
51 E 42nd St   212/661-4242
Manhattan Mall, Ave of the Americas at 33rd St (lower level)
212/594-1830
Hours vary by store

You can't beat this outfit for quality and value! Founded in 1889, Modell's is America's oldest family-owned and -operated sporting goods chain. The stores specialize in menswear, women's wear, sporting goods, footwear, luggage, and sundries. Prices are right, especially on shoes.

PARAGON SPORTS
867 Broadway (at 18th St)   212/255-8036
Mon-Sat: 10-8; Sun: 11-6:30

This is truly a sporting goods department store, with over 100,000 square feet of specialty shops devoted to all kinds of sports and fitness equipment and apparel. There are separate departments for team equipment, athletic footwear, skateboards, ice skates, in-line skates, racquet sports, aerobics, swimming, golf, skiing and snowboarding, hiking, camping, diving, biking, sailing, and anything else that is done in the great outdoors. There are also gift items, and the stock is arranged for easy shopping.

Golf

NEW YORK GOLF CENTER
131 W 35th St (bet Seventh Ave and Broadway)
212/564-2255, 888/465-7890
Mon-Sat: 10-7; Sun: 11-5 (April-October)

This shop is the ultimate hole-in-one for the golfer! In premises that provide the largest selection of quality brand-name golfing merchandise in the area, they offer goods at prices that average 20% below list. There are clubs, bags, clothing, shoes, accessories, and novelties . . . everything except one's own hard-won expertise. The folks here couldn't be nicer or more helpful.

Guns

JOHN JOVINO GUN SHOP
5 Centre Market Pl (at Grand St)   212/925-4881
Mon-Fri: 9-6; Sat: 9-3

These folks have been in business since 1911 and are recognized leaders in the field. They carry all major brands of handguns, rifles, shotguns, and accessories, including ammunition, holsters, bulletproof vests, knives, and scopes. Major brands include Smith & Wesson, Colt, Ruger, Beretta, Browning, Remington, Walther, Glock, Winchester, and Sig Sauer. Jovino is an authorized warranty repair station for gun manufacturers, with two licensed gunsmiths on the premises.

Horseback Riding

MILLER HARNESS CO.
117 E 24th St   212/673-1400
Mon-Sat: 10-6 (Thurs:10-7)

Miller's is a super place to find gifts for both horses and owners. The Miller symbol of two boots is displayed in hundreds of shops across North America. The exclusive Miller line can cover a rider from head to hoof. Sizes suit men, women, children, stallions, mares, and foals. The haberdashery offers proper English riding gear and saddles. Hermes' saddles, incidentally, are registry-numbered and sell for $3,400 and up! There are boots, helmets, riding shirts, breeches, and riding potpourri.

Marine

WEST MARINE
12 W 37th St (at Fifth Ave)   212/594-6065
Mon-Fri: 9-6; Sat, Sun: 10-4

West sells marine supplies as if it were situated in the middle of a New England seaport rather than the heart of Manhattan. The staff sometimes looks like a ship's crew on leave in the Big Apple, and they are actually that knowledgeable. They carry marine electronics, sailboat fittings, big-game fishing tackle, lifesaving gear, ropes, anchors, compasses, clothing, clocks, barometers, and books. Foul-weather suits are a star attraction, and there is also a line of clothes for yacht owners.

Outdoor Equipment

TENT AND TRAILS
21 Park Pl (bet Broadway and Church St)
212/227-1760, 800/237-1760
Mon-Wed, Sat: 9:30-6; Thurs, Fri: 9:30-7; Sun: 12-6

Whether you are outfitting yourself for a weekend camping trip or an ascent of Mt. Everest, Tent and Trails is the place to go! In the urban canyons near City Hall, this 6,000-square-foot store is devoted to camping. The staff is experienced and knowledgeable. There are boots from Asolo, Merrill, Vasque, Hi Tec, and Nike, and camping gear from Madden, Patagonia, Fabiano Clothing, Camp Trails, Moonstone, JanSport, Gregory Packs, Mountainsmith Packs, Eureka Tent, Coleman, Moss Tent, Timberland, and NorthFace. You'll find backpacks, sleeping bags, tents, down clothing, and much more. Tent and Trails also rents camping equipment.

Running

ATHLETIC STYLE
118 E 59th St (bet Park and Lexington Ave)   212/838-2564
Mon-Wed, Fri, Sat: 10-6; Thurs: 10-6:30; Sun: 12:30-5:30

Athletic Style is one of the top outlets in the city in terms of quality, value, and service. The 59th Street store has evolved into a custom outlet offering embroidery and laser engraving. Owners Vic and Dave are always on the job. Bloomingdale's was so impressed that they opened a branch in their store. Footwear includes many famous names. They also carry a good stock of clothing, including logo merchandise and personalized T-shirts, caps, and sweats.

SUPER RUNNERS SHOP
1337 Lexington Ave (at 89th St)   212/369-6010
360 Amsterdam Ave (at 77th St)   212/787-7665
1246 Third Ave   212/249-2133
Mon-Fri: 10-7 (Thurs until 9); Sat: 10-6; Sun: 12-5

Co-owner Gary Muhrcke was the winner of the first New York City Marathon in 1970. Entry blanks for local races are available in the stores. The stock includes a superb selection of men's and women's running and racing shoes, in addition to performance running clothes. The informed staff, who are themselves runners, believes that each person should be fitted individually in terms of sizing and need.

Skating

BLADES BOARD & SKATE
120 W 72nd St   212/787-3911
160 E 86th St   212/996-1644
128 Chambers St   212/964-1944
659 Broadway   212/477-7350
1414 Second Ave   212/249-3178
Chelsea Piers, Pier 61   212/336-6299
Sky Rink, Pier 61   212/336-6199
Ave of the Americas at 32nd St   212/563-2448
Daily: 10-8 (varies somewhat by location)

All kinds of skates, skateboards, ice-hockey equipment, and snowboards are rented and sold at Blades Board & Skate. Classy apparel and accessories are also available. A repair shop is on the premises, and party rentals are a specialty.

PECK AND GOODIE
917 Eighth Ave (bet 54th and 55th St)   212/246-6123
Mon-Sat: 10-8; Sun: 10-6

Peck and Goodie offer equipment and apparel to skaters who need the best with minimum fuss. The store offers a complete stock of roller and ice skates, in-line skates, skateboards, and accessories. With skates costing upwards of a hundred dollars a pair, it's wise to patronize an expert. Boot-fitter Mike, who works at Peck and Goodie, is a self-proclaimed skate doctor!

Skiing

SCANDINAVIAN SKI AND SPORT SHOP
40 W 57th St (bet Fifth Ave and Ave of the Americas)   212/757-8524
Mon-Sat: 10-6 (Thurs until 6:30); Sun: 11-5

Despite its name, this shop is really an all-around sporting-goods store. They stock a full range of goods, from skis and skiwear to bikes and skates. They also offer repairs and advice, as well as outfitting and ski and bike trips.

Soccer

SOCCER SPORT SUPPLY COMPANY
1745 First Ave (bet 90th and 91st St)
212/427-6050, 800/223-1010
Mon-Fri: 10-6; Sat: 10-3

Max and Hermann Doss, the proprietors of this half-century-old soccer and rugby supply company, claim that half their business involves importing and exporting equipment around the world. Visitors to the store have the advantage of seeing the selection in person, as well as receiving guidance from a staff that knows the field (excuse the pun) completely.

Tennis

MASON'S TENNIS MART
56 E 53rd St (bet Park and Madison Ave)   212/757-5374
Mon-Fri: 10-7; Sat: 10-6

Mason's is the only tennis specialty store left in Manhattan. Mark Mason offers a superb collection of clothing with all the best brand names: Fila, Elesse, Tail, LBH, Lotto, Wimbledon, Adidas, Prince, and more. U.S. Open products are carried from May to December. Besides clothing, you will find ball machines, bags, and every other kind of tennis paraphernalia. They will match any authorized dealer on racquet prices and will special-order any tennis product a customer may want. Mason's carries the latest hypercarbon Wilson racquet, as well as titanium racquets from Head, Prince, Yonex, and Volkl. Same-day stringing is offered, and twice-yearly half-price clothing (except children's) sales take place in mid-August and mid-January.

Hoops enthusiasts can find basketball gear and other overpriced items at the new **NBA** store (666 Fifth Ave, 212/666-NBAI). In my opinion, this store is more for browsing than buying.

Stationery

JAM PAPER AND ENVELOPE/HUDSON ENVELOPE
111 Third Ave (bet 13th and 14th St)   212/473-6666
611 Ave of the Americas (at 18th St)   212/255-4593, 800/8010-JAM
Open 7 days a week

This outfit has grown to become the largest paper and envelope store in the city and perhaps the world! Even so, you can purchase as few as a 100 sheets of paper and 25 envelopes. Their inventory includes over 150 different kinds of paper, with matching card stock and envelopes. They also have a vast selection of presentation folders. Close-outs and discounted items provide excellent bargains. Ask for their free catalog!

JAMIE OSTROW
876 Madison Ave (bet 71st and 72nd St)   212/734-8890
Mon-Sat: 10-6

For contemporary personalized stationery and invitations, you can't do better than Jamie Ostrow. They design and manufacture items to the specifications of individual customers, and they also carry Crane stationery and wedding invitations. A good selection of boxed Christmas and holiday cards is shown, and personalized Christmas cards are a specialty.

KATE'S PAPERIE
561 Broadway (bet Prince and Spring St)   212/941-9816
Mon-Thurs: 10:30-7; Fri, Sat: 10:30-8; Sun: 11-7

8 W 13th St (at Fifth Ave)   212/633-0570
Mon-Fri: 10-7; Sat: 10-6; Sun: 11-5

1282 Third Ave (bet 73rd and 74th St)   212/396-3670
Mon-Fri: 10-7; Sat: 10-6; Sun: 11-6

Here you will find one of the largest selections of decorative and exotic papers in the country. Kate's has thousands of kinds of papers, including papyrus, hand-marbled French paper, Japanese lace papers, handmade paste papers, and just about anything else you can think of. But that isn't all that's available at this unique store. There are leather-bound photo albums and journals, classic and exotic stationery, boxes, wax seals, rubber stamps, rice-paper lamps, pens, and desk accessories. They will do custom printing and engraving, personal and business embossing, custom and corporate gift selection, gift wrapping, and photo restoration.

MRS. JOHN L. STRONG
699 Madison Ave (bet 62nd and 63rd St), 5th floor
212/838-3848
Mon-Fri: 10-5 and by appointment

Several barriers must be crossed to reach this high-end stationery establishment in a fifth-floor room. First, a claustrophobic elevator. Then a locked door. When you are buzzed in, the atmosphere is strictly high-altitude, as are the noses of some of the salesladies. Strong sells very high-quality papers, invitations, and announcements—with very high prices to match. If you are looking for the best, this is the place to splurge.

PAPIVORE/MARIE-PAPIER
117 Perry St (bet Hudson and Greenwich St)   212/627-6055
Tues-Sat: 11-7; Sun: 12-6

This is the New York outlet for fine designer stationery from the house of Marie-Paule Orluc in Paris. Unusual note pads, writing papers, notebooks, photo albums, address books, portfolios, cards, and envelopes are available here in an enormous range of colors and textures. Custom printing is a specialty. Prices range from under a dollar to over $100.

PURGATORY PIE PRESS
19 Hudson St (bet Duane and Reade St), Room 403   212/274-8228
Mon-Fri: 10-2:30, by appointment only

I don't know who chose the rather strange name, but the people at Purgatory Pie know what they are doing. They have created quite a following, particularly with the printing of invitations. In addition, they do book production, custom hand bookbinding, yearly date books, coasters, artists' books, and handmade paper with uniquely designed watermarks.

REBECCA MOSS
510 Madison Ave (at 53rd St)   212/832-7671
Mon-Fri: 10-6; Sat: 10-5:30

If you are in the market for pens, this is the place! Moss carries the largest selection and the latest items from Montblanc, Parker, Waterman, Aurora, Pelikan, Omas, Lamy, Sheaffer, and all the other big names. Moreover, the personnel are informed and friendly. It is a family-owned business, and customers are treated as part of the clan. The late Rebecca Moss would be pleased at what her grandson is doing!

Tiles

IDEAL TILE
405 E 51st St   212/759-2339
Mon-Fri: 9-5; Sat: 10-3

Ideal Tile imports ceramics, porcelain, marble, granite, and terra cotta from Italy, Spain, Portugal, and Brazil. They have absolutely magnificent hand-painted Italian ceramic pottery as well. This outfit guarantees installation of tiles by skilled craftsmen. They also offer marble and granite fabrication for fireplaces, countertops, window sills, and tables.

TILES—A REFINED SELECTION
42 W 15th St (bet Fifth Ave and Ave of the Americas)   212/255-4450
Mon-Fri: 9:30-6; Thurs: 9:30-8; Sat: 1-5 (closed Sat June-Aug)

If you are in the market for quality tiles, try Tiles' "refined selection." There are American art tiles, slate, granite, molded tiles, marble and limestone mosaics, glass tiles, and a large assortment of handmade tiles. Design services are available, and the selection is tops.

Some places where you can buy fashionable tiles:
Ceramica Arnon (134 W 29th St, 212/807-0876)
EX: Inc. (155 E 56th St, 212/758-2593)
Fyji Tile Co. (55 Hester St, 212/219-1184)
Solar Antique Tiles (306 E 61st St, 212/795-2403)

Tobacco and Accessories

BARCLAY-REX
7 Maiden Lane (nr Broadway)   212/962-3355
Mon-Fri: 8-6

70 E 42nd St (bet Madison and Park Ave)   212/692-9680
Mon-Fri: 8-6:30; Sat: 9:30-5:30

570 Lexington Ave (at 51st St)   212/888-1015
Mon-Wed: 8-6:30; Thurs, Fri: 8-7:30; Sat: 9:30-5:30

3 World Financial Center (Winter Garden)   212/385-4632
Mon-Fri: 8-7; Sat: 11-5; Sun: 12-5

This is a tobacco connoisseur's shop, and a specialty shop at that. The specialty is pipes (cigars are anathema and cigarettes more so), and third-generation owner Vincent Nastri knows the field inside-out. His shop is prepared to create a pipe from scratch, fill it with any imaginable type of tobacco (including a good house brand), repair a pipe if it should break, and offer advice on proper pipe care and blending of pipe tobacco. Nastri has a good reputation for prompt quality repairs and reasonable prices. It might pay to buy a new "irregular" pipe, which can be had for a surprisingly low price. As with most specialties, esoteric models are available at astronomical prices. If you have $1,000 to send up in smoke, Nastri will come up with something extraordinary.

CONNOISSEUR PIPE SHOP
1285 Ave of the Americas, concourse level   212/247-6054
Mon-Fri: 10-6

Edward Burak has assembled a beautiful collection of hand-carved pipes that range in price from $27 to over $3,500. His store features natural unvarnished pipes, custom-made pipes, custom-blended tobacco, and expert repair of all kinds of pipes. Burak will also do appraisals for insurance purposes. If your pipe came from Connoisseur, you'll get admiring glances from those who know quality.

J.R. TOBACCO
11 E 45th St (at Madison Ave)   212/983-4160
Mon-Fri: 7:45-5:45; Sat: 9-3:45

1 Wall St (bet Beaver and Pearl St)   212/269-6000
Mon-Fri: 8-8; Sat: 9-4

For years Lew Rothman has claimed to offer the world's largest selection of cigars and pipe tobacco at the world's lowest prices. Over 3,000 brands of cigars are stocked. Prices are 20% to 70% off regular retail.

Choosing the Right Cigar

A wrapper ties an entire cigar together and gives it character. Cigar wrappers come in six basic colors:

Double Claro: green
Claro: tan, neutral in flavor, often from Connecticut
Colorado Claro or Natural: light brown to brown leaf
Colorado: reddish-brown color and rich flavor
Maduro: dark brown, oily, with a rich and strong flavor
Oscuro: dark brown or black, grown in Connecticut, Mexico, Nicaragua, and Brazil

---

Toys, Trains

General

CHILDREN'S GENERAL STORE
2473 Broadway (at 92nd St)   212/580-2723
Mon-Sat: 10-6; Sun: 12-5

Grand Central Station (nr Lexington Ave entrance)   212-628-0004)
Mon-Fri: 8-8; Sat-Sun: 1-6

Located in the lobby of Playspace, an indoor playground for children on the Upper West Side, and now along the Lexington Avenue access tunnel to Grand Central Station as well, this is a terrific all-purpose toy store. The emphasis here is less on space-age wizardry and battery-operated gizmos and more on basic, well-made toys designed to encourage creative and imaginative play. While the Grand Central Station location is significantly larger and easier to shop in, the cozy space on Broadway is a bit more child-friendly. At both places, the diverse stock is chosen by people who clearly know and love children.

CLASSIC TOYS
218 Sullivan St (bet Bleecker and 3rd St)   212/674-4434
Daily: noon-6:30

Classic carries old and new toys that have proven popular with generations of youngsters. It is also a haven for collectors and those (like your author) who just like to browse toy shops. Here you will find the largest selection of die-cast vehicles in New York, with pieces of old Matchbox, Dinky, and Corgi that go back to the 1930s. Over a hundred years of toy soldiers are on display, as well as stuffed animals, Christmas tree ornaments from Europe, and a great selection of antiques that will charm parents and children. They thoughtfully maintain a list of stores for shoppers who can't find what they want here!

DINOSAUR HILL
306 E 9th St   212/473-5850
Daily: 11-7

At Dinosaur Hill you can travel the world through toys! There are marbles from England, tin windups from China, papier-maché masks from Mexico, wooden pull toys from Greece, and solid wooden blocks made right here in the U.S.A. In addition, there is handmade clothing in natural-fiber fabrics for infants through four years and a wonderful assortment of hats, music boxes, monkeys, moons, and mermaids!

ENCHANTED FOREST
85 Mercer St (bet Spring and Broome St)   212/925-6677
Mon-Sat: 11-7; Sun: 12-6

The Enchanted Forest physically and philosophically matches its name. David Wallace and Peggy Sloane, a husband-and-wife team of owners, hired theatrical set designer Matthew Jacobs to create an enchanted-forest backdrop for a col-lection of toys, whimsies, and artwork. The shop purports to be a "gallery of beasts, books, and handmade toys celebrating the spirit of the animals, the old stories, and the child within." The emphasis is on the gallery aspect and it really isn't a great place for energetic small children. You can enter a crystal cave that transforms into an old wooden wardrobe through which you then pass into a small Victorian room. Other featured items include a fine selection of fairy tales, mythologies, children's stories, and various eclectic gems. This place truly is enchanted!

F.A.O. SCHWARZ
767 Fifth Ave (at 59th St)   212/644-9400
Mon-Sat: 10-6; Sun: 11-6

Ask any kid where he or she wants to go in New York, and the answer will likely be F.A.O. Schwarz! It is on the cutting edge of the toy business, because most manufacturers want to get their items stocked here first. But it is more than a retail establishment. Youngsters grow wide-eyed at the enormous selec-tion and exciting demonstrations. The store now has three levels arranged into small shops that specialize in stuffed animals, bears, games, electronics, dolls, soldiers, Star Wars, Barbie, and all that you'd expect in a first-rate toy emporium. There is even a counter by the door where those in a hurry can pick up a last-minute gift to take home. Just don't expect bargains. We're talking top-of-the-line!

GEPPETTO'S TOY BOX
161 Seventh Ave S (bet Waverly Pl and Perry St)   212/620-7511
Mon-Sat: 11-8; Sun: 1-7

One of the great pleasures of New York is walking into a store because of its window display and having it turn out to be a magical place, like this West Village toy store. Although the owners clearly have become more consumer-savvy, stocking trendy favorites, the heart of this store is its exceptionally high-quality teddy bears, jack-in-the-boxes. snow globes, marionettes, and other whimsical toys and games. Moreover, it's obviously run with great passion and care. You'll also find a variety of interesting items made by local artists and a small but carefully chosen selection of books. If you're a toy collector, have a child in your life, or simply like a store with class and grace, make a visit to Geppetto's a top priority.

KIDDING AROUND
60 W 15th St   212/645-6337
Mon-Fri: 10-7; Sat: 11-7; Sun: 11-6

68 Bleecker St   212/598-0228
Mon-Sat: 11-7; Sun: 11-6

Amid a rather routine selection of Ambi toys, Ravensberger puzzles, and the like, you'll find some of the most interesting riding and rocking toys I've ever seen at Kidding Around's 15th Street location. While that store is bigger and brighter, I prefer the coziness of the Bleecker Street store. Both stores carry an unusual and fun selection of natural-fiber clothing for infants and small children, as well as lots of things for Curious George fans.

WEST SIDE KIDS
498 Amsterdam Ave (at 84th St)   212/496-7282
Mon-Sat: 10-7; Sun: 12-6

The motto of this West Side institution is "well-chosen toys," to which I would add arts, crafts, and books, as well. This store has a great stock, a roomy and kid-friendly space, and lots of fun activities and contests scheduled for children of various ages. It can get a bit chaotic and noisy—which is just another way of saying that West Side Kids is clearly a well-loved local favorite. They even have a resident cat.

Gifts and Accessories

LITTLE EXTRAS
676 Amsterdam Ave (at 93rd St)   212/721-6161
Mon-Fri: 10:30-6:30 (Thurs until 7); Sat: 10:30-6; Sun: 11-5
(closed Sun in July and Aug)

Whether you're looking for a personalized bathrobe, the perfect picture frame, a baby present, or hand-painted furniture, this cheerful store is teeming with gifts and accessories for infants and children. Owner Terry Siegel's great taste shows in everything. Make sure to look up at the mobiles and other things hanging from the ceiling! An added bonus: Little Extras offers a wide selection of discounted birth announcements and will deliver them in Manhattan when ready.

WYNKEN, BLYNKEN & NOD'S
306 E 55th St   212/308-9299
Mon, Wed, Fri: 11-6; Tues, Thurs: 10-7; Sat: 11-6:30

The owner of this little gem left the practice of law to open up shop here on the quiet east side of midtown. Wynken, Blynken & Nod's is a celebration of Deborah Kleman's eclectic, whimsical good taste. From the unique children's furniture (much of it antique) to the clever puppets, games, and other toys, this relatively small shop is filled with something for every budget. Kleman buys stock from local artists, so much of what you'll find here—including some beautiful clothing for infants and small children—is unique.

Specialty and Novelty

ALPHABETS
115 Ave A   212/475-7250
Mon-Thurs: 12-10; Fri: 12-12; Sat: 11 a.m.-12 a.m.; Sun: 12-7

This crowded little place is really not so much a toy store for kids as a novelty shop and a stroll down memory lane for grown-ups. If you're looking for a Desi Arnaz wristwatch, a Gumby and Pokey piggy bank, some kitschy ceramics, or a T-shirt with the Velveeta logo on it, this is the place to come. It's also a great source for moderately risqué greeting cards, pasta in the shape of anatomical parts, and other R-rated novelty items. That's not to say Alphabets doesn't have some great toys for children—e.g., the kit for making balloon animals—but most younger kids wouldn't understand much of what's in here and most parents wouldn't want them exposed to it.

BEAR HUGS & BABY DOLLS
311 E 81st St (bet First and Second Ave)   212/717-1514
Tues-Sat: 11-6; Sun: 12-5 (closed Sun in summer)

"Beary" novel is the best description for this unique store, which features teddy bears and collectible dolls. They have over 300 teddies, including an array of handmade artist originals. You'll find many famous names: Steiff, the Muffy Vander Bear collection, and Madame Alexander dolls. They even have a seamstress who can custom-make doll and bear outfits.

BIG CITY KITE COMPANY
1210 Lexington Ave (at 82nd St)   212/472-2623
Mon-Fri: 11-6:30 (Thurs until 7:30); Sat: 10-6;
Sun (seasonally): 12-5

You would expect New York to have a store dedicated to kites, and it is a great one. Big City's David Klein sells kites for people's houses: i.e., mobiles and wall hangings. He sells custom-made specialty kites and brilliantly colored fighter kites made of tissue paper. He also offers a kite-repair service. Prices begin at about $2 and go as high as $300. The staff's genuine devotion is most evident in the community programs it sponsors. There are kite festivals, exhibitions, and even "kite-ins." They also carry a full line of darts, dartboards, and accessories for recreational and competitive use.

BURLINGTON ANTIQUE TOYS
1082 Madison Ave (at 82nd St)   212/861-9708
Mon-Sat: 11-6; Sun: 12-5

Anyone who has been to Forbes Gallery knows that toy soldiers are not just for children. At Burlington Antique Toys, toy soldiers are serious antiques, as is virtually everything else in the store. That roll call includes toy cars, airplanes, boats, and other tin toys. There is a "used car lot" specializing in out-of-production, die-cast car models. Best of all, Burlington proves that not only fabulously rich men can afford to play with toy soldiers or float their own armadas. This is a place for everyone, and the folks here couldn't be nicer. Crawford Doyle Booksellers is upstairs.

CHIMERA
77 Mercer St (bet Spring and Broome St)   212/334-4730
Daily: 11-6 (winter), 11-7 (summer)

Soho is full of stores with lots of stuff that nobody really needs. This one is no exception. That said, however, its buyers are a little more clever than most and have found a niche in the novelty market with animals: purses, backpacks, coffee mugs, hair clips, slippers, and even toothbrushes in the shapes of gorillas, turtles, cows, and other animals. Perhaps because they could not find enough animal-related novelties to fill the store, Chimera also has a great selection of hats, purses, and sweaters in the back.

DISNEY STORE
210 W 42nd St   212/221-0430
Mon-Tues: 10-9; Wed-Sat: 10-midnight

711 Fifth Ave   212/702-0702
Mon-Sat: 10-8; Sun: 11-6

39 W 34th St   212/279-9890
Mon-Sat: 10-8; Sun: 11-6

141 Columbus Ave   212/362-2386
Mon-Sat: 10-9; Sun:11-6

If the "malling" of New York hasn't gotten you down, these stores—particularly the one on 42nd Street—can be fun places to shop. Unlike the staff at a lot of the huge stores that have been popping up all over New York in recent years, the folks here really know their stock and are personable to boot. If you don't have a Disney Store back home and are looking for kids' luggage with Mickey Mouse on it, backpacks in the shape of Winnie the Pooh, or any other Disney-related item you can imagine, visit one of these locations.

DOLLHOUSE ANTICS
1343 Madison Ave (at 94th St)   212/876-2288
Mon-Fri: 11-5:30; Sat: 11-5

Dollhouse Antics, a shop dedicated to miniatures, is straight out of childhood dreams. Dollhouse-making is serious business here. The most popular orders are for replicas of ancestral homes, and you can bet your made-to-order miniature needlepoint rug that these dollhouses aren't for eager little children. Dollhouses come in kit form, but if money is no object—or when the fun of assembling it yourself wanes—the store will put it together for you. Like real houses, these models need to be furnished, too. I just hope you can afford the scaled-down Oriental rugs, custom upholstery, special wallpaper, electrical supplies, and made-to-order furniture.

E.A.T. GIFTS
1062 Madison Ave (bet 80th and 81st St)   212/861-2544
Mon-Sat: 10-6; Sun: 12-5

It's impossible to sum up what this store offers in a few sentences. E.A.T. Gifts is a wonderland of imaginative party favors and stocking stuffers that must be seen to be believed. From the tiny tea sets, party supplies, and invitations to the piñatas on the ceiling and seasonal holiday items, you'll want to inspect every square foot of this store. Indeed, it's the kind of place where you inevitably spot just one more thing as the salesperson is totaling up your purchases! The focus is mostly on kids and items you'll remember from childhood, but there is something for just about everyone at this wonderful store. As the Madison Avenue address suggests, there's nothing inexpensive about what you'll find here. But if you want to put together a special party bag or seasonal stocking, or send a gift basket, this is *the* place to go.

Can't Find Something?

Here is a very useful service! **Anything on Earth** (800/928-7179) is one of the oldest and most experienced full-service custom acquisition firms in the country. They will help locate and acquire any item, product, or service in a professional and cost-effective manner. A free consultation is followed by a free preliminary investigation to estimate the cost and time required to locate what you want. The final fee is based on time spent, a percentage of purchase price, or a combination of both, plus applicable expenses.

MANHATTAN DOLL HOUSE
236-A Third Ave (bet 19th and 20th St)   212/253-9549
Mon-Fri: 11-6:30 (Thurs until 7:30); Sat: 11-5; Sun: 12:30-5

Edwin Jacobowitz operates the Manhattan Doll House, which boasts the city's largest collection of dolls (including Madame Alexander), dollhouses, and related furniture and paraphernalia. The store is also a hospital where most injured dolls can be made healthy again.

RED CABOOSE
23 W 45th St, basement level   212/575-0155
Mon-Fri: 11-7; Sat: 11-5:30

Owner-operator Allan J. Spitz will tell you that 99% of his customers are not wide-eyed children but sharp-eyed adults who are dead serious about model railroads. The Red Caboose claims to have 100,000 items on hand. That includes a line of 300 hand-finished, imported brass locomotives alone. It doesn't begin to cover the tracks or track gauges available. Spitz claims that the five basic sizes—1:22, 1:48, 1:87, 1:161, and 1:220, in a ratio of scale to life size—will allow a model railroader to build layouts sized to fit into a desk drawer or a basement. They also carry an extensive line of plastic kits.

STUYVESANT TRAINS & HOBBIES
345 W 14th St (bet Eighth and Ninth Ave), 2nd floor
212/254-5200
Mon-Fri: 12-6; Sat: 11-4

Bigger isn't always better, and Stuyvesant proves it. They claim to be the smallest store with the largest inventory around! This place is for the young and young at heart. The stock of train and hobby supplies is superb. You'll find Lionel products, Mike's Train House, Dept. 56 items, Atlas (O) trains, and HO, N, and Z gauge trains. What you don't see, they will special order for you.

TOY BALLOON
204 E 38th St   212/682-3803
Mon-Fri: 9-5

The Toy Balloon sells balloons individually or in multitudes of up to 50,000.

There are graduations in diameter, thickness, style, and type (including Mylar balloons). Sizes range from peewees to blimps, while shapes include dolls, hearts, dachshunds (they're often used to advertise hot dogs), and extra-long shapes. Helium, ribbon, balloon clips, and balloon imprinting are also available. Most of this whimsical business is done for advertising campaigns.

UNIQUE SCIENCE
410 Columbus Ave (bet 79th and 80th St)   212/712-1899
Mon-Sat: 11-7:30; Sun: 12-7:30

"Discover what you've been looking for" is the motto of this relatively new shop for junior scientists (and amateur grown-up ones, too) directly behind the American Museum of Natural History. The atmosphere is both welcoming and helpful, and the stock runs from inexpensive toys for preschoolers to chemistry sets, sophisticated magnifying glasses, and real microscopes. Whether it's rocks, bones, planets, or worms you want to study, this welcome addition to the neighborhood will likely have just the thing to help.

WARNER BROTHERS STUDIO STORE
1 E 57th St   212/754-0300
Mon-Sat: 10-7; Sun: 12-7

1 Times Square Plaza (42nd St, bet Seventh Ave and Broadway)
212/840-4040
Mon-Thurs: 11-10; Fri-Sun: 10-midnight

I experience sensory overload whenever I walk through this place, but tourists, especially from foreign countries, flock to it. So do children. If you're a Warner Brothers fan, you'll be hard-pressed not to find something here: hats with Daffy Duck, infant clothing with Porky the Pig, mugs with Bugs Bunny . . . you get the idea. If the character originated at Warner Brothers, expect to find at least a dozen items bearing its likeness. For more serious collectors, original animation production cels are available. Recently the store more than doubled its size to 75,000 square feet, adding the Moving Pictures Cafe (on the fifth floor) and a space for birthday and other private parties (on the ninth floor). The Times Square location is smaller but equally busy.

Don't miss the former "Ladies Mile" shopping area, with great stores like these:

Barnes & Noble (675 Ave of the Americas)
Bed Bath & Beyond (620 Ave of the Americas)
Filene's Basement (620 Ave of the Americas)
Old Navy (610 Ave of the Americas)
T.J. Maxx (620 Ave of the Americas)

WNET'S STORE OF KNOWLEDGE
1091 Third Ave   212/223-0018
Mon-Sat: 10-7; Sun: 11-6

The Mall at the World Trade Center   212/321-2855
Mon-Fri: 7:30-7:30; Sat: 10-6; Sun: 12-5

These big, roomy, kid-friendly stores are just the sort of places you would expect from WNET, New York City's award-winning public television station. Whether you're looking for videotapes of a favorite PBS or BBC series, a science experiment, or a book on yoga, these are great places to look. But their real strength is in the children's sections, where you'll find a terrific selection of educational videos, toys, and games based on the Teletubbies, Arthur, and other PBS characters, as well as arts and crafts for the young ones.

Travel Items

CIVILIZED TRAVELLER
864 Lexington Ave   212/288-9190

No Big Deal in maps + Books

2003 Broadway (bet 68th and 69th St)   212/875-0306
Mon-Sat: 10-9; Sun: 12-7

Satellite Ticket Office
1 E 59th St   212/702-9502
Mon-Fri: 8:30-6; Sat: 9-5

For the person on the go, these stores are the most helpful places around! Books, maps, and videos are specialties of the house, but you will also find unique and handy travel items like personal grooming pieces, pocket tailors, shoe kits, water purifiers, packable rainwear, slippers, travel-size games, travel alarm clocks, luggage on wheels, world-time calculators and clocks, translators, doorknob burglar alarms, and automobile tool kits.

Variety, Novelty

CBS STORE
1691 Broadway (at 53rd St)   212/975-8600
Mon-Sat: 10-8; Sun: 12-5

Just down the street from the Ed Sullivan Theater (where David Letterman's *Late Show* is filmed), this store stocks T-shirts, mugs, and all sorts of other merchandise with the CBS logo or images from the network's television shows.

DISNEY STORE
141 Columbus Ave (at 66th St)   212/362-2386
Mon-Sat: 10-8; Sun: 12-6

Just as the Disney Store next to the Amsterdam Theater is home to more *Lion King* merchandise than anywhere else, this Disney Store at the ABC Studios stocks a wide array of merchandise related to ABC's network TV shows, especially its soap operas (all of which are taped here). If it's an *All My Children* sweatshirt you want, look no further!

MARCOART
186 Orchard St (at Houston St)   212/253-1070
Mon-Sat: 8-7; Sun: 10-6

Owner Marco specializes in art that's imprinted on "anything that will sit still!" This includes art on canvas, clothing, watches, and murals. You'll find funky designs on T-shirts, knit hats, baseball caps, jackets, bags, mouse pads, and ties!

NBC STORE
30 Rockefeller Plaza (49th St, bet Fifth Ave and Ave of the Americas)
212/664-5354
Tues-Fri: 9-7; Sat-Mon: 9-5

Positioned perfectly for those waiting to start or just having finished the NBC tour, this store is in the network's lobby. It stocks T-shirts, mugs, keychains, and other merchandise with the NBC logo or images from its television shows.

NEW YORK 911
263½ Lafayette St (bet Prince and Spring St)   212/219-3907
Mon-Sat: 10-6

For police buffs, this place is heaven! Cops and just plain folks can find police T-shirts, caps, pins, shirts, kids' clothes, gifts, and toys. New York 911 is truly a one-stop cop shop!

ODD JOB TRADING
390 Fifth Ave (bet 35th and 36th St)   212/239-3336
66 W 48th St (bet Fifth Ave and Ave of the Americas)   212/575-0477
149 W 32nd St (bet Ave of the Americas and Seventh Ave)
212/564-7370
10 Cortlandt St (west of Broadway)   212/571-0959
465 Lexington Ave (bet 45th and 46th St)   212/949-7401
601 Eighth Ave (at 39th St)   212/714-0106
36 E 14th St (at University Pl)   212/741-9944
Mon-Fri: 8-7; Sat, Sun: 10-6

Odd Job consistently comes up with good buys on quality merchandise. What differentiates this long-lived chain from others is that its stock is more current. Anything from book racks to perfume may turn up, but it's always interesting. It's also the perfect place to buy gifts for the folks back home; they'll never know how little the cost unless you tell. Odd Job has a reputation as the best of the close-out stores.

STAR MAGIC
745 Broadway (bet 8th St and Astor Pl)   212/228-7770
1256 Lexington Ave (bet 84th and 85th St)   212/988-0300
Mon-Sat: 10-10; Sun: 11-9

Stepping through Star Magic's door is like entering a time warp into the future. From its midnight-black ceiling with suspended galactic spheres to its spacecraft-like walls, Star Magic is designed to make a visitor forget contemporary New York and enter a timeless universe. The motto "Yesterday's magic is today's science" describes the eclectic selection of what owner Shlomo Ayal calls "space-age gifts." There are toys and items for anyone with a scientific bent. Books have been chosen for their ability to make a reader "ponder the cosmos." Star Magic offers minerals and prisms, scientific instruments to explore the universe, high-tech toys, and new-age music that is positively futuristic.

TIMTOUM
179 Orchard St (bet Houston and Stanton St)   212/780-0456
Daily: 1-8

Eclectic is the word for this place! You'll find some good values here in handbags, new and vintage clothing, hats, and new and vintage records and tapes. Why they chose this mix of items is a mystery, but it does make for a unique shopping experience. Ask for Erika!

Videotapes
BLOWOUT VIDEO
1521 Broadway (at 45th St)   212/764-7070
Daily: 10 a.m.-midnight

The big news here is the large selection and low prices. You'll find a stock of new and used movies that will make your pocketbook happy.

EVERGREEN VIDEO
37 Carmine St (at Bleecker St)   212/691-7362
Mon-Thurs: 10-10; Fri: 10 a.m.-11 p.m.; Sat: noon-11; Sun: noon-10

Here you will find more than 10,000 titles, including New York's largest rental collection of silent films; films of the 1930s, 1940s, and 1950s; and foreign-language titles and documentaries. Evergreen is particularly popular with folks in the arts and media.

VIDEO ROOM
1487 Third Ave (at 84th St)   212/879-5333
300 Rector Pl (South End Ave at W Thames St)   212/962-6400
Mon-Thurs: 10-10; Fri-Sat: 10 a.m.-11 p.m.; Sun: 12-10

At Video Room, you'll find a large selection of foreign films and classics, along with a highly competent staff of film students motivated to help inquiring customers. There is also an in-depth selection of new releases, home pickup and delivery service, and a special order department for hard-to-find films.

Visual Aids

LIGHTHOUSE INTERNATIONAL
111 E 59th St (bet Park and Lexington St)   212/821-9384
Mon-Fri: 10-6; Sat: 10-5

This is a wonderful place for the visually impaired and the blind. They also carry items for seniors who have mobility problems. Over 200 articles are displayed, including reading and writing supplies, large print books, canes, talking appliances, and electronic devices to enhance vision.

Watches

Don't be taken by the watch peddlers along Fifth Avenue, near Bloomingdale's, and on side streets in midtown. Most of what they purport to sell is fake, and you have no recourse if there are problems.

YAEGER WATCH CORPORATION
578 Fifth Ave (at 47th St)   212/819-0088
Mon-Sat: 10-5

Over 2,000 discounted watches are carried here. Choose from name brands retailing from $100 to $150,000 in a store that has been in the same family since 1970. Watch repair and warranties are offered.

New York's best watch stores include **Cellini Fine Jewelry** (509 Madison Ave, 212/888-0505), **Kenjo** (40 W 57th St, 212/333-7220), **Tourneau** (500 Madison Ave, 635 Madison Ave, and 200 W 34th St; 212/758-3265). and **Wempe** (700 Fifth Ave, 212/397-9000).

VII. Where to "Extras"

When I research and write a new edition of this book every two years, I'm always struck by how much information I have that doesn't fit neatly into any of the other chapters. That's why I came up with this chapter of "Extras." Where to go dancing, what to do with kids, where to spend a romantic evening, and where to host a special event. Those are just some of the questions that this chapter seeks to answer.

Annual Events

While stores, museums, restaurants, and the like are open all year, some special events are held only during certain seasons or once a year. (The "Resources" section in this chapter tells where to look for what's happening at any given time and the "Telephone Numbers and Web Sites" section provides numbers of most venues listed below.) You'll find a brief list of special events in the front section of the Manhattan Yellow Pages. In addition to shows, fairs, and festivals, I've included several particularly big or worthwhile sales in the following list.

JANUARY – All of the city's Christmas decorations come down in early January, but there's still time to catch the last few performances of the annual Christmas Spectacular at Radio City Music Hall. Check out the ice skating at Rockefeller Center and in Central Park's two rinks, or go see the Ice Capades at Madison Square Garden toward the end of the month. On New Year's Day, the Polar Bear Club takes a dip in the Atlantic Ocean out on Coney Island. The National Boat Show is held at the Jacob K. Javits Convention Center in the middle of the month, and the prestigious Winter Antiques Show at the Seventh Regiment Armory (Park Avenue at 66th Street) begins at the end of the month. Golden Gloves boxing begins at Madison Square Garden and runs through March. Depending on the lunar calendar, the Chinese New Year falls between the middle of January and the middle of February. Chinatown is definitely the place to be for the celebration. January is also winter sale time. One of the best is at Saks Fifth Avenue.

FEBRUARY – February is Black History Month, and New York has all sorts of official and unofficial celebrations. In early February, the Westminster Kennel Club's Dog Show moves into Madison Square Garden for two days, while the National Antiques Show moves in later in the month. Look for the New York

International Motorcycle Show at the Jacob K. Javits Convention Center. On Valentine's Day, the chapel on the Empire State Building's 80th floor is the site of a giant wedding ceremony for all comers. In the middle of the month, some of the city's more energetic sorts participate in the Empire State Building Run-Up (that's right—*up* the stairs, from the lobby to the 86th floor!), an invitational event sponsored by the New York Road Runners Club. Snow or no snow, there's a wonderful Winter Festival on Central Park's Great Lawn in the middle of the month. President's Day, the third Monday in February, is a huge sale day at department stores, electronics stores, clothing stores, and just about everywhere else. The Art Dealers Association of America holds an exhibition for member galleries at the Seventh Regiment Armory (Park Avenue at 66th Street) late in the month.

MARCH—The most famous New York event this month is the March 17 St. Patrick's Day Parade, a 200-year-old march up Fifth Avenue from 44th to 86th streets. The Greek Independence Day Parade is held a week later, also on Fifth Avenue. The International Cat Show is held at Madison Square Garden early in the month, as is the Spring Armory Antiques Show at the Seventh Regiment Armory (Park Avenue at 66th Street). Ringling Brothers and Barnum & Bailey Circus hits town in March, preceded by a hush-hush march of the biggest animals into Manhattan from Long Island City via the Queens-Midtown Tunnel in the middle of the night. Cirque du Soleil, an unusual and innovative circus with no animals and lots of contortionists, begins its run in Battery Park City late this month. The Golden Gloves boxing finals are held at Madison Square Garden in March, as are the Big East and the National Invitational Tournament (NIT) college basketball tournaments. The New York Flower Show is held at Pier 92 (51st Street at the Hudson River) in mid-month. The Film Society of Lincoln Center and the Museum of Modern Art co-sponsor the New Directors/New Films series this month as well. Depending on when Easter falls, you can also visit the Easter-egg exhibit at the Ukrainian Museum or the Easter lily displays in the Channel Gardens at Rockefeller Center and the Winter Garden at the World Financial Center. The Macy's Spring Flower Show is held at Macy's Herald Square for several weeks beginning around Palm Sunday, and the Greater New York Orchid Show opens this month at the World Financial Center's Winter Garden. An Easter-egg roll and other events for children are held in the East Meadow in Central Park on the Saturday before Easter, and an informal Easter parade is held on Easter Day on Fifth Avenue around St. Patrick's Cathedral, beginning at 11 a.m. You can catch the annual Easter Show at Radio City Music Hall throughout the Easter season.

APRIL—The month opens with the International Auto Show at the Jacob K. Javits Convention Center. April also marks the beginning of baseball season, so check the home schedules for the Mets and Yankees. The year's first outdoor festival is held on the third Sunday in April at Stuyvesant Square Park, on both sides of Second Avenue from 15th to 17th streets. You can browse rare autographs, manuscripts, and first editions at the New York Antiquarian Book Fair at the Seventh Regiment Armory (Park Avenue at 66th Street). Also visit the beautiful spring flower displays at Rockefeller Center, the World Trade Center, Macy's Herald Square, and the Winter Garden at the World Financial Center.

MAY—The Ninth Avenue International Food Festival is held the third weekend in May along Ninth Avenue from 37th to 57th streets. The Ukrainian Festival, on 7th Street between Second Avenue and Bowery, is usually held the same weekend. The American Ballet Theater begins its nine-week season this month at the Metropolitan Opera House in Lincoln Center. The Martin Luther King, Jr. Parade is held along Fifth Avenue this month, and the Spanish and Portuguese Synagogue on the Upper West Side holds a Sephardic Fair on a Sunday in the middle of the month. The Coast Guard and Navy sail into town the week before Memorial Day for Fleet Week. Look for festivities at the Intrepid Air-Sea-Space Museum. Over Memorial Day weekend and into early June, look for the Washington Square Outdoor Art Exhibit at the foot of Fifth Avenue in Greenwich Village. And keep an eye out for the Lower East Side Jewish Festival, held on a Sunday late in May.

JUNE – A number of cultural events that last all summer and are free to the public begin in June: Shakespeare in the Park, at the Delacorte Theater in the southwest corner of Central Park's Great Lawn; performances by the Metropolitan Opera Company and New York Philharmonic in Central Park and other parks throughout the city; the Midsummer Night Swing concerts at Lincoln Center Plaza; Central Park SummerStage performances; and Monday night movies in Bryant Park are some of the highlights. Although some museums along Fifth Avenue's Museum Mile offer free admission one night a week all year, almost all of them offer free admission one evening in mid-June during the Museum Mile Festival. Half the city turns out as Fifth Avenue between 82nd and 102nd streets becomes a pedestrian mall. An Italian street fair to commemorate the Feast of St. Anthony of Padua is held in Little Italy during two weeks in June, and street performers show up en masse for the Lower Manhattan Cultural Council's Buskers Fair in the middle of the month. The annual Salute to Israel parade is held along Fifth Avenue above 59th Street in the middle of the month, and one of the nation's largest gay and lesbian marches is held on the last Sunday of the month to commemorate the 1969 raid on the Stonewall Inn in Greenwich Village. The Texaco New York Jazz Festival kicks off early in the month, while the JVC Jazz Festival opens a bit later with events at Bryant Park, Carnegie Hall, and other locations throughout the city. Both the Lesbian and Gay Film Festival at the Public Theater and the Human Rights Watch Film Festival at the Walter Reade Theater are held this month.

JULY – The Fourth of July goes off with a bang at the Macy's fireworks display, launched from barges on the East River. FDR Drive from 14th to 51st streets is closed to traffic, so you can get really terrific views. An all-day Fourth of July Festival is held on Water Street from Battery Park to John Street in lower Manhattan. Lincoln Center Plaza, on Columbus Avenue between 62nd and 65th streets, comes alive with the American Crafts Festival during the first two weekends of the month. You'll also find free concerts galore in July: Metropolitan Opera Company and New York Philharmonic performances in Central Park and other parks throughout the city; jazz in the Museum of Modern Art's Sculpture Garden; concerts at South Street Seaport; and chamber music in Washington Square Park, at the foot of Fifth Avenue in Greenwich Village. Also look for the enormously popular Mostly Mozart concerts at Avery Fisher Hall in Lincoln Center, and the Midsummer's Night Swing in Lincoln Center Plaza.

AUGUST – August has never been New York's best month. It's usually hot and humid, and piles of garbage on the city's streets make the whole island smell. The city is relatively quiet, particularly on weekends, because a lot of New Yorkers head for summer homes or go on vacation. That said, however, there's still lots to do. In early August, the Uptown Chamber of Commerce sponsors a week-long salute to Harlem's past, present, and future. You'll find outdoor performances as part of the Lincoln Center Out-of-Doors Festival throughout the month in Lincoln Center Plaza, off Columbus Avenue between 62nd and 65th streets. A big crafts fair is held there on weekends at the end of the month and the beginning of September. Look for the Festival Latino's concerts, films, and other events at the Public Theater and other locations. As any tennis fan knows, the U.S. Open begins in late August and runs through Labor Day weekend. It's lots of fun, though traffic is pretty dreadful!

SEPTEMBER—Labor Day weekend is the last breath of summer, and roads in and out of the city are a nightmare on Monday evening. If you're in the city that weekend, check out the art fair in and around Washington Square at the foot of Fifth Avenue in Greenwich Village. My favorite event is the New York Is Book Country fair on the fourth Sunday of September. I haven't missed one yet, and we've made a tradition of releasing new editions of this book there! Fifth Avenue is closed to traffic between 48th and 57th streets, and there's something for just about everybody. The Third Avenue Festival, on Third Avenue between 68th and 90th streets, is usually held the same day. Little Italy comes alive with the Feast of San Gennaro. For 11 days, beginning in mid-September, there's food, fun, and family reunions. Alice Tully Hall at Lincoln Center is home to the New York Film Festival, beginning the third week of the month. The New York Philharmonic begins its long season this month at Avery Fisher Hall in Lincoln Center. Look for lots of "Back to School" sales at the end of the month as well as the "Broadway Cares/Equity Fights AIDS" flea market and auction in Shubert Alley.

OCTOBER—The NBA's Knicks and the NHL's Rangers open their seasons this month at Madison Square Garden, and there are three big parades: the Columbus Day Parade, the Polish Day Parade, and the Hispanic Day Parade. Look for the Soho Arts Festival in early October, when more than 100 galleries host open houses. Keep an eye out for the Fall Antiques Show at Pier 92 (52nd Street and the Hudson River), arguably the most prestigious antiques show in the country. Get a jump on winter as ice skating begins in Rockefeller Plaza. Finally, assuming recent controversy about size and rowdiness hasn't led to its demise, there's a Halloween Parade in Greenwich Village, for which the mostly grownup participants line up at Avenue of the Americas just north of Houston Street in the early evening. Don't expect much else for Halloween, however, since concerns about safety and a lack of space mean that most kids in Manhattan wander through their apartment buildings rather than neighborhoods. The sporting event that draws more spectators than any other in the world (well over 2.5 million at last count) is the New York Marathon, held on a Sunday in late October or early November. The 26-mile course runs through all five boroughs, starting on the Staten Island end of the Verrazano Narrows Bridge and ending at Tavern on the Green, on West Drive in Central Park. Call the New York Road Runners Club for the date and viewing suggestions.

NOVEMBER—Christmas is still more than a month away, but Manhattan gets decked out in its seasonal finery in November. The first sure sign is the annual Radio City Music Hall Christmas Show, beginning in the middle of the month. The Christmas windows in major department stores go up the week before Thanksgiving. Saks Fifth Avenue (at 50th Street) is just one of the many ones worth seeing along Fifth Avenue. Santa Claus arrives at Macy's Herald Square the day after Thanksgiving and stays through Christmas Eve. Of all the Santas to visit Manhattan, Macy's is one of the best, year in and year out. Check out the crafts and antiques at the Triple Pier Show on Piers 88, 90, and 92 (along the Hudson River between 48th and 55th streets). Look for the annual Home Show at the Jacob K. Javits Convention Center early in the month; the Corel/WTA Women's Tennis Tournament at Madison Square Garden in the middle of the month; and the Margaret Meade Film Festival at the American Museum of Natural History. Of course, it wouldn't be November without the Macy's Thanksgiving Day Parade. The parade starts on Central Park West at about 79th Street and winds down to Columbus Circle; from there, it heads down Broadway to Macy's Herald Square. For a real treat, let the kids stay up late to watch the giant balloons being inflated on Central Park West the night before!

DECEMBER—December means Christmas in New York, and it's hard to turn around without seeing advertisements for performances of Handel's *Messiah* and the *Nutcracker* ballet. The best of the former is arguably the "Messiah Sing-In" at Avery Fisher Hall, while the best *Nutcracker* is usually the one staged at the New York State Theater. They're both in Lincoln Center. The famed Christmas tree at Rockefeller Center, just off Fifth Avenue between 49th and 50th streets, is lit on the late afternoon of the first Monday in December, and Fifth Avenue in midtown is closed off two Sunday afternoons this month for holiday shoppers. Other great trees can be found in the Plaza at Lincoln Center, in front of the New York Stock Exchange, at the Metropolitan Museum of Art, and at South Street Seaport. The Brick Presbyterian Church has caroling accompanied by an organ and brass quartet early in the month; Central Presbyterian Church offers a blessing of pets on Christmas Eve; and the Church of the Heavenly Rest on 90th Street has an enormous Christmas Pageant on Christmas Eve. Check out the crafts fair in Ferris Booth Hall at Columbia University on Broadway at 115th Street, and look for the wares of a lot of the city's museum shops on display at a Christmas bazaar in Grand Central Station. You can do some shopping (window and otherwise) in midtown—assuming you can stand the crowds, which seem overwhelming even by New York standards on the weekends leading up to Christmas. Peek at the shops at Citicorp Center for a wonderful model-train exhibit. The eight nights of Chanukah are commemorated with the lighting of candles on a giant menorah at sundown in Grand Army Plaza (Fifth Avenue at 59th Street). Both the Jewish Museum and the 92nd Street Y host lots of Chanukah events. Kwanza is celebrated at the end of the month with a variety of events throughout the city, including storytelling at the Museum of African Art. Finally, if you must go to the annual New Year's celebration in Times Square, crowds begin to gather in the early evening. If you want to celebrate the turning of the calendar in a more family-friendly atmosphere, try the very popular series of events associated with First Night New York at locations throughout Manhattan; the Concert for Peace at the Cathedral Church of St. John the Divine (Amsterdam Avenue at 112th Street); or fireworks, a midnight run, and other events in Central Park.

Atriums and Other Public Spaces

If the hustle and bustle of the city makes you want to rest your weary feet, Manhattan has lots of beautiful atriums and public sitting areas. Indeed, the lobby of seemingly every big building in midtown has a waterfall and tables. Some, including the Equitable Center and the Philip Morris Building, are also home to small galleries. Others, including the Ford Foundation, offer magnificent flowers and plants. Still others, such as Citicorp Center and the World Financial Center's Winter Garden, are often the sites of concerts, special events, and family workshops. I've put together the following list of some of my favorite atriums, public spaces, and popular sitting areas in midtown and other parts of the city.

Citicorp Center, 53rd St at Lexington Ave (indoors)
Conservatory Garden, in Central Park, just off Fifth Ave at 105th St (outdoors)
Crystal Pavilion, 50th St bet Second and Third Ave (indoors)
Equitable Center, Seventh Ave bet 51st and 52nd St (indoors)
Ford Foundation Gardens, 42nd and 43rd St bet First and Second Ave (indoors)
Galleria, 57th and 58th St bet Park and Lexington Ave (indoors)
Grace Plaza, Ave of the Americas at 43rd St (outdoors)
IBM Garden Plaza, Madison Ave at 56th St (indoors)
James P. Grant Plaza, 44th St bet First and Second Ave (outdoors)
Margaret Meade Green, Columbus Ave bet 79th and 81st St (outdoors)
Metropolitan Museum of Art, front steps, Fifth Ave bet 80th and 84th St (outdoors)
Museum of American Folk Art, Columbus Ave bet 65th and 66th St (indoors)
New York Public Library, front steps, Fifth Ave bet 40th and 42nd St (outdoors)
Olympic Tower, 51st St off Fifth Ave (indoors)
Paley Park, 53rd St bet Fifth and Madison Ave (outdoors)
Park Avenue Plaza, 52nd and 53rd St bet Madison and Park Ave (indoors)
Parker Meridien Hotel, 56th and 57th St bet Ave of the Americas and Seventh Ave (indoors)
Philip Morris Building, Park Ave at 42nd St (indoors)
St. Luke's-in-the-Fields, Hudson at Grove St (outdoors)
Sony Plaza Arcade, Madison Ave at 56th and 55th St (indoors)
Strawberry Fields, Central Park, near Central Park West and 72nd St (outdoors)
Sutton Place Park, Sutton Place at 57th St (outdoors)
Trump Tower Gardens, Fifth Ave bet 56th and 57th St, levels 4 and 5 (outdoors)
United Nations Plaza, First Ave bet 45th and 46th St (outdoors)
Vivian Beaumont Theater Plaza, Lincoln Center, 65th St bet Broadway and Amsterdam Ave (outdoors)
Vietnam Veterans Memorial Plaza, Water St north of Broad St (outdoors)
Winter Garden, World Financial Center, bet West St and Hudson River (indoors)
World Trade Center, various plazas (outdoors)

Book Talk

Despite dire predictions of its demise over the last decade, the written word is alive and well. Books are selling briskly, bookstores (at least the chains) are thriving, and book talks and reading groups are very popular. That's probably more true in New York than anywhere else. After all, this is the publishing capital of the world, and almost every author turns up here sooner or later.

If you want to sit in on a book talk or find others who share your interests, the following are all great places to start. You might also try various museums, societies, and churches throughout Manhattan. The Museum of the City of New York, for instance, sponsors a group that meets at sites complementing a given book's theme. In addition, *Time Out New York* has an excellent day-by-day list of book talks, poetry readings, and the like in its "Books & Poetry" section. Most events are free or inexpensive.

Barnes & Noble—The literary equivalent of The Gap in terms of number of stores, this longstanding bookstore chain offers a diverse range of authors, discussions, and panels. Locations are scattered throughout the city, but the Barnes & Noble Events Line (212/727-4810) will let you know what is going on and where.

Borders—This nationwide chain attracts interesting authors, most of them on book tours. Its New York branches include 5 World Trade Center (212/839-8049) and Park Avenue at 57th Street (212/980-6785).

New York Public Library—All sorts of interesting and erudite discussions take place at the library's main branch on 42nd Street. Other New York Public Library branches throughout the city offer interesting events and series of their own as well. (212/869-8089)

92nd Street Y—This amazing community resource consistently attracts leading authors for its lecture series. The 92nd Street Y is at 1395 Lexington Avenue (212/996-1100).

Partners & Crime—Meet-the-author events and other fun things go on at this mystery bookstore on Greenwich Avenue at Charles Street (212/243-0440).

In addition to the daily listing in *Time Out New York,* look for poetry readings and discussions at the **Knitting Factory Poetry Series** (74 Leonard St, 212/219-3055) and the **Unterberg Poetry Center** at the 92nd Street Y (1395 Lexington Ave, 212/996-1100).

Dancing and Other Night Life

Whether you want to go out for an evening of elegant dining and dancing, rock and roll till the wee hours, drop in on a set of jazz, or catch some stand-up comedy, New York's club scene offers plenty of choices. For descriptions of places to go and information about who is playing where, look under "Night Life" in the front of *The New Yorker* or under specific listings in the back of *New York* magazine and throughout *Time Out New York.* I've listed several popular places in each category to get you started. Most levy a cover charge, many offer at least a light menu, and a few require reservations and jackets for men. As with so many other things, it is wise to call in advance.

Dancing

Decade—Dancing and mingling for an upscale, over 35-crowd at 1115 First Avenue (212/835-5979)

Limelight—If dancing in a former church doesn't give you pause, the doors of this legendary 1980s disco at 660 Ave of the Americas are open again. Call 212/807-7780 for more information.

Mother—Hip and happening, this popular club in the Meatpacking District (432 West 14th Street) caters to everyone: gay, straight, and in between. Call 212/366-5680 for more information.

Rainbow Room—This world-famous restaurant is under new management and recently got a facelift. You'll now find dancing here nightly. Both the Rainbow Room and Rainbow & Stars, an intimate and classy supper club, are located on the 65th floor of 30 Rockefeller Plaza. Call 212/632-5000 for more information.

Roseland—This enormous place has faded a bit but remains quite popular for rock music and ballroom dancing (obviously not on the same nights). It's located at 239 West 52nd Street. Call 212/247-0200 for more information.

S.O.B. – The letters stand for "Sounds of Brazil and Beyond," and this enormous club at 204 Varick Street (at Houston Street) is a favorite eating and dancing club for New York University students and those who favor Latino, Caribbean, and other international forms of music. Call 212/243-4940 for more information.

Supper Club – An older, more elegant crowd comes here for dinner and dancing in a pre-war atmosphere complete with big bands on Friday and Saturday nights. The club is located at 240 West 47th Street. Call 212/921-1940 for more information.

The Tunnel – If your idea of fun is going deaf in the sweaty company of 3,000 other people, this club near the entrance to the Holland Tunnel (220 Twelfth Avenue) is just the place. Call 212/695-4682 for more information.

Windows on the World – This amazing place atop 1 World Trade Center has dancing every night except Sunday. Call 212/938-1111 for more information.

Finally, if you're a fan of swing dancing, call the **New York Swing Dance Society** to find out about their Sunday night dances and other events (212/696-9737).

Probably the most *refined* (?) topless bar in the city is **Billy's Topless** (729 Ave of the Americas). In fact, it is more a bikini joint, but then . . .

Drinks

Aquavit (13 W 54th St, 212/307-7311)
Bemelman's Bar, Carlyle Hotel (35 E 76th St, 212/744-1600)
Cub Room (131 Sullivan St, 212/677-4100)
King Cole Bar, St. Regis Hotel (2 E 55th St, 212/753-4500)
Fifty-seven Fifty-seven, Four Seasons (57 E 57th St, 212/758-5757)
Soho Grand (310 West Broadway, 212/965-3000)

Cabaret Rooms

Bemelman's Bar, Carlyle Hotel (35 E 76th St, 212/744-1600)
Cafe Carlyle, Carlyle Hotel (35 E 76th St, 212/744-1600)
Danny's Skylight Room (346 W 46th St, 212/265-8133)
Don't Tell Mama (343 W 46th St, 212/757-0788)
Eighty-eight's (228 W 10th St, 212/924-0088)
Firebird (363 W 46th St, 212/586-0244)
Michael's Pub, Parker Meridien Hotel (119 W 56th St, 212/758-2272)
Oak Room, Algonquin Hotel (59 W 44th St, 212/840-6800)
Triad (58 W 72nd St, 212/799-4599)

Jazz and Other Music

Birdland – One of the few jazz clubs outside Greenwich Village, this restaurant and bar is a favorite among older and more mellow fans. It moved from the Upper West Side down to 315 West 44th Street but hasn't lost one bit of its class and style. Call 212/581-3080 for more information.

Bitter End – A longtime showcase for soon-to-be-discovered folk-rock musicians, this club is located at 147 Bleecker Street. Call 212/673-7030 for more information.

Blue Note – You'll find two and sometimes three sets a night of great jazz at this supper club. It's located at 131 West 3rd Street. Call 212/475-8592 for more information.

Bottom Line – Depending on the night, this perennially popular showcase club offers rock, jazz, soul, folk, and country music. It's located at 15 West 4th Street. Call 212/228-7880 for more information.

Iridium – A relative newcomer to the jazz scene, it's nonetheless among the best. The club is beneath the Merlot Bar and Grill, a restaurant at 44 West 63rd Street, across from Lincoln Center. Call 212/582-2121 for more information.

Knitting Factory – An alternative rock and jazz club with a basement space (the AltaKnit Room) for all sorts of interesting experimentation, the Knitting Factory is in Tribeca at 74 Leonard Street. Call 212/219-3055 for more information.

Metropolitan Museum of Art – The Met started a big trend at New York museums by offering live music on Friday and Saturday evenings. The Great Hall Balcony Classical Quintet performs at a wonderful space in the Great Hall balcony. Drinks are available. The museum, on Fifth Avenue between 80th and 84th Streets, stays open until 8:45. Call 212/535-7710 for more information.

Museum of Modern Art – The museum's Garden Cafe plays host to a variety of jazz musicians on Friday evenings. A menu and drinks are available. The museum is at 11 West 53rd Street. Admission to the museum is "pay-what-you-wish," and lines are sometimes incredibly long. Call 212/708-9480 for more information.

Small's – Another newcomer, this late-night jazz club is down among the giants in the Village at 183 West 10th Street. Call 212/929-7565 for more information.

Solomon R. Guggenheim Museum – The Guggenheim offers live jazz with an international flavor in its rotunda on Friday and Saturday evenings for part of the year. A light menu and drinks are available. The museum is on Fifth Avenue at 88th Street. Call 212/423-3500 for more information.

Sweet Basil – This club is among the elite for serious jazz fans. It's in the West Village at 88 Seventh Avenue South. Call 212/242-1785 for more information.

Village Vanguard – A Greenwich Village institution for well over half a century, this jazz showcase for established names and up-and-comers alike is located at 178 Seventh Avenue South. Call 212/255-4037 for more information.

Comedy Clubs

Caroline's Comedy Club – The site of the Arts and Entertainment channel's *Caroline's Comedy Hour* series, this popular place attracts such comedians as Jerry Seinfeld and Billy Crystal. An Italian restaurant as well as a comedy club, it's located at 1626 Broadway. Look here, too, for afternoon comedy hours aimed at kids and families in Caroline's Kids Klub. Call 212/757-4100 for more information.

Comedy Cellar – Known for its relaxed atmosphere, this place sometimes finds established comedians trying out new jokes. It's located at 117 MacDougal Street. Call 212/254-3480 for more information.

Dangerfield's – As in Rodney. This magnet for suburban comedy fans is located at 1118 First Avenue. Call 212/593-1650 for more information.

Gay and Lesbian Clubs

A Different Light—A cafe and bookstore that specializes in gay and lesbian literature, videos, and the like, this is also a very informal and popular meeting place. It's located at 151 West 19th Street. Call 212/989-4850 for more information.

Boiler Room—An East Village institution, the crowd here is very mixed. It's at 86 East 4th Street. Call 212/254-7536 for more information.

Bowery Bar—A big favorite of the fashion (and fashionable) crowd, this bar is at 358 Bowery. Call 212/475-2220 for more information.

g—A relative newcomer to the Chelsea bar scene, this gay bar nevertheless has become a big hit. It's at 223 West 19th Street. Call 212/929-1085 for more information.

Meow Mix—A very popular lesbian bar in the East Village, this one is at 269 Houston Street. Call 212/254-1434 for more information.

— Millennium Note —
The first recorded Chinese immigrant in New York was Ah Ken, a Cantonese who arrived in 1858 and opened a cigar store on Park Row. He lived on Mott Street.

Holidays

2000

January 1	New Year's Day
January 17	Martin Luther King's birthday (observed)
February 5	Chinese New Year
February 14	Valentine's Day
February 21	Presidents Day
March 17	St. Patrick's Day
April 2	Daylight Savings Time begins (set clocks ahead!)
April 16	Palm Sunday
April 20	Passover begins (eight days)
April 21	Good Friday
April 23	Easter Sunday
May 14	Mother's Day
June 18	Father's Day
July 4	Independence Day
September 4	Labor Day
September 30	Rosh Hashana begins (two days)
October 9	Yom Kippur
October 9	Columbus Day (observed)
October 29	Daylight Savings Time ends (set clocks back!)
October 31	Halloween
November 7	Election Day
November 11	Veterans Day
November 23	Thanksgiving
December 22	Chanukah begins (eight days)
December 25	Christmas Day

2001

January 1	New Year's Day
January 15	Martin Luther King's birthday (observed)
January 24	Chinese New Year
February 14	Valentine's Day
February 19	Presidents Day
March 17	Saint Patrick's Day
April 1	Daylight Savings Time begins (set clocks ahead!)
April 8	Palm Sunday
April 8	Passover begins (eight days)
April 13	Good Friday
April 15	Easter
May 13	Mother's Day
June 17	Father's Day
July 4	Independence Day
September 3	Labor Day
September 18	Rosh Hashana begins (two days)
September 27	Yom Kippur
October 8	Columbus Day (observed)
October 28	Daylight Savings Time ends (set clocks back!)
October 31	Halloween
November 11	Veterans Day
November 22	Thanksgiving
December 10	Chanukah begins (eight days)
December 25	Christmas Day

Manhattan at Night

New York bills itself as "the city that never sleeps," and a sizable number of those who live here are night people. They include not only actors and artists but also those who clean and maintain the huge office buildings; who work for answering services; who put together morning newspapers and newscasts; who work the night shift at hospitals and other businesses that never close; and secretaries, transcribers, and editors who must make sure paperwork is ready overnight.

The following list includes an array of emergency services and other places that are open at night. **Unless otherwise noted, they are open 24 hours a day, seven days a week.** This list is not intended to be inclusive but rather to give you some choices throughout Manhattan. In general, stores and restaurants in Soho, Tribeca, and Greenwich Village stay open later than ones in the rest of the city. The restaurants and mom-and-pop operations along Broadway on the Upper West Side, and on Lexington and Third avenues on the Upper East Side, also tend to keep late hours. As with everything else, call before setting out for any of these places to make sure that they are still keeping the same hours.

BANKS—Assuming you have a compatible card, thousands of automated teller machines (ATMs) are open at all hours of the night. Look on the back of your bank card for a phone number you can call to find the ATM nearest you. **Western Union** (212/354-9750), at 1440 Broadway, is open 24 hours a day on weekdays (Friday until midnight), from 7 a.m. to midnight on Saturday, and from 8 a.m. to midnight on Sunday.

BOOKSTORES—The following bookstores stay open until at least 11 p.m.

(some close earlier on Sunday): **B. Dalton Bookseller** (396 Ave of the Americas, 212/674-8780, and other locations); **Barnes & Noble**, 2289 Broadway, 212/362-8835 and other locations); and **Tower Books** (383 Lafayette St, 212/228-5100).

CAR RENTALS—All major car-rental companies have offices in New York. Different locations, however, often have varying hours. The **Avis** office at 217 East 43rd Street (800/331-1212) is open 24 hours and the **Hertz** office at 222 East 40th Street (800/654-3131) is open Monday through Saturday until midnight. All of these companies have locations at Kennedy and LaGuardia airports that stay open all night.

CLEANERS—Although it's located in Long Island City, **Midnight Express Cleaners** (212/921-0111) will pick up and deliver in Manhattan and can turn things around in a day. Moreover, they cost a fraction of what hotels charge. Midnight Express can pick up and deliver between 9 a.m. and around 10 p.m. on weekdays (depending on your location) and between 9 a.m. and 3 p.m. on Saturday. **Meurice Garment Care** (212/475-2778) will pick up, deliver, and turn clothes around in two hours at any time of the day or night for $200.

DELIVERY AND MESSENGER COMPANIES—If it "absolutely positively has to be there" at any time of day or night, call **Moonlight Courier** (212/473-2246). You can also try **Able Motorized Deliveries** (212/687-5515).

DENTIST—For late-night referrals, call the **Emergency Dental Service**'s referral line (212/679-3966). The **Beth Israel Medical Center** (First Ave at 16th St, 212/420-2000) also can handle dental emergencies.

DOCTORS—If you need to find a doctor who makes house calls at all hours of the night, contact **Doctors on Call** (212/737-2333). Also see the listings under "Emergency Rooms."

ELECTRICIANS—If you need an electrician in the middle of the night, try **Altman Electric** (212/744-7372).

EMERGENCY ROOMS—The citywide emergency number is 911. An ambulance called through 911 will take you to the nearest hospital—which may or may not be the one you want. If you are well enough to get to an emergency room under your own power, the following major hospitals offer 24-hour service:

Bellevue Hospital: First Ave at 27th St, 212/562-4141
Beth Israel Medical Center: First Ave at 16th St, 212/420-2000
Columbia Presbyterian Medical Center: 622 W 168th St
Doctors Hospital: 170 East End Ave, 212/870-9000
Lenox Hill Hospital: 100 E 77th St, 212/434-2000
Mount Sinai Medical Center: Madison Ave at 99th St, 212/241-6500
New York Hospital/Cornell Medical Center: 510 E 70th St, 212/746-5454
St. Luke's-Roosevelt Medical Center: Ninth Ave at 58th St, and Amsterdam
   Ave at 114th St (212/523-4000)

ENTERTAINMENT—For clubs that stay open all night or close to it, look in the "Dancing and Other Night Life" section of this chapter. Here are some other suggestions:

Chelsea Billiards (54 W 21st St, 323/989-0096) is open all night.

Bowlmor Lanes (110 University Pl, 212/255-8188) is open on Friday, Saturday, and Monday from 10 a.m. to 4 a.m.; on Sunday, Tuesday, and Wednesday until 1 a.m.; and on Thursday until 2 a.m.
The **Chess Shop** (230 Thompson St, 212/475-9580) is open until midnight.

FOOD — You can always find a deli or bagel shop open in the middle of the night along Broadway on the Upper West Side and on Lexington and Third avenues on the East Side. However, you aren't going to find an elegant dining experience at two in the morning. But you will find a surprising number of decent places open at least that late or later, including:

Around the Clock Cafe: 8 Stuyvesant St, 212/598-0402
Azure: 830 Third Ave, 212/486-8080
Blue Ribbon: 97 Sullivan St, 212/274-0404
Carnegie Delicatessen and Restaurant: 854 Seventh Ave, 212/757-2245
Chelsea Square Restaurant: 368 W 23rd St, 212/691-5400
Clementine: 1 Fifth Ave, 212/252-0003
Coffee Shop: 29 Union Sq W, 212/243-7969
Comfort Diner: 142 E 86th St, 212/426-8600
Cooper Square II: 87 Second Ave, 212/420-8050
Cosmos Diner: 395 Second Ave, 212/679-1290
Empire Diner: 210 Tenth Ave, 212/243-2736
Florent: 69 Gansevoort St, 212/989-5779
French Roast: Ave of the Americas at 11th St, 212/533-2233, and Broadway at 85th St, 212/799-1533
Han Bat: 53 W 35th St, 212/629-5588
Kiev: 117 Second Ave, 212/674-4040
Milou: 92 Seventh Ave S, 212/414-9824
Moondance Diner: Ave of the Americas at Grand St, 212/226-1191
Morning Star Restaurant: 401 W 57th St, 212/246-1593
Odessa: 119 Ave A, 212/253-1470
Silver Star: 1236 Second Ave, 212/249-4250
Skyline Coffee Shop: 1055 Lexington Ave, 212/861-2540
Tick-Tock Diner: Eighth Ave at 34th St, 212/268-8444
Tramway Coffee House: 1143 Second Ave, 212/758-7017
Washington Square Coffee Shop: 150 W 4th St, 212/533-9306

GROCERY STORES — Although Manhattan does have chain supermarkets that vaguely resemble the kind found in the suburbs, the shortage of space in the city and exorbitant rents mean that Manhattan is full of smaller mom-and-pop grocery stores. Sometimes you'll find as many as three on one block — and chances are at least one will be open all night or close to it.

The chain supermarkets in Manhattan include **Food Emporium, Sloan's,** and **D'Agostino** (or Dags, as New Yorkers call it). Most are open seven days a week, from early in the morning until at least 11 p.m. Some are open 24 hours. Many New Yorkers strongly feel that one chain is far superior to the others, but I've found that quality depends more on the individual stores and their management than on the chain.

GYMS — If you need to work out in the middle of the night, try **World Gym** (Broadway at 64th St, 212/874-0942), **Crunch Fitness** (Lafayette St bet 4th St and Astor Pl, 212/614-0120), or the decidedly downscale and relatively cheap **Johnny Lat's Gym** (17th St at Fifth Ave 212/366-4426).

HARDWARE—Whether you need nails or a new toilet in the middle of the night, try **Home Depot**, on the Brooklyn side of the Brooklyn-Battery Tunnel (550 Hamilton Ave, 718/832-8553).

LOCKSMITHS—Three things can be said of most locksmiths in Manhattan: they stay open all night, they put a lot of "A"s before their name so they'll be near the top of the list in the Manhattan Yellow Pages, and they're unlikely to give you a good deal. For reputable service, try **Manhattan Locksmiths** (212/877-7787), **AAA Locksmiths** (212/840-3939), or **Night and Day Locksmith** (212/840-3939). Make sure you get an estimate!

NEWSSTANDS—Although there are some newspaper boxes in Manhattan, most people who don't get home delivery buy their newspapers and magazines at newsstands, which are all over the city. In addition to local newspapers, they sell a wide range of magazines and cigarettes. These days, even New York's newsstands are being "gentrified," but they're usually on street corners and hard to miss. The vast majority are open late into the evening seven days a week. Those at the following locations are open all night:

- Second Ave at St. Mark's Pl
- Ave of the Americas at 8th St
- Broadway at 42nd St (the first dropoff spot for the *New York Times*)
- Eighth Ave at 42nd St (Port Authority Bus Terminal)
- Broadway at 50th St
- Central Park West at Columbus Circle
- First Ave at 63rd St
- Broadway at 72nd St
- Columbus Ave at 81st St
- Broadway at 116th St

PLUMBERS—Read what I said about locksmiths. Though the same holds true here, you can try **Kapnag Heating and Plumbing** (212/289-8847) for honest, reliable service. All plumbers must be licensed by the city's Department of Buildings. Make sure to get a written estimate before any work is done.

PHARMACIES—Manhattan now has a handful of pharmacies that can fill prescriptions 24 hours a day, seven days a week: **Kaufman Pharmacy** (212/755-2266), off the lobby of the Beverly Hotel at Lexington Avenue and 50th Street; **Duane Reade** (Broadway at 57th Street, 212/541-9708); and **Rite Aid** (212/727-3854) at Eighth Avenue and 24th Street. Several other Duane Reade stores are open 24 hours day (including those at 2465 Broadway and 378 Avenue of the Americas, as are several other Rite Aid stores (including those at 138 East 86th Street and 408 Grand Street).

PHOTOCOPYING AND COMPUTER RENTALS—Part of a national chain, **Kinko's** stays open all night and offers photocopying services, Macintosh computer rentals (you use them there), and basic office supplies. Call 800/2KINKOS to find the Manhattan location nearest you.

PHOTO DEVELOPING—Try **K&L Custom PhotoGraphics** (212/661-5600), at 222 East 44th Street, or **Duggal** (212/242-7000), at 3 West 20th Street.

POST OFFICE—Although money orders cannot be purchased between 6 p.m. on Sunday evening and Monday morning, you'll find windows open all night long, seven days a week, at the main post office on Eighth Avenue between 31st and 33rd streets (212/967-8585).

RECORD, TAPE, AND CD STORES—The Virgin Records Megastore at 1540 Broadway (212/921-1020) is open from 9 a.m. until 1 a.m., Sunday through Thursday, and until 2 a.m. Friday and Saturday. **Tower Records** stores at Broadway and 4th Street (212/505-1500) and Broadway at 66th Street (212/799-2500) are open daily until midnight.

VETERINARIAN—Emergency care for pets is available at the **Animal Medical Center**, at 510 East 62nd Street (212/838-8100).

VIDEO STORES—More hotels are putting VCRs in their rooms. If yours has one, check with the front desk to see if the hotel has a video library. Otherwise, you can become a member at a local video store with a credit card. **Blockbuster Video,** a huge national chain open nightly until midnight, has become a dominant force even in Manhattan. Check the phonebook for the nearest location. **Tower Video,** at Lafayette and 4th streets (212/505-1166), is also open until midnight.

Manhattan for Children

When I first began writing this book, I did so from the perspective of an adult who comes to New York without children. I quickly learned, however, that many people bring kids to New York, whether they're coming for business or pleasure. New York can be a little overwhelming for kids (the same is true for adults!), but it can also be a wonderland if you know where to go.

The "Kids" pages in the back of *New York* magazine and *Time Out New York,* and the "For Children" column in the Friday *New York Times* Weekend section are great places to look for upcoming events and activities for children in and around New York City. Also look in toy shops and bookstores for one of the several free parenting magazines currently published in New York.

I've listed the best places for kids in several categories: birthday parties; entertainment; museums and sights; play spaces, art centers and classes; restaurants; and toy and bookstores. (If you are a New Yorker with children or bring children here often, I urge you to look under "Parenting Resources" in Chapter IV as well.) When a specific place is described in another part of the book, in many cases I've simply included the address and phone number and marked the entry with an asterisk (*). When the place isn't described elsewhere, I've provided a little more information. Of course, different children are interested in different things, so I've included places that one child will love and another might find boring. I'll let you be the judge of that!

Birthday Parties

In addition to most of the play spaces listed later in this section, the following are great venues for children's birthday parties:

*Chelsea Piers—Whether you want in-line skating, rock-climbing, or gymnastics at your next birthday party, the amazing Chelsea Piers facility at the far west end of 23rd Street can probably accommodate you. Call 212/336-6666 for more information.

*Central Park Wildlife Conservation Center—Throw a party for children between 4 and 12 amid the animals in Central Park, off Fifth Avenue at 64th Street. Call 212/439-6538 for more information.

*Children's Museum of the Arts—This child-centered art exploration and play space is available for children's birthday parties. It's located in Soho at 182 Lafayette Street. Call 212/274-0986 for more information.

*Linda Kaye's Birthdaybakers, Partymakers—A mom turned birthday party genius, Linda Kaye has been putting on unique parties for children since I first began writing this book. Call 212/288-7112 for more information.

*New York Transit Museum—For surprisingly reasonable prices, you can throw a party for as many as 50 children in what can only be described as a train-lover's heaven. Activities include train videos for preschoolers, workshops for older kids, and ice cream for everyone from Peter's Ice Cream Parlor. Call 718/243-3060 for more information.

*Party Poopers—These folks had a private party space for kids long before such things became trendy. They do theme parties at their place or yours. Call 212/587-9030 for more information.

*Serendipity 3—You can have your child's birthday party for up to 70 guests in this perennially popular and decidedly upscale East Side ice cream parlor. Rates are high but the food is great. Call 212/838-3531 for more information.

*Screening Room—The birthday boy or girl can sit in an *Alice in Wonderland*-inspired throne at the head of a banquet table while watching a favorite movie or television show in this popular restaurant/movie theater's party room. Rates are surprisingly affordable, and catering is available. Call 212/334-2100 for more information.

Tortoise and the Hare—If your little girl likes to have her hair done and her nails painted, this East Side salon for children puts on "glamour parties" for girls age five and up. The price tag is a bit much, but partygoers get to be in a fashion show and are given a bag of hair accessories. Call 212/472-3399 for more information. Similar parties are also available at **Cozy's Cuts for Kids,** with locations on the East Side (212/744-1716) and West Side (212/579-2600).

Warner Brothers Studio Store—Birthday parties for children on the ninth floor of this in-your-face Warner Brothers wonderland on Fifth Avenue include a film, party favors and a cake. There's nothing cheap about them, but they do seem to be a great hit with kids. The space is also available for private functions and parties for grownups. Call 212/754-0300 for more information.

Entertainment

*ARTime—Run by art historians, this organization offers tours of Soho and Chelsea art galleries geared for elementary schoolchildren and their families. Call 718/797-1573 for more information.

Arts Connection Center—Various kid-friendly performances and very reasonable ticket prices can be found at this location (120 West 46th Street, 212/302-7433), near Broadway.

*Bryant Park—Assuming warm weather, kids (and adults) can rent such games as Scrabble and checkers for $4 an hour. Sailboats to sail in the fountain cost $2 an hour.

Caroline's Kids Klub—The kid-friendly version of Caroline's Comedy Club operates at the same spot in the afternoon (1626 Broadway, 212/757-4100).

*Central Park—Particularly during the spring and summer months, Central Park is full of events and activities for children. In addition to the marvelous Wildlife Conservation Center, there are activities for children on Saturday and Sunday afternoons at Belvedere Castle (212/772-0210), near 79th Street on the

West Side; a puppet theater on weekday mornings near the 62nd Street playground (call The Dairy at 212/794-6564 to make reservations); a marionette theater near 81st Street and Central Park West (212/988-9093); and story readings at the Hans Christian Anderson Statue, at the Conservatory Water near 74th Street and Fifth Avenue, on Saturday mornings. Make sure to call ahead, as some events require reservations and/or a small fee, and the hours and locations may vary. You might also stop by the Charles A. Dana Discovery Center (212/860-1370), in the northeast corner near Fifth Avenue and 110th Street, to borrow fishing poles or attend a family workshop. Every day from 10 to 7 (except Saturday) in warmer months, you can rent a small sailboat to sail in the Conservatory Water Pond (north of the 72nd Street entrance, off Fifth Avenue). If you're looking for an unusual way to see the park, try a two-hour bicycle tour (call Bite of the Apple Tours at 212/541-8759 for more information). You can find out what is happening on any given day in Central Park and other parks throughout Manhattan by calling 212/360-3456.

*Circle Line Sightseeing Yachts—Pier 83, Twelfth Avenue at 43rd Street (212/563-3200). For more information, see the "Tours" section in Chapter III.

Donnell Library Children's Center—Another branch of the New York Public Library, this one (20 West 53rd Street, 212/621-0636) houses a special room for children with more than 100,000 books, magazines, and recordings. Also look here for the original stuffed animals upon which Winnie the Pooh and his friends were based; they're in a display case on the second floor. It's open from noon to 6 on Monday, Wednesday, and Friday; 10 to 6 on Tuesday; noon to 8 on Thursday; and noon to 5 on Saturday.

IMAX Theater—Inside the American Museum of Natural History, on Central Park West between 77th and 81st streets, this theater shows films on such topics as African animals and tornados. The screen is enormous and the films well conceived. Call 212/769-5034 for more information.

Kaye Playhouse—Started by Danny Kaye and his wife Sylvia, this wonderful theater always has something fun going on. It's located on 68th Street between Park and Lexington avenues; call 212/772-4448 for more information.

Movies—The Museum of Modern Art (212/708-9805) has a weekly family film series, the Walter Reade Theater (212/875-5610) sometimes has movies and other programs for children, and the Donnell Library Center (621-0636) shows kids' movies for free! (For movies aimed at tourists, see other listings below.)

*New Amsterdam Theater—Part of the revitalization of 42nd Street, this renovated theater once housed the Ziegfeld Follies and is now home to the wildly popular Disney production of *The Lion King*. It's located on 42nd Street near Seventh Avenue; call 212/282-2900 for more information.

New Victory Theater—This theater (209 West 42nd Street, 212/564-4222) is entirely devoted to productions for children and families.

Sony IMAX Theater—This eight-story, 3-D movie screen is located on the top floor of Sony's wildly popular theater at Broadway and 67th Street, north of Lincoln Center. Call 212/336-5000 for more information.

Story Hours—Several children's bookstores—including Books of Wonder (on Sunday at 11:45 a.m.), Barnes & Noble, Jr. (Tuesday at 10:30 a.m. and Thursday at 5:30 p.m.), the children's section of the Upper West Side Barnes & Noble (Tuesday at 10:30 a.m.), and West Side Kids (Monday at 11 a.m.)—have story hours for young children. There's also a story hour at the Wildlife Conservation Center in Central Park, and all sorts of story hours and other kid-friendly events at Donnell Library's Children's Center. Check times and age requirements before setting out.

Museums and Sights

*Abigail Adams Smith Museum and Gardens—421 East 61st Street, 212/838-6878.

*American Museum of Natural History—The hands-on Discovery Room is open on weekend afternoons, and tickets are handed out on a first-come, first-serve basis in late morning (Central Park West between 77th and 81st Street, 212/769-5100).

*Central Park Wildlife Conservation Center—Central Park behind the Arsenal (Fifth Avenue at 64th Street, 212/861-6030).

*Children's Museum of Manhattan—(212 West 83rd Street, 212/721-1234).

*Ellis Island—In New York Harbor, off Battery Park, 212/363-7620.

*Empire State Building Observation Deck—Fifth Avenue between 33rd and 34th Streets, 212/736-3100.

*Fraunces Tavern Museum—54 Pearl Street, 212/425-1778.

*Intrepid Sea-Air-Space Museum—Pier 86, Twelfth Avenue at 46th Street, 212/245-0072.

*Metropolitan Museum of Art—Although not everything here is for children and strollers are not admitted on Sunday, the Egyptian mummy exhibit and the gallery full of arms and armor will be big hits (Fifth Avenue between 80th and 84th Streets, 212/535-7710). Call the Education Department (212/570-3756) for information about films and other special events for children.

*Museum of the City of New York—1220 Fifth Avenue, 212/534-1672.

*Museum of Television and Radio—25 West 52nd Street, 212/621-6600.

*National Museum of the American Indian—1 Bowling Green, at the foot of Broadway, 212/668-6624.

*New York City Fire Museum—278 Spring Street, 212/691-1303.

*NBC Studio Tour—Not for children under six, but a big hit with older kids. Daily except Sunday. Call 212/664-7174 for more information.

*New York Historical Society—Look for the new "Kid City" exhibit (Central Park West between 76th and 77th Streets, 212/873-3400).

*New York Transit Museum—Boerum Place at Schermerhorn Street, Brooklyn, 718/243-3060.

*Roosevelt Island Tram—The tram leaves from a station on Second Avenue, between 59th and 60th Streets.

*Sony Wonder Technology Lab—Madison Avenue at 56th Street, 212/833-8100.

*South Street Seaport—Located at the eastern end of Fulton Street (212/669-9400), the Seaport has a seasonal schedule of activities for children and families, plus a special interactive museum for children.

*Statue of Liberty—On Liberty Island in New York Harbor, just off Battery Park.

*United Nations—The visitors' entrance is on First Avenue, between 45th and 46th Streets (212/963-7713). Strollers are not allowed on the grounds, and children under five cannot go on the tour.

World Trade Center Observation Deck—1 World Trade Center, top floor, 212/435-7377.

Play Spaces, Art Centers, and Classes

Arts Connection—This wonderful place (120 West 46th Street, 212/302-7433) devotes Saturday mornings to creative and thoughtful art workshops for children and Saturday afternoons to storytelling. Reservations are required and parents must stay with their children, but prices are reasonable and quality is extremely high.

Children's Museum of the Arts—This friendly Soho spot is a big favorite with children who like to create and explore with their hands. Designed for children between 18 months and 10 years, this low-key, child-centered museum has various workspaces where children can explore different media. Workshops for children of different ages are held throughout the day, and scheduled classes and a morning drop-in program for toddlers and preschoolers are also available. The museum is open Wednesday from 10 to 7 and Thursday through Sunday from 10 to 5. You'll find it at a great new location in Soho (182 Lafayette Street). Look for the friendly zebra in front! Admission is $5 per person. Call 212/274-0986 for more information.

*Children's Museum of Manhattan—This museum (212 West 83rd Street), has great play spaces for toddlers, preschoolers and kids in early elementary school.

Craft Studio—For kids who like crafts, this studio (1657 Third Avenue, 212/831-6626) is a fun place.

Field House at Chelsea Piers—You name it and Chelsea Piers teaches it to kids. Classes for children six months and older are offered. The field house is near the entrance of the Chelsea Piers complex, at the far west end of 23rd Street. Call 212/336-6500 for more information.

Little Shop of Plaster—This store (431 East 73rd Street, 212/717-6636) allows children to paint, glitter, and varnish pre-made plaster shapes.

My Favorite Place—A big hit with little ones, this Upper West Side "play space" (265 West 87th Street, 212/362-5320) combines a low-key toy store with a safe play room for toddlers and studio space for toddler and preschool art, movement, and music classes.

92nd Street Y—This amazing institution (92nd Street at Lexington Avenue, 212/415-5611) offers classes for infants (two months and older) and children through its Parenting Center. Prices are a bit high, but the quality and new-mom networking opportunities are great.

Our Name Is Mud—A fun place for painting pottery on the East Side (212/570-6868), the West Side (212/579-5575), and in Greenwich Village (212/647-7899).

Outdoor playgrounds—Manhattan has lots of safe, imaginative, and relatively clean public playgrounds. Look in Central Park along Central Park West or

Fifth Avenue, on the promenade outside the World Financial Center, or call the Manhattan Department of Parks and Recreation at 212/360-8111 for the location of a playground near you.

PlaySpaces—Part of a trend in New York and elsewhere, PlaySpaces offers safe, indoor free-play areas for children between six months and six years of age (2473 Broadway, 212/769-2300).

Restaurants

*America—A big restaurant (9 East 18th Street, 212/505-2110) with large portions and lots of French fries.

*Avenue—A little bit of Balthazar on the Upper West Side (520 Columbus Avenue, 212/579-3194). Take the kids here for Sunday brunch.

Barking Dog Luncheonette—Good food and lots of dog knick-knacks to look at in this popular Upper East Side spot (1678 Third Avenue, 212/831-1800).

Benihana of Tokyo—The 120 East 56th Street location (212/593-1627) consistently gets high marks from pre-teens for all the action, the antics of the kid-friendly Japanese chefs, and the good food.

Brooklyn Diner USA—One of many theme restaurants in midtown, this diner (212 West 57th Street, 212/977-1957) has the basic foods that will make kids happy and parents nostalgic.

Bubby's—This southern outpost in Tribeca (120 Hudson Street, 212/219-0666) has great ambience and food. Be sure to save room for dessert.

*Carnegie Delicatessen and Restaurant—Expect huge portions, rude waiters, and bench seats at this bustling New York institution (854 Seventh Avenue, 212/757-2245).

*Cowgirl Hall of Fame—Small children can be entertained for hours looking at the walls of this low-key spot at 519 Hudson Street in the West Village. Call 212/633-1133 for more information.

*EJ's Luncheonette—A friendly neighborhood place (447 Amsterdam Avenue, 212/873-3444) with basic food at good prices.

Gray's Papaya—Cheap and delicious hot dogs and other such foods are served at this downscale, hurried spot at the corner of Broadway and 72nd Street (212/799-0243).

*Hard Rock Cafe—This popular location (221 West 57th Street, 212/459-9320) is part of a wildly successful international chain, and kids and teenagers eat it up. Look for a line to get into this one.

*Jackson Hole Burgers—You'll get great, juicy hamburgers and lots of thick fries and onion rings at this restaurant, which has several locations, including 232 East 64th Street (212/371-7187).

Jekyll & Hyde Club—There's usually a long line, but that's because kids love to dine in this not-too-scary haunted house, complete with talking heads (1409 Avenue of the Americas, 212/541-9505).

*John's Pizzeria—Many New Yorkers swear this is the best pizza around. The original John's is in the West Village at 278 Bleecker Street (212/243-1680), but new locations are popping up all over the city.

Mars 2112—For all the aspiring astronauts and science-fiction buffs out there, this theme restaurant on 51st Street at Broadway (212/582-2112) has Crater Masters instead of waiters.

McDonald's—Kids love McDonald's, and the one at 160 Broadway certainly lives up to all generic expectations, but it also has a store inside selling Ronald McDonald dolls and items with the McDonald's logo. They also offer table service on the second floor in the back. The store is open seven days a week from 11 a.m. to 7 p.m.

Motown Cafe—Yes, another theme restaurant (104 West 57th Street, 212/581-8030). And yes, it's wildly popular. Look for the lines.

Nick & Toni's Cafe—An Upper West Side newcomer (100 West 67th Street, 212/496-4000), this pleasant place has all the basics and does them well.

*Planet Hollywood—This is one of the older theme restaurants (140 West 57 Street, 212/333-7827). Stars come out nightly, as do tourists.

*Serendipity 3—The East Side's favorite ice cream parlor is Serendipity 3 (225 East 60th Street, 212/838-3531). It is the home of Frozen Hot Chocolate and other wondrous desserts, as well as good but overpriced meals.

*Tavern on the Green—The chef at this beautiful spot in Central Park (Central Park West at 67th Street, 212/873-3200) has five children of his own and has put together a terrific children's menu. Reservations are usually necessary.

Two Boots—A favorite pizza place that loves kids (and vice versa). The original location is at 37 Avenue A (212/505-2276), but locations are popping up all over the city (including the newly refurbished Grand Central Station).

Toy Stores and Bookstores

*Bank Street Bookstore—A tremendous source for children's books, as well as resources for parents and teachers, up near Columbia University (2875 Broadway, 212/678-1654).

*Barnes & Noble, Jr.—86th Street at Lexington Avenue (212/427-0686) and locations in Barnes & Noble stores throughout the city.

*Books of Wonder—A legend among children's bookstores, known especially for its *Wizard of Oz* collection (16 West 18th Street, 212/(989-3270).

*Classic Toys—For people who believe that good toys don't need to change every season or even every generation (218 Sullivan Street, 212/674-4434).

*Disney Store—The one on the corner of 42nd Street and Seventh Avenue (212/221-0430) is the best of several in town.

*FAO Schwarz—The grandfather of all toy stores, at Fifth Avenue at 58th Street (212/644-9400). Crowded and overpriced, it's nonetheless a fantasyland.

*Geppetto's Toy Box—A special place run by people who really care about toys and children, young and old (161 Seventh Avenue South, 212/620-7511).

*Tootsie's—A warm and inviting store (555 Hudson Street, 212/242-0182).

*Unique Science—For all those budding scientists out there. Behind the American Museum of Natural History (410 Columbus Avenue, 212/712-1899).

*Warner Brothers Studio Store—A store, tourist attraction, and theme park rolled into one (Fifth Avenue at 57th Street, 212/754-0300, and in Times Square 212/840-4040).

*West Side Kids—About as kid-friendly as a toy store gets (498 Amsterdam Avenue, 212/496-7282).

Just as there are some things that are all the more fun done with kids, there are others that you *shouldn't* do with them. Museums like the Frick Collection, the Grolier Club's gallery, and the Morgan Library, for example, are not places to bring small children. Indeed, children under ten are not allowed in the Frick, children under six can't go on the NBC Studio Tour, children under five are not welcome on the tour of the United Nations, and children under four are not allowed in most Broadway theaters. If you're going shopping at a perpetually crowded place like Zabar's or Fairway, don't take kids along or make sure you keep a firm grip on their hands if you do. The latter holds true just about everywhere in New York—it's very easy to get lost in a crowd! And remember that kids tire more quickly than adults. Chances are you'll be doing a lot of walking, and they're taking two or three steps for every one you take! As the *New York Times* once put it, "Baby miles are like dog years."

Finally, a word of warning: it's a real challenge to tote an infant or toddler in New York. While hundreds of thousands of children are born and raised in the city, visitors who are accustomed to carting their children through malls in strollers and around town in car seats may have trouble here. Many places, including the subway system, are not exactly stroller-accessible. A few, including the United Nations, the Forbes Magazine Galleries, and the Metropolitan Museum of Art (on Sundays), ban them altogether. Taxis with functioning seatbelts have become much easier to find in recent years, but ones with car seats are a rarity. Only a few public restrooms have changing tables, and I've yet to hear of a store that has followed the Nordstrom chain's example and set aside space for nursing mothers.

Manhattan for Free

There's no way to get around it: New York is expensive. Even the most frugal and resourceful visitors often feel like they're bleeding money ("Didn't we just get $200 out of the cash machine yesterday!?") after a couple of days here. Still, you can find some good deals and do a lot of sightseeing for free. Look in *Time Out New York's* tremendous weekly listings of events throughout the city for boxes noting ones that are free. You can also try some of the following:

Book Talks—If you're a reader, don't forget you're in the publishing capital of the world. Look for free lectures and discussions with all sorts of authors at bookstores and libraries including Barnes & Noble (212/727-4810), Borders (212/839-8049), the New York Public Library (212/254-9628), and Posman Books (212/533-BOOK).

Concerts and Other Performances—On Monday nights in summer, Bryant Park hosts (and HBO sponsors) free movies. Also in the summer, Central Park comes alive with free concerts by the New York Philharmonic (212/875-5700), operas by the Metropolitan Opera (212/362-6000), Shakespeare in the Park (212/598-7100), and all sorts of performances on the SummerStage (212/360-2777). Call 212/360-3456 for recorded information about events in Central Park and other parks throughout the city. There's also the Midsummer Night Swing concerts at Lincoln Center Plaza (212/875-5400), concerts on Thursday and Friday evenings at South Street Seaport (212/669-9400), and chamber music in Washington Square Park, at the foot of Fifth Avenue in Greenwich Village, every Tuesday night. Thanks to a pay-what-you-wish admission policy at the Museum of Modern Art on Friday night, you can enjoy an evening of live jazz in the museum's Sculpture Garden and cafe throughout the year without paying a dime. For information about concerts and other performances at the Winter Garden in the World Financial Center, call 212/945-0505.

If you're interested in discount tickets for concerts, the theater, and other performances, make sure to look in the "Tickets" section of Chapter III. Also check out the significant discounts on various museum admissions, performing arts tickets, and other events available through American Express's Culture Pass (877/278-7277).

Museums and Sights—In alphabetical order, the free museums and sights in Manhattan include the American Bible Society's gallery, the American Numismatic Society, the Americas Society gallery, the Cathedral Church of St. John the Divine, the Commodities Exchange, Dyckman Farmhouse, the Equitable Center Gallery, Federal Hall National Memorial, the Forbes Magazine Galleries, the Ford Foundation Gardens, Grant's Tomb, the Grolier Club's gallery, the Hispanic Society of America, the Municipal Art Society's Urban Center Gallery, the Museum of American Folk Art, the Museum of American Illustration, the National Museum of the American Indian, New York Public Library, the New York Public Library for the Performing Arts, the New York Stock Exchange, Newseum/NY, the Nicholas Roerich Museum, the Paine-Webber Gallery, the Rose Museum at Carnegie Hall, the Schomburg Center for Research in Black Culture, the Skyscraper Museum, the Sony Wonder Technology Lab, Trinity Church's small museum, and the Whitney Gallery and Sculpture Garden at Philip Morris. Some of these places accept donations, but none pressures visitors for them.

Several other museums are technically free but make a point of telling you that they expect a "suggested contribution." These include the Alternative Museum, the American Museum of Natural History, El Museo del Barrio, the Museum of the City of New York, and the New York Historical Society.

It used to be that the museums along Museum Mile offered free admission to everyone one night a week. Unfortunately, that tradition lives on only one night a year in late June. Some museums in the city do offer pay-as-you-wish admission on different evenings throughout the year, however. They include the Cooper-Hewitt (Tuesday between 5 p.m. and 9 p.m.), both branches of the International Center of Photography (Friday between 5 p.m. and 8 p.m.), the Jewish Museum (Tuesday between 5 p.m. and 8 p.m.), the Museum of Modern Art (Friday between 4:30 p.m. and 8:30 p.m.), the New Museum of Contemporary Art (Thursday between 6 p.m. and 8 p.m.), and the Whitney Museum of American Art (Thursday between 6 p.m. and 8 p.m.).

Children under 12 are admitted to a lot of places for free. Smithsonian Associates are admitted without charge to the Cooper-Hewitt. Although it isn't free, you can go to both the Cloisters and the Metropolitan Museum of Art on the same day and pay only one admission price. Finally, CityPass gives discount admission to the Empire State Building, the observation deck on top of the World Trade Center, the American Museum of Natural History, the Metropolitan Museum of Art, and several other places for roughly half what the combined admission to these places would cost. Call 707/256-0490 for more information.

Tours — The very best bargain in this category is the personalized tour offered free of charge by the city through its Big Apple Greeters program. A close runner-up is the marvelous free tour of Grand Central Station offered every Wednesday at 12:30 p.m. by the Municipal Art Society. Other free tours include ones of the neighborhood around Grand Central Station, the Federal Reserve Bank, the New York Public Library, Penn Station, the Schomburg Center for Research in Black Culture, Times Square, the area on and around 34th Street, the Lower East Side, and Trinity Church. The Urban Park Rangers also conduct a variety of free tours in the city's parks. For more detailed information about tours, see the "Tours" section of Chapter III.

Views — The best bargain on a view of the New York skyline is a trip on the Staten Island Ferry. The trip is free and the ferry leaves nearly continuously from the end of Whitehall Street in Battery Park. Another bargain view of the city can be had on the west side of Roosevelt Island. A trip on the tram (Second Avenue between 59th and 60th Streets) costs $1.50 each way. For $2, you can climb the 22-story bell tower at Riverside Church (212/870-6700) and gaze down on the Hudson and the city. And for nothing at all, you can walk for 1.2 miles along the Battery Park Esplanade.

Walking — It doesn't cost a dime to just walk around. Some of the more pleasant walking areas include Fifth Avenue in midtown, Soho (on Saturday afternoon and early evening), South Street Seaport and Central Park (particularly on weekends), Fifth and Madison avenues on the Upper East Side, the Lower East Side (on Sunday), the Lincoln Center area, and Greenwich Village (particularly on weekends). Take a look at the "Flea Markets" section of Chapter III; most of them cost nothing to browse and can be lots of fun!

Who says there's no free lunch? You can spend hours listening to music and playing with CD-ROMs at the Virgin Megastore superstore in Times Square; read a book in a comfortable chair at Barnes & Noble on Broadway at 82nd Street (or just about any bookstore in town these days); or park for up to four hours in lots maintained by the Lower East Side Business Improvement District at the foot of the Williamsburg Bridge. You can also take free classes on how to use the Internet at the New York Public Library's new Science, Industry and Business Library. For $25, you can join one of the city's recreation centers (there are 29 of them) for a year. For $3, you can see a first-run movie at the Cineplex Odeon's Worldwide Cinema (50th Street between Eighth and Ninth Avenue). For $2, you can swim in the clean, beautiful pool at Riverbank State Park (Riverside Drive at 145th Street). And for the price of a token, you can get to LaGuardia Airport (on the M60 bus) or Kennedy Airport (on the A train).

Finally, a couple of money-saving tips: travel at off-peak hours, spend a Saturday night, and consider coming off-season as well. Look for package deals and seasonal specials. Buy snacks at a deli down the street rather than from the minibar in your hotel room. Pack light and save the money you would otherwise spend on tips for bellmen. Walk or take public transportation, particularly when you're going a short distance in midtown or anywhere at rush hour.

Manhattan for Lovers

Whether you're falling in love for the first time or celebrating your golden anniversary, New York can be one of the most romantic places in the world. If you're in the mood for love or want to create a mood that's just right for romance, try the following:

- A getaway weekend swaddled in the first-class luxury of the Four Seasons Hotel, at 57 East 57th Street.
- Warming up in one of the suites at the Regency, a great hotel at 540 Park Avenue.
- A night at the always-elegant Plaza Hotel, overlooking Central Park from its southeast corner at 59th Street and Fifth Avenue.
- An intimate dinner at the small and sophisticated Sonia Rose, at 150 East 34th Street (between Lexington and Third Avenue).
- Dinner amid the flowers in the French elegance of La Grenouille, at 3 East 52nd Street.
- Drinks by the fireplace followed by dinner at One If By Land, Two If By Sea, at 17 Barrow Street (between Seventh Avenue and 4th Street).
- A summertime dinner in the garden at Barbetta, 321 West 46th Street (between Eighth and Ninth Avenues).
- Dinner in the discreet and classy March, at 405 East 58th Street (between First Avenue and Sutton Place).
- Dinner in Tavern on the Green's sparkling Crystal Room, in Central Park off 67th Street on the Upper West Side.
- Dinner at a window table at Columbia University's excellent Terrace restaurant, at 400 West 119th Street.
- A late-night visit to the Empire State Building Observation Deck, on Fifth Avenue between 33rd and 34th Streets.
- A picnic lunch looking out over the Hudson River from the Cloisters.
- Listening to jazz great Bobby Short in the Carlyle Hotel's intimate Cafe Carlyle.
- A stroll through the splendid lobby of the Waldorf-Astoria.
- A weekend evening spent listening to classical music in the Metropolitan Museum of Art's Great Hall balcony.
- A wintertime visit to the warm, lush greenery of the Ford Foundation's Gardens, at 320 East 43rd Street.
- A Friday evening of jazz in summer at the Museum of Modern Art's sculpture garden.
- A nighttime sail around Manhattan.
- A springtime stroll through Central Park on some of its less traveled paths.
- A picnic dinner gazing at the Manhattan skyline from Lighthouse Park, on Roosevelt Island.
- Cozying up in a love seat to watch a movie at the Screening Room (54 Varick Street).
- A rowboat or gondola ride on Central Park Lake.
- An evening carriage ride through Central Park in winter, just after a fresh snow has fallen.
- A visit to the "Kissing Gallery" in Grand Central Station, in what is now the basement of the Bank of America building on 43rd Street (directly across Vanderbilt Avenue from the station).

If you are looking for good entertainment along with good food (and hopefully good company), try the **Tatou** (151 East 50th Street, 212/753-1144). Housed in a former opera house, this romantic establishment features dinnertime shows on Tuesday through Saturday.

Manhattan on the Water

Although it's easy to forget, Manhattan is an island surrounded on all four sides by water. Boat trips around the island (or even part of it) not only help convey a better sense of how the city is laid out but can also be lots of fun. Look for a special "Boat and Yacht" section in the back of *New York* magazine if you're interested in chartering a private boat. Otherwise, I suggest one of the following:

Atlantic Kayak Tours—If you have a lot of courage and a bit of skill, this company offers kayaking tours of New York Harbor and even a paddle around the island of Manhattan. The views must be stunning! The company also offers lessons for students at all skill levels. Call 914/246-2187 for more information.

Circle Line—One of the most pleasant ways to see the city (and cool off on a hot summer afternoon), the standard Circle Line sightseeing cruise lasts three hours and circumnavigates the entire island. Other tours are available from Pier 83 on the Hudson River and Pier 16 at South Street Seaport. See the listing under "Tours" in Chapter III, or call 212/563-3200 for more information.

NY Waterway—90-minute New York Harbor cruises, a harbor cruise combined with a "hop-on, hop-off" bus tour (with New York Apple Tours), an abbreviated version of the same tour leaving from South Street Seaport, twilight cruises, and more are available from NY Waterway (Pier 78, 38th Street at the Hudson River, 800/533-3779). All but the harbor cruise are available in warmer months only.

Spirit Cruises—If you're interested in a two-hour buffet lunch cruise or a three-hour buffet dinner cruise on the Hudson River in warmer months, these folks on Pier 61 at the Chelsea Piers complex have numerous scheduled sailings (212/727-2789). Prices are higher on weekends and for dinner. All have cash bars.

Staten Island Ferry—There are two great bargain ferries left in the world, and the Staten Island Ferry (718/390-5253) is one of them. (The other is the Star Ferry in Hong Kong.) It runs 24 hours a day, seven days a week, all year round—and now, thanks to a decision in 1997 to eliminate the 50-cent fare, is totally free! The loading terminals (in Battery Park at the foot of Whitehall Street in Manhattan and at the end of Bay Street on Staten Island) aren't very nice and can get smelly in the summer, but the views from the water during the 22-minute trip are spectacular.

World Yacht—This is the upscale cousin of the Circle Line sightseeing trips. (They're owned by the same company.) You can have lunch, brunch, or dinner on board, and there is dancing at night. Some trips last longer than others, and prices vary accordingly. World Yacht cruises leave every day except Christmas from Pier 81, 41st Street at the Hudson River (212/630-8100).

New York for New Yorkers

Although New Yorkers often think there's nothing an outsider can tell them about their city, I've yet to meet one who has done all of the following things. Culled from years spent finding it, buying it, and eating it in New York, this list represents what I believe to be the very best experiences this magnificent city has to offer:

• Riding the tram to Roosevelt Island and strolling along its west side.

- Climbing the seemingly endless set of stairs inside the bell tower at Riverside Church to reach one of the city's prettiest views.
- Going to Ellis Island and retracing the steps taken by many of our brave ancestors.
- Enjoying a quiet afternoon at the Cloisters.
- Gazing around the Rockefeller Rooms, on the fifth floor of the Museum of the City of New York; perusing Mr. Morgan's Library at the Morgan Library; or gaping at the Venetian Room in the old Whitney Mansion, just down the street from the Metropolitan Museum of Art.
- Spending an evening listening to Bobby Short at Cafe Carlyle.
- Taking the vertical tour of the Cathedral Church of St. John the Divine.
- Walking the length of Central Park on a spring weekend.
- Exploring the ins and outs of Grand Central Station on the Municipal Art Society's free Wednesday afternoon tour.
- Wandering through the Lower East Side Tenement Museum and the Eldridge Street Synagogue on a Sunday afternoon.
- High tea at the Peninsula New York Hotel.
- Lingering over a glass of wine on an early-fall afternoon at the Roof Garden atop the Metropolitan Museum of Art.
- Relaxing on the benches overlooking the Hudson River and the Palisades in Fort Tryon Park.
- Sunrise from the pedestrian walkway on the Brooklyn Bridge or aboard the Staten Island Ferry.

— Millennium Note —
The first "pastrami-on-rye-to-go" slid over the counter of a Delancey Street delicatessen in 1888.

New York-ese

"The City," "the Island," "the Village," and "the Garden." I have a friend from Oregon who spent the first several weeks after she moved to Manhattan wondering what city, what island, what village, and what garden everyone was talking about! Anyone who has spent time here knows the answers: New York City, Long Island, Greenwich Village, and Madison Square Garden. But to the uninitiated, it often seems that New Yorkers are speaking in tongues. So that you aren't caught off-guard, here's a quick list of "New York-ese":

- **B&T Crowd:** Bridge and tunnel crowd, often used disparagingly by New Yorkers to describe visitors from New Jersey
- **Bloomie's:** Bloomingdale's
- **The City:** New York City, specifically Manhattan
- **Coffee regular:** coffee with milk but not sugar
- **The FDR:** Franklin D. Roosevelt Drive, an expressway running the length of Manhattan's East Side, beside the East River
- **The Garden:** Madison Square Garden
- **The Island:** Long Island
- **Houston:** a street in lower Manhattan (pronounced HOUSE-ton)
- **The Met:** either the Metropolitan Museum of Art or the Metropolitan Opera
- **MoMA:** the Museum of Modern Art
- **Noho:** the area immediately north of Soho

- **Slice:** a piece of pizza
- **Soda:** any carbonated beverage
- **Standing on line:** nobody in New York seems to stand *in* line!
- **Upstate:** anywhere in New York north of the Bronx
- **The Village:** Greenwich Village (Note: if you want to sound like a native, call it "the Village," "the East Village," or "the West Village," but definitely *not* Greenwich Village.)
- **Zagat's:** a pocket-sized restaurant guide relied on by many New Yorkers.

Resources

If you're planning in advance, I suggest doing a couple things before packing your bags and heading for New York. First, call the New York City Convention and Visitors Bureau (800/669-7810) to request their vacation planning package. It contains information on sights, Broadway shows, hotels, and various other places of interest in New York. (A $4.95 shipping and handling charge must be billed to a credit card.) If you want to talk with someone about your trip, call one of the bureau's travel counselors at 800/692-8474 between 9 and 5 on weekdays or between 10 and 3 on weekends. Second, look through both the "Tours" and "Tickets" sections of Chapter III to see what among the things you want to do requires advance reservations. Finally, write the New York City Transit Authority (Customer Services, 370 John Jay Street, Brooklyn, NY 11201) for maps and brochures about the public transportation system so you'll be ready to go from the moment you hit town. Make sure to ask for the wonderfully useful "Token Tips," a brochure that lists information about how to get to scores of the city's cultural institutions using public transportation.

Whether you're planning a trip in advance or are sitting in your hotel room trying to figure out what to do tomorrow, get copies of *The New Yorker, New York* magazine, *Time Out New York,* and the *New York Times.* All but *Time Out New York* are generally available throughout the country (although the various editions of the *New York Times* are smaller and less comprehensive than the metropolitan one). *The New Yorker* (in the front), *New York* magazine (in the back), and *Time Out New York* (throughout) carry detailed information about current theater, movies, gallery and museum exhibitions, concerts, dance, and New York nightlife. Be forewarned that the free magazines in hotel rooms are paid for by advertisers and are not particularly useful (although the maps and information about such topics as current museum exhibitions can be helpful).

If you don't have everything planned when you arrive, I'd urge you to drop by one of several visitor information centers in Manhattan. The New York City Convention and Visitors Bureau recently opened a state-of-the-art tourist information center on Seventh Ave at 53rd Street. Open from 8:30 to 5:30 on weekdays and from 9 to 5 on weekends, it has a multilingual staff and information about everything from current Broadway shows to ice-skating rinks in Manhattan. Other tourist information centers can be found in Pennsylvania Station, Grand Central Station, the mezzanine level of 2 World Trade Center, the Lower East Side (261 Broome Street), and just north of Times Square in the restored Embassy Theater (Seventh Ave between 46th and 47th Streets). Macy's and Bloomingdale's also maintain tourist information centers for their customers.

The front section of the Manhattan Yellow Pages is a good place to look for information and ideas. In addition to useful telephone numbers, it includes diagrams of major concert halls and sports stadiums. It also includes a short calendar of major annual events and maps of the subway and bus systems. Finally, the World Wide Web has made accessing tourist information about

New York as easy as clicking a mouse. For the most useful Web sites, check the "Telephone Numbers and Web Sites" section at the end of this chapter.

Restrooms

Nothing can ruin your trek around New York (or anyplace else, for that matter) more quickly than not being able to find a bathroom when one is needed. By law, public buildings are required to have public restrooms. They are not, however, required to be clean and safe.

The following list ought to give you some ideas of bathrooms in specific areas that I've found to meet at least a minimum standard of safety and cleanliness. You may need to ask for directions or a key at some of them, but all are free to the public. As a general rule, however, try major hotel lobbies, department stores, schools, theaters, churches, libraries, and even hospitals. The Barnes & Noble and Starbucks locations that have mushroomed in recent years throughout the city are also good bets. Of course, if you have small children in tow, the manager of just about any store or restaurant will likely take pity.

Wherever you end up, be sure to follow a few safety tips. Leaving anything on the floor in a public restroom is a mistake: purses, packages, and everything else have a bad habit of disappearing while you're otherwise occupied! The same is true of items left hanging on the back of a stall door. It's also a good idea to stay away from deserted bathrooms. No matter how badly you need to go, avoid bathrooms in parks (except the ones listed below) and most subway stations.

Below 14th Street

- **National Museum of the American Indian** (1 Bowling Green)
- **World Trade Center**
- **World Financial Center**
- **McDonald's** (160 Broadway)
- **Federal Hall National Memorial** (Wall St at Nassau St)
- **South Street Seaport**
- **City Hall** (Broadway at Chambers St)
- **Lower East Side Visitors Center** (261 Broome St)
- **K mart** (770 Broadway)
- **Strand Book Store** (828 Broadway)

Between 14th and 42nd streets

- **Barney's** (Seventh Ave at 17th St)
- **Supreme Court of the State of New York** (25th St bet Madison and Park Ave)
- **Manhattan Mall** (33rd St at Ave of the Americas)
- **Macy's Herald Square** (Broadway at 34th St)
- **Science, Industry, and Business Library** (Madison Ave at 34th St)
- **Sheraton Park Avenue Hotel** (Park Ave and 37th St)
- **Grand Hyatt Hotel** (42nd St bet Park and Lexington Ave)
- **New York Public Library** (Fifth Ave bet 40th and 42nd St)
- **Bryant Park** (42nd St bet Fifth Ave and Ave of the Americas)

Midtown

- **United Nations** (First Ave bet 45th and 46th St)
- **Embassy Theater Tourist Information Center** (Seventh Ave bet 46th and 47th St)
- **Waldorf-Astoria Hotel** (301 Park Ave)

- **Rockefeller Center** (bet Fifth Ave and Ave of the Americas from 49th to 51st St)
- **Olympic Tower** (bet Fifth and Madison Ave from 51st to 52nd St)
- **Park Avenue Plaza** (55 E 52nd St)
- **Trump Tower** (Fifth Ave bet 55th and 56th St)
- **Henri Bendel** (712 Fifth Ave)
- **Omni Park Central** (870 Seventh Ave)
- **Sony Wonder Technology Lab** (56th St at Madison Ave)
- **Warner Brothers Studio Store** (57th St at Fifth Ave)

Upper East Side
- **McDonald's** (Third Ave bet 57th and 58th St)
- **Bloomingdale's** (1000 Third Ave)
- **Hunter College Student Center** (Lexington Ave at 68th St)
- **Asia Society** (725 Park Ave)
- **92nd Street Y** (1395 Lexington Ave)
- **Museum of the City of New York** (Fifth Ave bet 103rd and 104th St)
- **Charles A. Dana Discovery Center** (Central Park, Fifth Ave at 110th St)

Upper West Side
- **Avery Fisher Hall** (Lincoln Center, 64th St at Broadway)
- **New York Public Library for the Performing Arts** (Lincoln Center, 65th St at Broadway)
- **Museum of American Folk Art** (Columbus Avenue bet 65th and 66th St)
- **Barnes & Noble** (Broadway at 82nd St)
- **Cathedral Church of St. John the Divine** (Amsterdam Ave at 112th St)
- **Hispanic Society of America** (Audubon Terrace, off Broadway bet 155th and 156th St)

— Millennium Note —
The first bagel baked in New York emerged from a cellar at 15 Clinton Street in 1896, according to Label Vishinsky, inventor of an automatic bagelmaker and a leading authority on bagels.

Special Events

If you're looking for the perfect spot to hold a wedding reception, bar mitzvah, or gala event for thousands, New York inevitably has the right place . . . and the people to put it together for you. The trick, of course, is finding them. (The other trick is paying for them!)

Note that you will not find museums, restaurants, or hotels in the following list. Many museums, including the Abigail Adams Smith Museum and the Roosevelt Rotunda of the American Museum of Natural History (complete with its dinosaur display), do rent space for parties and other events. Many restaurants have spaces for private parties, as do most hotels. Some of my favorite private party rooms in New York are at **Adrienne** (Peninsula New York Hotel, 700 Fifth Ave), **Barbetta** (321 W 46th St), **Firebird** (365 W 46th St), the **Four Seasons** (99 E 52nd St), **Fraunces Tavern Restaurant** (54 Pearl St), **Gramercy Tavern** (42 E 20th St), **Hard Rock Cafe** (221 W 57th St), the **Hudson River Club** (World Financial Center), **La Réserve** (4 W 49th St), **Le Cirque 2000** (New York Palace Hotel, 455 Madison Ave), **Le Périgord** (405 E 52nd St),

Lutèce (249 E 50th St), **Montrachet** (239 Broadway), **One If By Land, Two If By Sea** (17 Barrow St), **Primavera** (1578 First Ave), the **Rainbow Room** (Rockefeller Center, 65th fl), **Serendipity 3** (225 E 60th St), **Seventh Regiment Armory** (643 Park Ave), **Tavern on the Green** (Central Park W at 67th St), **The Terrace** (400 W 119th St), **The Tonic** (108 W 18th St), **Tribeca Grill** (375 Greenwich St), and **Windows on the World** (1 World Trade Center). If you want to throw a party at your favorite museum, restaurant, hotel, or bar, by all means ask.

Before you jump ahead with planning a party in New York, be forewarned: it's going to cost a great deal of money. I'm talking *really* big bucks. You can save some money by avoiding Saturday evenings, keeping your numbers down, and throwing your party in the off months of July and August or between January and early April. Some places and services will negotiate on their prices. But don't expect any great or even particularly good deals. And make your reservations at least a couple months (and as many as two years) in advance.

The following list is intended to give you an idea of what kinds of spaces are available rather than a comprehensive list. If you're interested in caterers, look under "Catering, Delis, Food to Go" in Chapter IV. If you're interested in florists, look under that heading in Chapter VI. And if you're interested in photographers, look under "Photographic Services" in Chapter V.

Boathouse—In the middle of Central Park at about 74th St, this indoor-outdoor cafe and garden pavilion (212/517-3623) looks out on the lovely Central Park Lake. Catering is included in the rental charge.

Burden Mansion—It was once given to a Vanderbilt as a wedding present. You provide the catering (7 East 91st Street, 212/722-4745).

Creative Edge Caterers—An elegant and versatile space run by a very popular catering company (639 Washington Street, 212/741-3000). Catering is included in the rental charge.

Glorious Food—A converted 1903 garage, complete with a terrace and open-air roof space, this place (522 East 74th Street, 212/628-2320) is run by a very fashionable caterer. Catering is included in the rental charge.

MacKenzie-Childs—The two rooms here are quite small but not to be missed if you have lots of money and are hosting a luncheon or similar event. Catering is included in the rental charge. Call 212/535-5564 for more information.

Museum Club at Bridgewaters—This club in the Fulton Market Building at South Street Seaport (212/608-8823) has stunning views of the Brooklyn Bridge and New York Harbor. Catering is included in the rental charge.

New York Botanical Garden—This new building comes complete with a ballroom and outdoor terrace at this wonderful spot in the Bronx (718/220-0300). Catering is optional.

New York Carriage House—Once the Rockefeller family's carriage house, this elegant space has a fountain, lots of marble, and an enclosed patio. You provide the catering. Call 212/399-0944 for more information.

New York Public Library—This magnificent main branch of the New York Public Library, on Fifth Avenue between 40th and 42nd streets, has several spaces available. You provide the catering. Call 212/930-0730 for more information.

Pier 60—Famed New York caterer Abigail Kirsch created this new spot at Chelsea Piers with spectacular views of the Hudson River (212/366-6060). Catering is included in the rental charge.

Pratt Mansion—You can't ask for a better location: across the street from the Metropolitan Museum of Art (1026 Fifth Avenue, 212/717-1130). Catering is optional.

Puck Building—One of the hottest properties in New York, Saturday nights at this elegant downtown building are booked at least a year in advance (Lafayette and Houston Streets, 212/274-8900). You provide the catering.

Studio 450—This renovated industrial building (450 West 31st Street, 212/290-1400) overlooks the Hudson River. You provide the catering.

Tribeca Rooftop—A great loft space complete with roof deck and a mezzanine overlooking the dance space (212/625-2080). Catering is included in the rental charge.

The Upper Crust "91"—A very flexible space with elaborate lighting and exposed bricks (91 Horatio Street, 212/691-4570). Catering is included in the rental charge.

Telephone Numbers and Web Sites

Emergencies and Hotlines

AIDS hotline	212/447-8200
Alcoholics Anonymous	212/647-1680
Ambulance	911
ConEd (gas leaks and power outages)	212/683-8830
Fire	911
Gamblers Anonymous	212/903-4400
Poison Control	212/764-7667
Police	911
Police (sex-crimes hotline)	212/267-7273
Suicide Help Line	212/532-2400
Travelers' Aid Society	212/944-0013
Victims' Services Crime Victims' Hotline	212/577-7777

Entertainment

Broadway Babies (theater information hotline)	888/411-BWAY
Central Park Visitors Center (The Dairy)	212/794-6564
Department of Parks and Recreation	
Permits and information	212/360-8111
Recording of special events	212/360-3456
Information	411
Jacob K. Javits Convention Center (recording of upcoming events)	212/216-2000
Lincoln Center (recording of upcoming events)	212/546-2656
Macy's Herald Square (recording of upcoming events)	212/494-4495
Madison Square Garden (recording of upcoming events)	212/465-6741
Movie Phone	212/777-3456
New York City Convention and Visitors Bureau	800/692-8474
NYC/Onstage	212/768-1818

Rockefeller Center (recording of upcoming events)........212/632-3975
World Trade Center (recording of upcoming events).......212/435-4170
World Financial Center (recording of upcoming events)....212/945-0505

Information and Complaints

Hospital Audiences Hotline (access information for people
    with disabilities 888/424-4685
Lesbian and Gay Community Service Center.............212/620-7310
Manhattan Borough President........................212/669-8300
Marriage Licenses (City Clerk's office).................212/669-2400
Mayor's Office for People with Disabilities..............212/788-2830
New York City Board of Elections (Manhattan)...........212/886-3800
New York City Department of Consumer Affairs..........212/487-4444
New York City Department of Health (complaint line).....212/442-9666
New York Public Library (branch information)............212/621-0626
U.S. Post Office (general information)..................212/967-8585
U.S. Customs (regional office).......................212/637-7914
U.S. Passport Agency...............................212/399-5290

Transportation

Airports
Air-Ride (transportation information)...................800/247-7433
Kennedy Airport
    General information...............................718/244-4444
    Lost and found..................................718/244-4225
LaGuardia Airport
    General information...............................718/533-3400
    Lost and found..................................718/533-3988
Newark Airport
    General information...............................973/961-2000
    Lost and found..................................973/961-6230

Mass Transit
Metropolitan Transit Authority
    (Customer service)................................718/330-3322
    General information on buses and subways............718/330-1234
    General information in foreign languages.............718/330-4847
    General information for people with disabilities.........718/596-8585

Taxis
Taxi and Limousine Commission......................212/221-8294

Trains and Buses
Amtrak/Metroliner 800/872-7245
Grand Central Station
    Metro North general information.....................212/340-3000
    Metro North lost and found........................212/340-2555
Long Island Railroad..............................718/217-5477
New Jersey Transit................................973/762-5100
Port Authority Bus Terminal.........................212/564-8484

Miscellaneous
Bridge and Tunnel Construction Information.............800/221-9903
On-street Parking Information........................212/442-7080

Towing (involuntary)................................212/971-0774
Vehicle Registration and Licenses..................... 212/645-5550

Web Sites

Central Park...............................www.centralpark.org
City Search...........................www.newyork.citysearch.com
Digital City (American Online)...........www.newyork.digitalcity.com
League of American Theaters and Producers........www.broadway.org
Lincoln Center.............................www.lincolncenter.org
Mayor's Office and City Services...www/ci.nyc.ny.us/html.om/home.html
Metropolitan Transit Authority...................www.mat.nyc.ny.us
Movie Phone..............................www.moviephone.com
New York City Parks and Recreation..............www.nycparks.org
New York City Convention and Visitors Bureau.......www.nycvisit.com
New York State (tourist information)...www.iloveny.state.ny.us/newyork.
New York Times (events information)...............www.nytoday.com
Theater Development Fund...........................www.tdr.org
Theatre Direct International...................www.theatredirect.com
Ticketmaster...............................www.ticketmaster.com

Index

NOTES

NOTES

NOTES

NOTES

NOTES

L.S. Collection — office supplies   very nice   p 449 | Met is at 79

~~Gracious Home~~ n/02   **NOTES**
  → expensive   French linens

CITY KNICKERBOCKER LAMPS

Haggstrom Maps

ONE SHUBERT ALLEY   bet B'way + 8th
                                794

Bread — St. FAMOUS   9th Ave at 56th
H + H Bagels, p259 (2nd Ave/ 80-81

Civilized Traveler, p303
Doorway to Design (Tours), p 231
Big Apple Greeter, free(!?), p 232
CAROLE STUPPELL